GOOD PARENTS, BETTER HOMES, AND GREAT SCHOOLS

GOOD PARENTS, BETTER HOMES, AND GREAT SCHOOLS

SELLING SEGREGATION BEFORE THE NEW DEAL

Karen Benjamin

THE UNIVERSITY OF
NORTH CAROLINA PRESS
CHAPEL HILL

© 2025 Karen Benjamin
All rights reserved

Designed by April Leidig
Set in Arno and Karla by Copperline Book Services

Manufactured in the United States of America

Cover art: Birmingham racial zoning map, 1926.
Courtesy of the Birmingham Public Library.

Library of Congress Cataloging-in-Publication Data
Names: Benjamin, Karen, author.
Title: Good parents, better homes, and great schools : selling segregation before the New Deal / Karen Benjamin.
Description: Chapel Hill : University of North Carolina Press, [2025] | Includes bibliographical references and index.
Identifiers: LCCN 2025001968 | ISBN 9781469684932 (cloth ; alk. paper) | ISBN 9781469684949 (paperback ; alk. paper) | ISBN 9781469684956 (epub) ISBN 9781469687391 (pdf)
Subjects: LCSH: Discrimination in housing—Southern States—History—20th century. | Discrimination in housing—Southern States—History—19th century. | Discrimination in housing—Law and legislation—Southern States. | African Americans—Segregation—Southern States. | Segregation in education—Southern States. | Parenting—Political aspects—Southern States. | BISAC: SOCIAL SCIENCE / Ethnic Studies / American / African American & Black Studies | POLITICAL SCIENCE / Public Policy / City Planning & Urban Development
Classification: LCC HD7288.76.U62 S683 2025 | DDC 363.5/1—dc23/eng/20250417
LC record available at https://lccn.loc.gov/2025001968

For product safety concerns under the European Union's General Product Safety Regulation (EU GPSR), please contact gpsr@mare-nostrum.co.uk or write to the University of North Carolina Press and Mare Nostrum Group B.V., Mauritskade 21D, 1091 GC Amsterdam, The Netherlands.

CONTENTS

List of Illustrations vii

Author's Note xi

INTRODUCTION
Selling Segregation 1

CHAPTER 1
Parenting Helps Build a Foundation for Lasting Segregation 17

CHAPTER 2
Affluent Parents and the Suburban Residential Park 41

CHAPTER 3
Residential Parks, Jim Crow, and School Inequality 63

CHAPTER 4
Residential Parks and the Rise of Segregation Ordinances 81

CHAPTER 5
Black Schools and the Rise of Segregation Ordinances 103

CHAPTER 6
Black Activism and the Battle for Better Schools 123

CHAPTER 7
The Segregation Ordinances versus Racial Zoning 149

CHAPTER 8
Racial Zoning and Schools 181

CHAPTER 9
The Best Possible Environment for the Growing Child 207

CHAPTER 10
Child-Centered Zoning and *Euclid* 233

CHAPTER 11
De Jure Segregation after *Euclid* 251

CHAPTER 12
An Enduring Legacy 281

AFTERWORD
Moving Forward 293

Acknowledgments 299

Notes 303

Bibliography 397

Index 413

ILLUSTRATIONS

FIGURES

0.1. *Planning the Home* by Norman Rockwell xiv

1.1. Topsy and Eva by John R. Neill 27

1.2. "Family Record: Before the War and Since the War" 28

1.3. Neighborhood Union's elementary class in childcare 30

2.1. Buena Vista Annex advertisement: girl exiting the gate 43

2.2. Ansley Park advertisement: "The Sandman Comes" 48

2.3. *Birmingham News* advertisement: "Do It for the Kiddies" 50

2.4. Palos Verdes Estates advertisement: "To a Certain Mother in Los Angeles" 51

2.5. Buena Vista advertisement: "It Is a Natural Instinct to Want to Provide a Home" 53

4.1. Plat map for Columbia Heights 93

5.1. Ira Street School boarded up 121

6.1. A classroom in Atlanta's Pittsburgh School 128

6.2. The Storrs School 130

6.3. Comparison of the Summer Hill School and Ashby Street School 144

7.1. "Topsey-Turvey" political cartoon 161

8.1. "An Example of an Excellent School Site" 185

8.2. Students crossing industrial railroad tracks 195

9.1. Central Terrace advertisement: "Home, Sweet Home" 213

9.2. Henry Holmes OYOH advertising copy 214

9.3. "Own a Home for Your Children's Sake" 215

9.4. "Dey's All Got Debbils!" (*Parents' Magazine*) 224

9.5. "For Better or Worse—Servants Influence Children" (*Parents' Magazine*) 224

9.6. "Americans in the Making" (*Parents' Magazine*) 226

9.7. Fleischmann's Yeast trading card 227

9.8. Photographs from *The Brownies' Book* 228

10.1. River Oaks advertisement: "A Real Homeplace for the Family of Modest Income" 237

10.2. "Too Late to Begin Being Careful" political cartoon 244

11.1. Photograph of the addition for Booker T. Washington High School 260

11.2. River Oaks advertisement: "A New and Wholesome Environment for Your Children" 263

11.3. Birmingham racial zone map 270

13.1. "The Children," Garden Hills (Atlanta) 294

MAPS

3.1. The development of the Raleigh school system 68

4.1. East Fourth Street neighborhood, Winston-Salem 92

5.1. Racial transition in Baltimore 106

5.2. Schools and residential development in Atlanta 109

5.3. Schools and residential development in Winston-Salem 116

6.1. Schools and Raleigh's College Park 126

7.1. Final zone map, Atlanta 162

7.2. Tentative zone plan, Atlanta 167

8.1. Raleigh annexation map and the school building program 200

11.1. Houston wards and the school building program 255

11.2. "Proposed Race Restriction Areas," Houston Planning Commission 257

11.3. "River Oaks" High School 265

11.4. Birmingham's school building program 272

11.5. Winston-Salem racial zone map 276

TABLES

7.1. Percentage of Black residents in the total population, 1900–1930 175

7.2. Population within city limits, 1900–1930 175

8.1. School surveys, 1910–1928 184

AUTHOR'S NOTE

In 2004, while reading through manuscript collections at Duke University as part of my dissertation research, I found a letter written in 1926 by a Black woman accusing the Raleigh school board of attempting to segregate Black residents through school site selection. I wasn't sure how this letter might fit in with my dissertation on curriculum reform, but I knew it was important, and so I made a copy of it for my files. This serendipitous discovery would eventually lead to "Suburbanizing Jim Crow," an article I wrote for a special issue on schools and suburbanization in the *Journal of Urban History*. The article examined how the Raleigh school board used its building program from the early 1920s to advance residential segregation. Jack Dougherty had kindly invited me to participate in the special issue, and Matthew Lassiter served as the editor. This project would not exist without their support and encouragement.

After receiving positive feedback for "Suburbanizing Jim Crow," I decided to expand my research beyond Raleigh rather than transform my dissertation into a book. I applied for and received a National Academy of Education/Spencer Foundation postdoc, and since then, the Spencer Foundation has generously supported this research with two additional grants, allowing me to write a larger regional history set within the national context. When I began presenting my preliminary research at conferences, I realized that it was not enough to demonstrate that school systems were intentionally promoting residential segregation. Some discussants wondered whether the school issue was simply a side effect of other segregation laws and strategies. Thus, I set out to determine why this tactic seemed to work so well and whether it was the key to maintaining segregation over time.

As my research focus shifted, criticism of "helicopter parents" seemed everywhere in the media, and since I was a mother of young children, I paid attention. Those editorials helped me see the connection between parenting styles, housing choices, and school quality in the more distant past. What started out as a book on residential segregation in the South had become more complicated: some threads—including the development of intensive parenting—began in the Northeast, while others—including the widespread use of racial covenants, segregation ordinances, and racial zoning—began in Jim Crow cities farther south. I also realized that the zoning movement was more responsible for the ties between school and residential segregation than local school boards. Planning commissions were eager to work with board members and school administrators who shared their vision of "better" cities surrounded by homes, schools, and playgrounds for white, middle-class children.

Scholars have rarely, if ever, discussed the child-centered nature of planning, which helps explain why schools are not simply one more tool from a larger toolkit. Early-twentieth-century planning documents are laced with references to middle-class child-rearing as well as to schools. Planning consultants zoned cities to safeguard suburban residential parks that catered to affluent white families. The outcome, if not the objective, was to design the perfect environment for child-rearing for some, while excluding children of color and those whose parents could not afford to move into strictly zoned areas—all under the guise of protecting childhood.

The chapters that follow rely heavily on Black and white newspapers, which served as diaries for my cities. They are full of rich detail rarely found in other sources. Moreover, multiple, competing newspapers provided a range of viewpoints, furnishing a more complete picture of the various controversies surrounding residential segregation, school building programs, and zoning. Because the articles and editorials were meant for public consumption, their contents often provoked reactions that helped document how diverse residents responded to unfolding events. When examined from the perspective of individual owners or editors and doublechecked through archival sources, they are invaluable. With that said, many of the quotes taken from newspapers should be read skeptically: reporters at the time were more likely to capture the essence of what was said rather than the exact wording. When possible, I quoted from official statements, resolutions, advertisements, editorials, or letters to the editor rather than from summaries of events. And to improve readability, I corrected obvious spelling errors and minor grammatical mistakes.

I also capitalized the word "Black" when it means African American but not "white," which, historically, is a more inconsistent category. Although genetic sequencing has obliterated the myth of biological race, the powerful legacy of racism, which was advanced by both scientists and social scientists until well into the twentieth century, created historical categories that continue to shape people's lives, as this book demonstrates. Who is classified as "white" has changed over time, sometimes arbitrarily or in reaction to larger historical events, with "white" being defined mostly by who was excluded rather than who was included. For example, "white" usually describes people of European descent, but a person of European ancestry with just "one drop" of African "blood" would have been excluded by law in certain states. Similarly, Jews and immigrants from the wrong parts of Europe were excluded during the late nineteenth and early twentieth centuries yet were welcomed into the ranks of "white Americans" after World War II when they were finally invited to move out to the suburbs.

**GOOD PARENTS,
BETTER HOMES,
AND GREAT
SCHOOLS**

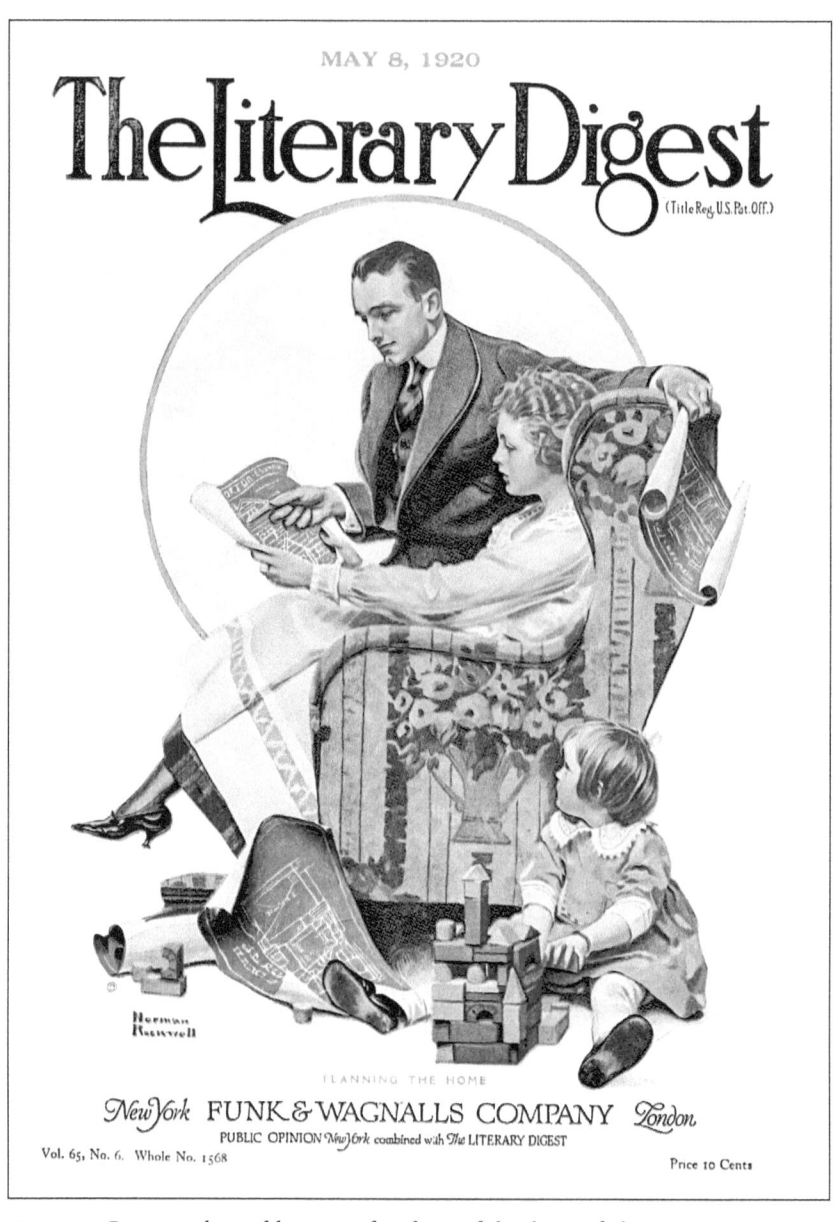

FIGURE 0.1. Business-class publications often depicted the choice of a home as an important decision, mostly in terms of child-rearing. Norman Rockwell, *Planning the Home*, illustration for *Literary Digest*, 8 May 1920. Scan courtesy of Andrew Sobol.

INTRODUCTION

Selling Segregation

A young, well-dressed couple carefully studies the blueprints of at least four different house plans with a toddler sitting nearby, constructing her own house out of wooden blocks while gazing at the object of her parents' rapt attention.[1] *Planning the Home* was a 1920 Norman Rockwell cover for *Literary Digest*, a newsmagazine popular with the American business class. It captured the cozy relationship between middle-class parenting and a modern, single-family home, a combination that had already begun altering the nation's residential development at the time.

Even now, the well-worn phrases "good parents" and "better homes," particularly when combined with "great schools," evoke images of whitewashed suburbia, which indeed, was their original meaning when they became ingrained in the middle-class psyche more than 100 years ago. Commitment to these ideals is rooted in the faith that, collectively, they are the principal engine of upward mobility for one's children. At the turn of the twentieth century, developers of residential parks—those carefully planned and heavily restricted subdivisions on the outskirts of town—understood the psychology of middle-class child-rearing. They capitalized on white parental ambitions and insecurities to promote profitable suburban development.

The profit motive of a few could not have controlled residential development in a democracy without convincing government officials, the courts, voters, and, above all else, homebuyers to embrace their rationale. In this, they succeeded remarkably well, especially in securing the acceptance of both deed restrictions and single-family zoning, which at the time made little sense to most citizens outside the context of child-centered arguments. Child-rearing was one of the few cultural concepts that superseded the sanctity of property and other American ideals related to individualism. From the nation's founding, prosperous parents had acted on the assumption that they must sacrifice their own interests for the sake of their children, not only to provide them with opportunities for upward mobility but also to safeguard the nation's future.[2]

At first, many resisted the new housing standards, which were less convenient and more expensive, but developers were soon able to convince affluent parents that single-family houses, landscaped yards, quiet streets, well-endowed parks, and superior schools were well worth the sacrifice. They also adopted a host of deed restrictions to exclude the uses and users of property they viewed as incompatible with "family life." Before long, multiple layers of government—from city councils, school boards, and planning commissions to state legislatures and the federal bureaucracy—agreed that residential parks deserved taxpayer support because they would nurture and protect the nation's most valuable resource: its children.

But racial covenants and other forms of de jure segregation excluded Black children, in particular, from the very benefits touted as essential to raising strong, healthy, well-educated, and productive citizens. The fundamental motivation behind residential segregation was little different from other race regulations: white Americans wished to preserve a racial hierarchy that benefitted them and their children. Since the interests of the white middle class dominated social, political, and economic norms, middle-class child-rearing became the key factor in segregation's entrenchment in cities across the nation. Not all white parents sought segregation and not all homeowners were parents, of course, but concerns over child-rearing so powerfully shaped the housing market that it was in every white homeowner's financial interest to share a similar vision of what a neighborhood should offer the children who lived there. Once racial exclusion became embedded within the dominant idea of what "good" parents, "better" homes, and "great" schools were, it became far more difficult to address the destructive legacies of segregation, even after opinion polls began suggesting that most whites opposed it, at least in theory.[3]

Certainly, other factors mattered, too, as expressed in the multipronged rationale advanced by segregation's supporters. As many scholars have shown, white homeowners expressed worry about falling property values, concerns over the threat to racial purity, despair over the loss of status, and the desire to preserve a suitable "home environment."[4] But at a fundamental level, middle-class child-rearing lay at the core of all four. It helps explain the high demand for housing in some residential areas but not others, which shaped property values; it helps explain why violence and the proliferation of antimiscegenation laws were not seen as sufficient to prevent "amalgamation" close to home; it helps explain why status was tied to the local school as much as it was to the neighborhood; and it helps explain what property owners meant when they laid claim to the "home environment." Most importantly, emphasizing the links to child-rearing helps explain why efforts to undo residential segregation have accomplished so little: segregation remains baked into white ideas of responsible parenting, and few families with the resources to choose where they want to live—whether Black, white, or any other racial or ethnic group—are willing to experiment with their children's lives.

This study also illustrates how the conventional wisdom on the superiority of single-family homes set apart from other areas of the city was neither a natural tendency nor inevitable. In 1982, near the height of residential segregation, historian Alan Trachtenberg dismissed Gwendolyn Wright's valuable contribution *Building the Dream* as "merely belaboring the obvious" in its analysis of the "middle-class ambition for a private, detached home in the suburbs."[5] Yet this "American dream" was carefully crafted and promoted through a powerful private-public partnership. It was packaged and sold for profit, and along with it, race and class segregation, urban sprawl, and increased anxiety about parenting. The social, economic, and environmental consequences have been staggering. We ignore at our peril "what has been under our noses all along," in the words of historian William Cronon.[6]

The Child-Centered Residential Park and Federal Housing Policy

At the turn of the twentieth century, a robust private-public partnership of residential developers and local officials devised a suburban package that seemed irresistible to upwardly mobile white families in the decades before New Deal housing programs expanded access to white families with lower incomes.[7] One prosperous suburban mom proudly described how her home's location facilitated good parenting by providing safe, spacious places for her children to play, which helped spark their creativity: her son fashioned "a hut from packing-boxes" in the "vacant lot next door," and her daughter made a birdhouse to "lure" bluebirds to their yard. In contrast, she believed their former home in the city had hindered her children's "complete development."[8] During the Depression, the newly established Federal Housing Administration (FHA) sought to increase the number of families who could benefit from suburban homeownership through guaranteed mortgages that allowed banks to extend substantially better terms. The FHA then published an *Underwriting Manual* (1936) as a guide for those assessing risk for the new mortgage program.[9]

The *Underwriting Manual* demonstrated the extent to which the nation's dominant cultural ideas about parenthood had become imbedded in the price of residential property. It required valuators to consider the appropriateness of the surrounding environment for child-rearing when evaluating homesites. "The husband and wife who own a home or are prospective purchasers of a dwelling might be willing to tolerate certain adverse conditions affecting themselves," it explained, but "an altogether different attitude will be taken when the welfare of their children is endangered." "Parents wish their children to have all available advantages for physical and cultural development and those areas offering the most will be the places in which they will prefer to live." It concluded, "The Valuator will reflect true conditions in his rating of this feature only when he includes in his consideration" the effect of the "presence or lack of advantages for rearing children."[10]

Similarly, the manual instructed appraisers to investigate the condition of the local school, which was another important aspect of a property's appeal. In areas where parents must "drive the children in the family automobile to and from school," a rating would be "adversely affected since the inconvenience will reflect unfavorably on the desirability" of the property. The manual cautioned that the social standing of the students attending the school was even more significant. "The social class of the parents of children at the school will in many instances have a vital bearing." Even if the "physical surroundings of a neighborhood area may be favorable," it warned, when "the children of people living in such an area are compelled to attend school where the majority or a goodly number of the pupils represent a far lower level of society or an incompatible racial element, the neighborhood under consideration will prove far less stable and desirable than if this condition did not exist." It further advised appraisers that the opposite was true as well: "In many instances where a school has earned a prestige through the class of pupils attending, it will be found that such prestige will be a vital element in maintaining the desirability of the entire area comprising" the school's attendance district.[11] This advice closely adhered to the conventional wisdom for residential property valuation backed by esteemed developers such as J. C. Nichols of Kansas City, Robert Jemison Jr. of Birmingham, and Hugh Potter of Houston.

Perhaps no one idealized the intersection between housing and parenting more than President Herbert Hoover.[12] The culmination of his efforts to advance better child-rearing in single-family, suburban houses came in 1931 when his White House Conference on Home Building and Home Ownership convened only one year after his White House Conference on Child Health and Protection. Many of the participants and topics overlapped by design, as his announcement of the second conference made explicit: "A principal object of home construction and homeownership is to provide the best possible environment for the growing child." He expounded on this idea in his remarks to the conference's planning committee: "Adequate housing goes to the very roots of the well-being of the family, and the family is the social unit of the Nation. It is more than comfort that is involved, it has important aspects of health and morals and education and the provision of a fair chance of growing childhood." Although his foremost concern was expanding white access to racially restricted residential parks, the needs of Black families were not wholly excluded. In a separate meeting, he acknowledged the "important" and "unselfish" work of the Committee on Negro Housing, although his message to its members did little more than applaud "self-help" within a purely segregated context.[13]

Hoover's two conferences capped a decade of activity in which he had championed single-family homeownership along with the parent education movement, insisting both would ensure that the nation's future was safely guarded by a strong, white middle class. He believed this goal required proper child-rearing, in a proper home, within a proper neighborhood. As the nation's commerce secretary, Hoover had endorsed "Own-Your-Own-Home" (OYOH) campaigns and the Better Homes in America movement (BHA) to pressure families with children to purchase single-family houses. He argued that parents would not only be providing their children with greater opportunities for upward mobility but they would also be teaching them better citizenship. In addition, Hoover convened an "Advisory Committee on Zoning" to facilitate the acceptance of zoning ordinances, including single-family districts that mainly benefitted affluent residential parks. With Hoover's assistance, the planning movement convinced both the courts and voters that strict single-family zoning was essential to the nation's future because it would preserve childhood from an assortment of urban threats. The elimination of even "two-family" duplexes was necessary to ensure vigor and virtue in the next generation of Americans, which the movement narrowly defined as white and middle class. Ultimately, the Supreme Court adopted this argument in *Euclid v. Ambler* (1926). The majority ruled that single-family zoning regulations promoted the general welfare by preserving "a more favorable environment in which to rear children."[14]

With single-family zoning secure, developers next sought ways to make homeownership more affordable. The National Association of Real Estate Boards (NAREB) had been seeking federal help to expand the mortgage market for years. In 1923, the creation of its Home Builders and Subdividers Division opened an avenue for residential park developers to dominate the organization. Far too many Americans, they believed, either could not afford to own a single-family house or preferred the convenience of renting. The national hunger for land ownership was part of an agrarian tradition that had not translated well to the urban environment. While ownership of a farm meant independence from wage work, fostering upward mobility, ownership of a house could interfere with one's freedom to seek better employment elsewhere or simply acquire a larger house, impeding mobility. Consequently, the United States was above all a nation of renters after World War I. According to the 1920 census, "The proportion of owned homes" inched upwards from about 38 percent in 1910 to almost 41 percent in 1920, a real increase to be sure, but nearly 60 percent of households were still renting. In individual cities, rates of homeownership could be far lower: 28 percent in Birmingham, 27 percent in Chicago, and only 25 percent in Atlanta. Cities with smaller industrial workforces such as Austin—a small city with a larger number of white-collar employees working for the University of Texas or the state government, had higher rates of homeownership, but even in Austin, renters comprised more than 50 percent of households.[15]

The rapid expansion of child-friendly residential parks after World War I had led to a robust suburban housing market between 1921 and 1925, but that market began to soften in 1926 with too many unsold lots in too many new developments.

To boost sales, developers began selling houses along with their lots; however, this required more investment capital, and the market for affluent homes was still too limited to take on the additional risk. When the entire housing market collapsed during the Depression, falling housing starts and a growing number of foreclosures provided NAREB with the opportunity to pull the federal government into large-scale residential development—on terms dictated by NAREB's leadership.[16]

Before developers could advocate for new federal housing programs, they first had to reshape the values of rank-and-file members. During the 1920s, most realtors had business concerns that conflicted with the residential vision of prominent developers. The majority rented houses, speculated in lot sales, and opened smaller "additions" that lacked the child-centered amenities of residential parks. Moreover, they scorned single-family houses as the least valuable use of property, hoping to resell their residential properties for more lucrative uses as the commercial center expanded outwards. Nichols, Jemison, Potter, and other renowned developers wanted to prevent these small-scale operators from "damaging" the adjacent property to their painstakingly planned developments, which represented hundreds of thousands of dollars in improvements. They supported strict regulation of additions platted as many as five miles beyond the city limits and hoped that requiring licenses and mandatory real estate courses would lead to the professionalization of the industry.

Working in collaboration with the YMCA and the Institute for Research in Land Economics and Public Utilities, NAREB endorsed a series of eight textbooks published between 1923 and 1927 for its "Standard Real Estate Course." The textbooks presented the principles of proper residential development to the nation's less enlightened practitioners by sublimating the work of the developer into a moral crusade.[17] The first volume reminded subdividers—including those primarily selling lots at the block level—that they were supplying the "homes for the families that are the hope of the nation," tapping into Hoover's rhetoric about raising white middle-class children to take the reins of society. Another volume expounded upon the importance of reserving "proper spaces for schools and playgrounds," calling for "10 percent of every subdivision [to] be set aside by law for parks." It further advised planning commissions to undertake the siting of schools and playgrounds to ensure their "proper" placement at "the center" of small "communities of homes" in new residential areas.[18]

Because residential developers well understood that they could not ignore the concerns of parents—their key buyers—if they wished to increase the price of residential lots, the textbooks recommended explicit references to child-rearing in advertising campaigns. The first volume suggested that advertisements ask parents if they had provided the surroundings for their children that would "safeguard their childhood and assure their future." It also proposed ads depicting the residential park as a "fairyland" affording "room to grow as nature intended" with "minds attuned to beauty and purity." A later volume described advertisements that explicitly targeted parents as "almost irresistible." "No appeal is greater to a mother or father than proper presentation of the advantages real home life will offer children," it lectured. "When a child comes into a household the entire family regime changes. Every thought is centered in the child. Its comfort and future are almost the sole objects of the parents' life." The volume further prompted developers to sell exclusion along with play space: "Perhaps it is the right sort of playmates for their growing children" that buyers "wish to purchase." J. C. Nichols, the nation's most celebrated developer, frequently relied on such appeals in advertisements for his famed Country Club District in Kansas City. One of his early ads guaranteed that "children will get the benefit of an exclusive environment and the most desirable associations."[19]

When developers promised that every child living in a residential park would make a fine companion, they were implying that the children would one day become likely marriage partners or business associates and, thereby, deliver additional avenues for economic mobility. They were also echoing the rhetoric of parent educators who warned that young innocents were often led astray through lax parenting and that those who were already debased might corrupt those from "good" homes. For example, child psychologist Edgar Doll cautioned the middle-class readers of *Literary Digest* that "many of the undesirable activities of children" were "the result of imitation of other children whose social training" had been "neglected or unsuccessful."[20] Thus, newspaper and magazine articles joined advertisements in persuading affluent white families to move to exclusive residential parks to limit their children's associations both at home and at school.

Adopting deed restrictions that barred residents who might "lower" the status of the community provided an effective tool for assuring affluent white parents that their children would have only the best companions.[21] Even so, most developers imposed restrictions not simply to appeal to parents but to protect their substantial investment in improvements during what was often a lengthy period of lot sales, which sometimes took decades. They feared that an introduction of "incompatible" uses or users during this precarious phase of development might damage the beauty or prestige of the residential park, and as a result, lead to plummeting prices on the unsold lots. Since most Americans despised others restricting what they could or could not do with their own property, developers began selling their "restrictions" as "protections," especially those that could be tied to more effective child-rearing. Consequently, the connection between property values and exclusion became fixed to parental concerns about childhood acquaintances and upward mobility.

Residential Segregation and Child-Centered Residential Parks

Minimum house values and other economic restrictions could not prevent affluent people of color from purchasing property, a "problem" some developers hoped to solve by imposing race restrictions. Racial covenants targeting Black Americans and Irish immigrants first appeared in northern cities before the Civil War, but ratification of the Fourteenth Amendment in 1868 made the continued use of race restrictions risky. If the courts invalidated them, then it might threaten the whole range of deed restrictions that developers were using to keep lot prices high, and the United States Circuit Court had already found racial covenants targeting Chinese residents in Ventura, California, to be unconstitutional.[22] Still, local officials in Jim Crow cities continuously pushed the boundaries of the Fourteenth Amendment by employing the states' police power to enforce a range of segregation laws during the late nineteenth and early twentieth centuries. Within this context, the use of racial covenants was simply another regulation in a long line of controls placed on Black residents across the South and into the border states. As more developers adopted them without incident, race restrictions spread quickly during the first decade of the twentieth century. After World War I, they sped through northern cities, too, where developers had been more restrained by the Fourteenth Amendment.[23]

Nonetheless, one cannot assume that racial exclusion was the principal lure of residential parks, which were selling a larger child-centered package that also included new schools, well-equipped playgrounds, and a less urban environment.[24] For example, a real estate article in the *Houston Post* urged parents with "high ideals for their children" to consider how the city had "completely surrounded" their homes "with business buildings, hotels, apartments, filling stations, etc." It enticed white families to move to developing residential areas by touting the newly completed schools that would soon serve the suburban residential parks the article was promoting. "Our children are the basis of our ambitions," it reminded them. "If we stop a minute and analyze our ambitions we find first that we want to give them a good start in life, which is an education." The article certainly praised exclusiveness as well—advising that "the proper daily association will serve to mould them into a better generation"—but only as one aspect of a child-friendly environment that was not overtly racialized.[25]

At the same time, the traditional block-level segregation patterns of most Jim Crow cities had long meant that Black and white homes were rarely far apart, yet the increased use of racial restrictions along the outskirts of town was altering the desirability of mixed-use, mixed-race neighborhoods.[26] Once the prospects of white middle-class children became tied to the broad range of restrictions in residential parks, unprotected property came to be seen as less desirable for child-rearing, and therefore, less valuable. White families who either could not or would not move to the suburbs soon found that the houses surrounding them were far more attractive to Black families seeking better housing in which to raise their own children than to other whites. Even so, the remaining white residents still expected the norms of Jim Crow to hold. According to the dictates of white supremacy, it was acceptable for white and Black families to live close by so long as Black families were forced into inferior housing around the corner or on a back alley, but it was not acceptable for them to live on the same block as equals. When an affluent Black family purchased a vacant house on a "white" block, their new white neighbors did not simply fear a loss of status; they also worried that their own children might become romantically involved with the attractive, well-dressed, and well-educated Black adolescents moving next door.[27] For them, an interracial relationship remained a taboo that would disgrace the family.

Starting with Baltimore and then spreading to other Jim Crow cities, racial transition in established neighborhoods sparked calls for segregation ordinances to prevent more Black families from moving onto majority-white blocks.[28] From their inception, the ordinances were largely doomed to fail because they could not force white, middle-class parents to buy houses that no longer met the standard for white, middle-class child-rearing, regardless of who lived next door. Therefore, selling a home in an older part of the city to the highest bidder usually meant selling to a Black family, particularly when the house was near a Black school, since the cities that passed segregation ordinances also had school systems racially segregated by law. With fewer options open to them, Black parents simply valued the houses more; they, too, wished to raise their children in healthier and safer surroundings. Accordingly, the *Dallas Express* protested laws designed to confine "our people to the undesirable parts of the city where the environment for the rearing of children would be anything but pleasant."[29]

The US Supreme Court in *Buchanan v. Warley* (1917) sided with the home sellers rather than their former white neighbors or even the Black protesters who condemned the ordinances as violations of the Fourteenth Amendment. The court could not seriously confront residential segregation without threatening *Plessy v. Ferguson*'s "separate but equal" doctrine, which it was unwilling to do. Instead, it ruled that the ordinances created unsalable properties, and thereby, interfered with the constitutional right to alienation.[30] *Buchanan*, however, did not end the desire to preserve white housing in areas that no longer met the national standard for white, middle-class child-rearing, especially after the "Great Migration" again turned de jure segregation into a national issue.[31]

Across the country, white residents living in aging neighborhoods without racial covenants launched a new wave of violence once local officials and the courts appeared unwilling to prohibit Black families from purchasing the home next door. While interest in segregating a broader spectrum of households remained, it was concern over preservation of the nation's Black-white hierarchy that stoked the hysteria during and after World War I. Indeed, the US military only segregated Black soldiers during the war. Benjamin Davis, the editor of Atlanta's most influential Black newspaper, lamented, "There is no nation on earth that hates a part of itself as the white man hates the Negro in this country."[32] Within that context, urban whites throughout the nation watched with intense interest as local officials in southern cities continued to test the boundaries of what a nominally democratic nation would bear. Southern experimentation might provide cover for segregation efforts in northern and western cities as the number of Black residents living outside the South continued to expand.

Experts from the zoning movement seemed more than willing to help local officials find a solution to the "Negro problem."[33] Planners claimed that both the demand for segregation ordinances and the violence that followed their defeat demonstrated that de jure segregation was necessary to maintain peace and promote the general welfare. Some wondered whether racial zoning, as part of a comprehensive zoning plan, might survive judicial review by promising Black families better housing opportunities. The segregation ordinances that had been declared unconstitutional were meant to impede racial transition on individual blocks, which denied Black families access to better homes when white residents moved out to the suburbs. In contrast, racial zones would include residential districts for Black middle-class child-rearing on undeveloped land or in designated transition areas.[34]

In 1924, Atlanta became the first city to adopt a zoning ordinance that included explicitly defined "colored districts." Eminent planner Robert Whitten, who helped design the nation's first comprehensive zoning plan in New York City, served as the consultant. Supporters were disappointed, if not surprised, when the Georgia Supreme Court applied *Buchanan* to racial zoning as well, but hope remained.[35] While de jure segregation through legal mandate—a specific law—was a dead end, de jure segregation through intentional government action—policy and practice—was still a possibility worth pursuing and one that might appease Black activists if "colored districts" received equal amenities.[36]

Consequently, even after racial zoning failed its first judicial test, the racial districting maps continued to provide important tools for distributing child-centered resources such as schools and playgrounds.[37] Although the race districts could no longer be enforced through police power, the public amenities placed within them served as particularly strong inducements for middle-class homebuyers focused on upward mobility for their children, creating an ideal opportunity to manipulate where families lived. Developers and planners—overlapping groups by the 1920s—had long understood the value of child-centered amenities to profitable residential development. In 1927, esteemed planner Lawson Purdy used the extensive investment in schools and parks in Westchester County, New York, to illustrate the connection between child-rearing and property values: "Westchester County has the means to provide these parks, schools and private playgrounds, and they in their turn attract families of wealth who increase the buying power and add to the value of land."[38] Strong demand among affluent white families was also the most effective way to maintain exclusion since homeowners would not feel compelled to sell their homes to families whose social status was lower than their own.

As with other early twentieth-century race regulations, the manipulation of schools and playgrounds to cement permanent racial zones began in Jim Crow cities—where it was strikingly effective. First, southern cities were far more likely to publish informal race districting maps even after it was clear that racial zoning would not pass judicial review. Second, state-required segregation allowed local governments to manipulate school sites for maximum effect with few obstacles. Third, southern elites purposefully undermined public-school funding, which limited the number of brick schools blessed with modern toilet facilities—even in urban areas—well into the twentieth century; if all neighborhoods had had access to modern school buildings, then new schools would not have served as the lures to residential parks that they would become. And fourth, during the 1920s, southern cities were growing at a faster rate than those in other regions, resulting in an unprecedented drive for new schools. While the South had only seven of the nation's fifty largest cities during the First World War, the number would double by the second, when the percentage of southerners living in urban areas finally matched that of Americans as a whole back in 1890. The region's rapid urbanization turned small, wooden schoolhouses into overcrowded firetraps. Frustrated middle- and working-class parents, both Black and white, demanded safe, modern school buildings that were spacious enough to accommodate every student.[39]

The ensuing building programs frequently coincided with the passage of comprehensive zoning ordinances in southern cities. Education experts and planning consultants alike agreed that the building programs required close collaboration between school boards and planning commissions. Both favored the interests of local developers, who often sat on one committee or the other. Board members almost always assented to locating new white schools near recently platted residential parks, facilitating the population shift of white residents out of mixed-race, mixed-use areas with antiquated, poorly maintained schools. Simultaneously, they located new Black schools "deep" within areas that had been set aside for Black development, facilitating the population shift of Black residents away from "white" residential areas, where Black schools were closed with increasing regularity. Because southern districts did not yet furnish transportation, living in an area with no school for one's race led to long, hazardous commutes for young schoolchildren, which parents tried to avoid. This strategy was so successful, it would be emulated in cities across the nation experiencing demographic shifts from the Great Migration.[40]

By the end of the 1920s, the building programs had markedly increased the distance between Black and white schools in Jim Crow cities, launching a process of ghetto formation that would have been ruled unconstitutional under any other form of government action. They also funneled children into different schools based on the affluence of individual residential communities, adding socioeconomic status to the draw of certain schools.[41] This advantage helped keep prestigious residential parks in high demand among affluent white families; and so long as those properties remained in demand, homeowners had no reason to sell to Black buyers. Similarly, the shift of Black homes to the opposite side of town meant that developers had little cause for concern from Black "interlopers" seeking to purchase homes too near the entrance of a residential park. Most Black parents refused to live in a neighborhood located far from the friends and institutions they cared about, let alone one in which their children had no access to a convenient and well-maintained school.[42]

With that said, modern schools were not a magic bullet for saving "white" homes in areas considered undesirable for middle-class child-rearing any more than segregation ordinances had been. But such experiments were rarely tested, since educational experts and planners insisted upon the purchase of oversized school sites along the outskirts of town, while discouraging the replacement of aging white schools in the established, mixed-use areas where most children lived. Thus, white families in those areas found that racial covenants failed them as well, even though the Supreme Court would declare them to be enforceable private contracts in *Corrigan v. Buckley* (1926).[43] In neighborhoods with traditional development and an inferior white school, racial covenants quickly turned "white" houses into unsalable properties because their demand among middle-class white homebuyers was low. Affluent white parents had been taught for more than a century that their primary responsibility was to ensure their children's future success. Homes in older areas of the city could no longer compete with residential parks. Many homeowners in those neighborhoods came to regret signing a racial covenant when they could not find a white buyer for their homes, a phenomenon not limited to the South.[44]

During the economic boom years following World War II, federal housing policies born during the New Deal guaranteed inexpensive amortized mortgages to less affluent whites who could not afford to purchase a suburban home during the interwar period. Pushed forward by residential park developers who controlled NAREB, this new entitlement invited them to abandon their old neighborhoods near downtown and move out to the suburbs. There, they could enjoy at least some of the benefits of the more prestigious residential parks, including new schools and, thanks to *Corrigan v. Buckley* and the *Underwriting Manual*, racial exclusion as well.[45]

For their part, Black middle-class families realized that, despite their exhaustive efforts to build child-centered neighborhoods, their dreams of nurturing their children in thriving residential parks remained just as elusive as ever. All the promises made by planners and local officials fell flat: informal racial zoning did not unlock new opportunities for homeownership either in the areas left behind by whites or in those set aside for Black development. Instead, the practice of "redlining" denied many Black families access to affordable mortgages through the Federal Housing Administration's mortgage insurance program. The 1936 *Underwriting Manual* urged federal valuators to downgrade properties that lacked appeal to white parents. By that time, racial exclusion had become so entrenched within the dominant norms of white child-rearing that the presence of a few affluent Black families was enough for federal valuators to rate an entire area as undesirable. Even properties in all-Black residential parks with owner-occupied, single-family homes and new schools were denied access to the benefits of an inexpensive mortgage, despite the strong demand for stand-alone houses among Black families.[46]

In the end, the loss of investment in Black neighborhoods—along with continued municipal neglect, economic isolation, overcrowding, and unenforced zoning protections—confirmed the worst fears of Black activists. They had warily accepted the assurances that Black residential areas would receive equal investment to white ones, even though their past experiences had made that doubtful. What other options did they have?[47] Unlike prosperous white parents, Black families lacked the political power to consistently shape residential development to their children's advantage.

Although the New Deal represented a watershed in federal housing policy, it did not substantially change the dynamic between parenting, housing, schooling, and residential segregation beyond expanding its reach to more white families.[48] Thus, rather than wade into the more well-tread, post–New Deal history of segregation, this study reaches back to the nation's founding to determine how this dynamic first formed and why it became entrenched in dominant, middle-class norms long before Franklin Roosevelt's election. It also examines the role that residential park developers, planning consultants, educational and social science experts, southern officials, and the courts played in the process.[49]

Social Class and Residential Segregation

A larger proportion of whites gained access to the suburban version of the "American dream" after World War II, but before then, socioeconomic status framed disputes over residential development as much as race did.[50] Members of the affluent, white middle class who embraced the dominant ideas about parenting and domesticity belonged to the business and professional classes that manifested a strong desire for upward mobility. This segment of the population could afford to purchase a home that met the standards of the parent education movement. The men held salaried "positions" that required an increasing level of education while their wives stayed home to pour their time and energy into raising children. Together, they expended their financial resources to provide their offspring with the advantages they believed were necessary for success in a stratified, urban economy.

Certainly, the concept of a "normative" family left out many households that did not fit its narrow definition, yet practically all lives were affected by the dominance of households comprising two parents with children, or at least the expectation of children. Government resources supported and encouraged them, housing development catered to their needs, and residential property values reflected each neighborhood's suitability for white, middle-class child-rearing. In taking seriously the ubiquitous rhetoric surrounding the "family," which almost always meant the presence of children, this study writes parenting back into the narrative of urban development and residential segregation.[51]

Of course, white working-class families wanted their children to have decent homes and to attend modern schools as well, but they still wished to live close to work and liked their neighborhoods. Fathers, mothers, and sometimes children worked outside the home in low-wage jobs that required physical labor and less education. All members of the family contributed to the household income in whatever ways they could, and parents did not "baby" their children but, rather, gave them free range of the city.[52] In between the affluent middle-class and working-class families were the "less affluent," lower-middle-class parents who lacked the resources needed to move into residential parks or to fully engage in the child-rearing strategies of better-off parents. During the early twentieth century, they were more likely to side with the white working class, expressing outrage that de jure segregation could not "protect" their blocks from racial transition. They were also furious that residential parks received superior schools to the ones in older areas of the city where their children lived.

White elites, on the other hand, had little reason to worry about the future social standing, political influence, or economic success of their children and so had less motivation to concern themselves with the tedium of day-to-day parenting. Their children's status was secure, regardless of where they lived or who their companions were. Still, elites usually chose to associate with one another. Together, they controlled urban development through a series of interlocking directorates, which included the boards of local banks, construction companies, utilities, insurance companies, real estate companies, and a host of other interconnected industries that made money from residential park development. They also served in leadership positions in the chamber of commerce, a powerful organization that frequently overshadowed local government.

Although the rise of residential segregation was a national story, southern developers and their allies in government eagerly led the parade. Black southerners made up a much larger percentage of far smaller urban populations than those in the North or West. Plus, the region had a more clearly defined tradition of mixed-race housing patterns that made it more difficult to create the vast, isolated ghettos that would come to define twentieth-century urban America—North, West, and South. As historian Kevin Kruse found in his postwar study of Atlanta, whites who wished to restrict where Black citizens lived were "less successful than their counterparts in the North," for "the black population they challenged was both larger and stronger."[53]

Consequently, the Black middle class in many Jim Crow cities served as an impressive counterbalance to white supremacy. Both women and men established civic clubs, neighborhood associations, and professional networks to challenge racial subjugation as well as the economic and social dominance of the white middle class. Sometimes fathers worked in skilled occupations that were more typically associated with the white working class, and mothers were much more likely to work outside the home. But they shared a strong desire for upward mobility: they engaged in intensive parenting strategies before and after exhausting days at work, and they pooled their resources to purchase single-family homes that would furnish better surroundings for their children. A smaller network of businessmen and professionals filled the ranks of the Black elite, who represented middle-class interests in Black-owned newspapers and in the leadership positions of civil rights organizations such as the Odd Fellows and NAACP. Affluent and highly educated, they sat on the committees that negotiated with the white power structure to obtain modern schools and other tax-supported services for Black families. Black elites also led the fight to obtain equal treatment under the law.[54]

This small Black elite joined with the larger Black middle class to fight for "better homes" and "great schools" for Black children. As part of the effort, they launched a parent education movement among Black working-class families to encourage "good" parenting, at least as defined by middle-class reformers. Nevertheless, residential park development undercut their herculean efforts. White families moved to segregated areas on the outskirts of town and then used their tremendous political, social, and economic power to acquire a disproportionate number of public resources for themselves. Economic development almost always followed them, creating lopsided metropolises that gutted opportunity for Black children in the name of increased mobility for white ones.[55]

CHAPTER 1

Parenting Helps Build a Foundation for Lasting Segregation

In 1788, Jacques Pierre Brissot, the leader of a moderate bourgeois faction in revolutionary France, visited the United States as part of his antislavery work. While in Boston, he recognized the extraordinary worth placed on progeny, admiringly describing Bostonians as "almost idolatrous parents."[1] A century later, Chinese immigrant Yan Phou Lee noted, "Americans lay more stress on the duty of parents towards their children, while the Chinese insist too much on the duty of children towards their parents."[2] These two observations bookended the emergence of a distinctly American style of parenting that flourished among the urban middle class. Affluent parents adopted new, "intensive" child-rearing strategies that demanded far more of their time, energy, and resources, requiring them to sacrifice their own desires in favor of their children's interests.[3]

As Brissot's remark suggests, the roots of intensive parenting date back to the Revolutionary period. Wishing to put Enlightenment theories into practice, the founding generation tied child-rearing to citizenship. The concept of "republican motherhood" designated the affluent white home as the key institution for developing a virtuous citizenry that would carry forth the nation's political experiment and safeguard its future.[4] Building on that foundation, white, middle-class parents further embraced intensive parenting during the market revolution to help ensure that their children would land safely in the competitive, free-market economy. Although industrialization would lead to greater income inequality, it also created more avenues for upward mobility. Together, a republican form of government and a capitalist economy produced an enticing combination of opportunity and risk. Within this context, the new middle class had the most to gain as well as the most to lose. Without the potential for economic and social advancement, the nation would not have generated such an intense class of strivers, whose tastes and values would come to dominate American culture. At the same time, expanding income inequality made the possibility of downward mobility a greater threat. Anxious parents felt that they must pour more resources into each child to nurture economically successful offspring. Intensive parenting combined with higher levels of education could ensure that one's children did not fall into the ranks of low-paid workers, who generally lacked the wherewithal to give their children an upward boost.

Intensive parenting was available to any family with the resources and knowledge to engage in it, the financial ability to withdraw their children from the labor market, and the means to control fertility. Affluent Black parents had more incentives to adopt these strategies because their task had been made infinitely harder through racial subjugation. During the nineteenth century, slavery was increasingly justified through scientific racism, which placed all Black children at the bottom of the nation's social hierarchy whether they suffered enslavement or not. Even though upward mobility remained possible, Black families struggled against racial barriers aimed at them regardless of their achievements, intelligence, or respectability. Affluent Black families used intensive parenting strategies to push back against scientific racism, even as one of the core impulses for promoting intensive parenting—the development of good citizens—excluded their children.

As the nineteenth century came to an end, rapid urbanization raised new concerns about less privileged children, at least from the perspective of the middle class, who were appalled by the "free-range parenting" of the working class. Meanwhile, working-class parents—and especially immigrants—spurned many of the assumptions of middle-class child-rearing. They lacked the means to withdraw their children from paid labor, let alone arduous household chores, and criticized "American" parents for babying their offspring.[5] Consequently, reformers sought solutions that bypassed working-class parents: children would acquire middle-class values in public schools and on playgrounds where they would unlearn the "aberrant" behavior that not only threatened the nation's future but might also corrupt respectable children living nearby.

Both Black and white reformers advanced "child-saving" campaigns that included compulsory school attendance, child labor laws, and supervised playgrounds in an ambitious effort to mold the behavior of working-class children, but white reformers showed far less concern for Black children. They failed to see them as burgeoning citizens, unlike the working-class children of European immigrants who might outvote middle-class whites one day. During a time when scientists obsessed over racial hierarchy, many whites rationalized their actions by claiming that Black children would not benefit from child-centered reforms because they could not advance beyond the limits of their race.[6] Thus, Black middle-class reformers—with far fewer resources than their white counterparts—assumed practically sole responsibility for the reform efforts targeting Black working-class families. They knew that uplifting impoverished Black children was crucial to providing opportunity to their own since the negative depictions of the poorest Black child would still affect the characterizations of even the most affluent and respectable.

The limited reforms accomplished in the name of working-class children were largely overwhelmed by the lasting damage accomplished through the intensification of segregation at the end of the Progressive Era. Because most advice manuals urged parents to shelter their children from the adult world in single-family homes for as long as they could afford to do so, the stage was set for child-rearing to become a central factor in the growth and persistence of residential segregation. Before the Civil War, most families made individual housing decisions as distinct actors, even when encouraged by popular moralists to consider the responsibilities of child-rearing when choosing a home. After the turn of the century, affluent white parents acted collectively when selecting home sites, thereby transforming residential development in ways that drove the expansion of segregation.

The Goals of Parenting Transformed

The early English colonists of Massachusetts Bay would not have understood the child-centered home of nineteenth-century, middle-class New England, where intensive parenting first emerged. They depended on their children for household production, which entailed hard work and genuine responsibility at young ages. Child labor was not only essential for the day-to-day survival of most families, but pious parents also considered hard work essential to keeping their children out of Satan's reach. Concern for the afterlife was much more important than concern for the present since they believed their main duty was to shield their offspring from eternal damnation. And because they thought all babies were born with the stain of original sin, parents implemented strict discipline, including corporal punishment, to foster obedience to God and, thereby, spare their beloved children from an eternity in hell. With child mortality highest for the youngest members of the family, it was never too early to "conquer" a baby's will. Famed minister Cotton Mather warned parents, "Better whipt, than damned."[7]

As the eighteenth century progressed, new ideas of childhood innocence slowly began to challenge old ideas of infant depravity. Philosophers such as John Locke and Jean Jacques Rousseau argued that children were born pure and malleable. Locke insisted that virtue developed more thoroughly from patient nurturance than from fear and the suppression of will. In challenging the belief that the devil must be beaten out of even small children, Locke advised parents to inspire their children's curiosity and use reason to shape their character. Seventy years later, as the chain of events that led to the American Revolution began, Rousseau advanced a concept of childhood in which children—or at least boys—would be permitted to play freely. He admonished those who worried about the dangers of idleness: "You are alarmed to see him consume his early years in doing nothing. What? Is it nothing to be happy? Is it nothing to jump, play, and run all day? He will never be so busy in his life." William Blake's *Songs of Innocence and Experience*, published in 1789, further popularized the idea that childhood was a special time in life.[8]

It was within this context that the American Revolution further transformed parenting by offering married women with children a pronounced role in the new republic. Although denied the right to vote or even own property, they were encouraged to accept "republican motherhood." They would educate their young children according to the ideals of the Enlightenment by modeling virtuous behavior and teaching the values of citizenship through patient guidance and nurturance. The hope was that Mother's diligence would ensure that the passion for the American experiment would outlive the revolutionary generation.[9]

The dawn of republican motherhood coincided with the beginning of America's centuries-long drop in the fertility rate of affluent white women. According to historian Susan Klepp, the nineteenth century's well-documented decline in fertility began during the revolutionary era. Between 1740 and 1760, the sky-high fertility rate of colonial women was a wonder even to contemporaries. Soon thereafter, women began rejecting decades of childbearing. The reason remained unclear, although dislocation caused by a decade of war and its aftermath certainly had an impact.[10] Once the new nation recovered, the fertility rate continued to drop, perhaps as a rational response to the mounting burdens of child-rearing. While republican motherhood elevated the status of young mothers, the Lockean idea of childhood placed immense pressure on them, as they frequently attested to in their diaries and letters. For example, in 1829, Abigail Hyde of Bolton, Connecticut, described herself as "so far" from "meeting the high responsibilities" of motherhood that the "conviction" of her "deficiency" was "sometimes overwhelming."[11] If children were, indeed, born "blank slates," their mothers understood that the blame for any character flaws should fall directly on themselves as the primary caregivers; thus, they worked hard to avoid incriminating outcomes.

Immigrants were often astounded by the selfless devotion of American mothers. In 1837, educator and journalist Francis Grund, a Bohemian immigrant, worried that the anxiety of "overparenting" was dooming young women "to an early decay." The "principal cause of this sudden decline" was "the great assiduity with which American ladies discharge their duties as mothers." "This continued application to the most arduous duties, the increasing care and anxiety for the progress and welfare of their children," he cautioned, "undermine constitutions, already by nature sufficiently delicate." He feared that "health and beauty" were being "sacrificed" for the children's sake. No human could "ever requite the tender cares of a mother," he reasoned. "But it appears to me that the Americans have, in this respect, obligations immeasurably greater than those of the inhabitants of any other country."[12]

By midcentury, intensive parenting had become the established norm for middle-class child-rearing, as urban mothers devoted more time to their children and less time to other aspects of housekeeping. T. S. Arthur, whose frequent articles in *Godey's Lady's Book* helped define the boundaries of proper middle-class deportment, published a popular advice book to teach mothers "The Right Way and the Wrong Way" to parent, as its not-so-subtle title suggested. He prodded middle-class mothers to hire domestic help for "all the complicated duties of housekeeping" so they might focus their energy on child-rearing. The use of domestics would enable a mother to "be careful of her strength, her health, and her life, *for her children's sake*" (emphasis in original). Only then might she "give herself more exclusively to" her children's "highest and best interests" as a "sentinel" who would "never sleep at her post."[13]

The political rhetoric of virtuous citizenship merged nicely with the economic interests of the nation's rising middle class, which developed alongside the market revolution. In the urban areas most affected by the changing economy, intensive parenting strategies—including formal schooling and a childhood extended through adolescence—were remarkably effective at endowing children with an advantage in the nation's more stratified economy. Middle-class fathers departed each morning for the well-paid and relatively stable white-collar jobs that supported market production. The mothers stayed at home where their primary responsibility was childcare, while the children spent most of their time at play or in school where they learned the disposition, habits, and skills needed for success in the market economy.[14]

Even as consumerism replaced household production and reduced the complexity of middle-class housekeeping, the demands of intensive parenting could more than offset the gains. T. S. Arthur supposed that mothers of "olden time" could manage "without failure" the "operations of the needle, the mysteries of culinary science, and all the complicated duties of housekeeping" alongside child-rearing. Yet, because "the structure of society" had changed, the modern "division of labour" required "new and extended effort" from "educated" mothers.[15] Preparing one's children for middle-class life demanded greater knowledge and new skills, which meant eschewing hired caregivers. Catharine Beecher, one of the most influential advocates of the new domesticity, thought it was "to be regretted" when mothers relinquished influence over their children to domestics, whom she believed had a "pernicious" effect on the young. A mother simply could not trust someone who lived in poverty—an immigrant at that—to furnish a proper moral example to her children or model the characteristics vital to economic success.[16] But middle-class families did hire domestics to accomplish the household drudgery, freeing up Mother's time and attention for child-rearing while also allowing middle-class children to spend more of their days free from toil. According to historian Jeanne Boydston, "Laundry, housecleaning, and some cooking were among the particular chores that had traditionally been performed by younger females in the family, but from which the emerging middle class was increasingly withdrawing its daughters in favor of education and the development of more refined social skills."[17]

Although religion remained central to the lives of middle-class families, child-rearing and education became less about religious duty and more about nurturing exceptional children who would achieve worldly success in a competitive economy. In prior generations, authoritarian parenting was intended to keep children from "falling" into sin. Now, intensive parenting would keep children from "falling" into the factory. Education took on new meaning as well. During the colonial period, Protestants supported educational endeavors to train ministers and to teach their children to read the Bible; neither agricultural pursuits nor home production required schooling. Amid the market revolution, however, education became the means to achieve upward mobility.[18] The nation's first public high schools were popular with middle-class parents who understood that prolonged schooling would allow their children to land more safely in a stratified economy, while reassuring them that they were doing right by the less fortunate, who, if talented enough, might also gain entry. The key was to keep one's sons in school and out of the workforce for as long as possible, despite the financial sacrifices it would entail. Likewise, middle-class girls attended high school so they could marry well and then help educate their children for upward mobility.[19]

As the expectations for middle-class parenting expanded, the number of children per family continued to decrease. This trend did not extend to southern states since patriarchal households remained stronger there and the market revolution did not produce a significant urban middle class, at least not during the antebellum period. For the remainder of the country, though, the average number of babies born to white women dropped by 50 percent between 1800 and 1900, from 7.04 to 3.56. The number would fall by an additional 41 percent between 1900 and 1936. According to Susan Klepp, middle-class parents saw smaller families as "a positive good," which was a major change from the colonial period when small families would have been seen "as a personal and social misfortune." Fewer babies and more space between conceptions allowed parents to maximize the advantages they were willing and able to bestow upon their children. In this way, they could facilitate upward mobility in a cutthroat economy that sometimes resulted in far more losers than winners, particularly during "panics" and other periods of economic decline.[20]

Simultaneously, the advent of Western childhood added a more righteous justification for coddling one's children. William Wordsworth's "Ode: Intimations of Immortality from Recollections of Early Childhood" (1807) fundamentally changed the child's place in western culture. "Heaven lies about us in our infancy!" the ode proclaimed, erasing once and for all the stain of original sin. According to literary critic Barbara Garlitz, "The Ode was to the first half of the nineteenth century what *The Origins of Species* was to the second half." Building on themes from the Enlightenment, Wordsworth made a powerful appeal for adults to treat children well. As heavenly creatures, each was a gift delivered straight from God, and thus, each child perfectly reflected His goodness. In 1841, well-known art and literary critic Henry Tuckerman described the seismic influence the ode had on his generation: one could "scarcely look upon the young with indifference. The parent must thence derive a new sense of the sacredness of children, and learn to reverence their innocence." Soon after, idyllic views of innocent childhood—draped in praise and sentimentality—appeared everywhere.[21]

As children became the nucleus of middle-class domesticity, parents organized their households, daily routines, and calendars around their offspring. Even Calvinists were foregoing threats of physical punishment in favor of moral suasion. In 1834, Elizabeth Dwight Sedgwick published a popular story titled "The Christmas Box" that extolled the benefits of molding children's behavior through affection rather than fear. In the story, "either one parent or the other was with the children nearly all the time." The father participated in active parenting as well as the mother. They engaged their children in conversation, walked with them, told them stories, read aloud to them, and participated in their games. Moreover, they rewarded good behavior with presents, illustrating consumerism's rising impact on intensive parenting, which encapsulated the growing tension between restraint and indulgence that affluent parents navigated. Their belief in the natural goodness of children led them to err too much on the side of indulgence to avoid inadvertently dimming their children's spirits. As a result, summer vacations, birthdays, and Christmas became new opportunities to celebrate their children.[22]

Perhaps no fictional character represented the glorified position of the affluent child better than golden-haired Eva St. Clare of *Uncle Tom's Cabin*, the most successful novel before the Civil War.[23] Eva's father suffered profoundly after her death, having realized that all his "interests and hopes" had "unconsciously wound themselves around" his daughter. His sorrow perfectly captured the sentiments of nineteenth-century middle-class parenting: "It was for Eva that he had managed his property; it was for Eva that he had planned the disposal of his time; and, to do this and that for Eva,—to buy, improve, alter, and arrange, or dispose something for her,—had been so long his habit, that now she was gone, there seemed nothing to be thought of, and nothing to be done."[24] In devising the character of Augustine St. Clare, Harriet Beecher Stowe placed her urban, middle-class view of parenting onto a southern slaveholder. St. Clare's lack of purpose after losing his angelic daughter depicted the child-centered home that Stowe's sister, Catharine Beecher, espoused in her writings on domesticity. In fact, Beecher, who never married, moved in with her sister's family to care for the children while Stowe finished her masterpiece.[25]

Catharine Beecher's most influential work, *A Treatise on Domestic Economy*, had been so popular that it was reprinted almost annually between 1841, when it first appeared, and 1856. It instructed mothers to keep their children "in a happy state of mind" through "constant effort" and a "steady course." Mothers should "take the attitude of advisors," using "gentle and kind remonstrances" while avoiding "severe and angry tones." They must also shun indulgence, which reflected parental indolence, and instead play with their children to strengthen the maternal bond. "Those, who will join with children, and help them along in their sports," Beecher counseled, "will learn, by this mode, to understand the feelings and interests of childhood; while at the same time, they secure a degree of confidence and affection, which cannot be gained so easily, in any other way."[26] Parenting rooted in perpetual attention and patient care necessitated that mothers stay home and remain focused on their children. This "ideal" was certainly not what all middle-class women wanted, but it quickly became normalized. More and more parents responded by having fewer children.[27]

As with other moralizers, Beecher imbedded her ideas about middle-class domesticity in a comfortable cottage set picturesquely in semirural surroundings. The conventional wisdom was that a single-family house in a peaceful neighborhood would shelter children from the noise and filth of the city and its morally suspect inhabitants. Its extravagant yard would furnish children with a healthy space to play while remaining under the close supervision of their parents. In 1853, the Reverend William G. Eliot maintained, "The foundation of our free institutions is in our love, as a people, for our homes. The strength of our country is found, not in the declaration that all men are created equal, but in the quiet influence of the fireside."[28]

The single-family house was further tied to intensive parenting because reformers thought it could extend childhood. Most immigrant and working-class children left home during adolescence, but middle-class children remained pampered in their childhood homes significantly longer. Native-born sons from affluent families often postponed marriage until their thirties, continuing to live with their parents until they had completed their education and had the wherewithal to support a family at an economic level comparable to what they had grown accustomed to as children.[29] Parenting advice suggested that even adult children should be prevented from "encountering prematurely the seductive wiles that the wicked world" would "throw around them."[30] The single-family house could also address the lack of privacy almost all experienced before the nineteenth century. Separate bedrooms would postpone the end of innocence by creating a distinctly asexual childhood.[31]

It did not take long for schools to be sentimentalized in the same vein as single-family houses. For example, famed nineteenth-century architect Gervase Wheeler compared the ideal school to an idyllic home: just as a single-family house could ensure that "the inducement to wander from it would have but little allurement," schoolhouses could be designed as "cheerful, smiling homes of the heart" that "children would love to linger around." He bemoaned the "severe temples of learning" that were "rude, often incommodious, and generally situated in by no means a pleasant site" with "only their admirable intention to recommend them."³² Thus, antebellum experts and reformers combined schooling and detached housing with intensive parenting in ways that helped fuel upward mobility for middle-class children. At the same time, the romanticized notions of childhood made extensive efforts to provide opportunities for one's offspring, even at the expense of other children, appear more noble—as a moral duty to God and country rather than as an act of selfishness.

The Racialized Limits of Intensive Parenting

Black middle-class parents often adopted a more vigorous and disciplined form of parenting because their children encountered dangers within the city that were mere phantoms for the white, middle-class child. For them, intensive parenting was based on a politics of respectability that left no room for error. Although affluent Black parents also sought single-family homes in good neighborhoods, they rarely had the luxury to engage in the democratic forms of child-rearing embraced by affluent white parents, who were encouraged to prepare their children for white-collar work as well as democratic citizenship. In Black families, a child's behavior was a matter of life or death. Some authoritarian strategies remained necessary to keep children safe in the face of extreme racial violence. Still, Black middle-class parents eschewed corporal punishment and, instead, "counseled with" their children.³³

While the worst abuses of slavery were usually condemned in the North, even there, Black and white abolitionists who demanded equal citizenship for Black Americans were labeled "zealots," "madmen," "fanatics," and "political incendiaries" who sought "amalgamation" and a "black government." Most white northerners supported segregated schools, the disfranchisement of Black men, and laws that would bar or at least strongly discourage Black Americans from settling in "their" states, which included those in abolitionist New England. An 1835 petition to the Connecticut legislature revealed that many of New Haven's white residents opposed abolitionist agitation because they presumed emancipation would result in the state being "overrun with an abandoned and desperate population," although competition for good jobs seemed more of a concern than poverty. Current Black residents, they warned, were already "plucking the bread from the mouth of the white laborer" and "determined to become our Lawyers, Physicians, Divines and Statesmen." The petitioners also claimed that Black neighbors would lower property values, "for who," they asked, "will have a negro neighborhood" and allow his "wife and children" to "be driven from the pavement." The remedy sought was not residential segregation but laws preventing African Americans from entering the state at all as well as de jure efforts to "drive out" the existing Black population.³⁴

Black middle-class youth seemed particularly unwelcome. Just a year before the above petition was signed, the white residents of Canterbury, Connecticut, attacked Prudence Crandall for operating a school for Black girls. It had originally served white students, but parents withdrew their daughters after Crandall admitted a Black pupil. Fearing that the school might attract more Black families, local officials passed a law in 1833 making it illegal to teach Black youth from outside the state. Crandall remained unintimidated but was forced to close the school the following year after white residents began violently harassing her students.[35] That same year, Boston's mayor "induced" a "very respectable and clever" Black student to "withdraw" from the highly acclaimed Boston Latin School after strong "opposition to his admission" emerged. The adolescent had enrolled in the school so that he would be able to seek "higher employment." His sister, an esteemed schoolteacher, also experienced threats when she attempted to move to a better "quarter."[36]

By midcentury, the exclusion of Black children from "white" schools was largely accomplished. In *Roberts v. Boston* (1849), the Massachusetts Supreme Court agreed that the school board could segregate Black and white children, despite the small number of Black families living in Boston at the time.[37] The states of the "Old Northwest" also excluded Black students, even though the US Congress had granted property owners living in the territories the right to send their children to township schools regardless of race. In Indiana, a delegate attending the state's 1850 constitutional convention claimed that white residents had risen "en masse" to expel Black students from the public schools, shouting, "Your children shall not go to school with our children." He argued that their uprising represented "a higher law" than the Constitution.[38]

Such outrages reflected the nation's dominant macro culture, which rarely portrayed Black children as innocents in need of protection. Historian Robin Bernstein traced the idea of the "pickaninny"—the Black child forced to bear the burden of a full range of hideous Black stereotypes—to Topsy, the most degraded character from *Uncle Tom's Cabin*. Although Harriet Beecher Stowe allowed Eva, the epitome of the sentimentalized white child, to redeem Topsy to her natural state of innocence, the influential stage adaptation stripped her of all humanity. By the end of the century, Topsy had become the ubiquitous pickaninny commonly depicted in advertisements and popular culture. According to Bernstein, "angelic white children" were often "contrasted with pickaninnies so grotesque as to suggest that only white children *were* children."[39]

Before World War I, roughly 90 percent of Black Americans still lived in the South, where Black parents struggled to protect their children from inhuman violence, harsh working conditions, sexual assault, demeaning stereotypes, and the humiliation of Jim Crow's evolving rituals of subjugation. During Reconstruction, mothers did their best—usually against the wishes of hostile landowners—to withdraw from the fields to focus their energy and abilities on providing their children with more opportunities for upward mobility, while fathers made every

FIGURE 1.1. During the late nineteenth and early twentieth centuries, influential illustrators such as John R. Neill portrayed Eva as the embodiment of the romanticized child in contrast to Topsy, who was characterized as a hopeless mess. Bannerman, *Story of Little Black Sambo*, 51. Courtesy of Illinois State University's Special Collections, Milner Library. Used with permission.

effort to support their families as the lone breadwinner (see figure 1.2). Black women also limited their fertility so they could concentrate their efforts on fewer children and gain more control over their lives.[40] Additionally, Black officeholders and their white allies pushed through legislation for the South's first public school systems. In the feudal society of the antebellum South, education had been available only to the wealthy, who sent their children to expensive private academies. Because the slave codes had made literacy a crime for the enslaved, parents and children alike thronged to the new schools.[41]

Despite these efforts, Black children confronted the daily threat of arbitrary attacks against them or someone they loved. Horrific acts of violence—usually in the form of public lynchings—were meant to terrorize Black communities as part of a continuing effort to preserve white supremacy. According to those who defended the barbarity, lynching was necessary to protect white womanhood from Black "fiends," but in reality, Black girls faced a far greater risk of sexual assault because the criminal justice system rarely, if ever, protected them.[42] As had been true for centuries, white men envisioned Black women as sexually aggressive, so much so that white men believed consent was implied no matter the circumstance. As soon as a Black child hit puberty—and sometimes even earlier—she was cast as the Jezebel who was always available to white men.[43]

FIGURE 1.2. After the Civil War, more Black parents were able to embrace the middle-class ideals of domesticity. "Family Record: Before the War and Since the War" (1880). Courtesy of the Library of Congress.

Young Black girls who worked in white homes were especially vulnerable to rape, but the law afforded them little, if any, relief. In 1895, a member of Kentucky's state legislature opposed raising the age of consent because of what he called the "natural complaisance" of Black girls, who supposedly reached womanhood earlier than white girls. He argued that assault against children as young as eleven should not be considered rape since a man could "easily satisfy his desire without violence." He insisted that raising the age of consent would be "a terrible weapon for evil" when "placed in the hands of a lecherous, sensual negro woman, who for the sake of blackmail or revenge would not hesitate to bring criminal action even though she had been a prostitute since her eleventh year!"[44]

Black middle-class parents attempted to shield their offspring from the ubiquitous stereotypes that left all Black children vulnerable. Intensive parenting helped protect them from harm while furnishing additional avenues of opportunity, especially when white parents denied Black children access to both good housing and modern schools. Most Black middle-class mothers valiantly cared for other people's children in addition to the prodigious efforts they undertook on behalf of their own. They recognized that the fate of their children was tied inextricably to that of impoverished Black children, who often suffered the greatest degradation under white supremacy.[45] While white, middle-class mothers might worry that unruly children would corrupt their own, they never feared that another child's behavior would reflect badly on how their own offspring were perceived within the dominant society. In contrast, Black middle-class parents understood that the conduct of any Black child would shape society's judgment of their own. They were especially concerned about the upbringing of children whose mothers worked in white homes from before sunrise, when domestics cooked breakfast for their white employers' children, to after sunset, when the dinner dishes were done.[46]

The volunteers of Atlanta's Neighborhood Union launched what became perhaps the nation's most exhaustive effort to improve the lives of impoverished children. Atlanta University's annual conference on child welfare had inspired the founding of the Gate City Free Kindergarten Association in 1905 and then the Neighborhood Union shortly thereafter. The association sponsored the city's only nurseries open to Black toddlers as well as the "Mothers' Clubs" that helped educate their parents. In the words of Louie Shivery, who served as the secretary of the Neighborhood Union's executive board, the goal was to "enlighten the parents in the use of love and patience as a means of" discipline rather than "force and authority only."[47] For its part, the union targeted older children through free health clinics, daycares, and playgrounds to make "the West Side of Atlanta a better place to rear our children." It also established a series of "lecture courses" to "instruct and help the mothers of the neighborhood in the proper care of themselves and their infants" and "to impress upon them the importance of fresh air, light, and cleanliness in and around the home." Proposed topics included "Habits and Habit

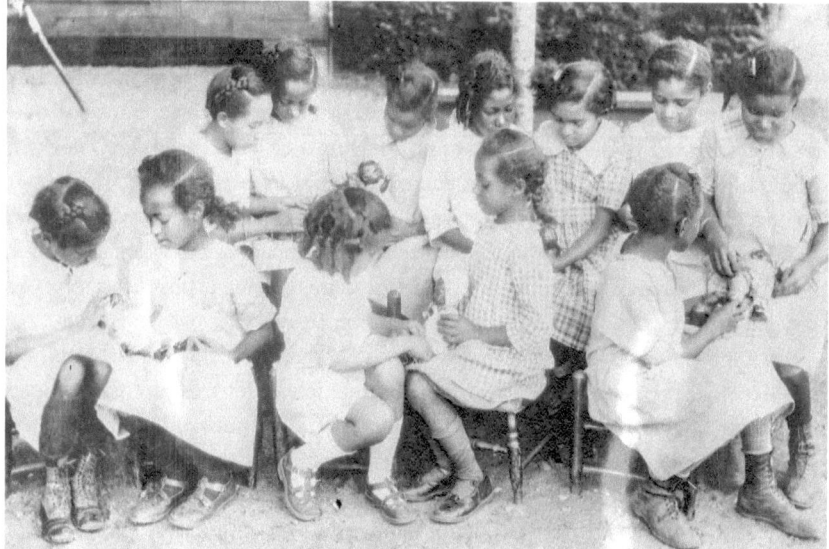

FIGURE 1.3. The volunteers of the Neighborhood Union taught childcare classes to young girls along with their mothers. Elementary Class in Childcare, circa 1910, Neighborhood Union Collection, Atlanta University Center Robert W. Woodruff Library. Used with permission.

Formation (Discipline)," "Play," "A Cross Section of a Child at 5 Years of Age," "A Cross Section of a Child at 11 Years of Age," and "The Problems of Adolescence." The volunteers organized classes for children, too, such as "cooking, sewing, millinery, manual training and general home making," which included childcare (see figure 1.3). They also taught children to play "beneficial sports and games" and disseminated "good literature among the young" to "encourage wholesome thought and action."[48] These after-school programs helped keep working-class children off the streets and engaged in more productive activities.

The Neighborhood Union hoped to temporarily fill the gap created by the negligence of white agencies and government institutions, but their repeated efforts to build coalitions across the color line received painfully little encouragement, as was the experience of Black clubwomen throughout the nation.[49] During the late nineteenth century, the National Association of Colored Women (NACW) had, in vain, sought support from the white members of the newly formed National Congress of Mothers, the forerunner to the National Parent Teachers Association. NACW vice president Frances Ellen Watkins Harper addressed the first annual meeting of the congress in 1897. She agreed with the call "to teach neglected and ignorant mothers how to make their homes the brightest spots on earth" and viewed "an enlightened parenthood" as essential to "train children for useful citizenship" for "the sake of the nation." But when she closed her address, she asked her white audience, "Have you no debt to be paid to the colored motherhood of the country?" "Let us be tried by the same rules and judged by the same standards as other people," she implored. "I ask that you will do what you can to create a public opinion which will not class the worthy and the worthless together" or say "the color of your skin must be a badge of exclusion," and "no valor nor any virtue can redeem you."[50]

A similar message was offered year after year. At the Third National Congress, the unflappable Mary Church Terrell, then serving as president of the NACW, lectured white women on the difference between Black and white motherhood, at least for the middle class: "As a mother of the weaker race clasps to her bosom the babe which she loves as fondly as you love yours, her heart cannot thrill with joyful anticipations of the future. For before her child she sees the thorny path of prejudice and proscription which his little feet must tread." She beseeched them, "In the name of the children of my race, Mothers of the National Congress, I come, asking you to do all in your power by word and deed to give them the opportunities which you desire for your own."[51] At the 1905 convention, Anna Murray, representing the Colored Women's League, pressed white attendees to consider all children "the jewel of our civilization," not just the white ones. Nonetheless, few white reformers, whether mothers or not, extended their efforts to Black children. Historian Marcia Chatelain found that even the youngest Black child "failed to inspire widespread concern or compassion" among most white Americans.[52]

The Child-Centered City

Although white reformers regularly ignored the needs of Black children, they actively imposed their middle-class view of parenting on white working-class families who often resisted their efforts. Because manufacturing work was unsteady and poorly paid, parents relied on their children's labor to round out the household economy. They simply could not afford to withdraw their offspring from the labor market for either school or play. And though industrialization tended to shrink the size of middle-class families, it had the opposite impact on those at the lower end of the income scale. Before the market revolution, the poorest Americans had the fewest number of children because their lives were hard and constricted. Relentless toil reduced the amount of time spouses could spend together, and in some cases, husbands had to leave home for long periods to find work. Death and desertion rates were also much higher for those with less economic security. By the end of the nineteenth century, however, poorer women had the nation's highest fertility rate. The expanding number of wage opportunities for prepubescent children meant that they could contribute directly to the family's subsistence.[53] Therefore, having a larger number of children made economic sense. As one immigrant father explained, "A family's wealth depends on the number of hands it has." Given that viewpoint, intensive parenting merely infantilized children who were old enough to contribute to the family economy.[54]

From the perspective of middle-class reformers, working-class parents who allowed their children to have virtual free range of city streets demonstrated "pathological" behavior. Unsupervised boys, in particular, filched small items and damaged property, knocked over displays and signs, and started fistfights with each other.[55] For working mothers, however, the streets were far safer than unsupervised homes, which poor design and maintenance could turn into fire hazards. Even when parents were at home, working-class dwellings furnished little room for children to play; reformers were rarely sympathetic. "When five hundred boys may vent their energies upon five square miles of hill, wood, and greensward around their town we may leave their doings to their parents," one protested. "When those five hundred must play upon a street a quarter-mile long, crowded with traffic, shops, and saloons, the city should, and *must*, have something to say about the conditions that shall exist on that street."[56]

Reformers organized the early-twentieth-century playground movement to address the problem of free-range children. In a 1912 article for *Outlook* magazine, Arthur Minturn Chase argued for supervised playgrounds to keep working-class children off the streets, where they were often left to "work out their destinies largely according to their own ideas" while "burdened by few rules." His depiction of the problem would have resonated well with his largely middle-class audience: the free-range child sat around on the "cold pavement," ate "over-ripe" food found along the street, and became "intimately enough acquainted with dirt and germs to drive a careful parent distracted." The city "cannot be safe if its children are neglected," he reprimanded. "For the future of the city is in their hands." After all, "the character of the children to-day is a most potent factor in determining the character of the city in years to come."[57]

Mass-produced automobiles further raised the stakes. Chase also described the "pitiful frequency" of automobile accidents that involved a child, who "too heedless" and "too helpless" was "struck down," never to "rise again." According to statistics from the National Highways Protective Association, 183 children were killed and another 384 seriously injured in 1911 alone.[58] Ten years later, the exponential growth in automobile use had made the streets even more dangerous. Between 1921 and 1923, the National Safety Council reported that 14,000 children were killed by automobiles. Reformers believed that supervised playgrounds, when combined with school safety programs and compulsory attendance, would rightfully turn over the streets to the automobile.[59]

Despite evidence that playgrounds would keep kids safe, city councils routinely denied Black children access to them. Between the turn of the century and US entry into World War I, the number of public playgrounds skyrocketed from

100 to almost 4,000. Yet, Harlem-born reformer Ernest T. Atwell, the director of the Playground Association of America's Bureau of Colored Work, discovered that only 3 percent of playgrounds were open to Black residents in 1921.[60] Of the 428 cities that participated in his survey, just 14 permitted both Black and white children to use the same space. Sometimes integration was unintentional. Atwell suggested that local officials in Newport, Kentucky, found themselves in an embarrassing situation when they completed the city's first "small but well equipped playground" for Black children. "Adults of both races" scrambled to determine "what means they might employ" to prevent white children from using "this most alluring spot." "But while the old folks debated the problem," he chuckled, "a mixed group of white and colored youngsters shared and enjoyed the equipment together without fear of friction."[61]

The lack of playground space for Black children extended well beyond the South. North Harlem still had no playground facilities despite multiple petitions, including one with 5,000 names. Atwell admonished his white counterparts: "Colored people are intensely human; live in similar environments; have similar aspirations; require the same infusion of influence and impulses to promote joy; and need preventives and curatives as advocated for other groups." He lamented the "comparatively small provision" of playgrounds relative to the "keen desire on the part of colored people for proper recreation facilities."[62] Even when public space was provided to Black children, the whims of government might take it back at any moment. For example, in 1913, Washington, DC's Willow Tree Playground opened for the benefit of the neighborhood's Black children. By 1925, the immensely popular park had a generous amount of playground equipment, a "shelter house," fountain and wading pool, and sports fields, but all was bulldozed in 1938 to make way for the new Social Security Administration building.[63]

In Atlanta, the Neighborhood Union established the city's first Black playground on Spelman College's campus after local officials refused to act. According to Louie Shivery, the union's recording secretary, members worried about the hundreds of Black children on the streets "at all hours of the day because of the pernicious 'double' and 'triple' sessions practiced in the elementary schools," which "left helpless little children exposed to vice and crime and other evils attendant upon 'sidewalk education.'" A "double" session meant that half the students attended school in the morning and the other half in the afternoon, while "triple" sessions divided the students into three shifts. Both resulted from grossly inadequate school funding. Union volunteers responded by recruiting Black children to help clean up vacant lots that were then converted into supervised playgrounds. Shivery noted that this effort inspired the establishment of Atlanta's first tax-supported playgrounds for white as well as Black children.[64]

In 1914, Atlanta's park commissioner asked the city council to allocate $1.3 million to further expand the number of playground sites. According to the *Atlanta*

Constitution, the aldermen thought the commissioner "was joking." A special committee including representatives from the chamber of commerce, the Associated Charities, the Atlanta Women's Clubs, the Parent-Teacher Associations, the library's board of trustees, and the school superintendent joined the commissioner in pressuring local officials to double the number of white playgrounds from nine to eighteen and to increase the number of Black ones from two to five. The committee also hosted neighborhood meetings with speakers who blamed the lack of playgrounds for serious childhood injuries and much of the city's juvenile delinquency. Statistics from the police and health departments showed that dozens of children had been injured or killed while playing on Atlanta's streets the previous year. The vast majority were "run over by automobiles," but five were "stabbed by playmates," another five were "shot by playmates" (most of them accidentally), and three more "ate injurious articles." By contrast, no child "was hurt on the playgrounds beyond a scratch or two." Atlanta's general manager of parks, Dan Carey, expressed particular concern for "a thickly congested section" of the city "with many children and small yards."[65]

Local officials responded by reluctantly funding a fraction of what had been requested. They opened two new white playgrounds, both in lower income neighborhoods including the one that especially concerned Carey and the committee. They refused to authorize a single additional playground for Black children, even though Black residents made up fully a third of Atlanta's population. A few years later, the city council failed to renew the appropriation for playground attendants, and as a result, $6,500 worth of play equipment was stored in the basement of city hall for three years while Atlanta's playgrounds remained closed. By the 1920s, most cities such as Atlanta simply relied on schools to supply playgrounds for working-class children, thereby avoiding the extra expense of a separate playground budget.[66]

Such decisions were made easier when children seemed uninterested in supervised play or in using the equipment as intended. At the Fourteenth National Conference on City Planning (1922), Lee Hanmer, the director of the Department of Recreation for the Russell Sage Foundation, offered his own cynical observations: "I have seen well equipped playgrounds in crowded neighborhoods practically deserted when the streets and alleys were teeming with children.... When the children were asked why they were not on the playground the answer usually was 'nothing doing there.'" When the kids did use the playground, the most popular game was to dodge the supervisor as he chased them "with a cudgel" for standing up on the swings. Hanmer's assessment was especially damning since he had spent his entire career traveling from city to city advocating for supervised playgrounds as the solution to the nation's most pressing urban problems.[67]

While reformers were souring on playgrounds as the panacea for reforming working-class domesticity, middle-class parents were heeding the advice that they primarily play with their children at home. Elaborate "Home Play Weeks"—often sponsored by parent-teacher associations—encouraged parents to build complex play structures in their backyards to keep their children safe at home.[68] Soon thereafter, manufacturers of playground equipment began selling apparatus designed specifically for the home market. The first backyard "Jungle Gym" was patented in 1923 at the peak of the "Home Play Week" movement, furnishing yet another reason to live in a single-family house on a large lot.[69]

Advocacy of backyard playgrounds quickly eclipsed the support for public ones. During the peak of the playground movement, housing reformer John Ihlder was already arguing that backyard play spaces were not only superior to "the best public playground ever dreamed of," but they would also shift the financial burden from the municipality back to parents. "In the happier cities, and even in the happier parts of the most unhappy cities," he contended, "it is still possible to keep the best possible playground, the one that entails no expense upon the public treasury for purchase or maintenance or supervision, a yard surrounding the single-family house." In a "sheltered back yard," he continued, a child "might be out of doors nearly all day long and still under the eye of a mother." As an added benefit, the backyard would allow parents to control who their children's playmates were at all times.[70]

The rapid shift in support from public to personal playgrounds revealed how reform rhetoric often swayed middle-class parenting strategies more than working-class domesticity. After all, the main audience was, admittedly, middle class. Arthur Minturn Chase had originally advocated for supervised playgrounds so that impoverished children would learn something other than idleness, dishonesty, rowdiness, and a "great familiarity with dirty gutters," but his language fed middle-class anxiety rather than concern for the poor. At the time, social science experts were repeatedly warning parents that impressionable children would soak up their surroundings, amplifying middle-class fears that irredeemable children would corrupt their own. Similarly, when Chase raised the alarm about the death toll from automobile accidents, he failed to note that affluent children were more at risk of injury as passengers *inside of* cars than as pedestrians on the street.[71] Since middle-class parents already carefully supervised their children's play, the message was not necessarily targeting them, but nonetheless, they concluded that they must move away from the bustle of the city to protect their kids. As the distance between their homes and those of the working class expanded, they showed less concern for other people's children.

The Ideal Home for Child-Rearing

The depictions of the single-family house as the ultimate place to raise a child sprang from the same literature that had advanced intensive parenting strategies during the nineteenth century. Advice manuals attacked both apartments and townhomes as being poor substitutes for a proper home, with the implication that respectable parents would not want their children associating with those raised in an inappropriate environment. In *Home Life* (1864), Unitarian minister John F. W. Ware instructed, "We should all be grateful that we have so pure a model as the ideal Anglo-Saxon home." "Every family should be brought up distinct from every other family" in a house where "the blessed sun and air should not be cut off" by "the intervening of any other house." His denunciation of the "cramped homes of the city" included a rebuke of the father who "prefers his child should be educated in the street," "refuses for his children even a garden or a yard," or "sacrifices his children's good to his desire" for "a more costly abode" that worked "against the best life of his child." He insisted, "Nearness to one's business, or any thing that could be urged in favor of such a residence, would not weigh as a feather with what could be urged against."[72]

Influenced by the Progressive Era preoccupation with "race suicide," white reformers often cast the single-family house as a distinct need of the Anglo-Saxon child. For instance, A. F. Weber of Cornell University declared, "To the Anglo-Saxon race, life in the great cities cannot be made to seem a healthy and natural mode of existence. The fresh air and clear sunlight, the green foliage and God's blue sky are dear to the heart of this people, who cannot become reconciled to the idea of bringing up their children in hot, dusty, smoky, germ-producing city tenements and streets." Likewise, social reformer Helen Campbell, who authored one of the nation's first home economics textbooks, expounded upon the importance of the single-family house to the Anglo-Saxon: "To-day we are studying the child and recognizing" that "in the soul of the child lies the future of the race, and that the future is built upon the homes of the race, homes developed and perfected by every means that science and art together may bring to bear."[73] For Campbell and other reformers, "the race" embodied whiteness, but it also served as a synonym for nation and the common good, further tying suburban domesticity to national advancement.[74]

With new houses increasingly constructed with middle-class child-rearing in mind, the rambling and hard-to-clean Victorian rapidly fell out of favor during the early twentieth century. The scorn heaped on Victorian houses could be scathing. Eminent reformer Charlotte Perkins Gilman condemned the "horrifying" houses that seemed designed "to *exclude* children." "Our houses are built and planned entirely and exclusively for adults," she scolded, "and in the more expensive ones children are frankly objected to—often prohibited."[75] "Modern" houses, by contrast, were smaller and simpler and, thus, easier to clean. Moreover, their floorplans catered to children's activities by including playrooms and even bedrooms that siblings no longer had to share. Popular toy construction sets, which prepared boys for the urban world that reformers were rejecting, required space, as did the doll furniture and toy appliances that prepared girls for domestic life.[76]

The difficulty and expense of modernizing old Victorian houses further led to their abandonment by middle-class families who flocked to the suburbs to build new houses with modern heat, sanitation, and electricity. Because utilities inflated the cost of construction by 25 to 40 percent, the typical middle-class house of the early twentieth century shrank in size and became more standardized. Consequently, the space dedicated to child-rearing became more prominent in the modern home, which was typically half the size of its sprawling Victorian counterpart. Reformers maintained that the smaller rooms of the modern house were beneficial to family life. Architects especially prided themselves on their use of scientific expertise to design efficient houses that would produce happy mothers, who would then in turn nurture happy, healthy children.[77] In his classic work *The Bungalow Book* (1910), Henry Wilson promised families that a bungalow would mean "the problem of easy housekeeping and homemaking" would be "reduced almost to an exact science." Architect Ekin Wallick agreed that "there has never been a time" when "the various problems of housekeeping have been thought out on such a scientific basis." As for the earlier Victorian "atrocities," he sneered, "fortunately, to-day we are no longer forced to accept the ideas of uneducated men in our house designs."[78]

Such a battering surely persuaded many to build bungalows and foursquares farther from downtown. The grand Victorians were then carved up into multiple dwellings, their large size and many rooms easily converted into boarding houses or tenements. Absentee owners frequently neglected them until their formerly respectable streets turned into slums. The resulting "blight" fed the call for additional middle-class families to retreat, creating a cyclical pattern.[79] Sometimes the old homes were torn down and replaced with modern apartment buildings, which led to an even larger outcry among the champions of detached, single-family homes. Their disapproval appeared most vehement when affluent families welcomed the convenience of "palatial" apartments, which had all the amenities of suburban houses but were much closer to downtown and required far less maintenance.[80]

Critics argued that even modern apartments would rob children of a nurturing home life. In his contribution to *The Child Welfare Manual* (1915), the Reverend Henry Cope asserted that a "diminutive pigeon hole" where "the natural free intercourse of the family is crowded out" could never serve as "a real home." He asked, "What sort of associations and memories can children hold of home when it has meant, not the cottage with roses twining about the door and the garden of play and happy toil in the back with 'mother's room' and 'my room,'" but instead, "an immense filing-case in which they had one partition?" "We must not allow our mad rush for things convenient to blind us to the greater importance of things beautiful, lovely, [and] character determining," he chided. "We must secure to every child his right to play-space, to grass and flowers and some touch with real nature."[81]

The next year at the Fifth National Conference on Housing (1916), one expert after another testified about the dangers of apartment living to the nation's future. Otto Davis of the Civic and Commerce Association of Minneapolis claimed that the "intelligent parent" should move from an apartment as soon as the first child arrives: "As we have been told here to-day, it is a rare person indeed who would advocate the apartment house as a place to bring up children." He declared that the "monster barrack" undermined "what we have been accustomed to regard as the foundation of the community, the state, and the nation—the American home." Dr. J. N. Hurty, the Indiana State Health Commissioner, agreed that "child life is of state concern." He argued, "Children cannot grow into good citizens if forced" to "dwell in gloom" in multifamily housing, which leads to "ill health, retarded physical and mental growth, vice, crime and disease."[82]

Similarly, childcare expert Mary Mills West tied the increasing popularity of apartments to the spread of contagious disease. In her advice manual written for the US Children's Bureau in 1918—the year 120,000 American children died during the influenza pandemic—West presented the "choice of a home" as the foundation for all other aspects of childcare. With little evidence, she blamed multifamily housing for fueling the pandemic: "The growing use of flats and apartments with tight doors and windows and modern heating systems is partly responsible for the alarming spread of diseases of the throat and lungs." She advised parents to take advantage of "the extension of the trolley lines" and "decreasing cost of motor cars" to buy a home in the suburbs.[83]

Not surprisingly, advertisements for single-family houses often repeated the warnings of the parenting advice books. For example, the Architects Small House Service Bureau included the familiar rebuke of apartments in its book of house plans. "The growing child needs for its best development a true home with plenty of sunshine and fresh air, privacy, and plenty of room indoors for wholesome play." "Any room" in a single-family house could be "a healthy playroom" and offer ample opportunity for "parents and children to engage in common activities and get to know each other better"; the "apartment child," on the other hand, was forced to play "in the noise, dust, and confusion of crowded buildings and crowded streets." If the next generation was "condemned to grow up in tenements or in ugly, unsanitary, ill-kept rented houses," it cautioned, "our national progress" would be "definitely retarded."[84]

Other nations that similarly espoused "Western childhood" did not develop a comparable tradition of intensive parenting or the preoccupation with the stand-alone house that came to characterize the American middle class.[85] Although the Progressive Era has often been identified with child-saving reforms, the most significant child-related trend of that period was the movement of affluent white families out of the central city and into new suburban developments, vastly accelerating segregation by race and class. Deed restrictions ensured that neither working-class families nor families of color would be allowed to follow. Suburban developments appealed to affluent white parents precisely because the urban hazards that reform was meant to address were banned.[86] Thus, parents could provide their offspring with an environment that fostered upward mobility while worrying less about the conditions other children still faced. Even as urban reforms nominally helped children who remained locked in the city, segregation within the suburbs enabled prosperous white families to lay claim to the best housing and best schools. Yet, the assertion that intensive child-rearing in single-family homes was the incubator of good citizenship made the outcome seem more democratic.

During the early twentieth century, few white, working-class families showed much interest in moving out to the suburbs anyway. It would have meant leaving behind their communities and private institutions, and they could ill afford the cost of commuting to work. Moreover, many believed that increased middle-class support for their unionization efforts would be far more beneficial to their children than the inculcation of middle-class values. They soon discovered, however, that the best child-centered amenities, including modern schools and elaborate parks, were being moved out to recently platted, suburban areas while the worst hazards of urban development were being concentrated close to their neighborhoods.

Meanwhile, Black families, regardless of income, remained almost entirely excluded from white reform efforts along with the housing developments that were less exposed to environmental harm. Even the wealthiest Black parents lacked all but the most trivial say over urban development or the local school system. Consequently, neither intensive parenting nor charitable outreach to Black working-class families could transcend the effects of systemic racism and widescale segregation. Years later, a disappointed Louie Shivery remarked that the recreational, educational, and housing needs of Black families remained "so great" that "the present achievements" of the Neighborhood Union seemed "as nothing."[87]

CHAPTER 2

Affluent Parents and the Suburban Residential Park

Advertisements for Houston's Woodland Heights, the city's first suburban development with race restrictions, informed potential buyers that they would not simply be buying a residential lot but an entire neighborhood. One claimed, "Every man with right instincts demands that his home be more than a house and grounds." A second maintained, "The character of the neighborhood and the class of people by whom you will be surrounded are matters of much importance and not to be overlooked in the selection of a home site. An atmosphere of morality and culture is essential for the development of the best qualities in yourself and children, and it is only among congenial people of integrity and intelligence that these refining influences are to be secure." Since affluent parents—the targeted buyer—would not move into an area without access to a modern school, ads also reassured them that "ample school facilities" were "forthcoming," which would be "regarded as a considerable advantage by those families who have children and wish to place before [them] as many educational advantages as possible."[1]

By the early twentieth century, the most important selling point of a meticulously planned residential development was that it would provide an idyllic environment for child-rearing, including access to a good school.[2] Through this assertion, suburban developers enticed a growing number of white families to inconvenience themselves by moving farther from the commercial center, their places of employment, and their religious and social institutions. It was not a difficult case to make since affluent parents already believed that they must sacrifice for their children's future, and advice manuals had long insisted that being a good parent required living in a sheltered, single-family house.

Developers sometimes used the term "residential park" to describe highly restricted subdivisions that promised a parklike atmosphere with spacious yards, curving streets, and charming, single-family homes. A residential park could be distinguished from the average "addition" by its full range of deed restrictions designed to preclude the type of hodgepodge growth that had supposedly marred past urban development. Advertisements suggested that children who lived in these suburban "fairylands" would not need to stay home to remain safe from physical danger or moral temptation. For example, a 1922 ad for Winston-Salem's Buena Vista depicted a young girl exiting the gate from her family's lush yard while her mother and baby sibling watched her set out alone (see figure 2.1). The ad assured anxious parents, "Buena Vista offers home seekers the fullest advantages of city life" without the "dangers of down-town conditions."[3]

Although affluent white parents would make most residential parks a financial success, developers understood that their profit was tied to sustaining the demand for unsold lots for an indefinite number of years, depending on the future economic conditions. Before the introduction of mass-produced housing, infill could take decades to complete. Subdividers were still selling lots rather than houses, making a lengthy period of infill risky. The value of unsold lots would plummet if affluent white families no longer wished to live there. Thus, ensuring that the property remained appealing for middle-class child-rearing was crucial to protecting the immense investment in amenities that would turn subdivisions into residential parks.

Careful planning was critical because the first buyers were usually speculators whose early lot purchases raised the capital needed to pay for the improvements that would ultimately make the endeavor a lucrative one. Most families were unwilling to build a house in a new development before all the improvements had been installed, and speculators might care less about preserving the environment for child-rearing than future homeowners. Consequently, developers embraced deed restrictions to prevent buyers from devaluing the other lots through the construction of commercial enterprises, apartments, or inexpensive dwellings. To persuade buyers to accept significant limitations on their property rights, subdividers convinced them that deed restrictions were necessary to create an ideal environment for child-rearing, the key to sustaining future demand for lots within the development. For instance, setback requirements would result in big yards with plenty of space for backyard playgrounds, minimum house values and race restrictions ensured offspring would have "respectable" playmates, and use restrictions offered safe surroundings for children to explore.[4]

Much remains to be learned about the spread of racial covenants, but it seems safe to conclude that their extensive use began in cities where laws requiring other forms of segregation existed. Some precedents arose before the Civil War: a development in wealthy Brookline, Massachusetts, barred Irish and Black residents, and one in Baltimore barred Black and Asian residents. But after ratification of the Fourteenth Amendment (1868), most developers hesitated before adopting racial covenants since they did not wish to expose their entire set of restrictions to a legal challenge stemming from racial discrimination.[5] In the South, however, the Fourteenth Amendment generated far less restraint; some developers in Jim Crow cities seemed willing to experiment with race restrictions, which

"See the Rest—Then Choose the Best"

BUENA VISTA

Offers home seekers the fullest advantages of city life without the dust, noise and dangers of down-town conditions. It's a fact that after you see the other properties offered for home sites near Winston-Salem you'll be all the more impressed with the Buena Vista properties. That is why we advise everybody to see them all—then Buena Vista. You'll appreciate better the generous size of the building sites—the magnificent and valuable trees — the altitude — the bracing air — the fine wide streets and sidewalks (now being laid) — the improvements that are usually to be had only with inside city lots — the easy access to the city by frequent and comfortable Buss service — the reasonable prices on the lots that remain on sale. Original Buena Vista purchasers have made money on their investments — those who buy now will also make money. For a home or investment you can't beat Buena Vista.

The following leading Real Estate agencies of Winston-Salem are exclusive representatives of the developers:

C. E. Johnson Realty Co., Masonic Temple, phones 251 or 93; Home Real Estate, Loan & Insurance Co., No. 511 Liberty St., phone 121; A. V. Nash & Sons Co., Jones Bldg., Liberty St., phone 1351; James-Conrad Co., first floor Masonic Temple, phone 1718; Poindexter-Montague-White Co., Merchants Bank & Trust Bldg., phone 2129; The Realty Bond Co., 202½ N. Liberty St., corner Liberty and Third, phone 2177; Home Builders Co., Wachovia Bank Bldg., phone 814; Pilot Real Estate Co., Wachovia Bank Bldg., phone 1453; Franklin Real Estate Co., Masonic Temple, phone 225; Spaugh Realty and Insurance Co., 3rd St.; Atlantic Coast Realty Co., Wachovia Bank Bldg.

Buena Vista Annex

(INCORPORATED)

FIGURE 2.1. Many developers portrayed their residential parks as ideal environments for child-rearing. In this advertisement, the mother has no reason to worry about her young daughter's safety when she leaves home all alone. *Twin City Sentinel*, 21 October 1922.

opened the door for their eventual spread to other parts of the country. In *Corrigan v. Buckley* (1926), the US Supreme Court ruled that the Constitution barred discrimination by state actors only, not by individuals using private contracts, giving a green light to subdividers across the nation. The Supreme Court would not declare racial covenants unenforceable until 1948.[6]

Property Restriction vs. Protection

A few years after the Civil War, Frederick Law Olmsted, the celebrated designer of New York City's Central Park, was hired to plan Riverside, an idyllic neighborhood in Chicago's distant suburbs. In his preliminary report for the project, Olmsted identified "domesticity" as "the essential qualification of a suburb." According to his plan, Riverside would contain only "the most attractive, the most refined and the most soundly wholesome forms of domestic life," with each family "well provided for in regard to its domestic indoor and outdoor private life." Olmsted also set aside some of the "best" property for parks and playgrounds to promote "harmonious association," which he believed required a homogeneous population of affluent, white, Christian families.[7]

The domestic principles laid out by Olmsted in 1868 continued to guide suburban development into the twentieth century. At the 1916 National Conference on City Planning (NCCP), J. C. Nichols, the renowned developer of Kansas City's Country Club District, expounded upon the potential economic value of "greater home interest." He illustrated his argument with an advertising card that portrayed a particular residential street as "a quiet place where the children" could nap. Such imagery produced "value" by keeping "people interested in the property." "We will never get the best valuations in residence subdivisions unless we get more home feeling," he urged.[8]

The problem, though, was that the array of amenities that would turn vacant land into a high-priced residential park required a substantial capital outlay from the outset. An advertisement for Palos Verdes Estates, a coastal residential park in suburban Los Angeles, bragged that "more than one million dollars" had "already been expended" for improvements with "a million and a quarter" more pledged for the coming year. Similarly, advertisements for Houston's River Oaks touted smooth asphalt streets, "wide and curving drives" with ornamental lights, sidewalks, "a system" of parks and community buildings, landscaped esplanades, as well as "light, telephone, water, gas, storm and sanitary sewer connections," even though River Oaks was well beyond the city limits when originally platted. Few would be willing to purchase an expensive house lot—let alone build their family home on it—with little more than a description of what the area might look like someday in the future.[9]

To raise the needed capital, developers auctioned off some of their lots to speculators, who then resold the property once land values increased, usually after all the improvements had been completed. For example, when Edwin Ansley initially opened Ansley Park in 1905, he advertised "pioneer prices," calling the purchase of one of his lots "the best and safest speculation now on the market." The following year he claimed, "Scores of purchasers of Ansley Park lots have sold at profits ranging from 25 to 300 percent, and many regret having sold at the profits named." Three years later, Ansley was still asking potential buyers to envision the future: "The present appearance of the park is only a slight indication of what it will be in the next few years." During the 1920s, Garden Hills, located due north of Ansley Park, capitalized on Ansley's ability to lure speculators. An early advertisement reminded potential buyers of Ansley Park's steep climb in value: one empty lot that had "sold for $9500 in 1911" was then "purchased in 1913 for $14,000 as the site of a handsome home."[10]

In most cases, developers would need to sell 75 percent of their lots to break even. The more prestigious and ambitious the development, the more important it was to guard the remaining lots from a decline in value before the full vision of a child-centered residential park could be realized. This precarious period typically lasted a decade or two, especially if the opening of the development coincided with an economic disaster, as had happened to many residential parks when "hard times" set in during the panics of 1873, 1893, 1907, or the long-lasting real estate slumps of World War I and the Great Depression. Chicago's Riverside became a financial failure after the economy collapsed in 1873.[11]

Even during periods of prosperity, infill posed worrisome risks: an individual property owner's "selfish" actions might damage the desirability of the lots that remained unsold. Thus, developers used deed restrictions to safeguard their considerable investment in improvements. The restrictions were basically laundry lists of what property owners either had to do or could not do—such as build a fence in the front yard or raise chickens in the back. In Atlanta's Inman Park, minimum house requirements meant that "nothing less than a three thousand dollar house" could be built. An 1890 advertisement boasted, "This fact insures the very best class of people, and makes the property very desirable." Desirable property, of course, was valuable property. In 1925, Kansas City's J. C. Nichols confirmed, "We have been able, in the long run, to get a better price for our land" in developments "where such restrictions" were "carried to such detail."[12]

Even as developers concocted new restrictions to protect their investments (the River Oaks Corporation would impose *thirty-three* on its buyers), most Americans remained hostile to the idea of someone interfering with their property rights.[13] They considered it un-American to have anyone, including the developer, tell them what they could or could not do with their own property, and some even insisted that suburbia should be significantly less constrained than the city center. In addition, quite a few of the restrictions were intended to halt land speculation, which remained a timeless way to acquire wealth in the land of opportunity. Many property owners thought it advantageous for a residential lot to eventually transition to commercial use since its value would rise dramatically. Aging homes might also be divided into tenements, which generated new income opportunities as well. These buyers disliked restrictions because they would not allow the normal evolution of urban property to take place, limiting their ability to profit from future development.[14]

Moreover, even though developers and reformers constantly assailed "blighted" residential areas, neighborhood change did not bother most Americans because mobility was an important part of American culture. Decades earlier, French philosopher Alexis de Tocqueville noted that "in the United States a man builds a house to spend his latter years in" but then "sells it before the roof is on." Three quarters of a century later, J. C. Nichols complained about the same phenomenon: "To me it is a deplorable thing" that "any man will offer his home for sale." "His wife and daughter may have carefully planned it, with the aid of the best architects and landscape artists." Yet, "some fellow comes along and says, 'Will you sell your home?' 'You bet your life; I will sell anything I have except my wife and children.'" With one-fourth to one-third of all households relocating during any given year, a stable neighborhood was simply not a priority. Between 1880 and 1910, the typical block in Atlanta experienced a 75 percent turnover of residents each decade, with some blocks as high as 100 percent. Only those streets housing the wealthiest residents experienced something closer to stability.[15]

Such attitudes left many developers cautious: too many restrictions might repel buyers rather than entice them. During the first decade of the twentieth century, Atlanta developer Joel Hurt hired the Olmsted brothers—Frederick Law Olmsted's sons who were prominent landscape architects in their own right—to help design Druid Hills. When they pressed Hurt to increase the number of restrictions in his development, he resisted: "There is a natural abhorrence in this democratic region to restrictions, and the longer they appear, the more abhorrent."[16] A strategy was needed to convince potential buyers that deed restrictions were as beneficial to the individual homeowner as they were to the subdivider.

The most promising approach was to tie restrictions to the protection of one's offspring. In 1914, the developers of Raleigh's Cameron Park justified their restrictions by asserting, "No one who appreciates the influence of environment on the child life will build his home in a community where conditions are uncertain. For the above reasons it has been thought best to place such restrictions on the property as will properly safeguard" the families who reside there. Likewise, a 1922 ad for J. C. Nichols's Country Club District featured an imagined conversation between a fictional "Judge Wilson" and his junior partner, who was then seeking to purchase a residential lot. The judge recommended one in the Country Club District, but the junior partner worried its restrictions would make building a house there too expensive. The judge responded by warning him that it would be a "great mistake" to buy a lot that was *not* "protected by restrictions like those in the J. C. Nichols sub-divisions." "You have children; think how much it will mean when you send them to school, to know that they will play and study with the children of other home-owning families." As a parent, he advised, "you can't afford to live anywhere else."[17]

This strategy helped make deed restrictions standard practice within about two decades. In 1925, Nichols explained, "We had to go through a period of education and I will admit to you that in our own properties it was quite a long period too before we could convince the buyer that restriction was good service, for which he could well afford to pay." The following year, developer Chester Chase similarly described the transformation in an article he wrote for *House Beautiful*: "Springfield [Massachusetts] property twenty years ago was difficult to sell if heavily laden with restrictions. The prospective buyer felt that he was being imposed upon if he could not do exactly as he pleased on his own property. But today the home-seeker demands the highest and most detailed restrictions as part of his right." After all, he "wants his family protected with every precaution that past experience has shown advisable. Colony Hills was planned and built, therefore, primarily for women [mothers] and children."[18]

The first "protection" sold to parents was a promise to safeguard their children's health. At the turn of the century, high infant mortality rates allowed subdividers to exploit parental fears of disease.[19] In 1894, the editor of the *Manufacturer's Record*, a booster magazine devoted to southern industrialization, urged the developer of Baltimore's Roland Park to use the "deaths of children" as an effective means to "keep up an interest" in the new development.[20] A 1909 advertisement for Atlanta's Ansley Park employed a similar strategy: "No poor little wan-faced youngsters" could be "found in this Garden Spot of Buttercups, Poppy, Forget-me-nots." For the "happy homes" of Ansley Park had no "wee, thin, tiny bodies and staring, sleepless eyes—the kind of city-bred babies and kiddies—that Drive Loving Parents Where the Lonesome Land of Heart-Ache and the Sea of Sorrow Meet" (see figure 2.2).[21] Along with being further from the filth of city streets, residential parks had large yards that would provide ample space for healthy, outdoor recreation. A 1914 ad for Atlanta's Peachtree Heights described its "big shady" lots "with room for the kiddies to play and grow strong" as the "ideal situation for a home" while "a cramped up city lot" was "a poor place to raise a family." In another example, an ad for Detroit's Greater Wayne District featured a mother throwing a ball to her son in the family's front yard. It prodded, "The invigorating atmosphere is particularly inviting to the mother who wishes to rear her children where they will have play space to romp and play and grow up—strong and sturdy."[22]

The advertisements linked healthy, suburban living to upward mobility as well. One ad for Raleigh's Cameron Park advised parents to "compare the ruddy cheeks

Do You Happen to Know What Bed-Time Means When the

Sandman Comes Hurryin' and Skurryin'

out of the Purple-Blue Mountain Mist that with every Twilight hangs over the Beautiful

Home in Ansley Park

to fill the eyes of Dear Little, Queer Little Folk with the sticky mixture that shows it's Sleepy Time? Why it means that all of these loving little Tots have just left the

Blinckywink Gardens Where Dreamikins Grow

and are doing their very best to keep the Sandman away until after

Daddy Comes for His Good-night Kiss

to take the Shut-eye Train to the Land of Nod. Oh, there's no poor little wan-faced youngsters to be found in this

Garden Spot of Buttercups, Poppy, Forget-me-not

with wee, thin, tiny bodies and staring, sleepless eyes—the kind of city-bred babies and kiddies—that Drive Loving Parents

Where the Lonesome Land of Heart-Ache and the Sea of Sorrow Meet

Oh, it's not this sort of children at all you'll find—they all belong to the other kind—for in Ansley Park each bed-time means a hurried trip to the Land of Dreams

From This Beautiful Park of Pleasure and Play

that comes at the Close of a Tired Day, hearing the Dinky-Bird's songs so sweet, or the Rock-a-by Lady of Hush-a-by Street, sing Droopy-droop Eyelids fast asleep while Katy-dids chirp "she did, did she," 'neath the shade of the Amfalula Tree.

Atlanta Is Growing Better and Greater

more rapidly than ever before. People are coming from every direction and best of all, wee, little citizens are arriving on the wonderful

Dreamships That Sail From Beautiful Harbor of Mother-Love

Looking into the unknown future, wouldn't you rather arrange for Homes where Blossoming Flower Gardens, Broad Plazas, Miniature Parks, Golf Links, Tennis Courts and Piedmont Park adjoining, prevent all possible chance of future crowding and afford every opportunity for Bi-cycling, Roller Skating and

All of those Good, Old-Fashioned Outdoor Games

that mean strong bodies and strong brains? Or do you prefer taking chances in the hot, stuffy, crowded thoroughfares of a city that will soon have Half a Million Population and the possibility of some time—when the Shadows Deepen at Noonday—

Find Yourself Living On Lonesome Streets

and everything so terribly quiet because your own Dear Little Stubby-Toe has gone to join Little Boy Blue and his Faithful Band? And all be-cause he or she hadn't been given the chance to start right with the strength that lies only in

Good Wholesome Air and Pure Georgia Sunshine

Honestly, are there not some things really worth while more than all else and worthy of the most serious consideration? A chance for

Just the Right Sort of Happy Homes In the Open

is offered in

The Fifth Annual Spring Auction Sale of

63 Lots In Ansley Park

Wednesday, April 28, 2:30 P. M.

Offers just the right chance to secure a home with all of these unequaled advantages, either as a residence or investment.

When These Are Gone There Will Not Be Any More

TERMS: One-fourth cash, balance 1, 2 and 3 years at 6 per cent. For plats and full detailed information, apply to Ansley Park Office. Bell 2917 Ivy, or either—

FORREST & GEORGE ADAIR,
Century Building.

REALTY TRUST COMPANY,
EDWIN P. ANSLEY, President
67-71 North Forsyth Street.

FIGURE 2.2. Early advertisements for Ansley Park warned parents that they were gambling with their children's health in the "hot, stuffy, crowded" city, which might end in tragedy with their "Dear Little Stubby-Toe" joining "Little Boy Blue and his faithful band." *Atlanta Journal*, 27 April 1909.

of the out-of-doors children with the pallid faces of the shut-ins," a reference to the fact that middle-class parents did not give their children free range of the city. "Tomorrow these children will be men and women battling for the mastery of the business world." It asked, "Which will you bet on?" The development's motto then provided the answer: "Cameron Park is the place for children." In the same vein, the *Birmingham News* encouraged homeownership with a full-page ad titled "Do It for the Kiddies." It instructed Father to "go out into the beautiful suburbs" where the kids can enjoy "open spaces," "sunshine," and "fresh air." Such an environment would "assure the future of your children" and give them "the best birthright—the chance to grow up strong in mind and body—to attend the sort of schools that will make intelligent men and women of them" (see figure 2.3). Birmingham developer Robert Jemison privately thanked the editor for "rendering a most valuable service" with the ad.[23] His ambitious residential park, Redmont, would begin selling lots later that year.

The triumph of such advertisements led to ever more elaborate declarations of the child-centered nature of residential parks. In 1924, a full-page ad for Palos Verdes Estates was addressed "To a Certain Mother in Los Angeles," indicating exclusion without directly referring to the restrictions. It depicted the new development as "the ideal place for their children," which would, thereby, grant mothers "freedom from anxiety" (see figure 2.4). To bolster its case, the ad posed the following question: "Wouldn't you like to live where your little girl may skate along the sidewalk, safely ride her bicycle or play a game of old fashioned 'hopscotch'; where blue skies and grassy hillsides form her playroom walls, and where ocean air, warm sunshine and vigorous outdoor play, safe from traffic, guide every childish thought into its happy natural channel?" The ad additionally promised that the children would have access to "good neighbors," "culture and refinement," and "good schools."[24]

Houston's River Oaks, which also began development in 1924, used many of the same themes in pursuit of affluent buyers. One ad guaranteed "an ideal environment for children during their health-building, character-forming years" by offering "the combined advantages of the city and of the country, with none of the disadvantages of either." "Here they can romp and play in protected freedom," it boasted. "They can breathe pure, health-building air, associate with the right companions, [and] know the joys which come only to children reared in a community like River Oaks" (see figure 11.2). In another example, a promotional booklet included a picture of five little girls enjoying an impressive playhouse. The caption encapsulated the spirit of idyllic childhood: "A miniature house where work is made play and play is made easy."[25]

These advertisements consistently portrayed the "right companions" as just as important to effective child-rearing as safe streets or healthy air. The assertion resonated especially well during the early twentieth century because children were

FIGURE 2.3. The editors of the *Birmingham News* created this full-page advertisement to promote its real estate pages. The ad encouraged parents to "go out into the beautiful suburbs" so they could "assure the future" of their children. *Birmingham News*, 15 July 1923.

FIGURE 2.4. By the mid-1920s, developers depicted their affluent residential parks as perfect child-centered havens for affluent white families. According to this full-page advertisement, "hundreds of mothers" had already "chosen" Palos Verdes Estates "as the ideal place for their children." *Los Angeles Sunday Times*, 3 February 1924.

beginning to spend more time with their peer groups.[26] A 1910 ad for Kansas City's Country Club District assured parents, "Your children will get the benefit of an exclusive environment and the most desirable associations." In another example, an ad for Raleigh's Cameron Park wove an intricate tale of parental regret: "Lack of Friendship is often given by ruined men as the cause of their downfall. When boys, their fathers moved so often, they were not able to keep the friendship of good people and so drifted into the careless crowd. Better own your home."[27]

Tying a residential park's fate to its suitability for child-rearing meant that the development's access to a new school was usually its most indispensable amenity. Developers understood that their lot sales could not make the leap from speculator to homebuyer without one. In a 1916 article written for the *Atlanta Constitution*, a local realtor acknowledged that "a fatal objection to most of the outlying sections" was the "lack of school facilities." "This question comes directly home to the family with growing children," he elaborated, "the kind of family most likely to seek a location in the outlying district." Frederick Law Olmsted Jr., in his presidential address before the 1919 National Conference on City Planning (NCCP), pronounced it "a matter of enlightened self-interest" to "plan for a suitable school and playground site," which was an absolute "necessity" for "a successful residential neighborhood." Indeed, a new school was such "a matter of keen interest to a clear-thinking" developer that he should "take the initiative in negotiations with the school authorities looking towards its establishment." Ideally, he advised, the "tributary to a single school" should be an individual residential park to ensure childhood exclusivity at school as well as at home.[28]

That same year, King G. Thompson, the developer of Upper Arlington in suburban Columbus, Ohio, informed his fellow subdividers that he instructs his salesmen to answer questions about high lot prices by reciting the benefits of an exclusive school. "We hammer the social advantages that the children will have, and that always appeals to a man, this argument about associates and the school advantages," he expounded. "You have your strongest argument in the apparently instinctive desire for good surroundings for the man's children." He claimed that this strategy was what allowed them to sell houses "for twelve thousand dollars" while admitting that the same properties "could have been bought for eight thousand dollars two years" earlier.[29]

Advertisements frequently promised that an assigned public school would serve only those children lucky enough to live within that particular residential park. For instance, an ad for Bloomfield Village in suburban Detroit celebrated its new school, located "within the boundaries of" the development: "Being in the center of a neighborhood carefully restricted to good families, Bloomfield Village children enjoy the advantages of a private school atmosphere—but without the expense of tuition." It further reminded parents, "Children at plastic ages are influenced by their associates. Their playmates must be from families

Affluent Parents and the Suburban Residential Park | 53

FIGURE 2.5. According to this Buena Vista advertisement, it was a "natural instinct to want to provide a home" for your family: a single-family house in an "ideal location" with access to good schools and "ample playgrounds for the children." *Winston-Salem Journal*, 26 March 1922.

of the right sort."[30] Similarly, a 1922 ad for Winston-Salem's Buena Vista Annex announced that its home lots would adjoin the grounds of "the new High School now in process of construction" (see figure 2.5). It also hinted that an elementary school would "likely be built on the same grounds," making it "possible for your child to pass from grammar grades all the way through the High School, never leaving home, or having any great distance to travel until he or she is ready for college."[31] The reference to higher education was obviously aimed at upwardly mobile families, but the mention of a probable elementary school was likely aimed at them, too, since it implied that Buena Vista children would not have to interact with working-class children at school or at home.

The Rise of Racial Covenants

The success of restricted residential parks not only extended class segregation far beyond what had existed previously, but it also led to the rapid expansion of racial segregation, which was in keeping with the developers' goal of exclusivity. While the vast majority of subdividers agreed that a homogeneous population was essential to profitable development, how best to accomplish that objective remained open to debate. Most seemed hesitant to impose racial covenants after ratification of the Fourteenth Amendment, especially after the US Circuit Court struck down an 1886 race restriction targeting Chinese residents in Ventura, California. They worried that subsequent court challenges might threaten the whole array of deed restrictions. In 1893, the developer of Baltimore's Roland Park sought legal advice before imposing race restrictions against African Americans. His lawyer responded with a warning that the Fourteenth Amendment "assured" Black citizens "the enjoyment of all the civil rights that are enjoyed by white persons." Why risk creating a legal problem from the very outset?[32]

Besides, developers could rely on several other strategies to prevent people of color from purchasing property. First, the threshold for building a home was high in affluent residential parks. At the time, few Black Americans or recent immigrants could afford the minimum construction costs, or at least that is what subdividers said to one another for reassurance. Second, they could simply refuse to sell lots to those they considered undesirable. A 1909 advertisement for Raleigh's Boylan Heights invited "every white man and lady in and around Raleigh" to enjoy "free Barbecue" at an upcoming auction. By restricting who was welcome at the sale, they limited who could purchase a lot.[33] Third, if that somehow failed, developers understood that the ubiquitous threat of violence, which had long been used to control the movement of Black Americans, would work in their favor, as was demonstrated at the 1919 meeting of the "Developers of High-Class Residential Property." Hugh Prather, the developer of Dallas's Highland Park, told his peers that if any property owner rented a house to a Black tenant, "the next morning he would be hanging to a flag pole," although Prather was ambiguous about who would be responsible for the violence.[34]

Because the political climate in southern cities was less restrained by the Fourteenth Amendment, southern developers began experimenting with racial covenants as part of a larger effort to restrain Black movement in Jim Crow cities. Although the beginning of the Great Migration is often associated with World War I, the "other great migration," in the words of historian Bernadette

Pruitt, began decades earlier.[35] Black southerners deserted cotton fields to seek better work, education, and housing opportunities in nearby cities, leading to an increased effort to confine their movement through Jim Crow laws mandating segregation on streetcars and in other public spaces. Furthermore, white supremacy campaigns worked to eliminate the possibility that Black voters could shape urban development. Raleigh subdividers Dan Allen and Frank Ellington were actively involved in the city's "White Supremacy Clubs" as young men. In 1900, a local newspaper reported that both had volunteered to serve on the precinct committees tasked with guarding "the interests of Anglo Saxon North Carolina" on election day.[36]

Jim Crow laws and disfranchisement campaigns often preceded the development of restricted residential parks, as was true in Raleigh, but the inverse was true in the twin cities of Winston and Salem, which would not merge into a single city until 1913. My research suggests the first race restriction in Winston was recorded back in 1889, when Henry Starbuck, a wealthy lawyer and future judge, began selling off the vacant properties he had just inherited from his father. Starbuck placed race restrictions on three separate lots that were adjacent to other pieces of property which either he or his sister had planned to keep for personal use. According to the deeds, the purchasers could "not sell, convey, rent or lease, said premises or part thereof or any building that may be erected thereon to negroes, nor to any person or persons who will not assume this condition with the land." If the "condition" was broken, then the property would revert to the seller.[37]

It is not clear what inspired Starbuck—an attorney—to include language that would restrict property sales in perpetuity. His father did not use race restrictions in his land transactions, and apparently, Henry only used them on three occasions, despite participating in dozens of real estate transactions during the late nineteenth and early twentieth centuries.[38] From what I have been able to determine, the only known use of race restrictions between the passage of the Fourteenth Amendment and Henry Starbuck's use of them in 1889 was the short-lived attempt in Ventura in 1886. Would Starbuck have known about a race restriction targeting Chinese Americans in California even before it was declared unconstitutional in 1892, three years after he began using them? How common was it to restrict individual parcels of land before then? Historian Colin Gordon has found that the first use of a race restriction in St. Louis was in 1893. What about elsewhere? To answer that question, one would have to search through recorded deeds, one by one, for each county in the nation, a massive undertaking to say the least.[39]

What is clear is that Starbuck's business partners and friends who were engaged in residential park development, including on hundreds of acres previously belonging to the Starbuck family, began using racial covenants routinely in 1890. The first covenants were adopted by Winston's West End Land Co., which restricted the lots for five years rather than in perpetuity, as Starbuck had done. The brief time designation provides further evidence that the restrictions were intended to protect the developer's investment rather than the future homeowners' interests.[40] It might also suggest some worry over the acceptance of the restrictions among potential buyers and, possibly, over the legality of race restrictions period.

During the next two years, an interlocking directorate of some twenty industrial titans embraced racial covenants as a strategy to segregate residential areas across the twin cities. This group included household names such as the Hanes family of Hanes underwear and R. J. Reynolds of Reynolds tobacco. Most of them inherited their wealth and then chose to consolidate their power and status through intermarriage.[41] They socialized together in various civic clubs, and many of them shared the same summer retreat in Blowing Rock, North Carolina. In August 1889, Henry Starbuck was there with his law partner, A. H. Eller, as well as the powerful Fries brothers who had inherited a textile empire from their father. Both Eller and the Fries would soon be involved in the development of residential parks with racial covenants. Though no evidence exists proving that Starbuck and Eller discussed deed restrictions with the Fries that summer, it is easy to imagine them sharing their real estate triumphs over drinks at the Wautaga Hotel.[42] After all, during the preceding five months, Starbuck had completed all three of his property transactions involving race restrictions, including one with Eller as the coseller.

Members of the interlocking directorate were involved in the local banking industry as well. Most directors for the West End Land Co. also served as directors for at least one of the three principal banks granting mortgages in the metropolitan area. John C. Buxton was the president of the Winston-Salem Building and Loan Association and a director for the Wachovia National Bank and Wachovia Loan & Trust. The Fries brothers, who were related to Buxton through marriage, served as directors for the first two banks and chartered the Wachovia Loan & Trust Company in 1893, just in time to provide mortgages for the new residential parks surrounding the city.[43]

Residential development in the twin cities was remarkably coordinated. Using a handful of land companies, various members of the directorate began selling home lots in developments on all four sides of the city. While the most prestigious one was located on Winston's west side, a second residential park—Washington Park—was located on Salem's south side. Developed by the Winston-Salem Land and Improvement Company, it used similar racial covenants to those in West End, only this time the deeds excepted "family servants." Both development companies included minimum house values for every lot.[44] In contrast, the new addition established in East Winston was aimed at lower-middle-class families. An 1891 advertisement described the development as an opportunity for "Accessible Elevated Healthy Cheap Homes for White People."[45] The deeds included five-year race restrictions but required no minimum house values. The lots sold for about $400, substantially less than those in West End or Washington Park, which often sold for three times that amount or more. On Winston's north side, working-class families could purchase even cheaper home lots adjacent to an industrial area. Those lots sold without restrictions for $50.[46]

Additionally, members of the interlocking directorate formed the Inside Land and Improvement Company to create Columbia Heights, a residential park for affluent Black families located in the far southeastern corner of the metropolitan area. The same engineer who platted West End and Washington Park also platted Columbia Heights (see figure 4.1).[47] Members of the directorate sold the lots to Black families and to each other as investment properties. During the 1890s, the lots ranged in price from about $300 to $600, comparable to those in East Winston, although those in Columbia Heights increased in value far more rapidly because Black middle-class families had far fewer alternatives.[48]

The news that racial covenants were used routinely in Winston and Salem did not take long to spread to other cities. For example, two of the directors for Winston's West End development company lived in Raleigh where they participated in the interlocking directorate responsible for the capital city's first two full-fledged residential parks, Boylan Heights and Cameron Park. One of the two directors, Richard Raney, sat on the board of Raleigh's Commercial and Farmers Bank with three of the developers for Cameron Park. The other director, J. R. Chamberlain, was also involved in Cameron Park. In addition, he sat on the board of directors for Raleigh Banking and Trust with Charles Busbee, whose brother and law partner, Fabius Busbee, was president of the development company for Boylan Heights.[49]

Furthermore, Raleigh elites William Boylan and Alexander B. Andrews were among the first investors in Winston's West End, meaning both were aware of the development's racial covenants well before the first race restrictions appeared in Raleigh fifteen years later.[50] William Boylan owned the land that eventually became Boylan Heights, and Alexander B. Andrews's son, William J. Andrews, was the vice president of the Glenwood Land Company, which was responsible for Raleigh's first racial covenants. In 1906, it was his signature that appeared on the city's first deed containing a race restriction, and his brother, lawyer A. B. Andrews Jr., notarized the document.[51] Although these interweaving business connections do not necessarily reveal the exact path of racial covenants in North Carolina, they do help us imagine how information spread quickly from one city to the next.

By 1910, racial covenants had become common enough within Jim Crow cities that the source of their proliferation was much less of a mystery. J. C. Nichols, perhaps the most influential subdivider in US history, adopted them in 1908, after a few of Kansas City's more modest additions began using them as early as 1900. Racial covenants appeared in Los Angeles no later than 1905, despite the court ruling against their use in Ventura a dozen years earlier. Except for southern California, however, the routine use of racial covenants would not spread beyond Jim Crow cities until after World War I and the beginning of the Great Migration.[52]

Early on, even developers inside the South seemed hesitant to openly publicize race restrictions, but their caution faded with widespread use. Ansley Park did not explicitly advertise its racial covenants when the lots went on sale in 1905, but four years later, the initial advertisements for Peachtree Heights did. One ad touted a "handsome park" and "playground for the children" along with the assurance that "no lot" would "be sold to negroes." Likewise, newspaper ads for Houston's Woodland Heights referred only to "wise" restrictions without publicly identifying its racial covenants, although a privately distributed brochure plainly stated, "You are also protected from colored neighbors." When the same developer opened a second residential park—Eastwood—in 1912, the newspaper ads were as explicit as the Woodland Heights brochure had been. One ad suggested that Eastwood would have "none but the best class of people," before adding that the development would be "free from such things as blacksmith shops, corner groceries, saloons, livery stables, negroes, etc." By insinuating that affluent Black families were "nuisances" along the same lines as saloons or stables, the ad crudely implied that the purpose of racial covenants was different from the restrictions fostering class exclusion.[53]

Evidence also suggests that nonwhite children were viewed as more objectionable than their parents, which is why advertisements promised that affluent white children would only have "associates" from equally "good homes." In 1916, a general contractor named Frank Carozza sought to purchase property in Guildford, a residential park in suburban Baltimore. According to the company's "exclusion" file, Carozza was "an intelligent rather high type of Italian," who wanted to "get his children in a different neighborhood." But even though Italians were not specifically excluded through the deed restrictions, they remained suspect. Thus, the following note was added later to Carozza's file: "I happened to see the children," and "I really think they would be undesirable residents for Guilford; their dress and looks are very much the Italian type and I am satisfied that the neighbors would object to them." In the end, the Carozza family was banned from the development despite the fact that the father—the actual buyer—seemed to pass muster. The children were the principal focus of concern because their "foreign" appearance could make them questionable companions for white, native-born offspring.[54]

Even the children of servants, who would make no claim to social equality with the homeowners' children, were unacceptable. In 1902, the Olmsted brothers advised Joel Hurt, who was then developing Atlanta's Druid Hills, that—though it was common to permit "gardener's and coachman's cottages" on single-family lots—it would be wise for him to "prohibit even houses for servants employed on the property." They insisted, "The raising of negro children, even those of gardeners, coachmen," and other servants, was "almost certain to result in disagreeable conditions through the noise which they are apt to create even if not through trespassing, pilfering, and other criminal acts."[55]

Although sentimentality paired childhood with innocence, in the real world, children frequently got into trouble, which was why childhood needed protection and other people's children needed to be restrained. The Roland Park Company repeatedly attended to grievances stemming from children's behavior. In 1908, residents complained that "some of the children" were "building dams in the gutters," which "in addition to being unsightly," created "a breeding place" for mosquitoes and caused "the gutters to overflow." A few weeks later, "property owners in the neighborhood" objected to a group of boys who were "playing ball on the grounds south of the Roland Park School" without permission.[56] The following year, a sardonic essay in *The Atlantic Monthly* humorously described the challenge of shielding one's property from the neighbor's children while also shielding the neighbors' property from one's "own plump, blue-clad little rascal." "We live in a cottage set with many others in one wide, communistic lawn, over which our children, collectively and individually, scamper freely," the author lamented. "They sample Mr. Wheaton's prize strawberries, they merrily swing upon Mrs. Harness's clothes-reel, pausing to plant a muddy foot on a bleaching tablecloth" and then "admire my white iris and snap off the largest flower."[57] Though an endless source of irritation, white children's trespassing and pilfering were merely annoying, yet they became "criminal acts" for Black children, in the words of the Olmsted brothers. While the childish antics of affluent white children would be tolerated, the curiosity and mischievousness of nonwhite children were wholly unwelcome and might even be viewed as threatening.

Since racial hostility might end in violence against Black children or their families, Black parents with the resources to afford class-based restrictions showed little, if any, interest in moving into white residential parks, with or without racial covenants. Instead, they sought single-family homes in Black communities on the outskirts of town where their neighbors would treat them with respect, although white encroachment could sometimes imperil their hard-earned enclaves. For instance, at the turn of the twentieth century, the developers of Baltimore's Roland Park began appropriating the city's northern suburbs, disregarding the Black communities that already existed there.[58] Similarly, Oberlin was a flourishing village of Black homeowners and businesses located west of Raleigh's city limits. A 1909 article in the *Raleigh Times* gushed, "All the property is owned by the negroes, and from the appearance of their homes and gardens, they are all good workers." It added, "A nice school building stands among the large number of houses and it is said that it is one of the best attended schools in the city."⁵⁹ The next year, the opening of nearby Cameron Park, which was soon followed by other racially restricted residential parks, started pressing in on Oberlin. Likewise, Houston's San Felipe District was a growing enclave of Black homes and businesses that dated back to Reconstruction. When white developers established River Oaks just west of it, they quickly turned their sights towards dismantling the community, as will be discussed in chapter 11.

In places where white encroachment was not a problem, isolation almost always was. Winston-Salem's Columbia Heights was a prime example. Although white elites supplied most of the investment capital, the project was a labor of love for educator Simon Atkins. He was happy to accept assistance from white "benefactors" to achieve his dream, despite their dubious motives. An anonymous letter to the editor of the *Union Republic* extolled the new community, sounding much like an effusive ad for a residential park. It described Columbia Heights as a "beautiful and progressive little village" with "a climate pure and wholesome." The "neat and attractive little cottages" available only to "people of good moral habits and industrial pursuits" were contrasted to the "crowded and ill-appointed homes of the city."⁶⁰ Yet even with the support of white elites, local officials still failed to furnish the improvements needed for the community to prosper. White residential parks were often annexed to the city before platting began, while Black enclaves were left to languish beyond the city limits without adequate fire protection or convenient transportation to downtown.⁶¹

Independence Heights, which was located north of Houston's city limits, further illustrates the dilemma Black middle-class families faced. A white real estate developer from Ohio purchased the property in 1905 and then began selling home lots to Black buyers. After about a dozen families moved in, local leaders requested a school from the county, and in 1915, residents incorporated the thriving village, which had reached a population of about 400. By 1920, the all-Black community had a healthy business district, and about 145 of its 183 families owned their homes. Despite a promising beginning, the citizens of Independence Heights voted for annexation to Houston in 1929, hoping to gain access to modern city services.⁶²

Before that fateful election, the *Houston Informer*'s uncompromising editor, Clifton Richardson, told the citizens of Independence Heights that seeking annexation would be "civic suicide." He correctly predicted that residents would receive few if any services, considering the long neglect of Black homes already within the city limits. His warning highlighted the core dilemma of racial separation for Black citizens: because they lacked political representation, they could not effectively vie for tax-supported services. In his editorials, Richardson repeatedly asked, "How long shall colored residential districts be conspicuous by the absence of passable and decent streets, electric lights, drainage, bridges and other modern conveniences and civic improvements?" He scolded, "Very few Southern cities make any civic provisions for the sections (ghettoes) of the city occupied by colored residents, and virtually all the money is spent in making improvements in the part of the cities occupied by the more favored and fortunate race."[63] The problem was compounded by the fact that economic development almost always moved in the direction of affluent white neighborhoods where politically-connected members of the chamber of commerce usually resided.

By 1920, most residential park developers agreed that their profit margins were tied to the assertion that they were not simply selling home lots but a better environment for child-rearing. The business class was steeped in the nation's dominant middle-class culture, including intensive parenting practices, which made the connection to residential development—along with the financial prospects of those who stood to profit—difficult to miss. Therefore, advertisements plugging lucrative investment opportunities to speculators soon gave way to ads that painted residential parks as havens for children. The success of these advertising campaigns generated wealth for investors, contractors, engineers, landscape architects, insurance agents, and the bankers who supplied the mortgages.

In the process, residential parks dramatically altered traditional urban development by offering something new to affluent white families: restrictions that guaranteed total segregation through the complete exclusion of other people's children. In the past, urban lots were largely developed one by one or, perhaps, block by block.[64] In that context, a next-door neighbor living in a comparable house implied a level of equality that suggested suitability for friendship or even marriage. Because residential parks developed hundreds of acres into a single neighborhood with like residences, they extended the concept of "neighbor" much further. A person living five blocks away would still be in a position of social equality as a suitable companion for one's children. As realtors began selling neighborhoods rather than individual home lots, they assured parents that anywhere in a residential park was virtually as safe as the home. Nuisances and dangers were banned, and only those people who lived in the neighborhood would have reason to be there, beyond those who provided services directly to the homeowners.

Ivan Allen, who served as Atlanta's mayor from 1962 to 1970, revealed the long-term effect of total segregation when he described the shared childhood of Atlanta's powerful business class: "When I looked around to see who was with me in this new group of leaders, I found my lifelong friends. Almost all of us had been born and raised within a mile or two of each other in Atlanta. We had gone to the same schools, to the same churches, to the same golf courses, to the same summer camps. We had dated the same girls. We had played within our group, married within our group, partied within our group, and worked within our group." He expressed pride in the results: "We were white, Anglo-Saxon, Protestant, Atlantan, business-oriented, nonpolitical, moderate, well-bred, well-educated, pragmatic, and dedicated to the betterment of Atlanta."[65] The outcome he described was the plan from the beginning. Advocates of the city's northside residential parks had made certain that the children who would one day inherit the reins of the city were as homogeneous in interest and thought as they were in religion, race, and social class.

Born in 1911, Ivan Allen was part of the generation most affected by the shift from block-level segregation to total segregation in and around residential parks. He saw the result as a positive gain for the civic body, in much the same way that those who originally promoted it claimed it would be. In 1921, the Raleigh *News and Observer* identified a parallel phenomenon emerging in the prestigious development Hayes Barton: "This section will in due time be the fashionable residential district in Raleigh" since most "Hayes-Barton homes will be occupied by prominent local citizens who now reside in different parts" of the city.[66] Once that goal was accomplished, property values and residential segregation began rising together, largely because affluent white parents were willing to pay a premium for the "right" environment for their children. The construction of public schools for individual residential parks would further accelerate the process.[67]

CHAPTER 3

Residential Parks, Jim Crow, and School Inequality

In 1904, social critic E. S. Martin quipped, "There isn't really such a vast choice in schools; but so far as there is a choice we want our children to have the best."[1] Modern schools were prized by all parents but especially those from the middle class. They believed sending their children to a good school—usually measured in relative terms—was essential to good parenting since it would provide their children with additional avenues for upward mobility. Subdividers were interested in schools, too, because they simply could not ignore the wishes of their key buyers. This imperative explains why J. C. Nichols not only served as chair of the Developers of High-Class Residential Property but also as chair of the Kansas City School Board. He reminded his fellow subdividers, "The first thing inquired about in selling a man a home" was transportation to downtown, and "the second" concerned the schools.[2] Parents needed assurance that the breadwinner could get to work and their children would have convenient access to a high-quality, modern school.

Consequently, developers learned to manipulate school location to their advantage. One strategy was to donate attractive school sites within their residential parks. For instance, a 1910 advertisement for Houston's Woodland Heights boasted that "an entire block" had been donated for the newly constructed Travis School, allowing for "unusually large play-grounds." It also claimed that Travis was "one of the best built and most modern of Houston's fine system of public schools."[3] Another strategy of the developers was to serve on school boards, planning commissions, or city councils to ensure that their projects received superior school facilities, almost always at the expense of children in older neighborhoods. Developers understood that new schools in suburban locations would facilitate segregation by class and—particularly within Jim Crow cities that had large Black populations—by race, too. Just as the acceptance of racial covenants spread outward from the South, the systematic use of schools to increase racial segregation began in southern districts, which under state law, could force children to travel long distances to the nearest school for their race.

The relationship between schools and housing became further pronounced after technological advances in electrical, plumbing, and heating systems transformed the expectations for a "modern" school, much as it had for houses. By World War I, new techniques for fireproof construction and the expectation for auditoriums, gymnasiums, and cafeterias meant that the difference between schools built before and after 1910 was stark. Some children attended class in antiquated wooden buildings that resembled a half-dozen one-room schoolhouses cobbled together, while others attended class in fireproof brick buildings loaded with every amenity available. When possible, parents changed addresses in hopes of sending their children to the safest, most well-equipped school.

Because modern schools acted as magnets for affluent families who had greater housing options, the newest school could quickly become overwhelmed with students, a significant dilemma for local school boards since middle-class patience with less-than-ideal conditions was rare. In 1913, a white, middle-class mother complained to the *Atlanta Constitution* about the overcrowding in her child's brand-new school: "I cannot see why the people in this section of the city should be so treated," she fumed. Her daughter had "been five weeks sitting against a dirty blackboard." Though she was pleased with her neighborhood, she threatened to relocate if conditions were not soon remedied: "The homes are new and well constructed and ornamental, but there will be many of us who will feel like moving away unless there are school facilities for our children."[4]

As racially restricted residential parks pulled more affluent families out to the suburbs, the dynamic between Jim Crow schooling and residential segregation began to change. In earlier decades, the predominance of block-by-block segregation patterns meant that both Black and white schools frequently served the same mixed-race neighborhoods. Indeed, it was more common for them to be located near each other than for Black schools to be any considerable distance from white homes. During Atlanta's 1910 building program, the school board sited a new Black school just two blocks from an existing white one and two white schools only a few blocks from existing Black ones.

In such cases, Black and white students could scarcely avoid interacting with each other at various points during the day. For instance, Houston's Booker T. Washington and Nathaniel Hawthorne elementary schools sat close together on the same street. During the city's sweltering summers, Black and white children from both schools watched silent movies projected on an exterior wall at Hawthorne.[5] Likewise, Raleigh's first white public school, the Centennial School, was nestled between two Black schools, one public and the other a private grammar school run by Shaw University. Jonathan Daniels—son of Josephus Daniels, secretary of the navy under Woodrow Wilson and the city's most prominent citizen—attended Centennial between 1908 and 1913. He later claimed to have spent so much time playing on Shaw's campus that he considered himself "practically an alumnus of its juvenile department."[6]

Interracial playmates were once common among young children, especially in southern cities; suburban residential parks, however, would make such friendships rarer and much less acceptable.[7] Not only would deed restrictions exclude certain children, but school boards also gave into the developers' demands for new schools to serve recently platted residential parks. This practice often denied similar facilities to children in older, mixed-race areas, particularly in perennially cash-strapped southern school districts, pushing more white families into the suburbs. Additionally, board members agreed to close Black schools near residential parks so that developers could control the racial demographics of the surrounding property as well. Since Jim Crow school systems could compel even young children to make long, hazardous commutes across industrial areas to the closest school for their race, the location of Black schools strongly influenced where Black families lived.

Raleigh is a good example of this process. Between 1900 and 1920, the all-white school board agreed to move Black schools away from white residential parks, shifting the Black population away from the western half of the city. As the location of new schools gradually whittled away at mixed-race housing patterns, increasing levels of segregation justified the further concentration of Black schools in Raleigh's southeastern corner. This strategy was remarkably effective because the area set aside for Black development was neither isolated from the rest of the city nor in the path of white middle-class homes. As a result, residential segregation evolved gradually without sparking strong resistance from either Black or white families.

Jim Crow Schooling and Residential Development in Raleigh

Jonathan Daniels's childhood in a mixed-race neighborhood shaped Raleigh's history in subtle ways. His father owned the formidable Raleigh *News and Observer*, the editorial mouthpiece of the state's white supremacy campaign, which effectively disenfranchised the vast majority of Black North Carolinians for more than half a century. Unlike his famous father, Jonathan embraced a more liberal view of race relations, one he credited to his interracial experiences as a boy. Although many white children still had Black playmates during the earliest decades of the twentieth century, Jonathan grew up among the faculty and students at Shaw, absorbing a more complex view of Black America than most whites. In 1933, he assumed the helm of the *News and Observer* when his father began serving as ambassador to Mexico during Franklin Roosevelt's administration. Jonathan softened the racist rhetoric of his family's influential newspaper, but the type of interracial experiences that once shaped his childhood had already grown rare.[8]

In 1920, Josephus Daniels moved his family further from downtown Raleigh to prestigious Hayes Barton, where they would be "protected" by covenants that excluded all Black residents and any white families who could not afford the class-based restrictions. Josephus's grandfather had built the family's ancestral home near the first governor's mansion, in what was once a fashionable part of town. During the early twentieth century, "Negroes and questionable white people came more and more to live in the neighborhood," in the words of Jonathan. Deed restrictions would block the same pattern from occurring again in Hayes Barton and the adjacent residential parks. Residents could feel secure that their new community would remain unchanged, making Jonathan's boyhood experiences unlikely for the children of future generations.[9]

This outcome was further guaranteed by government actions that extended segregation far beyond the borders of individual residential parks. Most developers believed that simply controlling who lived within their developments was not enough to protect their profits, so they sought ways to safeguard the edges as well as the center. That way, every lot would remain valuable as the city grew out and around them. To accomplish this goal, they pressured school boards to close Black schools near recently platted residential parks in hopes of shifting Black homes to another part of the city. In Raleigh, the combination of targeted Black school closures and the concentration of new Black schools in the city's southeast quadrant helped push the Black population away from Daniels's new home. Not only would race restrictions prevent Black and white children from playing together in Hayes Barton, but the city's downtown would separate them as well.

Prior to the appearance of residential parks, public school location was not used explicitly to promote residential segregation. The popularity of various neighborhoods rose and fell over time, and the construction of schools tended to follow that trajectory. The location of Josephus Daniels's ancestral home on the southside of Raleigh represented prestige during the antebellum period, but the city's northeast became increasingly fashionable during the late nineteenth century. Prosperous politicians and businessmen built gracious Victorian homes in the Oakwood neighborhood located northeast of the capitol. In 1883, the new governor's mansion was completed on North Blount Street, reflecting the neighborhood's rising status. In 1887, the district opened its second white school, Murphey, for the emerging community. But even as upwardly mobile white families were shifting the city's growth to the northeast, block-level segregation remained the norm. Raleigh's second Black college, St. Augustine's, was founded in 1867 just five blocks east of Oakwood. In 1896, the college established the St. Agnes Hospital and School of Nursing, the city's only institution affording medical care to Black citizens at the time.[10]

Soon after Murphey welcomed its first students, the Raleigh Land and Improvement Company platted Idlewild, a new addition just south of Oakwood Cemetery (see map 3.1). Idlewild's fifteen investors included Josephus Daniels, longtime school board member Needham Broughton, and local heavyweight A. A. Thompson. Conveniently enough, Thompson served as both mayor and chair of the school board between 1887 and 1891, when the investors were hoping to take full advantage of Murphey's appeal to white families. After completing his second term as mayor, Thompson remained on the school board during Idlewild's peak period of sales. Advertisements painted its prospects in rosy terms: "THE FUTURE OF IDLEWILD is assured. You run no risk in buying one of these lots. We have made it a rule to sell these lots only to desirable people. Soon this will become the most beautiful and popular suburb that has ever been built up around this city."[11]

But unlike the residential parks that would soon appear on the west side, Idlewild had no property restrictions to enforce the ads' promises of exclusivity; instead, Idlewild's modest development followed traditional mixed-race housing patterns.[12] In 1922, the year the school board launched a large building program to provide schools for the city's new westside residential parks, half of Idlewild's eighteen or so horizontal blocks were mixed race, four were all Black, and five were all white. Between 1907 and 1922, the percentage of white residents increased on four of its blocks and decreased on only one.[13] Once the school district started favoring the west side, however, Idlewild transitioned into a predominantly Black neighborhood.

During the late nineteenth century, many Black families preferred the west side, where all three of the city's Reconstruction-era Black schools were located. The industries stretching along the railroad tracks west of the capitol provided plentiful employment.[14] In 1865, the Friends' Freedmen's Aid Society of Pennsylvania opened the Johnson High and Normal School. Four years later, the American Missionary Society of New York established the Washington School, and that same year, a school opened in Oberlin Village, a prosperous community of Black homeowners located significantly west of the city limits (see map 3.1). When Raleigh's school district was formerly organized in 1876, it assumed control over all three. At that time, Johnson was the largest Black public school. It offered courses in Latin, algebra, and chemistry in addition to the traditional grammar-school subjects. The school was located in St. Paul AME Church at the center of an area that would one day become the gateway to Raleigh's most prestigious residential parks, including Hayes Barton and Cameron Park.[15]

Early on, the district had far more Black schools than white ones—even though white residents made up about 60 percent of the city's population—because the board would not invest in substantial school buildings for Black children. While makeshift schools created hardships for Black students and teachers, the scattered

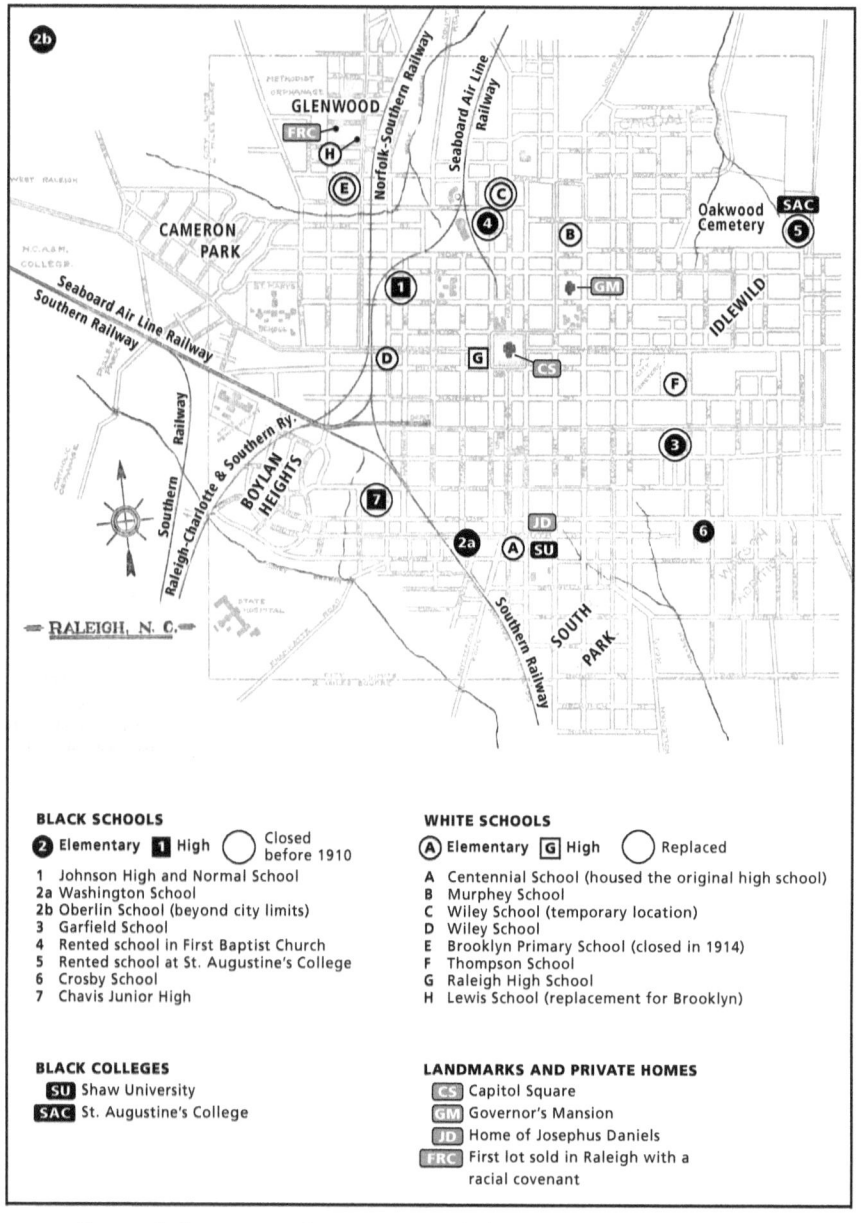

MAP 3.1. During the late nineteenth century, most Black schools were located on Raleigh's west side where the railroads provided ample employment. By 1910, the school board had begun concentrating Black schools in the southeastern corner of the city. On the above map, the schools are numbered or lettered in the order in which they first opened, demonstrating an increasing link between Jim Crow schools and residential segregation. Courtesy of the Louis Round Wilson Special Collections Library, University of North Carolina at Chapel Hill.

sites were convenient for Black families who lived throughout the city. Still, the district did not furnish a Black school on the east side of town until 1880 when it opened Garfield School on what was then an all-white block. The board also operated two additional schools in Black churches on the west side, but as the new century approached, it ended its practice of renting space in Black churches and, thus, its policy of scattered sites. The failure to maintain a Black school in the northern half of the city was the district's first move toward racial consolidation. The next two Black schools were built in Raleigh's southern corners: Crosby in the southeast in 1897 and Chavis in the southwest in 1903. Chavis was organized as an industrial junior high, partially replacing the defunct Johnson High and Normal School, which the board had discontinued.[16]

In the meantime, the district opened its first white school west of the capitol. At the turn of the century, Raleigh's development extended twice as far to the east as it did to the west since its railroad trunk line had slowed growth in that direction. In 1898, when the board added Wiley to relieve the overcrowding at Murphey and Centennial schools, it initially used a temporary site on the city's north side not far from Murphey. Two years later, Wiley's new westside building was finally completed. An editorial in the *News and Observer* called it "a tardy act of justice to the patrons of the western part of the city." In the coming years, Wiley's innovative building made it a popular school, helping Cameron Park establish itself as a full-fledged, child-centered residential park.[17]

In 1907, a successful bond issue allowed the board to further expand the number of schools in the district, starting with a new white high school near Capitol Square. The central location afforded access to the local and state libraries and was convenient to students throughout the city.[18] The board then built an additional white school for the east side, this one named for former mayor and school board chair A. A. Thompson, who was also one of Idlewild's earliest investors. The white children living in the southern half of Idlewild were assigned to Thompson while those from the northern half continued attending Murphey. Although Thompson's block was all white, those surrounding it were mixed-race, and Garfield, which served Idlewild's Black children, was just two blocks away.[19]

Once residential parks started appearing on the west side of town, the district began aggressively consolidating Black schools in the southeastern corner of the city, which reversed an earlier commitment to placing schools "within easy reach" of the children, as described by the *News and Observer*. In 1908, board members closed Chavis, discontinuing the only public school in Raleigh that provided Black students with courses above the grammar-school level. The following year, they asked the board of aldermen for permission to sell Chavis and Garfield to "consolidate the colored schools of the city." The board planned to use the combined proceeds from both sales "to enlarge and improve" Crosby, claiming Garfield needed "extensive repairs" that the district could ill afford.[20] The following year, it built a brick school on Crosby's lot. The board then transferred Garfield students to the new school, and from that point on, Black children living near St. Augustine's College walked past the white Thompson School on their long walk to the consolidated Crosby-Garfield School. Meanwhile, no provision was made for Chavis's students on the west side.[21]

No doubt the district was struggling through a painful financial crisis when Garfield and Chavis closed, but the city's powerful business class routinely dictated the school system's financial health by granting or withholding the tax money needed to keep the district afloat. Therefore, most financial crises in school districts, whether in Raleigh or elsewhere, were manufactured. It worked something like this: When residential parks needed schools, the chamber of commerce supported bond issues or tax increases to pay for them. But after the district furnished new schools for affluent white suburbs, local elites cried poverty before school improvements could be extended to the older neighborhoods. This cyclical pattern continued during the large school building programs of the 1920s. Schools would not have been able to guide residential development nearly so well without significant inequality; if all areas of the city were equally well provided for, then parents would have had far less incentive to relocate.

In North Carolina, the immediate financial crisis in 1907 was caused by a vote to abolish the state's alcohol dispensaries during the last week of December. Since a portion of the money helped fund the public school system, Raleigh's school district lost a considerable portion of its budget midway through the academic year. To replace the missing revenue, the board proposed a special tax as an emergency measure, but voters rejected it at the polls.[22] James Wynne, a real estate investor, led the opposition, which he portrayed as a "good government" campaign. To celebrate his victory, he wrote a letter to the *Raleigh Times* applauding the "good citizens" who defeated the tax while chiding the board for its profligacy. The election, he wrote, "was intended as a rebuke to extravagance, and not because people object to paying a reasonable tax." The following year, he won his campaign for mayor with a platform that promised "to reduce the tax rate as soon as possible" and to "run the city as economically as a large and successful business is run."[23]

At the time, Raleigh's mayor also served as the chair of the school board, which meant that Wynne was chair when the board auctioned off Chavis. The sale was just weeks after advertisements for Raleigh's first residential park, Boylan Heights, began touting its "careful restrictions" and other advantages.[24] The Chavis School was only two blocks outside the entrance to Boylan Heights along the main artery connecting it with downtown. Wynne's business associate was Frank Ellington, the principal developer. Wynne and Ellington served as president and vice president of the two real estate firms that managed Boylan Heights sales. Since Wynne ran for mayor as a government reformer, he took care to avoid the appearance of a conflict of interest, but it strains credulity to suppose his connections to Ellington were meaningless.[25]

And even if the closures of Chavis and Garfield reflected no more than the pronounced racism of a Jim Crow district starved of funds, that action undoubtedly contributed to the concentration of Black residents in Raleigh's southeast corner. According to the attendance figures for 1880, 734 Black students attended five public schools west of the capitol—including three operating out of Black churches—while only 170 attended Garfield, the one Black school located east of the capitol. Between 1909 and 1916, the period when Raleigh's westside residential parks began emerging, the situation largely flipped. The Crosby-Garfield School was the city's newest, largest, and most modern Black school while Washington School and Oberlin still had small, nineteenth-century buildings with smaller enrollments (see map 3.1).[26]

In 1916, a second bond issue helped rectify the imbalance somewhat. Two years before, fires had destroyed two of Raleigh's white schools, spawning a movement for fireproof construction. As a result, Washington received "several new rooms" to relieve "its crowded and dangerous condition," and Oberlin acquired a brick building. The following year, the number of students at Oberlin increased by 6.7 percent, the largest enrollment gain at any Black school in the district, but its modern building still had a limited impact on Raleigh's overall development for two key reasons.[27] First, a nationwide real estate slump lasting from 1914 to 1921 slowed the drawing power of the school.[28] Second, Oberlin was a remote enclave largely inaccessible due to poor roads. In 1920, a white minister beseeched the board of county commissioners to answer the pleas of the residents and improve Oberlin Road, "the only line of travel from the village to the car line." "For a great portion of the year," he chided, the road was "either very dusty or very muddy." The shameful conditions caused "embarrassment" for the "industrious and prosperous" Black families forced to endure it.[29] Thus, although Oberlin did receive a brick school, the community's isolation made it less appealing to Black parents who worked in town. For them, South Park—a new mixed-race addition convenient to the Crosby-Garfield School *and* the commercial center—was a more attractive option.

The two white schools built from the 1916 bond issue influenced Raleigh's development to a much greater extent. The fireproof replacements for Murphey and the three-room primary school that served Glenwood-Brooklyn were a response to safety concerns after fires destroyed both wooden schools. The Brooklyn community, located in the far northwestern portion of the city, dated back to 1905; neighboring Glenwood, Raleigh's first residential development with racial deed restrictions, opened the following year (see map 3.1). Because of the prolonged real estate slump, a majority of the development's houses were not constructed until the 1920s. Nonetheless, the district's two new brick schools enjoyed a significant jump in enrollment while every other white school lost students that year. Murphey, which served a long-established community, grew by a respectable 16 percent, while Lewis, serving Glenwood-Brooklyn, exceeded the original building's enrollment by more than 250 percent.[30] Lewis's gain was remarkable even when considering it had become a full-sized elementary school.

Glenwood-Brooklyn's rapid growth after the completion of Lewis demonstrated the importance of modern schools to residential park development regardless of the existence of racial covenants. Lewis experienced a dramatic increase in enrollment only after receiving a modern, brick building, even though the first racial covenant recorded in Raleigh was on a lot just three blocks from the original Brooklyn School. That deed was signed more than ten years before the area's small, wooden school was replaced (see map 3.1).[31] Most developers understood that parents valued a well-constructed and well-respected school far more than deed restrictions, so they made sure that their residential parks were first in line for new schools.

Residential Parks and School Inequality

This dynamic quickly turned residential parks into a driving force for school inequality.[32] Developers understood that the key to selling residential lots at a premium price was not just access to a school but access to a superior one. For that reason, they pressured local officials into building new schools for nascent communities even as schools in older neighborhoods were left to deteriorate. In most cases, the push for superior facilities led to rapid overcrowding as middle-class parents scrambled to enroll their children in the newest school with all the latest amenities. A prime example is Ansley Park, Atlanta's first racially restricted residential park, which acquired a new school in 1907, just two years after lots went on sale. But residents had to share the school with families who lived outside the development. When the school quickly filled beyond capacity, Ansley Park parents began pushing for a separate school *inside* the borders of their exclusive residential park.

Because Edwin Ansley was a novice developer, he, at first, neglected to set aside some of the property for a separate Ansley Park school. Instead, he focused his attention on the negotiations for the storied Piedmont Park—a 185-acre private park that ran alongside the entire eastern edge of his development. The park's stockholders had recently presented it as a gift to Atlanta, but the mayor hesitated before accepting it. The city would also inherit its substantial debt, and some opponents accused the park's stockholders of attempting to dump it on local taxpayers just before the bonds matured. Hence, the mayor refused to accept the "gift" unless the city could annex North Atlanta, including Ansley Park, to help pay for it. After all, nearby families would be the primary beneficiaries. Edwin Ansley enthusiastically supported the deal both to secure the park and to obtain a city school for the annexed area.[33]

Other elites joined him, believing annexation would protect property values in North Atlanta. Robert Maddox, an early investor in Ansley Park who was then president of the chamber of commerce, insisted, "We all know how property would depreciate if a guano factory should be established at Piedmont Park.... I am sure the residents of North Atlanta would rather have their property incorporated than have a guano factory" next door. Other advocates argued that a large, child-centered park would not simply be an improvement over a possible fertilizer plant but would, indeed, be the best possible outcome. The *Constitution* extolled the virtues of the park's "breathing places" that would permit children to "play as long as they please and as wildly as they please without fear of cars and other dangers of a large city."[34]

Still, North Atlanta's wealthy property owners would not accept annexation without a guarantee of certain "reciprocal benefits." Not wanting their political representation diluted through Atlanta's rough-and-tumble ward-based political system, they demanded entrance into the city as a distinct ward with full representation on the city council, which in turn could help them obtain a top-notch school. The mayor resisted, responding that the whole area contained "only about 125 voters" and, therefore, did not deserve "to come in on the same footing with wards of 2000 inhabitants." Instead, he advised that "North Atlanta should come in and take her chances along with other sections of the city." As for the school, he recommended that the old Cotton Exposition building in Piedmont Park be remodeled. Affluent parents recoiled at the suggestion that their children attend school in "an old barn" situated in "a sporting park." They rejected annexation to an existing ward as well, which would dilute their political power and make it more difficult to acquire a school on their terms. From the perspective of Atlanta's working class, such demands were blatantly selfish. The city attorney, who lived in a majority working-class ward, protested, "It would be unfair to have that section with so few inhabitants come in and get one-eighth of the city's revenue." During a hearing on the annexation bill, he warned local officials not to allow "the great metropolis of Georgia" to be "lost sight of behind this small crowd of big men."[35]

Despite widespread opposition from less affluent citizens, North Atlanta's politically connected property owners won their fight. They received a generous school site in "one of the most desirable locations of the city," in the words of the *Constitution*. Additionally, they entered Atlanta as the new Eighth Ward, receiving full representation on the city council. Ansley Park lots went on sale the following year, although most of the property was not annexed until 1908. This pause allowed speculators to avoid paying city taxes while they waited for improvements that would enable them to sell their investment lots for a profit. The completion of Tenth Street School in 1907 further advanced the goal by attracting families who were ready to build a home. A 1908 advertisement celebrated, "All of Ansley Park is now in the new city limits and will have electric lights, schools and all city conveniences."[36]

In keeping with the demand for a superior school, Tenth Street School received a unique innovation that the district touted as important for child development. Its basement was transformed into a gymnasium fully equipped with apparatus designed to "develop strong men and women" for the "rising generation." According to the *Constitution*, the Tenth Street teachers were "united in praising the experiment," which they said "helped in the work of the school room" and encouraged "regular attendance." While the district's "director of physical culture" promised, "where possible," such "rainy day playgrounds" would be "instituted in some of the older school buildings," the board failed to deliver, largely because it was facing other dire needs. For instance, multiple schools still had sanitation facilities dating back to Reconstruction.[37]

Tenth Street School's shiny new accommodations helped draw families to Ansley Park. By 1909, demand for the lots had increased so much that families wishing to purchase a lot struggled to find an owner willing to sell, even as prices soared. During the following decade, the population of the greater "Ansley Park residential area" exploded from 5,465 in 1910 to 13,527 in 1920, representing the largest increase for any of Atlanta's designated residential areas.[38] In 1913, board members moved the attendance line for Tenth Street School further north to accommodate Ansley Park families. The children living farther south were then sent to an aging school with outside toilets, resulting in "a great hue and cry" from their parents. The president of the Parent-Teacher Association complained that "many children" had to walk "more than a mile" to school "though living, perhaps, within a few blocks" of the Tenth Street School.[39]

Nonetheless, the din from Ansley Park parents grew louder. The PTA passed a resolution complaining that the Tenth Street School was "the worst sufferer" in the district. A delegation of businessmen appeared before the city council to denounce the conditions, which they claimed made their "children sluggish and unable to do good work." Ansley Park families demanded that the school board provide a separate school "in the park" for the exclusive use of their children. One mother wailed, "If the board does not give us the Ansley school, I don't know what we are going to do." When the parents began objecting to insufficient toilet facilities, an exasperated Fourth Ward councilman had heard enough. He scoffed, "If the children of the Tenth Street school had to meet toilet conditions now existing in [the Boulevard] School, their parents would not quarrel—there would be a riot.

On the other hand, if the condition of the Tenth Street school were transferred to [Boulevard], those people would consider it a blessing."[40]

In response to the rising chorus of criticism from Ansley Park's well-heeled residents, the board hunted for a suitable location for a second school. Edwin Ansley, having realized his mistake in not setting aside an appropriate site, offered to donate an $8,000 lot, but board members concluded that the residential park's own restrictions prevented them from building a school there. After a frustrating eighteen-month search, the board finally asked the city council to carve out a site from Piedmont Park fronting 300 feet along the eastern edge of Ansley Park. To justify the controversial request, one of the board members implied that the proposed site would promote the common good: "Instead of some lonely horseman riding by this overgrown portion of Piedmont park once a day we could have there 1000 happy children attending a model public school." The park board refused to go along, however; it convinced the city council that Piedmont Park could only be used for recreational purposes.[41]

With the east side of Ansley Park blocked, the school board then turned to the west side. In 1913, it purchased a site on neighboring Spring Street, although a school would not be built there until 1919 because the area's residents could not agree on the location's suitability (see map 7.2). Ansley Park parents continued to demand that the school be built "in the park" exclusively for their children, but parents living along the prestigious Peachtree Street corridor wanted the school built on the Spring Street lot, which the district already owned. One of them was Ivan Allen Sr., then president of the chamber of commerce and father of Ivan Allen Jr., future mayor. Allen reminded the city council that the purchase of the Spring Street site had "prompted many people to purchase property and move to that neighborhood so their children would be near the school." He pleaded, "We have been waiting a long time for the school and in the meantime residents of that section have been obliged to send their children" to the "badly overcrowded" Tenth Street School.[42]

Yet even after the Spring Street School opened at last, Ansley Park families continued angling for a school "in the park," which they never received. This failure would ultimately contribute to the development's decline in prestige, especially once an exclusive public school became the standard for residential parks. Apparently, the only site available within Ansley Park would have required extensive improvements to make it accessible, an expensive proposition even with the Ansley Land Company donating the property. Residents' constant irritation with local officials led many of them to advocate for a new city charter. They believed a commission-style government would give them more control over the city's resources than the current ward-based system.[43] Some even opposed bond issues for city improvements, including schools, until their demands were met. The mayor condemned their selfishness: "There have been a few, not many, who would cripple the city because they could not run it." He optimistically concluded that they could "safely be ignored, for in time their own sense of shame will overwhelm them."[44] But when it came to schools, affluent white parents had little shame.

Consequently, many subdividers sought ways to avoid Ansley's rookie mistake by ensuring that future residents received all the advantages promised in their advertising campaigns. Selecting one of their own to serve in local government during the critical years of development could remove the uncertainty of lobbying. In Winston-Salem, the same men who developed the city's first residential park, West End, created Winston's public school system. The original school board included three directors of the West End Land Co., one of whom was also the firm's president. Not surprisingly, the board placed the city's only white school—the West End School—right next to the residential park. Another director, John C. Buxton, served as mayor for eighteen months, just long enough to receive credit for establishing the school district. He then served as the school board chair for a quarter of a century.[45] During his first year on the board, advertisements for West End emphasized its school advantage: "THIS IS WORTH THINKING ABOUT— The schools will begin in a few days. Have you children to send? If so, are you convenient of the School House? If not get yourself a lot near it."[46]

Atlanta developer Aquilla Orme also participated in local government specifically when public "service" could help his North Boulevard Park become a child-centered haven. Earlier, he had been one of the frustrated parents of the Tenth Street School. At a protest meeting in 1915, he laid the "blame for conditions" on the city council, arguing that "they had managed to get money for other propositions and could just as easily" find the funds for "improvements" at his children's school. The next year he ran for city council, announcing his candidacy just one month after North Boulevard Park began advertising home lots; at the time, Orme sat on the development company's board of directors.[47]

On the city council, Orme's priority was securing the child-centered amenities that would ensure North Boulevard Park's profitability. To take full advantage of its auspicious location along the eastern border of Piedmont Park, Orme procured a public bridge over the railroad tracks that separated the development from the adjacent recreational facilities (see map 5.2). A 1917 ad boasted, "Residents of Boulevard Park can walk across the bridge to enjoy" music, boating, swimming, and "the beautiful playgrounds that are always under police protection."[48] In 1918, Orme became the city council's representative on the school board, where he joined the "finance and buildings" committee. The following year, the board permanently closed the Virginia Avenue School—which had long served northeastern Atlanta's Black students—because it was too near the southern edge of North Boulevard Park. Thus, Orme and the other developers sought the school's closure for much the same reason that the developers of Raleigh's Boylan Heights sought the closure of Chavis School. That same year, the Atlanta school district began planning a multimillion-dollar building program, which included a new school for North Boulevard Park on Virginia Avenue.[49]

As was common in most southern cities, the austerity brigade soon began chipping away at the list of schools the superintendent had deemed essential to the building program. When the mayor announced the final list of projects, it included only half of the superintendent's original recommendations, but the school for North Boulevard remained on the list. Little more than a week later, Orme declined to run for reelection since he had accomplished his goals as councilman.[50] In 1922, he became vice president of the Atlanta Trust Company where he managed the mortgage bonding department. Three years later, he oversaw the expansion of North Boulevard Park after being named president of the development company. A glowing article in the *Constitution* described the fashionable residential park as within "the shadow of the Samuel M. Inman school," the very school Orme had helped secure while in office.[51]

By the 1920s, local planning commissions offered another path for developers to influence the location of new schools. William Hogg became chair of the Houston planning commission soon after launching River Oaks. From that position, he coopted the district's multimillion-dollar building program. School administrators reluctantly agreed to build a school for his residential park despite voicing concern that greater needs existed elsewhere.[52] When the building program ended, the per-pupil cost of the River Oaks School and its fifteen-acre site—purchased directly from the River Oaks Corporation—was far larger than that of any other elementary school built at the time. Even before the school opened, advertisements for River Oaks had begun describing it as "second to none in the city" and emphasizing its accessibility to all River Oaks families.[53]

Other developers simply donated a site, which gave them control over the school's location and future enrollment. Local officials sometimes balked at requests to build new schools out on the edge of town before the population warranted it, but they hated to decline an outright gift. For their part, developers understood that they could easily recoup the value of the property since a school would enable them to sell their lots at substantially higher prices. Although Baltimore developer Edward Bouton failed, at first, to orchestrate a public school for Roland Park, he soon corrected his mistake. Most early residents were sending their children to Baltimore schools, which required them to provide transportation and pay tuition since the development had not yet been annexed to the city. When parents began pushing for a school within Roland Park, Bouton helped bully the county commissioners into providing one. The county board had already renovated an existing school hoping to end "the objections" of the "Roland

Park people" to "sending their children" there, but it did not. To help move things along, the company donated a site under the condition that it could approve the design, landscaping, and "any additions or changes made within the next ten years." The county agreed, and the school opened later that year.[54]

In the same vein, Atlanta developer Eretus Rivers worked to convince county officials to build a school for Peachtree Heights, located just north of the city limits, by donating an "ample tract" as well as the building materials. Even so, it still took six months to persuade the reluctant school board to move forward with the project. Ten years later, the community thanked him by officially changing the school's name from Peachtree Heights to E. Rivers. According to a congratulatory article, "Mr. Rivers perceived early the need of a school, but it was with some difficulty that he convinced the county school authorities." Later, Rivers acknowledged the important role the school had played in Peachtree Heights' success: "When the movement for the Rivers grammar school first started, the residents of that section were told that the child population would not warrant the school, but when the school was built, the number of students increased so fast an annex had to be built."[55]

Parents' desire to send their children to the best public school available pushed up real estate values in neighborhoods enjoying the most recently constructed schools—with all the bells and whistles that made them "modern." By the second decade of the twentieth century, school location was frequently shaping housing patterns as much as or more so than housing patterns were determining school location. Unequal school facilities fueled this dynamic. Per capita spending on education shot up during the early twentieth century, but it was rarely spent per capita, especially in the penurious school districts of the South.[56] After residential park investors finagled superior schools for their developments, the local power structure frequently began accusing the school board of extravagance before schools in the older parts of the city could be replaced. This cycle allowed developers and their allies in local government to create a new form of de jure segregation by limiting the number of modern schools, especially in Jim Crow cities where class was layered onto race.

As affluent families became concentrated in fewer and fewer schools, they could better use their political heft to insist that their children continue to receive preferential treatment. Even ward-based school boards found it much easier to deny working-class children adequate facilities than push back against business-class parents with ties to the powerful chamber of commerce. Consequently, the modern schools built for racially restricted residential parks helped draw white residents out of established areas where antiquated schools still served neighborhoods with traditional block-level segregation.

When affluent white parents no longer viewed older neighborhoods as appealing environments for raising children, Black middle-class families gained additional housing opportunities. They frequently moved into homes recently vacated by whites relocating to the suburbs, especially in those neighborhoods nearest the best Black schools. These changes placed a strain on block-level segregation almost immediately. White families who were unwilling or unable to move out to suburban residential parks became increasingly angry that the rules of the game seemed to have changed overnight. In response, they asked local officials to provide them with at least some of the benefits of residential parks. The protection of block-level segregation topped the list along with calls for modern schools in the older areas of the city.

CHAPTER 4

Residential Parks and the Rise of Segregation Ordinances

In 1910, Milton Dashiell, an attorney and father of three daughters, ages two to fifteen, lived on McCulloh Street in northwest Baltimore. That year, George McMechen, a Yale-educated attorney, moved his young family onto Dashiell's block. Rather than welcome McMechen as a fellow father and attorney, Dashiell responded by brashly writing the nation's first segregation ordinance, which barred Black residents from moving onto majority white blocks and vice versa.[1] Because George McMechen was Black, his family's presence on McCulloh Street threatened Dashiell's desire to raise his children according to the dominant child-rearing norms of the middle class, which included limiting who his daughters' companions would be.

Restricted residential parks had already begun disrupting previous notions of acceptable neighborhood standards by redefining expectations for the proper environment to raise white children, especially in Jim Crow cities. Developers were tying the single-family house to racial segregation in new ways that went far beyond traditional, block-level segregation. They sold upward mobility to white families by excluding children who would not make likely marriage partners or business associates in the future. Those exclusions extended throughout the development, which could include hundreds of homes, meaning that every family within the bounds of the same residential park acquired a comparable social status. Neighbors were no longer simply those within shouting distance on the same block.

Soon, the growing popularity of residential parks meant that the convenience of traditional patchwork development fell out of favor with affluent whites. Older neighborhoods such as Dashiell's, in which Black and white blocks coexisted together and where social and environmental hazards might be just around the corner, were no longer considered acceptable for white child-rearing. This transformation also affected the conventional wisdom about property values. Once child-centered arguments made residential parks fashionable, the value of those home lots climbed while white interest in aging neighborhoods plummeted.[2]

This dramatic shift in housing preferences increased segregation by preventing traditional block-level segregation patterns from expanding outward along with the city limits. For example, in 1910 the *Atlanta Journal* reported that owners of "an immense area of valuable land" north of the city limits had agreed to impose covenants banning "Negroes, cemeteries, hospitals, and sanitariums."[3] As housing options for Black residents narrowed, more Black families settled in centrally located neighborhoods that lacked restrictions. In 1910, only two of the attendance districts for Atlanta's forty-one white schools were more than 90 percent white. Even Ansley Park's attendance district was just 83 percent white. By 1920, however, fourteen districts had exceeded the 90 percent threshold, including one new district that was 99.9 percent white. Meanwhile, Black residents living in the Ansley Park district shrank from 17 percent of the population to about 8 percent as the footprint of the area's residential parks continued to expand.[4]

The white middle-class preference for suburban residential parks, at first, offered potentially positive outcomes for the Black middle class. When white parents deserted their old neighborhoods and headed for the suburbs, affluent Black families eagerly purchased their former homes. Black parents hoped to raise their children in a better environment than the crowded alleys and slums where white people still expected them to live. Likewise, once modern transportation, heating, lighting, and sanitation became standard, Black families were less willing to live in outlying enclaves that lacked city services, much as white middle-class families were less willing to live in urban areas that lacked all the amenities of residential parks.

The white residents who remained in unrestricted neighborhoods panicked when mixed-raced housing patterns began to collapse. In the past, block-level segregation followed the dictates of Jim Crow with Black families living in clearly inferior residences that preserved the appearance of social inequality. Evidence suggests that the hasty passage of segregation ordinances was a direct response to white middle-class parents from transitional neighborhoods who demanded local officials do something to preserve traditional block-by-block development. Historian Elizabeth Herbin-Triant found that calls for segregation laws were louder in areas where Black homeowning was increasing.[5] In other words, the objections arose in areas where Black middle-class homeowners were living next door to white middle-class families.

White families stayed behind in these mixed-race neighborhoods for multiple reasons. First, they appreciated the convenience of living near jobs, stores, religious institutions, friends, and family members, and they believed their proximity to Black laundresses and day laborers was a benefit. Second, not all agreed that traditional development lowered property values. At the turn of the century, property evolution continued to be the most common way to profit from real estate; the transition from residential to commercial use almost always raised property values, which many white owners applauded. And third, not all who considered themselves middle class could afford to move to a residential park. After all, the very purpose of many of the deed restrictions was to exclude those with lower incomes than the targeted buyer. The remaining white families soon turned to local officials to provide some of the racial "protections" afforded by residential parks.[6]

Traditional Residential Patterns in the Urban South

During the early twentieth century, Black residents in Jim Crow cities made up much larger percentages of far smaller urban populations than those living in the North or West, which meant that most Black and white residents lived and worked near each other. The most prominent addresses were along grand avenues close to downtown, while cross streets and alleys might contain a range of different property uses and users. Frequently, working-class, mixed-race communities were adjacent to the industries where the residents worked while middle-class storeowners and professionals remained close by to cater to their needs. White families usually hired Black domestics and day laborers living nearby and sometimes increased their income by renting inexpensive shacks on their property to Black tenants.[7] Black homes also lined the interstitial spaces of the city along alleyways, railroad tracks, and streams, creating the honeycomb residential patterns numerous historians have identified.[8]

A report produced by the UK Board of Trade in 1911 documented the mixed-race housing patterns that characterized most southern cities at the time. In Memphis, landowners "erected cottages (known as shanties) of two and three rooms for the accommodation of negroes" on "every available space," especially along low-lying hollows and "backways." In New Orleans, white and Black residents lived "in close proximity" all along the area "between Magazine Street and the river bank." It was only farther inland from the Mississippi River that Black and white residents were "separated to any considerable extent." In Savannah, Black tenants occasionally resided in basement apartments of older homes while the upstairs was "occupied by fairly respectable white people." In Atlanta, "no large districts" were inhabited solely by Black residents: while "portions of certain streets and clusters of houses here and there" had "only coloured occupants, in no case would it be necessary to traverse more than a few yards in order to come again to the dwellings of the other race."[9] As long as Black homes appeared outwardly inferior to white ones, mixed-race housing patterns did not challenge white supremacy.

In areas with block-level segregation, white and Black "districts" were much smaller than in residential parks controlled by racial covenants. In fact, a "white district" might be a single block—defined as two sides of the same street between two cross streets—or even half of one. White and Black "districts" sometimes alternated along the same street or, more often, intersected at crossroads. Other

Black homes, businesses, and institutions formed small enclaves, many of them dating back to Reconstruction or even earlier. These "colonies," as whites sometimes called them, were a tiny fraction of the size of midcentury "ghettoes." They were dispersed throughout the city and usually connected to one another by Black homes stretching along creeks, bayous, alleys, or railroad tracks. Thus, it was unusual for Black and white residents to live completely isolated from one another. According to Howard Beeth and Cary Wintz's study of early twentieth-century Houston, "Most black families continued to have at least one white family living across the street or down the block" well into the 1920s.[10]

Since city services were only grudgingly extended to Black "districts," the condition of Black blocks could be reprehensible; consequently, local officials sometimes championed the extension of services to Black homes to hinder fast-moving epidemics in mixed-race areas. In 1910, an Atlanta reporter praised "waterworks officials" for the "great wisdom" of extending city water to two densely populated Black blocks that had sewer facilities but no "water to flush them." "The negro women living in this neighborhood take in washing," he explained. "In the backyard of each place is a surface well and close by is a surface closet [outhouse]. The dirty water from the tubs is poured into the yards and trickles into the street, forming foul and slimy pools in which the little negro children play." In the same article, the mayor warned, "There's no telling how much disease has been distributed about the city from the unsanitation in these backyards."[11] The detailed description of the children's appalling play space was meant to gain support from white taxpayers through disgust rather than sympathy; as was typical, improvements to Black streets were almost always made in the name of protecting white families.

Black families, of course, were concerned about the impact of those conditions on Black children. Beginning in 1908, the volunteers of Atlanta's Neighborhood Union conducted regular house-to-house surveys to document the environment in which Black families were forced to live. They reported streets "badly in need of improvement," with many having "insufficient lights," which they worried would "breed crime." They also recorded "little to no sewerage facilities" so that "the water supply consisted mostly of surface wells." Worse yet, local officials did not seem to care "how houses for Negroes were thrown up," so unscreened "surface toilets" were often located near kitchen doors. In response, Union members advocated for regular garbage removal, better street maintenance, and more frequent visits from the "sanitary man" to service the outhouses. They also begged local officials to stop burning the city's garbage near their homes, which caused so much "stench and smoke at night the children could not sleep."[12]

As the number of Black residents increased in southern cities, the conditions on crowded Black blocks grew worse. Clifton Richardson, the courageous editor of the *Houston Informer*, wrote an "Open Letter" to the mayor and city commissioners objecting to the routine neglect of Black homes. Using all capital letters to emphasize his point, he wrote: "Sirs, as long as thousands of your citizens are compelled to live in hog wollows, on mud alleys, with little, or no, police or fire protection; with shacks jammed together like sardines in a can; with no park facilities and playground activities; with stagnant, foul and polluted water breeding and giving sustenance to disease-producing and health-destroying pests and insects, the health, well-being, safety and perpetuity of the entire community and combined citizenry are jeopardized, menaced and in constant peril."[13] He hoped a reminder that the health of white residents was also at stake might prod local officials to act, but intensifying segregation made this less likely. While Black activists understood that racial separation could be a strategy for combatting Jim Crow's daily insults, most opposed formal segregation because they understood that the disregard for Black blocks would only worsen if white people lived further away.

In the meantime, some white southerners saw no need for expanding residential segregation so long as Jim Crow laws effectively maintained the racial hierarchy. According to historian LaKisha Simmons, southern whites traditionally understood "place" in relation to "social performances" rather than as racially distinct space. Block-by-block segregation required educating Black and white children on the dictates of Jim Crow, an especially traumatic process for young Black children, whose own safety depended on learning the mortal dangers of offending white sensibilities. Black middle-class parents walked a difficult line between shielding their young children from America's caste system and protecting them from the violence that would immediately befall if they did not fully comprehend what lay at the core of white supremacy. Whites would viciously attack even young Black boys who innocently suggested some level of romantic interest across race lines, what whites obliquely referred to as a desire for "social equality."[14]

The hysteria about interracial sex was rooted in the fear of a white woman giving birth to a "Black" child and thereby throwing the boundaries of white supremacy into chaos. For hundreds of years, the racial status of the child had followed that of the mother. Therefore, a Black woman giving birth to a biracial child was never a threat to the system, making Black women frequent targets of sexual assault. The exception was the "legitimate" offspring of a legal marriage, which granted biracial children rights to their father's property and social standing. Antimiscegenation laws, some of which dated back at least to the eighteenth century, were designed to thwart legal marriages between Black women and white men and *any* sexual relationships between white women and Black men. After the Civil War, as Black men gained wealth and status, lynching became the preferred method for policing white supremacy, since terror was more effective and immediate than antimiscegenation laws.[15]

Preventing a Black family from living next door to a white one was another tactic used to foil interracial relationships, although this one was tied more directly to parenting. While the goal of both violence and antimiscegenation laws was to defend the boundaries of white supremacy in general, residential segregation hit closer to home. White parents especially feared the possibility that an interracial relationship might involve *one's own* daughter. A secondary concern was that *one's own* son might become seriously involved with the attractive, educated, well-dressed, and accomplished young Black woman living next door, even as the sexual assault of Black women and girls was a problem unworthy of their concern. Although miscegenation was often couched in terms of threats to the white race, the problem for individual parents was seeing their own children become social outcasts. Traditional, mixed-race housing patterns worked only where Jim Crow enabled whites to remain dominant: white families constituted the majority within the neighborhood and controlled the routes to their institutions, Black families lived in clearly inferior housing, and Black children attended clearly inferior schools.

Residential parks offered white families a more foolproof remedy for preventing miscegenation by limiting the acquaintances of one's children throughout the development. They also afforded parents the additional comfort of escaping questions about the morality of enforcing racial subjugation within a supposedly democratic meritocracy. Many white southerners wanted segregation to seem natural and to believe that it was good for everyone, Black and white. But each time Black residents refused to yield the sidewalk, sat where they wished on the streetcar, or challenged discrimination in Jim Crow schools, parks, hospitals, libraries, or other institutions, it compelled well-mannered whites to think about the system, to remember that Jim Crow was not natural but a product of their history, and to recognize its hypocrisies and inconsistencies. Thus, racial covenants allowed affluent white parents to shield their children from social ostracization as well as to shelter them from the discomfort of ever needing to ponder the gross injustices of the system. Those injustices would occur far from the enchanted borders of the residential park, where the children of the enlightened could live in peace and prosperity without seeing anything that might upset them.[16]

Affluent Black parents also longed for neighborhoods that would protect their children and provide more opportunities for upward mobility, although the stakes for them were much higher. Jim Crow sometimes pushed Black middle-class families into racially separate areas beyond the city limits, where they were less likely to suffer the dangers or indignities of racial subjugation.[17] With the rise of the residential park, however, suburban areas increasingly became closed off to Black families while commercial centers chipped away at the older housing stock. Black residents had little choice but to crowd onto the dwindling number of blocks with available housing. Rapid urbanization further added to the severe overcrowding on Black blocks.

Deteriorating conditions combined with an increasing number of vacancies on white blocks prompted affluent Black families to challenge the norms of block-level segregation. They rejected housing along unimproved alleys, beside open sewers, or in low-lying "hollows" that lacked drainage and, thus, imperiled their children's health. Instead, they purchased homes previously belonging to white families. In most cases, modern amenities could only be obtained on what were once "white" streets. Parents also wished to shelter their children from moral hazards, since local officials usually steered vice districts into areas near Black blocks. According to Booker T. Washington, "When a Negro seeks to buy a house in a reputable street he does it not only to get police protection, lights and accommodations, but to remove his children to a locality in which vice is not paraded." "If the Negro is segregated," he chided, the "'undesirables' of the other race will be placed near him, thereby making it difficult for him to rear his family in decency."[18]

In Search of Child-Friendly Streets

During the early twentieth century, segregation ordinances were devised explicitly to tackle the "problem" of upwardly mobile Black families moving into the single-family houses that had been recently vacated by upwardly mobile white families. Traditional block-level segregation was beginning to splinter because too many prosperous white families no longer wished to live in established, urban neighborhoods to sustain the old, single-family homes as white middle-class properties. Residential park advertisements had effectively diminished them in the eyes of white parents. Smaller yards, higher densities, nearby apartment buildings, stores, heavier automobile traffic, and unpredictable acquaintances now made them unsuitable for child-rearing.

Not all whites preferred residential parks, though. Some could not afford to move, others liked the convenience of the city, and still others sought upward mobility in established neighborhoods with long-standing reputations for affluence.[19] Yet, as demand decreased, the aging homes could no longer attract residents with the same status as those who left. Meanwhile, Black businessmen and professionals were willing to pay more for those houses than white buyers, and most property owners wished to sell to the highest bidder, regardless of race: the more profit from the sale of a previous home, the more money to build a dream house in the suburbs. Worried about the looming collapse of block-level segregation, the remaining whites hoped to restore the racial balance of their neighborhoods by pressuring local officials to pass segregation ordinances that would allow them to maintain control over their streets and institutions.

This cycle helps explain the relatively sudden appearance of the nation's first residential segregation law, passed in Baltimore in 1910. W. Ashbie Hawkins had purchased a house on McCulloh Street and rented it to his Yale-educated law partner, George McMechen. McMechen and his wife, a well-respected schoolteacher, sought "to rear their children in as good environments as they could secure," in Hawkins's telling of events. The presence of the McMechen family enraged Milton Dashiell and about fifty other white homeowners, who then formed the McCulloh Street, Madison Avenue, and Eutaw Place Property Association to organize a response. Improvement associations became popular during the early twentieth century to help residents advocate for their rightful share of city services, including schools, so they might better compete with residential parks for public resources. Many of them also became strong proponents of de jure residential segregation.[20]

Members of the McCulloh Street association appointed Dashiell to write a segregation ordinance as a possible remedy, even though the McMechen and Dashiell homes were already in a mixed-race area only one block from what a legal scholar has called the "worst" slum in Baltimore. In an interview with the *New York Times*, Dashiell defended the law by asserting that Druid Hill Avenue, which ran parallel to McCulloh Street one block over to the west, had been a "a white residential street" a "few years" before but was "now practically given up to the negro." The ordinance was intended to halt further racial turnover, a process Dashiell oversimplified as "the negro came in [and] the white man got out." He did not analyze how or why Black families "came in" or why it was acceptable to live so close to Druid Hill but not on the same block as the McMechen family.[21]

The rationale he gave to a local newspaper provided further insight into his reasoning. "If in our public schools colored and white children are legally kept apart for five hours a day," he argued, "why should it not be legal for us to have a law to keep the two races from living in the same block, where they will be forced to intermingle 24 hours a day."[22] His oldest daughter turned sixteen just two weeks after the improvement association first met, and his youngest daughter turned three soon after he uttered those words.[23] Dashiell and his white neighbors seemed most worried that their offspring's opportunities might be limited if their children interacted with the McMechens as equals. They revealed similar concerns every time they referred to the infiltration of Black *families* rather than Black homeowners or tenants. Their new neighbors had children, which they viewed as a threat to their own, especially in a society that increasingly assumed that the current and future happiness of white middle-class children was tied to living in an exclusive environment.

Since Dashiell seemed unwilling to acknowledge the new reality that residential parks had created, George McMechen was left to clarify the economics of the situation. "I think it is erroneous to say that the colored people have tried to push their way in among the whites," he explained to the *New York Times*. "All that they have done is merely to occupy the vacant houses when it has been found impossible to obtain a white tenant. As the white people move out into the suburbs or into apartment houses, many blocks are left practically vacant; it is into these districts that the well-to-do colored people move." His reference to "apartment houses" was a good reminder that "palatial" apartments were a popular rival to residential parks, one that housing reformers vociferously condemned as inappropriate for children. Those who did choose to move into apartments, including empty nesters, struggled to find young, white, upwardly mobile families willing to purchase their former houses because those families preferred residential parks.[24] His law partner, W. Ashbie Hawkins, further expounded on the economic impact of "the opening and development of large suburban tracts" for "the middle class of whites." "Baltimore was for years without any great suburbs, but with the coming and development of her cable and electric cars reaching out in every direction, these have grown with great rapidity and often at the expense of city market values."[25]

About fifteen years before the passage of Baltimore's segregation ordinance, the developers of Roland Park had begun targeting middle-class parents with an advertising campaign that criticized traditional mixed-use development. One ad urged parents to safeguard their children from "the drain of vitality, possibly unseen now" that "comes from the noise and dirt and dust and lack of sewers" in the city. A few days later, an ad suggested parental responsibility for a child's poor health unless families took "every possible precaution to prevent it." Parents who moved to Roland Park were "simply fulfilling their duty" by selecting "an ideal home" rather than being "cooped up in a narrow, prison-like house in a long row," like the brownstone-lined streets that Dashiell's improvement association sought to defend. The following year, another ad proclaimed, "The happy children of Roland Park furnish an object-lesson for parents," providing homes with "all of the comforts, but none of the dangers, of city life."[26]

Roland Park did not use racial covenants when Baltimore's first segregation ordinance became law, although residential parks further south already used them consistently, and the Roland Park Company had considered adopting them as early as 1893.[27] Whether Dashiell and his neighbors knew they existed before the McCulloh Street property association began pressing for a segregation law makes little difference. Residential park developers easily controlled who purchased their lots, thereby establishing whole neighborhoods that were widely recognized as whites only. Moreover, Black families had little desire to live in distant neighborhoods with no schools for their children. Therefore, it is unlikely that the use of racial covenants inspired the first segregation ordinance; instead, it was the rising number of vacancies caused by white families moving out to the suburbs.

Unlike Baltimore, Winston-Salem's earliest racial covenants were more than twenty years old when the city's segregation ordinance was initially proposed in 1912. By 1892, white residential areas were being developed on three sides of the metropolitan area along with Columbia Heights, a residential park for prosperous Black families in the far southeastern corner of the city, as described in chapter 2. Together, these residential areas allowed for significant racial and class sorting to occur even before the turn of the twentieth century. But because white investors in Columbia Heights did not advocate for improvements for Black homeowners as they did for white residential parks, Columbia Heights remained cut off from downtown without either street improvements or convenient access to public schools fully twenty years later.[28] As a result, when white middle-class families moved out to suburban residential parks, affluent Black families gladly purchased their old homes to gain access to more city services.

Calls for a segregation ordinance began after James Timlic purchased a home for his family at 617 East Fourth Street. He was the proprietor of a successful blacksmith shop as well as a director for the prestigious, Black-owned Forsyth Savings and Trust Company. The Timlics were not the first Black family to move onto the block.[29] Two and a half years earlier, during the summer of 1909, Charles Jones, a Black grocer and the vice president of Forsyth Savings and Trust Company, had already purchased two home lots, keeping one for himself and selling the other to Dr. Cleon Lee, a Black dentist.[30]

As with Baltimore's original ordinance, Winston-Salem's applied only to the specific part of town that was first aggrieved. In this case, the law designated East Fourth Street for white residents and one of its more industrial cross streets—Depot Street—for Black residents. Within a month's time, this law was replaced by another that barred Black residents from moving onto a majority-white block anywhere in the city. Local attorneys had determined that this version would be more likely to survive judicial review because it treated all parts of the city equally, following the same trajectory as Baltimore's multiple segregation ordinances.[31]

The two cities diverged when it came to the role that racial covenants played in the segregation law. White residents living along East Fourth Street claimed that deed restrictions existed on their properties, prohibiting racial transition either with or without a segregation ordinance. Some preferred seeking "relief" in court rather than betting on a constitutionally vulnerable law. To test the strategy, J. W. Carter, one of the previous owners of 617 East Fourth Street, brought a lawsuit against Timlic.[32] Carter had purchased the property back in 1901 from a Carolina Stewart, who had purchased it from Henry Starbuck in 1889. Her property was one of the three that Starbuck had encumbered with a race restriction, likely the first used in Forsyth County, as discussed in chapter 2.[33] Even so, that property's block was not part of the East Winston development, which did, in fact, use racial covenants.

The lawsuit against Timlic essentially ended before it began.[34] The property had gone through eight owners since Starbuck had inserted the race restriction in its deed. With so many prior owners and occupants, there was no clear path of enforcement, although Carter seemed to believe that the title should revert to him after the covenant had been broken. Minnie Craver, the person who had purchased the property from Carter, subdivided it into three home lots, which she then sold to white buyers without race restrictions (see map 4.1). From that point on, the lot in question changed hands three more times before Timlic purchased it in 1911.[35]

Carter and the others insisted that every lot along East Fourth Street had race restrictions, which was categorically false. When Starbuck originally sold his property on the western portion of the block in question, he imposed no deed restrictions. That property was eventually divided into four house lots. Over time, various owners erected dwellings on each one, most of which became rental properties. As discussed in chapter 2, Starbuck likely added the deed restriction to the eastern portion of the block to "protect" the adjacent property that was still owned by his sister. In 1912, Starbuck declined to enter the fray. Once his sister sold the adjacent property without restrictions, the family lost interest in who eventually lived on that corner.[36]

The Sanborn map for this block illustrates important differences between traditional housing patterns and a residential park. Because house lots were carved out of the block at different times and by different owners, they were irregularly shaped, affording some properties awkward access to the street if at all. The block also contained businesses, such as the store at the corner of Fourth and Maple and the boarding house at the corner of Fourth and Linden. Residential parks, on the other hand, did not leave subdivision up to chance. An engineer designed the plat map so that the entire property would be divided into rational lots, which were all covered by identical deed restrictions that prohibited businesses and other uses viewed as incompatible with child-rearing.[37]

As residential parks became the norm, traditional blocks fell out of favor with white buyers. Even before Charles Jones, a successful Black businessman, began purchasing houses on the 600 block of East Fourth Street, the properties had already experienced high turnover rates and falling property values. Most houses on the northern half of the block changed occupancy almost every year, and in more than one case, owners sold their properties for a loss.[38] Rather than destabilizing the block, Black homeowners brought stability and rising home values. Indeed, only one white property owner, Eugene Watkins, lost money after Black families began moving in.

Watkins purchased the lot at 617 East Fourth Street in 1909 one week before Charles Jones purchased the adjacent property from a white absentee landowner

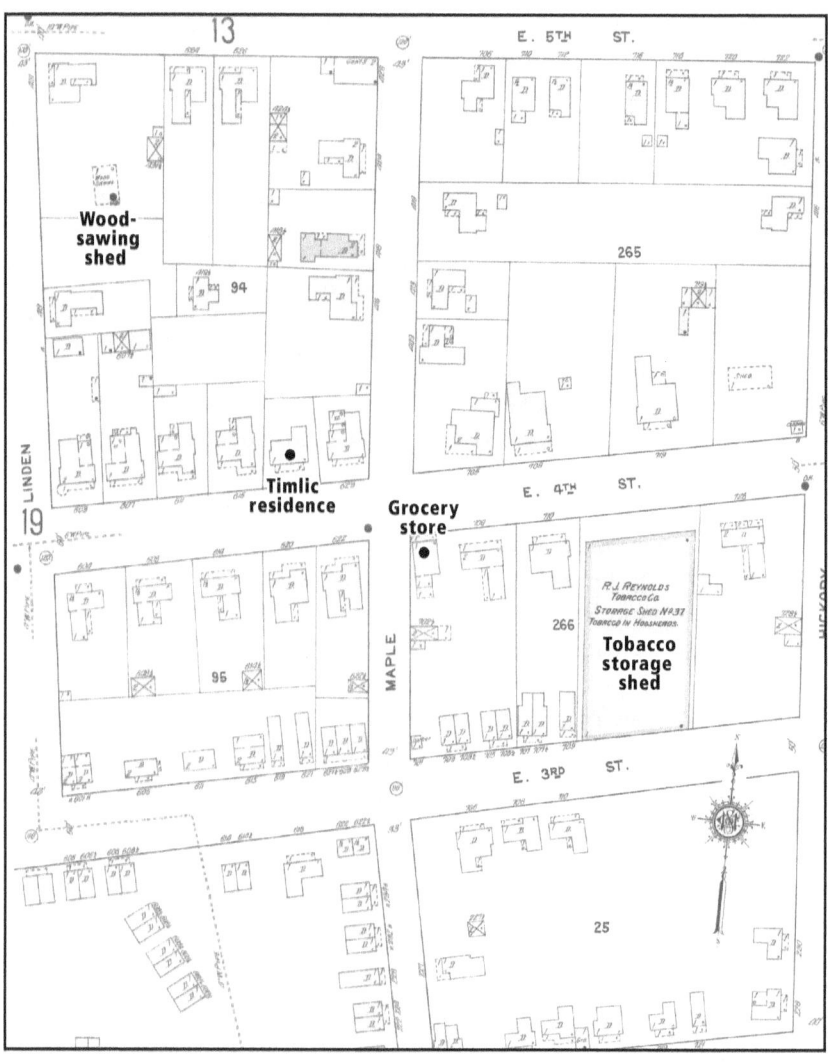

MAP 4.1. The East Fourth Street neighborhood that sparked Winston-Salem's 1912 segregation ordinance illustrates traditional mixed-use, mixed-race development. Note the tobacco storage shed on East Fourth Street, the grocery store down the block, the wood-sawing shed on Linden, and the small, attached dwellings on East Third Street. In addition, irregular lots, the awkward placement of buildings, and the lack of street access for some lots further marred the appeal of the block (compare to the Columbia Heights plat map, figure 4.1). Sanborn Fire Insurance Map, Winston-Salem, North Carolina, 1912. Courtesy of the Library of Congress.

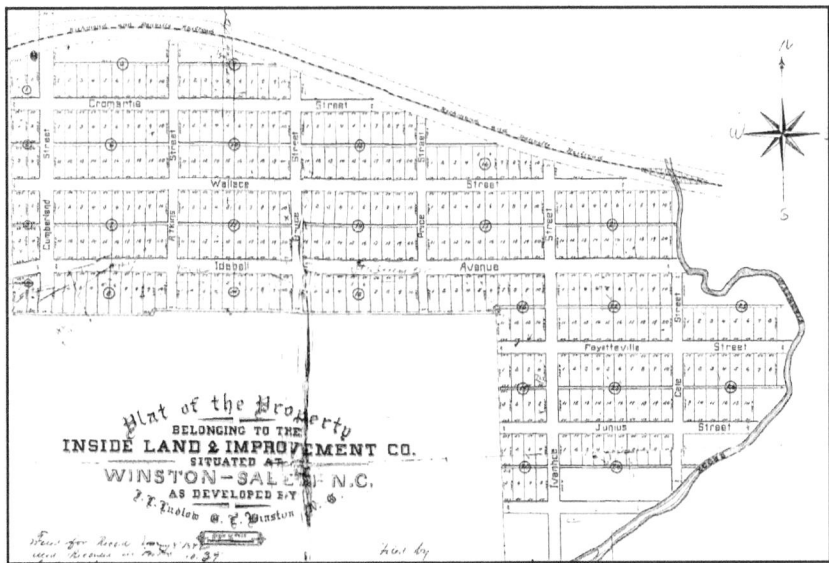

FIGURE 4.1. Unlike the jumble of buildings on many urban blocks (see map 4.1), Columbia Heights had uniform lots with equal access to the street, as illustrated by its plat map. The engineer who designed Columbia Heights also designed many of the affluent, white residential parks on the opposite side of town. Forsyth County Deed Book #39, p. 401, Forsyth County, NC, Register of Deeds Online Records Systems, Property Deed Books and Index, www.co.forsyth.nc.us/rod/online_lookup.aspx.

who was then living in New York. Watkins built a house for his wife and little girl straightaway. When Jones moved his family next door, Watkins immediately sold his new house at a loss to the Renigars, a white couple who already owned property on the block. Watkins's panic was most likely the catalyst for the segregation ordinance, although he himself was not directly involved. At forty years old, he died of a heart attack less than a year after selling the property. Before his death, he was the secretary-treasurer of the Winston Development Company, which had opened East Winston back in 1891. Thus, Watkins would have known about the racial covenants in that development, which was just east of his home. Perhaps he even knew about the deed restriction on his own property, which is why he quickly dumped it on the Renigars.[39] Or perhaps he felt he was not at liberty to sell the property to a Black family because local realtors had made an agreement not to sell "white" houses to Black buyers.

Regardless, the Renigars, who owned a working-class "saloon" on nearby Third Street, had no similar qualms about selling to a Black buyer but rather saw an opportunity to reap large profits. They more than doubled their money when they sold the property the following year to the Timlics.[40] A few months later, they sold 607 East Fourth Street to a Black grocer, after previously cycling through at least four white tenants during the preceding six years. They continued to use their residence on the corner as a white boarding house until 1918. They then sold the property and two additional lots to Charles Jones, who established a hotel, a smart investment since hotels serving Black customers were rare in the Jim Crow South.[41]

Throughout the entire uproar over the segregation ordinance, Timlic and his neighbors remained on East Fourth Street patiently waiting for the divisive law to wend its way through the courts. During the two years the law remained in effect, Winston-Salem's Black middle class did not publicly protest its passage. Instead, they played the long game, recognizing that a positive outcome in the courts would better safeguard their rights. After all, local officials did not see them as constituents in the same way they viewed white residents, including those who continued to call for a segregation law. Berating the board of aldermen would only jeopardize their petitions for desperately needed schools and street improvements.[42]

With that said, prominent Black businessmen under the leadership of Charles Jones and others organized a campaign to defeat Silas Bennett, the man who submitted the segregation ordinance to the city council (and who likely wrote it). An upstart lawyer well outside of Winston-Salem's elite circle, Bennett ran for a seat in the state legislature the same year he introduced the ordinance. Whites rallied to his cause to block Black citizens from influencing the election, which would have challenged a core tenant of white supremacy. For their part, Black citizens hoped to preclude Bennett from pushing forward a state enabling law that would have made it easier for Winston-Salem to defend its segregation ordinance in court. Bennett won his election, but the state legislature voted down the controversial enabling law nonetheless.[43]

In 1918, the year Charles Jones purchased the property for his hotel, the northern half of the block had one remaining white resident, a tenant who had been renting a house on the corner since 1911. The absentee landlord was Minnie Craver, the widow who had originally subdivided the property into house lots. In 1907, she remarried and moved to Spartanburg, South Carolina. For much of the decade, the same white tenant lived in peace next door to the Timlics. The adjacent block on East Fourth Street was still all white as was the cross street, making the corner house the racial dividing line. In 1918, Minnie Craver (Haddan) sold the house to a Black teacher, allowing the north side of the block to fully transition to Black property ownership, while the south side remained all white. This stalemate continued for a few years until the south side transitioned as well.[44] Even when white tenants were willing to stay, the demand from Black homebuyers was too great; simple economics would eventually push out any persistent whites.

Atlanta's first segregation ordinance, like those passed in Winston-Salem and Baltimore, was also born out of an effort to protect a single neighborhood that had fallen out of favor with white, middle-class families. Unlike events in the Twin Cities, however, Atlanta's Black businessmen publicly opposed the ordinance rather than relying solely on the courts. They immediately informed local officials that the ordinance was unconstitutional. With arguments echoing those of Baltimore's Black protesters, they lectured whites on the economics of the housing market and questioned both the wisdom and morality of those who supported the law.

Benjamin Davis, the unyielding editor of the *Atlanta Independent*, engaged his white "neighbors" in "a heart-to-heart talk" through a series of editorials published soon after the ordinance passed. He doubted whether they had fully considered the consequences of the law, which would stifle the city's real estate market and prevent Black residents from bettering themselves, a goal whites often alleged to espouse. If Black residents could not buy the housing stock that whites had rejected, he asked, then "who are to use the homes that the white man's means have outgrown? If we are not to leave the alleys, slums, backyards and the factory tenements, as we become able with a view of establishing a pure home life, then how are we to help ourselves?" Davis reminded his white "friends" that they, like him, had been "taught that a boy cannot rise above his home; that man is the creature of his environments." If those words were true for white children, then why not for Black ones? "How are we to improve each generation if we must continue to stay packed in back alleys and in tenements unfit for horse stables?"[45]

Davis reassured whites that Black families were not interested in white residential parks. A white lawyer named Eugene Mitchell, a staunch supporter of the ordinance, had illogically suggested that restricted communities would not be safe without the protections offered by the ordinance. He warned, "The time is near when negroes will be invading the Ansley Park, Druid Hills, Boulevard and Brookwood Sections," claiming that the ordinance "provided the only relief." Davis's trenchant response left little room for misinterpretation: "The Negro does not want a home in Ansley Park, Inman Park, Druid Hills, Peachtree Street, or in any other exclusive settlement" where "he cannot have a neighbor," but "he does contend for and has money to buy and pay for homes in settlements far superior to the places" where Black families were usually "confined." "Druid Hill, Peachtree Heights, Peachtree Place, Inman Park, and a dozen other settlements" had been "set aside for white homes," he argued, making it time for the larger community to "do its duty" and "provide settlements commensurate with the Negro's progress and intelligence."[46]

Eugene Mitchell had recently moved from Jackson Hill in the lower Fourth Ward residential area, where the appeals for a segregation ordinance had started. When he lived on Jackson Street, Mitchell had served as Fourth Ward's representative on the school board, and he remained unusually concerned about the fate of his old neighborhood after he moved. Once a relatively prestigious address, Jackson Hill lacked the restrictions of a residential park, and thus, commercial properties were threatening the residential quality of his former block, even though it was not undergoing racial transition. While Black middle-class families were moving onto nearby streets, his block retained enough cachet that it could continue to attract white families.[47]

Ignoring the multifaceted reasons that the larger neighborhood was no longer seen as appropriate for middle-class child-rearing, Mitchell helped his former neighbors advocate for a segregation law. But his effort to rouse support from suburban homeowners failed to consider the basic underpinnings of the housing market. White families living in residential parks, including those without racial covenants such as Druid Hills, needed neither reassurances nor segregation laws to feel secure. High demand meant that none of their neighbors would feel compelled to sell to either a Black family or someone from a lower economic stratum.[48] Consequently, they either stayed out of the fight or openly opposed the ordinance because it would make it more difficult to sell residential property in the older areas of the city.

The Value of Property

The assertion that whites seeking segregation ordinances were primarily concerned with falling property values has remained widespread in the literature on residential segregation.[49] Although the rhetoric about falling property values was common during the early twentieth century, it should not be taken at face value or understood in abstract terms but rather analyzed according to the key factors driving the housing market. The priorities of affluent parents had become affixed to residential real estate values, causing the demand for houses that were no longer seen as appropriate sites for white, middle-class child-rearing to plummet in both relative and absolute terms as *white* properties. Given that affluent Black families were eager to purchase them despite being forced to pay significantly higher prices than a white buyer, the shrinking demand among white families did not reduce the overall value of the houses.

As early as 1903, an article in *The Nation* had already identified how the process worked, at least in northwest Baltimore. Once white middle-class families began rejecting aging rowhouses on traditional urban streets, it became increasingly difficult to find white tenants at rents that would sustain them as middle-class properties. Accordingly, "the decline in value" made "large progress before any negroes appeared in the neighborhood." As the number of vacancies grew, Black middle-class residents who had achieved greater "education and culture" and aspired "for their children and themselves better surroundings" began purchasing the properties.[50]

Perhaps the proponents of the various segregation ordinances did not fully understand the forces that had originally pulled affluent white families out of their neighborhoods. After all, declining property values in formerly middle-class areas could create the illusion that Black neighbors diminished property values. Moreover, the presence of Black families living alongside white families as equals challenged the basic tenets of Jim Crow; white residents who stayed would lose status.[51] Still, plenty of evidence suggests that those who embraced the property-value argument understood its hollowness but thought it would help segregation laws survive judicial review.

When Dashiell began searching for a solid defense of his ordinance, he approached the subject as an attorney rather than as a father. From the beginning, Dashiell seemed much less concerned about financial loss than about finding a legal argument that would bar Black families from becoming his neighbors. Even the most ardent advocates of segregation laws doubted their constitutionality, especially since the legality of racial covenants had not yet been determined. Dashiell, therefore, devised a strategy he imagined would be more sympathetic to the courts. "If it could be shown that a negro moving into a neighborhood causes property values to decrease," he reasoned, "I am of the opinion that the adjoining property owners could protect themselves, and obtain a writ of injunction and keep the colored people from moving in." Soon, he was making wildly unsubstantiated claims that the presence of a single Black family in "a white residential district" would "depreciate the value of that property fully one-half."[52]

Baltimore's mayor then followed Dashiell's lead. He maintained that the ordinance would "prevent the depreciation which is of necessity bound to follow when the colored family" moved into "a neighborhood that had hitherto been exclusively occupied by white people." To prove his point, he asserted that a Black property holder would "no more think of occupying or leasing that property to another negro than a white man would—simply because he knows that such an act would result in the depreciation of the value of his property perhaps one-half."[53] This claim was laughable since George McMechen had rented the house in question from his law partner, W. Ashbie Hawkins. In other words, the ordinance existed precisely because a Black property owner had rented the house to a Black tenant.

Their faulty argument enabled advocates of the segregation law to insist that Black neighbors initiated suburban flight rather than vice versa. One proponent fumed, "We cannot blame our suburbs. Unpleasant negro neighbors have forced white residents to go outside the municipal city limits, where they are protected. This proposed ordinance is all that is necessary to settle the question." Yet, the idea that a segregation law would end the appeal of suburban residential parks was as much a fantasy as the contention that it would somehow lead absentee landlords to tear down "the old houses now occupied by negroes" and rebuild them "with handsome residences" that would attract affluent white families.[54]

New standards for the proper environment for white, middle-class child-rearing extended well beyond the presence of Black families, as demonstrated by the success of residential parks in cities with small Black populations.

Fortunately for those white families aspiring to move to the suburbs, Black parents were prepared to rescue them from financial loss by paying a premium for their former homes. In his interview with the *New York Times*, George McMechen countered the property-value argument by reminding his white neighbors that Black residents paid more for their homes: "As for property deteriorating on account of our advent into that neighborhood, I know it cannot be so, because all of us are paying higher rental than the white occupants who immediately preceded us." The *Atlanta Independent*'s Benjamin Davis also challenged the idea of declining property values, explaining, "The whites sold these homes to the Negroes at very attractive and remunerative prices." Even white newspapers often conceded the point. The *Winston-Salem Journal* acknowledged that Black families were "willing to pay much more for real estate than the average white man can, and more than the property is actually worth, in order that they may establish their residences in the more favorable location."[55]

Proponents of segregation laws also understood that Black residents raised property values since they frequently blamed selfish whites for the appearance of Black families on their blocks. They hoped the ordinances might stop "greedy" white property owners and real estate agents from profiting off of racial transition, capitalism be damned.[56] Judge E. B. Jones, the attorney who represented the white delegation pushing for Winston-Salem's ordinance, went so far as to charge "certain real estate dealers" with "robbing the white people" by attempting to sell them houses at the "exorbitant prices" that Black homebuyers were willing to pay. In Baltimore, an aggrieved white resident made a similar denunciation: "It is not the negro that I condemn, it is the white man who, to make a few dollars, will sell his property to a negro who should be condemned."[57]

As the rhetoric became more heated, white elites began distancing themselves from the ordinances. After one of Dashiell's especially alarmist speeches in which he alleged that "millions of dollars" would "be lost in real estate values unless the mayor and city council" acted immediately, a wealthy citizen accused Dashiell of "doing more harm than good." In a thoughtful letter to the editor, he admonished, "We must not lose sight of the fact that some of our wide streets naturally develop into negro neighborhoods, and that the negro occupation has been a boon rather than a loss to the property owners thereon. As the white people on some of the unpretentious wide streets move to newer and more modern neighborhoods, the colored occupant becomes the only hope of the unfortunate owners." He further warned that Dashiell's irrational assertions would set up a self-fulfilling prophecy. The more he howled about property values being cut in half, the more white homeowners would engage in panic selling. This argument was essentially the same as the one Black activists had been making all along, but his letter emphasized the stakes for white residents if the hysterical nonsense continued.[58]

Winston-Salem elites lacked enthusiasm for their city's segregation ordinance as well.[59] Rather than enforce laws that were clearly unconstitutional and which would create unsalable properties, they saw voluntary segregation through residential park development as a better proposition. After the segregation ordinance was ruled unconstitutional in 1914 by the North Carolina Supreme Court, the "Columbia Heights plan" was born. Editorials in the *Winston-Salem Journal* began insisting that residential segregation could be accomplished in the city "without any law on the subject whatsoever." Columbia Heights, which the present owners of the *Journal* had invested in during the late nineteenth century, would serve as the model. "There is ample proof right here in Winston-Salem of the fact that negroes can, and actually do, live better to themselves than when mixed with white people," one editorial declared. After all, the residents of Columbia Heights own their homes and take "pride in the fact that this is their section and that its progress and development rest with them."[60]

The obvious flaw in their reasoning was that James Timlic, whose move onto East Fourth Street had originally sparked the segregation ordinance, also owned a large home lot in Columbia Heights. He nonetheless chose to live on Fourth Street because it was close to his business and the only public school that served Black children beyond the fourth grade. Fourth Street also enjoyed modern sewerage, curbs, and sidewalks, which Columbia Heights lacked. Residents had repeatedly petitioned for improvements, including "better fire protection," "more frequent visits from the sanitary wagon" to service their outhouses, and "another outlet to town" beyond "the poor one" that they were then forced to use.[61] Nevertheless, twenty years after the development opened, Columbia Heights' families continued to suffer from civic neglect.

In plugging the new "voluntary" segregation plan, members of the *Journal's* editorial board interviewed prominent Black citizens about their preference for living in homes formerly occupied by white people rather than in Columbia Heights. The board learned what should have been obvious: conditions in Columbia Heights remained far below those of white middle-class communities. An editorial confessed, "We cannot—the Board of Aldermen cannot—expect the negroes of this community to be content to reside in a section where there are no paved streets, where there are no sidewalks, where city water cannot be had and where sewer lines are unknown." It recognized that "the big temptation" for Black families "of means" to "move into a white community" was so they "may have a sidewalk to walk on, paved streets to drive on, water gushing into their home and ample sewer facilities to protect them from disease and death."[62]

The *Journal* blamed local officials and their white constituents. "They are to blame because they are in full control of the machinery by which existing conditions may be remedied, so that the matter of segregation would cease to be a problem," it chided. "If the aldermen will give due regard to the wishes of the people of negro communities in appropriating funds for making public improvements, we believe it will be but a short time before there will be no need of an ordinance on segregation."[63] Another editorial admitted that the "best colored people in Winston-Salem" will not remain segregated in Columbia Heights "if present conditions are not remedied." It asked the "white people of Winston-Salem" if they could honestly "expect negroes who have money and are able to supply themselves with modern city conveniences to be content to reside in a section" without them.[64]

In the end, the segregation laws served no one's interests. Even Milton Dashiell was frustrated with later versions of the Baltimore ordinance that were not written by him. He unsuccessfully fought a change that excluded mixed-race blocks. Elites and others engaged in the real estate industry had encouraged local officials to revise the law, which Dashiell understood would mean the exclusion of his own street since Black families had already moved onto it.[65] He expected the ordinance to roll back Black gains on previously "white" blocks, but this was unrealistic, especially since enforcement on mixed-race blocks rendered some houses unsalable. According to W. Ashbie Hawkins, Baltimore's law had caused a "loss to many white property owners" who could not "sell or rent their property for want of white buyers or tenants."[66]

For that reason, the ordinances could not save block-level segregation for white families, even if the US Supreme Court had found them to be constitutional. Residential parks had changed the calculus too much: the properties had already lost their value for white middle-class child-rearing, which was why they were available for Black middle-class families to purchase. The *Independent*'s Benjamin Davis explained this reality when local officials first passed Atlanta's ordinance: "We are progressing. We are building up corporations, businesses, farms, and we have got to have homes to live in. We have and are making the money to buy them with, and the real estate agents and landlords have them for sale and we are going to buy them, segregation laws, peanut politicians, demagogues and hypocrites to the contrary notwithstanding."[67]

Ultimately, the efforts to pass segregation ordinances merely sped up the process of racial transition. In publicly declaring their neighborhoods unfit for white, middle-class families, advocates triggered a panic that accelerated the evolution of aging, middle-class neighborhoods rather than stabilizing them. Their dire predictions about the perils of Black neighbors merely encouraged more white families to pack up and move out to residential parks. Furthermore, white advocates demonstrated how utterly ineffective local government was at providing them with the "protections" that residential parks guaranteed through their deed restrictions. The multiple iterations of each ordinance revealed that transitory laws could not safeguard their long-term interests.

Residential park promoters could not have written better advertisements for the suburbs, illustrating how the relationship between segregation ordinances and racial covenants went both ways. While the emergence of residential parks helped kindle the demand for segregation laws, the effort to pass those laws further increased the popularity of racial covenants. Moreover, the affluent whites who had already moved out to the suburbs did not understand the objections of those they left behind. What was there to protect on streets that, in their view, were simply too urban for child-rearing? Why not sell one's home to a Black buyer, who was willing to pay top dollar for it, and then move to a residential park? The answer to that question was not so simple. Not everyone wished to leave the conveniences of the city or could afford to move into a residential park, especially one that offered the amenities that might balance out the hassle of living farther from their jobs and social and religious institutions. For those folks, the shifting residential landscape generated resentment against the developers who were changing the status of the traditional urban neighborhood, which they continued to value.

CHAPTER 5

Black Schools and the Rise of Segregation Ordinances

Historical analyses of Baltimore's segregation ordinance almost always begin with George McMechen's move onto McCulloh Street, which overlooks the importance of earlier resistance to the opening of Black schools in that neighborhood.[1] Those protests shaped the subsequent calls for a segregation ordinance along with the arguments used to justify it. Even after passage of the ordinance in 1910, white residents continued to oppose the conversion of white schools to Black ones, causing the school board president to lament, "The location of colored schools is a most difficult problem. It matters not in what locality we decide to place these schools, some objection will be raised."[2]

During the first decades of the twentieth century, white protests in Baltimore and in other Jim Crow cities made the opening of desperately needed Black schools a rare event. Most Black schools dated back to Reconstruction or soon thereafter, when interracial coalitions created the South's first public school systems.[3] Once residential parks halted traditional block-by-block development from expanding outward, provisions for additional Black classrooms began to stall, despite the growing number of Black children needing seats. Consequently, mixed-race areas that did have a modern Black school, or at least one with advanced coursework, experienced rapid racial transition. Again and again, the clamor for segregation ordinances arose in those areas blessed with the best Black school. Such was the case in Baltimore, Atlanta, and Winston-Salem, as well as in St. Louis where *Buchanan v. Warley* (1917)—the Supreme Court case that ultimately nullified the ordinances—originated.[4]

White residents understood how quickly a new Black school would undermine block-level segregation. A large influx of Black families into mixed-race areas would make it more difficult to confine the movement of Black children, leading to a loss of control over "white" blocks. Most white residents did not want Black children traveling past their homes to and from school since they were far less tolerant of youthful behavior coming from Black children than from white ones, as the developers of residential parks well understood. White parents also wanted to limit contact between older Black children and their own, especially interactions that would imply some level of "social equality," as discussed in chapter 4.[5]

White disputes over the location of Black schools frequently resulted in questionable sites or, all too often, no school at all. Under unusual circumstances, Black families could exploit white discord to assert some power over the location of their schools, as in Winston-Salem. In most cases, however, they had few options since Black citizens were largely locked out of local government. Therefore, affluent Black parents were willing to pay a premium for houses near modern Black schools, particularly those that offered a high school curriculum. In the process, they turned white homes into Black ones, sparking new laws intended to save block-level segregation.

Efforts to preserve white schools in mixed-race areas also prompted demands for segregation ordinances. In Atlanta, increasing disparities between white schools led to a shift in population that initiated the collapse of block-level segregation, fueling calls for the city's first residential segregation law. In Winston-Salem, whites hoped to increase support for a segregation ordinance by arguing that the recent investment in their "great white school" would be lost if white children no longer lived in its attendance area. One resident warned, "You have built a fine school building in our section of the city, but unless you check this intrusion of the colored race, we shall be obliged to turn this over to the negroes."[6] Similarly, the outrage in Baltimore over conversion of white schools to Black ones was as much about the loss of educational access for white children as fears of neighborhood transition. In each case, white protesters hoped that a segregation ordinance would defend their school as well as their homes.

Black Schools, White Fears, and the Property Value Argument

The white residents who designed the nation's first segregation ordinance knew just where to lay the blame for the "problem" northwest Baltimore then faced. One advocate told the school board that it had "made a serious mistake when it transferred the Colored High School" to their neighborhood. He demanded to know "why this change was made." Almost ten years before, the board had relocated the city's sole Black high school from its downtown location to the northwest section.[7] Its new building, a former English-German bilingual school that was no longer needed by the district, was not far from the house on McCulloh Street in which George McMechen moved his family in 1910, thereby triggering the segregation ordinance.

Back in 1901, the board's decision to relocate the high school had led to "vigorous protests" by the local improvement association, whose members had urged the board to leave the school at its original downtown site. They made their case through a property value argument that set the precedent for Milton Dashiell's defense of the segregation ordinance almost a decade later. At a hearing sponsored by the board, a spokesman for the white delegation stated that the complaint was not "actuated by race prejudice" but instead the desire "to preserve the value of our property." The residents feared that a Black high school "would attract a great many more colored people" to the neighborhood, and the resulting "negro invasion" would lower home prices by as much as 75 percent. As evidence, they claimed that their homes had already "depreciated because of the heavy colored population." Unconvinced, the board president asked whether the Black high school had also had "a disastrous effect on property values" downtown. The spokesman responded that "the conditions" were "not the same" because downtown was "full of offices," while the proposed site was on a commercial street where white merchants lived "over their stores" with their families. Hence, their children were "in closer touch with the crowds" walking along the street.[8]

The explanation for why the new site was a property value killer when the downtown site was not demonstrated that the important underlying context of the property value argument, even then, was white, middle-class child-rearing. Many of the white residents on McCulloh Street had selected the area because they believed it would provide upward mobility for their children.[9] Motivated by the reputation of the neighborhood before affluent whites started leaving for suburban residential parks, they failed to recognize that white, middle-class interest in the area had already plummeted, which was why they could afford to purchase a house there in the first place. Racial transition was an outcome of falling demand rather than the cause of it.

By 1903, the area surrounding the high school had become majority Black, as expected, so the board planned to convert another white school—grammar school No. 46—to serve the rapidly growing number of Black children living nearby. Board members felt it was a logical decision since No. 46 was around the corner from the Black high school, yet their action soon ignited a controversy that dwarfed the earlier one (see map 5.1). White residents accused the board of having intentionally concocted a scheme to empty No. 46 of white children so that they could then convert it to Black use. First, they argued, board members implemented a new policy that allowed students to transfer to another school within the larger attendance area. Next, the district's building program ignored No. 46's antiquated facilities, which occasioned a large number of transfers after the new schools opened. Then, the board began permitting students to stay longer at their primary schools if they had younger brothers or sisters who needed help getting to and from school. This policy further depleted the population of grammar schools like No. 46 that would have otherwise served the older siblings.[10]

Residents complained that these "most undemocratic" practices favored "class distinction" since only affluent parents had the wherewithal to send their children to a school farther from home.[11] Statistics provided by the board supported

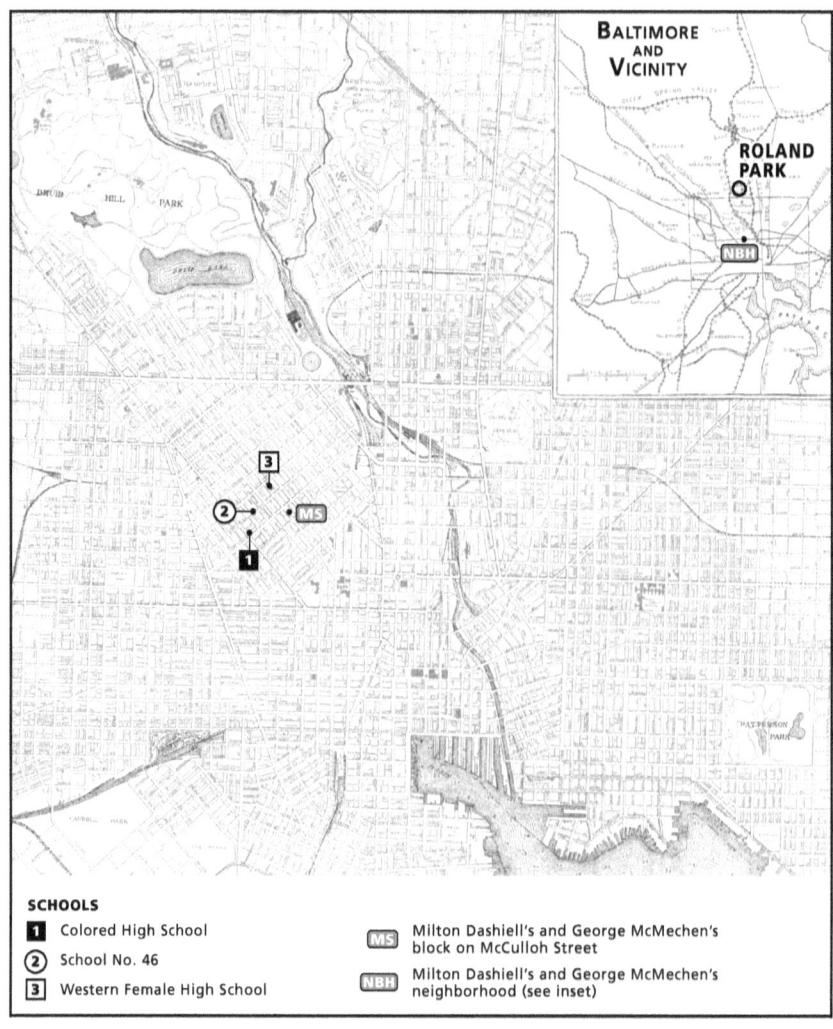

MAP 5.1. School No. 46 sparked an intense battle over the school board's plans to convert it to Black use. The block on McCulloh Street that triggered Baltimore's first segregation ordinance was only a few blocks from the school. Courtesy of JScholarship, the digital repository of the Sheridan Libraries of Johns Hopkins University.

their allegations. From 1898 to 1900, No. 46's enrollment was steady at about 750. The first big drop occurred in 1901, the year the board implemented the transfer policy and relocated the city's Black high school. The following year, No. 46 took a second hit with the completion of the building program.[12] The board insisted that the large number of transfers simply reflected the reality that No. 46 was in a Black district, but several hundred "indignant" white residents signed a petition disputing that characterization of their neighborhood. "There is not a school in the northwestern section of the city near which some negroes do not live," they asserted. They chimerically predicted a whiter and wealthier future so long as no more Black schools opened nearby: "It is natural that in a beautiful neighborhood, convenient to the business section, railroad stations and parks, there will be a demand for better residences, which will not long be unheeded. The presence of a colored school would certainly interfere with any such progressive plans that may be contemplated."[13]

Parents also objected to the imminent displacement of more than 500 white students who still attended No. 46, providing further evidence that the underlying issue was about children rather than property. Among the resolutions that outlined their grievances, the first was "the inconvenience and discomfort incurred by the white children" who would lose their school. A doctor residing in the neighborhood stated that all twelve children who lived on his block attended No. 46 precisely because it was "convenient" to their homes. They "didn't have far to go in bad weather," and they could return home for lunch each day. Protesters expressed further outrage that the needs of Black children would be prioritized above their own. One seethed, "We are to stand by and see our children turned out of a school that had always been a school for the white children of this neighborhood and to see it turned over to a lot of negroes."[14] Facing intense resistance, the school board soon yielded to the pressure from white parents.

Although the patrons of No. 46 won in the short term, the dream of reestablishing a neighborhood attractive to white, middle-class families was futile. Retaining the school would not reverse the larger trend: No. 46 still faced the challenge of its deteriorating condition and the area's mixed-use development. Even so, this win encouraged white residents in other neighborhoods to resist the board's strategy of using school conversions to save money. One month later, members of a different improvement association adopted similar rhetoric when opposing the conversion of "their" school: "If given over to the use of colored children," the school would surely "prove an attraction for colored persons" and encourage them to "move into" the neighborhood.[15]

In 1907, anger over the district's plans to increase the number of Black schools led to calls for a segregation ordinance by yet another improvement association. The superintendent's "placid discourse on the educational system of Baltimore" culminated in "the stormiest meeting in [the association's] history." Worried about losing future fights over the location of Black schools, angry attendees sought alternative ways to stop Black families from moving next door. One proposed an ordinance that would bar Black residents from moving onto a "block occupied entirely by white people without the consent of a majority of the residents" and vice versa. According to the *Baltimore Sun*, the underlying motivation was linked to "fears of contamination of children." An irate parent unabashedly asked, "Shall we allow our toddling tots to associate with negro children? Shall we let them suffer the contamination that ensues?"[16]

Schools and Racial Transition

As in Baltimore, white residents living in Atlanta's older neighborhoods first attempted to manage block-level segregation by restricting the location of Black schools, especially once residential parks began threatening the continued sustainability of traditional urban development. Three years before passage of the city's 1913 segregation ordinance, white residents of the lower Fourth Ward attempted to push Morris Brown College out of the neighborhood (see map 5.2). At the time, the college had a growing enrollment, serving about 850 high school and college students. Most Black colleges, including Morris Brown, operated high school departments to help fill the gaps left by the public schools. Morris Brown was also Atlanta's sole institution of higher education controlled entirely by African Americans.[17] Since 1881, it had peacefully shared a block with both white homeowners and the white Boulevard School.

Articles in the *Atlanta Journal* suggested, without evidence, that the impetus to remove the college was conflict between Black and white youth at Morris Brown and Boulevard, the neighboring white school; instead, it appears the real issue was Black middle-class families purchasing the vacant homes of whites who had moved out to residential parks, thereby threatening block-level segregation. White residents suspected that Morris Brown was the reason Black families were buying homes on nearby "white" streets. One proposal advised relocating Morris Brown to a site adjacent to Spelman Seminary on the opposite side of downtown. Another recommended moving the school "out to the open country" where it would no longer be "cramped up on a limited space in a populous residential section occupied by white people." The effort went nowhere since Morris Brown's leadership chose to expand rather than to leave the area.[18] The following year, the lower Fourth Ward received the only Black school built from a $600,000 bond issue to construct new schools for the city's eight wards.

Local boosters understood that modern schools, along with the extension of other city services, were essential to Atlanta's future growth and development. During the buildup to the election, the president of the chamber of commerce, F. J. Paxton, galvanized voters with the vision of an ideal city designed for childrearing: "We want our city so healthy, so attractive, so wholesome and full of charm in every respect that people will come here because it is the best place to live and to educate their children." At the time, boosters sold the building program as an opportunity to promote fairness across wards rather than favor certain neighborhoods. A resolution of support passed by the City Federation of Women's Clubs declared it "unpatriotic, unwise, and unjust" for "one section of the city to have the most modern and sanitary school facilities" and another

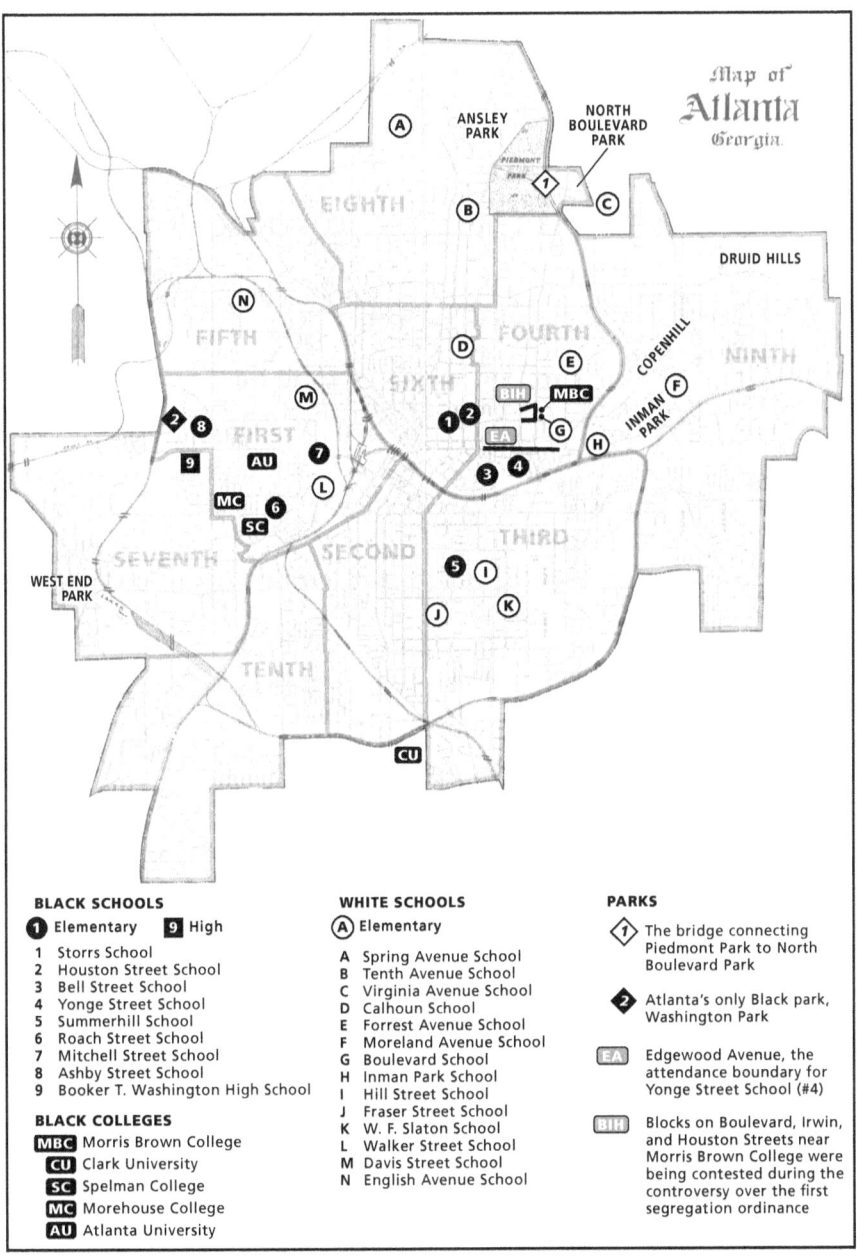

MAP 5.2. Schools influenced residential growth as much or more so than residential growth influenced the establishment of schools. With that said, Atlanta's ward-based political system tempered the extent to which affluent residents could control the location of new schools. Thus, the 1910 building program favored the industrial west side rather than the more affluent east side. Courtesy of the Kenan Research Center at the Atlanta History Center. Used with permission.

"to have inadequate and insanitary" ones.[19] But from the perspective of white families living in the lower Fourth Ward, the building program accomplished just the opposite. They were denied better school facilities even though a leaky roof, outside toilets, and missing blackboards placed their school at or near the bottom of all the city's white schools.[20]

The neighborhood *did* receive the only Black school completed during the building program. The bond commission had originally pledged to build two Black schools and renovate three others. In response, Black citizens had organized election rallies throughout the city to ensure that they received the critical improvements. But after the bonds passed easily, the promises shriveled down to a single Black school: lower Fourth Ward's Yonge Street School.[21] The *Atlanta Independent* had been lukewarm about the bond issue from the start. Ten days before the election, Benjamin Davis had hesitantly endorsed it with the defiant declaration, "We do not admit that this is a white man's country." But he was not naive about the district's priorities: "We do not expect the white folks to provide for us until they have amply provided for themselves, and whether it is right or just, it is what we expect. The fairness and equity of the question is a matter we leave up to their conscience." Still, he feared Black citizens would forfeit their portion of the bonds if they sat out the election. Therefore, he cynically directed Black voters to "help carry these bonds, so our neighbors can provide for themselves as early as possible and get to us."[22] No editorial appeared the next week reminding Black voters to go to the polls. Perhaps Davis's motivation was to shame local officials into carrying out their pledge since he doubted their sincerity.

By then, playing hot potato with Black schools had become the primary means for white residents to control block-level segregation within their neighborhoods. Before Yonge, Fourth Ward remained the only ward without a Black public school. The large number of Black families living along Auburn Avenue sent their children to aging Sixth Ward schools, which dated back to Reconstruction (see map 5.2). Still, the location of Yonge reflected the interests of First Ward boosters more so than Black parents. The whites who had been most vocal about building a Black school in Fourth Ward were those who had been engaged in a year-long campaign to stimulate *First* Ward's development through the construction of a $100,000 viaduct connecting the area to downtown.[23] They worried that a new Black school might alter the existing racial dynamics of the ward, thereby threatening their plans to expand white residential development. The district's "special committee on needed school improvements" included one of the ward's biggest boosters, attorney W. H. Terrell, who was then secretary of the West Side Improvement Club. His committee falsely reported that Fourth Ward contained "the largest negro population of any ward in the city," although Fourth Ward had fewer than 3,000 Black residents and First Ward had more than 12,000.[24]

The *Atlanta Journal* enthusiastically advanced the west side's booster projects, including the proposed $100,000 viaduct and two new white schools. A political cartoon on its front page titled "Why Keep Them Apart?" pictured the paradoxical situation of a white middle-class woman pitifully separated from the downtown retail district. Behind her loomed the large factories of the ward, which apparently did not detract from the zeal for further residential development. Supporters of traditional urban growth understood that industry was the reason the ward was "thickly populated" despite its isolation from downtown.[25] The *Journal*'s effort to boost First Ward included the advocacy of a new Black school for *Fourth* Ward on the opposite side of Atlanta. One editorial asserted that Fourth Ward had "more colored children than all the rest of the city put together," further exaggerating the already inflated claims put forward by Terrell's committee.[26] The westside boosters ultimately achieved their goals for the school bonds, even though the costly viaduct was never completed. Along with a Black school for Fourth Ward, First Ward garnered two new white schools—one of which it plainly did not need—while no improvements were made to either of the ward's severely overcrowded Black schools.

First Ward's boosters were not the only ones who played hot potato with Black schools. Fourth Ward whites pushed the new Black school down to the southern tip of the ward, and then white property owners in Third and Ninth Wards vetoed potential sites along the border. When Terrell's committee recommended a site on the edge of Ninth Ward, Joel Hurt, the developer of Inman Park, objected because he thought it was too near Inman Park School (see map 5.2). The committee was then given two additional weeks to "select a site suitable to [the white residents of] the fourth, ninth, and third wards." Hurt himself volunteered to help find "a suitable place."[27]

The site finally selected was in a mixed-race slum peppered with industrial and commercial businesses—hardly an ideal location for a new school from the perspective of educational experts, let alone middle-class parents.[28] It was about a block north of infamous Decatur Street, described by one of Atlanta's "best citizens" as a "leprous spot upon the face of our fair city" with its "foul fish stalls" being "an offense against high heaven and the nostrils of all Atlanta." The *Journal Magazine* styled it as "the home of humanity as it is." Vaudeville theaters dotted the street, pawn shops sold articles stolen by diverse criminals, and Pat's near-beer pool hall catered to construction workers who "were thrown out of employment on account of the weather." The colorful street also attracted struggling rural families who came to town in "prairie schooners," many carrying "several jugs of 'moonshine,' right from the mountains."[29] Louie Shivery, the executive secretary for the Neighborhood Union, characterized the street's "dens of vice, slums, pawnshops, pool rooms, bar rooms, cheap eating places, row houses, second hand clothing shops, junk shops," and jail in much the same way.[30]

Even considering its disreputable surroundings, Yonge School's attendance boundary was what truly betrayed Black middle-class voters living near Auburn Avenue. The official attendance district was frozen between Edgewood Avenue to the north and Decatur Street to the south, an area far smaller than those served by every other Black school in Atlanta. Before Yonge opened, the families of affluent Black businessmen and professionals who lived near the intersection of Auburn and Butler Street—a prosperous Black community dating back to the Civil War—were assigned to Sixth Ward's rundown and dangerously overcrowded Houston Street School (see map 5.2). The school's attendance area was enormous, including all of Fourth Ward and parts of Sixth, Eighth, and Ninth Wards.[31] Yonge helped shrink Houston's attendance area somewhat, but the middle-class homes near Auburn Avenue and the transition properties by Morris Brown were excluded from Yonge's attendance district. Most likely, its location and attendance boundaries were meant to prevent further racial turnover farther north.

Regardless, the board did allow exceptions for some well-connected parents who lived north of Edgewood Avenue. Affluent Black families hoped their children would attend the new school rather than the dilapidated Houston Street School. For instance, Henry Rutherford Butler, a Harvard-trained doctor, lived at the intersection of Auburn Avenue and Yonge Street, which was only a few blocks from the new school but still outside its small attendance area. The Butlers would not have considered moving closer to the notorious Decatur Street slum, but they were permitted to send their child to Yonge Street School, nonetheless. This exception allowed Selena Sloan Butler to establish the nation's first Black PTA at the new school in 1911, the year it opened.[32]

Because Yonge was Atlanta's only modern Black school at the time, it dramatically altered the racial mix of the lower Fourth Ward. Between 1910 and 1913, the three blocks on Boulevard Street between Decatur and Edgewood Avenue transitioned from 18 percent Black to 84 percent. Before the bond election, those blocks contained thirty-one white households and just seven Black ones. Once the board publicly announced the site, the number of individual residences grew to fifty as Black families sought housing near the new school. Accordingly, Black households rose from seven to twenty-two, while white households decreased slightly from thirty-one to twenty-eight. After Yonge's first full year in operation, the number of Black households climbed to forty-seven, while the number of white ones plummeted to nine.[33]

For most of the decade, Yonge enjoyed the best Black school facilities in Atlanta, but the deteriorating Boulevard School endured some of the worst, at least among white schools. The combination of a superior Black school and an inferior white one further undermined the mixed-race housing patterns in the lower Fourth Ward. Between 1910 and 1920, the percentage of the white population in Boulevard's attendance district dropped from 73 percent—higher than the percentage of the white population in the city as a whole—to 24 percent, the smallest percentage of white residents living in any of the forty-one white attendance districts. At the same time, the number of Black residents skyrocketed from 1,155 to 7,792, representing, by far, the largest Black gain in any white attendance district.[34] The Butlers were part of this shift. In 1914, they purchased a house on Boulevard from a white owner soon after Dr. Butler had begun teaching nursing classes at nearby Morris Brown.[35]

Furthermore, the attendance boundary for Forrest Avenue School—the new white school completed for Fourth Ward out of the 1910 bond issue—dipped south into Boulevard's old attendance district. As a result, most of Boulevard's middle-class children were transferred to the new school (see map 5.2).[36] Although Fourth Ward's white families did not live in residential parks, the parents had started to believe that their children should grow up in a comparable environment. The desire to send their kids to a modern school with other children from a higher socioeconomic class meant that Forrest Avenue School quickly became overcrowded. The board then attempted to balance out enrollments between the two schools by readjusting their attendance boundaries, but most middle-class parents refused to send their children to Boulevard, hastening racial transition in the lower Fourth Ward.[37]

The subsequent plunge in Boulevard's enrollment raised alarm bells. One councilman blamed the school's depopulation on "class prejudice" and the board's reluctance to "offend certain parents." An editorial in the *Constitution* agreed, claiming it was "nothing less serious than CRIMINAL NEGLIGENCE" to refuse to relieve overcrowded schools by better utilizing Boulevard's ample space. The mayor also entered the fray. He charged board members with permitting "'class distinction' to stand in the way of a fair and just distribution of pupils to the Forrest Avenue and Boulevard schools" because their "method of districting" had "resulted in an exodus of school children from the south side to the north side.'" "The Boulevard and Forrest Avenue school districts adjoin each other," he admonished, yet "the children of the poorer classes are forced to attend the Boulevard school, while the children of parents who are financially able to dress their children a little better than the poor kids on Decatur and Lucy streets, are allowed entrance in the Forrest Avenue school." "If the parents of children object to them going to school with youngsters of the less fortunate let them establish a private school," he scolded, although he stopped short of recommending that improvements be made to Boulevard's crumbling facilities.[38]

Fourth Ward councilman Claude Ashley wanted to balance the enrollments between the two schools as well. As the author of the city's first segregation ordinance, which was introduced just four months before the school controversy, he did not want the lower Fourth Ward emptied of white middle-class families, even though white demand for the homes had already crashed. The final catalyst for the so-called Ashley Ordinance was the sale of a house on Houston Street to a Black family. Although the property was around the corner from "white" blocks near the Boulevard School, it was also less than half a block from Morris Brown. In response to the proposed law, Benjamin Davis defended the right of Black families to live in any home that afforded their children access to better educational opportunities, shrewdly arguing that "white people ought not to insist upon living around negro churches and negro school houses."[39]

In the same vein, Black real estate agent Holland McGahee explained to the white readers of the *Constitution* that Black homebuyers only sought property "in sections where their interest" lay. In a letter to the editor, he identified four blocks in the lower Fourth Ward where Black middle-class families were willing to pay top dollar to secure a home, including the block that had incited the segregation ordinance (see map 5.2). According to the 1908 directory, those four blocks were all white, although at least one of the adjacent blocks was already mixed race. In 1913, McGahee's four blocks still had no Black residents, but the number of vacancies was growing. The purpose of the segregation ordinance was to "protect" those vacancies from Black buyers, though McGahee reasoned that white proponents of the ordinance were simply hurting themselves: "Any attempt at segregation will work a worse hardship on the white people who have property to sell than it will on the colored people, as white people can always buy in sections where colored people will never think of wanting to purchase"—meaning white residential parks.[40] The ordinance could do nothing to change the fact that Black middle-class families valued the homes near Morris Brown and Yonge Street School far more than white families or that most white property owners did not want to sell or rent their houses for a loss.

Black Activism and White Conflict

In Winston-Salem, Black parents also aspired to live in neighborhoods with decent housing and a good school for their children. As the city's segregation ordinance began wending its way through the state court system in 1913, Black middle-class families used a quarrel between whites to challenge the school board's effort to relocate their high school to the outskirts of town. One white faction hoped that the new ordinance would sustain block-level segregation while the other promoted a "voluntary" segregation scheme with schools as the principal appeal, thereby avoiding the "need" for a controversial segregation law. Black activists effectively manipulated this dispute to keep Depot Street School at its current location near their homes, which many had purchased precisely so that their children could be near the city's only school with a curriculum that extended beyond the fourth grade.

The story began in 1883 with the selection of a site for Winston's first Black school. White residents opposed the board's initial choice, alleging that the central location would "depreciate the valuation of their property." A local newspaper suggested that "somewhere in Bahnson town would be a better choice, as most of the negroes live[d] in that section." That assertion, however, should not be read literally to mean that most of Winston's Black children lived in Bahnson Town, a small enclave of only sixty or seventy residents out of a Black population of about 1,250.[41] Instead, the newspaper was advocating for a school site in an area frequently characterized as a place where whites did not belong. For example, another article described the accidental shooting of a "young white girl" when she and "her colored Adolphus" were "fooling with a pistol at her home near Bahnsontown." Reportedly, the young man was "lodged in jail," awaiting "the results of his wounded mistress."[42] Although this denigrating account must also be treated with skepticism, at the time, it did serve as a cautionary tale against interracial relationships, the underlying context for why white residents opposed locating a Black school near white homes.

Back in 1875, the founding of the R. J. Reynolds Tobacco Company had launched a racially lopsided population explosion that stirred several efforts to produce residential segregation, including the one analyzed above. Between 1870 and 1890, the population of Winston climbed from less than 500 to more than 8,000. Because the tobacco industry heavily recruited Black workers, the Black population expanded faster than the white one, increasing from 21.4 percent of the population to 58.4.[43] This rapid growth made block-level segregation difficult to establish in the emerging city. The resulting scramble to control where Black families lived explains both the appearance of racial covenants as well as the racialized opposition to a school site so soon after the end of Reconstruction.

Since Bahnson Town was not yet part of the school district, board members chose an adjacent site on Depot Street at the far northeastern edge of town close to the tobacco factories employing many Black residents. This decision adhered to the dictates of block-level segregation because it forced Black children to leave their mixed-race neighborhoods to attend school in an industrial section with fewer white homeowners. During the next three decades, Depot Street School attracted large numbers of Black families, helping to form a densely populated Black neighborhood near Bahnson Town, as originally intended. At the turn of the century, the Timlics were one of many Black families who built homes in the area (see map 5.3). Then in 1912, they moved to a home on East Fourth Street, which they had purchased from a white couple. Their new residence was still within easy walking distance of Depot Street School, but it removed the children from the slum conditions that overcrowding and civic neglect had created in their old neighborhood. This classic example of upward mobility triggered the first segregation ordinance, as discussed in chapter 4. White residents wished to prevent further racial "incursion" along East Fourth Street, even though the Timlics were not the first Black family who moved onto the block.[44]

The following year, the school board attempted to relocate Depot Street School

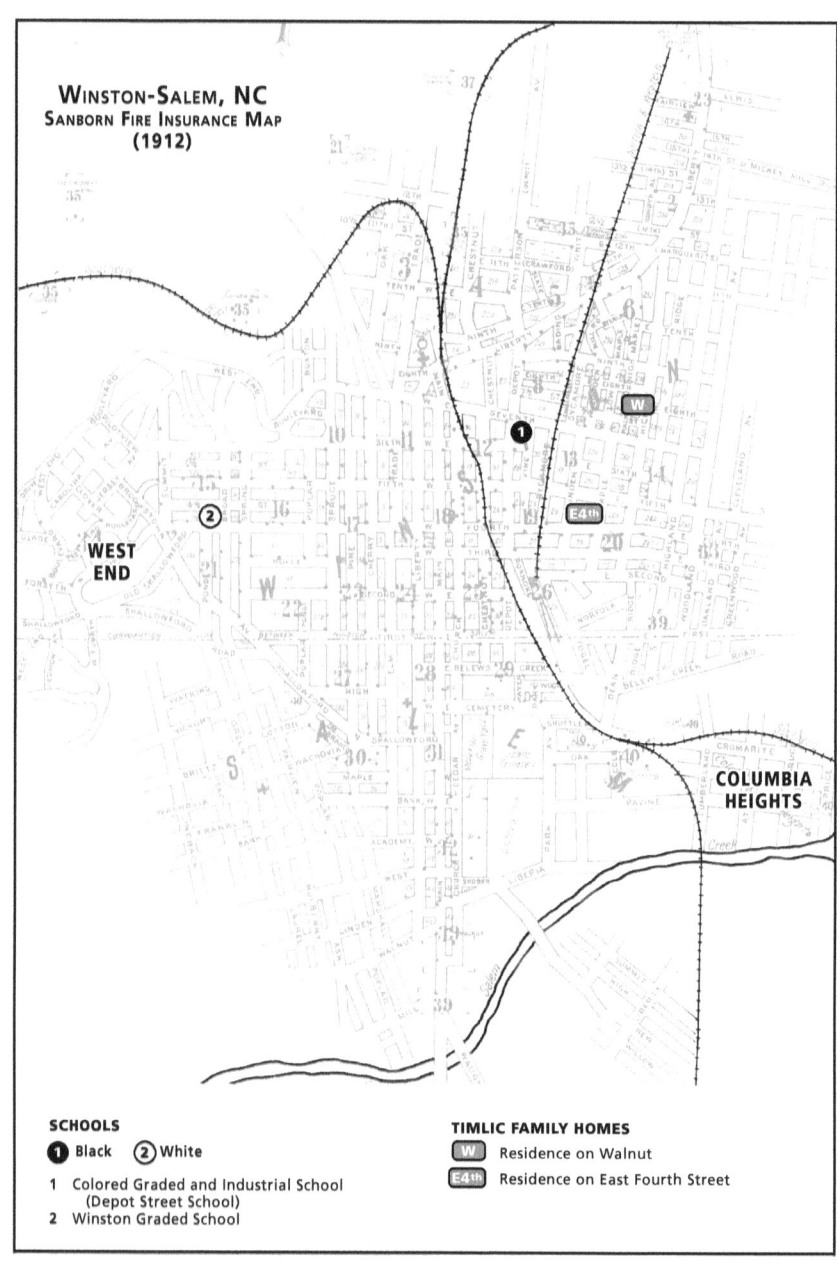

MAP 5.3. During the late nineteenth century, Winston's first Black school, the Depot Street School, and its first white school, the Winston Graded School, dramatically shaped residential development in the city, especially in terms of residential segregation. Sanborn Fire Insurance Map, Winston-Salem, North Carolina, 1912. Courtesy of the Library of Congress.

to a site further from the mixed-race neighborhoods near downtown, a decision affluent Black families vehemently opposed. Somewhat surprisingly, the advocates of the segregation ordinance joined Black residents in protesting the actions of the board, which was dominated by white elites, the purported allies of the Black middle class. "Ex-Judge Jones"—one of the most outspoken supporters of the segregation ordinance—represented a group of Black businessmen hostile to the plan to move the school.[45] Meanwhile, John Buxton, the longtime chair of the school board, would soon serve as the lawyer who would successfully challenge the ordinance before the North Carolina Supreme Court. During the Depot Street School controversy, he was already representing George Penn, a Black grocer who had been denied a permit to erect a house near the proposed site for the new school.[46] In addition, Buxton's close friend Henry Fries, the former vice president of Columbia Heights' development company, was on the school board as well. Both men were held in high regard by Simon Atkins, the visionary behind Columbia Heights. He would later praise Buxton and Fries for "making the negroes feel that Winston-Salem" was a place "they could dwell in peace and safety and prosperity—they and their children."[47]

Buxton and Fries shared extensive personal and business ties that prompted their mutual interest in the school board. They had been involved in residential development since the early 1890s. In 1912, the year the Depot Street controversy began, they formed a new partnership to launch Central Terrace, a child-centered residential park on the south side of town. Buxton and Fries also shaped the city's mortgage industry. Both were affiliated with the Winston-Salem Building and Loan Association, which had financed more than 800 homes in the metropolitan area before 1913.[48] The Wachovia Bank and Trust Company, the largest bank in the state, was another example of their deep connections to the industry. The behemoth was created in 1910 when Wachovia Loan & Trust—founded by the Fries family—merged with the Wachovia National Bank. Buxton had served as a director for the two banks before the merger, with Henry Fries remaining on the board afterwards. Buxton and Fries shared family ties, too: Buxton's wife was Fries's first cousin, and the Buxtons honored this relationship by naming one of their daughters Caro Fries Buxton.[49]

Other members of the school board also had links to industries that were likely to benefit from residential park development. Washington A. Wilkinson was the manager of the insurance department of Wachovia Bank and Trust, and Thomas Maslin was the vice president and cashier of Merchants National Bank. W. E. Franklin was the president of the Winston Realty Company, and Fred Fogle was the secretary of Fogle Brothers, a construction company that sold lumber, doors, blinds, and other materials used in home building.[50]

In addition, Henry Fries owned the largest share of the *Winston-Salem Journal*, while its other investors read like a who's who among the interlocking directorate responsible for the city's residential parks.[51] As explained in chapter 4, Fries's newspaper was first to suggest that the solution to the race "problem" was not a segregation ordinance but rather "voluntary" segregation, beginning with Columbia Heights. The proposal's fatal flaw was that Columbia Heights was in a remote corner of the city, far from Depot Street School. One editorial acknowledged that the community needed a better "outlet to the business center of the city." The single "makeshift" road between Columbia Heights and downtown intersected the railroad tracks at grade crossing, making it "dangerous for the children to traverse" when going to and from school.[52] Most affluent Black families, including the Timlics, preferred living near downtown. Once they were invested in that location, they opposed all efforts to relocate the school.

The board promised to build a modern high school, which it insisted the city could not afford without selling the Depot Street site. Board members guessed the downtown property would bring as much as $20,000, allowing them to build a sixteen-room brick high school with a thousand-seat auditorium. Multiple newspaper articles repeated their claim: unless the Depot Street site was sold, Black students could not obtain a modern high school to replace the "dangerous and disgraceful" building then in use. The mayor maintained that the city was simply "not in a position to go to the expense of tearing down" the present school "to erect a new one" on its current site.[53]

When Black activists disputed this characterization of the city's finances, they engaged in a bold gamble, hoping to call the board's bluff. Depot Street School was, in fact, an old wooden structure that desperately needed replacement, yet 500 Black citizens audaciously signed a petition arguing that a town as prosperous as Winston-Salem could afford to rebuild the school on its original site. "A large delegation" of "prominent colored professional and business men" presented the petition to the board of aldermen. After rebuffing the board's offer of "crumbs from the table," it proposed using the Black students' share of the per capita allotment of the state school and county building funds to construct a modern high school on Depot Street. Although the present site was in an industrial area, Black churches surrounded the school, and "many of the best homes" were close by. Furthermore, a delegation of Black businessmen had recently convinced the city government to pave the blocks leading up to the school, though the streets near the proposed site remained unimproved. Children would "have to wade through mud, shoe top deep" to travel to school under those conditions. The petition also reminded local officials of "the many fine, modern school buildings" and "splendid equipment" that had "been provided for the boys and girls of your race." "We cannot believe that the honorable" school board "would have decided to move our central school" if board members had understood "the express wishes" of "8000 faithful, toiling citizens and taxpayers of our noble city," it implored. "We will not believe that you will refuse to give us a suitable school building."[54]

A few days later, Frederick Fitch, the owner of a Black funeral home, expounded on the petition's assertions in a letter to the *Winston-Salem Journal*. He questioned "why a few of our white friends" would want "to deprive us of the pleasure of having a centrally located high school in a colored community, where all the land [was] owned by colored people." He also challenged the wisdom of moving "the school into a community where a colored dentist" had been "indicted under the segregation ordinance" for building his family's home near the proposed site. Fitch was certainly no friend of the segregation law. He had recently led the campaign to prevent the election of the law's sponsor, Silas Bennett, to the state legislature. Yet he had no problem exploiting the law's existence to protect the Depot Street site.[55]

As Fitch implied, the board's motivation was murky. In November 1912, strong opposition from Black parents had effectively halted the initial attempt to relocate Depot Street School. After Fries was appointed to the board during the spring of 1913, the issue was revived once again, this time more forcefully. Advocates insisted that the suburban, northwest site was "the logical location" for a Black high school since "the center of the colored population" would "be around the proposed building site within the next decade."[56] Of course, placing the high school on that site would all but guarantee that it would become the future nucleus of Black residential development, as had happened with Depot Street School decades before. Moreover, consolidating two schools on a single site, as they were proposing to do, followed the same approach to racial concentration that was then being implemented in Raleigh, the state capital.

To win the fight, Black activists brilliantly argued that moving the school would force the students to walk "through a white community," thereby undermining the tenets of traditional, block-level segregation. To reach the new site, dozens of Black children would need to trek outward from downtown along all-white blocks rather than walking just a few blocks inward. That possibility grabbed the attention of many of the supporters of the segregation ordinance. White protesters who disliked the idea of Black children parading past their homes twice a day demanded that Depot Street School remain where it was. Local officials soon yielded to the pressure from white residents, as Black activists knew they would.[57]

At least for the time being, the Black middle class had successfully played the two white camps off each other: elites helped defeat the segregation ordinance in court, while proponents of the law helped defeat elite efforts to relocate the Black high school to the outskirts of the city, where it would advance residential segregation in an area more convenient to downtown than Columbia Heights. But before local officials would be able to shift Black families out of the mixed-race neighborhoods near downtown, they would first need to extend street improvements, parks, and other amenities to Black homeowners in the suburban areas. In the coming decade, white elites would offer affluent Black parents a pared-down version of child-centered development to encourage greater acceptance of "voluntary" segregation.

In most Jim Crow cities, white residents pleaded for modern school facilities for their own children while protesting *any* school facilities planned for Black children living close by. Consequently, neighborhoods near the handful of Black schools that remained soon became overcrowded. The most affluent Black families then pushed outward to adjacent "white" blocks with vacant homes for sale. Thus, white refusal to support the expansion of Black educational access created the very dynamic that white residents in mixed-race areas dreaded most. In Baltimore, Atlanta, Winston-Salem, and elsewhere, the calls for a segregation ordinance began in the neighborhoods with the city's best Black school.

Meanwhile, local officials responded to the lobbying efforts of developers and their well-heeled customers by placing new schools along the outer rim of the city while neglecting white schools in older sections. The resulting disparities led to rapid overcrowding in the newest schools, causing an uproar among affluent families. One Atlanta parent from a newly annexed residential park complained, "It is very disheartening to a mother to send her children from a very healthy environment in the morning into a school room which is not only overcrowded, but which has poor equipment at best for the comfort" of her children.[58] Such objections callously ignored the appalling conditions in older white schools, let alone Black ones, and indicated a growing consensus among affluent white parents that their offspring should have superior schools because their children had grown accustomed to living in better housing.

In some cities, board members hoped to save money by simply converting antiquated white schools in mixed-race areas to Black use. They saw little incentive for making improvements to them, since worsening conditions would work in their favor to accelerate racial transition. The deteriorating white schools would contribute to the collapse of block-level segregation while new, modern schools helped facilitate a rush to the suburbs. When neighborhoods with decaying white schools lost additional white families, Black parents paid inflated prices for the vacant houses. The whites who remained understood that the board would then recommend the conversion of "their" school to Black use, exactly as had happened with Atlanta's Bell Street School after Yonge Street School opened only a few blocks away.

This cycle of racial conversion generated an even greater outcry over the drawing power of Black schools, however, making it increasingly difficult for board

Black Schools and the Rise of Segregation Ordinances | 121

FIGURE 5.1. During the 1920s, the Atlanta school board closed the Ira Street School rather than convert it to Black use. This photograph, taken during the 1940s, was used by the Urban League to document the district's egregious neglect of Black children who continued to endure severe overcrowding at their schools. Ira Street School, circa 1942, Atlanta Urban League Papers, Atlanta University Center Robert W. Woodruff Library. Used with permission.

members to continue converting white schools to Black use. For example, during Houston's large building program of the 1920s, the superintendent wished to convert three white schools but admitted that the board faced "a touchy situation in suggesting that they be made negro schools." Only one would become a Black school during that decade. For the same reason, Atlanta's school board closed the white Ira Street School, claiming it was too near an industrial area, but it refused to convert the school to Black use, despite petitions from Black residents begging for additional classrooms. Instead, the superintendent ordered the building sold under the condition that it was "not to be used for negro property." When the school district could not find a white buyer, the city simply left Ira Street School to rot.[59]

The situation would not change for more than a decade. As late as 1938, a report commissioned by the Atlanta Chamber of Commerce admitted that providing modern schools for white children in older, mixed-race neighborhoods would "not be so serious" a blunder if they "could be turned over to negro use" when no longer desirable for white children. Yet, "the state of public opinion" meant "that such transfers must wait for practically the last white family to move from the territory." For example, the school board finally closed the Davis Street School to white children in 1940, when only 164 students remained, but it did not reopen Davis as a Black school until the 1947–48 school year, when it served an overflowing enrollment of 730 students.[60] Racial conversions in southern school districts would not become routine again until after the Federal Housing Administration began helping more white residents move out to the suburbs after World War II.

Ultimately, the effort to halt Black school expansion failed to protect block-level segregation, but it had a devastating effect on Black education. Even in Winston-Salem where Black activists won their immediate fight, Black children never received a new school on Depot Street. Instead, students and teachers endured in the same old, ramshackle building until the board permanently closed it, less than ten years later, to carry out the original plan.[61] The further deterioration of overcrowded, Reconstruction-era buildings meant that school conditions rapidly declined. In the coming years, this stagnation would lead to one of the first successful civil rights efforts of the twentieth-century South: the demand for modern schools and increased access to secondary education.[62]

CHAPTER 6

Black Activism and the Battle for Better Schools

During the antebellum period, middle-class families looked to schooling to help their children navigate the new opportunities and greater risks generated by the market revolution. The key was to keep their children in school for as long as possible, despite the financial sacrifices the family would need to make. By the turn of the twentieth century, the industrial revolution had made prolonged schooling even more important for a secure livelihood, with high school a crucial status marker for the upwardly mobile. During the period of rapid industrialization between 1890 and 1918, the number of high school students grew by 711 percent, far outstripping the 68 percent increase in the nation's overall population. Urban districts struggled to furnish accommodations for the rapidly increasing high school population. Underfunded Jim Crow districts especially lagged, often failing to stay ahead of rising enrollments even in the lower grades.[1]

From the moment Reconstruction ended and the "redeemers" wrested control over the region's embryonic school systems, southern elites had conspired to keep tax-supported expenditures on education at or below a bare necessity. The result was too few classrooms for the needs of an urbanizing population. According to historian Gavin Wright, because the South was "a low-wage region in a high-wage country," powerful elites reasoned that investments in education for the masses would not pay since workers with more than a rudimentary education would leave the area in search of higher salaries elsewhere. They undermined public education at both the state and local level to keep their workers trapped at the bottom of the South's low-wage economy. Wright explained, "However desirable it may have been to upgrade the educational system, southern employers had reason to doubt that they or the region could actually capture the benefits."[2] Consequently, the ex-Confederate states plus Kentucky still constituted the twelve lowest ranking school systems in the nation in 1926, based on their shockingly low expenditures per pupil.[3]

While the curtailment of district resources created difficulties in most white schools, it led to unconscionable conditions in Black ones. Despite the *Plessy* decision (1896), which notoriously declared separate-but-equal facilities constitutional, the courts soon forgave grossly unequal schools, too. In the landmark case *Cumming v. Richmond County Board of Education* (1899), the US Supreme Court ruled that districts were not obligated to provide equal schooling to Black and white children if a school board claimed it lacked the resources to furnish equivalent facilities for both. The case was filed after a Georgia district discontinued its only Black high school, alleging insufficient funds. The court accepted this excuse, finding that the district's actions did not interfere with the rights of US citizenship under the Fourteenth Amendment because public education was a power belonging to the states.[4] Afterwards, most Jim Crow districts closed Black high schools or refused to open them in the first place while accepting disgraceful conditions in Black elementary schools. With many white parents dead set against the expansion of Black schooling near their homes, extreme overcrowding—often with more than a hundred students per teacher—produced unsafe conditions for children forced to attend class in aging, wooden firetraps.

As conditions worsened, Black middle-class parents organized campaigns for new schools with modern heat, lighting, and sanitation. In a nation that had long tied virtuous citizenship to education, they believed an adequate number of classrooms in modern schools would permit all Black children to earn their rightful place as citizens. They also hoped access to secondary education would protect their children from grueling, low-paid labor with few, if any, opportunities for advancement. In one of the many petitions sent to local officials by Black activists, Atlanta's Neighborhood Union expounded upon the importance of good schools to Black parents: "The question of the education of his children lies close to the heart of the Negro. He is interested in securing school advantages for his children above everything else, and when he is unable to get his child in school and the child is unable to get a fair opportunity for training, a spirit of dissatisfaction and a feeling of restlessness immediately possess the parent." Union members cautioned that more Black families would leave the city, thereby threatening the local economy, if the district did not ameliorate school conditions.[5]

In addition to the petitions and elected delegations representing their interests, the Black middle class tested new ways to compel elected officials to act. Their strategies included the use of voting blocs to defeat unjust bond issues along with the creation of interracial networks to sidestep Jim Crow. Through it all, the Black press sustained pressure on local boosters, challenging their narrative of racial accord. White working-class families also sought convenient and comfortable schools, but white battles over limited resources almost always ended in favor of the affluent. In contrast, Black middle-class parents pursued upgrades in *all* Black schools, not just those serving their own children. They understood that racism tied their offspring's prospects to the majority's perception of even the most impoverished Black child.

The Battle Begins

In 1903, white residents in northwest Baltimore successfully blocked the conversion of a school from white to Black, as discussed in the previous chapter. Following that win, white residents in *southwest* Baltimore upped the ante by attempting to bully board members into giving white children the new Black school then under construction. According to the *Baltimore Sun*, the protesters worried that the school would "prove an attraction for colored persons" who would then "move into that neighborhood." They justified their selfishness by contending that Black families did not actually want the school because they had not shown up at the meeting "to be heard." In response, the *Baltimore Afro-American* beseeched Black residents to take a stand: "If the colored people do not" let the board "know that they are interested in the education of their children," then "they deserve" to lose any "school that the white people may take a notion to protest." In the coming weeks, Black parents heeded the call and submitted a petition "protesting against the action of the Southwestern Improvement Association." The board then moved forward with its original plan, handing the victory to Black families.[6] As block-level segregation continued to fall apart, such triumphs grew increasingly rare.

Many early campaigns for additional Black schools were simply ignored. For example, a Black educator named Charles Hunter led the effort against Black school consolidation in Raleigh. Between 1910 and 1917, he served as the principal of the esteemed Berry O'Kelly Training School in Method, but he lived in East Raleigh near Garfield School. After the district closed Garfield in 1909, Hunter began petitioning the board for another school to serve Black homeowners like himself who lived northeast of the capitol.[7] At that time, students either paid to attend a private school run by St. Augustine's College or walked past the white Thompson School on their way to the consolidated Crosby-Garfield School in the southeastern corner of the city. One of St. Augustine's future presidents, James Boyer, remembered other boys throwing rocks at him as he walked "way across town" to school, although he did not specify the race of his tormentors.[8]

In 1911, white developers platted College Park just south of St. Augustine's and began selling lots to Black buyers, heightening the need for a Black school in that section (see map 6.1). Since white residential parks had narrowed Black housing options on the west side, demand for lots in College Park remained strong, especially among those affiliated with the college. By 1920, 300 of its 325 lots had already been sold, even though fewer than 8 percent had access to piped water. The city refused to annex the addition until 1929, largely because the developers would not advocate for Black homeowners in the same way they did for white families living in restricted residential parks.[9] Consequently, Black families were on their own in the effort to obtain public services, including a school.

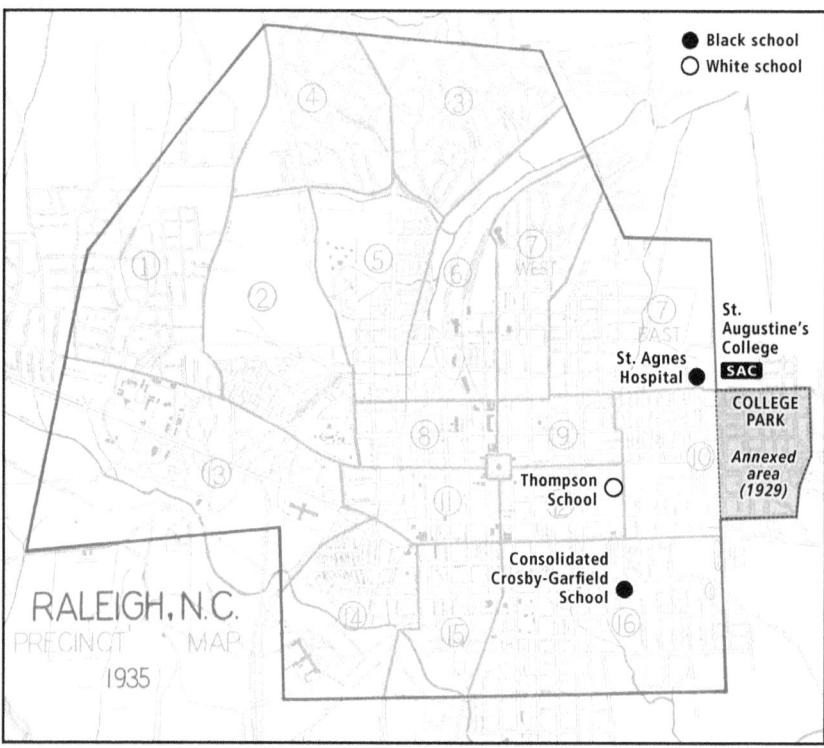

MAP 6.1. Black homeowners in or near College Park, a Black addition that opened in 1911, repeatedly petitioned local officials for a school for their neighborhood. They never received one, and College Park was not annexed to the city until 1929. Note the distance between St. Augustine's College and the Crosby-Garfield School. Courtesy of the Louis Round Wilson Special Collections Library, University of North Carolina at Chapel Hill.

In 1915, Hunter believed that the district's proposed bond issue would finally rectify the situation. Although Raleigh's turn-of-the-century disfranchisement campaign had suppressed the Black vote, bond elections remained open to all registered voters, Black and white, who were current on their poll taxes. These elections were particularly vulnerable to defeat by a small group of determined voters because the number of citizens who participated in them was usually low while the hurdle for passing them was kept high by design. In Raleigh, a successful bond election required a majority of *registered* voters rather than a simple majority of *actual* voters. Since staying at home could endanger the bonds as much as casting a negative ballot, even a modest number of Black voters could still influence the results. Thus, when Hunter joined several other Black leaders to petition the board for a new school, they were given vague assurances that their request would be met. One of the board members was B. F. Montague, an investor in both

College Park and Cameron Park, the city's most child-centered residential park at the time. Montague privately persuaded Hunter to support the bonds while insinuating that the board could not publicly commit to a new Black school without jeopardizing white support. With this faint encouragement, Hunter launched a voter registration drive to help pass the bonds. Yet, no school was built for College Park residents after the issue succeeded at the polls.[10]

In Atlanta, Black middle-class residents were also disappointed with the outcome of a building program in which more was promised than granted. Before the 1910 bond election, the district had pledged two new Black schools along with substantial improvements in three more. But when the funds for the bond issue had all been spent, Black children had received only a single school, the Yonge Street School, and no other improvements. In response, the Neighborhood Union launched a campaign to upgrade the city's Black schools. Since its founding in 1908, Union members had worked to improve children's lives by opening playgrounds, operating free health clinics, and promoting better housing. Addressing the appalling condition of Black schools seemed a logical extension of their previous efforts.[11]

In 1913—merely three weeks after passage of the city's first segregation ordinance—the Union launched a survey of Atlanta's Black schools. According to Louie Shivery, who served as a member of the coordinating committee for the Union's school campaign, 100 "leading colored women" participated. They documented the city's ramshackle Black schoolhouses, which together provided a total of 4,102 seats for an enrollment of 6,163 children. Additionally, they sent a petition to the school board condemning the disgraceful neglect of the southern part of the city. One school housed the students "in three unsanitary shacks" that were "widely separated from each other," making it "impossible for the teachers to co-operate with each other to the best advantage." Shivery characterized the school as "a patchwork of sheds" that had been cobbled together "by the residents gratis" because board members refused to provide them with proper facilities.[12]

The Union publicized its findings through a series of "mass meetings" complete with a slideshow presentation. Committee members sought white allies by soliciting aid from white as well as Black ministers, reaching out to influential white clubwomen, and petitioning local officials. One called for "the Board's prayerful consideration" in correcting the "very unsanitary" condition of the schools and ending the "double sessions" in which half the children attended school in the morning and the other half in the afternoon. Members further reminded the board that the middle-class "taxpayers" living near Clark University, one of Atlanta's six Black institutions of higher education, had no school at all, even though the bond commission had promised them one. The district, instead, sent the children to a rural school run by the county board, which forced them to provide free janitorial services to "pay" for their attendance at a public school.[13]

ILLUSTRATION NO. 94.

PITTSBURG SCHOOL.—A second floor classroom in a fire trap annex. Note how the teacher's chair has already been partially burned away from coming in too close contact with the overheated stove. The immediate replacement of these inadequate provisions by a modern school building is recommended.

FIGURE 6.1. In 1913, the Neighborhood Union documented the appalling conditions at the Pittsburgh School. When this picture was taken in 1922 for Atlanta's official school survey, few improvements, if any, had yet been made. Strayer and Engelhardt, *Survey*, 142.

When the Union contacted the white press, the *Constitution* eagerly embraced the movement, but its exposé widened the focus from Black schools to all schools, resulting in a cooptation of the Union's campaign. Their articles galvanized delegations of "determined" white parents who lobbied hard for new schools for *their* children. A spokesman representing the working-class parents of the Davis Street School declared that their "building was unfit for the housing of children and could be used more advantageously as a barn." Along with "defective toilets" and "broken floors," the stoves used to heat the classrooms were "broken and crumbled with age" and had "to be tied together with wires to keep them from falling apart and setting the building" on fire. Two months later, a Davis mother painted "a grotesque picture of conditions" in the school. "The smoke and soot in the classroom" were "so dense at times," it was "impossible for the children to see the teacher or for the teacher to see the children." She fumed, "Parents have found it to be much more comfortable and safe to send their children through the cold over a distance of more than a mile to a modern school than to send them to" that "rattletrap." Another parent warned that "unless something" was done directly, families would be "compelled to leave."[14] Nonetheless, the Davis School received few improvements, let alone a modern building. During the years that followed, white families gradually moved away from the neighborhood. Between 1910 and 1920, the white population surrounding the school dropped 34.5 percent.[15]

An important reason that Davis School was not replaced was because affluent white families, once again, cut in line. They argued that their children's health would deteriorate more rapidly under subpar conditions since their children were accustomed to a superior home environment. The *Constitution*'s editorials sympathized with white, middle-class parents who sent their children from homes "constructed along the most modern lines" to overcrowded classrooms where children might "breathe and rebreathe poisoned air." One editorial dramatically predicted "DEATH AND DISABILITY" if something were not done to help the children at the new Highland School, which served nearby Copenhill Park. Although Copenhill dated back to the late nineteenth century, it had developed slowly at first before it was annexed to the city and given a school during the 1910 building program, after which it boomed.[16]

The affluent parents of Inman Park similarly jumped into the fray. "One of the most advantageous things" that could "be done for the property owners in Inman Park and the children who live there," a "prominent business woman" declared, would be "the erection of a commodious schoolhouse *in the heart* of Inman Park" (emphasis added). She predicted "a decrease in the value of real estate" without "better school facilities," complaining, "We have lost the sales of three residences in Inman Park to persons who wished to buy, but would not do so on account of the school facilities, or rather the lack of school facilities." She identified all three potential buyers as belonging to "as desirable a class of citizens as can be found." While developer Joel Hurt had originally secured the Inman Park School for the community, by 1913 its antiquated building sat too close to an industrial area and could no longer compete with the city's recently constructed schools (see map 5.2).[17]

As the clamor for new schools led to calls for an ever-larger bond issue, local officials and the chamber of commerce balked. School board member James Key insisted that "the whole situation had been exaggerated" and the schools were "not as bad as they [had] been painted." He wanted to know who had started this "agitation." The chair of the Board of Lady Visitors, an appointed group of affluent white women who advised the all-male board, replied that "she did not know who had started the movement," but "she would feel honored to have been the originator."[18] Surely she did know, however, since Union members had reached out to the Board of Lady Visitors as soon as they had completed their survey. Yet by this point, the Union's efforts to improve Black schools had already been forgotten in the scramble among white parents to have their needs met first.[19]

The initial response to the Union's survey had been more encouraging. The board chair had appointed a committee to investigate, and the majority report had stated honestly, "A decent regard for the opinions of mankind demands that

FIGURE 6.2. Before Atlanta's 1920s building program began, the antiquated Storrs School was used for the overflow enrollment at the Houston Street School, which had an enormous attendance area covering most of the Fourth and Sixth Wards. Strayer and Engelhardt, *Survey*, 134.

the present condition of these schools be remedied, if it was not necessary from the standpoint of health and safety. We will not say more—we ought not to say less." It recommended six new Black schools plus a modern "toilet annex" for the Houston Street School (see figure 6.2). The superintendent then wrote a lengthy letter to the *Constitution* requesting a large bond issue to rescue Black schools and upgrade white ones. He lectured, "Our failure to grant the negroes even semi-respectable schoolhouses is a great mistake and injustice. Every negro who is made a good citizen by education is a protection to the life, liberty, property, and happiness of every man, woman and child in society." He cast the issue as a matter of basic self-interest for whites: "I consider better school facilities for the negro children necessary, not only for their own usefulness, but also as a protection to the white race. It is justly claimed by sociologists and philosophers that education wields a great force as a preventive of vice and crime." Likewise, the *Constitution* framed the "alarming" situation in Black schools as a danger to white children, suggesting, "The sick negro is a menace to the white child."[20]

Evidently, most whites failed to see the issue as one of self-interest and were willing to tolerate abysmal conditions for Black children. When local officials adopted a policy of strict austerity, the school board responded by abandoning the movement, addressing the overcrowding in Black schools by shortening their academic program from eight grades to six.[21] At the time, the district offered no high school coursework to Black youth even though it operated four white high schools. Black parents were left to defend what they had rather than advocate for more. Another round of petitions successfully prevented further catastrophe, but the physical condition of Black schools continued to deteriorate while enrollments kept climbing.[22] White schools, too, stumbled along, also falling victim to an elite establishment that refused to invest in modern facilities for children in the older areas of the city.

Looking back, Louie Shivery acknowledged that "the immediate direct gains" of the 1913 school campaign were "not great." The Union's original petition had asked modestly for one additional school to relieve dangerous conditions and "make our children good citizens." But in 1914, board members voted to reapportion the $5,500 balance left over from the construction of Yonge Street School—all the money that remained for Black schools from the last bond issue—to help build a white school for a new residential park. A month later, the incoming board reversed the decision by only a single vote. Under pressure from Black parents, it used the money for a small Black school on the campus of Clark University, which donated the site. The school was neither fireproof nor even connected to the city sewer system, although it did provide a few urgently needed classrooms.[23] That year, the board also converted Bell Street School, a decaying white school located two blocks east of Yonge Street School, to Black use. That decision eased overcrowding at the Black schools serving children in the Sixth and Fourth wards, but Shivery thought so little of the gesture that she ignored it in her history of the Union's larger school campaign.[24]

Postwar School Building Programs in the Urban South

US entry into World War I halted almost all local construction projects, including schools. During the war, southern farmers enjoyed monocrop agriculture's final hurrah before a lasting depression descended in the 1920s. The collapse of cotton fueled unprecedented urbanization throughout the South as agricultural workers sought brighter prospects in nearby cities, especially Black workers who suffered most under labor exploitation. Many migrants from the South's impoverished countryside took advantage of new employment opportunities in northern factories, while others sought opportunity closer to home.[25]

Rapid urbanization meant that thousands of new students would further strain the region's habitually underfunded school systems. As the tide of children poured into urban districts, administrators scrambled to accommodate them. The overcrowding was compounded by increasingly rigid compulsory attendance laws, which southern states began enacting decades after they appeared in other regions. Massachusetts was first in 1852 and Mississippi dead last in 1918, with Georgia's law taking effect just one year earlier. Ten days before it kicked in, Atlanta's superintendent warned of the impending crisis. He had no idea where he would put the additional students since some areas were already "so crowded" that "no seat" could be "found in three or four contiguous [white] schools."[26]

The years directly following the war brought more concerns: labor was costly, supplies were limited, and inflation was high. The situation was especially dire in the South, where districts had long suffered from a critical shortage of classrooms. Between 1914 and 1921, Atlanta's school population had risen from 20,000 to 35,000, but only three small elementary schools had been built to accommodate the increase. The superintendent begged, "We have got to build schoolhouses or crash. The system can't stand this strain much longer." Other cities were also stretched to the bursting point. In 1921, the *News and Observer* reported that Raleigh's public schools lacked capacity for one-third of the district's enrolled students. Children sat on the floor in crowded classrooms despite the use of double shifts. In Houston, 12,000 students were already without seats while the population continued to soar. Principals carved makeshift classrooms from basements, hallways, and stairwells. The gravest conditions were found in Black schools. One in Birmingham housed more than 1,000 students even though its capacity was 360. In Atlanta, some Black schools maintained *triple* shifts with each student attending class, at most, three hours a day. Double and triple shifts made it nearly impossible to enforce the new compulsory attendance laws because it was difficult to know when students were supposed to be in school.[27]

The physical structures were equally shocking. In 1921, the *News and Observer* reported that Raleigh's wooden schools were "dangerous to the lives of the hundreds of children taught there." Birmingham's 1923 school survey described various white schools as "miserably planned," "insanitary," "unsafe," "unfit for school purposes," and "injurious to the health of children," but they were still superior to most of the city's Black schools. One was housed "over a rickety old vacant store" in a building that was "leaning" as if it might "tumble over" at any moment. Local officials in Memphis were also guilty of a staggering level of neglect. According to historian Lynette Wrenn, Black children endured "conditions that health officers would not have permitted to 'exist even in the case of livestock:' cracker box seats, leaky roofs requiring the use of umbrellas indoors, and classes meeting on school steps."[28]

Atlanta's most shameful schools were no better, despite the city's reputation as the epicenter of the "New South." In 1921, an editorial in the *Constitution* described two of the city's high schools as "dull, dreary, insanitary and disease breeding, tumbledown structures not fit for stables for mules and cows." The following year, the district's own survey offered plenty of evidence to substantiate the newspaper's denunciations. It identified fire hazards "appalling in number and degree," charging that even the newest schools had "not been built according to the fire protection standards" that had been "progressively embodied in school building construction in the leading cities in the country [in other words, northern cities] since 1900." Indeed, between 1918 and 1920, three of Atlanta's schools suffered fires so severe that the board had to assign the students to other schools while repairing the buildings.[29]

The rhetoric comparing Atlanta's schools unfavorably with those of more "progressive" cities tapped into one of the key drivers of the school building boom. The "progressive" label—associated with "scientific government" and expertise during the 1920s—helped cities compete for national recognition and acceptance. As southern cities vied for entry into the nation's larger industrial economy, local boosters found an "unprogressive" school system to be an embarrassing impediment to future growth. The *Houston Chronicle* worried that their city's schools ranked "far below other progressive cities in the country." In the same vein, a "leading" citizen of Raleigh cautioned, "If Raleigh, by unprogressiveness, hands over educational leadership to other cities, we shall have only ourselves to blame."[30]

Within this context, local elites no longer cried poverty when parents and school administrators begged for new schools. Instead, they organized campaigns to pass large bond issues in unprecedented amounts. Atlanta booster Frank Inman, son of one of the city's wealthiest investors, embraced the spirit of competition. "The city of Cincinnati recently completed a high school costing as much money as Atlanta's entire school system," he attested. "Cleveland recently did the same. Birmingham is planning, in the next three months, to build a $1.5 million high school. Nashville has a high school that cost half as much as every school in Atlanta put together." Likewise, US congressman W. D. Upshaw goaded Atlantans through unflattering comparisons: "I confess that I have been in many towns of from 10,000 to 50,000 inhabitants that boast of better school buildings, and especially better high schools, than Atlanta has today."[31]

Because affluent parents expected nothing less than the best for their children, the consensus view of the chamber-of-commerce crowd, many of whom wished to profit from housing development, was that the economy would suffer without immediate and substantial investments in the school system. A prominent businessman from Raleigh wrote a letter to the editor alerting his fellow citizens, "The progress of the city is at stake, for I verily believe that people who come to look around and locate here would seriously consider some other place if they were to examine all of our school buildings." Boosters in Houston shared similar concerns. According to an editorial in the *Chronicle*, one of the first things newcomers did was inquire about the schools: "If Houston has to answer that it has an old, antiquated and dilapidated school system, it can not expect people to become enthusiastic over coming here to make Houston their home. But, if it can show the finest school system in the state, or the South, it then has a tremendous asset added to its commercial and industrial prestige as a drawing card." Atlanta's mayor agreed: "Whether you have a child in school or not, I stand here and tell you our failure to have a first-class public school system is going to hurt every business and every foot of real estate in Atlanta."[32]

Action

As business-class boosters launched their impassioned rivalry for population growth and economic expansion, the emerging consensus afforded a new opportunity for Black citizens to demand greater educational access. This campaign was part of a larger movement for civic improvements that would benefit Black children, including parks and playgrounds, better housing, and safer streets. The timing coincided with the Great Migration, which provided Black activists with substantial leverage. White elites feared that the exodus would not only damage the economy but would also contradict their assertions that Black residents were content under Jim Crow. In leaving the South, Black southerners protested a wide spectrum of injustices from trifling wages to the unspeakable horrors of lynching, with grossly inferior schools a key impetus as well.

At the same time, Black veterans were returning home from World War I resolved to live in a democracy. Their determination inspired Black activists who circulated petitions and then elected committees to represent their interests before local officials, much as earlier movements had done. They also opened branches of the NAACP and skeptically joined interracial committees. By this time, most white boosters were projecting a façade of interracial harmony to attract outside investment, which furnished Black activists a small opportunity to question the whitewashing of local race relations.[33] Yet activists understood that below the façade was the ever-present threat of violence whenever white supremacy was challenged. The trick was to corner whites into making significant improvements without unleashing the mob.

At the 1919 Emancipation Day celebration in Raleigh, members of the local NAACP introduced a set of resolutions that reflected this renewed spirit. According to the *News and Observer*, speakers directed Black parents "to instill into the hearts of the negro children that to be black is no disgrace." They also demanded "that equal opportunities of education be given our people" as well as "full representation in the ballot." More than 1,000 participants unanimously adopted the resolutions. A few months later, the Twentieth Century Voter's Club bravely put forth an all-Black ticket for mayor and the city commission.[34]

Four days after the election, white elites moved to reestablish the color line at a "mass meeting" welcoming home Raleigh's Black soldiers. Governor Thomas Bickett spoke before the gathering and offered the veterans some "sound advice and friendly suggestions," in the words of the *News and Observer*. Worried about rumors of growing militancy among the soldiers, he warned them to be on their best behavior or suffer disastrous consequences, drawing "the parallel of the Indian people" and "calling attention to the extinction of the red man who would not accommodate himself" to the white man's law. The Black organizers of the event thanked the governor and the other white speakers "for their cheering words" and assured them that the "returned soldiers" would "make good as citizens."[35] Intimations of "extinction" were particularly persuasive as widespread violence swept the nation during the "red summer" of 1919. Massacres in Tulsa in 1921 and in Rosewood, Florida, in 1923 demonstrated the seriousness of the threat.

Within this perilous context, Black citizens courageously advanced an agenda to ensure their children would not be further left behind as southern elites finally committed to investing in modern schools and other civic improvements. To be successful, the movement had to tap into white self-interest by making white people feel a little pain. In Atlanta, Black voters had lukewarmly supported bond issues in the past hoping that local officials could be shamed into building schools for Black children as well as white ones, but their repeated appeals for modern elementary schools, let alone a Black high school, went nowhere.[36] This time, they were determined that whites would receive no new schools or other public improvements until Black citizens were guaranteed their fair share of resources.

The leadership of Atlanta's recently established NAACP was optimistic that a voting bloc might work because bond issues could be defeated relatively easily by a small number of organized voters, reflecting elite interests in keeping municipal expenses low. Bond issues in Atlanta required a *two-thirds* majority of actual voters in addition to a majority of registered voters, whether they stayed home on election day or not.[37] And unlike the elections governed by "all-white primary" laws, Black voters could participate in bond elections if they were current on their poll taxes, which remained the biggest obstacle as it was designed to be. Until the Twenty-Fourth Amendment declared the tax unconstitutional in 1964, Atlantans were required to pay each year before registering.

When local officials announced the impending bond election in 1919, they offered only vague promises as to what improvements Black schools would receive if the bonds passed. In response, the Atlanta Colored Teachers Association submitted a petition to alert the school board that it would have to do better: "Again and again the colored people have been promised more schools and better schools, but these promises have been so slow in fulfilling that the people are restless and distrustful. THEY WANT ACTION." "If ample provisions were proposed and the colored people were advised definitely in advance as to the number and locations of the school buildings," it pleaded, "we are confident that ninety percent of the registered colored voters" would support the bonds.[38]

Despite the forewarning, local officials failed to produce a plan for Black schools. As a result, the NAACP launched a voter registration drive that would create a formidable voting bloc. Because the poll tax was cumulative from the first year of eligibility, the South's low-wage economy rendered it an especially prohibitive requirement. During the previous bond election, Black citizens comprised only 5 percent of registered voters, even though they made up a third of the total population. An effective voting bloc would require a much larger Black electorate, but postwar inflation made paying the tax that much harder. The *Independent's* Benjamin Davis, who served on the NAACP's executive committee, pushed Black citizens to make the financial sacrifice in honor of Black soldiers: "Since our boys went overseas and played such a mighty part, reflecting such credit upon their country and race, we owe it to them as well as ourselves, to show our appreciation and gratitude by paying our taxes and registering."[39]

After the war, membership in the local branch of the NAACP swelled to 1,700, providing a sturdy foundation for the registration drive. The leadership sent out a letter to members reminding them that Atlanta was "the only city of her size" with "as great a Negro population" that did not "at least pretend to give high school facilities to Negroes." It worked. According to Vice President T. K. Gibson, "Within one month we had registered more than a thousand names" with "many people paying as much as fifteen, twenty, and even twenty-five dollars, in back [poll] taxes." They had served notice "upon the white people of the city" that Black citizens would have "to be reckoned with in municipal affairs."[40]

Election day took the city's white boosters by surprise. Although white newspapers had acknowledged the heavy registration among Black voters, they had assumed the drive was in *support* of the bond issue, a belief that required an extraordinary level of collective denial. When it became evident that Black citizens were voting against the bonds, the alarm bells began to peal. At midday, headlines screamed, "Bonds Declared in Danger—Don't Fail to Vote" and "Big Negro Vote against Bonds Is Peril to Election." The acting mayor also issued a statement to the press. "It is reported that negroes are voting in large numbers against the bonds," he warned. "I wish, in the absence of the mayor, to urge the people of this city who love Atlanta to go to the polls and vote for the bonds and save their city from dire calamity."[41]

In the days that followed, local officials were swift to blame Black voters, even as they struggled to understand the motive. The chairman of the bond commission was Aquilla Orme, one of the developers of Boulevard Park, which was slated to receive a school thanks to Orme's maneuvering. He advised the city council to ask the state legislature to overturn the election since "white voters overwhelmingly supported" the bond issue. In his statement to the press, he alleged that "Negros flocked in droves" to defeat the bonds because they had been "misinformed." The acting mayor, equally befuddled, suspected the influence "of certain white people" who had wielded "a subtle influence" he had "not been able to trace." This explanation was more palatable than recognizing the NAACP's remarkable accomplishment; it also reflected a long tradition of blaming effective Black resistance on white phantoms.[42]

Benjamin Davis's trenchant response in the *Independent* shredded those assumptions. "We plead guilty to the soft impeachment, and are proud of our day's work," announced his front-page editorial. "But we deplore the effort . . . to stir up race strife and race hatred by attempting to make it appear that it was a race question. Why was it any more of a race question for the Negroes to vote solidly against the proposition than it was for the white people to vote solidly for it?" Davis also lambasted their effort to circumvent a lawful, democratic election so they could "impose a heavy, high and arbitrary tax upon the taxpayers, without their consent or knowledge." Moreover, he pilloried the supposition that shadowy white men were behind "the Negro vote." "The Negro is a citizen, entitled to his own opinion, clothed with the right to exercise it as a free man," he scolded. "When he votes, he acts of his own free will and volition, expressing by his ballot his honest convictions, arrived at after due consideration of every municipal interest, just like the Mayor or any other white man." He then assured them that the only white men who tried to influence the Black vote were advocating *for* the bonds.[43]

The leadership of the NAACP attempted to correct any confusion through an open letter to "the city at large." Written so "that there may be no misunderstandings of the position of colored citizens," it informed white Atlantans that "colored men themselves" were "responsible for their own actions, which resulted from decisions arrived at after full, frank and free discussion among themselves." Along with a description of their grievances, the letter requested modern school buildings, the elimination of double sessions, equal pay for teachers regardless of race, and a high school that was "no sham" or "make believe" but would properly prepare children for higher education. Other demands included playgrounds, swimming pools, a library, and a hospital, as well as streetlights, sewers, regular garbage pickup, and paved streets to make the blocks where Black families lived healthier and safer. "We too believe in bonds, but when they are issued they should carry specific and unalterable provisions for a division of the funds," the letter instructed. "We are willing to pay for these things. But when we increase our taxes for the purpose of getting what we want, we want to understand exactly ALL the terms of the bargain."[44]

The many candid articles, editorials, and statements that summarized their position fell on deaf ears. Local officials and boosters blindly offered Black voters the chance to humiliate them all over again just six weeks later. When the white press announced a second election, the *Independent* reiterated the stance of Black voters: "We adhere to the same proposition, based upon the same principles, which actuated us to vote for the defeat of both propositions before." Their goal remained unmistakable: "We are not going to vote any more money for white people to spend for themselves to the exclusion of Negro people, and the authorities had as well sit up now and take notice."[45]

The authorities did, indeed, take notice, but they were deluded about what was required to induce Black voters to support the bonds. Further, they were talking to the wrong people if they wished to achieve a different outcome. According to the city's white press, the mayor and school board invited a "colored delegation" to discuss the election, but it did not represent the position of the NAACP. Instead, the delegation's chair reportedly told officials that "the committee had come to be spoken to rather than to speak." The board obliged. One member, a real estate developer, obtusely admitted that "he did not see how voting against the tax would remedy the inequalities and deficiencies of the past." The board did, however, reveal "tentative plans" to give Black students Fourth Ward's decrepit Boulevard School along with another equally disgraceful white school.[46]

As usual, the *Independent*'s reply did not mince words. Davis called the offer "ridiculous" and "beneath the dignity of an enlightened and progressive municipal corporation." To insinuate that "old dilapidated, antebellum school houses" were "an inducement" to vote "for new schoolhouses and new water mains in white communities for the benefit of white people" was "a little less than an insult to the intelligence, wealth and respectability of the Negroes of this city." If "old second-hand, out-of-date, unsanitary schoolhouses are unfit to teach white children in, they are unfit to teach Negro children in," he scoffed. "Such inducements as these will only drive self-respecting votes away from both propositions." He also questioned the authority of the "colored delegation." "We take it for granted that they represent themselves only and do not pretend to represent anybody else."[47]

Rather than negotiate with the NAACP, local officials and their booster allies chose to concentrate their efforts on increasing white voter turnout. In the days before the election, the *Journal* published a series of articles written by school board member W. H. Terrell meant to rally white voters: "I, for one, would be pleased to have [white] high school buildings that the Chamber of Commerce could picture and describe in its literature and to which it could point with pride when boosting Atlanta." He argued that a palatial school that was "the best building in the neighborhood" would always "make money for the real estate man, merchant and banker." The mayor made a similar statement: "A prosperous successful and efficient school system will add to the value of every piece of real estate, every business and every profession in Atlanta." Likewise, a "mother" hoped her letter to the *Constitution* would galvanize white men since women did not yet have suffrage. If Atlanta seeks to attract "a desirable class" of citizens "as home makers and business men," she advised, "she must make her schools the best in the south." The "rivalry among towns in this respect is very keen."[48]

These assertions merely convinced Black voters that the objective was to build show-palaces for white children rather than decent classrooms for their own. The *Independent* rallied Black voters with the opposite purpose in mind. "Let us go to the polls on the 23rd, as we did on March 5th and defeat bonds and higher taxation as a rebuke to those who have wantonly disregarded our constitutional rights," an editorial prodded. "Vote against higher taxes until we have a library, better school houses, high schools, playgrounds for our children, parks for recreation, police and fire protection and a square deal as citizens of Atlanta."[49]

Unsurprisingly, the result of the second election was the same as the first, the reaction of white supporters just as dense, and the *Independent*'s response just as incisive. The precinct for the lower Fourth Ward, which included the racial transition area that had sparked the city's original segregation ordinance, handed boosters the largest rout. The president of the Atlanta Teachers Association, which represented only the district's white teachers, captured the characteristic view of white Atlantans after their second thrashing at the polls: "The pathetic thing about the election is the fact that the ignorant element, the very persons needing good schools, are the ones who defeated the proposition."[50]

Benjamin Davis's retort was edifying but measured. He stressed the irony of suggesting that Black voters should support bonds for new schools because they needed them most while simultaneously denying their offspring access to decent schools. In an open letter to the *Atlanta Georgian*, he asked, "Have you taken the time to think that 'if the blackest, most stupid and ignorant ward in the city' is the fourth ward, there is a cause for it that is not far to find, and that is in the failure of the city of Atlanta to provide for the educational advancement of the Negroes within its bounds?" "If they are 'ignorant and stupid,'" he lectured, "it is not their fault, but the fault of those who have oppressed, lynched, burned and kept from them what they are due—education in civic duties." He further asked, "Do you think it 'ignorance and stupidity' on their part to not vote for bonds to beautify [a park] into which they can not go; to increase the facilities of a library they dare not enter; and to build more high schools for the children of the white race, while they have not one for themselves?" He then explained, once again, how whites could "secure every Negro vote in the city of Atlanta": "Build some decent school houses and equip them properly, in which the Negro girls and boys can be educated; build two high school buildings like you have for yourself, for Negro boys and girls; build and support a library for the Negro public, and do away with all this ignorance for which you are responsible, before you condemn us for it."[51] Soon thereafter, local officials began negotiating with the NAACP.

In the coming years, events in Atlanta would inspire those in Houston. Clifton Richardson also used his newspaper as a bully pulpit to demand modern Black schools as well as greater access to city services, especially those that would benefit Black children. When Richardson launched the *Houston Informer* in 1919, he set forth a ten-point platform for the paper. "Democracy, both domestic and foreign" topped the list, reflecting Black priorities during the war, but "playgrounds for colored children" was second and "better educational facilities" third. Richardson's focus on school improvement seemed to have stemmed from his role as a parent. His initial exposé was of his son's school. On the front page, he printed four pictures of the standing water that almost completely submerged the schoolyard because the street lacked a drainage system. He blamed the near-constant flooding for the unhealthy conditions at the school, maintaining that his own child was just recovering from a two-week illness.[52]

Following the announcement of a $3 million bond election in 1923, the *Informer* began hounding local officials to include Black schools in the proposed building program. Richardson published a list of "totally inadequate" schools including five with "antiquated frame structures." He depicted his son's school as "situated in the center of a young lake" and another as "likely to fall with a good gust of wind." After directing Black citizens to vote against the bonds if local officials earmarked less than $500,000 for Black schools, he added, "People seldom get all they ask for and where they ask for nothing, nothing they shall receive."[53]

Richardson joined nine other leading businessmen to form a "colored citizen's committee" of "large taxpayers" to communicate their priorities to the school board. Five of the men were currently serving on the executive committee of Houston's NAACP, and two more, including Richardson, were former members. Although Houston was one of the first southern cities to open a Black public high school, by 1923 it languished in disrepair, with only 500 seats for 900 students. Committee members called for a new high school that would "reflect credit upon our great city, inspire our children and serve as one of the places of interest to visitors." They also requested a second high school equipped with a manual training department for the city's industrial east side. As in Atlanta, they were abundantly clear that Black voters would not support a bond issue without a pledge, in advance, detailing exactly how the money would benefit Black children.[54]

When local officials designated more than $500,000 to Black schools, the *Informer* enthusiastically endorsed the bonds, but white hostility, led by the *Houston Post*, sunk them anyway. Evidently, the promises made to Richardson and the other members of the citizen's committee supplied extra ammunition to the opponents of the city's appointed school board. The *Post* charged Richardson with "presumptuousness and insolence" and accused board members of buying Black votes with a half-million-dollar bribe. Editorials claimed that all essential repairs to the city's (white) schools should cost no more than $1 million instead of the proposed $3 million bond issue. Furthermore, the paper alleged—inaccurately—that African Americans were not qualified to vote in the election.[55]

In response to the *Post*'s outburst, the *Informer* began a series of articles associating Black out-migration with educational neglect, most likely as a thinly veiled threat. One cautioned, "If we thought that the good white people of this community would oppose and vote against a bond issue for schools, merely because it was apparent colored children would get better and larger school buildings and more modern facilities and equipment, this paper would advise every colored person to sell out his belongings and seek a home in some other community." The following week, a front-page headline proclaimed, "Negro Exodus Stirs Dixie: Northern Migration Seriously Affecting South's Labor Mart." The accompanying article argued that educational improvements were the best means to prove that white southerners wanted their Black employees to stay.[56] A similar headline announced, "Atlanta Tries to Combat Negro Exodus by Extensive School Program—Spending $1,179,270.59 for Colored School Buildings—Fireproof and Modern Construction."[57] A few months later, Richardson reminded his readers, both white and Black, that out-migration along with the strategic use of voting blocs helped convince local officials to improve Black schools in Atlanta. He then condemned Houston's "rat-trap called a colored high school building," declaring it would "reflect discredit upon Podunk Creek." Close by, a second editorial ordered, "Pay your poll tax and pay it right now!"[58]

Inspired by the NAACP's victory in Atlanta, Richardson called for a voting bloc when local officials announced a subsequent bond election without specifying how Black residents would benefit. "Why vote for increasing your taxes and getting nothing in return but a tax receipt?" he questioned. "The *Informer* is not opposed to civic progress and municipal growth, but this paper is tired of such progress and growth at the expense of our group, while we get nothing in return for our support and taxation—not even promises." Two weeks later, he urged, "Until the city officials see to it that colored residential sections get some civic considerations from such bond issues, the colored voters in this city should go to the polls en masse and vote against every bond issue," asserting that it was often "necessary to vote negatively to get an ultimate positive result." Whether Black voters were instrumental in defeating the bonds remains uncertain, but all six propositions, including those for paving, drainage, and the library, were defeated. An editorial in the *Post*—which had heartily endorsed *this* bond issue—grumbled hypocritically, "The great majority of the people are progressive, and stand ready to support every reasonable forward program in the way of municipal improvements," but "those opposed" were more "aggressive." What was "undoubtedly a minority group in Houston carried the day, thereby halting Houston's progress."[59]

When officials tried again two months later, they combined the proposed bonds from the last election with the school bond issue defeated the previous year. After the plans for the building program were made public, Richardson expressed disappointment with the paltry allotment for black schools. Out of $3 million, the board earmarked only $70,000 for a single makeshift high school. Since Black Houstonians were 25 percent of the population, the money designated for Black children was less than a tenth of an equitable per capita distribution. Richardson pushed for another citizen's committee to petition the board, but other leaders thought it unwise to make an ultimatum considering the disastrous outcome of the 1923 election.[60]

This time, Houston's boosters took no chances. An appointed bond committee from the chamber of commerce recruited more than thirty white civic clubs to advance the cause, and on the night before the election, a "huge parade of school children," representing every white school in the district, marched through downtown accompanied by each of the white high school bands. On election day, a "brass band" paraded through downtown with banners reading, "Progressive Houston is Calling You—Vote for the Bonds." It worked. Houstonians cast 11,000 ballots, more than three times the number that would be cast in the next bond election.[61]

Once the building program was underway, Richardson derided the "miniature school building" that was supposed to serve as the new Black high school. It would barely seat 300 students, and even the board described it as "a small affair." Meanwhile, construction began on seven white senior and junior high schools that would each house 900 students. Richardson challenged Black citizens to abandon their cowardice and apathy. He asked why parent-teacher associations and citizens' committees had not petitioned the board. Upbraiding the entire community, he admonished, "Blessed is he that expecteth nothing, for nothing he shall receive." The *Post* answered Richardson's strong rebuke with a headline exclaiming, "'Houston Informer,' Negro Weekly, Hits City School Board." In the article, district administrators defended the size of the high school and praised its attractive site.[62]

But Richardson would not back down. In his next editorial, he accused the board of making a "serious blunder," calling the school "a monumental joke, a misnomer, a gratuitous insult to our racial pride and civic fidelity and a horrible reflection upon the fair name of Miss Houston." That October, he credited Black school improvements in Dallas to a group of tenacious citizens who had petitioned the school board, and he again implored Houston's Black leadership to step up. Two weeks later, he praised his friend R. T. Andrews, a successful grocer, for his speech at the new high school's dedication ceremony. Andrews proudly affirmed that, although whites might only throw crumbs, Black citizens would "ever insist upon and contend for bread." Not surprisingly, the written copy of Andrew's address was the one speech not placed inside the canister tucked behind the school's cornerstone.[63]

Results

The following year, Richardson's harsh words began to pay off. When local officials started campaigning for another bond issue, the *Informer*'s front page announced that "for the first time in [Houston's] history," the board had circulated, in advance, the specific improvements contemplated for Black schools. After the bond issue succeeded at the polls with the help of Black voters, the board expanded the seating capacity of the new Black high school and awarded contracts for several modern elementary schools. Richardson graciously acknowledged the "tangible consideration" shown Black families, and then the district's business manager reached out to the *Informer* to convey his appreciation for the flattering editorial. He also outlined several more projects that were being planned for Black schools.[64]

A year and a half later, officials pledged an additional $500,000 if a third bond issue passed. The *Informer* again endorsed the bonds, and the election met with overwhelming success. Between the three bond issues, the district would spend more than $1.3 million on Black schools, including a third high school and a new junior high. The amount fell far short of a proportional 25 percent of the total $11 million building program, but Richardson still found much to celebrate: "When the *Informer* was launched there was not a decent public school building in Houston for colored children.... This paper exposed the problem and practice pursued by the school boards, which spent all bond money on and for buildings for white children." "After nine years," he boasted, "we are delighted to observe that several new and modern school buildings for colored children have been erected."[65]

By 1930, Houston was educating more than two and a half times as many Black high school students as in 1924; Black enrollments represented almost 20 percent of the district's total number of secondary students. Lorenzo Greene, a research associate for Carter G. Woodson's Association for the Study of Negro Life and History, provided a glowing report of Houston schools while traveling through the city that year: "Houston has the best Negro school system in the South. It comprises about twenty schools, including three senior high schools. They are all large, airy, brick or stucco buildings. This is especially true of the Phillis Wheatley High School, which for sheer artistic beauty, surpasses any colored school that I have seen yet."[66]

The triumph in Atlanta was perhaps even more inspiring. When a large bond issue finally passed with the support of the Black electorate, Black families received the high school they wanted as well as four modern elementary schools with cafeterias and libraries. Although the completion of Booker T. Washington High School was their greatest victory, it was not the most immediate. The initial win was Ashby School, which board members turned over to Black students as a

ILLUSTRATION NO. 85.

SUMMER HILL SCHOOL.—A school, with an old house used as an annex for classroom work, located on a site which is totally unsatisfactory for school purposes. Both school house and annex are falling into decay.

ILLUSTRATION NO. 86.

ASHBY STREET SCHOOL.—The main entrance of this school, erected in 1915, one of the best school buildings for colored children. Note how the concrete surfacing has broken away and refer also to the pictures of the interior of this building, such as Nos. 90, 91 and 92.

FIGURE 6.3. The Summer Hill School (*top*) dated back to Reconstruction while the Ashby Street School (*bottom*) opened in 1911 as a white school. Although Ashby still needed a few repairs, it was one of only two modern schools that served Atlanta's Black children in 1922 when the building program began. Strayer and Engelhardt, *Survey*, 133.

peace offering following the back-to-back shellackings they received during the prior two bond elections (see figure 6.3). Ashby was built out of the 1910 bond issue after First Ward boosterism had yielded two new white schools but no new Black schools, despite the ward's Black majority. The school was just a few blocks from Atlanta University, but the property farther west remained largely undeveloped. The ward's tradition of block-level segregation had led boosters to believe a school would spur the construction of white housing there, even though Atlanta University had long attracted Black homeowners to the area and industry lurked nearby.[67]

The year Ashby opened, small-scale developers launched a modest white addition, Sunset Park, with limited success. By that time, traditional mixed-race, mixed-use development had already begun to fracture, making the property near Ashby less desirable for white, single-family homes. Then in 1914, the beginning of a nationwide real estate slump caused further stagnation, producing the oddity of a new school without students to fill it.[68] Still, despite the dire need for more Black classrooms, First Ward whites refused to give up Ashby in a futile attempt to prevent block-level segregation from collapsing completely.

Instead, they hoped a second segregation ordinance would preserve traditional development. Atlanta's first ordinance, which was triggered by fears of racial transition in the lower Fourth Ward, was declared unconstitutional by the Georgia Supreme Court in 1915. Supporters of the second ordinance believed enough changes had been made to the original law for it to pass judicial review, but the US Supreme Court soon ruled all segregation ordinances unconstitutional in *Buchanan v. Warley* (1917). This decision ended the dreams of First Ward boosters including W. H. Terrell, who by that time was serving on the school board.[69]

As block-level segregation continued to crumble, the attempt to maintain Ashby as a white school failed, too. The school board eventually pushed through Ashby's conversion, although board members postponed the transition for an additional year "to allow the white residents of that section to sell their homes." This decision granted white homeowners more time to relocate at the expense of Black children who would continue to endure unconscionable overcrowding at nearby schools. Still, the *Constitution* reported that the announcement "aroused a storm of protest" from white homeowners "who appeared before the board and registered strenuous objections to the plan." Board members considered reversing course, but white members of the Committee on Church Cooperation (CCC), an organization with representatives from dozens of Atlanta's Protestant churches, requested that they convert Ashby straightaway into a Black junior high, which the board agreed to do. Only W. H. Terrell and the board chair voted against the proposal. The CCC remained involved in interracial work during the 1920s, pressuring local officials to fulfill their promises to Black voters. Negotiating with a white delegation allowed the board to remain within the bounds of white supremacy when making decisions their white constituents opposed.[70]

Once Ashby's conversion was made final, white developers wasted no time rebranding their lots. Within days, the developers of Sunset Park began advertising the opening of Ashby Heights, which they characterized as a "Beautiful Residence Section for Colored Citizens." Ads assured that "one house and only one can be built upon one lot." Similarly, developer Edgar Craighead advertised West Hunter Park by prominently featuring Ashby School, as well as other city improvements such as paved roads, access to the car line, and connections to city water and sewers—the remains of white development. The following year, J. R. Smith and Jones Ewing began advertising a new addition with "exceptional school advantage" for "high class colored residents." Soon thereafter, Smith launched Morningside Park, an affluent, white residential park located on the opposite side of town from his Black development, further expanding the size and scope of segregation in the city.[71]

Nonetheless, Black middle-class families were not opposed to the latest plans for the west side. Heman Perry, the Black entrepreneur most associated with residential development west of Ashby Street, wished to build a prosperous Black community that would enjoy the same child-centered amenities as white residential parks. In 1923, he placed his development on the market after purportedly selling Booker T. Washington High School's twenty-acre site to the school district the year before.[72] Perry's aim of creating a full-blown Black residential park was aided by the gift of Washington Park, which would remain Atlanta's only Black park until after World War II. The CCC donated the park's twenty-one-acre tract less than three months after convincing the school board to convert Ashby to a Black school. John Manget, a wealthy cotton broker, was a powerful member of the CCC. He would soon establish the Manget Realty Company with his partner Edgar Craighead. In the coming years, they would develop a modest white addition on the city's east side. Apparently, helping pull Black families to the west side had financial benefits for some of the most influential white men involved with Washington Park and the conversion of Ashby School.[73]

During the early twentieth century, relentless pressure from Black activists resulted in tangible improvements for Black schooling. In 1928, the Associated Negro Press recognized that Black education had "made more progress in the past nine years than in any like period of history." Between 1916 and 1929, the number of publicly funded Black high schools in the former Confederate states climbed from only 38 to well over 900. Of this number, about 370 were four-year academic high schools and 60 percent were in urban areas, even though fewer than a third of Black southerners lived in cities at the time.[74] In many cases, improvements in urban Black schools far outstripped those in white schools during the same time period. This dynamic was especially true for white schools in rural areas but also in older urban neighborhoods with block-level segregation.[75]

The victories made in Black education during the 1920s were all the more impressive given the threatening context in which they occurred. Clifton Richardson faced death threats because of his frank editorials, but as an independent businessman, he was mostly shielded from threats to his livelihood, unlike the majority of Black parents who worked for white employers.[76] Teachers were the largest group of Black professionals during the first half of the twentieth century, and they took extraordinary risks with relatively good employment when they protested the treatment of Black schools, as the Colored Teachers' Association did in Atlanta and Charles Hunter did in Raleigh.

In the end, the cost of modern Black schools was a vast expansion in the size and scope of residential segregation. Black middle-class parents recognized the Faustian bargain they were making, but they hoped for the best. Even though increased segregation might very well trap their children and their children's children in neglected and overcrowded neighborhoods, they simply had no better alternative. How else could they create the proper environment in which to raise their children? At the very least, *Buchanan v. Warley* (1917) offered some assurance that segregation laws could not be used to further limit their housing options.

CHAPTER 7

The Segregation Ordinances versus Racial Zoning

As Black middle-class efforts to obtain modern schools and better housing achieved some success, local officials in Jim Crow cities rushed to find new ways to control Black development while also appeasing Black activists. They found their opportunity to do both through the zoning movement then sweeping the nation. During the 1920s, hundreds of cities adopted zoning plans to separate industrial, commercial, and residential areas. In 1922, Atlanta became the first to adopt a zoning ordinance that included explicitly defined "colored districts." The scheme followed the prescriptions of the national planning movement, which called for homogeneous residential development.[1] Robert Whitten, a well-known planning expert who had helped devise the nation's first comprehensive zoning plan for New York City, served as the consultant.

This chapter limits the term "racial zoning" to only those regulations that were part of a comprehensive zoning law as opposed to previous studies that included segregation ordinances under the same umbrella.[2] Even though both used the states' police power to enforce segregation, racial zoning had a different approach and purpose. Block-level segregation went against the interests of large-scale real estate companies that were then marketing high-priced suburban lots to white families and wished to sell the older housing stock to Black families at inflated prices. They hoped restricting larger areas of the city to a single race would be less capricious and were much less concerned when racial zones erased many of the white blocks that the segregation laws had tried to "protect." Thus, the supporters of the segregation ordinances did not necessarily endorse racial zoning, which threatened their neighborhoods, just as the supporters of racial zoning did not necessarily endorse the ordinances, which stymied business by generating unsalable properties.

Elite representatives of the Atlanta Real Estate Board and the chamber of commerce argued that incorporating "colored districts" into a comprehensive zoning ordinance could survive judicial review because it would facilitate the housing and educational needs of Black families rather than impede them, as the ordinances had done. Certainly, advocates of the original ordinances had attempted to preserve block-level segregation by preventing Black buyers from purchasing vacant houses and by disrupting plans to open additional Black schools. By contrast, advocates of racial zoning claimed that Black families would have access to their own residential parks complete with schools and other child-centered amenities, thereby affording equal treatment under the law.[3]

As evidence of their good intentions, local officials in Atlanta granted Heman Perry's Service Company a permit to begin construction of twenty-five single-family homes near Ashby School less than a week after Atlanta's tentative zoning scheme became public. The Citizens Trust Company, a local Black-owned bank, provided the financing as part of its goal to "supply every colored family" in the city "with a home of its own." That same week, the company signed a $50,000 contract for the "laying of sewers, sidewalks and paved streets on and near the tract."[4] Perry's firm planned to build 100 homes in the development, but this admirable goal came far short of addressing the dearth of modern housing for Black families.

Consequently, Black activists fought against racial zoning because they understood it would concentrate Black residents in limited areas of the city with no space for expansion as the population continued to grow. For Benjamin Davis, the editor of the *Independent*, little daylight stood between this scheme and the initial segregation ordinances. Both stripped Black citizens of their rights and made them targets of unequal treatment, especially the denial of public investment in their neighborhoods. Clifton Richardson, the editor of the *Houston Informer*, denounced the condition of majority-Black blocks, which were not paved, graded, drained, lighted, or policed, except when officers suddenly materialized to brutalize a suspect. "It is a sin to high heaven for human beings to be forced to live amidst the intolerable and unbearable conditions that prevail," he admonished.[5]

Although Black parents embraced the idea of Black residential parks, they never believed the fairytale that racial zoning would lead to better housing conditions. They recognized that de jure segregation in any form would result in overcrowding and neglect. Without access to paved roads, sidewalks, or playgrounds, Black children would still be forced to play in the muck. Using all capital letters for emphasis, Richardson lectured the powers that be for blaming children for the conditions that had been imposed upon them: "It is preposterous to make a child play in the dirt all the time and then expect that child to keep his clothes clean and unsoiled!" Strategically appealing to white self-interest, he cautioned, "There is no such thing as isolation these days—not even with segregation and zoning (more polite term for segregation); for unhealthy and unsavory conditions precipitated because of these public menaces and crime incubators will ultimately react upon the entire community."[6] Richardson assailed segregation through zoning just months before the Georgia Supreme Court declared Atlanta's racial zoning scheme unconstitutional under *Buchanan v. Warley* (1917), the US Supreme Court decision that had nullified the segregation ordinances.[7]

The Short-Lived Segregation Ordinances

During the height of Jim Crow, when *Plessy v. Ferguson* (1896) remained the law of the land, one might have expected the Supreme Court to find a way to declare the segregation ordinances constitutional. If compulsory segregation was sanctioned in schools, transportation, and elsewhere, then why not in housing? And if the goal of segregation was to reinforce the antimiscegenation laws, then housing segregation seemed logical; after all, children spent more time at home than in school. On that basis, advocates insisted that the ordinances were in line with other racial laws that the courts had already validated, regardless of the Fourteenth Amendment. The Supreme Court disagreed, despite its increasing tolerance for government action. Why?

Derrick Bell's theory of interest convergence helps clarify the logic of *Buchanan v. Warley* (1917).[8] According to Bell, Black Americans have only won gains through the US court system when their interests converged with those of affluent white Americans. Therefore, decisions that supported Black civil rights were most likely "the outward manifestation of unspoken and perhaps subconscious judicial conclusions that the remedies, if granted, will secure, advance, or at least not harm societal interests deemed important by middle and upper class whites." Ample evidence suggests that affluent whites had little love for the segregation ordinances because they ran counter to their financial interests.[9]

The impact that interest convergence had on the *Buchanan* decision is especially stark considering the impact that scientific racism had on the conventional wisdom of those making and interpreting the law. Prominent white scientists and social scientists not only theorized that race was a biological fact but that the evolution of the "black" race lagged far behind the "white" race and would require millennia to catch up. In the meantime, whites would continue to progress, keeping the racial divide constant so long as "amalgamation" did not stall "the advancement of the [white] race," a common expression during the early twentieth century. Scientists further alleged that biracial individuals, pejoratively referred to as "mulattoes," were both intellectually and physically weaker than either racially pure blacks or whites, accounting for their supposedly short life expectancy. If true, then a growing number of biracial children would endanger the nation's future, a convenient argument for the preservation of white supremacy. These false claims appeared in newspapers and popular magazines and eventually made their way into the defense of segregation laws.[10]

As Black intellectuals explained repeatedly, however, obvious contradictions raised questions about the extent to which white supremacists believed their own assertions: they promoted racial separation only in circumstances that threatened white power but not in those threatening their own comfort or convenience. It was fine for a Black adolescent to spend each afternoon with white children inside their home so long as she was cleaning it, but it was not fine for her to live next door or to attend school with them. Yale-educated attorney George McMechen, whose residency on Baltimore's McCulloh Street triggered the nation's first segregation ordinance, informed the *New York Times*, "Our women are certainly on much closer and more intimate terms with the whites than I, for instance, for they are thrown in the closest relations as cooks and nurses and maids. One hears no complaint about the contamination of the negro race for them; and yet if I, perchance, live on the same block with a white man he feels as though I had rubbed some of my color off on him. It looks very inconsistent to me." This hypocrisy was the reason most ordinances excluded servants from their provisions. Meanwhile, local officials did nothing to protect Black women, let alone adolescents or even young girls, from sexual assault, casting doubt on the seriousness of white beliefs in the harm of amalgamation.[11]

And despite the apocalyptic rhetoric, no evidence from Baltimore, Winston-Salem, Atlanta—or most likely any of the other two dozen or so cities that passed segregation ordinances—supports the conjecture that the laws were designed to hinder amalgamation at large.[12] Instead, in each case, white homeowners and renters demanded an ordinance after one or more affluent Black families moved onto *their* block. For instance, the purchase of a home by prominent educator William Windsor triggered the calls for an ordinance in Greensboro, North Carolina. According to historian Elizabeth Herbin-Triant, local whites described him as "a tall, exceedingly Light negro," as well as "a man of considerable intelligence." His new neighbors feared he "might easily pass among strangers for a white man," making "the close intermingling of our houses and association of our children ... extremely detrimental to both races."[13]

Although advocates of segregation ordinances hoped the new laws would deter their own children from falling in love with the charming and attractive Black youth living next door, they understood that an ordinance would have to promote the general welfare to be constitutional. Thus, they justified use of the police power by contending that segregation laws would prevent the degeneration of both races, a positive good for everyone. Because of the predominance of scientific racism, the argument had legs and even persuaded some courts. In *Harris v. City of Louisville* (1915), the Kentucky Court of Appeals affirmed, "Under the congested conditions of modern municipal life, there is practically as much, if not a greater degree of association among the children of white and colored inhabitants when living side by side than there would be in mixed schools under the direct observation of teachers." It continued, "All social organizations which lead to their amalgamation are repugnant to the law of nature. From social amalgamation is but a step to illicit intercourse, and but another to intermarriage."[14]

The assertions about public health and safety were more difficult to take seriously since the affluent Black families moving onto "white" blocks were among the most dignified citizens in the city. Black homeowners made clear that they primarily wished to move their children out of the unsanitary and overcrowded conditions of alleys and slums where Black Americans were expected to live. White claims that pushing them back into the slums would somehow promote public health defied credulity. Public safety was an equally tough sell because the violence that advocates alluded to was almost always an insinuation of *future* disturbances rather than evidence of *past* ones.[15] In pressuring Atlanta's government to pass a segregation ordinance, councilman Claude Ashley threatened, "I have been out among the people of the lower part of the fourth ward every night for several weeks imploring them to calm themselves and let council act. . . . I'll tell you frankly that I don't want to go out there tonight and tell the people that council would not relieve them." In Baltimore, violence did break out but only after the Maryland Supreme Court voided the city's first ordinance.[16] Such temper tantrums offered a weak foundation for convincing the courts that the ordinances were necessary.

Similarly, the oft-repeated allegations about preserving property values had little effect on either the state courts or the US Supreme Court. In fact, the courts that upheld the ordinances in Kentucky, Virginia, and Georgia concluded that the laws were so essential to racial integrity that they should stand despite their tendency to *lower* property values. According to the Georgia Supreme Court in *Harden v. City of Atlanta* (1917), "The fact that police regulations may limit the use of property in ways which greatly diminish its value does not necessarily render them void." In such cases, the courts often sided with renters who thought the property value argument worked against their interests. One Baltimore tenant complained, "The residents of a neighborhood and not the property owners should be the ones who should have the say regarding matters of the welfare of their neighborhood. The property owners' interest is purely one of the value of his property and the revenue he can obtain from it."[17]

In contrast, the courts that voided the ordinances emphasized property rights rather than the "general" welfare, siding with affluent whites over lower-income homeowners and renters. Although the North Carolina Supreme Court reiterated its unequivocal support for antimiscegenation laws and the segregation of public places, it ruled that the due process clause of the Fourteenth Amendment distinctly protected the right to acquire, occupy, and sell property—period.[18] In *Buchanan v. Warley* (1917), the US Supreme Court agreed that the justifications for the law did not negate the constitutional requirement to respect a citizen's right to own, use, and dispose of property—a right that Congress had extended to African Americans through the Fourteenth Amendment.

Buchanan was the result of a brilliant test case designed by the NAACP. The Black defendant, Charles Warley, withdrew from a real estate deal with William Buchanan because St. Louis's segregation ordinance would not allow him to move onto the block. William Buchanan then took Warley to court, alleging that he had improperly withdrawn from the real estate deal since the segregation law was plainly unconstitutional. By setting up a white plaintiff, the NAACP invited the justices to side with a white homeowner (who was, in fact, a real estate agent opposed to the ordinance) against a Black defendant (who was, in fact, the president of the local NAACP). It worked.[19]

The unanimous decision systematically addressed each justification for the segregation laws. First, it agreed that the prevention of "race conflicts" was a worthy goal but one that could not "be accomplished by laws or ordinances which deny rights created or protected by the Federal Constitution." Second, it dismissed the claim that "acquisitions by colored persons depreciate property owned in the neighborhood by white persons." This argument made little sense without first confronting the multiple advantages residential parks had over aging, mixed-use neighborhoods. Black residents were able to move onto "white" blocks precisely because most white, middle-class families no longer wished to live there. If an ordinance failed to address the presence of "undesirable white neighbors" or other "disagreeable though lawful uses," then it would not protect property values. Third, the justices rejected the belief that segregation was "essential to the maintenance of the purity of the races" since the ordinances did nothing to prohibit "amalgamation" or even "attempt" to do so. Because the laws were meant to preserve block-level segregation rather than to eliminate it, traditional mixed-race housing patterns would remain, undercutting the amalgamation argument.[20] This reasoning allowed the justices to thread the needle: they managed to leave *Plessy* intact while barring the one form of de jure segregation that harmed affluent whites, as the theory of interest convergence would have predicted.

Still, a ruling grounded in traditional property rights seemed somewhat out of step when zoning regulations and other restrictions on private property were beginning their ascent.[21] Most likely, the sloppiness of these hastily written laws made them difficult to defend even in sympathetic courtrooms, helping to explain their rapid demise. A crucial problem was that the initial ordinances failed to protect vested property rights, which meant that residents who already owned property before the law went into effect might not be able to occupy their homes. An amused W. Ashbie Hawkins chuckled, "There were some humorous incidents connected with the execution of the law which, as afterward proved, was most unskillfully drawn." He offered the following example: "A white person who had temporarily removed from his home while needed repairs were being made" learned that "this wonderful law had placed his house in a block 51 percent colored, and that to return to his own home would make him a criminal, subject to fine and imprisonment."[22] Local officials quickly scrambled to rewrite their ordinances to protect vested property rights.

A more serious blunder was the lack of maps identifying the racial makeup of each block when the laws were passed. Roanoke, Virginia, was the only city in which local officials bothered to produce such a map or even some type of inventory.[23] Thus, by the time a particular segregation case made it to court, the majority race might have flipped, but local officials lacked proof that the block had been "white" at the time of arrest. In striking down Baltimore's law, the Maryland Court of Appeals chided, "A practical difficulty in the enforcement" of the law was "the lack of any provision in the ordinance for some sufficient public notice of" which blocks were "to be white and which colored." It further clarified, "Unless there be some public record giving the necessary information there would probably be great confusion in the examination of title and passing on the rights of purchasers."[24] Despite this blunt warning, city councils failed to make inventories in almost all future attempts to formulate a workable segregation ordinance.

Perhaps the most significant weakness was the ordinariness of mixed-race blocks within traditional urban development. Typically, the laws were designed to stop Black or white residents from moving onto blocks with a *majority* of households from the "opposite" race. This language was intended to accommodate for the mixed-race blocks that remained common in cities with large Black populations. It soon became clear that attempts to eliminate mixed-race blocks would harm white property owners who wanted to sell or rent their houses on those blocks to the highest bidder. The laws also hurt white real estate agents who wished to profit from racial turnover.[25] Local officials came up with a variety of solutions to circumvent the problem. Baltimore's city council simply removed mixed-race blocks from the ordinance's purview, but this action undermined the claim that segregation promoted the general welfare. If mixed-race blocks inevitably led to amalgamation and violence, then why were the mixed-race blocks already in existence not a concern?

Atlanta's city council attempted to address the problem by adding an amendment that required persons moving onto a mixed-race block to obtain permission from the residents living next door if they were not of the same race, as determined by local authorities. The Georgia Supreme Court recognized the absurdity of such an arrangement. What if a homeowner lived between a Black neighbor and a white one? If the Black neighbor objected to a white buyer or tenant and the white neighbor objected to a Black buyer or tenant, then the homeowner could neither profit from nor dispose of the property, which was an obvious violation of the due process clause. Justice Samuel Lumpkin wrote a concurring opinion that acknowledged the state's interest in regulating private property, including the race of the occupants. Yet, he objected to Atlanta's ordinance because it permitted the whim of individuals to decide the appropriate racial category for a piece of property rather than a formal regulation rooted in the general welfare.[26]

Although Atlanta's second ordinance attempted to reduce the ambiguity and capriciousness of the law, the next legal challenge demonstrated it was no less absurd. Frank Harden, a Black man, purchased a house on a corner where a "white" block intersected a "Black" one, a familiar configuration in traditional mixed-race housing patterns. While his address was technically on the white block, he "nailed up" the windows and doors that faced it and "had his house listed" on the Black one. When his white neighbors tried to remove him from his new home, he challenged the law's constitutionality.[27] In *Harden v. City of Atlanta*, the Georgia Supreme Court found that local officials had made enough changes to the ordinance for it to be declared valid. The decision concluded, "If it be justifiable to separate the races in the public schools in recognition of the peril to race integrity, induced by mere race association, then we can not see why the same public policy can not be invoked to prohibit the black and white races from living side by side." By that point, *Buchanan* was already headed to the US Supreme Court, so the judges had little reason to risk ostracism at home with a provocative decision.[28]

Even so, the whites who most vigorously defended the segregation laws were those living on the blocks in contention. In 1915, Booker T. Washington questioned the extent of their popularity among white southerners. He surmised correctly that whites were hesitant to criticize them publicly—despite their limited support—for fear of being labeled traitors: "After such ordinances have been introduced it is always difficult, in present state of public opinion in the South to have any considerable body of white people oppose them, because their attitude is likely to be misrepresented as favoring Negroes against white people."[29] The laws were especially unpopular among whites who had a financial interest in the collapse of block-level segregation. Fortunes could be made pulling white families out to emerging suburbs and selling the single-family houses left behind to Black buyers. Nearly all elites were involved in residential development on some level, either outright or by sitting on the boards of banks, utilities, real estate companies, insurance companies, construction companies, or some combination thereof.

For example, the case against Winston's ordinance—passed before Winston and Salem officially merged into a single city—was argued by John Buxton, a member of the interlocking directorate that had begun imposing racial covenants on new residential developments back in 1890, as discussed in chapter 2. While actively fighting the segregation law, he was developing Central Terrace, a new, child-centered residential park. He was also president of the Winston-Salem Building and Loan Association and a partner in one of the city's most respected law firms.[30] With someone of Buxton's stature leading the defense, the North Carolina Supreme Court had no qualms shredding the ordinance, even implying that a person whose property became unsalable through the law "should have some compensation for his loss."[31] In this particular suit, Buxton represented William Darnell, who had purchased a home on a majority-white block with a Black elementary school and playground located directly behind it, which made the house especially attractive to his family. Buxton's Central Terrace was on the opposite side of town from the Darnells' new home, allowing the interests of an elite white residential developer and a Black homeowner to converge.[32]

In another example, the *Atlanta Independent*'s Benjamin Davis assured white elites that Black citizens would not contest segregation in restricted residential parks so long as they had access to good housing near good schools. In this regard, Davis blamed lower-income whites for blocking Black families' efforts to obtain better housing rather than local elites who imposed racial covenants. He asked, "If the white people on Johnson Avenue, Houston Street, Highland Avenue, or any other street or avenue, because of their superior means, build better homes in the parks and in the country, and desire to sell their old residences on crowded and unsanitary streets to Negro citizens, who are able to purchase them, why should the poor white trash who are renting and unable to buy the old homes of the wealthier whites object to the deal being consummated?"[33] The "wealthier whites" usually agreed that the ordinances unfairly deprived upwardly mobile Black families of decent housing.

The Next Chapter

Buchanan did not end white efforts to control where Black families lived. White Atlantans quickly latched onto another chance to enforce residential segregation when a disastrous fire struck Fourth Ward just months before the US Supreme Court invalidated the city's segregation ordinance. The fire burned 300 acres containing almost 2,000 homes. About 10,000 people—the majority African American—were left homeless. Despite the devastation, members of the Atlanta Real Estate Board, who had been unsuccessfully lobbying for a city plan, hoped to exploit the tragedy to redevelop the Boulevard section near Morris Brown into something more akin to a residential park. An enthusiastic editorial in the *Constitution* encouraged Atlantans to consider the fire "an opportunity of a city's lifetime." The centerpiece was a plan for "wide parks" to separate Black and white homes, settling "for all time the embarrassing problem" of Black and white families "living on the same streets" in Fourth Ward.[34]

City planning experts from across the country championed the proposal to rebuild the ward according to the standards of white, middle-class child-rearing. Consultant George Kessler saw the fire as a potential blessing, even for the displaced families who had lost everything: "As I understand it there is plenty of fine territory about Atlanta which can be used for the housing of those people whose homes had been burned, and in fact they would be better off out where there would be spacious lots for homes." Then the city "might use the former home lots for small park areas and playgrounds." A "well-known" architect from Salem, Oregon, who visited the city after the fire, painted a similar vision for the ward: "I blotted out this terrible wreck for a moment and pictured beautiful parkways, green with the life of spring, the joyous shouts of little children racing among the wonderful works of nature." Likewise, an engineer for the US Army advised Atlantans to "furnish playgrounds for the children."[35] The parks would not only offer attractive, safe, and stimulating outdoor play spaces, but they would also keep white and Black children apart, a core element of the idyllic image of white, middle-class children at play.

Not everyone was so enthused. According to the white press, many Black property owners worried that the latest segregation scheme would result in a "district set apart for negroes" that "would be deprived of city improvements." A meeting of Black homeowners at the famed Big Bethel AME Church passed a series of resolutions that "denounced" the "actions of the rebuilding commission." In addition, Benjamin Davis used the *Independent* to educate white people about the shortcomings of their judgment as well as their morality. "It is extremely unfortunate that the question of segregation should be raised while the city is in the throes of a great calamity" and "Atlanta's best is bending every energy to relieve the suffering and repair the loss." He reminded local officials that the scheme would certainly be declared unconstitutional: "Every court that has passed upon the question has voided the act and the principle as being in contravention of the inalienable rights of the citizens." He warned that such actions would contribute to the exodus of Black southerners, too. "The Negro understands segregation as practical confiscation and believes it is aimed at him, because he is a Negro, and he is inclined to leave any community where such heartlessness and savagery is inflicted."[36] As Davis predicted, the latest segregation scheme went nowhere. White residents from other wards refused to spend tax money on a project with no clear benefits for them.

Atlanta's next effort involved the creation of a zoning plan for the entire city. The chamber of commerce initially launched the endeavor before recruiting Mayor James Key to carry it forward. Key was an attorney and member of the school board representing the Fourth Ward. After the fire, he had drawn up legal documents for the white residents who wanted to impose racial covenants in the burned area, although that effort failed.[37] Then, at the beginning of his first term as mayor, he oversaw the city's defeat in back-to-back bond elections at the hands of the NAACP, followed by the negotiations to convert Ashby Street School to Black use. These experiences surely shaped his embrace of racial zoning as the answer to Atlanta's "race problem."

Mayor Key strategically appointed members to the planning commission who would give the body instant stature. Hoke Smith, who had served as a US senator from 1911 to 1920 and as Georgia's governor before that, supplied formidable political connections. Joel Hurt, the son of a large plantation owner, had developed the city's first two residential parks: Inman Park and prestigious Druid Hills, designed by the renowned Olmsted Brothers. A civil engineer, Hurt built Edgewood Avenue—a fast, straight road connecting Inman Park to downtown. He also started the city's first streetcar company, which furnished transportation for his residential parks. Charles Wickersham was the president of the Atlanta and West Point Railroad Company, which provided a connection to Atlanta's powerful railroads, and whose cooperation would be essential for carrying out any city plan. Former alderman Frank Pittman led the Pittman Construction Company. Under the motto the "Headquarters for Homes," Pittman's company built houses for speculation in Inman Park, Ansley Park, and other affluent developments. Fred J. Terry served as the token representative of the city's labor interests, another potent faction in the city. Employed in the mechanical department of the *Atlanta Georgian*, he afforded the commission a valuable link to a newspaper that had a less sophisticated readership than the *Constitution*'s.[38]

When Key first organized the commission in 1920, Wickersham, Smith, Pittman, and Hurt represented the older generation responsible for the city's past development rather than its present. Key likely chose them rather than members from the previous, informal planning commission sponsored by the chamber of commerce because their participation leant an aura of prestige without challenging Key's authority. Moreover, the group allowed the commission to appear above "politics," especially during the nasty fight over charter reform that eventually pitted Key against those very same members of the chamber.[39] Key seemed unbothered that the aging members of the commission remained aloof from the daily work of developing a city plan. In fact, throughout Hoke Smith's tenure, he stayed in DC earning money as a lobbyist. His absence, however, did not prevent him from buying around $350,000 worth of Atlanta-area real estate while serving on the commission. This lucrative investment suggests he was more interested in helping himself than the city, potential corruption that Key simply ignored.[40]

The most essential member was the chair, Robert Otis, who had served as president of the Atlanta Real Estate Board from 1913 to 1918. Under his leadership, the board had unsuccessfully pushed the city council to establish a planning commission first in 1915 and then again in 1917 during the debate over the burned district. After agreeing to chair the planning commission, Otis hired Robert Whitten, a zoning expert from Cleveland who had helped devise the nation's first comprehensive zoning ordinance. Otis selected him over the Olmsted Brothers, who were Joel Hurt's preference because of their earlier work on Druid Hills and Piedmont Park. Robert Whitten, on the other hand, was trained in municipal law, and if the goal was to create a racial zoning scheme, then the commission needed someone with legal expertise.[41]

As a lawyer, Whitten hoped to avoid the pitfalls of the discredited segregation laws. In considering what *not* to do, he consulted Atlanta's two segregation ordinances and Gilbert Stephenson's influential article "The Segregation of the White and Negro Races in Cities by Legislation" (1914).[42] As legal scholars indicated at the time, *Buchanan* had generated some optimism that a better designed law might survive judicial review, which explains why so many attempts continued to be made, including in Atlanta.[43] The justices could not challenge the constitutionality of segregation without overturning *Plessy*, which they had no appetite to do. Therefore, the unanimous decision emphasized property rights rather than civil rights while accepting the legitimacy of property regulation, demonstrating the growing momentum of the planning movement. Under that logic, de jure segregation remained fair game if local officials could accomplish the task without impinging on individual property rights. Whitten thought racial zoning might be the answer. Rather than a piecemeal segregation ordinance, zoning would treat all areas of the city "equally" within a single, coherent plan. In addition, it could facilitate racial transition, unlike the ordinances. A continuous appeals process would let property designations change over time, thereby eliminating the creation of unsalable houses, at least in theory.

Furthermore, zoning would address the concerns over property value and miscegenation more consistently. Black and white children would no longer live around the corner from each other, which would more effectively deter amalgamation and the conflict it inspired. And because racial zoning would be combined with single-family districting, it would also eliminate the difficulty of "undesirable white neighbors" and other "disagreeable" uses that lowered property values, in the words of the *Buchanan* decision. Thus, racial zoning was just one aspect of the protection zoning would bestow upon residential properties intended for white, middle-class child-rearing. Whitten justified banning apartments from "family home districts" for just that reason. "Apartments are good enough for adults," he argued, "but residences should be encouraged for the good of our future citizens. A child has no place in an apartment house for his full and satisfactory development."[44]

Only eight months after Robert Otis's first meeting with Whitten, Atlanta's tentative zone map was ready to unveil. According to the proposed plan, Black families not already occupying a house within a white district were prohibited from moving into one, and the same held true for white families and "colored" districts. The existence of traditional, mixed-race development meant that the racial zoning map needed a third category—racially "undetermined"—to avoid the thorny issue of unsalable property.[45] In some cases, majority-white areas received this designation if the commission believed the area would or should transition into a colored district at some point in the future.

FIGURE 7.1. This political cartoon, which first appeared the morning Atlanta's city council voted on the racial zoning ordinance, likened urban development without zoning or an effective city plan to the fictional character Topsy, who "just growed" without parental guidance: "Now this poor town, like Topsey grew, without a plan or survey." *American City*, June 1922.

Unlike the segregation ordinances, racial zoning did not always reflect what was but rather what Whitten and the commission thought should be. Some of the smaller Black enclaves, such as the one at Reynoldstown located south of Inman Park, were simply erased from the map as part of the larger effort to shift Black residents from the city's east side to the west side.[46] Planners also responded to the thriving community near Morris Brown and the growing number of

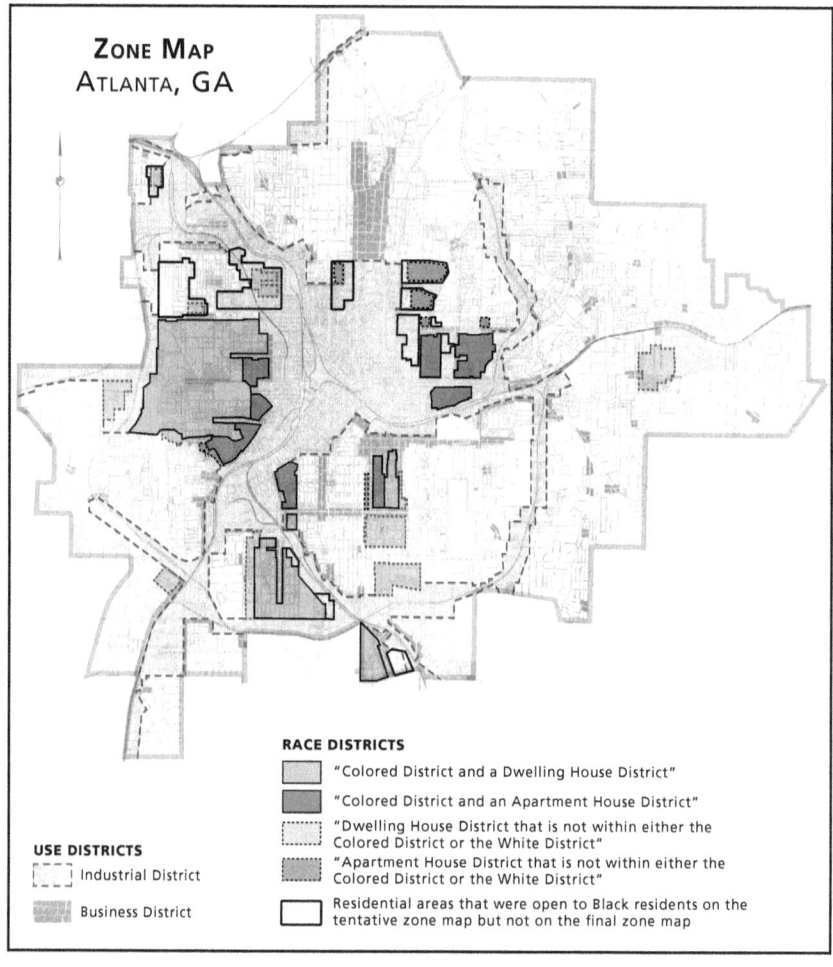

MAP 7.1. Note the large amount of space in Black and "undetermined" districts removed from the zone map before it was approved by city council. It is especially striking in Fifth and Fourth Wards, where the number of blocks designated for one and two-family homes also shrank dramatically. Courtesy of the Kenan Research Center at the Atlanta History Center. Used with permission.

professional and cultural institutions along "Sweet Auburn Avenue" by limiting Black middle-class housing in Fourth Ward. According to the zone map, only a handful of blocks were set aside for single-family homes within the fragmented Black districts envisaged for the area.

The largest Black district, by far, was on the city's west side. It encompassed Atlanta University, Ashby School, Washington Park, the proposed Booker T. Washington High School, and the largely undeveloped land west of Ashby Street.

Many hoped that this area would become a full-fledged residential park for the Black middle class. But even Atlanta's most favored Black neighborhood was not designated an "A1 area district" with a density requirement of at least 5,000 square feet per family, the typical designation for white residential parks. And although apartments were banned from the area, the ordinance permitted an industrial zone to hedge in Washington Park and the single-family houses that would soon be built around it.[47]

According to Whitten, a major difference between racial zoning and the segregation ordinances was that zoning set aside areas for future Black development. By pushing white families out of "colored" and possibly even "undetermined" districts, more housing would become available to Black families. Whitten defended his plan by insisting that it offered "adequate areas for the growth of the colored population," suggesting, "The colored people in these large homogeneous districts are given a better chance for the development of a more intelligent and responsible citizenship than was possible under former conditions."[48] Perhaps Whitten genuinely believed that they were accomplishing what Atlanta's Black middle-class families wanted. For two years, various interracial committees had been working behind the scenes to mitigate disputes over access to schools and housing. During those negotiations, Black parents had reiterated, again and again, a desire to purchase single-family homes near schools and parks in healthy neighborhoods fit for child-rearing.[49]

Nonetheless, Benjamin Davis informed Whitten and the other advocates of racial zoning that they were deluded if they thought Black citizens supported it. He decried the racial districts as "short-sighted" and even "suicidal" and reprimanded the commission for confusing reasonable zoning regulations with unconstitutional segregation. "Zoning laws ought not to mean segregation of the races, and should have no significance as such. And if used to deprive one group of citizens the rights and opportunities enjoyed by another group, the zoning regulation is unconstitutional and will not run the gauntlet of the courts," he lectured. "The object of law is the orderly regulation of society for equal protection of all; and the sooner the white man recognizes this fundamental of constitutional government, the better it will be for all."[50]

Despite Whitten's assurances to the contrary, Davis maintained that the impact of racial zoning would be little different from that of the segregation ordinances. "The Negro is hedged in from every point of compass and it is unfair and unjust to further hedge us in by zoning or other discriminating rules," he objected. In areas of contention in the Third and Fourth Wards, the zoning map had "completely bottled the colored man up," while the accommodations for future development were dubious at best. He predicted that "undetermined" areas would not furnish additional housing but would instead be snatched away by white residents refusing to share. In protest, he renewed the threats of Black migration. With "no outlet within the city limits in which to increase" their "housing space," Black families must "live in the country or migrate north," he warned. "Thousands of us want to remain in Atlanta and in the south, but we cannot unless we can have somewhere to live."[51] He then urged Black voters to oppose all bonds until their housing needs were met.

A few prominent whites also publicly challenged the proposed zoning law, despite strong support from the Atlanta Real Estate Board and the chamber of commerce. Some of the opponents had substantial investments in the city's rental market since 75 percent of Atlantans did not own a home.[52] M. L. Thrower, a real estate agent with significant investments in Black residential properties, called the plan "monstrous," declaring that its "worst feature" was that it was not "going to work." Still, the most "scathing attack," according to the *Constitution*, came from Judge E. C. Kontz, who denounced the plan as "class legislation" with likely "disastrous consequences." He upbraided the commission for going to "other states to get men to make a zoning plan for Atlanta." The outcome was a committee that "overnight" could "change the value of your property from $100 a foot to $1500, and vice versa. How much money wouldn't people pay to get on such a powerful committee?"[53]

While much of his critique was leveled at zoning in general, Kontz also condemned racial zoning specifically, which he argued was "a closed book" because the Supreme Court had already struck down earlier segregation laws. His position angered Mayor Key, who fired off, "Are you opposed to separation of whites and blacks?" Kontz shot back that he was only "stating the law and did not care to indulge in personal views." Kontz lived downtown in a mixed-race area, and the planning commission would soon approve his subdivision plat for Berkeley Park, a modest white addition located northeast of the city. Yet, it would be unfair to dismiss his criticism as mere self-interest.[54] He took a risk when denouncing racial zoning, which he thought unnecessary as well as unconstitutional.

Apologists for the plan, on the other hand, claimed it would extend the benefits of child-centered residential parks to areas that lacked deed restrictions. Forrest Adair, a prominent realtor, attempted to persuade critics with a lengthy defense published in the *Constitution*: "There are certain districts of Atlanta that have enjoyed the zoning plan for a number of years. Among them is Druid Hills. Everyone agrees that this section has benefitted more from [deed] restrictions than most any other section." Likewise, the president of the North Boulevard Park Civic League endorsed zoning with the assertion that "many of" North Boulevard's "residents had been driven away from other sections of the city because of undesirable surroundings growing up with no regulations to prevent [it]."[55]

In reality, most whites who remained in the areas with traditional urban development—the "undesirable surroundings" business-class Atlantans were fleeing—opposed the new zoning regulations.[56] They were stunned to learn that they no longer lived in "white" areas when the zoning map included many of their blocks in "colored" or racially "undetermined" districts. For instance, in working-class Bellwood, the zoning map had labeled blocks that were at least 50 percent white as "colored districts" and those that were more than 90 percent white as "racially undetermined" (see map 7.2). Bellwood was adjacent to the Atlanta University section then being targeted as the largest "colored district." It was also far enough from the city's white residential parks that the planning commission had set aside much of the area for future Black development, even though it was growing whiter. Between 1910 and 1920, the percentage of whites in Bellwood rose from 72.4 to 83.6 percent of the population as the number of white residents surged from 2,294 to 5,118—an increase of 123 percent during a decade when Atlanta's overall population had increased by just 30 percent.[57] Bellwood's white families had long viewed conventional development as inclusive of block-level segregation, but now the zoning law threatened to erase white households from their neighborhood.

Consequently, before the city council voted on the tentative zone map, white residents in Bellwood and in other working-class neighborhoods pushed Whitten and the planning commission to reduce the amount of housing available to Black residents, especially in "undetermined" districts.[58] The commission obliged. On the final zone map, the colored district near Bellwood disappeared into a much smaller undetermined district, while the original undetermined district shriveled down to a small fraction of its previous size. Fourth Ward's Black residents also lost territory on the final zoning map, including the few blocks that had been set aside for single-family housing. Additionally, the commission replaced the category "undetermined" with the verbose phrase "district that is not within either the colored district or the white district." Surely, this change appealed to the white residents who disliked the word "undetermined," an ambiguous term that seemed to imply that certain areas were marked for racial transition (see map 7.1).[59]

Moreover, Atlanta's ward-based political system enabled lower-income whites to quickly take the momentum back from the chamber of commerce. As chair of the planning commission, Robert Otis depicted the ward system as a problem that needed solving: "Civic improvements were handled by various self-appointed Ward committees," which resulted in "numerous political battles" that "were pitched upon the merit of improvements demanded in one section as opposed to another." Early in the debate, the commission gave residents from working-class wards few opportunities for input because most of the presentations took place at civic club meetings controlled by business-class Atlantans. The clubs then selected representatives to speak at the public hearings to ensure boosters dominated those debates as well.[60] Lower-income whites, however, were

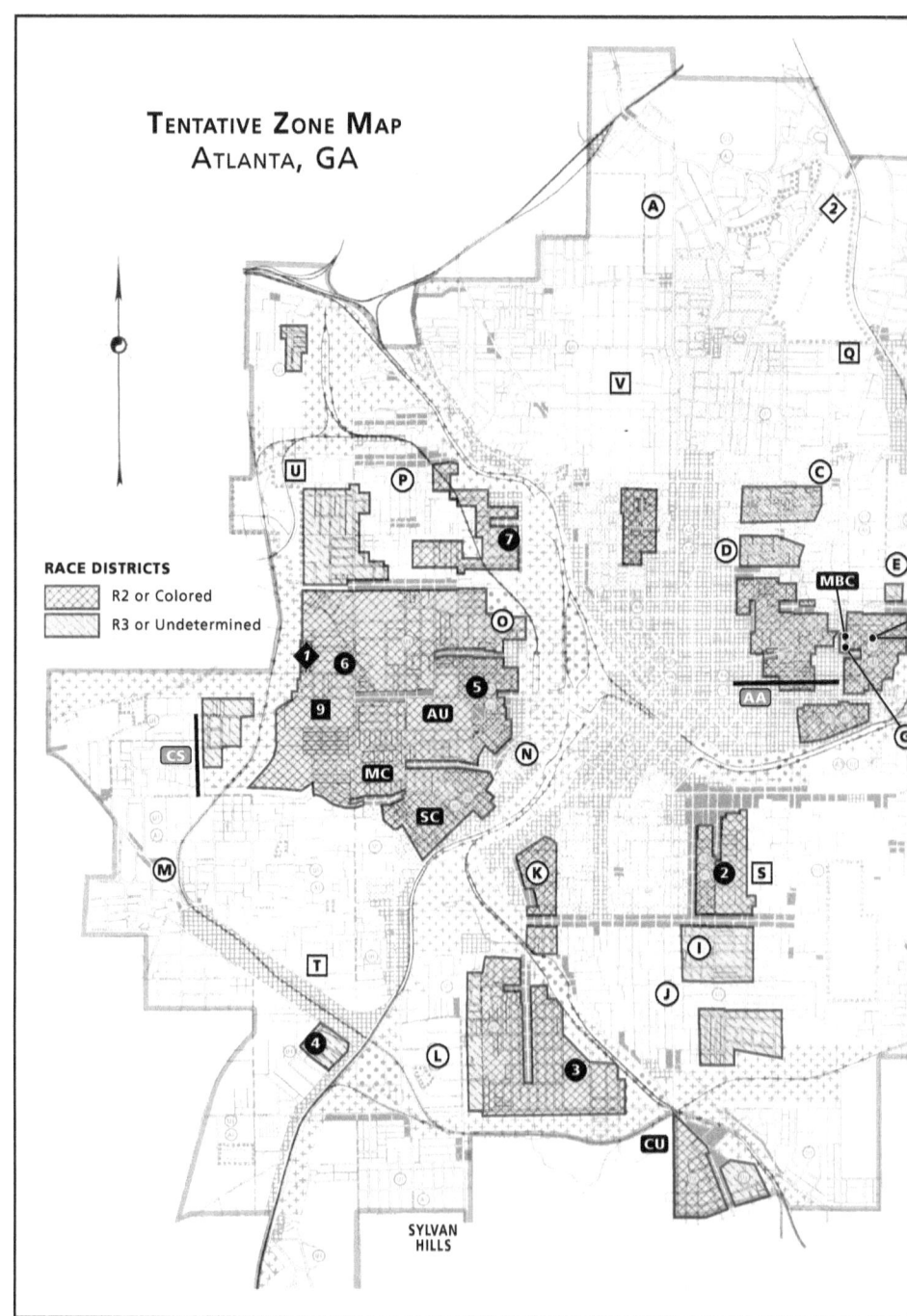

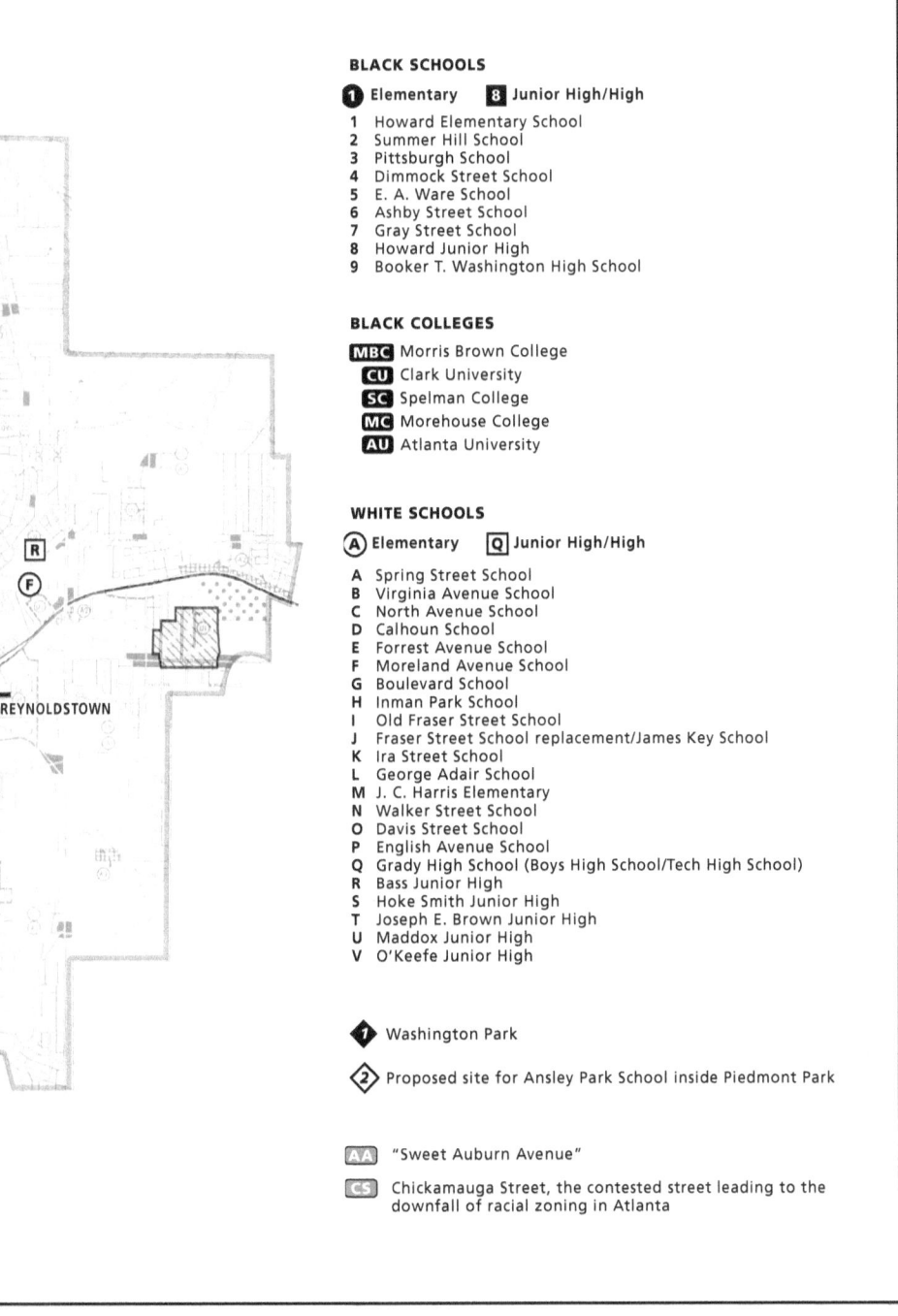

MAP 7.2. Even though racial zoning was declared unconstitutional, school sites selected in accordance with the tentative zone map—some purchased even before the map had been publicly vetted—would continue to shape residential patterns in the city for decades to come. Courtesy of the Kenan Research Center at the Atlanta History Center. Used with permission.

able to reassert the customary power of the wards during the ensuing election, which was influenced by the resurgence of the Ku Klux Klan. Councilman Walter Sims, a favorite with the local Klan, claimed he had "received literally hundreds of solicitations from citizens" urging him to run for mayor.[61]

After his election, Mayor Sims began undermining the zone plan almost immediately. He first asked for Robert Whitten's resignation, which he received without fanfare. The following day, he replaced Otis with a small-time realtor named John A. White, the president of the Fourth Ward Improvement Club. Next, Sims replaced Hoke Smith and Joel Hurt, which resulted in a much less prestigious planning commission. Sims then placed the commission under the authority of the city building inspector, leading to the resignation of the zoning engineer, who would not be replaced for almost a year. Council members also tried to add a representative from each of the twelve wards to the planning commission. Bellwood's councilman J. Allen Couch declared, "Every ward has its peculiar zoning problems and some wards their race housing question, and it is absolutely necessary that some one acquainted with local conditions as well as the city-wide problem should be on the board."[62]

Sims vetoed the measure despite its popularity with the Klan. As mayor, he still needed to work with the chamber of commerce, which was then enmeshed in a spirited campaign to shrink the power of the wards through charter reform. Councilman Claude Ashley, the author of the 1913 segregation ordinance, disdainfully referred to the chamber as the "Hemlock Crowd" and described the area north of Ponce de Leon Avenue, which included Ansley Park, North Boulevard Park, and Druid Hills, as the "fountain of Hemlock poison."[63] Sims hoped to pursue a middle ground that could satisfy his working-class constituents without alienating the formidable chamber, without which he could not govern. One way was to use his reconstituted planning commission to subtly transform Whitten's racial zoning map into an old-school segregation ordinance meant to safeguard white residential property in working-class areas.

Before Sims's election, the final zoning map had been amended to reduce the housing available to Black families only once. In that case, council agreed with the planning commission that a racially undetermined district serving as the westside border of "Pittsburgh"—a Black working-class neighborhood on the south side—should be pushed further east. This change would ensure that Black housing would not approach Stewart Avenue, the main artery leading to the modest residential parks being developed south of the city limits. One of them was Sylvan Hills, whose developer had recently launched a Black addition near Ashby Street School on the west side and who was then planning Morningside Park, a white residential park in the privileged northeastern section (see map 7.2). Council accepted the plat for Sylvan Hills only three months before agreeing to the change near Stewart Avenue. This adjustment was consistent with elite efforts to protect segregated residential parks.[64]

With Sims's election, council began to break away from the recommendations of the planning commission. First, it reversed course on a petition sponsored by chamber-of-commerce foe Claude Ashley, the Fourth Ward councilman who introduced the original segregation ordinance. His petition sought to change a racially undetermined apartment district to a white district explicitly to stop a local textile manufacturer from constructing a Black apartment building, for which he already had a permit. The petition had been at the center of a six-month fight in which the planning commission had consistently opposed the change. After Sims became mayor, an emboldened council pushed it through, preventing construction of the Black apartment building.[65]

During the remaining twenty months that racial zoning was enforced, Black citizens lost potential housing more than a dozen times. Five involved a change from a business or industrial zone to a white residential district. Since racial designations applied to residential districts only, anyone could move onto a block in a business or industrial zone. In each of these cases, either the petition to change the law or the debate surrounding it expressed clear racial intent. In some instances, the council minutes identified the blocks in question as racially undetermined residential areas even though the zoning map had included them in business or industrial districts.[66] On the flip side, council denied at least eight petitions that would have added Black housing in Atlanta's racial transition areas. In most of those cases, the relevant petitions involved changing a white residential district to a business district, but fears of further racial transition produced enough opposition to kill it—an outcome that stagnated business development as well the city's black housing stock.[67]

On the other hand, Black citizens gained access to areas initially zoned white just three times. In the first instance, the tentative zone map had labeled the street "undetermined" until white Bellwood residents forced Whitten and the planning commission to change it. This decision was ultimately reversed, but it took almost eighteen months. On the same day the petition was finally approved, council also accepted the plat for a residential park from the Black-owned Service Realty Company. The two actions were most likely related, reflecting the prior agreement that the area would become Atlanta's premier residential section for affluent Black families.[68] The next two instances involved overlapping blocks in Fourth Ward. The planning commission had first recommended the change seventeen months earlier; the council refused even though there were more Black residents on those particular blocks than white ones. Opponents had sought to freeze the status quo by preventing additional Black residents from moving onto the street, but the stalemate only created more vacancies.[69]

The other four changes that might have benefitted Black residents were all expansions of the business district, and in three of those, council merely reversed a previous decision that had resulted in unsalable properties. Even in those cases, Black residents were denied badly needed housing for months, and the gains failed to provide zoning protection. In the final case, the area simply reverted to its original designation on the tentative zone map, once again denying Black families desperately needed housing in the meantime. As Davis had predicted, the racial zoning scheme had become a tool for limiting where Black families lived rather than serving as an instrument to sort out the city with some fairness to Black citizens, as Whitten had promised.[70]

The National Debate over Racial Zoning

Evidently, Robert Whitten incited the ire of lower-income whites and their representatives on the city council even more than the chamber's "Hemlock Crowd." Alderman J. L. Carpenter warned that the zoning ordinance would destroy "the rights of the people" by putting "them where they will have to report to bosses," whom he described as "experts" with "hair parted in the middle and wearing toothpick shoes." "Where do they come from? From the North," he spat. "I'll fight 'em to the finish. I'll build to the moon if I want to." Carpenter was correct that Whitten and most other planning consultants placed northern concerns about high population densities onto southern cities with no such problems.[71] What is less clear is how much of the responsibility for racial zoning rested with Whitten as opposed to Robert Otis and the other Atlantans who had spent years pushing for a city plan. Local elites who wished to ease the transition of specific properties from white to Black were convinced that racial zoning was the answer. Most likely, Whitten was hired because he was willing to hazard his reputation by implementing their segregation scheme. He certainly had more to lose than local boosters since, in the end, he was the one left defending his actions.[72] Why did he agree to do it?

Even as a "toothpick-shoe"-wearing northerner, Whitten had experience with de jure segregation through his work on New York City's zoning ordinance. The plan reflected growing alarm over the large number of immigrants arriving from eastern and southern Europe. During the Progressive Era, a wave of "new" immigrants, many of whom were Catholic or Jewish, streamed into cities in the Northeast and Midwest. As a result, most of the nation's largest cities had a substantial immigrant majority, fueling middle-class anxiety over the rapidly changing ethnic composition of urban neighborhoods. Fears of "race suicide" led to support for eugenics and immigration restriction, along with an early interest in zoning.[73] New York's ordinance included height restrictions on Fifth Avenue intentionally designed to preclude the erection of factories over prestigious retail spaces. Storeowners worried that immigrant garment workers would drive away the affluent white women who were their primary customers.[74]

The creation of single-family residence districts was another attempt to exclude immigrants, this time by banning multifamily housing. In 1920, Bruno Lasker, an associate editor for *The Survey*, an important journal for the budding social work profession, was troubled by the potential impact of the nation's zoning laws. His editor in chief, Paul Kellogg, was an ardent champion of immigration restriction who viewed immigrants as a threat to the nation's Anglo-Saxon heritage.[75] Within that context, Lasker, a Jewish immigrant himself, characterized single-family zoning as another form of discrimination. "Why," he questioned, "in this country of democracy, is a city government, representative of all classes of the community, taking it upon itself to legislate a majority of citizens—those who cannot afford to occupy a detached house of their own—out of the best located parts of the city area, practically always the parts with the best aspect, best parks and streets, best supplied with municipal services and best cared for in every way?" Lasker suggested that the connections between zoning and segregation were not accidental. Consultants had convinced local officials that "no height restriction, street width or unbuilt lot area" would "prevent prices from tottering in a good residential neighborhood" without the exclusion of "whatever race most jars on the natives." As evidence, he quoted the city commissioner of Portland, Oregon, who claimed "an influx of foreigners" was the key motivation behind Portland's zoning plan.[76]

Lasker thought the best way to make America "safe for democracy" was to eliminate barriers between people rather than manufacture new ones. He argued that "a geographical separation of the population" by "tastes, habits and opportunities" was "un-American" and would destroy community cohesiveness, but as long as "the various social classes" had "occasional glimpses of each other," a "certain sense of civic responsibility" would persist. "As the distances increase[d]," however, "mutual knowledge and sympathy" would slowly vanish. Inevitably, separation would spread "erroneous ideas among the people of the way in which one class or another lives" and would "encourage those grotesque misconceptions and misunderstandings which aggravate every social problem." Ultimately, "the mutual ignorance thus engendered" would lead "to mutual distrust and open or suppressed hostility." "Every deepening of the gulf between the classes" would make it more difficult for "a later generation" to reestablish "saving contacts" across race and class, a prescient warning that now haunts housing policy in the twenty-first century.[77]

Just two weeks after Whitten began working as a consultant in Atlanta, he addressed Lasker's criticism at the 1921 National Conference on City Planning (NCCP). He reminded his audience that the primary objective of single-family zoning was "perpetuating and developing a breed of men and women strong physically, mentally and spiritually." In pursuit of that lofty goal, "a reasonable segregation of economic classes" was neither "undemocratic" nor "anti-social." Whitten attempted to paint social integration as the more undemocratic "arrangement" by tying traditional development to European feudalism, with "the mansion of the lord of the manor" surrounded by "the huts of his retainers." He dismissed Lasker's concerns about "misunderstandings and class hatred," proposing instead that "the so-called industrial classes will constitute a more intelligent and self-respecting citizenship when housed in homogeneous neighborhoods than when housed in areas used by all of the economic classes."[78]

Whitten assured skeptics that single-family zoning would have but little impact since the forces of segregation went well beyond his or anyone else's control. "A reasonable segregation is normal, inevitable and desirable and cannot be greatly affected, one way or the other, by zoning." But if such a claim were true, both single-family zoning and racial regulation would have been unnecessary. Whitten admitted this contradiction in a lecture before the Cook County (Chicago) Real Estate Board in 1919. While "the purpose of a zone plan" was "merely to strengthen and supplement" the "natural trend toward segregation," without zoning, those "natural forces" were "not strong enough to prevent the invasion" of "inappropriate" uses or users.[79] In other words, segregation was a natural phenomenon, yet planners needed to move quickly because it would not happen on its own.

Whitten's convoluted argument mirrored the assumptions of the planning movement. A report on the "Best Methods of Land Subdivision" presented at the 1915 NCCP described an old, blighted neighborhood that had once housed Philadelphia's "first families" but had since become "largely occupied by the foreign element." The "once handsome residences" had descended into "almost, if not quite, slums." Rather than blame the absentee landlords who had subdivided the houses and then neglected them, the report identified the ethnicity of the renters as the key reason for the area's decline. It concluded, "Land subdivision in itself, without proper control of the occupancy," would "scarcely have any large influence in raising the physical, intellectual or moral standards of a community."[80]

Chinese residents were the first immigrant group targeted by de jure segregation after passage of the Fourteenth Amendment. White Americans associated Chinese immigrants—and all people of color—with sexual immorality, disease, and drug or alcohol abuse. Their "foreignness" was also seen as a threat to Anglo-Saxon domesticity. According to historian Nayan Shah, "The fact that a variety of households and domestic arrangements existed was seized by city officials as definitive evidence that typical Chinatown domesticity contradicted the nuclear family ideal." Any household arrangements that diverged from the cultural standards of middle-class domesticity were seen as a threat to white child-rearing because they might tempt white adolescents away from "American" home life. It mattered little that US immigration restrictions and antimiscegenation laws had produced the very gender imbalance that made it nearly impossible for Chinese immigrants to recreate the middle-class ideal. During the 1920s and 1930s, Chinese American reformers championed the dominant norms of domesticity as an effective strategy for combating discrimination.[81]

As for European immigrants, those who accepted white, middle-class cultural norms found the American dream within far easier reach of their children. Even Jewish Americans, a common target for restrictive covenants, could undergo whitening after achieving economic success. At the 1919 annual meeting of the Developers of High-Class Residential Property, Hugh Prather, the developer of Dallas's Highland Park, sheepishly admitted that he had sold lots to a few "pet Jews," one of them being "old man Sanger." Prather reassured his fellow subdividers, "Everybody loves Mr. Sanger; he goes with the very best Gentiles in town," adding, "The people in Highland Park will be glad to have Mr. Sanger or that kind of Jew in the property." And indeed, they would have, since the Sanger family owned a chain of department stores worth $13 million at the time.[82] As bigoted and demeaning as Prather's comment was, it would have been inconceivable for a similar statement to have been made about a Black citizen, no matter how prosperous, brilliant, or public spirited. Across the nation, neither wealth, accomplishments, nor the embrace of the politics of respectability would alter the discrimination affluent Black families faced.

The segregation ordinances that had been aimed almost exclusively at Black middle-class southerners were declared unconstitutional just as the Great Migration picked up steam during World War I. As the exodus of Black southerners unfolded, the "colored problem"—a white euphemism for Black urbanization—expanded into a national issue that soon supplanted concern about immigrants, especially once new immigration laws reduced the flood of immigrants to a trickle.[83] Officials from both Chicago and Philadelphia wrote to Atlanta's mayor in the months before *Buchanan* to request "several copies" of the city's ordinance. They said that they were "now concerned with the problem of whites and negroes living in the same blocks," even though Black and white residents had long lived side by side, just in smaller numbers. The following month, the Chicago Real Estate Board asked local officials "to immediately pass an ordinance" prohibiting the further migration of Black southerners until "such reasonable restriction of leasing or selling" could be established to avert "race hatred, violence and blood-shed."[84]

After *Buchanan*, the Chicago Real Estate Board abandoned its flirtation with a segregation law and instead encouraged the use of racial covenants and "owners societies" to police "every white block" and ensure "mutual defense" in older areas of the city. A committee appointed to investigate the issue reported that "some feasible, practicable and humane method must be devised to house and school" the "great" number of Black residents arriving each day. The solution was to channel the "migrants" into a single, southside neighborhood and then manage its gradual expansion through neighborhood associations and discriminatory real estate practices. The committee advised, "Inasmuch as more territory must be provided, it is desired in the interest of all, that each block shall be filled solidly and that further expansion shall be confined to contiguous blocks, and that the present method of obtaining a single building in scattered blocks, be discontinued."[85]

Violence and the threat of violence were key to enforcing the plan. Between July 1917 and March 1921—just a few weeks before Robert Whitten's first day as Atlanta's consultant—fifty-eight bombs exploded in Chicago to warn Black homeowners that certain blocks were to remain all white. The bombs resulted in the deaths of two Black residents, an undisclosed number of injuries, and more than $1.5 million in property damage (2020 dollars).[86] Chicago was also one of the many cities to suffer bloodshed in 1919 during "Red Summer," which exploded across the country in important destinations of the Great Migration. Chicago's "riot" began when a white man killed a Black teenager who had floated across an invisible race line at a segregated beach along Lake Michigan. Black residents expressed anger that the police refused to take the perpetrator into custody. In retaliation, white mobs began hunting down Black victims to terrorize, while Black citizens did their best to defend their homes and families. The violence, which lasted more than a week, ended with 38 people killed and more than 500 injured.[87]

Illinois's governor established the Chicago Commission on Race Relations to investigate the underlying causes and make recommendations to prevent future atrocities. The 650-page report identified a range of issues, with housing prominent among them, but it recognized white aversion to amalgamation at root. The widespread mythology which insinuated that "the mind of the Negro child ceases to develop when he reaches the age of puberty" had, once again, ignited fears of miscegenation. "Always resident in the background of popular consciousness," the myth had "the same head and the same features in almost every clash of races." The report's recommendations were nuanced and complex, but local officials latched onto segregation as the principal solution.[88]

Promoting residential segregation was easier outside the South because Black newcomers could be funneled into segregated areas as they moved into the city. Black residents were a small fraction of the total population at the beginning of the century. When 50,000 Black southerners arrived during World War I, the percentage of Black Chicagoans increased from 2 percent of the population in 1910 to about 4 percent in 1920 and then 7 percent in 1930. Real estate agents, backed by the ubiquitous threat of violence, channeled new Black residents to the southside with breathtaking results. In 1900, only two of Chicago's thirty-five wards had a Black population above 10 percent, and almost a third of Black residents lived in areas that were no more than 5 percent Black. In 1920, the city still had no census

TABLE 7.1. Percentage of Black Residents in the Total Population, 1900–1930

City	1900	1910	1920	1930
Chicago	1.8	2.0	4.1	6.9
Atlanta	39.8	33.5	31.3	33.3
Houston	32.7	30.4	24.6	21.7
Raleigh	41.9	38.4	35.0	33.6
Winston-Salem	40.5	40	42.8	43.3

Source: Gibson and Jung, "Historical Census Statistics."

TABLE 7.2. Population within City Limits, 1900–1930

City	1900	1910	1920	1930
Chicago	1,698,575	2,185,283	2,701,705	3,376,438
Atlanta	89,872	154,839	200,616	270,366
Houston	44,633	78,800	138,276	292,352
Raleigh	13,643	19,218	24,418	37,379
Winston-Salem	13,650	22,700	48,395	75,274

Source: Gibson and Jung, "Historical Census Statistics."

tracts as high as 90 percent Black, but by 1930, two-thirds of Black Chicagoans lived in tracts with a Black population at or above 90 percent while almost one-fifth lived in tracts above 97.5 percent.[89]

Whites in the urban South, however, faced a more complicated task in achieving that level of segregation. Black southerners were a much larger percentage of far smaller urban populations, and they lived throughout the metropolitan area except for white residential parks. Because they constituted between one-fourth and one-half of the total population of most southern cities, they were powerful enough to make demands on the local power structure (see tables 7.1 and 7.2).[90] In an effort to control the movement of Black residents, white southerners experimented more readily with de jure segregation, remaining far less cautious about defying either the Constitution or the Supreme Court.

After *Buchanan*, racial zoning was the next significant effort at de jure residential segregation. By the 1920s, planning consultants from outside the South seemed ready to help since interest in the possibilities of segregation laws, by that time, extended well beyond Jim Crow cities. According to the librarian at the American City Planning Institute, Theodora Kimball, racial zoning "aroused wide discussion" among planners. The consensus was that African Americans were "the least assimilable of the many types" of urban inhabitants, so the published debate focused on the likelihood that racial zoning would survive judicial review rather than on its decency.[91]

Bruno Lasker, who had criticized the discriminatory nature of single-family zoning two years earlier, was one of the few whites who publicly condemned Atlanta's racial zoning scheme when it first became law. *The Survey* published his critique just twelve days after Atlanta's city council accepted Whitten's final zoning map. Lasker unequivocally denounced the plan as the "logical outcome" of zoning's tendency to "set up class divisions in areas marked for residential use." Such a scheme from "perhaps the most influential zoning adviser in the United States" would set a dangerous precedent. He worried that it would open "up the possibility of new zoning ordinances embodying restrictions against immigrants, or immigrants of certain races" and "against persons of certain occupations, political or religious affiliations, or modes of life."[92]

Whitten's response appeared two months later in the same journal. He dismissed Lasker's concern that Atlanta's zoning ordinance would set a precedent for other forms of segregation, calling an effort to separate households based on occupation, political affiliations, or religious beliefs "foolish and unjust" and doubting that it "would ever be seriously considered." He then justified racial zoning with the usual blather about property values. Without evidence, he suggested that the uncertainty of block-level segregation had led to "enormous economic loss," including "wiping out" the savings of "thousands of poor families" and leaving "hundreds of acres of land" either "undeveloped or poorly developed." He also insisted that widespread violence after World War I further demonstrated why the plan was necessary and good: "Atlanta in establishing colored residential districts has removed one of the most potent causes of race conflict" through "a common sense method of dealing with facts as they are."[93]

The Tulsa massacre had occurred only one month after Whitten's first meeting with the Atlanta plan commission. His work files for the project contained two newspaper articles on the attack clipped from his hometown newspaper in Cleveland, Ohio, a reminder that the massacre was national news and on Whitten's mind while he worked on Atlanta's zone map. Although racial violence was all too real, his assertion that residential segregation would deter it was disingenuous, at best. He could not have reasonably deduced from the two articles in his possession that segregation would discourage additional attacks on Black residents. Tulsa was more fully segregated than perhaps any other US city at the time, and some observers concluded that hypersegregation was a contributing factor to the violence.[94]

During the late nineteenth century, Black southerners began moving to Oklahoma in hopes of forming a Black state, or at least Black towns, where they could prosper out from underneath Jim Crow. Within this context, African Americans built Greenwood, an almost entirely separate community from white Tulsa. Greenwood's "Black Wall Street" housed one of the nation's wealthiest Black business districts, which benefitted from lucrative investments in the oil industry. In one of Whitten's clippings, W. E. B. Du Bois described the "complete separation there of the two races, so that a colored town has its own business streets, lined with stores, a very good modern hotel, moving picture theaters and all the details of a highly organized community."[95] When Tulsa officials adopted a segregation ordinance in 1916, hundreds of Black protesters passed resolutions condemning it, arguing that the law was wholly unnecessary: "There already exists in the city of Tulsa an almost complete and voluntary segregation of the races with no effort on the part of any member of the colored race to break over the line." They recognized the true intent was to transform their community from an achievement to a ghetto, and they accused the mayor of supporting the ordinance as a stunt to distance himself from the Black voters who had helped elect him.[96]

In 1921, Greenwood's marked prosperity was precisely what planners were promising Black residents through racial zoning, but the community's wealth and independence challenged white supremacy. The massacre began when the white press accused a young Black man of behaving inappropriately towards a white woman in an elevator, even though all charges against him were later dropped. As tensions rose, a couple hundred armed Black men went to the courthouse to avert a possible lynching. Soon thereafter, enraged whites began attacking Black homes and businesses. During the bloodshed, several planes were seen flying overhead; city officials claimed they were meant for "sightseeing" rather than striking Greenwood from above, as was certainly the case.[97] When the attackers finally withdrew, thirty-five blocks had been burned to the ground and hundreds had been killed, although an exact number is likely impossible to determine. Almost the entire population of Greenwood, as many as 13,000 people, were left homeless. While the city burned, the police and their deputies rounded up thousands of Black survivors and imprisoned them in makeshift camps. Many "wore their night clothes and were barefooted" when taken into custody. One of Whitten's newspaper clippings attempted to capture the desolation in the camps as the shell-shocked community tried to comprehend what had happened: "Here an old woman clung to a Bible; there a girl carried a wooly white dog and behind trotted a little girl with a big wax doll."[98]

Whitten must have known that hypersegregation would not prevent another tragedy from occurring. According to Du Bois, racial segregation facilitated the attack by allowing white Tulsans to destroy the economic wealth of the entire community and render more than 10,000 people homeless. Traditional development would have made it impossible to accomplish this level of devastation without destroying the homes, businesses, churches, parks, and schools of white people, too. Surely, Whitten understood this. The Tulsa massacre, like all racial violence, was meant to preserve white supremacy by keeping African Americans from rising.[99] This was true of the Atlanta "riot" of 1906, which had little to do with housing but rather the old canard about Black men assaulting white women, as in Tulsa. Alarmist rhetoric about social equality coming from Hoke Smith's gubernatorial campaign along with hysterical newspaper reports about a "carnival of rape" set off the white mob, which killed more than two dozen Black Atlantans.[100] In 1921, members of the Atlanta planning commission, including Hoke Smith, knew this.

In the end, Whitten's willingness to design the nation's first racial zoning scheme reflected the reality that Jim Crow cities were no longer exceptional, if they ever had been.[101] His hometown of Cleveland had also experienced demographic change during the war. Between 1910 and 1920, the number of Black residents jumped by more than threefold, from fewer than 9,000 to just over 35,000. Whitten completed zoning plans for both Cleveland and Cleveland Heights in 1921 while beginning his work as Atlanta's consultant. His address to the NCCP that year focused on Cleveland Heights and the need to protect "beautiful" single-family homes in white residential parks, especially in older developments where expiring deed restrictions could lead to changing conditions that resulted in a "a poor place to bring up a [white] family."[102] His experience at home likely made him sympathetic with the desire for a permanent solution to the nation's "colored problem."

Without the imprudent segregation ordinances of the prior decade, perhaps racial zoning would have survived judicial review as part of the comprehensive, single-family zoning plans that were eventually found constitutional, but *Buchanan* doomed the effort from the start. The Georgia Supreme Court swiftly declared racial zones unconstitutional in *Bowen v. Atlanta* (1924), only two years after Atlanta's zoning ordinance went into effect. The plaintiff was a white widow named Annie Bowen. Her deceased husband had subdivided an investment property into eighteen lots, which he began selling to Black buyers before the zoning ordinance became law. The ordinance placed his property in a "white" zone, even though it ran along the edge of an "undetermined" district about four blocks west of the new Booker T. Washington High School, which opened just a month before the case was decided (see map 7.2). When the law went into effect, Annie Bowen unsuccessfully petitioned to change the property's designation. Nonetheless, she still sold one of her lots to Luther Crittle, a Black investor who immediately built a house which he then rented to a Black tenant. When Atlanta's building inspector attempted to enforce the law, Bowen and Crittle went to court. Because Black residents already lived on the street, Bowen maintained that she was unable to sell the lots to a white buyer for a profit.[103]

Local officials refused to change the racial designation of the street in question, even though Whitten and the planning commission had promised that the zoning map could be amended if conditions warranted. Instead, the Klan-backed Sims administration used the zoning ordinance to safeguard white homes on the streets west of Bowen's property. City attorney James Mayson insisted that Bowen had no right to challenge the ordinance. The general assembly had granted Atlanta the power to zone "classes of residents" through the state's enabling law, and Bowen had failed to protest her property's classification at one of the public hearings held before the ordinance became law. Mayson further alleged that racial zoning did not harm Black residents because a "large section" near the Bowen's property was "devoted" to Black housing. The court disagreed. Citing *Buchanan*, the justices ruled Atlanta's racial zones null and void while leaving the rest of the zoning ordinance intact.[104]

Undoubtedly, any segregation law, regardless of its structure, would have generated unsalable properties if it failed to address the fundamental issue governing the value of residential property: the dominant norms for middle-class child-rearing. Simply labeling a street "white" did not make it appeal to white families, particularly if it lacked the amenities deemed essential for middle-class child-rearing, including access to a modern school. Likewise, "white" homes near a modern Black school were in such great demand by Black families that lower-income whites could not afford them. Atlanta's next and most enduring segregation scheme—its multimillion-dollar school building program—embraced this reality.

CHAPTER 8

Racial Zoning and Schools

Bowen v. Atlanta (1924) ended the legal enforcement of racial zoning only two years after it went into effect, but the tentative zone map continued to hold sway over Atlanta's development since it coincided with the city's multimillion-dollar school building program. The ability to determine the location of schools and playgrounds offered a unique opportunity to manipulate where families lived, especially in Jim Crow school districts that could force children to walk long distances to a segregated school. Although the connection between school sites and residential segregation was not new, a large-scale building program combined with more clearly defined racial zones allowed local officials to accelerate the impact. Existing Black schools helped determine the designation of "colored" districts, which could then determine the future location of new schools, leading to a greater concentration of Black residents. At the same time, planners advised against building new white schools in areas zoned for industry or commerce, even if most of the city's white children lived in those neighborhoods. Instead, they pressured local school boards to build the newest and most modern white schools in single-family districts that benefitted affluent whites at the expense of other children.[1] The fact that developers frequently sat on planning commissions, school boards, or both helped facilitate the effort, with the results working so well that legally enforced racial zones were no longer necessary.

In Atlanta, the planning commission teamed up with the school board to select sites according to the city's newly created race districts. Before launching the building program, they hired two additional outside experts: Columbia University's George Strayer and N. L. Engelhardt, both guiding lights in the influential progressive education movement. In city after city, Strayer and Engelhardt urged local officials to use "scientific data" obtained through elaborate surveys to predict future school needs, regardless of where students lived. As strong supporters of the planning movement, they included a copy of Atlanta's tentative zone map in the survey report and acknowledged its usefulness in determining their recommendations.[2]

The following year, Strayer presented "The School Building Program an Important Part of the City Plan" at the 1922 National Conference on City Planning (NCCP) while still serving as Atlanta's consultant. He cautioned, "The absence of a general city plan and of zoning must inevitably result in shifts in population and in the character of housing" that "would be difficult or almost impossible to forecast." Future shifts in school enrollment could be prevented if zoning laws determined where children lived, making it easier to forecast where to build schools. CBJ Snyder, superintendent of school buildings for New York City, responded to Strayer's talk by enthusiastically endorsing the proposition that schools and residential development should be planned together. The "location and construction" of a new school will increase the assessed value of adjacent homes "from 300 to 600 percent," he contended. "Nothing will develop a community more rapidly than the construction of schools in outlying and undeveloped sections."[3]

Planners and developers did not need convincing. They had long used schools as magnets for new residential parks. After all, "enlightened realtors" were in the "legitimate business of producing and selling what the ultimate consumer wants," Frederick Law Olmsted Jr. reiterated during his presidential address at the 1919 NCCP. He reminded his audience, "It has been fully established that a well located school and playground," incorporated within "the program of the school authorities, adds to the value of all the remaining land in the territory to be served by the school." "Under ideal conditions," the school would serve a single residential park so that careful restrictions would control who attended the school as well as who lived in the neighborhood.[4]

Atlanta was the first city with an official racial zoning scheme, but it was not the first to manipulate school sites with the goal of intensifying segregation. Local officials in Raleigh had been intentionally concentrating Black schools in the southeastern corner of the city for more than a dozen years. Their efforts accelerated during the 1921 building program, which overlapped with the creation of Raleigh's original zoning ordinance. Similarly, local officials in Baltimore and Winston-Salem initiated school building programs alongside other efforts to expand residential segregation. Because the mayor of Winston-Salem was the most forthright about his plan to foster segregation through strategic school sites, his city most likely influenced the others. Nonetheless, it is difficult to determine the full extent to which events in one city inspired those in others, although their reliance on the same pool of experts meant that local officials were at least aware of each other's actions. George Strayer served as a consultant for Baltimore and Winston-Salem before Atlanta hired him; zoning consultant Jefferson Grinnalds worked for Baltimore before moving on to Raleigh; and contractor C. V. York sat on Raleigh's planning commission while designing school buildings for Winston-Salem.

City Planning and the School Survey Movement

After World War I, the Labor Department urged municipalities to launch public works programs, including school modernization projects, to avoid a national recession. "During the war it was patriotic not to build. Now we can best show our patriotism by building," it encouraged.[5] In most cities, new schools were a priority, with a broad consensus emerging over the need for more classrooms and better buildings. In much the same way that Victorian homes in older areas of the city were being abandoned for modern housing in residential parks, relatively new schools were rejected as hopelessly out of date if they lacked electricity, plumbing, heat, or all the bells and whistles of progressive schooling. Still, auditoriums, gymnasiums, cafeterias, libraries, health offices, manual training rooms, and other nonclassroom spaces were contributing to the soaring cost of new buildings, which caused the austerity crowd to balk. But school architect W. B. Ittner admonished those who wished "to reduce the cost of school buildings" by sacrificing all the amenities of modern schooling. He and others insisted that "numerous small" schools would have to "give way to large and centralized units," which— intentionally or not—extended residential segregation by both class and race.[6]

In addition, the demand for high schools exploded during the early twentieth century with the percentage of adolescents attending high school rising from 20 percent in 1915 to 50 percent in 1928. In Atlanta, the number of high school students soared from 2,000 to 11,000 during roughly the same period. This impressive jump in enrollments reflected parents' desire to provide their children with economic security in the face of mounting income inequality. To meet the demand, taxpayers invested millions in new school buildings during the 1920s. According to George Strayer, the nation issued school bonds worth $240,000,000 in 1921 alone (almost $3.5 billion in 2020 dollars).[7]

Surveys allowed local officials to defend their decisions using "scientific" data that would be difficult to refute. Although surveys could cover all aspects of the district—from its finances to the curriculum—the stand-alone building survey reigned during the 1920s. Survey expert Hollis Caswell completed his PhD at Teachers College, Columbia University, where Strayer and Engelhardt were faculty members. His dissertation examined the emergent survey movement. He found that the number of "comprehensive" surveys completed between 1920 and 1928 had increased by a modest 22 percent over the prior decade, but the number of stand-alone building surveys had ballooned by almost sevenfold (see table 8.1). In 1916, Strayer and Engelhardt began developing a "highly technical procedure" to forecast population growth to improve school site selection. Their method of "mathematical prediction" relied heavily on the work of planners: they studied the "saturation of residential and industrial areas," recent trends in building permits,

TABLE 8.1. School Surveys, 1910–1928

	Comprehensive Surveys	Stand-Alone Building Surveys	Total
1910–1914	19	1	20
1915–1919	32	6	38
1920–1924	31	29	60
1925–1928	31	26	57
Total between 1910 and 1928	113	62	175
Total before 1920	51	7	58
Total after 1920	62	55	117
Percent growth between decades	21.57%	685.71%	101.72%

Source: Caswell, City School Surveys.

and the passage of local zoning ordinances. According to Caswell, "The analysis of population trends and residential developments" quickly became "an accepted part of nearly all school building studies."[8]

Consequently, school surveys opened the door for planners to oversee school site selection at the exact moment when they were helping local officials pursue a constitutional means to achieve residential segregation. Atlanta's consultant, Robert Whitten, applauded the surveys for placing "the main emphasis" on "population and its distribution rather than upon the condition and adequacy of present school buildings." George B. Ford, president of the National Conference on City Planning (NCCP), commended cities such as Cleveland, Detroit, and New Bedford for "locating schools so they would fit in with the rest of the city plan." Likewise, preeminent planner Edward Bassett argued that schools "ought to be" where "people resided" instead of "forced into a business district where land values are high, traffic congestion is great, noise is always present, and space is needed for merchandising and commerce."[9] Such assumptions advantaged residential parks and ignored the reality that large numbers of children still lived close to where their parents worked. True believers rarely, if ever, recognized the cultural assumptions baked into the scientific studies they touted.

One assumption was that no site could be too large, even as most parents continued to prioritize fairness and tradition in selecting sites. In his acclaimed study of the school "plant," Arthur Moehlman, professor of education at the University of Michigan, depicted "nearly all sites secured in the past" as "woefully inadequate." Expansive yards, he asserted, would provide the necessary space for structured play and future expansion. The recommended size for elementary sites was five to ten acres, for junior highs ten to fifteen, and for senior highs fifteen

AN EXAMPLE OF AN EXCELLENT SCHOOL SITE
Houston believes in giving its children plenty of light, fresh air, and playground space to develop strong and healthy bodies.

FIGURE 8.1. The final report on Houston's building program included multiple pictures celebrating the district's enormous school sites. The planning commission reprinted the images and applauded the school board for selecting sites that supported the larger goals of the zoning plan. Houston Independent School District, *Building Program*, 19, 29, 108; Houston City Planning Commission, *Report*, 88.

to twenty. Strayer went a step further, encouraging twenty-five acres for senior highs. Even with these princely recommendations—which were all but impossible in the older sections of the city—bigger was still better. In 1924, George B. Ford congratulated Palos Verdes, California, for supplying its junior highs with twenty-five acres and its senior highs with forty acres. Another "progressive" city secured fifty-six acres for a single high school![10] In the race that ensued, Houston's planning commission praised the immense sites purchased during the city's recent building program. Its 1929 report compared Houston High School's constricted downtown site unfavorably to the vast yard of the new Albert Sidney Johnston Junior High.[11]

Planners also sought larger sites so that cities could increase the acreage dedicated to playground space. The goal was a thoughtful system of parks and playgrounds within easy reach of every family, but the reality of city budgets often conflicted with this ideal. Planners had much better luck convincing school boards to purchase generous sites to remedy the gaping holes in their park proposals. At the 1922 NCCP, Lee Hanmer, director of the Department of Recreation for the Russell Sage Foundation, agreed that schools and playgrounds were a natural fit: "School playgrounds can be economically and effectively operated by the school board, not only during school hours, but after school, on Saturdays, and during vacations." Furthermore, "properly located" schools were "easily accessible to the children," which was exactly where "playgrounds should be."[12] Whitten, too, thought playgrounds should be "considered an adjunct of the school." "The same data" used "to determine the number, size and location of school buildings," he indicated, should "be used to determine the location and area required for playgrounds."[13]

The preference for park-like sites was not simply about providing schoolchildren with more space to play; it also boosted property values. Although residential parks were designed for families with children, planners and developers understood that other people's kids could be a nuisance, an important justification for deed restrictions. George B. Ford explained to his audience at the 1922 NCCP that schools sometimes had "a harmful effect on surrounding property values" because of "the noise" children made "going to and from school or during their recess periods." As a solution, he suggested that schools "should be built on sufficient ground to allow for a playground close to the school," which would then "be surrounded by a belt of park land." The primary purpose of the park would be to "act as a barrage, mitigating the noises" of the children while offering "a charming outlook and place of promenade" for "nearby property owners." He supposed "the benefit might be sufficient" to "pay the entire extra cost of the park belt."[14] In the long run, however, the additional acreage rarely resulted in parks for the community or even play space for children; they mostly served as expansive lawns requiring costly maintenance.

Since the largest school sites were usually in or near areas zoned for single-family houses, they were a boon to residential parks, further contributing to segregation by class and race. The trend occurred nationwide, but the connection between school and residential segregation differed by region. In cities transformed by the Great Migration, new Black residents were funneled into areas targeted for Black development; local officials then built schools at the center of racially identifiable areas and gerrymandered attendance districts. Through their efforts, school segregation *followed* residential segregation, at least during the 1920s.[15] The reverse was true in Jim Crow cities, where segregated schools had long shaped residential development, supplying a blunt instrument to push people into segregated areas and keep them there, regardless of the constitutionality of racial zoning.

Racial Zoning and Atlanta's Building Program

When Atlanta voters endorsed a $4 million bond issue in 1921, all decisions on how the money would be spent had to be approved not only by the school board and city council but by the planning commission and a recently appointed "bond commission" as well. Neither the chamber of commerce nor the Atlanta Real Estate Board trusted the ward-dominated school board—let alone a contentious city council—to make decisions that would align with the new zoning plan. Elites further reduced the power of individual wards by insisting that the district's "scientific" survey removed "politics" from the process. During previous bond issues, local officials had paid more attention to white residents who wanted resources distributed somewhat equally across the city. Some officials, therefore, thought newly developing residential parks should receive less of the bond money than the more populated areas closer to downtown. This reasoning irritated affluent residents who supported charter reform. They hoped a proposed city-manager plan would allow them to acquire more control over both the school board and city council, yet in 1922, the rising power of the Klan helped defeat their reform efforts.[16]

Despite the failure of charter reform, the use of outside consultants helped affluent residents sidestep democracy. The collaboration between Whitten and Strayer ensured that the location of new schools would be determined by the boundaries of outwardly imposed race districts rather than the needs of children. For example, the site for Booker T. Washington High School was located on the edge of the largest "colored" district near the new residential developments then targeting affluent Black families (see map 7.2). The far westside location worked well for Black middle-class students living near Atlanta University, Spelman, and Morehouse, but it was far less convenient for those living in Fourth Ward by Yonge Street School and Morris Brown. Before the bond election, Black middle-class activists were led to believe that they would be allowed to select the site for the new high school. Mayor Key had invited representatives from the local NAACP, the Congress of Colored Parents and Teachers, the Colored Women's Council, and the Neighborhood Union to a meeting with the school superintendent. He pledged that "every child would have a seat" and "a committee of Colored men and women would decide the kind of high school" they "would get." With those promises in hand, Black organizations worked tirelessly to help pass the bonds.[17]

After the election, the "colored bond commission" chose a site in Fourth Ward. Before they could make their recommendation, the school board had already purchased a site west of Ashby Street in Heman Perry's new development. Although those with a financial interest in the city's first Black residential park supported the site, most Black students would have to trek through heavy industrial districts, the downtown commercial center, or both to get to the high school. The board claimed their decision simply adhered to the survey, but local officials wanted a far westside site to reduce tension over racial transition in Fourth Ward and to discourage affluent Black families from moving closer to the white residential parks in the northeast section.[18] In fact, Atlanta would not have a second Black high school until 1947, despite extreme overcrowding at Booker T. Washington High School, which had almost 4,000 students but only fifty classrooms.[19]

The location of the new *white* high school also advantaged the residential parks in northeast Atlanta. Rather than select a central location in downtown, as had always been done in the past, the site was at the base of Piedmont Park in between the tip of Ansley Park and North Boulevard Park (see map 7.2). The board purchased the site before the school survey had been made available to the public or residents had been given a chance to respond to the final zone map. The *Constitution* celebrated the twenty-acre site, which faced "the beautiful" residential area "contiguous" with Atlanta's most esteemed recreational park.[20] Once again, local officials used expert consultants to defend their decision. Strayer argued that "an 'outer rim' school" would make "it possible for children to travel to and from school against, instead of with, the heavy traffic" of rush hour.[21] Perhaps that was the case for the affluent students living in the northside's "beautiful" residential parks, but it made little sense for those who would first have to travel through downtown to reach the school.

The construction of white junior high schools also favored residential parks at the expense of older areas of the city, creating an additional source of inequality among white children. By locating junior highs in the most segregated parts of town, board members and the planning commission encouraged families to desert mixed-race neighborhoods with traditional development. Their decisions went well beyond even Strayer's skewed recommendations. According to the survey, the district needed junior highs in the northwestern, northern, and southwestern sections of the city, where overcrowding was the most severe. Local officials disregarded his advice and located a junior high in the privileged *northeastern* section—with its newly developing residential parks—rather than in the northwest, where the population of working-class Bellwood was exploding (see map 7.2).

Before the election, the mayor had addressed Bellwood residents to assure them that their children would be well taken care of in the building program. The $4 million bond issue would "give every child in Atlanta a seat in a comfortable school house," and "this thing of stopping at the sixth grade" would "be eliminated," he maintained.[22] Once the bonds passed, however, Bellwood residents were furious to learn that they would not receive their promised junior high, most likely because the zone map had designated much of the Fifth Ward as either "colored" or racially "undetermined." It took multiple petitions just to receive a few wooden portables. After the portables burned to the ground, the students were forced to walk through an industrial area crisscrossed by railroad tracks to attend the northside junior high. The board ignored their repeated calls for a permanent building. Although Bellwood residents had successfully demanded changes to the racial zoning map before it was declared unconstitutional, they failed to acquire a modern junior high.[23] The planning commission had strategically designated the surrounding area for Black residential expansion to direct Black housing away from the city's affluent white residential parks. Denying Bellwood a junior high helped fulfill that goal even without enforceable race districts.

The Davis Street School was another example of extreme neglect in Fifth Ward. Soon after the conversion of Ashby in 1919, local officials planned to convert Davis, too, but white parents refused to hand over the school. When talk of a bond issue began heating up, a delegation representing 900 parents petitioned for "a modern school building on the same site to replace the dilapidated structure" then "housing the children." They ardently opposed any plans to "rebuild the school at another location" and "abandon the old school to the negroes." The petition explained that the present site was "convenient to the homes of the patrons and highly desirable because of the playground facilities furnished by Mims Park." It further reasoned, "The colored district lying to the south and west of the school has been there for thirty years and can come no nearer: nor can it ever surround the school or cut it off from its white patrons because of the railroad in front of the school and the Georgia Railway and Power company plant on the north."[24] Of course, under no circumstances would expert planners, let alone educators, describe a power plant or railroad tracks as suitable guardrails for a school, but the parents had the staunch support of their principal, Julia Riordan, who boldly challenged the mayor's decision. "The white citizens in the Davis Street district know that to give up Mims park to the negroes would deprive themselves and their children of all park and playground facilities," she protested. "There are 900 property owners and voters in that district who have pledged themselves to fight Mayor Key's plan."[25]

Other working-class whites were more accommodating of the racial zoning scheme. Third Ward's Fraser Street School was in an "undetermined" district near Summer Hill, a Black enclave dating back to Reconstruction. In 1923, local officials erected a new white school for the Fraser Street community on a different site fully within a "white" district, according to the zone map. With much fanfare, the children marched the three blocks from their old school to the new one, which was renamed in honor of Mayor Key. As part of the bargain, the board agreed not to convert the old building to Black use, even though it was desperately needed by Summer Hill families.[26] W. C. Caraway, the president of the Atlanta Federation of Trades and labor's token member on the bond commission, also accepted the plan to move white working-class schools into newly defined white districts. In 1921, he owned a house on a mixed-use, majority-Black block located south of the school. His wife was the president of the Davis PTA. Caraway had purchased the home before Ashby School's conversion. At the time, the block was all white but had small businesses scattered among the houses, devaluing it for white, middle-class child-rearing. In addition, the intersecting streets were majority Black, as was typical of block-level segregation. In 1922, the year the building program began, Caraway sold his home to a Black woman and then purchased a new house within a few blocks of Grant Park and the future Bass Junior High. Although the school did not yet exist, Caraway was in the know. Local officials were planning to shrink the Summer Hill community to safeguard the more affluent white homes near Grant Park, the most respectable residential area south of downtown.[27]

Other Davis families refused to give up so quickly, but like their compatriots in Bellwood, they discovered it was easier to change the zoning map than to alter the building program. According to the 1921 directory, the blocks south of Davis were majority Black while those north of it were all-white before becoming majority Black again as they approached the ward's only Black school, the Gray Street School. The zone map had initially included the white blocks within a "colored district" since Davis School would be converted to Black use. Davis patrons, nevertheless, succeeded in changing the section's designation from a Black residential district to an industrial one on the final zoning map (see map 7.1). Although Black families would still be able to move onto those blocks, white families would no longer live in a "colored" district, which seemed like an improvement to them even if the experts did not understand their logic.[28]

The election of Klan-backed mayor Walter Sims offered Davis patrons some hope that they would be able to keep their school. An empowered and sympathetic city council instructed the newly elected school board to "take immediate steps" so "that the Boys and Girls of the Davis Street School" would not "be housed" in a "fire trap."[29] Feeling encouraged, Davis patrons presented another petition to the reconstituted board, but the election had not changed the bond commission's commitment to the original zoning map. Thus, the new board consistently refused to invest in the school. All that Davis students would receive during the remainder of the decade was "a portable frame structure" in Mims Park.[30]

Middle-class child-rearing standards worked against the Davis families as well. In 1923, ex-councilman J. N. Renfroe, the sponsor of the city's second segregation ordinance, finally accepted reality and began constructing houses for Black residents between the Ashby and Davis Street Schools. The Fifth Ward Civic League immediately countered with a petition to have the area rezoned from a business district to a white residential district to prevent the construction of more Black housing, claiming that white patrons required "every available vacant lot" if the school was "to stand and remain white." Though this action pleased Davis parents, it rapidly led to more unsalable properties. Middle-class whites were simply unwilling to build homes along a busy commercial corridor, let alone in an industrial, mixed-race area. Seven months later, the decision was reversed once again.[31]

Black families were also determined that, this time, their children would receive their fair share of improvements from the building program. They obtained four modern elementary schools in addition to the high school, which represented about 25 percent of the total bond issue. The expenditures were far above the amounts previously spent on Black schools but still well below a proportional 33 percent. Moreover, because the district had closed more Black schools than it had opened, the building program did not lessen the number of children in double or triple sessions. The new Howard School in Fourth Ward had fewer than 1,000 seats, but it was replacing both Storrs and Houston Street Schools, which had a combined enrollment of 1,859. Likewise, First Ward's Ware School was replacing both Roach and Mitchell Street Schools yet had seats for only half the enrollment. The teachers and students from Mitchell occupied Ware in the morning, and those from Roach occupied the school in the afternoon. Even under that shocking arrangement, one class had 253 students, and the principal had to disband the kindergarten for lack of space.[32]

A "mass meeting" was quickly called to protest the conditions. Attendees elected a "citizens committee," which included the presidents of the Neighborhood Union and the Atlanta NAACP, to prepare a report that they intended to share with local officials. White members from the interracial committee asked if they might make the first appeal, and the Black citizens committee agreed. After negotiating in vain for three months, however, the white mediators grew discouraged. The citizens committee then handed over their report to Mayor Sims, the city council, and the school board along with a petition "asking that measures be taken as soon as possible to relieve the existing conditions." It acknowledged that the new schools were "architecturally beautiful, splendidly equipped, modern in appointments and in every way admirably and adequately suited to school work" and assured that "the Negroes of the city are proud of them and grateful for them and congratulate the school officials upon the brilliant achievements in their construction." But it also reminded them that the number of seats added through the building program was only "50 percent of the enrollment," representing a pitiful gain of just "1 percent in seating capacity." The petitioners concluded that "too great haste was had in getting rid of all the old school buildings before opportunity was afforded to ascertain if the new buildings" sufficiently met the need for more classrooms.[33]

When the initial $4 million bond issue proved insufficient to complete even a fraction of the proposed projects for either Black or white students, Atlantans supported a second bond issue to complete the program. Aquilla Orme, councilman for the posh Eighth Ward, was chair of the powerful finance committee, which had the authority to determine the size of the bond issue. He was also president of North Boulevard Park's development company. Through his earlier efforts, North Boulevard had acquired a school even though George Strayer had warned that $4 million would barely cover the cost of the new senior and junior highs, let alone "the worst needs of the elementary schools."[34] North Boulevard's school was on Virginia Avenue in an area that was still largely undeveloped. At the time of its procurement, Orme was the chair of the city council's Public Schools Committee, which allowed him to pressure the board into closing the original Virginia

Avenue School that served Black children living in the northeastern section of the city, as discussed in chapter 3.[35]

With talk of a second bond issue, Orme ran again for a council seat representing Eighth Ward's residential parks. After the election, Mayor Sims appointed him chair of the finance committee, and Orme fulfilled his responsibilities by repeatedly saying no to the school board, which he and Sims began accusing of "extravagance."[36] When the local Klan fell into disarray in 1924, Sims survived his reelection bid by moving closer to the elite faction promoting financial austerity. When the board requested a $6 million bond issue to provide a seat in a fireproof school for every child in Atlanta, Orme cut the amount down to $2 million. He had already procured a school for North Boulevard Park, and his constituents in Ansley Park were frustrated that charter reform had stalled. Orme agreed that they should not support a large bond issue that they could not control.[37]

Parents immediately challenged Orme's severe cuts to the building program; he compromised by setting the bond issue at $3.5 million, but organized labor rejected the patronizing gesture. In the past, labor leaders had almost always remained aligned with the chamber of commerce. This time, they refused to endorse a bond issue of less than $5 million. Jerome Jones, the editor of the *Journal of Labor*, warned that the smaller amount would "deny a seat to some one—to your child or to mine, perhaps." From prior experience, he understood, "Certain privileged sections will be cared for while others will receive a promise of relief from the 'next bond issue,'" betting that "some of our readers may be able to pick out in advance such districts." This time, he argued, the need was critical. Working-class children had already been harmed by earlier neglect: "We have stunted their mental and physical development; we have deadened their ambition and forced them into idleness at a time and under conditions most fertile for juvenile delinquency." He implored local officials "to cease dilly-dallying with the lives of our children." Yet despite the pleas for justice, the chamber of commerce endorsed the smaller bond issue and organized a mammoth campaign to ensure it passed. The day before the election, thousands of white children marched through the city accompanied by bands and parade floats promoting the bonds.[38]

Black voters joined in support of the campaign once local officials pledged $700,000 for Black schools, but that amount plunged to little more than $250,000 after the election. Benjamin Davis voiced the community's outrage: "It may be believable but unthinkable" that "white men" would deceitfully "tell a class of people that if you will help us put over a bond proposition, . . . we will see to it that no discrimination is inveigled against you—that you shall share equally and equitably" in its benefits. White members of the Atlanta Christian Council petitioned the board "to keep faith with our negro citizens and to do exact justice to them and their rights." They pleaded, "The negroes have no voice in directing the expenditure of the moneys raised by the sale of the bonds. They must rely on the good faith of our white race." An editorial in the *Constitution* conveyed further support for the petition, but Black children did not receive a single additional school.[39]

Consequently, the four Black elementary schools completed during the first bond issue continued to draw Black families to the very race districts that had been declared unconstitutional a few years earlier. Black children living outside those districts lost their schools altogether, worsening the overcrowding at the four new schools. For instance, Dimmock School was permanently closed, even though according to the survey report, the surrounding community was about 30 percent Black—essentially the same proportion of Black residents as the city as a whole (see map 7.2). When parents and their allies repeatedly petitioned the board for "some school facilities" for the "400 Negro children formerly housed in Dimmock," board members alleged that they could not find an appropriate site, the usual excuse given to angry parents.[40]

A white tantrum over the district's new Black high school and four new Black elementaries reinforced the board's inaction. Third Ward Alderman and future mayor William Hartsfield assailed board members for favoring Black children over white ones. He fumed, "Hundreds of innocent little grammar school children and white girls" have been "left in ramshackle, temporary buildings and insanitary firetraps," while "a great modern four-story Negro high school was being rushed to completion." In response, Dr. Henry R. Butler—husband of Selena Sloan Butler, the founder of the nation's first Black PTA—wrote a scathing piece for the *Independent* denouncing Hartfield's attack: "About the time I make up my mind that there are a large number of good white people in Atlanta here comes someone to kick the thing over and away goes it all." In a separate editorial, Benjamin Davis rebuked Hartsfield for failing to consider that "white children would not have modern school facilities, or that the bond issue would never have gone over, had the Negroes not put it over." Davis also reminded him that he was "our representative as much as" the "white man's."[41]

Fourth Ward's two councilmen followed Hartsfield's lead. John White was one of Mayor Sims's appointees to the reconstituted planning commission before he ran for councilman, and Claude Ashley was the sponsor of the city's original segregation ordinance. Both backed the Fourth Ward Civic Association's complaints that the ward's white residents had "not been given their share" of the bond money. After receiving nothing during the first round, they found a single appropriation for an auditorium insulting. The delegation insisted that parents wanted additional classrooms since Fourth Ward's white schools had "been congested for years" and "new families and homes" were "being added to the vicinity every day." Accusing the board of helping Black families at white children's expense, Councilman White seethed, "I cannot see why nearly $400,000 should be allotted to [Howard Jr. High] when the [white] children are in the basements." The delegation demanded that the money for Howard be reallocated to the area's white schools. The board agreed despite the fact that Black residents had already been promised an eastside junior high and Strayer's survey had predicted that the white population of the area would soon decline.[42]

Once the entire bond issue had been spent, the total number of Black schools had actually decreased. During the second round, Black families did not receive one additional school. Instead, Howard gained a modest annex allowing it to function as a junior high, though its appropriation had been reduced to appease Fourth Ward whites. The makeshift South Atlanta School received a brick building, and First Ward's Ashby School received a more spacious replacement when the original building tragically burned to the ground. The new building included ten extra classrooms, which expanded its capacity beyond the 600 seats that had heretofore been accommodating the school's 1,500 students.[43] The additional classrooms offered some relief, but fewer schools meant greater segregation.

A different vision for the building program had been put forward by the school superintendent when he first outlined the district's needs back in 1920. His recommendations had prioritized where children lived rather than where they were expected to live. Therefore, he not only requested a much bigger bond issue than the one eventually passed but also suggested two new Black schools in areas where none had previously existed, including one in the northern portion of Fourth Ward. As was true of Atlanta's population in general, more Black families were moving northward in the direction of Piedmont Park, but the old Virginia Avenue School had been closed at the behest of Councilman Orme, increasing the need for a Black school in the area. The plan never made it beyond the superintendent's initial report, however. Under the leadership of Mayor James Key, the school board fired the superintendent without cause and replaced him with someone more amenable to racial zoning.[44]

Schools, Zoning, and Segregation

When Strayer and Engelhardt arrived in Atlanta in 1921, they brought with them experience from another Jim Crow city interested in combining a school building program with zoning and residential segregation.[45] Their work began just months after they had completed a survey for Baltimore. Like Atlanta, Baltimore essentially opened no new Black schools during the decade when segregation ordinances remained in dispute. Not long after the *Buchanan* decision, the impasse broke when the city annexed a large expanse of suburban territory that almost tripled its size. The school board then hired Strayer and Engelhardt to help design the district's $7 million building program, which would furnish schools for the newly developing residential parks in the annexed area. Meanwhile, local officials hoped to convert white schools in the city's older neighborhoods to Black use, although first they would have to battle white residents determined to save block-level segregation.[46]

Racial Zoning and Schools | 195

FIGURE 8.2. The Urban League used this photograph, taken during the early 1940s, to document children being forced to cross dangerous railroad tracks on their way to the Gray Street School because no Black school existed in their mixed-race neighborhood. Gray Street Pupils en Route to School, Atlanta Urban League Papers, Atlanta University Center Robert W. Woodruff Library. Used with permission.

As in Atlanta, Baltimore's building program coincided with the passage of the city's first zoning ordinance. It did not include racial zoning, but the combination of single-family districts and new schools made racial designations unnecessary. Baltimore's annexed area was largely restricted to single-family houses in white residential parks while the old rowhouses were made available to Black buyers and renters. At the 1922 NCCP, Strayer's presentation explained how the location of Baltimore's new schools reinforced the zoning plan. Afterward, Jefferson Grinnalds, the city's zoning consultant, spoke on the symbiotic relationship between the "zoning campaign" and the building program, which were "carried out at the same time." The zoning map "indicate[d] where the residential areas" should be and, thus, where to build the schools.[47] In turn, the new schools would lure families to those residential areas.

That same year, local officials in Winston-Salem turned to Strayer and Engelhardt for help with their building program after passing a large bond issue. Upon the recommendation of the "Civic Council" of the local chamber of commerce, they, too, hired Pittsburgh planner Morris Knowles to complete the preliminary work for "a zoning plan to be taken up later." The chairman of the Civic Council, Robert Hanes, was the brother of the new mayor, James G. Hanes. Their father and uncle had founded Hanes Hosiery and Hanes Underwear, respectively. The Hanes family belonged to the powerful interlocking directorate that had controlled much of the city's residential development since the late nineteenth century. Likewise, James sat on the board of the Wachovia Bank and Trust Company, another household name, while Robert was the vice president and loan officer.[48]

Although Winston-Salem would not follow through with a zoning ordinance until 1930, Knowles's map helped determine the unofficial race zones that would guide the city's building program. Given that the officials who hired Knowles seemed to be in no hurry to pass a zoning law, it appears the primary goal was to foster "voluntary segregation" through carefully selected sites for schools and parks. Adopting the plan as a recommendation rather than a law allowed them to accomplish their objectives without risking judicial review, an important consideration since the North Carolina Supreme Court had invalidated the city's segregation ordinance only seven years earlier. Plus, the outcome could not be undermined through public hearings or an amendment process, as had happened in Atlanta.[49]

The "voluntary segregation" plan called for the construction of seven "school centers," with the Black schools placed in the far southeastern, northeastern, and northwestern corners of the city and the white ones placed in the outlying southern, northern, eastern, and western sections. Each center would receive a modern school along with a well-equipped park and playground that would, ideally, promote cohesive, self-contained communities. According to a resolution passed by the board of alderman, the "well-defined districts or zones" would "afford the members of each race" the "full opportunity to develop their own homes and institutions without interference from the other." A triumphant Mayor Hanes went farther, declaring the segregation problem "amicably solved" since the details of the plan had been hammered out during a series of "conferences" attended by "representative colored citizens," the school board, and "other leading citizens of the white race."[50]

The local press also championed the effort. One newspaper praised the "gradual shifting" of the schools to "more convenient locations," although it still felt compelled to add in all capital letters, "NOTHING RADICAL IN IT." Another suggested the solution was "a means of relieving forever any possibility of there ever arising a race problem in Winston-Salem" because of "definite plans" to give Black "districts every public convenience, and to extend water, sewer and sidewalks" on an equal basis with "white sections." It further called on "all the civic and commercial organizations" to help actuate the building program, which a third article boasted was receiving "nation-wide attention."[51]

Knowles's work no doubt shaped Strayer and Engelhardt's recommendations for school sites. In early 1922, the famed pair visited Winston-Salem on several occasions while they were finishing up Atlanta's survey. They continued to advise both cities during the remainder of the year. As usual, the experts encouraged generous sites with plenty of playground space. Local officials obliged with elementary sites as large as forty acres and a seventy-five-acre site for the white high school. In all, the building program would increase the total footprint of the schools from 19.5 to a whopping 306.5 acres, most of which was dedicated to the white "school centers," even though white residents made up only 60 percent of the total population.[52]

Since local elites sought class segregation as well, the plan included four distinct white residential areas despite the fact that the city's population had not yet risen above 50,000. The program began on the industrial north side. Residents in that largely working-class section were already upset that the board had located the city's sole white high school in West End where it was convenient only to the residential parks on the southwest side. The magnificent site had been a joint gift from the Hanes and Reynolds families, but northside students had no direct access to the new $750,000 school, named in honor of R. J. Reynolds. They would have to travel south to downtown before heading west. The principal of North School complained, "In going to the western part of the city," a student first had "to come to the square," and when "he reached this point," he remained "no nearer West End than when he left home." To make amends while preserving class segregation, local officials gave the north side a $250,000 combined elementary and junior high school, the first school completed during the building program.[53]

On the city's south side, white middle-class residents received two new schools after rejecting the board's initial plan. Many of the residents of Central Terrace—the residential park developed by school board chair John Buxton—preferred the current school location, even if it had a small lot that lacked an adjoining park. Local officials maintained that the site was unacceptable, but Central Terrace residents had enough political pull to obtain what they wanted. Board members agreed to purchase two southside sites: one inside the borders of Central Terrace and the second, envisioned as a "school center" on par with the other white districts, further south in an area that remained largely undeveloped. They rationalized the extra expense by claiming another school would soon be needed as the city expanded outwards.[54] Of course, locating a school and park at the edge of existing residential parks all but ensured that future development would match their expectations.

Officials also devised the segregation scheme to draw Black families away from the mixed-race areas east of downtown, where most Black residents still lived and worked. A decade earlier, Black parents had succeeded in keeping the Depot Street School at its original site, as discussed in chapter 5. In 1921, a "determined" board moved the high school out to Columbia Heights, the city's only Black residential park. This decision harkened back to the "Columbia Heights Plan"—the "voluntary segregation" scheme that inspired the current effort.[55] But the new high school failed to pull substantially more Black families out to Columbia Heights because the development remained just as isolated from downtown, a key reason why Black middle-class parents preferred living near the Depot Street School in the first place.

Instead, the most desired Black residential area would develop in the northeastern section where the board had acquired a twenty-five-acre school, park, and playground site surrounded by "high class" residential properties. The school and park were named for W. N. Reynolds, who donated the site. One newspaper article guaranteed "no unsightly buildings" would "be allowed to be built in the community." Another falsely assured a school "equal in every respect to the one" for white children, even though the new Black school would cost less than half of what the new white schools cost. It was still worth more than Columbia Heights High School, however, and the neighborhood was more accessible to downtown and offered more amenities to affluent Black parents seeking the best possible environment to raise their children.[56] The segregation plan would work less well for the working-class families who made up the majority of the city's Black residents. They could not afford to move further from the factories where they worked, let alone purchase a single-family home.

The same year that Winston-Salem elites implemented their plan, local officials in Raleigh launched their own zoning effort alongside a large-scale school building program. Raleigh's mayor appointed the first planning commission about a month before voters passed the first of two bond issues. He also supplied a direct link between the two endeavors by sitting on both the new planning commission and the school board. Unlike the industrial cities discussed above, Raleigh's population was still below 25,000, and its function as the state capital powered the local economy. The secretary of the Raleigh Real Estate Board, suburban developer Dave Fort, characterized the city as "short on factories, but long on education and inspiration." While boosting the city's new zoning ordinance, he told the Civitan Club, "I glory in telling the people of North Carolina not to compare or confound Raleigh with the spinning wheel or the tobacco factory [i.e., Winston-Salem], but to join us and help us preserve this city as a pure and spotless place where their sons and daughters may be trained to more lofty ideals."[57] Accordingly, Raleigh's sizeable middle class was in firm control of the local government. The city commissioners, who themselves were elected at-large, appointed prominent citizens to the school board, which enjoyed far more prestige than in cities such as Atlanta where members had to stand for election.[58]

Because segregation was easier to accomplish in a small city dominated by white, middle-class families, efforts in Raleigh were much less pronounced than in cities that had experimented with segregation ordinances, such as Winston-Salem, Atlanta, and Baltimore. Raleigh's plan was relatively simple: officials would continue concentrating Black schools away from the white residential parks on the north and west sides. Raleigh, like Baltimore, had annexed an immense area of undeveloped land just before its building program began. The newly annexed territory almost doubled Raleigh's size, and it shifted the center of the population in a northwesterly direction for the first time. The residential parks that would soon appear in that area received a disproportionate share of the resources from the building program as well as greater protection from its zoning ordinance.[59]

Raleigh had important ties to both Baltimore's and Winston-Salem's segregation efforts, which perhaps influenced this strategy. Jefferson Grinnalds began working as a consultant for Raleigh while completing his work on Baltimore's zoning ordinance. Raleigh elites were also paying close attention to the activities in Winston-Salem. About a month after Raleigh's mayor first appointed the planning commission, the *News and Observer* published an article titled "Race Segregation Problem Is Solved," which described Winston-Salem's plan to use schools to promote "voluntary" segregation. Six months later, the Winston-Salem school board hired contractor C. V. York, a member of Raleigh's planning commission, to construct the first school for its building program. Surely York and various members of the Winston-Salem school board exchanged details about the building programs and zoning efforts taking place in both cities simultaneously.[60]

Another connection was Gilbert Stephenson, the lawyer who defended Winston-Salem's segregation ordinance before the North Carolina Supreme Court. He also authored the best-known assessment of the segregation ordinances before *Buchanan*. Stephenson moved to Raleigh just after Mayor Hanes launched Winston-Salem's building program and just before Mayor Eldridge launched Raleigh's. At a meeting of the Raleigh Kiwanis Club, Stephenson "drew upon his experience" in Winston-Salem to "offer some timely advice" to his adopted city.[61] Such connections illustrate the ways that ideas flowed from one city to another, especially during this period of uncertainty with the courts when local officials were paying particularly close attention to the actions of their counterparts in other cities.

Even with ready advice coming from Winston-Salem, Raleigh's building program stumbled because local officials largely ignored the city's interracial networks when formulating the plan. Consequently, they disregarded the wishes of Black middle-class families living in College Park and Idlewild near Saint Augustine's. Residents had been petitioning for a school in that area since at least 1910. When the district began plans for the building program in 1922, the school superintendent assured them that, this time, they would receive a school. Longtime educator Charles Hunter sensed victory. He wrote to the superintendent to express his "great delight" that the administration supported his bid for the school:

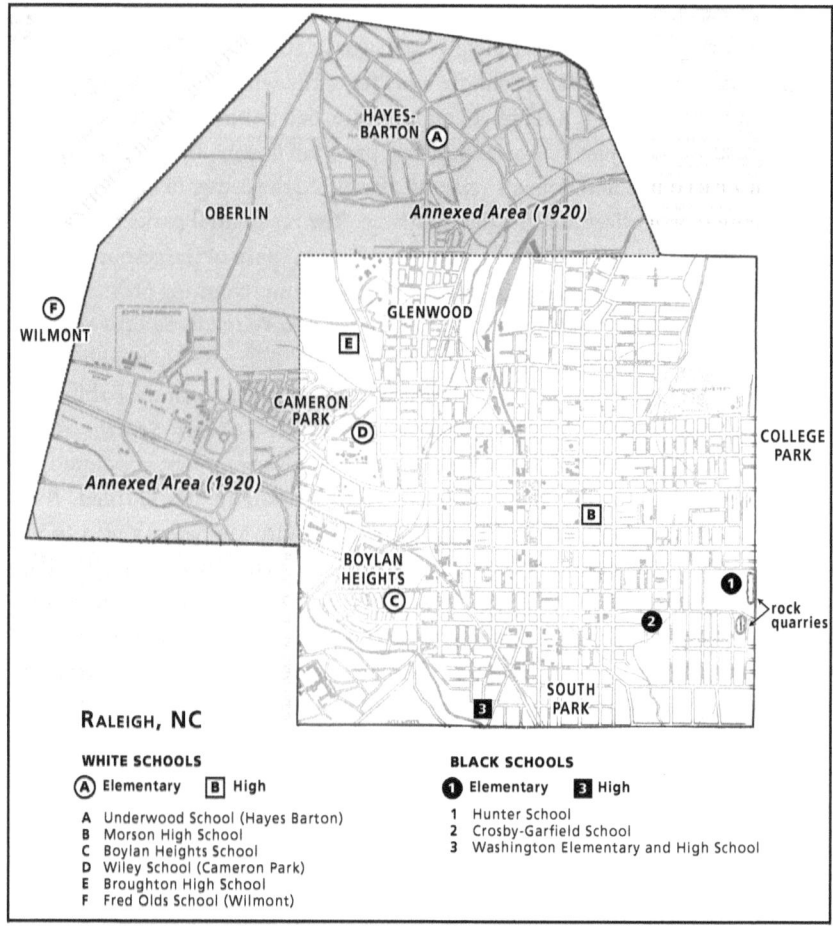

MAP 8.1. Raleigh's school building program was designed to serve the extensive area annexed to the city in 1920. Prior to this annexation, the city had always expanded the same distance outward from Capitol Square in all four directions, maintaining its perfect square shape. Courtesy of the Louis Round Wilson Special Collections Library, University of North Carolina at Chapel Hill.

"I have been laboring for this for quite a number of years and your approval gives the highest promise I have yet had of the fruition of my hopes."[62]

Nonetheless, after the bonds passed, the board announced its plan to expand Washington School into a much-needed Black high school, but it would be built on a new site only one block north of the city's southern border (see map 8.1). In the days before publicly funded school buses, the board's decision showed blatant disrespect towards the Black middle-class residents near Saint Augustine's, who believed their children would constitute a significant portion of the enrollment.

During the 1920s, a high school diploma had not yet become the norm for Black or white youth. Black middle-class families would continue to protest the high school's site long after it opened in 1924. As late as 1948, a Black citizens' committee compiled statistics showing that the school's location was convenient to just 17 percent of its students.[63]

The board expressed no intent to build even a primary school for the young children living in the single-family homes near St. Augustine's. Hunter fired off a letter to Clarence Poe, the editor of a popular newspaper, *The Progressive Farmer*, and one of the most influential members of the school board. Poe's response claimed that they gave "the most generous support possible to the building program plans for the negro schools," but it was "out of the question" to furnish a second Black school from the limited resources of the bond issue. The following spring, Black parents again petitioned for a school in or near College Park and were, once again, turned away.[64]

As was often the case, local officials proposed a second bond issue after the first one proved inadequate. They obtained support from Black voters by pledging to build an additional Black school. According to the *News and Observer*, 1,000 Black citizens registered to vote, representing about 22 percent of the total registration. At the time, about one-third of Raleigh's population was Black. Although the percentage was still disproportionate, it represented a strong showing considering the multilayered disadvantages of second-class citizenship.[65] Many Black families believed that they would finally get a school in the northeastern section of the city. Soon thereafter, they learned that the board had instead chosen an inexpensive site not far from the Crosby-Garfield School—the cornerstone of the district's earlier consolidation project. Among other problems, the site was "adjacent to the city dump," near a notorious "crime pit," and alongside "a rock quarry filled with stagnant water."[66]

Black citizens found the choice demeaning and wholly unacceptable. In a letter to the editor, Hunter implored, "With neither voice nor vote in deciding this question, we have only the sacred right of petition." A positive outcome would mean "Negroes would feel more like citizens and less like subjects."[67] A week later, the *Times* published a letter signed by a dozen prominent Black citizens and "four hundred others" censuring the board's lack of response to twenty years of patient and polite requests for a school near St. Augustine's. Without representation, they argued, Black residents could only "appeal to the Christian conscience of the Christian white people of the community" and ask them, "Would you locate a white school upon a site with similar conditions, to say nothing of the need of this same school in another locality?" The prior consolidation of Black schools had already initiated the process of concentrating Black families in the southeastern corner of the city, which the board then used as evidence to justify its decision to place an additional school nearby. Some suspected that more was going on than a callously undemocratic process for selecting sites. Charles Hunter's niece captured the sentiment in a letter to her uncle. "I am sorry our white people handed such a raw deal in the matter of [the] school," she commiserated. "You see, they are trying to get all the Negroes segregated."[68]

As further evidence, the new Hunter School served a substantially larger student population than the new white schools built for westside residential parks. In 1929, Hunter's enrollment was 828 compared with 570 at Hayes Barton and only 231 at Boylan Heights. Wiley School, which the board moved to a new site within Cameron Park, had 544 students, and West Raleigh, built for the recently platted Wilmont, had a mere 215. In fact, Hunter's enrollment was even greater than Broughton High School's 780 students.[69] Local officials had chosen to build a single, supersized school where they wanted Black families to live rather than two smaller schools in areas where Black families *did* live.

The building program also raised the ire of white residents in the city's older neighborhoods because it so overtly favored the westside residential parks. Ironically, the program began with a project intended to appease white working-class families on the east side, in much the same way that Winston-Salem's program began with a school for working-class residents who felt cheated by the location of the new high school. In Raleigh's case, the board was under intense pressure to replace the Thompson School, which served the children living in mixed-race Idlewild. During the last building program, the only "improvement" the school had received was a deep hole in the middle of the school yard. Years before, the hole was dug for a foundation for a new school, but then the board ran out of money before it could finish the project. Now, Thompson parents threatened to derail the whole bond issue if they did not receive a modern school right from the start.[70]

In the end, modern facilities for Thompson School did not avert a heated controversy over the location of the new white high school. A three-member "advisory committee of the Chamber of Commerce" was tasked with selecting the site. It recommended a location at the edge of Cameron Park, the city's most child-centered residential park at the time; since 1913, ads had been reassuring white parents that Cameron Park was "the place for children." The advisory committee included Charles Park, who would soon be appointed to the new planning commission. He was also the vice president of his brother's booster newspaper, the *Raleigh Times*, and his family resided in Cameron Park.[71]

White parents living in older, mixed-race neighborhoods expressed serious opposition to the site. Requests poured in for a more centrally located high school, and accusations intensified that the board had attempted to "put something over" on residents from the east side.[72] "Several hundred citizens" signed a petition pleading for the selection of an alternate site on Benehan Square, located a few blocks southeast of the capitol next to the emerging Black business district—

a site that would preserve block-level segregation. Their petition stated that Benehan Square met "the need for a high school centrally located with respect to the overwhelming large majority of the residents of the city." It predicted that future development in "the northern and northeastern and southern sections of the city" would necessitate a downtown site. "Even if the city should ultimately grow largely in the western and northwestern portions," it reasoned, "there would still be at least twenty-five thousand people or more who would need a high school located near the center of the present built up portion of the city."[73]

Not all elites agreed that white development was heading westward. School board member Clarence Poe owned an 800-acre estate just east of the city limits. He would begin developing this property into an affluent residential park named Longview Gardens soon after the controversy over the high school ended. Not surprisingly, he advocated for a northeastern site that would have been more convenient to his potential buyers once the lots went on sale.[74] Defending his selection as the best course to adequately serve the white population as a whole, he maintained, "A radius of one mile would take in practically all the more thickly settled white areas, while 1.5 miles, according to a map issued by the Chamber of Commerce, would include the remaining well-settled sections of Boylan-Heights, Hayes Barton, Cameron Park, and the new developments eastward." As evidence, he twice referred to a race population map produced by the chamber of commerce. It is likely that the map was completed by Jefferson Grinnalds as part of the zoning process, but it was not included in the final ordinance since both the state legislature and the courts had strongly opposed the passage of segregation laws. Apparently, the board used the map to make decisions about school sites, although Poe interpreted the data differently from those promoting residential parks west of the city.[75]

After a bitter year, officials agreed to build two white high schools despite Raleigh's small size. Morson High was located on Benehan Square near the Black business district, and the flagship Broughton High was on St. Mary's Street, which stretched about half a mile between the northern edge of Cameron Park and the southern edge of prestigious Hayes Barton (see map 8.1). The *Raleigh Times* hailed the westside site, declaring it would "bring this section of the city into prominence and enhance the value of the property." As mentioned previously, the *Raleigh Times* was owned by the Park brothers, including planning commission member Charles Park. Since he was a resident of Cameron Park and his brother, John Park, was a resident of Hayes Barton, the school would "enhance the value" of their homes as well.[76] The same article also prematurely demoted Morson to a "junior high," even though it would remain in use as the eastside high school for three more decades.[77]

Private real estate investments were typically the root cause of elite disagreements over residential segregation and the city's future development. With Poe's plans for Longview Gardens on the horizon, he did not want Black housing to extend further east. Therefore, he exploited his position on the school board to push Black schools farther south. The Park brothers disagreed. They supported Charles Hunter's effort to obtain a Black school near St. Augustine's: "It is a fact well-known that the northeastern negro section was due largely to the desire of better class negroes to escape the very Rock Quarry locality in which it is suggested the new school will take place." The editorial described the Black petitioners as "owners of their own homes" who had "built up with who knows what sacrifice a self-respecting and steadily improving community."[78] The Parks saw no harm in giving Black residents a school near St. Augustine's since they believed the white population would soon follow them to the newly annexed area on the opposite side of downtown—but to no avail. As was often true, white disagreements over residential segregation almost always led to a greater concentration of Black families in the least desirable section of town.[79]

During the 1920s, Black middle-class parents successfully obtained modern schools, including high schools, but at the price of greater residential segregation. Building programs had become a tool for city planners to promote segregation, especially in Jim Crow cities. School boards acted on the recommendations of local planning commissions well before zoning ordinances were accepted by the city council, let alone the courts. In the meantime, parents in older neighborhoods wanted fireproof replacements for their children's schools. Both Black and white parents were outraged when school boards neglected their communities and, instead, spent most of the bond money constructing modern schools along the outer edges of the district where fewer people lived. In some cases, white families in mixed-race neighborhoods did gain a new school or at least were able to hold onto what they had, but those "wins" did not alter the macro trend. White residents were defending neighborhoods that could not compete with the residential parks newly protected by strict zoning laws. In most cases, their efforts simply hurt Black families by delaying access to more classrooms and better housing.

The residential segregation that resulted from school building programs was particularly insidious because, in hindsight, the outcomes appeared largely inevitable. The programs had created self-fulfilling prophecies by locating modern schools in areas of desired growth. When families eagerly sought homes near a new school, they validated expert predictions and, thereby, helped justify similar decisions in future building programs. In 1952, the Atlanta Metropolitan Planning Commission prepared a confidential report for the school board that reinforced the idea that "properly located" schools were "a major factor in developing neighborhood and community identities and making them desirable places in which to live." Segregation was part of that goal. The report advised that "nothing substantial be done to develop additional Negro elementary school facilities in the North area," claiming that the number of Black children would not sustain a school there. The closure of the Virginia Avenue School in 1919, discussed in chapter 3, ensured that the Black population of that section would remain small for decades to come.[80]

The strategy was highly effective because experts had linked suburban school sites to the cultivation of future generations of healthy, intelligent, and productive citizens. Perhaps the experts truly believed that they were doing what was best for children. Indeed, George Strayer characterized the "splendid city planning movement" as "a movement for God and Humanity and the making of a better world." Raleigh's school superintendent likewise celebrated the building program's impact: "The importance of the lives of little children has been brought to the attention of our community. I am sure all have brighter hopes for public schools, better homes, and the highest types of patriotic citizens."[81] In the coming decade, an increasing number of parent educators soon joined the chorus of educational experts and planning consultants encouraging middle-class families to embrace this vison.

CHAPTER 9

The Best Possible Environment for the Growing Child

Since families with children were the key buyer of single-family homes, schools became an essential component of residential development. Targeting parents also meant convincing them that paying a premium for a lot in a residential park was a wise investment because the idyllic surroundings would benefit the children who lived there, which in turn would preserve the property's value. "The most important outside factor in the development of your boy or girl is environment," a 1912 ad for J. C. Nichols's Country Club District declared. "Boys and Girls Reared in a Place of Flowers, Lawns and Shrubbery of clean-air and sunshine have an unquestioned advantage over the children from closely built houses, apartments and dusty traffic streets."[1]

While parenting advice that romanticized the stand-alone cottage dated back to the antebellum period, the child study movement of the early twentieth century cemented the link between residential parks and the "one best way" to raise a child. Armed with scientific expertise and the arrogance that accompanied it, parent educators spread the gospel of "intelligent" parenting, placing a new spin on intensive child-rearing. Just as educational expertise included the school building and its site, parenting expertise included the home and its neighborhood. By the 1920s, an unyielding faith in the superiority of suburban living had become a core assumption of parent education, which then helped justify the zoning movement's preoccupation with the single-family residence district.[2]

Parent educators welcomed government assistance to help disseminate their work, much like the planners and educators who shared their admiration for residential parks. Local, state, and federal government entities partnered with a host of experts from psychology, social work, medicine, and home economics to determine "the best possible environment for the growing child," in the words of Herbert Hoover, one of the movement's biggest fans. Together, these private-public partnerships—which included the Own-Your-Own-Home campaigns and the Better Homes in America movement of the 1920s—tethered intensive parenting to suburban housing as the best means to support white, middle-class efforts to raise healthy and virtuous citizens.[3]

For most middle-class parents, however, the principal allure of "child study" was not the lofty rhetoric about citizenship but the desire to help one's own children navigate a shifting urban landscape and changing economy. In that sense, the appeal was not that different than it had been during the market revolution. Anxious white parents engaged in a new form of competitive parenting to promote upward mobility despite mounting income inequality and uneven economic growth. And by the early twentieth century, intensive parenting strategies were also deeply rooted in consumerism. In 1904, *Harper's Weekly* published a witty piece that encapsulated the mixture of scorn, awe, and understanding that greeted the rise of competitive parenting and the consumption that surrounded it. Columnist E. S. Martin quipped that the foremost incentive of the American businessman was providing his offspring with superior advantages: "What the advantages are doesn't greatly matter so long as they seem advantageous to the children." They might be "better clothes, or better schooling, or music lessons, or dancing lessons, or horseback exercise, or a bigger house in a better street," he teased. "Advantages are relative and depend upon what our contemporaries who live within sight of us are doing for their children."[4]

Black middle-class parents embraced intensive parenting strategies as well; however, racial uplift remained their primary focus, and the effort was far less competitive. By sponsoring parent education opportunities for working-class families, the Black middle class hoped to place even the least fortunate child on a path to full citizenship and better employment. Black parents also challenged the demeaning images in popular culture that stereotyped Black children as impoverished and ignorant, yet the broader parent education movement undermined their efforts by connecting "good" parenting to homeownership in racially restricted residential parks. Meanwhile, the rhetoric of interracial cooperation and tolerance imbued the parent education movement with a sense of racial fairness, which eased white consciences about the advancement of separate and unequal residential development.[5]

The Impact of Parent Education

Robert and Helen Lynd's classic study of American life during the 1920s, *Middletown* (1929), captured the impact of parent education on individual mothers. "Life was simpler for my mother," a "thoughtful" young woman confided. "In those days one did not realize that there was so much to be known about the care of children." Another admitted, "My mother never stepped inside the school building as far as I can remember, but now there are never ten days that go by without my either visiting the children's school or getting in touch with their teacher." Her efforts at the school were meant to augment those at home: "I always like to be here when they come home from school so that I can keep in touch with their games and their friends. Any extra time goes into reading books on nutrition and character building." The sheer quantity of time intensive parenting required led another to confess, "I accommodate my entire life to my little girl."⁶

The roots of the organized parent education movement date back to 1888 when a small group of mothers established a study circle to improve their knowledge of child development. They were inspired by the work of Felix Adler, a professor at Columbia University who was prominent in the tenement reform movement. At first, the mothers read Plato, Rousseau, Locke, and Spencer. Once the field of child psychology appeared, they added Froebel, Montessori, and G. Stanley Hall. More study groups soon formed, and then a central organization, the Federation for Child Study, was founded in 1908 to pool resources for the various groups, sponsor lectures and conferences, and conduct research. Its 1913 statement of purpose encapsulated the gravity of their work: parental "failure" could "only be avoided by unceasingly studying the problems of their children's lives; by understanding the ever changing school conditions and the ever varying influences which society is constantly bringing to bear."⁷

The organization received a handsome grant from the Laura Spelman Rockefeller Memorial in 1923, after which it became known as the Child Study Association (CSA). Sidonie Gruenberg, the longtime director, described the CSA's philosophy in scientific terms. "Wise parenthood requires more than good will and traditional ideas. It requires understanding based upon the studies of experts," she explained. Our grandmothers did "the best they could, and it was often a devoted and inspired best," but "we of today would prove unworthy of them if we did not go farther and bring to the care of our children the best knowledge that is now available." Gruenberg suggested that most discipline problems arose when parents placed their own concerns before the needs of their child. She chided, "It is the difficulties and desires and uncomfortable longings of the parents that bring about the problem which is attributed to the child," who invariably began life as a blank slate.⁸

As part of its mission, the CSA managed a consultation service that provided expert advice to anxious parents. According to CSA associate Dr. Ruth Brickner, the service targeted children below age nine whose parents were "already somewhat enlightened" but who still had "minor behavior deviations." They also lacked any "economic, social, [or] physical factors" that might be "so pressing" as to "obscure psychological processes." In other words, the consultation service was aimed at affluent white families experiencing fairly conventional problems with middle-class child-rearing. In one triumphant example, the service helped a mother who had grown exasperated by her young son's "insistence on being with her." The problem was diagnosed as insecurity that had been caused by "the mother's change in attitude from one of delight in her docile child to one of annoyance with his feminine characteristics." The assigned expert recommended that the mother "spend a daily half-hour" playing one-on-one with her son and arrange "supervised play groups" after school. The goal was to gain "insight into her own over-meticulous behavior" so she might "refrain from driving her son towards" the undesirable conduct. After three months, the mother reported improvement in her own behavior as well as the child's, and she promised "to continue her parent education through active participation in a study group." Her son's "feminine" qualities, of course, did not need fixing, but the solution—accepting responsibility for his individuality—called for "enlightened" parenting rather than empathy.[9]

The CSA's main competitor was the National Congress of Mothers, now known as the National Parent Teacher Association. According to Hannah Schoff, president from 1902 to 1920, the congress worked to "deepen the influence of fathers and mothers" through an "educated parenthood." Both President Schoff and Theodore Roosevelt, who served as chair of the organization's advisory council from 1900 to 1919, argued that childhood was being endangered by the Progressive Era's "new woman," a harmful outgrowth of an urbanized, consumer society. They viewed white women who pursued identities beyond that of mother as key factors in "race suicide," a belief that the decline in the white, native-born fertility rate was threatening the racial stock of the nation because of the relatively high birthrates among immigrant women. The PTA's conservative leadership believed education in "intelligent home-making and child-nurture" would strengthen the white middle class's dominance over society.[10]

The congress evolved into the PTA after its leaders found that each city's "well organized school system" furnished an efficient means to introduce child study into every home. This strategy led to a rapid expansion of the organization from fewer than 200,000 members in 1920 to nearly 1.5 million by 1930.[11] During that decade, Bulus B. Swift, president of the national organization, pressed local PTAs to use their growing influence to guide urban policy as well as to educate parents: "Count every Parent-Teacher Association a failure unless" it makes "our communities, cities, and state more wholesome places for rearing all children."[12] Indeed, school-based PTAs played a critical role in the success of the building programs of the 1920s. Black parents participated through their own parallel movement, thereby rejecting white paternalism. In 1919, Atlanta's Selena Sloan Butler formed the Georgia Congress of Colored Parents and Teachers with only minimal assistance from the national organization and then went on to establish the National Congress of Colored Parents and Teachers in 1926.[13]

Butler's accomplishments built upon the solid foundation laid by Atlanta's Neighborhood Union, of which she was a member. From its inception in 1908, the Union sponsored regular "mothers' meetings" with lectures on assorted topics related to child health and development. Members also taught gardening classes and handed out prizes for "the best kept backyard and front yard" as part of their effort to promote more attractive play spaces. According to Louie Shivery, the recording secretary, "comparatively few" parents understood the importance of "properly planned and supervised play" in "developing the physical and moral life of their children." Members tackled the problem by demonstrating an assortment of family games and then instructing mothers to engage their children in "wholesome recreation" for at least an hour each day so they "would remain at home instead of in the streets."[14] Other Black settlement houses soon followed the Union's lead. For example, the Southwest Settlement House in Washington, DC, partnered with Howard University to offer parenting classes.[15]

Black clubwomen supported parent education at the national level as well. Referring to child-rearing as a "science as exact as mathematics," the Women's Convention of the Black Baptist Convention encouraged its members to engage in the scientific "study of youth." In 1914, it formed a committee on "child welfare and juvenile delinquency." After reviewing the latest social science research, the committee concluded that delinquency was the consequence of poor parenting as much as inadequate schools or a lack of playgrounds.[16] Additionally, the National Association of Colored Women (NACW), of which Selena Sloan Butler was a founding member, sponsored a "program of adult education for mothers and fathers." The organization urged Black families to purchase single-family homes that would function as "places in which children may be born and have the proper cultural background." During the early 1930s, its "Department of Mother, Home and Child" distributed an extensive questionnaire on "home life" that included the following questions: "Are you a companion for your children?," "Do you visit the schools?," "Do you take the parent's magazine?," and "Do you own your own home?"[17]

Although rarely acknowledged, the work of southern Black clubwomen often preceded that of their white counterparts as parent education spread outward from New York.[18] Over the course of the 1920s, more and more southern PTAs organized child-study groups, invited guest speakers to their meetings, and participated in regional conferences.[19] In 1927, North Carolina's governor presided over the first State-Wide Institute for Parental Education, which drew more than 600 attendees. The Department of Public Instruction, the Board of Health, the Board of Charities and Public Welfare, and four public universities cosponsored the event, along with the North Carolina PTA and the Federation of Women's Clubs. The president of the PTA portrayed the movement as "a serious need" for the "best development" of the "school and community" as well as the child. She insisted, "Parents should know their jobs as parents as well as teachers know theirs as teachers."[20] Because parent education mostly appealed to middle-class adherents and was organized at the school level, its impact became concentrated in schools serving affluent families, usually within residential parks.[21]

It is difficult to disentangle the multiple ways that residential park advertisements and the parent education movement inspired each other, but developers unquestionably used parent education to their advantage, reinforcing the movement while also benefitting from it. A 1910 brochure for Woodland Heights highlighted its "Mother's Club" as a selling point.[22] Other ads assured young couples that moving to a child-centered residential park would make them better parents. For instance, a full-page ad for Winston-Salem's Central Terrace claimed that "happy" memories of one's "childhood home" would induce even "tired, worn and worried" fathers to "get down on the floor" and "romp and play" with their children as the parenting experts had advised them to do (see figure 9.1). In large font splashed across the middle of the page, it asked, "Have You Provided a Home for Your Own Babies?" In another example, an ad for Winston-Salem's Ardmore referenced parent education directly: "Students of child life say that children, during their impressionable years, are greatly influenced by their surroundings, and here in Ardmore there is nothing but what tends toward refinement and mental uplift. The pretty homes, beauty in environment [sic], clear skies and pure air are all certain to bring out what is best in the child."[23] Likewise, the *Baltimore Sun*'s real estate page promised that an owner-occupied, single-family house would entice children to remain safe at home. It asserted, "The child of the home owner is far more apt to be a home lover than the boy or girl reared in an apartment or rented house" and manifest "greater love for their community and country," too.[24]

A Friend in Washington

As secretary of commerce, Herbert Hoover encouraged the organizers of local "Own-Your-Own-Home" (OYOH) campaigns to incorporate the rhetoric of parent educators into their marketing materials.[25] Perhaps this advocacy is why the principles of child study so clearly pervaded the OYOH posters and pamphlets produced in 1922 by the Henry Holmes Company, self-described "specialists in real estate advertising." One poster showed a pleasant-looking white mother blissfully reading to her young children. The open window filled the room with fresh air and natural light, and the furnishings included round-cornered tables to prevent injuries, as parenting experts advised. The accompanying text reminded parents that "the character of a man" was built upon the "foundation of Home love" and "a Mother's care." In another example, a pamphlet asked parents, "Are you rearing your family in a home of your own—where surroundings and associations will develop the best there is in your children?"[26]

The National Association of Real Estate Boards (NAREB) had launched the original "Own-Your-Home" campaign just before US entry into World War I. In 1919, the Department of Labor's US Housing Corporation (USHC) revived the movement—renamed "Own-Your-Own Home"—in hopes of avoiding a postwar recession while addressing the national housing crisis caused by rapid urbanization during the war. The USHC disseminated OYOH literature, provided copy for newspaper and magazine articles, and concocted a variety of creative advertising ploys, such as contests designed to "stimulate the 'own-a-home' desire." Working

Home, Sweet Home

JOHN HOWARD PAYNE touched the tenderest chord in the human heart when he wrote "Home, Sweet Home." It is sung in every land and in every tongue. It brings back the happy days of childhood. It has been the means of bringing back thoughts of home ties that have made the wanderer return and the wrongdoer to change his life. It has done more, for it has put into the heart of every man and woman a desire for a home. No matter when or where you hear it, your pulses quicken and your heart leaps. Have you never gone home tired, worn and worried after a hard day in the office, factory or counting room, and after the evening meal go for a walk in the moonlight where you could be alone, away from everybody and everthing; where you could think as you walked and refresh and rest your frayed nerves and your tired mind, and suddenly came upon a cozy little home with hollyhocks growing before the door? Music greets you and it falls like a balm upon your ears, for the strains of "Home, Sweet Home" come floating to you on the night breezes, and as you pause you are rapt into a reverie. The tired look leaves your eyes, every wrinkle in your face is rubbed out, you are no longer a world-worn, tired man. A sparkle flashes into your eyes, your brow is shadowed again with brown curls that hang about your shoulders as gracefully as the delicate tendrils of the wild grapevine that climbs the highest tree, and you are swept back across the flood of vanished years to your childhood home. As you draw near you hear the old songs your mother used to sing, old familiar scenes half forgotten leap afresh into your memory and you walk up on the porch and gaze through the dusty widnow panes. Silence is there. Through the empty rooms come no sound save the echo of a suppressed sob as you awake and find it all a dream. But you are a better man for having heard this beautiful melody. Your step becomes light and firm, your heart beats a little faster and you go home. You are affectionate with your wife and babies; you get down on the floor and romp and play with your boy and girl, and you sleep better that night. Just the memory of your old childhood home brought all those lofty emotions and you became just a little more human.

Have You Provided A Home For Your Own Babies?

So that they too will know the blessings of a childhood home and cherish it as their fondest memory long after the sombre curtain of night has hidden you from their eyes. You can give them a home and have one for yourself when the evening of life comes, when you can forget the shadows, the rains, and the storms of life; a home for your wife and babies built by the hand of Love that will leave its reflection here to bless them after you have gone and will implant in their hearts the real significance of "Home, Sweet Home."

Start now and buy a lot in

Central Terrace
"The Beautiful Residence Section On Southside"

CENTRAL TERRACE is an ideal place to build and ideal home. It is removed from the din and dust of the city; exempt from city taxes and yet has all conveniences and advantages of the city—cement sidewalks, electric lights, sewerage, water, und a splendid street car service. Call Mr. Wright at Wright's shoe store. He will be glad to show you beautiful CENTRAL TERRACE, a home-like section for home-loving people.

FIGURE 9.1. The developers of Central Terrace used sentimental advertising to encourage fathers to buy a suburban home for their children: "Have You Provided a Home for Your Own Babies? So that they too will know the blessings of a childhood home and cherish it as their fondest memory long after the sombre curtain of night has hidden you from their eyes." *Winston-Salem Journal*, 29 April 1917.

FIGURES 9.2A AND B.
The Henry Holmes Company produced advertising copy for local Own-Your-Own-Home campaigns that mirrored the advice of the parent education movement: "With every father and mother rests the responsibility of having a Real Home, around which will cling associations and memories to mould and guide the future of their children." Courtesy of the Birmingham, Ala. Public Library Archives. Used with permission.

FIGURE 9.3. After World War I, the US Department of Labor printed a series of posters to stimulate homebuilding among working-class families. The appeals that specifically targeted parents were far more likely to be effective than those that promoted worker productivity or reflected the hysteria of the red scare. Courtesy of the Library of Congress.

in collaboration with the real estate industry and local boosters, it reached out to newspaper editors, school administrators, and bankers for help. Although the campaign experimented with various appeals for increasing homeownership, the chief strategy was to "make the family man who does not own his own home as uncomfortable as possible."[27] Thus, ties to child-rearing permeated much of the propaganda.

The campaign materials usually assumed husbands would be the ones purchasing most new homes, but other family members might be relied upon to apply pressure to the presumed head of household. For example, the USHC sought support from the General Federation of Women's Clubs to convince more families that "actual ownership offers the only channel through which" parents might ensure "a desirable neighborhood and proper environment in which to rear children." Much of the advertising copy followed the same line of thinking. One questioned, "What is there in renting to appeal to any thinking Mother and Home-Maker?"

"Nothing!" was the firm reply. "The neighborhood may be a thorn in your side; unfit to rear children in." Another spoke indirectly to parents through their offspring: "Your father and mother want you to be healthy and strong. Now, in Oakland, California a doctor measured a lot of little boys and girls not long ago, and the children whose fathers and mothers lived in their own homes were bigger and stronger and smarter than others whose parents were not so well situated." "When you live in a nice home you progress faster at school," it continued. The neighborhood will have "a lot of nice playmates, nice children your own father and mother will be glad to have you play and go with, if they choose it rightly."[28]

Despite the full-court press, the USHC's short-lived campaign did not dim the popularity of modern apartments. In some cities, the construction of apartment homes outpaced single-family houses. At NAREB's 1921 annual meeting, the housing committee called for a new OYOH campaign organized through local real estate boards. Herbert Hoover's Commerce Department enthusiastically backed the effort, especially the ongoing commitment to tying single-family housing to middle-class child-rearing.[29] The following year, the Atlanta real estate board sponsored an OYOH week coinciding with passage of the city's racial zoning scheme and the beginning of its school building program. The culminating event, a segregated "Own-Your-Home Exposition," was designed to attract families with children. One exhibit featured an "exquisite" playhouse "to be given away at the close of the show," causing a constant "crush" of children "about the display." The *Constitution* dedicated a whole paragraph to the "the little house," which it described as "complete in every detail, even to the roses which grow over the trellis before the door and beside the windows."[30]

The Birmingham Real Estate Board's 1925 OYOH exposition also targeted parents.[31] In publicizing the campaign, the secretary of the real estate board declared, "The primary value of a home lies in the safeguards and environment it throws about children while they are at the impressionable age." "The strongest argument in favor of home-ownership," he continued, was "the inevitable tendency of man to hark back to the associates and environment of childhood." A home in a residential park gave parents the "opportunity to develop in the child a character" that would "stand ready and resolute through the vicissitudes of later life." The real estate board optimistically expected 125,000 visitors out of a total population of only 200,000, with more than a third of those excluded because of their race. At the end of the week, the organizers hosted a "children's day" so that kids could explore the "veritable fairyland" of "model bungalows" on "landscaped miniature plots" while unrestrained by their parents, who would, in turn, be delighted by their children's excitement.[32]

The handbook *How to Own Your Own Home* (1923)—prepared by John Gries, chief of the Division of Building and Housing within Hoover's Commerce Department—further endorsed child-centered approaches. Hoover's foreword declared, "A family that owns its home" has a "more wholesome, healthful, and happy atmosphere in which to bring up children." On the first page, Gries insisted that "the buying or building of a home deserved serious consideration," not only because it was a "large" financial commitment but because it would "probably determine the neighborhood in which his [the homebuyer's] children will be reared." He advised parents to investigate the location of parks and playgrounds, reminding them that "wholesome outdoor play" was "the birthright that few care to see their own children deprived of." Conversely, traditional values such as living "close to relatives and friends" should *not* "be given too much weight." Instead, the "general type of people living in the neighborhood" was more important, especially for children "who should be brought up in the right kind of surroundings."[33]

Some who coopted the rhetoric of parent education did so primarily because it was effective at selling residential property, but others, such as Hoover, were true believers, convinced that scientific evidence had confirmed the advantages of suburban living for children. The industry insiders who promoted for-profit OYOH campaigns likely represented the former, but the nonprofit Better Homes movement represented the latter. In 1922, the popularity of OYOH weeks inspired Marie Meloney, editor of the popular woman's magazine *The Delineator*, to launch Better Homes in America (BHA). Her new organization received a $300,000 grant from the Laura Spelman Rockefeller Memorial, the principal funder of parent education. She also rallied support from the General Federation of Women's Clubs, local chambers of commerce, churches, schools, and the Girls Scouts. At its peak, BHA boasted 30,000 members participating in 9,000 cities and towns.[34]

Harvard sociologist James Ford, the former manager of Wilson's US Housing Corporation and the brother of internationally renowned planner George B. Ford, served as the executive director for BHA. He outlined the organization's mission in *The Better Homes Manual* (1931): "The first essential is that every growing child should be able to grow up in a private dwelling, located in a convenient, quiet, attractive and wholesome neighborhood. No tenement or apartment, even in the so-called 'model' class, can meet as well the deeper needs of childhood." Along with many parenting experts, he linked childhood experiences to the future success of the nation. "If we are to have social progress," he argued, children's "opportunities for good health and for physical, intellectual, and moral growth must be superior to those enjoyed by their parents."[35] In 1931, President Hoover demonstrated further confidence in the organization and its ideals when he tapped Ford for associate director of the White House Conference on Home Building and Home Ownership.

BHA was a classic example of Hoover's "voluntary associationalism," a philosophy that relied on an assortment of public-private partnerships to advance his priorities. Hoover served as president of BHA's board of directors, continuing in this role even after his election to the US presidency six years later. The board also included John Gries, chief of the Division of Building and Housing within the Commerce Department, who prepared *How to Own Your Own Home*; Grace Abbott, chief of the US Children's Bureau; and President Coolidge himself along with most of his cabinet, too. This impressive list of government officials was joined by industry representatives from the US Chamber of Commerce, the Architects' Small House Service Bureau, and the American Civic Association. Lawrence Veiller and John Ihlder, two prominent housing reformers with close ties to the planning movement, also served. Additionally, the board had representation from the General Federation of Women's Clubs and the American Home Economics Association.[36]

Perhaps the greatest achievement of the Better Homes movement was the annual competition to design, build, and decorate innovative demonstration houses for local exhibition. The national BHA awarded prizes for the best conceived homes. In 1924, the first-place winner, chosen from more than 1,000 entries, was "Everyman's House," designed by nationally known reformer Caroline Bartlett Crane of Kalamazoo, Michigan. Crane's goal was to build a "decent, attractive," and efficient "little house" that would function as "a modest-cost plan of comfort and convenience for a mother of several children, including a baby." The efficiencies incorporated into the architectural plan were intended to preserve the mother's energy for her most important duty: child-rearing. According to Crane, the "productive business" of homemaking required "a better place" for the mother's "part of the firm's business," which was "raising and cultivating their crop of children." Similarly, her architect referred to the house as "a plant for the manufacture of good citizens." The private bedrooms and a well-appointed recreation room were arranged to serve as "magnets" to keep the older children safe at home. "Mother likes to know where her" children are, Crane explained, particularly "the sex that mothers find the hardest to hold against the call of the wild streets and wilder bypaths."[37]

BHA also gave out awards for outstanding demonstration houses designed by Black committees, whose members received far less financial assistance for their efforts. Their white counterparts could thank an array of professionals and businessmen who donated virtually everything from the site and the blueprints to the building materials and the furnishings; after all, demonstration houses were golden opportunities to advertise to the tens of thousands of people who would tour them or, at the very least, read about them in the newspaper. By contrast, Black committees were forced to rely on help from school children to make modest improvements such as cleaning yards, painting houses, erecting fences, creating gardens, sewing curtains, or completing minor repairs. The national BHA sanctioned gross inequality when it presented awards to Black committees for relatively small renovation projects. One year it patronizingly recognized a committee from Little Rock, Arkansas, for upgrading a "run-down," three-room rental shack into "a creditable cottage."[38]

The Neighborhood Union's demonstration houses were different. Having already shown a tenacious commitment to improving Black housing long before the founding of BHA, the Union was a natural fit for the Better Homes competition. It had access to significantly more resources than other Black committees because of its well-established interracial networks and impressive record of accomplishments. The Union's 1924 demonstration house was located just a block from the new Booker T. Washington High School. Heman Perry's Service Realty Corporation contributed the lot and built the home. The Union also received donations from the Georgia Power Company, the telephone company, and local furniture dealers. The following year, Union members placed their demonstration house in a mixed-race slum, reflecting their deep commitment to improving all Black homes and not just those of the city's wealthiest Black families. The city council contributed to the effort by agreeing to pave the street.[39]

Each of the Union's demonstration houses were part of a larger collaboration with the Atlanta Better Homes Committee, which had representatives from various civic organizations and government entities including the local real estate board and the school district. Atlanta's entries received third place in 1923, second place in 1924, and first place in 1925. The first two award-winning entries encompassed three demonstration houses: the Union's contribution along with two white homes for families of different income levels. Beginning in 1925, the committee increased the number of "demonstrations" to five. The *Constitution* described "No.1" as a "home for white people," "No. 2" as an "Americanization apartment for our new citizens," "No. 3" as a "home for negroes," and 4 and 5 as racially segregated "school practice apartments." "No. 3," the Union's contribution, received much of the credit for Atlanta's success that year. The judges especially praised its backyard play space with a sandbox, a child's gardening set, and two windmills.[40]

In 1926, Councilman Orme's North Boulevard Park was selected as the site for Atlanta's "Better Home No. 1."[41] The *Constitution* styled the house as a "charming bungalow, situated [on] land offered for this purpose by A. J. Orme." Its lot sat idyllically "among tall pines" across from "one of Atlanta's little parks." The PTA of North Boulevard's Sam Inman School played "an outstanding part" in the creation of the exhibit. The BHA committee invited the school superintendent, himself a member of Inman's PTA, "to turn the first sod" at the public cornerstone laying while the president of the chamber of commerce served as master of ceremonies. The committee chair hoped the exhibit would help develop "the new idea of a small and compact community within a big city." She commended the residents of North Boulevard Park for displaying "all the charm and neighborliness of a small community, where everyone knows the other." After its triumph, the committee kept "Better Home No. 1" open for an extra week so that the delegates attending the annual meeting of the National Parent Teacher Association, which took place in Atlanta that year, could admire the house and its neighborhood.[42]

Parents' Magazine and White Liberalism

As BHA's influence peaked, child-rearing advice distributed through academic publications and the press began to eclipse the centrality of the informal mothers' groups in which parents shared wisdom they had gained through personal experience. The number of academic studies on child development increased from only a handful during World War I to 600 by 1930.[43] The executive secretary of the National Council of Parent Education, Flora Thurston, applauded the "spectacular increase in popular and scientific literature" in her subcommittee report for Hoover's 1931 Conference on Child Health and Protection: "Not more than ten years ago the books, bulletins, and articles devoted to the problems of parents numbered only a few each year. Five years ago they were available in dozens, while during the past year literally hundreds of books, pamphlets, and articles have been produced on a fairly wide variety of child and family topics." Popular women's magazines such as *The Ladies' Home Journal*, *McCall's*, and *Good Housekeeping* also regularly published articles related to parent education while local newspapers and radio broadcasts spread the message to even more families.[44]

The most influential outlet was *Parents' Magazine*, a new commercial publication that burst forth in 1926 to disseminate the latest research on child-rearing. As with most efforts related to parent education, a $50,000 grant from the Laura Spelman Rockefeller Memorial launched the magazine. Although the foundation avoided public association with the project, its board wished to preserve control over editorial decisions, which were to be grounded in scientific evidence rather than veer off into the consumer-driven world of women's magazines. CSA director Sidonie Gruenberg sat on the board of editors, along with five PhDs and one MD. In addition, several of the advisory editors served in government positions and overlapped with Better Homes in America, including Louise Stanley, head of the Bureau of Home Economics, and Grace Abbott, director of the Children's Bureau.[45]

Accordingly, the magazine's mission incorporated the motivation and assumptions of the larger movement. Publisher George Hecht's opening editorial stated, "If this publication does nothing more than make parents realize that the care and training of children is a complicated, difficult task, as well as a joy, one that challenges their best thought and requires a certain amount of specialized knowledge, it will, we believe, be more than justified."[46] The magazine was not just for mothers, either. A central goal of parent education was to prod fathers into taking a more active role in child-rearing. Articles such as "Can a Tired Businessman Be a Good Father?" were regular features from the first year of publication.[47] Despite the economic collapse that soon followed its debut, subscriptions soared; it was the only magazine to increase its advertising revenue and circulation every year of the Depression, demonstrating the extent to which its message resonated with middle-class families.[48]

Since parent educators worried that urbanization was weakening the home's appeal, single-family housing remained an essential facet of "the care and training of children," as Caroline Crane's reasoning for Everyman's House indicated. The experts agreed that the perfect antidote to free-roaming children was a well-endowed playroom or recreation room, depending on the children's ages. "Practically every house has space" if only "Mother and Father will realize the importance of doing so," one article prompted. "If you are planning a house, be sure to plan a playroom for the children. If you already have a house, see if you can't find a way to turn over a room for play." The author suggested an attic room as a possibility for small houses: "The cost of the attic is an important item, but where there are children, worth exceeds the cost." Another article described an elaborate basement recreation room set up to appeal to adolescents and their friends. It boasted such costly items as a dartboard, ping-pong table, and movie projector, even though it was the height of the Depression.[49] Such recommendations assumed that all child-rearing took place in a land of abundance.

From its inception, *Parents' Magazine* blended expertise and consumerism so thoroughly it became difficult to separate one from the other. By the 1920s, play had become irretrievably tied to consumption. The toy industry grew rapidly during the early twentieth century: Lionel electric trains appeared in 1906, Erector sets in 1913, Tinkertoys in 1914, and Lincoln Logs in 1916.[50] Toy experts encouraged middle-class children to explore the adult world through make-believe rather than learn gendered tasks by simply helping their parents. In the article "What Toys for Your Children?," the author praised "Jean's mother" for buying her daughter "a miniature washing set, tub, washboard, ironing board, small electric iron, clothesline and clothespins." "If you could see Jean playing," she gushed, "you would think it is the best kind of play." Jean and her friends "do all the things that Jean's mother does" and learned "to do them the right way" since her mother took the "time to play with them." In another example, *Best Toys and Their Selection* scorned "poorly made, inappropriate toys" as "an insult to the child for whom" they were purchased. Tucked within the pages of the article was an advertisement captioned, "Playthings *are* Textbooks of Childhood."[51]

In this way, the magazine's advertisements seamlessly copied the language of parenting experts. Ads for StromBecKer PlayThings echoed the advice of the articles they sat adjacent to: "Your children's playthings are the tools which they use to reconstruct their environment. Properly selected playthings develop the child's powers of imagination, concentration, comparison, selection, and creation."[52] Although CSA consultants frequently advised parents to provide stimulating toys that would spark curiosity, discovery, and experimentation, the toy industry's mimicry of child-rearing expertise alarmed Sidonie Gruenberg. She worried that parenting decisions were increasingly based on advertising rather than actual scientific research. "In the name of the children we are urged to buy all sorts of products," she lamented, "the chief merits of which seem to lie in the attractive labels reminding one of the latest scrap of scientific jargon."[53] Despite her concerns, the magazine's articles were more likely to persuade middle-class parents to fill their single-family homes with child-centered products than to question blind consumerism.

The racial attitudes presented in *Parents' Magazine* were equally conflicted. Though the National PTA embraced the more conservative aspects of parent education, CSA reflected the more liberal "cultural gifts" movement. According to historian Diana Selig, the movement involved "hundreds of thousands of Americans" who "welcomed heterogeneity as a source of strength for the nation," believing all cultural groups had "gifts" worth sharing. *Race Attitudes in Children* (1929), written by Gruenberg's friend Bruno Lasker, served as the unofficial handbook for the movement. Because race hatred was learned in childhood, enlisting parent education in the fight against prejudice seemed logical. Thus, Lasker cited Gruenberg's work multiple times, and she sat on the book's advisory committee. Their message spread quickly. Not long after the book was published, Lugenia Burns Hope, the founder of the Neighborhood Union, gave a talk titled "Race Attitudes in Children" to Atlanta's Commission on Interracial Cooperation.[54]

Lasker was also one of few white people to publicly criticize Atlanta's racial zoning scheme when it was originally proposed. Calling it dangerous and undemocratic, he argued that further residential segregation would increase racial hostility by preventing children from interacting with diverse people in ways that might break down stereotypes. Children were "born democrats," he explained, but their "observation of the way grown-up people live and behave" imparted a "knowledge of race differences" that led to animosity. When children saw "that people of dark skin are 'jim-crowed' or that they occupy a different part of town," they learned to "associate race and nationality with social status and, failing contrary experiences, to look upon that association as permanent, inevitable and part of the divine plan that rules the relationship of men." School segregation had an analogous effect: "The fact that children of another color do not go to the same school as they do is a lesson which is ineradicable if it extends through the whole period of school attendance."[55]

Parents' Magazine published several articles written by Lasker and other supporters of the cultural gifts movement. In one titled "How Children Acquire Race Prejudices" (1928), Lasker admonished, "The development of race attitudes in children normally represents the attitudes which society—or the section of society nearest them—wants them to hold." Interracial experiences, however, offered some hope: "Sometimes the miscellaneous lessons, that have, almost unconsciously, been absorbed from the environment in earlier childhood, are by the more intelligent adolescent, subjected to questioning." A reflective young person might ask, "Should I take my ideas of Jews from the comic strips or from the Cohens and other families of school fellows who I know quite well?" or "Why are Negroes barred from school?" Likewise, in an article titled "Should We Hand-Pick Our Children's Friends?" (1929), a different author scolded parents who would "unload on their children their particular prejudices." She encouraged parents to support childhood friendships with "Chinamen, Jews, Catholics, or Negroes" to actively confront society's pervasive stereotypes.[56]

Both CSA and *Parents' Magazine* taught tolerance to white families through articles written by white authors rather than disseminating the work of Black authors or cultivating real-world interactions across race. The CSA made some effort to maintain contact with Black parent educators, but few Black experts, if any, appeared in their monthly magazine, *Child Study*. Indeed, the CSA seemed more comfortable *studying* nonwhite groups than working with them. The organization had no Black staff, let alone Black leadership, although it did create an "Inter-Community Child Study Committee" to paternalistically "extend" segregated study groups to Black parents, ignoring the fact that Black clubwomen had long organized child study groups without their help.[57]

In many ways, *Parents' Magazine* perfectly illustrated the limitations of CSA's racial "work" as well as the limited goals of the cultural gifts movement.[58] Its more liberal espousals were almost always overshadowed by the articles and advertisements that uncritically accepted the racial stereotypes ubiquitous in popular consumer culture. One contributor who set out to prove that no child was "just naturally born bad" presented her case through demeaning stereotypes and assumptions. Portraying herself as an investigator, she went in search of a "born criminal" at a school serving the "second-worst slum" in town. The school's principal produced a boy named George Washington Woolly, whom the author characterized as "almost blue-black" with "a face that belongs with a luscious watermelon." She added meanly, "George Washington may have been a misnomer but Woolly was right."[59]

Her treatment of the boy's mother was even worse. She callously described her as "a Zulu warrior, nearly six feet in height, broad, black, fierce, a prowling panther of a woman," who had broken every parenting rule (see figure 9.4). She had "buried" ten children; she was ignorant (the author had her speaking in dialect); she used corporal punishment; she bought no toys for her children; and she denied them time to play since, as a poorly paid washerwoman, she needed their help. Worst of all, she rejected parent education: "You couldn't teach *her* anything about bringing up children." When the boy revealed that he had no toys that had been purchased specifically for him, poverty was not to blame, but his mother's

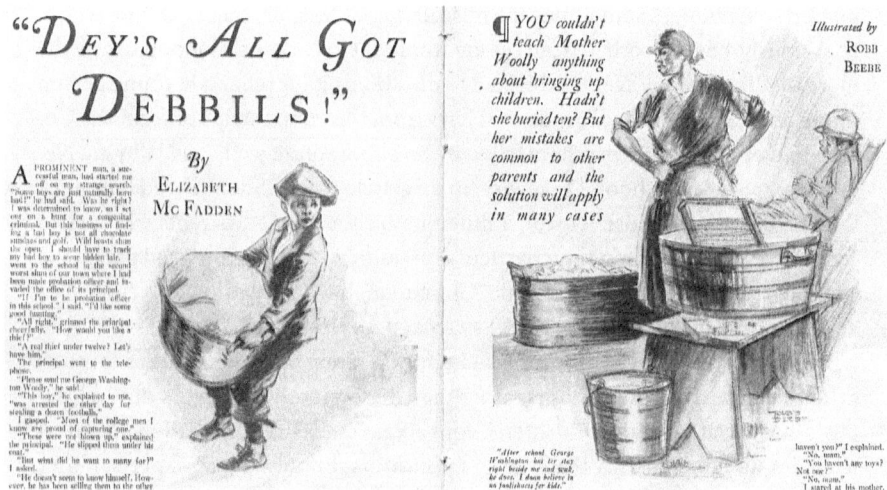

FIGURE 9.4. According to "Dey's All Got Debbils!," juvenile delinquency was the result of bad parenting since all children were born naturally good. The author built her case by ridiculing a Black mother who had supposedly ignored all the dictates of parent education. *Parents' Magazine*, October 1929. Courtesy of the Joseph Regenstein Library, University of Chicago.

FIGURE 9.5. In contrast to fig. 9.4, "For Better or Worse—Servants Influence Children" portrayed a Black "mammy" as soft, loving, and good-natured while she cooked for the white family and entertained the children. Of course, poorly paid domestics could not care for their own children while at work or afford to pay for childcare, a dire situation that led to the establishment of Black settlement houses such as the Neighborhood Union. *Parents' Magazine*, January 1929. Courtesy of the Joseph Regenstein Library, University of Chicago.

neglect. The author threatened to arrest her if she failed to buy her son a toy and let him play for at least two hours a day, supposing this would make him "a man of property" and "a responsible and happy citizen."[60] The author expressed no sympathy for how hard a washerwoman was forced to work or how negligible the pay was. Instead, she seemed clueless about the near impossibility of purchasing the costly toys marketed in *Parents' Magazine* or the fear Black mothers must instill in their sons to keep them alive in a nation governed by white supremacy.

This article contained the only mention of a Black parent during the magazine's first years of publication; most relegated Black adults to servile positions. For instance, "For Better or Worse—Servants Influence Children" reinforced the white assumption that Black women were servants rather than mothers. The accompanying illustration showed a "mammy," round faced and loving, holding a spoon in one hand with the other outstretched to the white children she was tending (see figure 9.5). As a servant, she was represented as soft and nonthreatening in contrast to the "fierce" and warrior-like mother pictured above. The purpose of the article was to advise white mothers on how best to foster a "satisfactory relationship" between their children and their domestic help so that a servant's "foolishness" would not undermine the hard work of enlightened parents. The author recommended "constant supervision of the maid" who was "much with the children." The "thoughtful modern woman," she lectured, must "sacrifice" her "time and energy" and exhibit "infinite patience" to keep her servant from corrupting her children.[61] Catharine Beecher could not have said it better.

Liberal parent educators were much more likely to sympathize with white ethnic immigrants and religious minorities than to recognize the effect of racial subjugation on Black families.[62] In 1927, the magazine celebrated the Fourth of July with a photo essay titled "Americans in the Making," which did, at least, acknowledge the diversity of American childhood (see figure 9.6). The captions depicted immigrant children as upwardly mobile while romanticizing Indigenous children as being "from one of America's first families." Black children, however, were portrayed as content in their ignorance and poverty with a denigrating caption that read: "Way down south in the land of cotton days are long and sunny and pickaninnies follow the example of Topsy who 'just growed.'" The barefoot children stood on the front steps of a house that would have horrified any urban reformer.[63] According to the "pickaninny" stereotype, even the youngest Black child felt neither physical nor emotional pain, and therefore, did not need protection, let alone safe housing or decent schools. Tragically, whatever the dominant society considered an absolute necessity for a white child was thought wholly unnecessary for a Black one.[64]

Consumer culture was responsible for some of the most humiliating and ubiquitous stereotypes; Black children could hardly avoid seeing the demeaning images along with everyone else.[65] During the late nineteenth and early twentieth

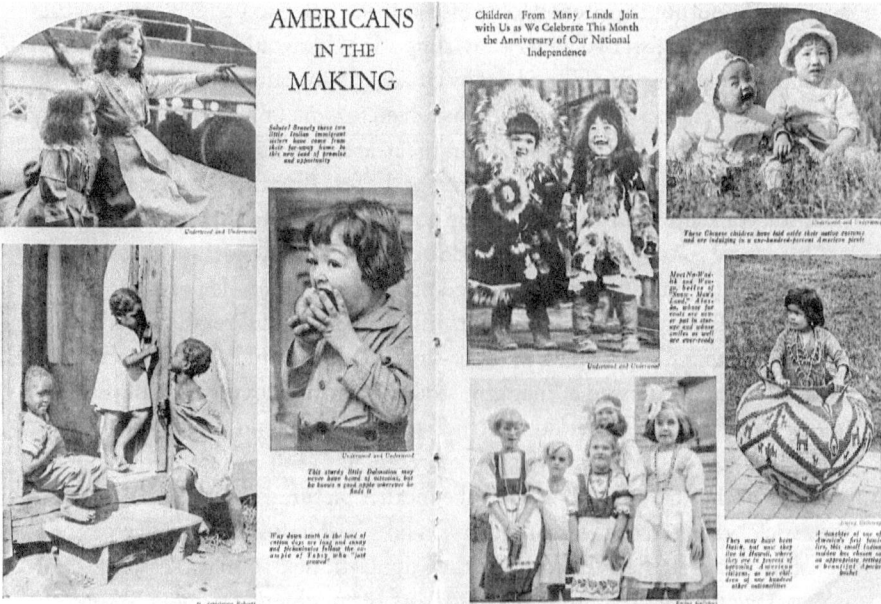

FIGURE 9.6. To celebrate Independence Day, "Americans in the Making" applauded various Americanization efforts aimed at young children, yet the Black children pictured on the first page were wholly left out of the citizenship project. Included as comic relief, their demeaning caption reinforced the typical disrespect shown to Black parents in other articles: "Way down south in the land of cotton days are long and sunny and pickaninnies follow the example of Topsy, who 'just growed.'" *Parents' Magazine*, July 1927. Courtesy of the Joseph Regenstein Library, University of Chicago.

centuries, "trading card" advertisements were meant to be collected and displayed. Advertisers selected artwork that would appeal to white, middle-class mothers—the targeted consumer—with sentimental depictions of white children alongside devastating depictions of Black ones. In one example, a turn-of-the-century trading card for Fleishman's Yeast pictured three young white girls in colonial garb: one English, one Dutch, and one French (see figure 9.7). The English and Dutch girls wear lovely dresses and carry beautiful dolls. The French girl, also beautifully dressed, holds a kitten for her "baby," making her the center of attention. A young Black child stands in the forefront of the image, removed from the other girls both physically and socially. She is ill-dressed and holds a shabby, homemade rag doll. A Japanese child is also present. She, too, is excluded from the white girls' intimate huddle, but she stands next to them, and her clothing and doll are equally elaborate. Her "exotic" image represents the divide between Eastern and Western civilization, but she is not altogether excluded like the Black toddler, who has no culture to guide her.[66]

FIGURE 9.7. This Fleischmann's Yeast trading card, which was printed at the turn of the century, encapsulates the exclusion of Black children from the sentimental ideals of childhood. Images such as this one helped normalize the policies and practices that promoted segregation. Courtesy of the Warshaw Collection of Business Americana—Yeast, Archives Center, National Museum of American History, Smithsonian Institution. Used with permission.

In 1920, W. E. B. Du Bois challenged the crushing stereotypes of consumer culture by expanding the children's page of *The Crisis* into a glossy monthly magazine titled *The Brownies' Book*, designed for kids aged six to sixteen. He wanted Black children to see reflections of themselves as happy, healthy, high achieving, and beautiful (see figure 9.8). The magazine contained games, artwork, the "race history of great Black Americans," stories, songs, and poetry—almost all of which were created by Black artists and authors, including a teenaged Langston Hughes. The column "Little People of the Month" highlighted the impressive accomplishments of Black children from around the country. One issue featured Helena Harper of Sacramento, who won an essay contest on "Why We Need New School Buildings," beating out 5,000 entrants of all races. In addition, each issue incorporated stunning photographs of well-dressed, playful children and, during the summer, portraits of smiling high school graduates. One of them was Langston Hughes, "class poet" and yearbook editor for his integrated Cleveland high school.[67]

The Brownies' Book was an important tool for Black middle-class parents, but

LITTLE PEOPLE OF THE MONTH

Little Fairies

YES, these are truly little fairies,— not the make-believe fairies of the story book, but real fairies who get lots of happiness out of doing good for others.

These little girls are members of Miss Amanda Kemp's Dancing Class and because they are so tiny and dance so well, they are known as Miss Kemp's Dancing Dolls.

There are many children in New York whose fathers are dead and whose mothers must go out daily to work in order to keep the home together and give the little ones a proper education. The mother can take her children, if they are under seven years of age, to the Hope Day Nursery where they are properly cared for during the day.

The nurses in attendance see that the children left in their charge have the best care, with three meals a day and plenty of milk to make them grow strong. A play teacher teaches them

FIGURE 9.8. W. E. B. Du Bois filled the pages of *The Brownies' Book* with images of well-dressed, accomplished Black children. In this photograph, a Black "fairy" challenges the assumption that only white children belonged in "fairylands," an important counterbalance to the romanticized depictions of white children in advertisements for racially restricted residential parks. Courtesy of the Library of Congress.

because of wage discrimination, a magazine subscription for their children was a luxury many could ill afford. Aspiration and the politics of respectability identified them as middle class more so than their income level, and Black middle-class mothers were more likely to work outside the home than their white counterparts. Their low pay provided limited resources for engaging in intensive parenting, which they did before and after exhausting days at work.[68] Consequently, the circulation of *The Brownies' Book* never rose above 5,000 copies, while 12,000 subscribers were needed for the magazine to break even, which was all that Du Bois asked. Although a labor of love, reproducing the large number of high-quality photographs essential to its mission was expensive. Short on funds, the magazine ceased publication after two years.[69]

The Brownies' Book was also an important tool for liberal white parents, who might have saved it. A white father from Cambridge, Massachusetts, wrote a letter of appreciation after the magazine taught his child "that little girls that look entirely different from [her] like just the same things and so are like her." "Two or three" of his white friends were also subscribers, and he suspected that "many thousand" more would like their children to learn the same "indispensable lesson."[70] But white parents did not support Du Bois's effort beyond those few subscriptions.

They did, however, subscribe to *Parents' Magazine*, which, in the end, helped rationalize the exclusion of Black children more than it promoted tolerance. An article in the first issue advised parents to "become interested in your neighbors' children as well as in your own, for no child is exempt from the influence of his companions."[71] The author's objective was to increase support for PTA-sponsored parent education programs to ensure that all neighborhood children were raised properly. But his message struggled to compete with residential park advertisements promising parents a slew of "wise" restrictions that would screen all the neighborhood children for them. Wasn't that easier? And the cultural gifts movement, which stopped well short of either confronting racial injustice or examining its consequences, accepted this solution, even though restrictive covenants virtually guaranteed that even the vilest stereotypes could not be questioned through interracial friendships. Lasker was one of the few whites who spoke out against segregation.

The emphasis on racial tolerance allowed liberal white parents to condemn cruder forms of oppression without acknowledging the harm that they themselves were imposing. Walter White, executive secretary of the NAACP, accused even racially "progressive" schools—those that embraced the cultural gifts movement—of rejecting Black applicants because affluent white parents wanted their children to have the proper "social contacts" to "marry favorably."[72] In a similar critique, Lasker recognized the "growing parental watchfulness over the social contacts of girls soon to enter the marriageable age."[73] He insisted that interracial friendships from the same social class were necessary to counter stereotypes, yet those were the very relationships that segregation was meant to thwart to prevent amalgamation. During the Progressive Era, a popular advice book had instructed parents that, although interracial marriages would not be "sterile," the children would be "sickly and shortlived" with a "mental inferiority" that would be "likewise apparent"; any (white) woman "who would willingly curse her offspring" had "thoughts unnatural."[74] For centuries, the taboo against interracial relationships between Black men and white women sat at the core of white supremacy and, therefore, school and residential segregation. This fear overshadowed the few white voices advocating for something more meaningful than tolerance.

Although parent education's emphasis on environment would shift the focus of child development away from scientific racism, most of Lasker's liberal white audience ignored his critique of segregation and concentrated on changing "individual attitudes" instead.[75] Lasker himself was pessimistic about a curriculum's ability to offset structural racism that remained intact and unchallenged. "Children learn most of all through the observation of adult attitudes in circumstances when grown-ups are least conscious of being studied," he cautioned. White children would learn who belongs and who does not when they failed to "meet colored people in the same circumstances in which" they met white people.[76] Regardless of what they had been told or what they had read, white children would conclude that Black people were inferior because their homes, schools, and occupations were inferior. Despite this warning, the cultural gifts program rarely questioned the policies of racial subjugation and, thus, failed to ask why some Americans were denied the opportunity to develop their "gifts" through the same residential, educational, and career opportunities that affluent white children took for granted. As a result, white children growing up in some of the nation's most liberal homes failed to grasp the extent to which segregation provided them with unearned advantages—advantages that almost always came at someone else's expense.

During the 1920s, affluent white parents increasingly focused on their own trivial parenting problems from within the confines of their single-family houses, located within exclusive residential parks. The popularity of deed restrictions combined with single-family zoning helped white, middle-class families isolate their children from the misfortunes of others rather than seek effective ways to eliminate urban problems for all, as they had done in the past. According to historian Molly Ladd-Taylor, "In contrast to the Gilded Age and Progressive Era, when the ideal mother was portrayed as a 'social' mother involved in women's clubs and charities, the exemplary mother of the 1920s was focused on her own children."

Historian Stephanie Coontz also found a "turning inward to the family," which included a "repudiation of responsibility for other people's children."[77]

Racial subjugation denied Black women the luxury of turning their time, energy, and resources inward towards their own children. Tethered to race regardless of class status, Black middle-class women worked tirelessly to uplift other people's children while making every effort to provide greater opportunities for their own. Because Black men and women both lacked the political power needed to influence urban development on a scale that could effectively protect Black children from harm, let alone cultivate upward mobility, their work made Sisyphus's task look easy.

Meanwhile, the preoccupation with enlightened parenting allowed white, middle-class families, in all good conscience, to rationalize their self-interest by blaming poor outcomes on negligent parents rather than on economic instability, the unequal distribution of city resources, or environmental hazards. After all, the new scholarly consensus held that deficient parenting rather than poverty or uneven urban development was to blame for delinquency.[78] Once fault was laid squarely at the feet of individual parents, it became easier to justify the exclusion of other people's children through deed restrictions, which exacerbated the harms those children faced in their unprotected neighborhoods.

In 1932, Sidonie Gruenberg expressed discomfort with the tendency of white, middle-class families to look inward. "Since the chief concern of parents is the welfare of children, we must expect parent education to make men and women aware of the fact that they cannot advance the welfare of their own children except as they are willing to consider the welfare of all children," she urged. "In the end the welfare of our own children must be definitely and disastrously limited by the suffering and privation and deterioration that we permit any children to endure."[79] This admonition went largely unheeded in white homes. Parent education was a civic project that connected well to affluent white families' self-interest; white parents all too gladly concentrated their energy on ensuring that their homes, neighborhoods, and schools provided superior opportunities for their offspring. In the end, the movement to which Gruenberg dedicated her life shaped residential development in ways that went far afield from what she herself advocated, especially when the assumptions of parent education were used to justify strict zoning laws that further codified segregation.

CHAPTER 10

Child-Centered Zoning and *Euclid*

The ascendance of "intelligent" parenting within expertly designed houses located in carefully planned residential parks shaped twentieth-century urban development in the United States as much or more so than any other factor. The social scientists, educators, and medical doctors of the parent education movement convinced white, middle-class parents that urbanization put their children at risk. The solution was to withdraw their families to child-centered utopias on the outskirts of town. During the 1920s, local planning commissions looked to zoning laws to facilitate the retreat by aggressively rerouting residential development away from traditional mixed-race, mixed-income, and mixed-use neighborhoods. Mimicking the single-family house itself, zoning laws divided the city into single-use areas and made alternative visions of development illegal. According to housing reformer Madge Headley, the result was a city "as orderly as a well planned house," where "the necessary activities of industry, or commerce, and of family life, each have their appointed place."[1]

This was no easy accomplishment. During the ten years between 1916, when New York City passed the nation's first comprehensive zoning law, and 1926, when the US Supreme Court declared zoning ordinances constitutional in *Euclid v. Ambler*, zoning remained controversial. Commercial and industrial usage increased the value of property, creating opportunity for small-scale real estate speculators looking to replicate the success of large-scale developers, most of whom had already made fortunes through various other investments before embarking on residential park development. Furthermore, zoning defied one of the basic tenets of the Constitution: the right to private property, including the right to profit from that property through its use. Thus, zoning, along with all restrictions on alienation and occupancy, seemed to challenge American liberty at its core.

To convince a skeptical public, planners defended zoning, and especially the single-family district, using many of the same arguments that had effectively sold deed restrictions. By the first decade of the twentieth century, developers had persuaded affluent white parents to forgo some of their property rights in exchange for a superior environment in which to raise their children. Thus, residential park advertisements assured buyers that deed restrictions were protective rather than restrictive. During the 1920s, advocates of zoning would embrace similar language. For example, Lewis Ryon, civic engineer for Houston's planning commission, described the "aim" of zoning as "protection, not restriction." The strategy worked because the primary goal of zoning in most small to medium cities was to protect child-centered residential parks from encroachment.[2]

Planners also hoped to convince the courts that even single-family residential districts did not impose unconstitutional restraints on private property. At first, they suggested that "incompatible" uses, including the incursion of multifamily dwellings into an area of single-family houses, would lower the property value of stand-alone homes. But their opponents worried about the effect of restrictions on their property's earning potential. The Detroit Property Holders' Protective Association predicted that the enactment of the city's proposed zoning ordinance would "destroy many millions of dollars of present property values" and questioned "Who gains? Who benefits?"[3] To counter accusations such as this one that zoning would damage property values as well as undermine property rights, advocates alleged that zoning was, instead, the only way to stabilize them. Nonetheless, the courts repeatedly ruled that the protection of property values was not a valid use of the police power.

Advocates needed evidence that zoning was somehow grounded in the general welfare. Meanwhile, parent education and the Better Homes movement were reinforcing the supposition that neighborhoods of single-family homes were the ideal environment for raising children and, therefore, vital to preserving the nation's future. This belief ultimately persuaded the Supreme Court that zoning's protection of child health, safety, morals, and welfare *did* warrant use of the police power. James Metzenbaum, the chair of the Euclid planning committee who served as the village's attorney in the *Euclid* case, turned his defense of single-family zoning into a crusade for rescuing the "growing generation." Echoing the rhetoric of parent educators, he argued that child-rearing in communities of single-family homes resulted in "better children": "It means not merely comfort but greater safety for the children" and "a more vigorous generation due to plentifulness of fresh air and sunlight" along with fewer "accidents for the young ones because they have a yard in which to play instead of being compelled to resort to the streets." Additionally, parents would have "a greater relationship to the schools," an assertion that recognized the close connection between school building programs and zoning during the 1920s.[4]

Zoning and the Limits of Deed Restrictions

Most likely, a considerable number of developers and even planners were not driven by the desire to improve parenting or avert race suicide but rather viewed child-centered appeals as the most expedient way to steer zoning through the courts, much as it had been used to sell residential lots. After all, fashioning suburban developments for middle-class child-rearing had undoubtably increased the property values within residential parks. Conceivably, the arguments made about child development and good parenting were the only ones that could have superseded American ideals about individualism and the sanctity of private property. Middle-class parents had long been told that they must sacrifice for their children, and developers well understood the financial benefits of explaining their deed restrictions through that angle.

By the time *Euclid* began wending its way through the courts, child-centered advertising was justifying even the most extreme restrictions, including regulating the aesthetics of a neighborhood. J. C. Nichols, developer of Kansas City's Country Club Estates, admitted, "It probably would have been impracticable in the beginning to have controlled the design of a home, its color, its location, its elevation on a lot." Indeed, for most homeowners, the "infliction" of a neighbor's garage placed in an "improper location" was surely of much less concern than relinquishing that much control over their property. Child-rearing experts helped developers rationalize impositions that previously would have seemed unfathomable. For instance, an article in *Parents' Magazine* prompted families to fill their homes with tasteful art to push back against the tawdriness of consumer culture and, thereby, allow their children to become "normally developed human being[s]." The effort might include "a little landscape gardening," "the harmonious arrangements of a room," or sweeping away "decorations" that the children "have learned to scorn as ugly." "Once they have learned to appreciate the best they are safe from the appeal of the inferior," the author insisted. Likewise, an ad for Palos Verdes Estates in suburban Los Angeles presented its architectural review of houses as desirable for child-rearing: "A permanent Art Jury" would review "every building plan" in the development so that children would "grow up where ideals of beauty are foremost."[5]

Residential parks did not need zoning ordinances to regulate construction within their borders, but developers remained concerned. As private agreements, deed restrictions had significant limitations. First, many of the restrictions expired well before developers and planners thought appropriate, and it was "a Herculean task," in the words of J. C. Nichols, to convince enough homeowners to renew them.[6] Developers who intended to expand their residential parks or plat new ones wanted their older developments to stand the test of time, which, in turn, would facilitate the sale of new lots at inflated prices. Lawrence Veiller, a housing reformer who would later serve on Hoover's advisory committee on zoning, suggested the need for government intervention to maintain ideal residential conditions over time. Few were "willing to invest their money in real estate" when private agreements subject to "conflicting decisions of the courts" were "the only guarantee of the stability of the residential character of the neighborhood."

He illustrated his point by emphasizing the absurdity of regulating "the purity of the milk supply" or safeguarding "the pedestrians on our thoroughfares and highways" through private agreements. "The time has come in America when we should call upon the state to use its great power and prohibit those things that we know are clearly injurious to the community," especially children.[7]

Second, because of the haphazard nature of urban growth, the development of adjacent property could undermine even the most stringent restrictions. As cities expanded out and around suburban developments, new "hazards" might appear if owners were able to exploit their unrestricted property in whatever way they wished. If they chose to introduce a use or user viewed as "incompatible" with the norms of white middle-class child-rearing, they might lower the value of single-family lots in nearby residential parks. As J. C. Nichols complained, "You never can be assured that the holders of the adjoining property will not do something to depreciate the value of your own." Nichols's Country Club District inspired the layout of Houston's River Oaks, which began development in 1924. The advertising director predicted that "within a very few years" Houston would "grow around it and be beautified by it."[8] The flip side, of course, was the understanding that River Oaks could be damaged through urban expansion.

To avoid financial ruin, Nichols recommended that residential parks be sufficiently large so that the most expensive lots could be shielded from "the border" problem; his own Country Club District boasted 1,000 acres. Following that example, River Oaks contained more than 1,100 acres with the most valuable lots nestled along Buffalo Bayou. Those lots were surrounded by increasingly smaller and less valuable ones, so that tasteful, middle-class houses would guard the development's grand estates, while upwardly mobile families could rub shoulders with local elites at the exclusive public school and parks (see figure 10.1). Still, the developers worried, if they could not control the actions of adjacent property owners, then they could not deliver on their motto "Protection Without and Within."[9] And even if "nice" single-family homes buffered the most expensive real estate, the border problem would continue to plague the more modest lots on the development's edge, where middle-class parents—who were most concerned about safeguarding their children's futures—would be the buyers.[10]

One remedy was to enter into an agreement with the adjacent property owners, but this idea remained tenuous, at best, particularly if the property changed hands. The Olmsted brothers, who helped design Atlanta's Druid Hills, were relieved to learn that the developer Joel Hurt would be able to "control the character of occupation" along the northern and eastern border. Nonetheless, they warned him about the property to the west and the "comparatively low ground" to the south. They advised him to "enter into a mutual agreement with [its] owners" to "keep the land vacant and inoffensive" until he could convince potential buyers to spend "a larger amount" on his lots than they might "consider prudent"

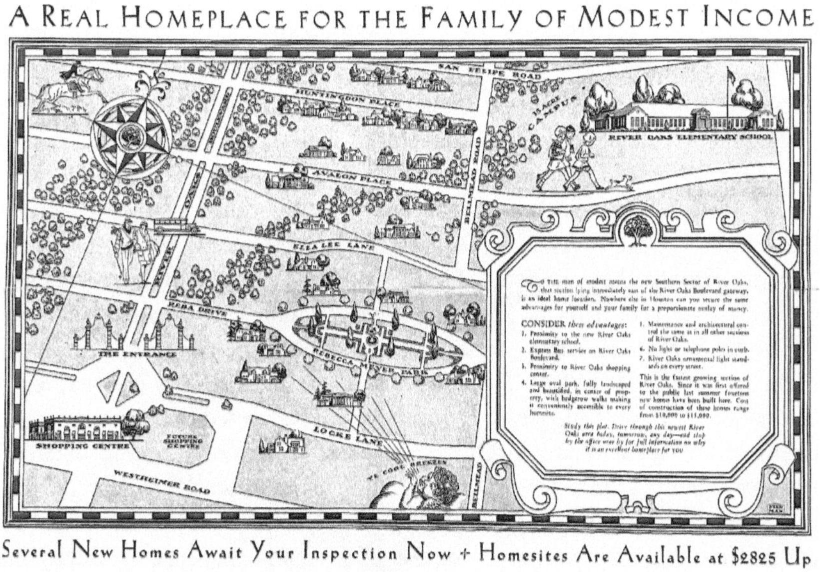

A REAL HOMEPLACE FOR THE FAMILY OF MODEST INCOME

Several New Homes Await Your Inspection Now ♦ Homesites Are Available at $2825 Up

FIGURE 10.1. The developers of River Oaks surrounded the most expensive lots with smaller ones for families of more "modest income." Child-centered advertisements such as the one pictured above resonated especially well with upwardly mobile, middle-class families who put a premium on child-centered "advantages" such as the new River Oaks Elementary School. MSS 0118, box 4, folder 19, Houston History Research Center, Houston Public Library. Used with permission.

if the "future character" of any border properties proved unpleasant. The Olmsteds hoped the adjacent property might stay "in the hands of a strong owner fully determined not to sell to undesirable purchasers" and financially capable of "holding the property" for "as long as he live[d]." But even if such an agreement relieved Hurt of some "immediate anxiety," they still cautioned it would not be "of a sufficiently permanent character" to function as a lasting solution.[11]

What was needed was a zoning ordinance guaranteeing that everything—and everyone—would remain in a suitable place, furnishing residential parks with a permanent remedy. Zoning ordinances were never meant to supplant deed restrictions but to enact legally enforceable restraints on neighboring property owners, with decreasing standards as one approached the city center. Developers and planners also pressed hard for zoning ordinances that would extend at least five miles beyond the city limits so they could ensure that future additions would not harm existing residential parks either.[12]

In most zoning schemes, the "best" residential districts were limited to single-family houses and the institutions that served them, which might include schools, churches, parks, and the "truck farms" that provided affluent children with fresh vegetables.[13] Charles Cheney worked as a zoning consultant for Berkeley, California, and Portland, Oregon, and he helped design Los Angeles's Palos Verdes Estates. At the 1919 National Conference on City Planning (NCCP), he championed the "Class I" single-family residential district, affirming that the zoning consultant's "most imperative duty" was "to foster and protect" communities of single-family homes, which he characterized as "the backbone of our nation." "God grant we shall always keep them foremost in our minds in whatever zones or plans we make," he preached. "Class II" districts, which permitted multifamily dwellings, would be reserved for "the renter class" with "few children."[14]

Skeptics regarded zoning's proposed restraints on property rights just as warily as many had regarded those imposed by deed restrictions. Only now, the regulations would blanket the entire city rather than be limited to voluntary agreements within residential parks. During the 1920s, resistance to zoning remained so fierce that it threatened to derail city planning altogether.[15] The Detroit Property Holders' Protective Association helped galvanize local opposition with a pamphlet asking, "Do you want a bureau of government agents, backed by the arbitrary police power of the state, to determine how you can use your property, even such meddling as to resolve the number of families that may live on an acre?" Frustrated zoning advocate Madge Headley complained, "Men still argue that every man's house is his castle, and that property rights give entire control of everything within the boundaries of any plot of land down through to China and up to the sky." Similarly, planning consultant Jefferson Grinnalds admitted that a zoning campaign would succeed only if supporters recognized "the psychology of land ownership which causes a man to believe he can do what he pleases with his own land."[16]

Small-scale real estate speculators were chief among zoning's most vociferous adversaries. For them, the greatest profits came from speculation when the downtown business area expanded, since commercial properties were worth far more than single-family lots. Only large-scale developers sought "stabilization" or "permanence." Consequently, the National Association of Real Estate Boards (NAREB), headed by the nation's most esteemed developers, endorsed a series of textbooks to convert small-time operators to their way of thinking before allowing them to join the "profession." James Metzenbaum, Euclid's attorney in *Euclid v. Ambler*, described the difference between a realtor and a real estate man as the difference between a "statesman and a politician." The professional "realtor," who must be a member of NAREB in good standing to use the trademarked title, cared about the future.[17] Fly-by-night real estate men only cared about making a quick buck with little regard for the property-owners next door. They were the devils that zoning restrictions were meant to stop, but first the public at large would need to be convinced that residential zoning laws were proper and necessary.

Child-Centered Planning

After Robert Whitten completed the tentative zone map for Atlanta, his next task was to sway public opinion in favor of the plan so it could become law. To convince the average citizen, he connected "the need for zoning" to effective child-rearing. He used the following vignette, included in his final report, to make the case: "Mr. Smith has purchased a home in an attractive neighborhood. All of the homes have large well kept yards. Mr. Smith believes that children, like plants, must have plenty of sunlight and room in which to grow. The location seems like an ideal one in which to live and raise a family. But there is a vacant lot next door. A speculative builder estimates that he can buy that lot, erect a four-story, sixteen suite apartment house thereon, rent the apartments, sell to some investor and clean up a handsome profit for himself."[18] Whitten's cautionary tale ended with "the value of Mr. Smith's home" being "practically destroyed" because "his light and air" was "cut off by the huge bulk of the apartment house." The tragedy was the decline in property value, but underlying that misfortune was the damage to the home's suitability for child-rearing. He had purchased this house to be a good parent, yet his laudable efforts had failed. Now, his children could not thrive like they would in a community of single-family homes, and no buyer would want to purchase his house for the same reason. His investment was, thus, "practically destroyed."

Tying zoning to child-rearing, much as Whitten had, ultimately became the planners' best weapon to refute those who obstinately refused to see how zoning advanced the general welfare. As Lawrence Veiller put it at the 1916 National Conference on City Planning (NCCP), "A restriction of this kind must not only be good, it must *seem* good," and wrapping single-family zoning around childhood was an effective means of making it "*seem* good." George Hooker, secretary of the Chicago City Club, revealed the playbook in his closing speech at the conference: "The most urgent of all national needs is for the oncoming generation. Generally speaking our cities are not conceived, planned or maintained as fit places for child life. City planning seeks to readjust them so that they shall be suitable for children." Almost a decade later, Charles Eliot, president emeritus of Harvard University, launched *City Planning*, the official organ of both the NCCP and the American City Planning Institute, with equally rousing language. "Planners will have a chance to provide the city population" with "wholesome and comfortable ways of living and bringing up children." "No large American city today provides the means for a family of small or moderate income of bringing up a family of children safely," Eliot lamented. "The children are not safe even in their schools, much less in the streets, which are their only playgrounds. To the rescue, therefore, all city, town and village planners!"[19]

The relationship between city planning and child welfare dated back to Progressive Era campaigns for housing reform, with Jane Addams and other well-known reformers being early supporters. Addams attended the first annual meeting of the NCCP (1909), which social worker and reform activist Benjamin Marsh had helped organize.[20] Internationally renowned planner George B. Ford also attended. He was the brother of Harvard sociologist James Ford, manager of the US Housing Corporation during World War I and, later, executive director of Better Homes in America. Ford's presentation depicted housing as "the most vital phase of city planning" because it was "the side which affects life at its most crucial period; that is, in the early years of childhood."[21] Four years later, the American City Bureau further elevated the emphasis on childhood with its traveling "City Planning Exhibition": "If you forgot the children when you planned your city, you'll have to plan it over again. An ordinary unplanned city—a group of houses, factories and office buildings hastily thrown together—furnishes an abnormal environment for children."[22]

Once residential developers began expanding their influence within the planning movement, the focus shifted from child welfare at large to a preoccupation with white middle-class child-rearing. Many social reformers left the movement, feeling disillusioned. By 1925, developers had gained substantial representation on the NCCP's board of directors and in other planning organizations, following the early examples of Kansas City's J. C. Nichols and Birmingham's Robert Jemison Jr.[23] Planning rhetoric continued to include some expressions of concern for less privileged children, but urban poverty was more often used to underpin efforts to plan separate, idyllic communities for affluent white children than to improve conditions for all.

Not surprisingly, the movement found a friend in Herbert Hoover, who helped build the case for zoning. In 1921, the commerce secretary appointed a committee to draft the language for a standard enabling act, which local planning commissions could then shepherd through state legislatures so individual cities would have the authority to pass local zoning laws. His "Advisory Committee on Zoning" included representation from the various planning organizations, the National Association of Real Estate Boards, and the National Chamber of Commerce. In 1922, the committee issued *A Zoning Primer* to teach local officials how to write zoning ordinances that would survive both public scrutiny and judicial review. This effort was followed by the publication of *A City Planning Primer* in 1928.[24]

Unlike most planners from outside the United States, members of Hoover's advisory committee demonized apartments, joining hands with parenting experts to rebuke those who failed to purchase a single-family home. The *City Planning Primer* denounced as irresponsible any parents who chose "this more cramped manner of living" simply to "avoid personal responsibility for upkeep of the dwelling" or "to have easier access to the city center." The solution was single-family zoning, which would reduce the number of children living in apartments by controlling the spread of multifamily housing: "Many existing dwellings in our cities do not conform to the standards of the single-family homes that most families would prefer. Wise city planning can do much to make one-family houses available to more families."[25]

In the same vein, committee member John Ihlder censured young couples who attempted to save money by living in a "furnished two-room flat" before moving into "that idyllic vine-covered cottage where love traditionally abides." He supposed their rationale might be economically sound, but "pure economics is a sterile soil which will not produce an adequate crop of babies." He worried that too many couples would be "living in their apartment, still thinking first of their own safety, their own comforts" when their children were largely grown. In those circumstances, "the nation may well ask why it was taxed to provide for their schooling, to protect their health, when they have been unwilling to pass on the heritage they received." "The first home of the young couple should be at least a promise of its future home," he moralized. "It may be beyond the means of many young married couples, but it is an objective to be approximated as closely as we—and they—can."[26] Ihlder's use of "we"—even before "they"—reflected the authoritative stance that planners assumed as the experts, much like the parent educators who distrusted parental instincts. "We" must encourage couples to do the right thing so that our "heritage"—white, Anglo-Saxon Protestant—might be passed on to the next generation. This goal justified prioritizing the homes of white middle-class families as the "first consideration." "With them lies the future," Ihlder concluded.

Such assertions were not new to the planning movement. In 1920, Charles Cheney reasoned, "We need some flats and apartments, but not scattered through every block of the city." Like Ihlder, he feared an abundance of apartments would discourage families—"the most important social unit"—from "living and developing" independently in detached, single-family houses. He believed zoning was "the only method so far devised" to limit the incursion of apartment buildings and, thus, secure "clean living conditions" and a "healthful environment." Andrew Wright Crawford, field secretary of the American Civic Association, defended zoning through an even more scathing attack on apartments; he wholly condemned "those child-devouring, family-destroying tenements we call by the fashionable name of apartment-houses" and counted families living in even "palatial apartments" as "nevertheless living in tenements." "An apartment is merely a tenement house with a college education, soon forgotten when the surroundings begin to go down," he scoffed. "People who have children and live in apartment houses are recreant in their duty to their children."[27]

Hoover's how-to planning guides overlapped with the founding of Better Homes in America (BHA), which further boosted single-family zoning with the assistance of local clubwomen. Several members of the zoning advisory committee also served on the BHA board, and Hoover placed James Ford, the executive director of BHA, on the zoning subcommittee for the White House Conference on Home Building and Home Ownership. Together, planners and their allies in BHA and the federal government urged newly enfranchised mothers to support zoning for the "Love of Home." Indeed, the *Zoning Primer* began with an appeal that seemed directed at the PTA. Page one asked, "Does your city keep its gas range in the Parlor and its piano in the kitchen?" An attentive mother would never let her daughter make "fudge in the parlor," it confirmed, "yet many American cities do the same sort of thing when they allow stores to crowd in at random among private dwellings."[28]

Local clubwomen did not disappoint in their support of the zoning movement. A member of Atlanta's League of Women Voters "led a discussion" on the "civic rights of residential sections" at a meeting in her home. Embracing Hoover's rhetoric, she applauded the zoning ordinance for protecting "against the encroachment of business or commercial interests," which would be "detrimental to the highest development of home communities, the especial environment of the children—our future citizens and lawmakers." That year, the mayor rewarded the efforts of the League of Women Voters and the Atlanta Woman's Club by appointing one of their own to the planning commission. Not long after, the city's zoning engineer wrote to the Woman's Club "pledging" his "unlimited support" for the "staging of Better Homes week," affirming that "a movement of this kind" was an "integral part of city planning."[29]

Protected Kid Zones

Convincing the voting public that zoning was "normal" and "necessary" meant little if the courts continued to invalidate strict zoning laws. In 1909, social reformer Benjamin Marsh helped introduce the concept of zoning to the United States by suggesting that government was "the most important factor in securing good living conditions and preserving the life, health, and well-being of all citizens." Ultimately, this language, which portrayed zoning as vital to the protection of people rather than property, would win over the courts, but professional planners were slow to understand the distinction. They continued to argue that zoning would stabilize residential property values, while the courts repeatedly declared—no matter how worthy that objective might be—the maintenance of property values was *not* a constitutional use of police power. In 1925, Jefferson Grinnalds voiced frustration when the Maryland Court of Appeals nullified Baltimore's zoning plan because "there was apparently nothing in the language of the ordinance which showed that it related to health, safety and general welfare."[30]

Similarly, Atlanta's zoning ordinance ran into further trouble with the Georgia Supreme Court in a case that had nothing to do with racial zoning, since the city's race districts had already been struck down. In *Smith v. Atlanta* (1926), the plaintiff, Corrine Smith, had petitioned for a zoning change that would have allowed her to build multiple stores at an intersection at the northern edge of Ansley Park. The original zone map had designated the other three corners of the intersection—all of which were outside the formal boundaries of Ansley Park—as a business district, but the Ansley Park Civic League still vehemently opposed the change. It insisted that the construction of a retail store, even at the northern most tip of the development, would damage the character of the neighborhood. After exhausting the appeals process, Smith built the stores anyway to test the validity of the law. The Georgia Supreme Court ruled in her favor: it was unconstitutional to ban retail stores from residential districts because stores had not been considered nuisances in the past. The authorities could only eliminate a business once it become a nuisance, not before. Moreover, if it was, in fact, in the public interest for no store to exist at that location, then the city must compensate the property owner using eminent domain rather than arrest her under the state's police power.[31]

As Atlanta's zoning law came under attack, its supporters continued to use child-centered arguments to save it. An editorial in the *Atlanta Journal* defended zoning as a requirement for any city wishing to be "known as a good place in which to rear children" and that sought "rarer values than mere money can express!" Another reminded that "discriminating homeseekers demand such protection, and prudent investors lay great store by it. Both know that a city which has not taken thought of its future development is not a desirable place, as a rule, for persons having children to rear or large interests to promote."[32] Following the *Smith* decision, the city's zoning engineer urged voters to support an amendment to the Georgia Constitution that would grant cities the power to create single-family residential districts. He pleaded, "In the protection of our homes, we create a better community spirit and rear our children under the best of circumstances, thereby making for better citizenship and health."[33]

Perhaps the same child-centered appeal used to persuade voters might also sway the courts. At the 1918 meeting of the NCCP, Lawson Purdy, who worked on the nation's first comprehensive zoning law in New York City, advised planners to "educate" the courts on the need for zoning so that judges would begin to sustain their efforts. He felt that the dissenting opinion of a Minnesota judge held the key. "When a man builds a house on a restricted street," the judge reasoned, he "does it for the protection of the health and morals and character of his children, and on such a street, land has a higher value than on a street not so protected, other things being equal, because that protection is worth money." He continued, "The value of the house may be practically destroyed by the erection of stores" since "the desired atmosphere for the rearing of the family is gone, and the man is just as much entitled to be protected in the value of his house" as "he is to the protection of the police to prevent burglars breaking through and stealing from

FIGURE 10.2. Although working-class children were far more likely than affluent children to be injured by an automobile while playing in the street, quiet streets were an important selling point for residential parks zoned for single-family housing. *Atlanta Constitution*, 24 February 1921.

him." Purdy proposed that his fellow planners "popularize that idea" so that other courts would "be ready to follow the good example of that judge."[34]

A common justification for the exclusion of multifamily dwellings from single-family districts was the danger posed by increased automobile use. The skyrocketing number of car registrations along with the attendant demand for roads, parking, and service stations had produced a municipal problem that seemed worthy enough to justify the entire expense of city planning. The 1920s was an especially deadly decade, as the number of cars on the road expanded faster than cities could adapt.[35] Playground advocate Angelo Patri criticized homeowners who "built to the street line and as far back" as the "fence permitted" but "made no provision for the play of children" who made the "house a home." Consequently, death took "his toll of a child a day" (see figure 10.2).[36] Like parent educators, planners touted residential parks as the safest place for children because the required setbacks guaranteed large yards, while generous provisions for parks and playgrounds provided additional space for play. Failing that, winding streets with low-density housing reduced the amount and speed of local traffic. J. C. Nichols questioned the shortsightedness of developers who had an "absolute disregard" for the obligation "to secure the safety of the streets for children." He wondered how they could "invite the most dangerous kind of traffic, and yet expect to sell the property on that street to parents with many little children."[37]

Supporters of single-family zoning embraced a similar argument, even though it was working-class children who were far more likely to be injured by a passing automobile and far *less* likely to live in a stand-alone house. The Illinois Chapter of the American Institute of Architects maintained that large single-family residential zones would protect "the life and limb of children and others who have to use the streets." Likewise, Charles Cheney promised that, once zoning laws were "settled," a "man with a family" could "feel that his children" were "safe and on a quiet street."[38] Many of those making these assertions seemed to care more about safeguarding the advantages of residential parks, however, since single-family zoning tended to increase traffic in the unprotected areas where most children continued to live.

Planners also emphasized the importance of tranquil streets for babies' nap schedules, which had become somewhat of an obsession for child-rearing experts who insisted that young children should sleep in hushed rooms, preferably alone, for healthy development. Planning consultant Herbert Swan reiterated that advice in "The Legality of Zoning" (1920): "Approximately one-fifth of the total population of a large city consists of children under five years of age. The necessity for quiet residence districts, so that these children can obtain a reasonable amount of sleep in the daytime, is apparent." Developers had adopted similar rhetoric and imagery to sell single-family home lots. At the 1916 NCCP, J. C. Nichols praised an advertising card that used "a picture of a quiet residence street" to portray the development as "a quiet place" for babies to nap.[39]

By the mid-1920s, court decisions had begun recognizing the special role that communities of single-family homes were supposed to play in child-rearing. The Massachusetts Supreme Court accepted a strict zoning law in Brookline that banned even "two-family houses" (duplexes) because of their presumed negative impact on growing children. The decision stated, "It may be a reasonable view that the health and general physical and mental welfare of society would be promoted by each family dwelling in a house by itself," thereby conferring "freedom for the play of children" among other advantages. Perhaps its most dubious finding was that the law did not discriminate against less affluent children since the "features of family life are equally essential or equally advantageous for all inhabitants, whatever may be their social standing or material prosperity." The court further dismissed the exclusionary nature of residential parks by concluding it was "common knowledge" that subdivisions with "modest single-family dwellings" were within reach "of the thrifty and economical" wage earner, ignoring the fact that the law did not treat those neighborhoods the same as it treated the more affluent ones.⁴⁰ While acknowledging that the protection of "family life" was "equally advantageous for all," the court did not require that all be given access to those advantages so long as areas within the same zoning category received equal treatment.

In 1925, the California Supreme Court unanimously upheld a similar ordinance based on the need to encourage family life in single-family homes. "We think it may be safely and sensibly said that justification for residential zoning, may, in the last analysis, be rested upon the protection of the civic and social values of the American home," the judges pronounced. "It is axiomatic that the welfare, and indeed the very existence of a nation depends upon the character and caliber of its citizenry. The character and quality of manhood and womanhood are in large measure the result of home environment." With a logic that surely warmed Hoover's heart, the court agreed that zoning could inspire even "those of moderate means to own their own homes," resulting in "better attention to the rearing of children" among other positive outcomes related to the "moral and mental make-up of the citizenry."⁴¹

Even if the judges in this case were not necessarily convinced that duplexes were a danger to child-rearing, they fully accepted the assumptions behind the superiority of the single-family house and the vilification of apartments. "It is needless to further analyze and enumerate all of the factors which make a single family home more desirable for the promotion and perpetuation of family life than an apartment, hotel, or flat," the judges surmised. "It will suffice to say that there is a sentiment practically universal, that this is so. But few persons, if given their choice, would, we think, deliberately prefer to establish their homes and rear their children in an apartment house neighborhood rather than in a single home neighborhood." Though the judges imagined that a two-family flat was less offensive than a ten-family apartment building, they left it up to the "municipal body" to determine at what point multifamily residences became such a threat that they should be removed from the district.⁴²

That same year, the Ohio Supreme Court reached a similar conclusion about the use of police power to restrict the location of multifamily housing. The judges accepted the proposition that "family life" was "promoted by the separation of families." Echoing Hoover's advisory committee, they expressed optimism that zoning could increase "public demand" for single-family houses to the point that developers "would be compelled to build" the one form of housing that contributed to "the maintenance" rather than "the deterioration of the American family."⁴³ Their validation of zoning certainly entertained other arguments, but it was the assertion about family life that convinced them that even the strictest forms of residential zoning should stand.

These three cases served as precedents for the landmark Supreme Court decision *Euclid v. Ambler* (1926), which gave a green light to single-family districts that excluded all other types of housing. The village of Euclid, a suburban community adjacent to Cleveland, Ohio, had enacted a zoning ordinance with residential districts banning all multifamily dwellings, including duplexes. Parks, public transit stations, and truck farms were all that it permitted. The important question was whether the police power could be used to defend such strict residential zones in the interest of the *general* welfare and not just those who lived there. The lower court had been unwilling to make such as leap. It found that single-family zoning discriminated against those with more modest incomes because they could not afford a single-family house with at least three rooms plus a modern bathroom, basement, and the required minimum-sized lot, in accordance with the law. As a result, they would be forced to live among the greater number of hazards that would become concentrated in areas with fewer protections.[44]

In a 6–3 decision, the Supreme Court disagreed. The majority ruled that Euclid's zoning law met the test since the regulations would "increase the safety and security of home life" by creating "a more favorable environment in which to rear children." According to the decision, multifamily housing—even if only for two families—monopolized "the rays of the sun" and interfered "with the free circulation of air." The "disturbing noises" from increased traffic would detract from the safety of the streets, while heightened "confusion" would "deprive children of the privilege of quiet and open spaces for play" that were "enjoyed by those in more favored localities." Consequently, the presence of multifamily housing would mean "the residential character of the neighborhood and its desirability as a place of detached residences" would be "utterly destroyed."[45]

After his triumph in *Euclid*, attorney James Metzenbaum wrote *The Law of Zoning* (1930) to address the large number of queries he received about the case. He explained how falling property values frequently revealed the "disregard" too often shown for the widely accepted standards of the "American home." "There is additional abundant evidence to substantiate the fact, that modern tendencies are rapidly destroying and undermining the continuance of separate and individual homes and residences," even though "the bulwark and the stamina of this country" have been "credited to the home-owning tendencies of our people." He repeated the supposition that heavily restricted, single-family residential areas were necessary for nurturing "a more vigorous generation": "It is generally conceded that the home owner who has the opportunity" to "rear his family in a house" was "one of the important factors in the sustaining of the American people and American ideals." He asked, "If homes and residences are not to find ready quarters in the suburban territories, where will they find themselves sheltered?"[46]

Planners outside the United States remained committed to the needs of working-class children even as American planners seemed to abandon them. The US movement appeared far more enraptured by the "Anglo-Saxon" single-family house than even British planners, who stubbornly insisted that children could flourish in well-designed apartments.[47] Paul Harsch, the developer of Ottawa Hills in Toledo, claimed that the "home spirit" was "essential to the Anglo-Saxon idea," even if "in England the home idea" was not "developed as highly as it" was in the United States.[48] This divergence was all the more striking because "German zones" came to the United States from Europe, and early American advocates of zoning such as Benjamin Marsh had sought to help the urban poor, first and foremost, by reducing congestion in tenement districts.[49]

At the third annual NCCP, housing reformer Lawrence Veiller suggested that requiring setbacks for working-class families would be counterproductive. He figured that they would not be able to afford the additional land, and, even if they could, they certainly would not plant "grass and flowers for the children" but would be more likely to use it to store garbage. "The idea of a beautiful flower garden for this class of population is Utopian," he expounded. "The ordinary laborer, working as he does ten hours a day, has little time for the cultivation of any garden nor does the woman of the average laborer's family have time either, if she gives to her children the attention they require." Instead of gardens, "dilapidated little outbuildings" would soon be "patched together with old boards and tin, and the whole place and neighborhood" would rapidly assume "a squalid and unkept appearance." Side yards, too, would become filled with refuse, blocking the light and air anyway.[50]

In contrast, J. C. Nichols characterized working-class families as the residents most likely to gain from zoning because they did not already benefit from restrictive covenants and their children were most in need of improvement, at least from the perspective of the middle class. Nichols imagined that zoning could effectively impose middle-class standards on the "working man" by appealing "directly to the strongest sentiment in him": the desire "to give his family better and more pleasant surroundings." Zoning protections, he theorized, would grant the working man's children access to playgrounds, modern schools, "air and sunshine," and "grass and flowers," although he acknowledged that this "class of buyer" would "require considerable education along these lines."[51]

Charles Cheney generally agreed. In 1920, he responded to Bruno Lasker's criticism of single-family zoning by arguing it would offer the "foreign-born worker an equal opportunity to live and raise his family according to the most wholesome American standards" in "a detached house of his own rather than in a tenement." The "poor man with a family" was just as "entitled to an opportunity to live in a home neighborhood restricted from flats, apartments, business and other undesirable buildings" as "the wealthy man, who builds his home in a privately restricted tract." As evidence, Cheney described a scene he witnessed at a hearing for Oregon's proposed enabling law. A "union labor leader" spoke before the body, charging, "You rich men live in protected and privately restricted home neighborhoods and let all the stables and public garages and other dirty businesses intrude into any block of the workers' home neighborhoods, to spoil all that they work and live for." Cheney supposed the man's objection was based on his "misunderstandings" of the law, given that the purpose of zoning was to shield the homes of "industrial workers" from those very stables and garages. Yet, the union leader was not the one mistaken; he accurately depicted the impact of residential parks on older areas of the city, a situation he knew zoning would only worsen.[52]

Ten years later, the debate was largely immaterial: it was clear that zoning's main goal had been to safeguard affluent, white families, who by then seemed much less inclined to worry about the welfare of those excluded from their neighborhoods. During the decade after *Euclid*, the number of US cities with zoning ordinances exploded from 76 to 1,322. Local officials passed many of these laws without coherent city plans, instead employing zoning mostly "to perpetuate status quo discrimination and whim," in the words of historian John Hancock. Every real or perceived nuisance banned from the strictest residential zones became concentrated in or near neighborhoods that were also denied a fair share of public resources. The deteriorating conditions ravaged the life chances of children who were excluded from the protections that had been promised to the next generation. Locked out of suburban areas through a combination of deed restrictions and zoning, they experienced greater harm so that affluent white children would be exposed to none.[53]

City planners, developers, and local officials—those who formed the public-private coalition controlling urban development—joined with parent educators to define the parameters of what the right kind of environment for child-rearing should be. They then sold this idea to white, middle-class parents who wanted their children to grow up with all the opportunities that would enable them to meet—or preferably exceed—their parents' economic and social success. Accordingly, the demand for homes in areas that were perceived as most advantageous to children drove up property values in nearby developments, guaranteeing their profitability. Likewise, zoning's ostensible benefits for children led to its acceptance by both voters and the courts and gave the planning movement a noble cause to champion.

Despite the lofty rhetoric, zoning did not result in an urban environment that was safer, healthier, or more appropriate for children—at least, not for all children. Rather, *Euclid* handed planners and developers exactly what they wanted: rising home prices within single-family districts. The absurdity of excluding certain children from the benefits of zoning under the guise of preserving childhood went almost wholly uncriticized by affluent white people beyond, perhaps, Bruno

Lasker. As he predicted, the most heavily "protected" neighborhoods also received the most tax-supported resources. Affluent white children thereby gained a monopoly over the best schools, the safest and most stimulating places to play, and the most well-connected neighbors because zoning enhanced the ability of deed restrictions to limit who would have access to those engines of upward mobility.[54]

No group of young people experienced exclusion as thoroughly or as consistently as Black children. Racial covenants were the most prevalent type of deed restriction, appearing even in subdivisions with lower thresholds of entry.[55] In *Corrigan v. Buckley* (1926), the US Supreme Court held that racial covenants, as private contracts, were a constitutional means of achieving segregation, even though they relied on the courts for enforcement. The decision, which was handed down just a few months before *Euclid*, ensured that the symbiotic relationship between zoning and restrictive covenants would flourish for decades to come. The NAACP had originally set up *Corrigan* as a test case to demonstrate that racial covenants caused harm like all other forms of de jure residential segregation. Since the key issue in *Buchanan v. Warley* (1917) had been alienation rather than discrimination, the NAACP decided that the most effective plaintiff would again be an aggrieved white person. This time the strategy did not work.[56] *Corrigan* combined with *Euclid* to magnify the size and scope of residential segregation. Together, the two decisions inspired renewed hope among some whites that racial zoning might yet survive judicial review, leading to a resurgence in experimentation with de jure segregation.

CHAPTER 11

De Jure Segregation after *Euclid*

Euclid v. Ambler (1926)—the landmark decision declaring residential zoning a constitutional use of police power—raised expectations among some that racial zoning might also be found constitutional, at least if embedded within a comprehensive zoning ordinance. Two years earlier, the Georgia Supreme Court had struck down the racial component of Atlanta's zoning ordinance in *Bowen v. Atlanta* (1924) before gutting what remained of the law in *Smith v. Atlanta* (1926).[1] But just eight months later, the US Supreme Court found that even the strictest forms of residential zoning did not conflict with the US Constitution, overruling the state decisions that had suggested otherwise.[2] At that point, some wondered whether *Euclid* might provide an opportunity for racial zoning to be found constitutional as well. Legal scholar George Hott certainly thought so. "If a municipality can prevent the establishment of a 'Piggly-Wiggly' store in a residential section, without violating any of the constitutional prohibitions," he reckoned, "it should follow that an ordinance" that excludes Black residents "from a 'white' zone and vice versa, should, in the absence of infringement of existing property rights, be constitutional."[3]

Euclid's sanction of single-family districts that banned all multifamily housing raised expectations even further. The lower court had concluded that single-family zoning *must* be invalid if racial zoning was. After all, the consensus among whites was that racial segregation would promote the general welfare far more than the protection of single-family housing.[4] When the US Supreme Court reversed the lower court's decision, some supposed that *Bowen v. Atlanta*—which struck down racial zoning—should also be reversed. In their calculation, the lower court's reasoning in the *Euclid* case could simply be inverted: if single-family zoning was valid, then racial zoning must be, too, since racial segregation promoted the general welfare far more than neighborhoods of single-family homes.

Others considered *Corrigan v. Buckley* (1926) more promising. Handed down by the US Supreme Court a few months before *Euclid*, the decision gave a green light to racial covenants, which segregationists hoped would work as "private racial zoning contracts" in areas of the city that lacked deed restrictions. With their acceptance by the Supreme Court, racial covenants could perhaps serve as effective replacements for the ill-conceived segregation ordinances. Andrew Bruce, a law professor at Northwestern University, believed that a new kind of "racial zoning" achieved through private covenants could "aid, rather than interfere with, the marketability and exchange of land."[5]

But even validation from the Supreme Court could not stop racial covenants from creating unsalable properties in older neighborhoods. The underlying dynamic had not changed: the piecemeal use of racial covenants in areas marked by traditional urban development could not stimulate white demand for those properties. At the same time, child-centered residential parks did not need them, as Baltimore's Roland Park and Atlanta's Druid Hills had plainly demonstrated. White homeowners would not consider selling their property to a Black family because numerous white buyers were willing to pay top dollar for the homes.[6] Recognizing this conundrum, the Dallas city council passed an ordinance that enforced racial covenants through criminal penalties. In *Liberty Annex Corp. v. Dallas* (1927), the court of civil appeals shot down the Dallas law, arguing that its criminal penalties rendered it a segregation ordinance falling under the prohibitions of *Buchanan* (1917).[7]

Others assumed that even old-school segregation ordinances might survive judicial review now that interest in de jure segregation had spread far beyond Jim Crow cities. Back in 1922, local officials in New Orleans had devised a segregation ordinance specifically to address the concerns over property rights expressed in *Buchanan*.[8] As the challenge to that law wended its way through the courts, Indianapolis passed a similar ordinance. In a letter to the editor of the *Indianapolis News*, the "Secretary of the White Peoples' Protective League"—aptly named Omer S. Whiteman—felt that the growing demand for segregation in northern cities was in and of itself justification for the new ordinance: "Ten years ago there was practically no public sentiment in favor of segregation of the races [in the North], now it is general."[9]

Yet in *Harmon v. Tyler* (1927), the Supreme Court let the lower court's prohibition of the New Orleans ordinance stand. In refusing to revisit the issue, the justices avoided the responsibility of delivering a clearer ruling on why de jure residential segregation, regardless of individual property rights, was offensive to the Constitution. Consequently, the decision emboldened some to presume that a tweaked ordinance might still survive judicial review.[10] Indeed, the Court's failure to write a second opinion helps explain why advocates of old-school segregation ordinances began characterizing them as racial zoning after *Euclid*. They hoped adopting the language of zoning might increase the likelihood of a favorable court decision.

Legal scholars, however, continued to differentiate between segregation ordinances and racial zoning with some claiming that race districts layered into a comprehensive zoning plan would not run afoul of *Buchanan*. Arthur Martin, an assistant professor of law at Ohio State, supported that position. Echoing Robert Whitten's defense of the Atlanta zone plan, he insisted that racial zoning would facilitate the growth of Black housing rather than prevent it, as the segregation ordinances had done. In the first place, he argued, racial zoning would alleviate the problem of overcrowding caused by white hostility to Black neighbors, which had resulted "in a density of population in negro quarters" that was "two to five times greater than the density of population in white sections." In the second, racial zoning could address the longstanding problem of white absentee landlords neglecting aging Black rentals while waiting to sell the properties for commercial or industrial use.[11]

Perhaps without the prior existence of the clunky ordinances, the court might have accepted this logic, but those were not the circumstances. Most zoning advocates acknowledged reality and moved on.[12] They knew further attempts would not survive judicial review and so fell back on a form of de jure segregation the courts had not nullified: the cooptation of school building programs to advantage segregated areas protected by single-family zoning. Convincing white home buyers that raising their children in restricted residential parks would make them good parents was vital to this strategy, as was furnishing suburban areas with superior schools. A 1927 article in *McCall's Magazine*, cowritten by its architectural advisor Marcia Mead and planning consultant George B. Ford, implored parents to "refuse to live in a neighborhood" that did not "provide proper school facilities." They also urged families to pressure local officials to hire experts who would select proper school sites only "where permanent residence districts will be built up."[13]

Racial Zoning and the Protection of River Oaks

Even if planners frequently sold zoning to the public as a means for the little guy to protect his modest home, developers wished to use zoning mostly to shield their residential parks from the less pleasant aspects of urban growth, often at the expense of other neighborhoods. For example, William Hogg, a member of Texas's legendary Hogg family, served as chair of Houston's planning commission to further the interests of his flagship development, River Oaks. The resulting plan so brazenly favored his development that it contributed to the wholesale rejection of zoning in the Bayou City. The planning commission, nevertheless, linked the city's school building program to an informal racial zoning scheme that successfully drew affluent white families to River Oaks while pushing Black families in the nearby "San Felipe District" to the other side of town.

Hogg's initial effort to combine residential park development with city planning was the purchase of 1,500 acres beyond the city limits that had previously served as the site of a military camp during World War I. He offered the land to the city at cost to be used for Memorial Park, which Hogg believed was the best means to protect the northern flank of River Oaks. J. C. Nichols had long advised his fellow subdividers to use parks as barriers "to injurious encroachment of unrestricted or lowly restricted property," and his Country Club District was the inspiration for River Oaks. Early on, the president of the River Oaks Corporation, attorney Hugh Potter, visited Nichols in Kansas City to "gain ideas." Potter then hired Hare and Hare, the father and son team who had risen to international fame for their work on the Country Club District.[14] Soon thereafter, Houston's planning commission hired the son, Herbert Hare, to produce a zoning plan for the city, further advancing the interests of Hogg's River Oaks.

Before *Euclid*, a pall had hung over Texas because the state supreme court had nullified Dallas's original zoning ordinance, which had been drafted by Robert Whitten before his work began in Atlanta.[15] As a result, most thought zoning was dead in the Lone Star State. When *Euclid* overturned the Texas Supreme Court in 1926, Hogg joined forces with other zoning enthusiasts in Dallas to lobby the state legislature to pass an enabling law that would allow them to proceed with confidence. Even though Atlanta's race districts had been declared unconstitutional two years before, the Texas enabling law, nonetheless, granted local officials the authority to segregate Black and white homes.[16] During the months between *Euclid* (1926) and *Harmon v. Tyler* (1927)—which nullified New Orleans's 1922 segregation ordinance—advocates had hoped that a Supreme Court amenable to single-family zoning might accept "equitable" racial zoning, too. The enabling law also permitted cities to enforce racial covenants with criminal penalties, although Dallas's attempt was declared unconstitutional later that year.[17]

Notwithstanding that minor setback, Hogg agreed to take the reins of the planning commission with greater assurance that his work would bear fruit. His primary aim was to protect the substantial investment in improvements then being poured into River Oaks. In this regard, his first accomplishment was to kill the proposed airport in Memorial Park; instead, planes would fly in and out of southeast Houston on the opposite side of downtown.[18] Next, he secured greater control over the zoning process by not only retaining Herbert Hare as the city's zoning consultant but also by adding John Staub, River Oaks's in-house architect, to the planning commission.[19] He then prevented Mayor Oscar Holcombe from interfering in the commission's affairs while he plotted to have a River Oaks insider, Walter Monteith, elected mayor in 1929, just in time to receive the completed zone plan.[20] That same year, Hugh Potter joined the planning commission as well. His job was to promote the proposed ordinance, which benefitted River Oaks in multiple ways. In addition to restricting the property adjacent to the development, the accompanying street plan increased access to and from the development's two entrances.[21] Most importantly, it included a new parkway along Buffalo Bayou that originated at the side entrance of River Oaks and terminated at the very site Hogg had chosen for the new civic center. When completed, the

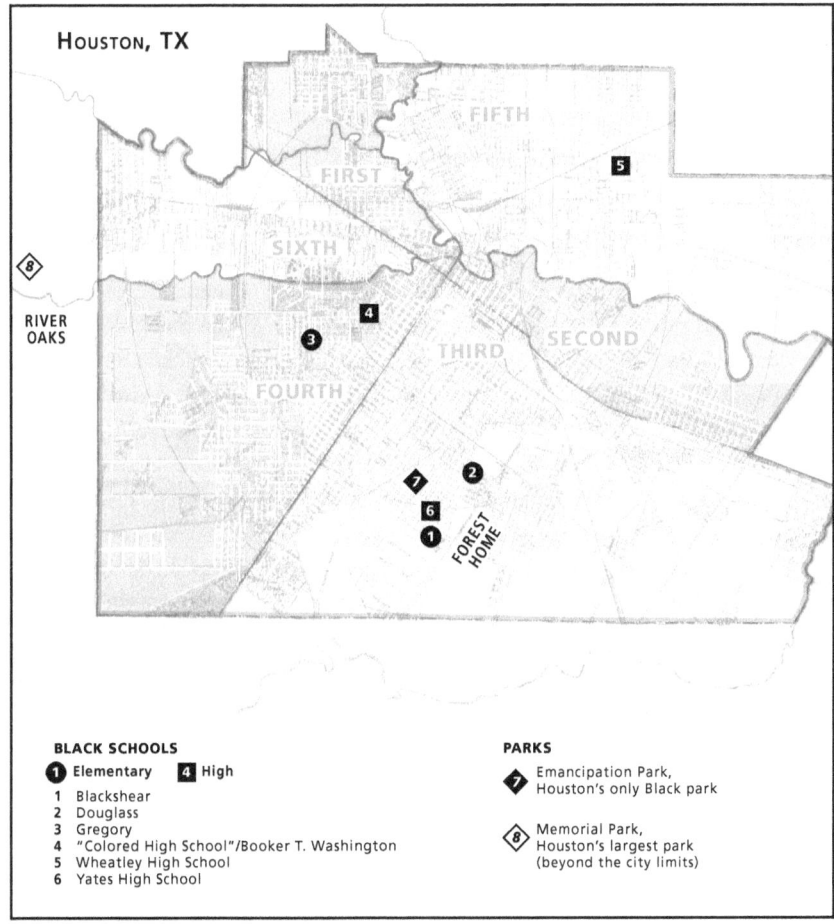

MAP 11.1. New Black schools and single-family houses facilitated the planning commission's effort to push Black middle-class families out of the San Felipe District, where Gregory Institute and the original "Colored High School" were located, into a largely undeveloped area across downtown from River Oaks, where Yates High School was built.

graceful parkway would allow River Oaks residents to reach downtown in under ten minutes.

Moreover, the zoning plan sought the elimination, or at least shrinkage, of the San Felipe District that stretched southward from Buffalo Bayou across the entire area separating River Oaks from downtown (see map 11.1). After the Civil War, freed people had entered Houston along the San Felipe Trail, establishing Freedmantown, which would later expand into the San Felipe District. Black residents spent decades building up a thriving community, which included the city's most important Black institutions: the elite Antioch Baptist Church; the only hospital, college, and Black high school in the city; and the Houston Colored Carnegie Library, which opened in 1913 on a valuable lot across from Antioch, not far from the high school. A committee of prominent Black professionals had purchased the expensive site. Hogg's effort to push San Felipe residents away from River Oaks and to stop Black property owners from "damaging" his planned parkway—even though they were there first—ignored the historic significance of the community.[22]

Houston's planning commission had already completed a "race distribution map" of the city even before Hogg took control.[23] He immediately launched a controversial survey of Black homeownership to "check" the map. Members of the commission met with the Houston Committee on Interracial Cooperation to coordinate the work. Hogg claimed that the survey's purpose was to determine the "community needs" of Black residents, and he promised to support the development of Black residential parks that would enjoy the same amenities as white ones. Many Black citizens correctly surmised that the real goal was to impose residential segregation rather than to ameliorate existing conditions.[24] C. H. McGruder, a Black member of the city's interracial committee, asked Hogg, "Will this survey result in the adoption of an Ordinance that will require the Colored population of the Fourth Ward [the San Felipe District] to sacrifice their homes at prices fixed directly or indirectly by the municipality?" "Hundreds" of Black property owners were questioning the true intent of the survey, and McGruder felt they deserved an honest answer before he asked for their cooperation. Hogg simply ignored the query; he was, in fact, interested in using eminent domain to fulfill his plans.[25]

The *Houston Informer*'s reply was forthright, as usual. After Hogg's first appearance before the interracial committee, a satirical column humorously described the irony of a planning commission plotting to dismantle Houston's most segregated community in the name of residential segregation. "Ef its seggergashun day dey wants, I'd lack ter no whare dey fine it better den its bin out dere in dat San Fillipy nayberhood," the author goaded, using dialect. "Dis bisness uv ever time dere's inny seckshun uv er town ter be maid ter look purty an zirabul, it do look mitey tuff, dat me an my fokes is gotter be tole dat we's gotter git up an git." The column then reminded Hogg and the other whites coveting the west side, "Us black fokes bin livin in dat nayberhood, Gus, fer de las 50 er 60 yeers, an dident vite nun er dem uther fokes ter cum out dere an live long side us."[26]

Two key pieces of evidence support their suspicions. First, when Hogg asked the engineer of the planning commission, Lewis Ryon, if a survey would be worth the expense, Ryon answered honestly that it would be "invaluable" from a "social services point of view" but of questionable worth "for segregation." On that advice, Hogg decided to skip it. After all, his racial zoning scheme did not require an accurate count of Black homeownership anyway.[27] Second, when he wrote to

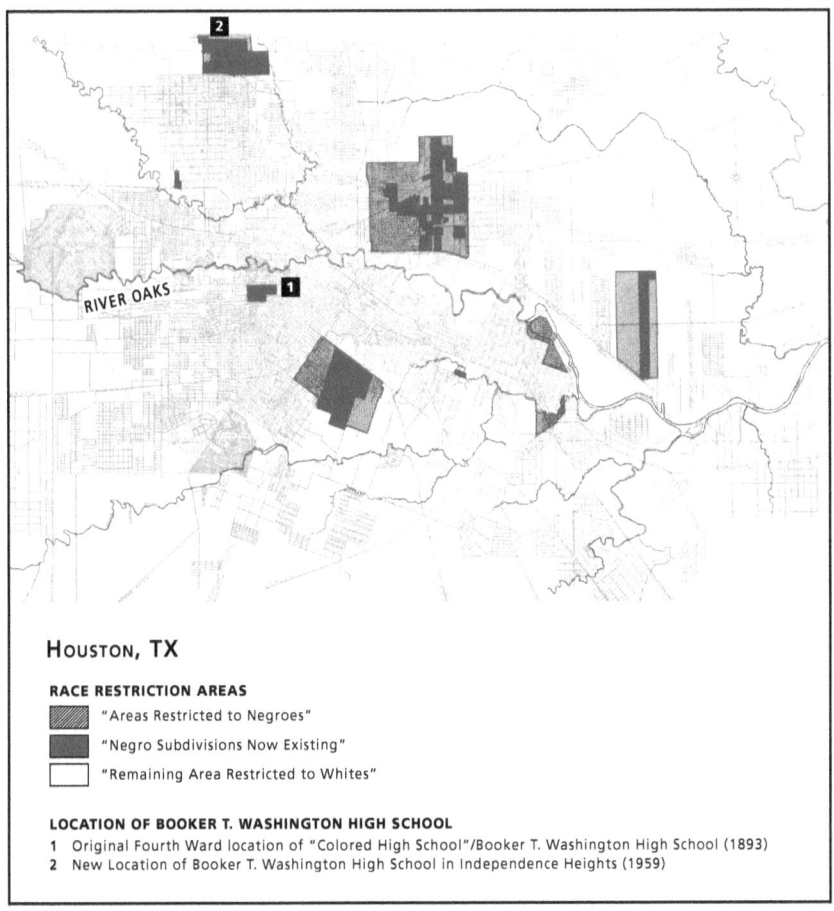

MAP 11.2. The Houston Planning Commission's map of "Proposed Race Restriction Areas" substantially reduced the size of Fourth Ward's San Felipe District while designating large areas on the opposite of downtown for Black expansion. Houston City Planning Commission, *Report*, 27. Scan courtesy of Matt Drwenski.

the mayor to inform him about the survey, Hogg sent a carbon copy of the letter to David Picton, one of the attorneys for River Oaks. In response, Picton warned Hogg that any type of segregation law "would be violative of the U.S. Constitution." Hogg snapped back that he was "aware of this" but supposed it would "not keep us from planning [an] ideal layout."[28] This "ideal layout" was soon revealed in a map of "Proposed Race Restriction Areas," which called for a significantly smaller Black presence in Fourth Ward, regardless of what had been or still was.

Just months before publication of the commission's final report, which included the informal racial zoning map, Hogg received a copy of Austin's new city plan. It supplied the necessary language to move his segregation scheme forward without generating a firestorm. As in Winston-Salem, Texas's capital city sought to promote "voluntary" segregation through enticements such as modern schools, parks, playgrounds, and other amenities that middle-class families had come to expect. And like Hogg's plan for Houston, the fundamental purpose was to shift Black residents to the city's east side, away from prestigious residential parks such as Pemberton Heights, which began development in 1927. The 1928 report expressed regret that "practically all attempts" at residential segregation had "been proven unconstitutional," but the city still faced a "race segregation problem." Black residents were "present in small numbers, in practically all sections of the city." As a solution, it designated one area to function as the "negro district" and recommended that "all facilities and conveniences be provided" for Black families in that section "as an incentive to draw the negro population" there. In recognition of the central role that schools would play in accomplishing this objective, the proposal appeared under the subheading "Schools": all Black schools in the appointed area would "be provided with ample and adequate playground space and facilities similar to the white schools of the city."[29]

Within days of receiving Austin's report, Hogg wrote a letter to Houston's zoning consultant, Herbert Hare, urging him to create a corresponding plan for the Bayou City. He copied Mayor Monteith and his allies on the planning commission, claiming to have "had in mind for many years" just such an idea. "If put up to the colored occupants properly, coupled with the right attitude of the City administration and the public to give each one of these colored communities civic justice, including sewerage, water, paving and other public utilities on the same basis as the white population, I have no doubt we would accomplish a great deal," he enthused.[30] Hare replied cautiously: "I believe your scheme of voluntary segregation of the races is the only feasible way of handling that problem, and I hope it can be worked out." He thought the improvements devised to safeguard and enhance the area near River Oaks would increase property values in the surrounding neighborhood, which, in turn, would "drive the colored population out of some of the localities now occupied by them." "Of course," he added, that would "necessitate providing suitable places for these people to go."[31]

By that point, the school board and planning commission had already accomplished much of the heavy lifting, even before Hogg took over the process. In 1924, the newly appointed commission began its duties by feting more than two dozen planners traveling to Los Angeles for the National Conference on City Planning. Robert Whitten was among the party, as well as George B. Ford, Edward Bassett, Harland Bartholomew, and John Nolan. Houston architect Alfred C. Finn was responsible for entertaining the guests. In addition to serving as a member of the planning commission, he was also running for school board. It seems unlikely that he—or anyone else for that matter—would have neglected to mention the large school bond campaign then under way. The visitors, for their part, surely would have encouraged the planning commission to coordinate the building program with their zoning effort. Finn's election to the school board would make this collaboration much easier: he remained on the planning commission while chair of the board's subcommittee responsible for selecting school sites.[32]

Indeed, the 1929 planning report thanked the school board for its cooperation and acknowledged the importance of the building program in furthering the commission's goals. "These activities of the School Board bear an important relation to the city plan as a whole and fortunately have, for the most part, fitted into the recommendation of the Planning Commission," the report commended. Board members carefully investigated each proposed site's "proximity to white districts" to establish a segregated attendance area while closing Black schools in the "smaller negro sections" that Hogg's commission sought to eliminate. Simultaneously, residential areas set aside for Black "expansion and satisfactory development" received ample school facilities.[33]

The neglect of the San Felipe District was particularly striking. The decision not to build the premier Black high school in Fourth Ward, where most Black middle-class students lived, ignored the expressed wishes of prominent Black leaders. A Colored Citizens Committee composed of ten highly respected Black businessmen, including Clifton Richardson and five members of the NAACP's executive committee, petitioned the board with a list of school improvements they found most urgent. Even though Houston was one of the first southern cities to open a Black public high school, by 1925, it was languishing in neglect.[34] The committee demanded a modern building that would "reflect credit upon our great city, inspire our children and serve as one of the places of interest to visitors." Along with a flagship high school for the San Felipe District, the committee called for a second high school in Fifth Ward, equipped with a manual training department to meet the needs of the working-class students in that industrial area.[35] Yet, board members chose not to replace the overcrowded and deteriorating "Colored High School." Instead, they simply provided an unadorned annex before changing its name to the more dignified Booker T. Washington High School (see figure 11.1). Washington High would not receive a modern building until 1959 when it was removed entirely from Fourth Ward.[36] Fifth Ward did receive an industrial high school, however it was placed in an aging white elementary school that had been converted to Black use as part of the effort to increase segregation in that section.

The site for the premier Black high school was in Third Ward, south of downtown (see map 11.1). It was named for the Reverend Jack Yates, the first pastor of Fourth Ward's esteemed Antioch Baptist Church; back in 1872, Rev. Yates led the effort to purchase Emancipation Park for Houston's annual Juneteenth celebration. Yates High School was just two blocks away in a newly developing area. During the nineteenth century, parks along the outskirts of town allowed urban

FIGURE 11.1. During the 1920s building program, Houston's original Black high school, which was located in the San Felipe District of Fourth Ward, received only an unadorned addition—pictured above—while the city's flagship Black high school was relocated to a largely undeveloped area of Third Ward. Houston Independent School District, *Building Program*, 120.

residents a chance to escape the crowds and noise of the city. It was finally absorbed by the public park system in 1918, although no significant improvements were made prior to the building program, which limited its usefulness and appeal to nearby families. A 1923 editorial in the *Informer* condemned the city's disregard: "Oodles of dough for additional park acreage for whites, while not even sanitary conveniences nor graveled driveways have been provided or contemplated for Emancipation Park!"[37]

After the planning commission launched the effort to shift Black middle-class development to Third Ward, Emancipation Park started receiving more amenities. Richardson then lambasted officials for the lack of park facilities for Black children in the other parts of town: "There are municipal parks all over the city for whites, while the only park for blacks is located in the Third Ward, miles away from the majority of the colored citizens of the city." A second editorial demanded a fully equipped playground along Hogg's proposed parkway for "the large colored population in the Fourth Ward."[38] Surely, he knew that any request involving Hogg's beloved parkway would be in vain, but he pointed out the hypocrisy, nonetheless.

In the meantime, the well-equipped Yates High School, which would also house the new Houston Colored Junior College, helped attract affluent Black families to Third Ward, especially in the rapidly developing area south of Elgin Street. In prior decades, most Black residents of the Third Ward lived east of downtown near St. Nicholas Catholic Church, Houston's first Black parish, while fewer lived near Emancipation Park (see map 11.1). Of the 109 residential addresses listed in the 1915 *Red Book*—a private directory of leading Black Houstonians—only two were south of Elgin Street, the future site of Yates High School. Thelma Scott Bryant, a Black teacher born in 1905 and raised in that neighborhood, described it as "very much like the country" when she was a little girl.[39] Moreover, as late as 1923, traditional mixed-race development continued to shape the area. The enrollment at Bowie Elementary, a nearby white school, grew by more than 40 percent between 1922 and 1923. The following year, board members requested Bowie's "possible relocation in a white district," although opposition from white residents prevented the district from acting at that time.[40]

The planning commission also championed the expansion of Black single-family housing in the Third Ward. Hogg clearly wished to shrink Fourth Ward's San Felipe District to benefit River Oaks, and another commission member, John Embry, had a financial interest in Third Ward's development near Yates High School. In 1923, he began selling lots in a new Black residential park named Forest Home. The *Informer* ran full-page advertisements suggesting it was "the highest class home addition ever put on [the market] for colored people in Houston." Unlike other subdivisions targeting Black homebuyers, the "sanitary sewer" and "water lines" were "practically completed" and work was "under way on the streets." The developers were also preparing "a large drainage ditch" so that Houston's swampy conditions would not flood the neighborhood.[41]

Even with the assurance of more single-family home lots, Black middle-class parents in Fourth Ward were disappointed with the school site, especially since it was not clear that Colored High School would remain open after Yates was completed. Along with many of his friends, Clifton Richardson lived and worked in the San Felipe District, and his children attended Fourth Ward schools. Upon learning that the flagship high school would be "stuck out there in Third Ward," Richardson questioned the site's accessibility: "Located at the far southeastern extreme of the city—far from the maddening city crowds—The Informer would like to know" how close "the street cars will run to the proposed site" and "how many of the streets will be shelled or graveled near or to the school." At the time, local officials had repeatedly broken their promises to improve Dowling Street, the main artery leading to Emancipation Park. During the run-up to 1924 bond election, Richardson had used the neglect of Dowling Street to galvanize Black voters to go "to the polls en masse" and vote "against every bond issue." "Not only is Dowling Street still unpaved," he scoffed, "but it is in worse shape than it has been in for years."[42]

By the time Yates welcomed its first students, the situation had flipped, and Richardson was complaining that Third Ward had received a disproportionate share of street improvements. "The Informer's attention has been called to the fact that most of the streets in colored residential sections that have been or are being graveled, are located in the Third Ward." "This paper does not begrudge seeing any Negro section graveled nor paved," he admonished, but "all the Houston Negroes do not reside in Third Ward, neither are all the home-owners and property-holders residents of that section, nor are all the colored churches and public schools located" on its streets.[43]

Third Ward's Emancipation Park neighborhood also received the district's finest Black elementary schools, including a new flagship elementary named for Frederick Douglass. The board spent over $155,000 on its building and site, almost $35,000 more than the next most expensive Black elementary and $5,000 more than the total spent on improvements for Fourth Ward's Colored High School. Between 1920 and 1930, Douglass's enrollment increased by 41 percent, from 738 to 1,039, while enrollment at Gregory—Fourth Ward's historic Black elementary school—declined from 923 to 909. Likewise, the board gave Blackshear Elementary, located only two blocks from Embry's Forest Home development, a new building with fifteen additional classrooms (see map 11.1). Its enrollment then soared by a remarkable 200 percent from 286 to 858, making it Houston's fastest growing Black school, by far.[44]

The improvements for Third Ward did not end there. The site for the new Houston Negro Hospital, which was also completed in 1926, was only a block from Yates High School, even though the hospital it was replacing was located in Fourth Ward. Wealthy oilman Joseph Cullinan, founder of Texaco and a longtime business associate of William Hogg, donated the money for the new building while the city donated the land. Alfred C. Finn, joint member of the school board and planning commission, was the architect for the project, while fellow planning commission member Dr. J. W. Slaughter helped determine the location. The initial site proposed for the hospital was in the San Felipe District near Hogg's planned parkway, but Slaughter rejected it. "I was doubtful of the wisdom of locating on that property because it is pretty close in, and should in time be very valuable," he confessed.[45]

The school building program also figured prominently in Hogg's efforts to attract affluent white families to River Oaks, despite its remote location. Hogg began corresponding with school administrators about potential elementary and high school sites in 1925, about eighteen months after publicly announcing the plan to develop River Oaks. He also met with an ally on the planning commission to discuss his preferred school sites before officially joining the commission later that year. The school board cooperated with his requests even though some administrators expressed concern that the "greatest emergencies" lay elsewhere. The impressive fifteen-acre site—which the company sold to the district for half price—was professionally landscaped by none other than Hare and Hare. River

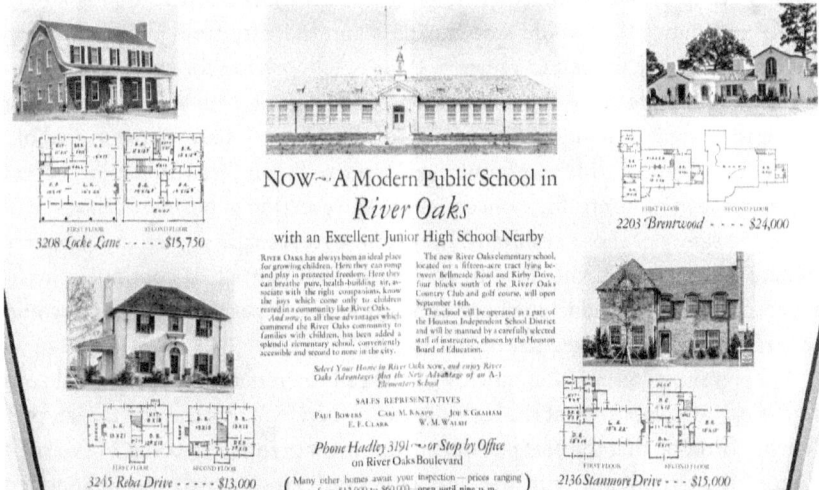

FIGURE 11.2. This River Oaks advertisement promised parents the trifecta that had come to epitomize the "ideal place for growing children": a single-family house, a modern school, and a restricted neighborhood that would shelter their children from the negative influences of the city, including the possibility of less-advantaged playmates. MSS 0012v8, Houston History Research Center, Houston Public Library. Used with permission.

Oaks was the only elementary with a per-pupil cost of more than $300, placing it more on par with the district's new junior highs than with its new white elementaries, which had a per-pupil average of just under $225.[46]

The River Oaks School welcomed its first students during the fall of 1929, the same year the building program ended. Local developers hoped that dozens of new schools would help counter the softening real estate market that was already heralding the nation's slide into depression. Earlier that year, advertisements for River Oaks began celebrating its "conveniently accessible" school, describing it as "second to none in the city" (see figure 11.2).[47] Similarly, the *Houston Post*'s real estate page urged parents to relocate near one of the district's new schools: "With several weeks left before the opening of school this fall, Houstonians will now begin to build homes near well located schools in many of Houston's finer subdivisions." It advised parents to "make arrangements to secure the proper location near adequate educational facilities" without delay, so that their "children may have every advantage possible" during the coming school year.[48]

Months later, the planning commission delivered its final report to Mayor Monteith. The published report was popular within professional planning circles—especially the "notable progress" in "planned park and school development"—but it stirred controversy at home. The first hint of trouble appeared a year earlier when a group of white homeowners petitioned the city council to pass a temporary ordinance that would stop business and industry from encroaching on their homes. They wished to preserve their neighborhood for child-rearing before it was too late since the completion of the zoning plan was taking longer than anticipated. "Owing to the nearness of the Albert Sidney Johnston school," the petition argued, "this community is attractive to families with children," yet an "increase in motor traffic, consequent to the erection of business houses, will affect the safety of those children." In response, real estate agents and property owners who expected the downtown commercial district to continue marching southward expressed vehement opposition to the petition because it would undermine real estate speculation in the area.[49]

The planning commission quickly dismissed the request for "piecemeal zoning," but Hare worried that the hostility unleashed by it was the real threat, predicting correctly that the protests were a harbinger of things to come. He warned Hogg, "The experience with the temporary ordinance which was abandoned (I believe fortunately)" demonstrated that "there will be considerable pressure" to zone "an undue amount of property for business, and I would not be surprised if this would also extend to apartment use."[50] After all, the purpose of zoning was to prevent commercial properties and multifamily housing from marring child-centered communities of single-family homes.

When the planning commission's final report became public, Hare's concern proved justified.[51] Although it was common for planners to feel some pressure to zone an excessive amount of property for commercial and industrial use, Houston's problem extended well beyond the typical pushback. Hogg had demanded complete secrecy while developing the plan and then abandoned the city before the public had a chance to debate it. He died while on vacation in Europe the following year. The newspapers agreed that shielding the process from the public eye had been a mistake because it had fomented distrust.[52] Too many Houstonians thought it was tainted by "the selfishness of owners of high-class residence sections," in the words of one critic. Moreover, Hogg had been so domineering that the other members of the planning commission beyond Hugh Potter were not invested in the final product and refused to defend it, while members of the real estate board were deeply divided.[53] Even Potter, who had served as president of the real estate board the prior year, was unable to moderate the discord. Consequently, the planning commission was forced to withdraw the plan for lack of support. Potter tried again the following decade, but that effort failed as well.[54]

He had more success overseeing the completion of a high school for River Oaks. Named for Texas revolutionary war hero Mirabeau B. Lamar, the new school would sit directly opposite the development's main entrance (see map 11.3). The location raised the ire of families in the southwestern section of the city who

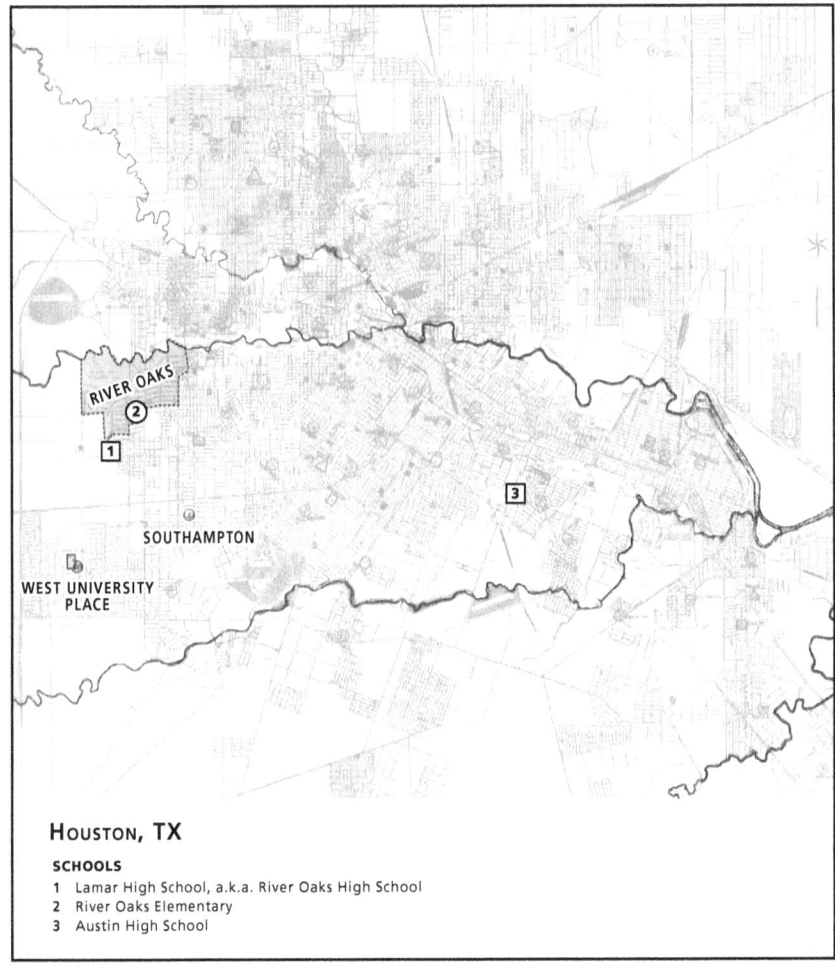

MAP 11.3. The residents of West University Place and Southampton had no direct access to Lamar High School when it first opened in 1937. Meanwhile, the children living in the more modest additions on the industrial east side attended the less prestigious Austin High School. Local History Collection, 917.641 H., Houston History Research Center, Houston Public Library. Base map used with permission.

accused the board of duplicity for having promised them a "Southwest High School" before the bond election. Affluent whites had been moving further south along Main Street to the residential parks near Hermann Park and Rice Institute—including West University and Southampton—for decades. The Southampton Civic Group passed a resolution of "deep regret," declaring the site to be "most unjust to the scholastics to be accommodated." As further insult, the plans had the school facing River Oaks with its "back toward our section of the city." Detractors dubbed it the "$1,000,000 school on the prairie" and contemptuously referred to it as "River Oaks High School."⁵⁵

While the site was only about two miles from the southwest suburbs as the crow flies, no existing road cut across that expanse, which was still part of the county. As a result, students would have to travel about eight miles through downtown to get to the school. "They don't want our kids there. They didn't build that school for us, but for River Oaks," one parent complained. "If they didn't, why don't they give us some roads to get to school?" "We have a fine new school for our children and no way to approach it," another grumbled. "The people of this community are going to continue to fight for what we think is due us and our children."⁵⁶ Hogg's vision for the original street plan included the extension of Kirby Street to connect the southwest suburbs to the proposed high school along with the River Oaks Shopping Center, which needed their business. But property owners along the route wished to develop the area into new residential parks and feared a "speedway" would damage their prospects. Thus, Lamar opened in 1937 with no road joining the two sections.⁵⁷

When the developers of Braeswood and Riverside Terrace—two new white residential parks on the south side—accused Hugh Potter of using his position as chair of the planning commission to benefit River Oaks at their expense, Potter addressed the attacks in a lengthy public rebuttal, which included a defense of the controversial high school site. "I had nothing whatever to do with the location of the Lamar School," he stated truthfully, but he omitted the crucial detail that William Hogg *had* negotiated the site more than ten years earlier. Potter explained that the company, instead, was merely being a good citizen by inviting the school district to connect Lamar to the River Oaks sewer system for free. He also reminded the other developers that River Oaks had requested annexation from the start, even though the corporation had paid for most of its own improvements. Potter's suggestion that River Oaks had given more than it had received quelled much of the uproar. The storm further evaporated once the opening of Buffalo Speedway efficiently linked the southwest residential areas to Lamar High School.⁵⁸

Even so, the advantages given to River Oaks irritated more than just the residents of the southwest section. "East End" was one of the most rapidly developing sections of the city during the 1920s because of an array of new, moderately priced additions. Nonetheless, the superintendent dubiously claimed that "their numbers" did not "warrant the erection of a new senior school" because "the pupils of the southeastern section" supposedly had "direct transportation" to the aging Houston High School located downtown.⁵⁹ When the area finally did receive a high school thanks to the same Public Works Administration funding that had helped build Lamar, parents were offended by the differences between the two schools. The *East Ender*, a weekly newspaper for the community, characterized

Lamar as "the superintendent's monument to injustice, inequality, and prejudice." While Lamar was "ultra-attractive, expensive and beautiful," their high school had been constructed of "cheap, ugly, undecorated brick" that made it look like a "penal institution." Indeed, Lamar's architect, John Staub, was also the in-house architect for River Oaks as well as a former member of the planning commission under Hogg. Staub's blueprints lined the walls of the school with "double glaze cream tile" and supplied it with an auditorium that had a modern heating and cooling system, among other unusual amenities. The board also furnished Lamar with $20,000 in landscaping for its 23-acre site but nothing for East End's smaller 13.5-acre site. The *East Ender* questioned "why the same was not provided for East End children."[60]

The short answer was that equal schools did not shape residential development nearly so well as unequal ones did. The beautiful new schools built for River Oaks drew affluent white families to the west side, while superior Black schools pulled Black families out from the San Felipe District, away from River Oaks and towards its rivals. The westside Gregory Institute—previously Houston's most distinguished Black elementary school—did receive a new building, but the board spent 23 percent less on it than on Third Ward's Douglass School, despite Gregory's larger and more affluent enrollment. Before long, wealthier Black families began relocating to Third Ward so that their children could attend the city's most well-equipped Black schools, including Jack Yates High School. According to Mary L. Johnson, one of the original teachers at Yates, "With the planting of an educational institution" in that section, "local conditions began to change and within a few years a new community had grown up around the school." It enjoyed "landscaped gardens, businesses, parks, new homes, and amusements." As for the once-thriving San Felipe District, by 1980 the population was well under half of what it had been in 1920, fulfilling one of the key goals of the planning commission.[61] And Houston never did pass a zoning law, making the city an instructive case. Ultimately, the benefits that child-centered residential parks acquired through the unequal distribution of schools and other public resources mattered more.

Morris Knowles and Racial Zoning

While Houston and Austin opted for "voluntary" de jure segregation, local officials in other southern cities continued to push the limits of the courts. Planning consultant Morris Knowles was ready to help: first in Birmingham, then back to Winston-Salem, and finally in Charleston. Local officials found it nearly impossible to uphold racial covenants in older neighborhoods without having a stronger enforcement mechanism. They wanted racial zoning to provide "permanent legal safeguards" in those areas undergoing racial transition. In Birmingham, members of the zoning commission first interviewed Robert Whitten to be their consultant, but in the end, they hired Morris Knowles. Apparently, Knowles was hungry enough for the job to be willing to experiment with racial zoning even after Atlanta's race districts had been struck down.[62] Plus, Knowles already had some familiarity with racial zoning: earlier that decade, he had drawn race districts for Winston-Salem as part of the preliminary work for a future zoning ordinance. Local officials then used his maps as the foundation for their school building program.

Although Knowles was a member of Hoover's advisory committee on zoning, a director of the National Conference on City Planning (NCCP), and the chair of the Pittsburgh planning commission, he still had less experience drafting actual zoning ordinances than Whitten. Therefore, he reached out to local heavyweight Robert Jemison Jr. for help securing the job. During World War I, Jemison and Knowles had worked together in the Housing Division of the Emergency Fleet Corporation.[63] Not long after, Jemison acquired a national reputation in the planning movement as a founding member of the American City Planning Institute before being named to the NCCP's board of directors. He was also the most powerful man in Birmingham. His father, the son of a wealthy plantation owner, had developed the city's first residential park and established the Birmingham Railway, Light and Power Company to facilitate suburban expansion. Jemison followed in his father's footsteps and began developing suburban residential parks in 1903.[64] When Knowles reached out to him for a recommendation, Jemison readily agreed to help; it would not hurt his business interests to have the zoning consultant in his back pocket.

As in Winston-Salem, Birmingham elites shaped residential development far beyond what was possible in more democratic cities such as Houston, Raleigh, and Atlanta. Birmingham's real estate board pressured local officials into drafting a state enabling law that would permit passage of an ordinance including the power to regulate the "different classes of inhabitants" in various sections of the city. Jemison participated behind the scenes by commenting on at least one draft. His thoughts on racial zoning were almost certainly influenced by Atlanta's efforts, since Whitten had sent him a copy of Atlanta's tentative zone map soon after it was completed.[65]

While the enabling bill made its way through the Alabama legislature, the debate over racial zoning in Birmingham began in earnest. According to the *Birmingham News*, a "delegation of prominent Negroes" appeared before the city commission to protest the effort to "fix upon the Negro by actual legislation, inferior living conditions." Their petition reminded local officials that the Supreme Court had already judged "such laws" to be unconstitutional and that, wherever segregation existed, there was "less police protection, poorer civic improvement and worse sanitary accommodations." The petition also tied inferior housing to the current Black exodus from the South, depicting "those going" as "the industrious, the thrifty and the intelligent"—the ones who made "good, reliable citizens" and who "labor and buy homes and are planning for a better life for their children." Benjamin Davis reprinted the entire article in the *Atlanta Independent* as part of his continuing fight against Atlanta's race districts, which were still being enforced at the time.[66]

Because Birmingham's industries relied heavily on Black workers, threats of migration were rarely dismissed. The *Birmingham News* not only published the petition in full, but an editorial criticized the racial component of the enabling act. Reflecting the views of the business class, the newspaper repeated the concerns that affluent whites had long expressed about segregation ordinances: "The creation of white and black zones would prevent blacks from improving their housing conditions, while making it harder for white property owners to dispose of their property when white demand diminished." Though local officials pressed forward with the original plan, the zoning commission agreed to sponsor segregated hearings to discuss "regulations for the negro districts" in hopes of gaining the "acquiescence" of the Black middle class.[67]

The final zoning ordinance included residence districts that banned all multi-family dwellings, including duplexes. The zoning commission argued unconvincingly that the "A" and "B" residential categories did not imply class distinction: "It is important to note that the term 'A residence' does not imply a more expensive development, or better style of architecture, than 'B residence.' These things, often controlled through private restrictions, are not attempted under zoning." The "residence districts" were then further divided into race districts, which included the exemptions typically found in other de jure segregation schemes. Along with servants and Black residents already living in "white" zones, the ordinance excluded vacant properties that would become unsalable if forced to transition to white occupancy.[68] In effect, Knowles had devised a plan to prevent further racial turnover, much as the segregation ordinances of the prior decade had unsuccessfully tried to do.

Some evidence exists that it was white residents in Birmingham's older, mixed-race neighborhoods—the ones who had repeatedly called for a segregation ordinance before *Buchanan* (1917)—who pushed hardest for racial zoning, which they expected to defend block-level segregation. The day after Knowles was hired as the city's consultant, members of the Graymont Civic Association asked the zoning commission to recognize the "zone line" they had "proclaimed" two years earlier. They wanted it enforced immediately as an "emergency measure," even though only two breaches of the color line had occurred in the past, with both cases involving "white persons wishing to erect negro houses." With the opening of the new Black high school just blocks away, the demand for Black homes

270 | Chapter 11

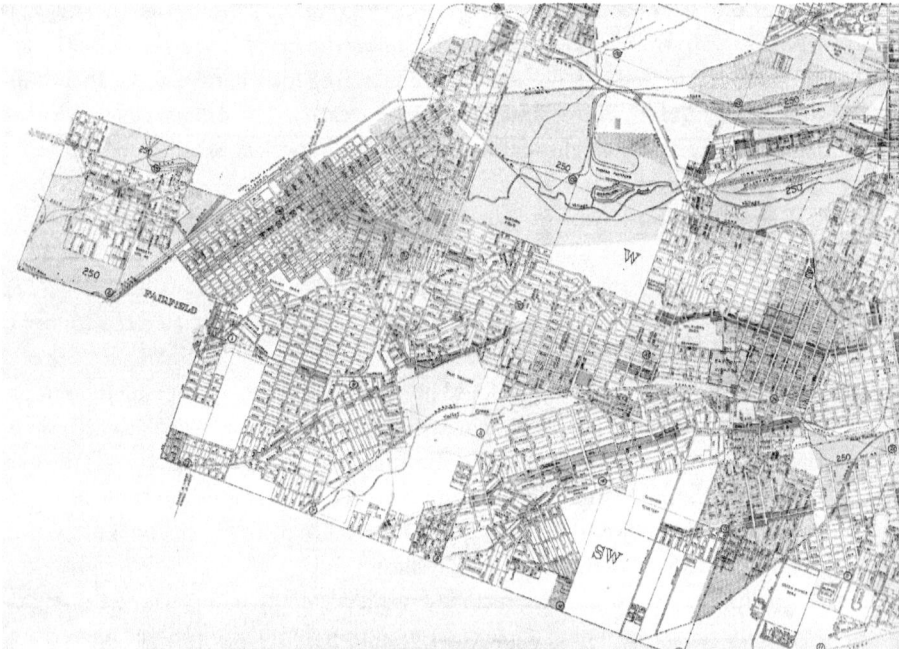

FIGURE 11.3. Birmingham's racial zoning map was approved almost two years after Atlanta's race districts were declared unconstitutional by the Georgia Supreme Court. Birmingham's

had begun to surpass the demand for white ones.[69] Thus, although the zoning commission refused to permit piecemeal enforcement, it did agree to incorporate their color line into the official zoning plan.

Even if the race districts had been a response to white residents in lower-income areas, the final zone map still generated widespread opposition. According to the *Birmingham News*, the hearings prompted the "filing of a large number of individual protests from residents of all sections of the city." For instance, a white delegation from "Pratt City," an industrial neighborhood near Pratt mines, attempted to alter the area's racial boundary to obtain more space for white homes. But unlike Atlanta's planning commission, Birmingham's would not budge, especially since the local real estate board had maintained steadfast control over the process. In addition to Jemison's influence behind the scenes, back-to-back presidents of the board had served as two of the zoning commission's five members. Upon their urging, the city commissioners passed the ordinance exactly as drafted—nearly two years after Atlanta's race districts had been struck down.[70]

The school building program made judicial review much less important to its implementation anyway. School sites would continue to produce segregation long into the future, mostly in ways that benefitted influential residential park

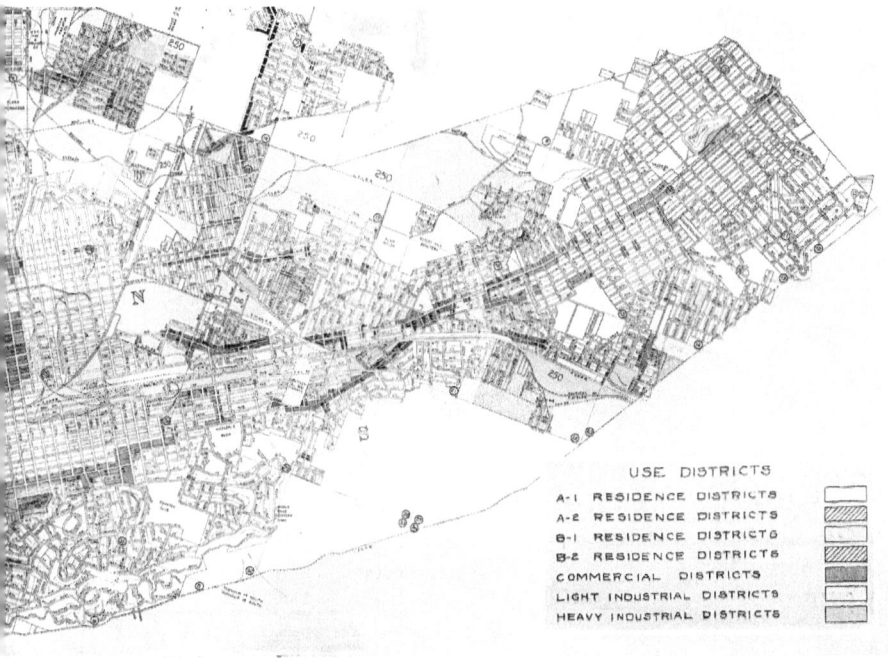

racial zones would not be declared unconstitutional until 1951. City of Birmingham v. Monk, 185 F.2d 859 (5th Cir. 1951). Courtesy of the Birmingham Public Library.

developers. Before the building program, Black schools were scattered across Birmingham, reflecting the mixed-race housing patterns of a city in which Black residents made up fully 40 percent of the population. During the building program, however, board members began concentrating new Black schools in the industrial northern and northwestern sections of the city, pulling Black families away from Jemison's residential parks on the south side.[71] Moreover, the one Black district that was zoned for single-family housing was favored with new schools. Along with the new Black high school, the old high school received a modern addition that transformed it into the city's largest elementary school. It would have more than 2,600 students by 1930, compared with fewer than 1,400 in the city's largest white elementary. North Birmingham's brand-new Lewis School was also not far from this "very desirable negro community," in the words of the school survey.[72]

In contrast, the district's two oldest Black schools, located between downtown and the prestigious residential parks on the south side, received no modern improvements (see map 11.4). The antiquated Lane School had a seating capacity of only 360 for an enrollment of more than 1,000 students. The survey recommended it "be replaced at once" in "a new location" because it straddled the attendance districts of two white schools serving nearby residential parks. Nonetheless, at the

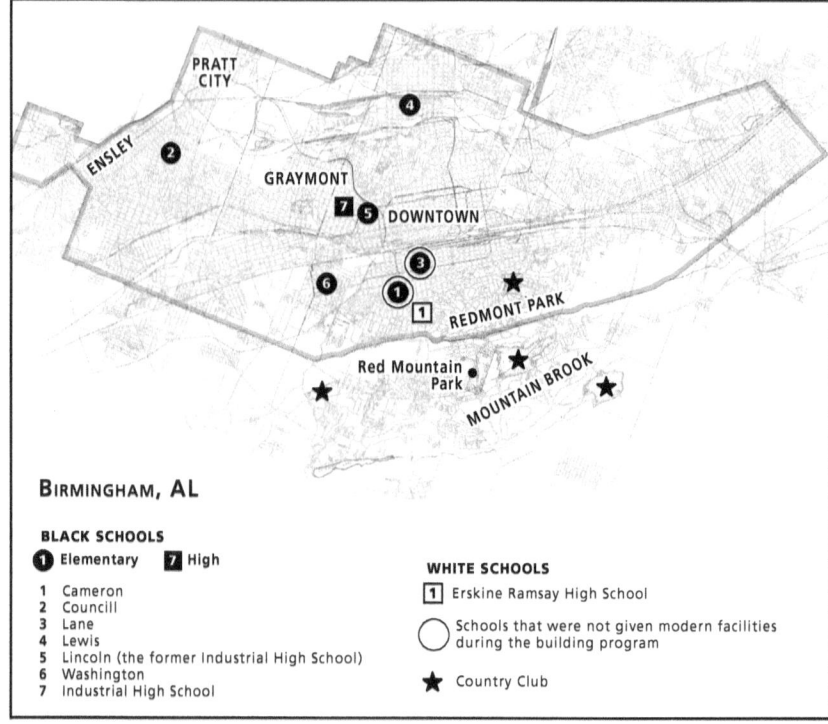

MAP 11.4. Birmingham's building program supported the planning commission's segregation efforts by pushing Black families away from the affluent residential parks on the city's south side. Courtesy of the Birmingham Public Library. Used with permission.

close of the building program, Lane still had not received a single improvement despite its appalling condition. The district's second oldest school, Cameron, was located on the south side as well. It received a two-room frame addition worth less than $2,300, raising its value to about $13 per pupil, a mere $2 more per pupil than Lane's shockingly low assessment. By comparison, the average for all Black elementaries was $68 per pupil, and the new Lewis School, built in North Birmingham, was $131 per pupil.

The building program's final report (1931) included a map of the district that labeled Cameron a "temporary" school and left Lane off completely, even though Birmingham's rapidly rising student population meant that both schools would remain in use. Rather than provide decent schools on the south side where they were needed most, the board gave Washington School, located in an isolated community farther west, a modern addition and the Black residents of Ensley—a working-class community in the industrial northwest section—a brand-new school (see map 11.4). According to the city's zone map, both schools were placed deep within large Black apartment districts.[73]

The neglect of Lane and Cameron had everything to do with Robert Jemison's real estate interests. Previously, he had developed several small residential parks in the southside "Country Club District," but his newest and most ambitious project was Redmont Park, which began selling lots in 1924, the same year the initial bond issue passed.[74] One advertisement promised "not simply a lot on which to build a house, but a neighborhood in which to build a home." Another advised, "Instead of asking yourself if you can afford to live in a select environment, where you and your family will find congenial friends and neighbors, you should rather ask yourself if you can afford to live" in a neighborhood where you will be unable to "rear your children in an atmosphere of culture and refinement."[75] By 1927, Redmont Park was an unqualified success, so Jemison launched Mountain Brook Estates, an even more exclusive residential park with Redmont keeping guard from the city below.[76] An ad assured parents, "Fortunate indeed is the boy or girl who can spend childhood's impressionable years in Mountain Brook's attractive home environment. For here is a children's paradise—trees to climb, woods to roam, brooks to wade in, [and] companions of their own social station to play with."[77]

Jemison's unique stature gave him relatively open access to most city officials, but he nevertheless arranged to have an insider placed on the school board. Erskine Ramsay joined the board as its new chair in 1922, when talk of a building program began in earnest. Ramsay had acquired his vast fortune from mining coal with enslaved convicts, most of whom were found guilty of the type of misdemeanors intended to entrap Black men in the state's deadly convict lease system.[78] He also sat on the board of directors for Redmont Park, and in 1926, became one of the two vice presidents for Mountain Brook Estates. As chair of the school board, Ramsay ensured that Redmont Park received a conveniently located high school, aptly named Erskine Ramsay High. The site cost over $400,000, an enormous sum equal to the entire amount spent on Black schools from the first bond issue. Furthermore, Ramsay guaranteed that no modern Black schools would "encroach" on either Redmont Park or other southside residential parks, even though Black residents had lived in the area since at least 1886 when Lane School first opened. Before Ramsay's interference, the board had followed the survey's original recommendation and purchased a $20,000 site for Lane's replacement. After Ramsay became chair, the decision was rescinded, and the building program ended without any substantial improvements to the two Black schools between downtown and Jemison's premier developments.[79]

Jemison's rise to national prominence peaked when he was elected president of the National Association of Real Estate Boards (NAREB) in 1926, the same year that *Euclid* was handed down and Birmingham's zoning plan became law. That year, he wrote an article for *Nation's Business*, the official organ of the US Chamber of Commerce, expounding upon the vital issues then facing NAREB. He commended Hoover's Commerce Department for fostering public-private partnerships in which "professional institutions" took the lead while the federal government stood back and provided moral advocacy and financial support.[80] He also encouraged a closer relationship between developers and planners, even though he did not share the latter group's idealism but instead considered harnessing the power of government essential to profitable development.

Jemison's extensive business files helped track the flow of ideas between NAREB and the NCCP, as well as from one city to the next. During the late 1920s, he remained in constant contact with the developers of many of the nation's most acclaimed residential parks: J. C. Nichols of Kansas City's Country Club District, Hugh Potter of Houston's River Oaks, Hugh Prather of Dallas's Highland Park, and Edward Bouton of Baltimore's Roland Park, among others.[81] They exchanged lists of deed restrictions, strategies for effective advertising, data about sales, and information on local zoning efforts. In addition, Jemison corresponded regularly with preeminent zoning consultants, including Knowles, who sent him the preliminary data and maps for Birmingham without the zoning commission's consent.[82] Knowles was willing to share confidential information with Jemison not only because he had helped Knowles get the job but also because he had extensive connections that might help Knowles obtain consulting work in the future.

After completing Birmingham's zoning plan, Knowles returned to Winston-Salem. Back in 1921, he had finished the preliminary work for a zoning plan with the expectation that he would complete the ordinance sometime later. Meanwhile, Mayor James Hanes used Knowles's maps and data to locate school and park "centers" as part of a "voluntary segregation" scheme to lure families to racially designated areas of the city, as discussed in chapter 8. Modern schools had reliably functioned as key inducements for residential development for decades, but Hanes's effort soon faltered. The most significant flaw was that local officials had chosen to place the new Black high school in Columbia Heights. During the late nineteenth century, Black educator Simon Atkins had dreamed of developing Columbia Heights into a child-centered residential park for affluent Black families. He readily accepted investment money from the city's powerful elite, even if their primary interest in the project was residential segregation.[83]

Although Columbia Heights' isolation appealed to segregationists, it made for an untenable location for affluent Black families, at least beyond those affiliated with Simon Atkins's Slater Normal School. Winston-Salem was a small city, but Columbia Heights required a thirty-minute commute to downtown by either jitney or streetcar—and that only after a ten-minute walk to the nearest station.

Black businessmen and professionals preferred the accessibility of the northeastern district. That area enjoyed the costliest Black school constructed during the last building program—a combined elementary and junior high with a twenty-five-acre site surrounded by a park and playground.[84]

Mayor Hanes also established a third school "center" near Kimberly Park in the northwestern section of the city. It, too, was less remote from the downtown business district, but mortgage lenders remained scarce. Without investment from white elites as Columbia Heights had had from the beginning, the area grew slowly. Furthermore, neither Columbia Heights nor Kimberly Park had minimum building standards, let alone zoning protection, so shacks and other types of substandard housing started to pop up in both neighborhoods.[85] In contrast, the northeastern section enjoyed good single-family housing that became available as white residents moved out to neighborhoods near the new white schools. The houses they left behind were on established streets, greatly reducing the risk that either poor housing or commercial use would damage the area's environment for child-rearing.

Mayor Hanes's "voluntary segregation" scheme effectively steered Black development away from the affluent residential parks on the city's southwest side, but it did not help white families in East Winston defend block-level segregation. The continued tension in racial transition areas led to a push for legally enforceable race districts, especially since the number of Black residents in the city was growing faster than the number of whites.[86] Consequently, many of the white residents living in East Winston believed a carefully designed segregation law might still prevent Black families from moving next door. This was the situation in 1928 when the board of aldermen agreed to rehire Morris Knowles to complete the zoning ordinance.

Whether or not racial zoning was inspired by the city's lower-income whites, local elites maintained firm control over the process, as was true in Birmingham. The chair of the zoning commission, Henry Fries, had long tied public service to residential development. He sat on the school board when home lots went on sale in Central Terrace, one of his southside residential parks. Now, his role on the zoning commission allowed him to further protect his investments, which included his family's bank, Wachovia, a major mortgage lender. Elites with ties to the housing industry used zoning to stimulate new home construction, an important reason why zoning efforts often overlapped with local own-your-own-home campaigns. By seeking a reshuffling of families, residential zoning could increase sales; Winston-Salem's ordinance was particularly strict, with three different types of residential districts layered onto its racial zones.[87]

Local officials also hoped to advance their goals through a second school building program, which did not protect block-level segregation as many white

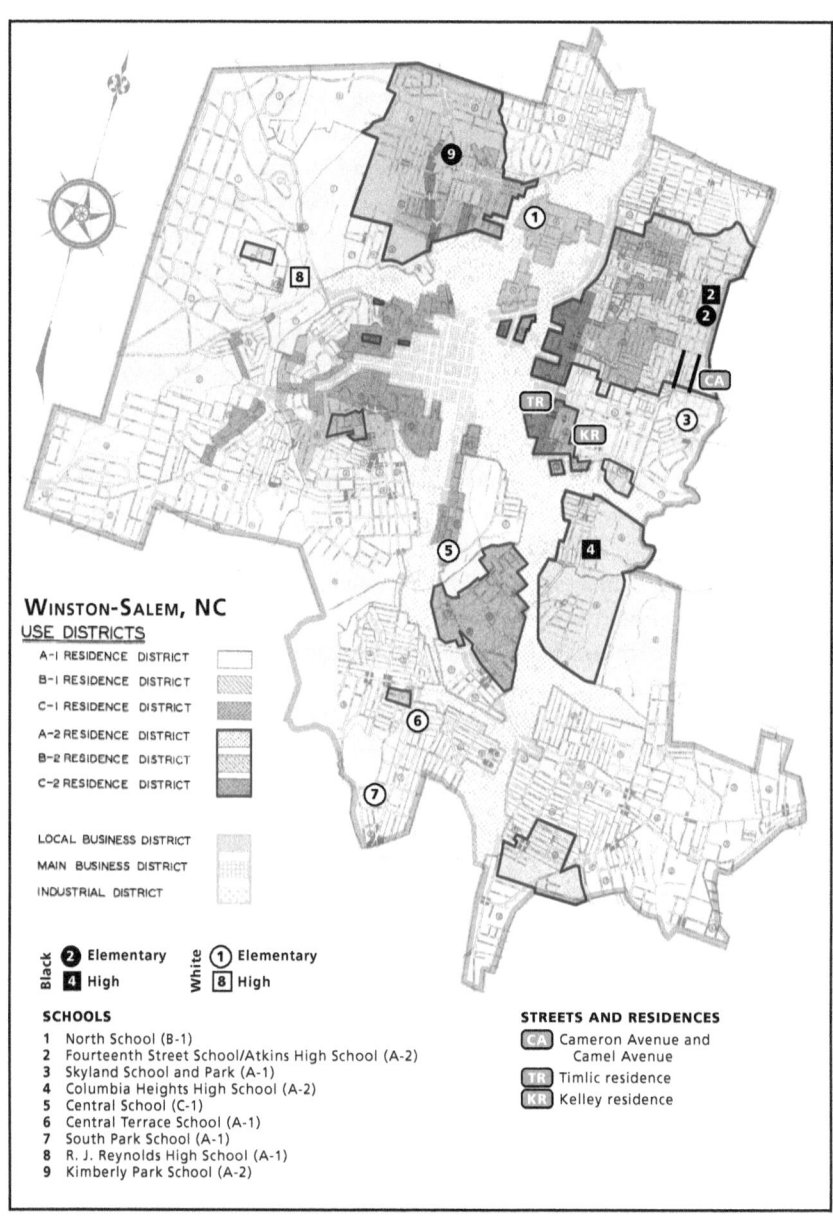

MAP 11.5. Winston-Salem's racial zoning map (1930) was completed after local officials had already initiated a "voluntary segregation" scheme, which relied on new schools to shift the population to segregated areas. The original plan, which was widely heralded in the press, likely inspired efforts in other cities. Courtesy of Forsyth County Public Library North Carolina Collection, Winston-Salem, NC.

residents had wanted. Several months before the board of aldermen approved the preparation of the ordinance, voters had passed a $2.5 million school bond issue. The resulting building program included a "state-of-the-art" Black high school completed with the aid of a $50,000 grant from the Julius Rosenwald Fund. The high school was built along Cameron Avenue on the same advantageous site as the flagship elementary-junior high school. Named in honor of Simon Atkins, it opened its doors in 1931. At the time, white families occupied every house below Tenth Street on Cameron and Camel Avenues (see map 11.5). The next year, the occupancy flipped: Black families lived in every house except one on the blocks above Eighth Street. Black parents wishing to live near the new Black high school had put those blocks in high demand, just as the zoning ordinance had anticipated. That expectation explains why all-white blocks were placed in a Black, single-family residential district even before the new high school opened.[88]

For the most part, the outlines of the racial zoning map corresponded to the 1922 voluntary segregation scheme that attempted to remake the mixed-race areas in the northern and eastern sections into sizeable white districts. Both sections had received impressive schools and parks during the earlier building program, yet neither a zoning law nor a new school could stop racial turnover on a block that was more attractive to Black residents than white ones any more than a segregation ordinance or racial covenant could. As a result, the block along East Fourth Street that had triggered the city's original 1912 segregation ordinance, predictably, was not far from the block that initiated the legal challenge to the 1930 racial zoning map. William A. Kelly Jr., a Black employee at RJR Tobacco, purchased a home in East Winston that had previously been occupied by a white tenant. At the time, Black tenants occupied eight of the ten houses.[89]

During the initial hearings on the ordinance, white residents had requested that the proposed race line in East Winston be shifted one block west, which placed Kelly's block on the edge of a white, single-family residential district. When the change was made, a grocery store and boarding house already marred the block for middle-class child-rearing; meanwhile, a Black housing shortage forced Black tenants to pay far higher rents than whites, generating a lucrative opportunity for absentee landlords. Accordingly, Black tenants started moving onto the block as early as 1935. Nonetheless, local officials did not begin enforcing the zoning law until after Kelly purchased a home in 1939, apparently because the block no longer had all-white ownership. The authorities ordered all Black residents to immediately vacate the block. Kelly and the white property owners then went to court, with Kelly asserting the right to live in his own house and the others asserting the right to profit from their property.[90]

The following year, the North Carolina Supreme Court declared the city's race districts unconstitutional in *Clinard v. Winston-Salem* (1940). The justices reminded the holdouts that the ordinance under review in the *Euclid* case "contained no provision for segregation of the races such as the one here challenged." Plus, they dismissed the argument that racial zoning when part of a comprehensive zone plan with "fairly apportioned" race districts belonged in a separate category from the segregation laws that had been ruled invalid in *Buchanan* (1917). "The law will not permit the indirect accomplishment of that which it directly forbids," they concluded, and racial zoning clearly would not be allowed to stand on its own.[91]

In the long run—whether found constitutional or not—racial zoning was just as unworkable as the other types of segregation laws. Winston-Salem's zone map placed East Winston in a white single-family district, but it was surrounded by Black residential districts of varying classes (see map 11.5). This dynamic resulted in vacancies all along the border, which included Kelly's block. In a paper presented at the 1929 NCCP, Ernst Freund, professor of law at the University of Chicago, questioned the ability of zoning to promote stable residential areas because of this very problem. Even if edge properties acted as buffers for the houses located deep within single-family districts, requiring the same residential use generated unsalable properties since the border would remain much less desirable to families who could afford to pay a sizable amount for a home.[92] Indeed, zoning appealed to residential park developers precisely because they wished to control the adjacent property: they secured the edges of their suburban developments with single-family zoning, schools and recreational parks, and convenient, fashionable shopping centers. So long as the buffers were also child-centered, edge properties would continue to attract affluent white homebuyers. Thus, residential parks that were fully encapsulated within large single-family districts and surrounded by child-centered amenities produced much more effective race districts than any segregation law.

Given that single-family zoning so clearly favored the affluent, Freund doubted that it protected the general welfare, and for that reason, he supposed it did not warrant use of the police power. He mused, "We find it argued that the one family home district is conducive to health, and to the cultivation of all kinds of civic virtues; would any one contend that under the police power the state might compel the well-to-do to bring up their children in such homes instead of exposing them to the blighting influences of hotel life?" His rhetorical question illustrated the absurdity of claiming that zoning's provision of a more wholesome environment for white, middle-class child-rearing somehow benefitted everyone else. Of course it didn't. Single-family zoning was inherently class legislation devised primarily to safeguard large financial investments in suburban residential parks.[93]

In 1931, Knowles followed up his efforts in Winston-Salem with a city plan for Charleston, South Carolina. Although he identified "probable future white and negro residence sections" in his preliminary work, he never intended to include them in the official zoning ordinance. Instead, he expected new schools and parks to mold the city's racial development. His final report explicitly recommended that Charleston's impending building program function as a substitute for racial zoning: "In the South, where separate schools are established for white and negro children, the logical location of schools may be an effective influence for the desirable development of the surrounding territory." He completed the school survey while also working as the city's zoning consultant. One of his recommendations was the provision of "proper facilities, such as schools, parks and playgrounds in logical locations" that would result in a "decrease in negro population in Wards 1 to 8." He also advised the conversion of "Buist School into a white elementary" to "greatly assist in maintaining a desirable character of development" and, thereby, "keep" the surrounding area "a white section." He hoped his suggestions might "point out the ways in which the location of school facilities" could "contribute toward guiding the development of property in accordance with the purposes of the zoning ordinance."[94]

The following year, Knowles publicly defended his contributions to residential segregation by distancing himself from local officials "in the South" who continued to pursue irresponsible segregation ordinances "under the guise of zoning." He thought any law that attempted racial segregation "without proper planning for equality of opportunities and municipal amenities" ought to be condemned. In contrast, he described actual zoning as "a science" requiring "accuracy and vision" and "an art" requiring "long and proper training."[95] For professionals such as himself, the creation of racial zones through the "scientific" distribution of schools and other child-centered amenities remained a positive good, even as his work further embedded racial segregation into white concepts of what it meant to be a good parent.

It was undoubtedly segregation's deep-seated connection to child-rearing—even beyond the schools that had acted as magnets for nearly all families with the resources to choose where they lived—that ensured it would endure long after other forms of de jure segregation had been abandoned. Schools would only advance residential segregation in areas otherwise deemed desirable for child-rearing and that provided reasonable access to employment. After *Euclid* and *Corrigan*, single-family zoning guarded the flanks of child-centered residential parks, turning whole swaths of the city into racial zones. High demand in those areas reinforced the idea that racial covenants supported high property values. Simultaneously, Black schools, parks, and single-family housing on the opposite side of town were supposed to help affluent Black families build equally nurturing neighborhoods in which to raise their children—or at least that was the promise. Despite the best efforts of Black parents, continued municipal neglect, lax zoning enforcement, inadequate space for population growth, exposure to numerous environmental hazards, a discriminatory mortgage market, and a decade-long depression shattered the dream of thriving residential parks dedicated to Black child-rearing.

CHAPTER 12

An Enduring Legacy

In 1929, researchers in Washington, DC, interviewed some 200 white residents who lived on blocks undergoing racial transition. Commissioned by the Interracial Committee of the Washington Federation of Churches and published by Howard University Press, the results provided some rare insight into the specific reasons why individual white families aggressively opposed Black next-door neighbors. The study dismissed the "mythical" property value trope that whites typically leaned on to avoid an honest discussion about race, but it sympathetically acknowledged that the subjects of the study were "victims of forces over which" they had "little or no control." It also pointed out the evasiveness of most answers. Only two of those interviewed admitted that they feared a daughter might become involved in an interracial relationship, although an additional twenty-three worried they might grow to like their Black neighbors. Many of those interviewed dreaded "the attitudes of the other members of white society" most. One woman complained that some friends refused to speak to her and her family after learning they had Black neighbors.[1] The researchers found that the respondents with children harbored the greatest hostility. For many white parents, the presence of other white children confirmed a block's suitability for white child-rearing whereas the presence of a well-dressed, well-behaved Black child signaled they were living at a "bad" address.[2] After all, affluent white residents had been living in racially restricted residential parks for decades.

During the 1920s, advertisements and articles in popular magazines insisted that a residential park was the only suitable place to raise a child. In promoting suburban development, racial exclusion was rarely presented as the most significant factor; instead, the emphasis was on the desirability of neighborhoods restricted to single-family homes.[3] In 1929, the director of advertising for the River Oaks Corporation applauded "the discriminating home-owner" who was "rapidly learning" what "the modern community builder" already knew: "the ideal place for a home" was in a neighborhood "where there are *only* homes."[4] Experts in the fields of parenting, city planning, and education regularly insinuated that those who did not move into residential parks were bad parents willing to endanger both their children's and the nation's future. Over time, the connection between who was a "good" parent and what was a "good" neighborhood seemed natural rather than a cultural construct worthy of historical analysis.

The ultimate child-centered amenity was a modern school, making new schools the most important centrifugal force in urban development. Because the location and condition of schools shaped housing decisions, school building programs were powerful tools for steering families to suburban housing, especially in Jim Crow cities where large-scale building programs overlapped with local zoning efforts. Indeed, long after the courts had banned racial zoning, new schools would continue to preserve residential segregation. Atlanta's success in combining zoning with its school building program influenced Robert Whitten to add school surveys to his repertoire as a consultant. In his 1932 survey report for Dobb's Ferry, New York, he recommended the placement of schools "be governed more by the future distribution of school children than by present distribution," setting up the same self-fulfilling prophecies that had benefited Atlanta's residential parks.[5]

Whitten was not alone in declaring that new schools and new residential development should be planned together.[6] In 1928, Helen Monchow of the Institute for Research in Land Economics and Public Utilities reinforced the belief that school sites and playgrounds were "among the most important" of the "community features" developers needed to consider. She cited Robert Whitten, who was then researching the plausibility of extending some of the advantages of the residential park to homes in older, urban areas through the "neighborhood unit," a concept credited to his colleague Clarence Perry. Whitten and Perry worked together on the 1929 regional plan for the New York metropolitan area.[7] Using the residential park as his model, Perry identified the essential components of a neighborhood as housing, a school, a park with a playground, and a convenient shopping center, as the residents of J. C. Nichols's Country Club District enjoyed. In fact, Perry cited Nichols along with Roland Park's Edward Bouton as his inspiration.[8]

Like the developers he admired, Perry felt that neighborhoods should cater to families with children. He had been heavily influenced by the social science arguments that had defined what the appropriate environment for child-rearing should be.[9] Perry agreed that the insulated communities within restricted residential parks not only enhanced child development but also helped to combat juvenile delinquency by shielding children from the urban problems that existed outside their neighborhoods. Housing "devoted to child-rearing families," he argued, was "peculiarly and vitally dependent upon the resources and character of the immediate vicinity," with a conveniently located public school the most indispensable resource for effective child-rearing.[10]

Perhaps the most innovative aspect of Perry's "neighborhood unit" was the possibility for redeveloping older areas of the city to reflect the child-centered advantages of a carefully planned residential park. Robert Whitten published an analysis of its feasibility two years before Perry's work appeared as part of New York's regional plan. Whitten, too, saw improving the environment for child-rearing as the primary goal. He warned that large cities endangered "the welfare of the children" whose parents "subordinated" young people's interests to either "convenience" or the "economic pressure resulting from increasing land values." Both Whitten and Perry had hoped that using the power of eminent domain along with other government resources would help pay the cost of redevelopment, but Whitten ultimately concluded that the cost would remain prohibitive.[11] In 1931, he published *Neighborhoods of Small Homes*, a volume that analyzed the cost of urban redevelopment for less affluent families. Whitten determined that low-income parents simply could not afford a single-family house. Still, he thought that implementing at least some of the features of the neighborhood unit might help provide more child-centered spaces for less-advantaged children.[12]

In 1931, the "Regional Plan of New York and Its Environs" (1929) helped frame the discussion at Hoover's White House Conference on Home Building and Home Ownership.[13] Its inclusion seemed logical since it had only recently been published and eminent planners such as Edward Bassett and Lawson Purdy had participated in its creation. Bassett had served as the chair of Hoover's "advisory committee on zoning," and Purdy had initially proposed using a child-centered argument to convince the courts of zoning's constitutionality at the 1918 National Conference on City Planning (NCCP), as discussed in chapter 10. Furthermore, Whitten, Perry, and Thomas Andrews, the "General Director of Plans and Surveys" for the 1929 regional plan, served on conference subcommittees: Whitten on "Subdivision Layout," Perry on "Housing and the Community," and Adams on "City Planning and Zoning."[14] Andrews also coauthored Whitten's *Neighborhoods of Small Homes*, which was cited frequently in the conference's final reports.

Still, residential park developers such as Hugh Potter and Robert Jemison were far more influential in the design of the FHA's mortgage insurance program and *Underwriting Manual* than the planning consultants and social scientists debating variations of the neighborhood unit at Hoover's conference.[15] Potter, representing Houston's River Oaks, was the president of the National Association of Real Estate Boards (NAREB) in 1934. During his term in office, he spent long stretches in Washington, DC, lobbying for the passage of the National Housing Act, which would establish the Federal Housing Administration (FHA).[16] Likewise, Hill Ferguson, vice president of Jemison's flagship development companies in Birmingham, began serving in FDR's administration in 1934, first as the deputy chief appraiser for the Home Owners Loan Corporation and then as the zone appraiser for the FHA.[17] During World War I, Hill Ferguson was given much of the credit for launching NAREB's original "Own-Your-Home" campaign before the US entry into the war. A debate over making home financing more affordable had been a key component of the movement from the beginning. Jemison himself was a former president of NAREB who had also served in leadership positions in the NCCP and the American City Planning Institute.[18]

Developers and their allies had grown adept at using local governments to fulfill their plans in ways that would not necessarily implicate them, and the federal government's new role in housing was devised in the same vein. If future projects met the FHA's minimum subdivision standards—standards that the developers themselves had written to reflect their own "best" practices—they would be practically guaranteed buyers who could obtain affordable mortgages. Not only would the subsidies substantially lower their risk, but the standards would lock out small-scale developers who they feared would "damage" adjacent property through speculation or carelessness. It also deprived those who specialized in older neighborhood housing of similar financing opportunities, further reducing the competition for potential homebuyers.[19]

In the wake of World War II, the policies that had been put in place during the Depression successfully launched a housing market dominated by federally subsidized, large-scale residential parks, making a home in the suburbs affordable for more white families. Even though developers had given themselves the tools they needed to shape residential development according to their plans, they publicly presented the new policies as a federal effort to help parents obtain a better environment for child-rearing and, thereby, stabilize home values. Potter's River Oaks began advertising the new program almost immediately. One 1935 advertisement assured, "The amortized payments on your own home will be less than the rent you'll have to pay next year." It encouraged renters "to buy or build now, especially if there are children in your family." "Every child deserves the sort of home-life that can only be had in a home of your own," with River Oaks being an exceptionally "desirable" place for children.[20]

White families with lower incomes had been resisting affluent visions of residential development for a quarter of a century. Before the New Deal transformed the housing market, many white residents who could not afford to move out to restricted suburbs sought ways to prevent racial turnover in their neighborhoods. To assist the effort, Atlanta's ward-based city council passed two additional segregation ordinances between 1929 and 1931. Both originated in the Fourth Ward, the birthplace of Atlanta's original 1913 segregation ordinance. The first law attempted to sidestep *Buchanan* by declaring that home seekers could not move onto a block if they could not intermarry with the majority of residents on that block. Since the Supreme Court had already upheld antimiscegenation laws, local officials believed this new ordinance might survive judicial review. The mayor disagreed, but his veto was unanimously overridden by the city council. After the courts quickly struck down the law, the next one banned Black residents from moving within *fifteen* blocks of a white school. This law reflected the much wider scope of segregation that had been established through residential park development; in 1920, it would have been difficult for a white Atlantan to travel even half a mile without passing the home of a Black family. The new law was also a response to white parents' ongoing fear that the school board would meet the intensifying demand for additional Black classrooms by converting more white schools to Black use. This law, too, was found unconstitutional. The following year, multiple bombings terrorized Black residents who moved onto blocks still hotly contested by whites, with most of the violence occurring in the Fourth Ward.[21]

Once the FHA made a home in the suburbs more affordable, less affluent white families could then leave behind the mixed-use areas they had previously defended. To facilitate the process, the FHA devised an advertising blitz during the mid-1930s to encourage young "white" parents to buy a home in the suburbs. The resulting "Better Housing News Flashes" placed child-rearing at the center of homeownership. In one clip titled "Where Do Your Children Play?," homeownership meant a "private playground" with "cool grass," a swing set, a sandbox, a dog, and a nearby field to play ball, all of which would lead to offspring with "sturdy bodies, alert minds, and happy hearts." The video assured parents, "In your city, there are countless spots where you can conveniently build a home under the National Housing Act or buy one already built, and around it provide a safe playground for your children."[22]

The FHA's child-centered arguments no doubt resonated with its intended audience. Developers and planners had long prepared for this day by educating children and adolescents about the superiority of suburban living. While many of their parents had looked askance at the extent to which American middle-class families "babied" their children, local developers and planners had set the stage for the next generation to take a different path. Along with the advertisements and child-rearing articles appearing regularly in newspapers and popular magazines, local "Own-Your-Own-Home" campaigns plastered their slogans everywhere, making them difficult to miss. They were seen on streetcars, in department store windows, on screens in local theaters, and even printed on the menus of popular restaurants.

Beyond the ubiquitous slogans, strategies directed specifically at students included home economics courses that stressed the proper environment for child-rearing, special textbooks on city planning such as those found in the high schools of Dallas and Chicago, and essay contests and debates on "the merits of home ownership." Some local campaigns went further than others. The New Orleans Real Estate Board awarded the school that produced the "the best essay on 'Why Every Family Should Own Its Own Home'" an impressive "little bungalow" for its playground. The organizers of Birmingham's annual Own-Your-Own-Home show sponsored a children's day meant to entice the "future home-owners of the city," and in Portland, Oregon, children whose parents already owned a home received "We-Own-Our-Own-Home" buttons from their teachers, a mean-spirited strategy that singled out children whose families could not afford to buy a single-family house.[23]

Although scholars have long recognized the child-centered nature of midcentury suburbs, what they were identifying was largely a change in scale rather than a new phenomenon. According to surveys at the time, 80 percent of suburban residents across the nation claimed they purchased their new homes specifically for their children.[24] Rising incomes and falling construction costs also aided suburban development, which in turn contributed to the nation's strong economic growth during the three decades following World War II. According to the work of economists Thomas Piketty, Emmanuel Saez, and Gabriel Zucman, the "income share of the bottom 90 percent" of the population soared during World War II before peaking during the 1970s. They concluded that between 1946 and 1980, "real macroeconomic growth" was "strong" and "equally distributed," with the bottom 90 percent of incomes increasing at a faster rate than the top 10 percent.[25] Relatively high taxes on the wealthy combined with union recognition, Veteran's Administration housing and education programs, and government-backed mortgages helped reduce income inequality substantially. Almost 85 percent of Americans identified as middle class, and suburban children grew up in a land of consumer abundance, much of it aimed at them.[26]

During the same period, the most vulnerable children—those whose welfare was most endangered by urbanization and industrialization—found themselves excluded from the government-endorsed solution: suburbia. The rhetoric of the planning movement had insisted that the purpose of zoning was "to help the child," in the words of renowned planner John Nolen. Yet, the combined effect of overcrowding and inadequate services caused lasting damage to Black children and others excluded from residential parks, with the FHA directly advancing segregation through its recommendations. The consequences have been devastating, as many parent educators might have predicted.[27]

During the 1920s, Black middle-class families had been hopeful, if skeptical. They had achieved dramatic wins, especially improved access to single-family housing and the expansion of Black secondary education. While they recognized that "voluntary segregation" was likely a trap, they had no better options than to work hard to make their communities what they hoped they would be, even if those efforts were systematically undermined. In 1923, E. Franklin Frazier, a prominent Black sociologist and the director of Morehouse College's Atlanta School of Social Service, questioned "how far" it was "possible for two fully developed, independent communities to exist in the same city." "For the present," at least, the Neighborhood Union was "ministering to the needs of the people and inspiring colored children to receive the heritage of American civilization."[28]

Increasing levels of residential segregation produced significant risks in terms of municipal neglect, but it also afforded some protection for Black children. Living among whites exposed them to a form of terror that was unimaginable to the white parents who sought to shelter their children away from the city. The most extreme forms of violence—including house bombings, lynching, and rape—could occur at any moment; Black Americans lived with the heavy burden of knowing that any day could end in torture and death, regardless of one's actions, reputation, or wealth. Parents could never fully protect their children from the nightmare of seeing a loved one brutalized or they themselves becoming the victim of tragedy.[29] Therefore, they purchased homes where they and their children could live in freedom from violence and humiliation. If necessary, those homes would be in racially separate neighborhoods where, ideally, Black businesses could pump resources back into the community, one that they would have the power to shape and nurture.

Even before the onset of the Depression, it was already becoming clear that informal racial zoning would not create separate-but-equal residential parks, as promised. The first problem was that the segregated housing market forced Black homebuyers to pay much higher prices for their homes. In 1930, the *Houston Informer*'s Clifton Richardson asked, "Why is it that Negroes must pay from 25 to 50 percent more for a home in Houston than do all other races?" "One has but to pick up the average daily paper to realize that the homes in the most modern white additions sell for many hundreds of dollars less than corresponding homes for Negroes in Negro additions. Even the price of lots is cheaper," he objected.[30] The second problem was that white absentee landlords could acquire wealth by encouraging multiple families to live in or on properties that had originally been intended for a single family, since decent housing for Black residents remained scarce. Many of the racial zoning schemes provided no avenues for expansion, as Benjamin Davis, editor of the *Atlanta Independent*, protested when he pointed out that the areas set aside for Black residents would not come close to meeting the needs of a growing population.[31]

Even in Black residential parks near Washington Park, Atlanta's first Black public park, middle-class standards for child-rearing remained elusive. In 1928, the city's park appropriation supported sixty-six parks containing 1,800 acres for white Atlantans but only one park containing a mere 21 acres for Black Atlantans, who made up one-third of the total population. Predictably, conditions in the park and especially the swimming pool rapidly deteriorated from overuse; Washington Park soon became a nuisance rather than a benefit to nearby families. Indeed, a survey by the Neighborhood Union found that a third of the Black families who lived in the single-family homes that faced the park wanted the city to close it because of its negative impact on the surrounding neighborhood. One resident had already moved from the neighborhood "on account of the Park," and another expressed "regret" to still be living nearby.[32]

The third problem was that zoning, too, failed to live up to its promises. When white property owners and realtors wished to speculate on real estate near commercial and industrial areas, they demanded unnecessary amounts of property be zoned for industrial or commercial use. Black families, once again, suffered most, even though planners had promised that zoning would protect their homes as much as white ones. Instead, the industrial nuisances and environmental hazards banned from white residential areas were allowed to endanger Black ones.[33] In Atlanta, members of the Neighborhood Union agreed to investigate the zoning laws "in the part of town" which they lived and "see to it that the requirements" were enforced, but usually to no avail.[34] During the brief period in which Atlanta's racial zoning law remained in force, the council allowed business or industry to encroach onto Black residential streets eight times, while denying a petition only once. The approved requests included changes that downgraded even Atlanta's Black middle-class residential parks west of Ashby Street. In one instance, the council allowed a white pharmacist to expand his business onto a residential home lot "opposite Washington Park," even though the planning commission had opposed the change.[35] A disgusted Benjamin Davis protested, "Any time a white man wants to put a factory, a garage or anything else in a Negro settlement, the zoning committee readily changes the rule" to permit it. "It matters not how exclusive the section is."[36]

Local officials also quickly reneged on promises to provide equal municipal services, especially once the Depression settled in. A 1939 editorial in the *Houston Post* chastised the city government for its negligence: "During [the] previous Holcombe administration, considerable work was done on streets and drainage in the negro areas, but during the Depression years maintenance work virtually was abandoned and the situation today is worse than at any time in the city's history." After reprinting an editorial from the *Informer* warning that epidemics would result from the poor conditions, the *Post* pleaded, "The needed improvements in negro sections should be provided, not as a gesture of charity, but because negro citizens are entitled to improvements because they pay taxes and have a right to live like human beings."[37]

Adding to the problems of Black residential development, the Depression had devastated Black-owned businesses, largely because their owners could not tap into public and private resources such as those provided by the chamber of commerce, which helped white businesses limp along. Plus, their smaller customer base was among the first fired and lowest paid, and their white competitors were more likely to benefit from economies of scale. After Black-owned banks and insurance companies began failing, Black residential development ground to a halt with little hope that an FHA intent on promoting discrimination would help.[38] Rapid urbanization during World War II further intensified the extreme housing shortage facing Black Americans in cities across the nation.

Locked out of most suburban developments and more likely to encounter redevelopment proposals that included bulldozing their neighborhoods, Black families were disproportionately in need of public housing units after the war.[39] Perry's and Whitten's proposals for redeveloping urban neighborhoods influenced the design of public housing by advocating for isolated communities with their own schools, playground, and public spaces, further exacerbating segregation. In 1934, they coauthored a report for the Advisory Committee on Housing in New York, which recommended that "each of the several initial housing projects should be large enough to form a self-contained neighborhood unit, with its full complement of community services and facilities—an elementary school, local stores, playgrounds, and probably other social and commercial activities." It also recommended closing certain streets to make "super-blocks" that would contribute to "the required play-park areas."[40]

Perry and Whitten thought isolated "projects" would help support the children who lived there, but in practice, public housing violated almost every principle promoted by the parent education movement. Because larger families struggled to find adequate housing in the private market and children were seen as more deserving of public largesse, housing authorities frequently filled public housing with children, including the high rises built at midcentury. The outcome was to create communities with sky-high ratios of youths to adults, reaching almost three to one in distressed developments such as Chicago's Robert Taylor Homes. According to historian Brad Hunt, the Chicago Housing Authority engineered "communities with youth-adult ratios several magnitudes greater than any previously seen in the urban experience," including Chicago's "worst tenement" district at the turn of the twentieth century or the "postwar, baby-boom suburbs." In both examples, adults still outnumbered youth, allowing the communities to maintain order.[41] Furthermore, the longstanding belief that families were islands unto themselves further damaged public housing communities by ignoring the role that collective efficacy plays in child-rearing.[42] The tragedy of high-rise public housing is only the most spectacular example of how federal and local governments conspired to give Black children the exact opposite of what experts insisted that children needed. The disastrous results further cemented white fears of Black children as threats to their own, increasing resistance to racial and economic integration.

Although the majority of Black families were not exposed directly to the shortcomings of public housing, even the most affluent Black children were still more likely to live in high poverty neighborhoods than impoverished white children. These neighborhoods lacked the resources that almost every white, middle-class child took for granted. White communities received infrastructure improvements whereas communities of color were treated as "sacrifice zones" for locating environmental hazards, a situation that could not have occurred without extensive segregation and sprawl. Even the wealthiest Black homeowners saw their property values tumble while less affluent whites saw their property values rise, further reinforcing the illusion that Black neighbors endangered the value of white homes. The postwar period's widening "home appreciation gap" contributed substantially to the persistence of the nation's racial wealth gap.[43]

Additionally, economic growth along with many of the jobs it produced followed in the direction of affluent, white residential areas, which were almost always strategically located on the opposite side of town from those areas set aside for Black development, leading to the lopsided growth that would endanger the economic health of many cities. Atlanta's wealth followed the affluent suburbs to the north side, leading to the parabola-shaped, traffic-choked metropolitan area evident today. Similarly, Houston's wealth followed River Oaks over to the west side and beyond, eventually reaching Cinco Ranch, located west of Katy. Birmingham's affluent neighborhoods moved northward over the top of Red Mountain while most Black homes remained south of downtown. In Raleigh, Black residents were clustered in the southeastern corner of the city while affluent suburbs stretched farther out to the north and west. Along with the strain on public utilities and roads, lopsided growth meant that isolation and neglect would become greater problems in the decades to come, a key reason why scholars have linked sprawl and residential segregation to low mobility rates. According to the findings of Harvard University's well-respected *Equality of Opportunity Project*, the places where children live largely determine their chances for achieving upward mobility. Economist Raj Chetty and his colleagues found that sprawling Atlanta, the nation's second-fastest-growing metropolitan area between 2000 and 2010, had mobility rates worse than bankrupt Detroit or Pine Ridge, the nation's most impoverished reservation, perpetuating intergenerational inequality in a city often praised for opportunity.[44]

The average postwar suburb was not nearly as child-centered as the earlier residential parks that targeted more affluent families. They contained less open space, and schools required transportation by either car or bus.[45] Indeed, many developments seemed designed for adults and their cars rather than children, a situation denounced by the Urban Land Institute (ULI). J. C. Nichols, Hugh Potter, Robert Jemison Jr., Hugh Prather, and other prominent developers were active in the ULI's Community Builders' Council after the war. The *Community Builders Handbook*, first published in 1947, criticized some of the newer developments for focusing less on child-rearing: "Developers have, in some cases, spent large sums to provide golf courses and similar facilities which have not provided for the juvenile population. The reason why most persons purchase a home is to raise a family in the right environment and to offer them all advantages within their means. Not to recognize this fact is a common mistake in many developments."[46]

Some of the newer subdivisions provided no recreational space at all. Because it had become easier to sell suburban homes with FHA subsidies in combination with decades of promotional literature touting the advantages for children, developers began cutting corners by offering smaller lots and setting aside less shared space. When suburban environmentalists became alarmed by the "bulldozer in the countryside" cutting down nearby forests or filling in attractive wetlands, they initially protested the loss of open space and park land that had provided play areas for their children. They also worried about worsening industrial water and air pollution, although segregation allowed them to protect the environment near affluent neighborhoods without promoting regulations that would have prevented environmental hazards period. Moreover, they accepted automobile traffic and metropolitan sprawl as the price of ensuring a safe and healthy environment for their offspring. Their shortsighted concerns created larger problems for future generations to solve.[47]

During the Progressive Era, before sprawl and segregation increased the distance between children of various racial and economic backgrounds, affluent parents were more interested in aiding other people's children. Black clubwomen, who understood that the fate of their offspring was inextricably tied to the fate of the poorest Black child, set a remarkable example of sustained commitment to the common good, especially as it related to children. After the progressive movement began losing momentum, affluent white parents increasingly turned inward toward their immediate families. In 1919, famed housing reformer Edith Elmer Wood scolded, "If we were not utterly blind and heedless, we would go to any length, make any sacrifice, to enable every child to spend his first five years, at least, while foundations of his health, his mind and his character are being laid, in an environment of pure air, sunshine, cleanliness and serenity."[48] By the end of the 1920s, Sidonie Gruenberg of the Child Study Association and social critic Bruno Lasker were also expressing alarm about the extent to which affluent white parents had become less concerned about other people's children. Even the most liberal white parents—those who embraced the rhetoric of racial tolerance—thought the exclusion of other people's children was necessary to properly raise their own. This narrative was reinforced by popular articles in the press, child-centered advertising for a wide range of products, and government on all levels.[49]

Once white, suburban homeowners fully embraced the developers' mantra connecting effective child-rearing to racial segregation and single-family zoning, the coupling was extraordinarily difficult to undo. What had begun as a turn-of-the-twentieth-century business venture had become a cultural and social reality that continues to shape our political discourse. During the 2020 presidential election, Donald Trump vowed to protect suburban families from policies that made it more difficult to prevent affordable housing in affluent, majority-white suburbs. At a press conference in the White House Rose Garden, President Trump warned that a Biden administration would strip "localities of federal affordable housing funds unless they change their zoning laws to fit the federal government's demands," which, he argued, would "abolish the suburbs." "Mothers aren't happy about that. Fathers aren't happy about that," he concluded.[50]

Yet, as we look around today, it is evident that excluding certain children from the most advantaged home environments did not lead to a stronger society, as Hoover and others promised it would. Instead, it weakened our social fabric, as Gruenberg and Lasker had foreseen, leading to a host of costly problems that seem impossible to solve without significant class and racial integration, something too many white Americans, including affluent liberals, still fight to prevent. As Lasker predicted, when children grow up isolated from the range of people who live in our larger communities, our ability to function as a society is substantially diminished. A century ago, developers and planners realized that they could not accomplish their vision without the use of government power, which resulted in government at all levels playing an important role in the creation of residential segregation.[51] Now, in the twenty-first century, only government has the power to reverse the damage, but the mythology tying race to dominant ideas about what makes a good parent, a better home, or a great school must first be unraveled.

AFTERWORD

Moving Forward

At the end of the twentieth century, urban planners began advocating for a return to traditional development patterns with diverse uses and users of property sharing the same block, yet steadfast resistance to mixed-income neighborhoods has continued into the twenty-first century. Thus, even as the old dynamic of an impoverished "inner city" surrounded by affluent "suburbs" is disintegrating in many cities, the shift has not led to substantially greater residential integration. Instead, it has produced a "Patchwork Metropolis," in the words of urbanist Richard Florida.[1] In 2021, researchers with the "Roots of Structural Racism Project" at the University of California, Berkely, found that segregation has again been rising in recent decades with additional headwinds making the efforts at achieving greater integration more difficult. The COVID-19 pandemic resulted in another wave of suburbanization while an acute lack of affordable housing, an alarmist discourse on urban crime, and challenges to diversity, equity, and inclusion programs seem to be taking us, once again, in the wrong direction.[2] Meanwhile, the ties between segregation and "responsible" white parenting remain strong, whether in an urban, suburban, exurban, or rural context.

Unraveling those ties will require greater attention to the concerns of parents as well as the needs of children. Derrick Bell's interest convergence theory suggests that the white middle class will not support policies that provide opportunity to Black children unless it helps their own. Legal scholar Sherrilyn Ifill, the former president of the NAACP Legal Defense Fund, agrees, reminding policymakers that we must demonstrate how integration benefits white children if housing policies are going to succeed. After all, as political scientist Desmond King has shown, white middle-class families with children are the most likely to live in segregated neighborhoods, despite their consistent claims that integrated communities are preferable. Parents will often make decisions that safeguard their own children's advantages even when they understand that preventing access to other children is wrong.[3]

If greater awareness of our society's inequities along with the critical challenges that come with them are not incentive enough to dismantle segregation, perhaps

FIGURE 13.1. When Garden Hills opened in 1925, its advertisements described it as a "fairyland for Garden Hills children—where youth may disport itself with never a dull moment. Slides, swings, seesaws, a miniature zoo, sand-piles, a gay little brook, wading pools." Since 2012, Garden Hills residents have passed by an elaborate sculpture aptly titled "The Children." It continues to reflect the child-centered spirit first invoked in the original advertisements. *Atlanta Constitution*, 5 May 1926; *Atlanta Journal-Constitution*, 22 December 2012. Photograph by the author.

the higher levels of anxiety and depression among young people in even the most affluent suburbs indicates that they are harmed, too. In recent years, social scientists have shown a renewed interest in intensive child-rearing practices among middle-class families. The rise of income inequality has led affluent parents to again expand the amount of time, energy, and resources spent on raising a smaller number of children. As in the past, the strategies are effective, so much so that they feed income inequality, which then provides further incentive to engage in intensive parenting. In a 2019 analysis of the ways in which "economics explains how we raise our kids," economists Matthias Doepke and Fabrizio Zilibotti found that American parents spent about an hour and forty-five minutes more *per day* interacting with their children in 2005 than they did in 1979. The shift was especially noticeable among college-educated parents, who were spending three more hours per week with their children—playing, talking, or reading with them and helping with their homework—than parents without a college education, adding to the achievement gap measured in schools.[4]

Parental spending also grew more unequal between 1970 and 2007. Sociologists Sabino Kornrich and Frank Furstenberg concluded that "both rich and poor" families had responded to "growing pressures to invest" in childhood by spending "greater shares of their income" on child-rearing expenses. Even so, upper-middle-class parents have dedicated a much larger portion of their disposable income towards "their children's futures," resulting in a gap in parental spending that is climbing faster than the gap in incomes, further exacerbating an achievement gap heading the wrong way. As the parental investment gap increases, so does the gap in standardized test scores, including high-stakes college admission exams such as the ACT and SAT. As a result, the expectation for childhood accomplishments has spiraled upward, making college admission more cutthroat and producing a trap for middle-class families who are squeezed in the middle. Fierce competition to get into a few dozen schools has also pushed up education costs with the most in-demand colleges able to charge whatever tuition the market will bear. So far, affluent families have been willing to absorb the soaring costs because prestigious schools can give their children an advantage in the race for a postgraduate degree, which is now needed to set them apart from the "growing herd of college graduates," in the words of Richard Reeves, a senior fellow at the Brookings Institution. Meanwhile, schools without billion-dollar endowments struggle to compete for students, often spending scarce resources on marketing and amenities that do not contribute to strong academic programming. In some cases, schools have eliminated core academic programs, and almost all have relied heavily on poorly paid, part-time faculty.[5]

Middle-class parenting strategies designed to promote upward mobility date back to the birth of the new republic, but many scholars and social critics recognize it as a more recent phenomenon.[6] Sociologists, economists, and psychologists often compare contemporary parenting trends to those during the 1970s, when "free-range parenting" was widespread. But that decade represents an outlier in the history of middle-class intensive child-rearing rather than an accurate starting point, because the less stratified economy enjoyed at midcentury was also an outlier. The economic stakes were much lower, so perhaps, middle-class parents responded by relaxing their parenting strategies and letting go of their children's fate, at least more so than in the past.

Between 1980 and 2014, the situation flipped. The bottom 50 percent of earners were "completely shut off from economic growth" whereas "income more than doubled for the top 10 percent" and "tripled for the top 1 percent."[7] Thus, the risks of downward mobility increased while the rewards for economic success skyrocketed. Economist Raj Chetty found that children born in 1940 who grew up during the prosperous decades following World War II had a 92 percent chance of earning a larger income than their parents, creating new expectations for the American dream. Children born in 1984, however, had only a 50 percent chance of earning more than their parents, with intergenerational mobility falling furthest for the middle class.[8] Adding to the economic pressure, higher education costs began to soar at a time when a degree had become essential for participation in the information economy and avoidance of the low-wage service sector. These two trends are likely related.[9] Expanding income inequality means that downward mobility has more dire consequences for one's children, creating greater incentives to prevent them from falling in the first place.[10]

Because income inequality depresses social mobility for everyone except those at the top, it generates anxiety even within affluent families. When income inequality rises, competition becomes more cutthroat, but the resulting push for higher achievement and productivity offers financial security only to the few. This upward spiral generates anxiety for those young people trapped within the larger cycle of needing ever more impressive accomplishments to compete for fewer rewards. Twenty-first-century critics of "helicopter" parenting have blamed irrational parents for causing their children's anxiety. For example, Kate Julian, senior editor at *The Atlantic*, lectured her middle-class readers that "a change in parenting styles may well help spare a child's mental health." Such criticism ignores the root cause of the anxiety.[11]

According to recent studies, what drives intensive parenting in the twenty-first century is not that different from the economic factors that motivated middle-class parents in the nineteenth century. Although critics worry about the negative effect on coddled children, the empirical evidence suggests that children are much more likely to profit from their parents sacrifices than they are to be harmed by them.[12] Intensive parenting may bring misery to exhausted parents, but it has major payoffs for children through greater academic achievement. Data from the 2012 PISA, an international test given to young high school students, revealed a strong correlation between a self-reported intensive parenting style and higher test scores, even when holding parental education levels constant. Economists Matthias Doepke and Fabrizio Zilibotti concluded that "having two highly educated parents only adds 7 points to the average math test score, while an intensive parenting style adds more than 20 points across parents of equal levels of education." The type of child-rearing they connected to higher academic achievement—parenting rooted in patient care and perpetual attention—has been the norm for affluent families of all races since the nation's founding.[13] This parenting style uses reason and persuasion to teach kids to negotiate, argue, and advocate for themselves within the family, helping children develop independence, creativity, and problem-solving skills. Despite fears that intensive parenting develops weak, anxious kids that lack grit and determination, these children are more likely to graduate from college and obtain postgraduate degrees.

Inspired by the work of Doepke and Zilibotti, *New York Times* opinion writer Pamela Druckerman confirmed what history has shown us: intensive parenting "works." In fact, it works so well it is contributing to economic inequality for the next generation.[14] Observers from other nations sometimes understand the enigma of US "meritocracy" better than Americans. A 2014 article in *The Economist*, "Relax, Your Kids Will Be Fine," identified the disparate impact from parenting styles based on class. On the "lower end," parents "struggle to provide enough support, especially in the crucial early years." They simply cannot keep up with affluent parents, who "try to do too much." Meanwhile, affluent parents "fear that unless they drive their offspring to Mandarin classes, violin lessons and fencing practice six days a week, they will not get into the right university." The article urged them to worry about their own children less while championing the expansion of government programs that provide assistance to financially struggling parents with young children.[15]

Studies have repeatedly shown that public investments in children more than pay for themselves through the lifetime of taxes contributed by the beneficiaries. According to economist Nate Hilger, rather than spending tax money when children "repeat grades," require "emergency healthcare," are incarcerated, or need income supplements, society could benefit from higher tax receipts, receiving as much as 30 percent of the future income of a child who has had greater opportunity.[16] Policies that help parents invest in child-rearing would both lessen the impact of income inequality and stimulate the economy, which would further benefit all. When incomes are distributed more equally, less-affluent Americans have more money to spend on consumption. They pump their earnings straight into the economy, promoting economic growth through increased demand, which typically benefits the middle class most of all. This dynamic was certainly true during the decades following World War II, when income inequality was at historic lows and a more relaxed parenting style became the norm.[17]

For those Americans who are worried about our nation's debt and tax burden, investing in children is an economic solution we cannot ignore. The research of Barbara Sard and Phillip Tegeler has demonstrated that high-poverty neighborhoods—where Black children are far more likely to live than white children regardless of parental income—hurt children's "cognitive development, school performance, mental health, and long-term physical health." Nathaniel Hendren of Harvard's *Equality of Opportunity Project* agrees that "every year a child spends growing up in a better neighborhood improves her outcomes in adulthood." And Nate Hilger adds that investing in children promotes school success for all: "When more children get the investments they need outside school to relax and concentrate inside school, teachers spend less time putting out fires and more time helping children master academic content, while kids themselves spend less time disrupting each other and more time collaborating." For those who remain concerned about the price tag, maintaining segregation costs more. Middle-class families cannot afford to pay the high price of housing and school exclusivity while also paying higher taxes for society's failures with the children who have been excluded.[18]

As the women of the Neighborhood Union understood, our children's quality of life is connected to the least advantaged child among us. If children are denied real opportunity, how will their limited choices affect us all? Why would we expect young people to play by the rules of a game that they recognize is rigged against them?[19] Could we support policies that help us function more as a society and less as a board game? At the end of the day, a nation of individuals will not be able to solve the problems we now face, let alone work with the rest of the world to address a refugee and climate crisis that will only get worse. How might we empower our children—all of them and not just our own—to build a future in which they wish to live?

ACKNOWLEDGMENTS

My citations do not convey my gratitude to the historians and scholars who have written on segregation, housing, parenting, the planning movement, and the history of education. Your work made this project possible, and I cannot adequately thank you for your contributions. This book would also not exist without generous funding from the Spencer Foundation and the National Academy of Education, which provided me with the opportunity for extended conversations with great minds from multiple disciplines. Judith Warren invited me to speak at UC Berkeley, where I met Richard Rothstein, who has been one of the most important mentors of my career. I also hold a huge debt to Matthew Lassiter, John Rury, and Jack Dougherty. I am so grateful for your guidance, assistance, and example. Thank you for believing in the worth of this project.

My faculty advisors and mentors in graduate school, including Bill Reese, Stephen Kantrowitz, Michael Fultz, Adam Nelson, Nan Enstad, Susan Johnson, Wanda Hendricks, and Catherine Miller, taught me how the world works and what it means to be a scholar: to ask meaningful questions and to turn over every stone in search of the answers. Most importantly, they taught me what it means to be a supportive teacher, advisor, and colleague. Your example has shaped my life in so many ways, and, to this day, my primary motivation remains the desire to pass it forward. Other mentors from graduate school include Seema Kapani, Rodney Horikawa, and Hazel Symonette. You, too, shaped my understanding of the world and how to live in it. My teaching, scholarship, and service owe much to your example.

In addition, I am in debt to several talented individuals who have improved this project. I am forever grateful for the creativity and wide-ranging abilities of Heather Meyer and Michelle Reidy. Thank you for always knowing how to find a solution to every setback, whether large or small. I would also like to thank the talented cartographers, artists, and geographers who helped with the maps and images. Erin Greb made all fourteen maps for the book. Thank you for your extraordinary effort to achieve my vision for each one. I know that wasn't easy to do. I also appreciate the assistance of Lindsay Starr and Madge Duffey, who helped prepare the cover and other artwork for the book, and Dajun Dai assisted with the design of the maps for Atlanta. Andrew Sobol and Matt Drwenski helped me scan the images that were not already digitized. Finally, many thanks to Carmen Cauthen, Lisa Boccetti, Bob Williams, and Tammy Brunner of the Wake County

Covenants Project. I appreciate the important work you are doing in Raleigh, and I am so grateful for your kindness and generosity.

I also lack the words to express my gratitude to my wonderful colleagues at the Saint Xavier University and Elmhurst University libraries, especially Sheila Murphy, Brenda Williams, Jody Malecha, and Allison Isztok. I know I kept them busy, but they never complained. Thank you for hunting down my many strange requests and for caring about this project. You always made the library feel like home to me. I am also grateful to the librarians and archivists from across the country who helped me find the golden nuggets that made this research so absorbing. Often the staff did more than I asked, which led to the serendipitous discoveries that made this book possible. I would especially like to thank Serena McCracken, Brooke Shilling, Katherine Budinger, Ted Nazur, Katherine Olson, Connor Marullo, Kris Ford, and Mark Schmitt for going above and beyond, especially over email or during a too-brief on-site visit. Similarly, the staff at the Houston Independent School District, Wake County Public Schools, and Atlanta Public Schools kindly welcomed me into their offices for weeks at a time when I know they had far more pressing concerns on their schedule.

The scholars who presented with me at conferences, served as a discussant, worked with me on a related project, or who simply helped me work through my ideas at various stages of the process have shaped my thinking in diverse and important ways. They include Elizabeth A. Herbin-Triant, Ansley Erikson, Marc VanOverbeke, Amy Shuffelton, Noah Sobe, Cynthia Taines, Valerie Farnsworth, Ariel H. Bierbaum, Willow Lung-Amam, Sarah Thuesen, Jeffrey Gonda, Tyina Steptoe, Bernadette Pruitt, Robert Nelson, Andrew Highsmith, David Gamson, Walter Stern, Alexander X. Byrd, Emily Straus, Laura K. Muñoz, Ruth N. López Turley, Brian D. Behnken, James Leloudis, LeeAnn Lands, David Freund, Neil Flanagan, and, especially, Tracy Steffes. Your honest, open, and thoughtful feedback and advice have been immeasurably helpful.

I am also forever grateful for my colleagues who have spent untold hours over the years listening to the latest news on my never-ending manuscript, offering encouragement to persevere, and responding to my concerns, questions, and ideas. Matt Costello, Mary Beth Tegan, Forrest Perry, Kathy Alaimo, Chris Fojtik, Amanda Lopez, Rob Butler, Connie Mixon, Andrea Krieg, Erika McCombs, Tracy Crump, Tim Hazen, Steven Kowal, and Andrew Das, among many others, have helped me celebrate every stage of this long process. You did not let me walk away when other demands seemed more pressing, and your sense of humor and concern always carried me through. At small teaching schools, our workload is great but so is our fellowship, which has allowed us to build an emotionally and intellectually supportive community for our students and for each other. These friendships have meant the world to me.

I am also grateful to Matt Costello, Michael Clark, and Rob Butler for serving as patient and good-humored department chairs. You have protected me when I needed it most and championed me when I needed that, too. I could not have done this without you. Thank you for caring about me and this project. Kathy Alaimo, Courtney Miller, and Dean Pribbenow—my deans—provided me with encouragement every step along the way and additional resources when possible. Thank you for supporting faculty scholarship even when the demands of a small school make it difficult. I also appreciate the grants from the Elmhurst University Center for Scholarship and Teaching, which paid for the maps and index. The resources from the Lester Brune and Joan Brune Endowed History Chair arrived just in time.

I love teaching at a small, liberal arts institution that values scholarship and recognizes that research allows us to create a more vibrant and stimulating learning environment for our students. It also means it has taken me a long time to complete the research for this book, but I believe the slow growth of my manuscript has improved it immensely. Since my project has been sustained over an extended period of time, I have been able to develop my ideas more fully through teaching a wide range of courses. Class discussions have helped me think about my argument and evidence in new ways, and student questions have sent me in directions that I had not previously considered. I know I would not be as effective in the classroom if I was not deeply engaged in scholarship, and I know my research project would not be as strong if my ideas had not had time to simmer in the classroom. My students have been a constant source of inspiration for me, and I hope that my work has inspired them. I would like to offer a special thank you to Lily Armentrout, Afaaf Amatullah, Melissa Morrissey, Katie Mulford, Jack Vavrinchik, Kyle Orczykowski, and Lindsey McAuliffe. Your interest in this project along with our rich conversations about the topic provided me with fresh insights and allowed me to make connections in new and meaningful ways.

Thanks as well to my incredible editors, Andrew Winters and Brandon Proia. Your patience with my delays and your encouragement when I lacked faith are the reason this project is now a book. It has been a long journey. Thanks, too, for allowing the number of pages, images, and maps to expand along with my understanding of the topic. I am also grateful to my careful copyeditors, Erin Granville and Alex Gergely, and the book's promoter, Sonya Bonczek. And thanks to the anonymous readers who stuck with this project over the years and pushed me to get it right. I am forever grateful to you for taking the time to challenge my assumptions, steer me in more fruitful directions, and correct my errors. Your comments have helped me create a more nuanced book. I hope you are happy with the results.

I would also like to thank to my muse and inspiration, the incomparable Sherry Williams, the founder of the Bronzeville/Black Chicagoan Historical Society. I admire your wit, imagination, integrity, and persistence as well as your deep contributions to both historical preservation and understanding—there is no fire you will not walk through. You have given me a sense of purpose that goes far beyond anything you might imagine. Thank you for showing me what matters.

And then there is my family, who has put up with eighty-hour workweeks, missed vacations, and the trials of attempting to complete a large project at a small school. Thank you, girls, for believing the book was worth your sacrifice. Thank you, Ella, for serving as my research assistant at NARA, Johns Hopkins, the Kenan Research Center, and Atlanta University Center. Your curiosity, acumen, and organizational skills allowed me to accomplish far more during those brief trips than I could have ever done without you (you made them far more enjoyable as well). Thank you, Lily, for your encouragement and deep insights over the years. The manuscript is your twin, born the same year you were. Thank you for believing in this project, even when it meant I was not by your side when I wanted to be. And thank you, Will, for your humor, wisdom, patience, and wide-ranging skills as a remarkable father and husband, excellent cook, and perceptive historian, all of which helped me persist through what sometimes felt like an endless process. I appreciate you sticking by me. I couldn't have finished the project without your love and support!

I would also like to thank my mom and sister for being my biggest cheerleaders. From the first moment I can remember, not a day has gone by when you didn't make me feel respected and valued. That love has carried me through fifteen years of a manuscript-in-progress—even during our brief visits when all you have ever asked from me was my company. Thank you for turning our family trips into research trips, offering your assistance whenever possible, hosting Ella and Lily during their spring breaks, and a million other thoughtful gifts and sacrifices that are too numerous to list. I hope this book makes you proud.

Finally, how do I thank my father for reading through every single draft of this book? The time commitment alone was far too much to ask, but your honest feedback pushed me forward and made me realize that I did not want to settle for just being done. Your questions always made me take another look at what I thought I had already figured out, and your suggestions strengthened what I wanted to say. Thank you for pouring so much time, love, and energy into this project!

Any errors or flaws are, of course, mine alone.

NOTES

Abbreviations

ACC Minutes
    City Council Minutes and Index, City of Atlanta Records, Kenan Research Center at the Atlanta History Center, Atlanta, GA

CH Papers
    Charles N. Hunter Papers, David M. Rubenstein Rare Book and Manuscript Library, Duke University, Durham, NC

Forsyth County Property Deed Book
    Forsyth County, NC, Register of Deeds Online Records Systems, Property Deed Books and Index, www.co.forsyth.nc.us/rod/online_lookup.aspx

HF Papers
    Hill Ferguson Papers, MSS AR56, Birmingham Public Library, Department of Archives and Manuscripts, Birmingham, AL

HH Collection
    Herbert Hoover Collection, The American Presidency Project, UC Santa Barbara, www.presidency.ucsb.edu/people/president/herbert-hoover

HS Collection
    Houston Subdivision Collection, MSS 118, Houston History Research Center, Houston Public Library, Houston, TX

Minutes of the Atlanta Board of Education
    Minutes of the Atlanta Board of Education, Atlanta Board of Education Archives and Museum, Atlanta Public Schools' Center for Leadership and Learning, Atlanta, GA

NAACP Branch Files
    John H. Bracey Jr. and August Meier, eds., *Papers of the NAACP: Part 12. Selected Branch Files, 1913–1939*, series A, *The South* (Bethesda, MD: University Publications of America, 1991), microfilm

NU Collection
    Neighborhood Union Collection, MSS 0050, Archives Research Center, Robert W. Woodruff Library of the Atlanta University Center, Atlanta, GA

Raleigh Minutes
    Minutes of the Raleigh Township School Committee, Wake County Public School System, Raleigh, NC (in author's possession)

304 | Notes to Introduction

RO Scrapbook
Series 1: Scrapbooks, River Oaks Collection, Houston History Research Center, Houston Public Library, Houston, TX

RPC Records
Roland Park Company Records, MS 504, Special Collections, Johns Hopkins University Sheridan Libraries, Baltimore, MD

RJ Papers
Robert Jemison Jr. Papers, MSS AR6, Birmingham Public Library, Department of Archives and Manuscripts, Birmingham, AL

RW Papers
Papers of Robert Harvey Whitten, 1920–1935, Frances Loeb Library, Special Collections, Harvard University Graduate School of Design, Cambridge, MA

Tentative Zone Plan map
Tentative Zone Plan, Atlanta, Ga., City Planning Commission, 1922, file FF 339, folder 5, series "Atlanta City Maps, 1853–1991, undated," Kenan Research Center at the Atlanta History Center, Atlanta, GA

USHC Records
RG 3 Records of the United States Housing Corporation, National Archives and Records Administration, College Park, MD

WHCCHP
White House Conference of Child Health and Protection

WH Papers
William Clifford Hogg Papers, Dolph Briscoe Center for American History, University of Texas at Austin

Introduction

1. Norman Rockwell, *Planning the Home*, illustration for the cover of *Literary Digest*, 8 May 1920.
2. Ladd-Taylor, *Mother Work*, 49–50, 55–56, 62.
3. Massey, "Still the Linchpin," 2.
4. For influential examples of each argument, see Cahn, *Sexual Reckonings*; Fennell, *Unbounded Home*; Brooks and Rose, *Saving the Neighborhood*; David Freund, *Colored Property*; Boger, "Meaning of Neighborhood"; Kenneth T. Jackson, *Crabgrass Frontier*; Lands, *Culture of Property*; Gotham, *Race, Real Estate*; among others.
5. Gwendolyn Wright, *Building the Dream*; Trachtenberg, review of *Building the Dream*, 670. For an analysis of the peak period of residential segregation, see Massey and Denton, *American Apartheid*. See also Cutler, Glaeser, and Vigdor, "Rise and Decline of the American Ghetto," 456, 470.
6. Cronon, *Changes in the Land*, 177.
7. Weiss, *Rise of the Community Builders*, 45; Glotzer, *How the Suburbs*.
8. Ethel Longworth Swift, "In Defense of Suburbia: A Reply to 'Is Suburban Living a Delusion,'" *The Outlook*, 4 April 1928, 543–44.

9. For an in-depth study of the creation of the FHA, see David Freund, *Colored Property*. See also Winling and Michney, "Roots of Redlining," 42–44.

10. Federal Housing Administration, *Underwriting Manual*, part 2, section 256.

11. Federal Housing Administration, *Underwriting Manual*, part 2, section 266 and 267.

12. Agran, *Herbert Hoover*, 146. According to Agran, Hoover's priorities reflected his two greatest passions: "development of better homes" and "development of child welfare."

13. Herbert Hoover, "Statement Announcing the White House Conference on Home Building and Home Ownership," 15 September 1931; Herbert Hoover, "Remarks to the Planning Committee of the White House Conference on Home Building and Home Ownership," 24 September 1930; Herbert Hoover, "Message to the Committee on Negro Housing of the White House Conference on Home Building and Home Ownership," 24 April 1931, all in HH Collection. See also WHCCHP, Committee on the Family and Parent Education, *Home and the Child*, 9–27; Gries and Ford, *Homemaking*; Gries and Ford, *Negro Housing*; Lands, *Culture of Property*, 131–33. In 1931, Selena Sloan Butler, president of the Negro National PTA, gave a presentation titled "The White House Conference from a Negro Mother's Point of View" before the Georgia Committee on Interracial Cooperation. Unfortunately, I have not been able to find a copy of her speech. "Program for Annual Meeting, Georgia Committee on Interracial Cooperation, Central Y.M.C.A., Luckie Street, Atlanta, Georgia," 14 January 1931, box 10, folder 20, NU Collection.

14. James Ford, "Planning and Equipping," 194–98, 200; Ladd-Taylor, *Mother Work*, 49–50, 55–56, 62; Agran, *Herbert Hoover*, 146; Hurley, "Shaping Housing"; Euclid v. Ambler Co., 272 U.S. 365; 47 S. Ct. 114 (1926). For local examples, see "More Home Building," *Atlanta Constitution*, 4 September 1921; "Own-Your-Home Drive Is Showing Results," *Atlanta Constitution*, 19 March 1922; and "Raleigh's Great Expansion Began Less Than Ten Years Ago," *Raleigh News and Observer*, 26 October 1927. During the 1920s, planners and developers often referred to duplexes as "two-family dwellings."

15. "Value of Realty for Investment Shown by Adair," *Atlanta Constitution*, 13 January 1921; US Department of Labor Information and Education Service, "Financing the Prospective Home Owner," 25 April 1919, Press Release no. 4-23A, "Own-Your-Own Home," box 295, folder 3, USHC Records; John Ihlder to "Mr. B.," 25 February 1919, box 295, folder 5, USHC Records; Weiss, *Rise of the Community Builders*, 47; US Census Bureau, "General Summary," in *Mortgages on Homes*, 38, 69.

16. Weiss, *Rise of the Community Builders*, 2; Hornstein, *Nation of Realtors*, 145–47.

17. MacChesney, *Principles of Real Estate Law*, iv. See also National Association of Real Estate Boards, *Session by Session Outline*. For a different perspective, see Winling and Michney, "Roots of Redlining," 48.

18. Ernest Fisher, *Principles*, 4; James, *Land Planning*, 204–5.

19. Ernest Fisher, *Principles*, 94; Gifford, *Real Estate Advertising*, 24, 113–14; Country Club District advertisement, *Kansas City Star*, 17 April 1910. See also Worley, *J. C. Nichols*.

20. "No Naturally Bad Children," *Literary Digest*, 31 October 1925, 21.

21. For analysis of the rise and fall of restrictive covenants, see Glotzer, *How the Suburbs*; Gonda, *Unjust Deeds*; Fogelson, *Bourgeois Nightmares*.

22. Glotzer, *How the Suburbs*, 52–53, 95; Gandolfo v. Hartman, 49 F. 181 (1892).

23. Jones-Correa, "Origins and Diffusion," 545–47, 550. See also Colin Gordon, "Dividing the City," 161; and Gotham, "Urban Space, Restrictive Covenants," 617–18.

24. Historian LeeAnn Lands convincingly argues that "park-neighborhood ideology"

created a new "culture of property" in Atlanta during the early twentieth century. Lands, *Culture of Property*. Likewise, Kevin Fox Gotham ties segregation to a "propagandizing effort of the real estate industry" to convince white homebuyers that "all-white racially homogeneous neighborhoods were a superior atmosphere for residential life and a requisite for protecting the homeowner's investment," but he does not define a "superior atmosphere for residential life." Gotham, "Urban Space, Restrictive Covenants," 621.

25. "Houston Parents Locate Near Public Schools Prior to Term Opening This Fall; Many Build," *Houston Post*, 28 July 1929.

26. For a broader discussion of suburban residential development and residential segregation, see Lands, *Culture of Property*, 135–57; Gotham, *Race, Real Estate*; Paige Glotzer, *How the Suburbs*; and Michney, *Surrogate Suburbs*.

27. Hirsch, "With or Without Jim Crow," 75. For an analysis of status and the nation's first segregation ordinance, see Boger, "Meaning of Neighborhood." See also Herbin-Triant, *Threatening Property*. Herbin-Triant argues that southern elites were much less enthused about the residential segregation ordinances than the middle class. For an analysis of white fears of interracial relationships, see Gordon-Reed, *Hemingses of Monticello*, 84–90; Cahn, *Sexual Reckonings*, 165; Robinson, *Dangerous Liaisons*; and Royster, *Southern Horrors*.

28. Power, "Apartheid Baltimore Style"; Silver, "Racial Origins of Zoning"; Lieb, "'Baltimore Idea.'"

29. "Citizens Organize to Segregate Colored People in Baltimore," *Dallas Express*, 20 December 1919.

30. Buchanan v. Warley, 245 U.S. 60 (1917). See also Lee, "Wall of Hate," 434–36; and Godsil, "Race Nuisance," 544–45.

31. Hirsch, "With or Without Jim Crow," 73–78.

32. "Take It Up or Put It Down," *Atlanta Independent*, 9 November 1922; "Immigration and the Races," *Austin American Statesman*, 6 April 1927.

33. Silver and Moeser, *Separate City*, 22.

34. Committee on Best Methods of Land Subdivision, "Report of Conference Committee," 247; Whitten, "Zoning of Residence Sections," 34–39; Whitten, "Zoning and Living Conditions," 27–28; Ihlder, "Housing and the Regional Plan." For a contemporary critique, see Bruno Lasker, "Unwalled Towns," *The Survey*, 6 March 1920, 675–80; and Bruno Lasker, response to Charles Cheney's "Removing Social Barriers by Zoning," *The Survey*, 22 May 1920, 279.

35. Bowen v. City of Atlanta, 159 Ga. 145 (1924).

36. For an analysis of the dubious distinction between "de jure" and "de facto" segregation, see Lassiter and Crespino, "De Jure/De Facto Segregation." See also Rothstein, *Color of Law*.

37. A growing body of literature has examined the power of schools to shape residential development. Robena Estelle Jackson, "Socio-Historical View"; García, *Strategies of Segregation*; Erickson, *Making the Unequal Metropolis*; Erickson, "Building Inequality"; Lieb, "'Shove Those Black Clouds'"; Stern, *Race and Education*. For an examination of how this strategy worked in northern cities, see Highsmith, *Demolition Means Progress*; Clapper, "School Design, Site Selection,"; Steffes, *Structuring Inequality*; and Todd-Breland, *Political Education*.

38. Purdy, "Land Values and Social Values,"258.

39. Benjamin, "Suburbanizing Jim Crow"; Gavin Wright, *Old South, New South*, 14, 80; Tindall, *Emergence of the New South*, 95, 111–12, 355; Smith, "Emergence of Cities," 27, 32–34.

40. Benjamin, "Suburbanizing Jim Crow." For northern examples, see Hirsch, *Making the Second Ghetto*, 119, 127, 196, 232–33; and Michael W. Homel, "Willis Wagons," *Encyclopedia of Chicago Online*, accessed 16 May 2024, www.encyclopedia.chicagohistory.org/pages/1357.html. See also note 37.

41. Dougherty, "Shopping for Schools"; Rury and Rife, "Race, Schools"; Rury, *Creating the Suburban*, 1–37.

42. "Segregation," *Atlanta Independent*, 14, 21 June 1913; Hanchett, *Sorting Out*.

43. Corrigan v. Buckley, 271 U.S. 323 (1926); Brooks and Rose, *Saving the Neighborhood*. Brooks and Rose make the argument that older, urban neighborhoods turned to restrictive covenants after *Buchanan*, but as Jeffrey Gonda demonstrates in *Unjust Deeds*, the covenants often failed to prevent racial transition.

44. William Henry Jones, *Housing of Negroes*, 74–79. See also Gonda, *Unjust Deeds*; and Fogelson, *Bourgeois Nightmares*.

45. According to historian Adam Rome, moderately priced subdivisions often lacked open space for parks and playgrounds as well as other child-centered amenities typical of early-twentieth-century residential parks. Rome, *Bulldozer in the Countryside*, 119–52.

46. The term "redlining" comes from the color-coded security maps prepared by the Home Owners' Loan Corporation (HOLC) for its mortgage rescue program. Since the maps were completed after HOLC had already extended most of its loans, little evidence exists that they were used to discriminate based on race. Instead, records suggest that Black buyers did receive a proportionate number of loans, although they continued to pay interest rates far above that of white borrowers. With that said, HOLC shared its maps with the Federal Housing Administration, which did promote discrimination against African Americans through its mortgage insurance program. The evidence is less clear whether the HOLC maps were used to make those decisions, since they were not shared externally. What we do know is that the HOLC maps accurately reflected existing racial discrimination in local real estate markets as well as the continued desire to increase residential segregation. Michney, "How the City Survey's"; Hillier, "Redlining"; Hillier, "Who Received Loans?"; Winling and Michney, "Roots of Redlining," 42–69. See also Freund, *Colored Property*, 114.

47. For an analysis of the impact of the Black middle class on housing conditions for Black working-class families, see Connolly, *World More Concrete*; and Smith, *Racial Democracy*.

48. Decades of research on the role that New Deal housing policies played in expanding residential segregation during the postwar period make an extensive retelling unnecessary here. Perhaps the most widely read overview of redlining can be found in Rothstein's *Color of Law*. Kenneth Jackson's *Crabgrass Frontier* is still a classic, and Freund's *Colored Property* provides one of the most thorough analyses of the federal role in the postwar housing market. For more nuanced analyses based on individual case studies, see Highsmith, *Demolition Means Progress*; Gordon, *Mapping Decline*; and Howell, *Making the Mission*. Along with Ocean Howell, Jennifer Light examines nationality in the production of security maps. Light, "Nationality and Neighborhood Risk."

49. Winling and Michney, "Roots of Redlining," 44. According to Winling and Mich-

ney, "the question of whether the government or private industry is more culpable for redlining" is "moot" considering the "elaborate" public-private partnerships that devised the policies.

50. Fishman, *Bourgeois Utopias*, 15; Herbin-Triant, *Threatening Property*.
51. Brody, "Constructing Professional Knowledge," 38.
52. Ewen, *Immigrant Women*, 98.
53. Kruse, *White Flight*, 12.
54. Dorsey, *To Build Our Lives*. For an analysis of how social class divided Black Americans' interests in residential development as well as segregation, see Connolly, *World More Concrete*; and Smith, *Racial Democracy*.
55. Reeves, *Dream Hoarders*; Cashin, *White Space, Black Hood*; Dorceta Taylor, *Toxic Communities*; Hurley, *Environmental Inequalities*; Sharkey, *Stuck in Place*; Jenkins, *Bonds of Inequality*; Massey, "Still the Linchpin."

Chapter 1

1. Brissot de Warville, *New Travels*, 52.
2. Lee, "Why I Am Not," 311.
3. Doepke and Zilibotti, *Love, Money and Parenting*, 51. Doepke and Zilibotti describe current "intensive" parenting strategies in ways that are similar to the advice given in nineteenth-century child-rearing manuals.
4. Norton, *Liberty's Daughters*, 242–50.
5. Ewen, *Immigrant Women*, 98. Garb, *City of American Dreams*, 148–76.
6. Bederman, *Manliness and Civilization*, 106; Leonard, *Illiberal Reformers*, 128.
7. Demos, *Past, Present, and Personal*, 13–14; Bernstein, *Racial Innocence*, 36–37.
8. Locke, *Some Thoughts Concerning Education*, 62–63; Rousseau, *Emile*, 107; Blake, *Songs of Innocence*.
9. Norton, *Liberty's Daughters*, 242–50.
10. Klepp, *Revolutionary Conceptions*, 6.
11. As quoted in Boydston, *Home and Work*, 80–81.
12. Grund, *Americans*, 35–37.
13. Arthur, *Mother's Rule*, 261.
14. Kerber, "Separate Spheres." For a discussion of the impact of the market revolution on middle-class families, see Larson, *Market Revolution*.
15. Arthur, *Mother's Rule*, 261.
16. Catharine Beecher, *Treatise on Domestic Economy*, 227–30; Sklar, *Catharine Beecher*, 151; Ryan, *Cradle of the Middle Class*. See also Nayan Shah, *Contagious Divides*, 89. For a concise description of the complexity of women's labor during the colonial period, see Ulrich, "Ways of Her Household."
17. Boydston, *Home and Work*, 80.
18. Degler, *At Odds*, 66; Demos, *Past, Present, and Personal*, 10; Lasch, *Haven*, 6.
19. Zelizer, *Pricing the Priceless Child*, 5; Mintz, *Huck's Raft*, 76–77, 91; Reese, *Origins*, 50–54; Boydston, *Home and Work*, 81.
20. Degler, *At Odds*, 182, 201; Klepp, *Revolutionary Conceptions*, 12; Larson, *Market Revolution*, 39–140.

21. Wordsworth, "Ode: Intimations"; Garlitz, "Immortality Ode," 639, 644. For an analysis of "Western childhood," see Gutman and Coninck-Smith, "Good to Think With."
22. Sedgwick, "Game at Jackstraws," 31; Mintz, *Huck's Raft*, 81; Nissenbaum, *Battle for Christmas*, 203–4; Gillis, "Islanding of Children," 321.
23. Bernstein, *Racial Innocence*, 15–16.
24. Stowe, *Uncle Tom's Cabin*, 327, 360.
25. Sklar, *Catharine Beecher*, 233.
26. Beecher, *Treatise on Domestic Economy*, 227–30; Sklar, *Catharine Beecher*, 151.
27. Wellman, *Road to Seneca Falls*; Mohl, *Abortion in America*.
28. As quoted in Kenneth Jackson, *Crabgrass Frontier*, 48. See also Chudacoff, *Children at Play*, 107–8.
29. Lasch, *Haven in a Heartless World*, 5; Deger, *At Odds*, 67.
30. As quoted in Ryan, *Cradle of the Middle Class*, 168.
31. Stearns, *Anxious Parents*, 42; Garb, *City of American Dreams*, 167–70.
32. Wheeler, *Rural Homes*, 277–78, 289.
33. Higginbotham, *Righteous Discontent*, 179–80; Davis, *Lifting As They Climb*, 98–99.
34. "Refuge of Oppression," *The Liberator*, 15 February 1834, 1.
35. Litwack, *North of Slavery*, 126–31; "Biographical/Historical Description," Prudence Crandall Collection, MS-021, Linda Lear Center for Special Collections and Archives, Connecticut College, New London, CT, accessed 30 June 2024, https://aspace.conncoll.edu/repositories/2/resources/45.
36. Abdy, *Journal of a Residence*, 169.
37. Bruce, "Racial Zoning," 705.
38. Indiana Constitutional Convention, *Report of the Debates*, 114–16.
39. Bernstein, *Racial Innocence*, 16. See also Wilma King, *African American Childhoods*, 129–31; and Webster, *Beyond the Boundaries*.
40. Klepp, *Revolutionary Conceptions*, 7.
41. DuBois, *Black Reconstruction*; Heather Andrea Williams, *Self-Taught*.
42. Field and Simmons, "Introduction to Special Issue," 2; Simmons, *Crescent City Girls*; McGuire, *At the Dark End*.
43. Morgan, *Laboring Women*, introduction and chapter 1; Cahn, *Sexual Reckonings*; Chatelain, *South Side Girls*; Holland, *From the Mississippi Delta*, 78–91. On the culture of dissemblance, see Hine, "Rape and the Inner Lives," 912–20.
44. Odem, *Delinquent Daughters*, 39.
45. Reed, *Not Alms but Opportunity*, 36–50; Webster, *Beyond the Boundaries*, 129–35; Hendricks, *Gender, Race*; Hendricks, *Fannie Barrier Williams*.
46. Commission on Interracial Cooperation, "Fact Finding Methods," undated, box 12, folder 18, NU Collection.
47. Georgia Swift King, "Mother's Meetings"; Selena Sloan Butler, "Need of Day Nurseries"; and Rosa Morehead Bass, "Need of Kindergartens"; all in series 2, number 2: *Social and Physical Condition of Negroes in the City*, 1897, 61–67, box 18, folder 2, Atlanta University Printed and Published Materials, MSS 0002, Robert W. Woodruff Library of the Atlanta University Center; "The Gate City Free Kindergarten," circa 1917, "Organizations Affiliated with the Neighborhood Union, 1914–1935," box 12, folder 24, NU Collection; Shivery, "History," 5, 14–17. Shivery became active in the union no later than

1913. Public School Campaign Monthly Time Book, 1913, minutes, 1914–1915, box 4, folder 4, NU Collection.

48. Minutes of the Neighborhood Union, 8 July, 23 July, 3 September, and 3 December 1908, 11 March, 9 September, 14 October, and 14 December 1909, 19 January and 25 February 1910, 10 August and 9 November 1911, box 4, folder 1; Charter of the Neighborhood Union, 1911, box 2, folder 3; Mrs. Edna E. Lamson to Mrs. Hope, box 2, folder 37, all in NU Collection; Shivery and Smythe, "Neighborhood Union," 109–17; Shivery, "History," 46, 72. See also Chatelain, *South Side Girls*, 15; Knupfer, *Toward a Tenderer Humanity*, 91; Driskell, *Schooling Jim Crow*, 131.

49. Ladd-Taylor, *Mother Work*, 56; Rouse, *Lugenia Burns Hope*, 66–68, 115.

50. Harper, "Afro-American Mother," 68–70. The congress was the forerunner to the National Parent Teachers Association, as discussed in chapter 10. See also Webster, *Beyond the Boundaries*, 137–40.

51. As quoted in Boris, "Power of Motherhood," 36.

52. Chatelain, *South Side Girls*, 5–6. See also Gutman, *City for Children*, 27; and Fitzpatrick, *Endless Crusade*, 139.

53. Klepp, *Revolutionary Conceptions*, 15–16, 47, 268; Boydston, *Home and Work*, 92.

54. Mintz, *Huck's Raft*, 204, 207–8; Ewen, *Immigrant Women*, 98. Quote is from *Huck's Raft*, 204.

55. Chudacoff, *Children at Play*, 107–8, 111; Gutman, *City for Children*, 16; Zelizer, *Pricing the Priceless Child*, 33–34.

56. Michael Davis, *Exploitation of Pleasure*, 3–4.

57. Arthur Minturn Chase, "Children of the Street," *The Outlook*, 27 July 1912, 688–89, 694.

58. Chase, "Children of the Street," 689.

59. Fritz Blocki, "The Most Dangerous Job in the World," *Independent*, 30 May 1925, 605–6.

60. Butler, *Pioneers in Public Recreation*, 160–67. See also Mintz, *Huck's Raft*, 179.

61. Atwell, "Playgrounds for Colored America," 87.

62. Atwell, "Playgrounds for Colored America," 84–85.

63. Austin, *Coming of Age*, 50, 64. See also Gutman, *City for Children*, 27–28.

64. Shivery, "History," 44–45, 68; Minutes of the Neighborhood Union, 19 October 1914, box 4, folder 5, NU Collection. See also the photograph of the Foundry Street Playground, 1912, series number 16, box 14, folder 38, NU Collection.

65. Dan Carey, "Campaign for Increased Recreation Facilities Is Growing in Atlanta," *Atlanta Constitution*, 20 December 1914. Since the city furnished no separate public parks for Black families at the time, the two existing public playgrounds were located on the grounds of two Black schools.

66. "A Bond Issue of $4,100,000 Is Plan of Sub-Committee to Care for Schools and Other Needs," *Atlanta Constitution*, 2 December 1914; "More Than 14,000 Children on Playgrounds Last Week," *Atlanta Constitution*, 21 July 1915; "Playgrounds Were Visited by Thousands of Children," *Atlanta Constitution*, 8 September 1915; "Approval Given Municipal Links and Playgrounds," *Atlanta Constitution*, 14 May 1920; "Money Sheet Task Now Is Completed," *Atlanta Constitution*, 15 January 1927; Consultant Service of the National Municipal League, *Governments of Atlanta*, 134, 287.

67. Hanmer, discussion of Henry Hubbard's "Parks and Playgrounds," 36–37; Butler, *Pioneers in Public Recreation*, 66. When rowdy children overran the limited facilities that

were available, it was not unusual for overworked and underpaid supervisors to throw up their hands in futility. Austin, *Coming of Age*, 65.

68. "Parent-Teacher Congress Sponsors Home Play Week," *Lincoln Star*, 22 June 1930; "Home Play Week Planned April 26–May 2: Commission Asks Co-Operation of Parent-Teachers," *Post-Star*, 3 April 1931; "Mayor Issues Proclamation," *The Times* (Munster, IN), 15 November 1922; "Home Play Week Is Arranged for City's Children," *Salem News*, 20 April 1923; "Waco Parents Urged to Observe Play Week," *Waco News-Tribune*, 25 January 1929; "New Home Play Week Comes Monday," *Monroe News-Star*, 15 May 1922; "Ask Parents to Take Part in Daily Play Life of Children," *Ithaca Journal*, 26 April 1928; "Play Week Starts Today," *The Times* (Shreveport, LA), 30 January 1922; "Come Play with Your Child," *Fitchburg Sentinel*, 21 December 1922.

69. Advertisement for the Playground Equipment Co., *Children: The Magazine for Parents*, April 1927, 41.

70. Ihlder, discussion of Henry Hubbard's "Size and Distribution," 297–98.

71. Chase, "Children of the Street," 690–94; Stearns, *Anxious Parents*, 176; Zelizer, *Pricing the Priceless Child*, 47–48; Weaver Pangburn, "Home Recreation," *Chatham Press*, 30 April 1927.

72. Ware, *Home Life*, 15–18, 23–25. See also Kenneth Jackson, *Crabgrass Frontier*, 54–72; and Mintz, *Huck's Raft*, 187.

73. Weber, "Suburban Annexations," 616; Campbell, "Is American Domesticity Decreasing," 96; Campbell, *Household Economics*, 24, 241.

74. Leonard, *Illiberal Reformers*, 109–28. During the 1930s, the American Eugenics Society promoted suburban residential parks as ideal places to raise a child. "Report of the President of the American Eugenics Society," American Eugenics Society, 26 June 1926, www.eugenicsarchive.org/html/eugenics/static/images/635.html; Lovett, "Eugenic Housing."

75. Charlotte Perkins Gilman, "Housing for Children," *Independent*, August 1904, 436.

76. Cross, *Kids' Stuff*, 54, 60–61, 71.

77. Clark, *American Family Home*, 153, 162–63.

78. Wilson, *Bungalow Book*, 3; Wallick, *Small House*, 13, 14.

79. Anderson, "Zoning," 155–56; Clark, *American Family Home*, 132. For a local example, see The Society for the Preservation of Historic Oakwood, "Neighborhood History," Historic Oakwood, accessed 26 June 2024, www.historicoakwood.org/neighborhood-history.

80. For example, see "Mackle to Erect Apartment House," *Atlanta Constitution*, 4 April 1919; and "Modern Apartment House Planned for Atlanta," *Atlanta Constitution*, 5 March 1922.

81. Cope, "Conservation," 20–21.

82. Davis, "Shall We Encourage," 335, 337; Hurty, "State and Housing," 170. See also Fairbanks, "From Better Dwellings," 25.

83. West, "Child Care," 7–8.

84. Architects' Small House Service Bureau, *100 Bungalows*, 18.

85. Gutman and Coninck-Smith, "Good to Think With," 13; Stearns, *Anxious Parents*, 13.

86. Gotham, "Urban Space, Restrictive Covenants," 618, 621. Gotham argues that the rhetoric of housing reformers and social workers contributed to the "segregationist real estate ideology."

87. Shivery, "History," 345, 369.

Chapter 2

1. "Post Yourself Thoroughly on Woodland Heights," advertisement, *Houston Post*, 29 September 1907; William A. Wilson Realty Company, Woodland Heights promotional booklet, 1910, box 2, folder 10, HS Collection.

2. For example, "New Park for Colored to Allow No Tenants," *Atlanta Constitution*, 11 June 1919. This advertisement promoted a "new residential park now under way for desirable colored people" that will assure one's "children will be reared in an atmosphere of refinement close to the largest educational institutions in Georgia."

3. Buena Vista advertisement, *Twin City Sentinel*, 21 October 1922.

4. Kenneth Jackson, *Crabgrass Frontier*, 58–59, 71; Gotham, "Urban Space, Restrictive Covenants," 618, 621.

5. Colin Gordon, "Dividing the City," 161; Gotham, "Urban Space, Restrictive Covenants," 617–18; Fogelson, *Bourgeois Nightmares*, 96; Glotzer, *How the Suburbs*, 52–55.

6. Corrigan v. Buckley, 271 U.S. 323 (1926); Shelley v. Kraemer, 334 U.S. 1 (1948). For an excellent study of the effect of *Shelley v. Kraemer*, see Gonda, *Unjust Deeds*.

7. Olmsted, Vaux & Co., *Preliminary Report*, 6–7, 26–28. While touring the South just before the Civil War, Olmsted was convinced that slavery must eventually come to an end for the sake of white morality, but he remained committed to white supremacy. Olmsted, *Journey in the Back Country*. See also White and Kramer, *Olmsted South*.

8. Nichols, "Financial Effect," 102–3. See also Stearns, *Anxious Parents*, 46.

9. Advertisement for Palos Verdes Estates, *Los Angeles Sunday Times*, 3 February 1924; Riddle, "'Homes to Last,'" 23; Fogelson, *Bourgeois Nightmares*, 54.

10. Hanchett, *Sorting Out*, 153, 172; "The Big Land Sale," *Western Sentinel*, 9 October 1890; "Ansley Park Lots for Sale," *Atlanta Constitution*, 12 March 1905; "Ansley Park: 14 Lots at Auction," *Atlanta Constitution*, 18 June 1906; "Edwin P. Ansley Purchases Additional Property Adjoining Ansley Park," *Atlanta Constitution*, 31 May 1908; Garden Hills advertisement, *Atlanta Constitution*, 5 May 1926.

11. Fogelson, *Bourgeois Nightmares*, 58; correspondence between J. C. Nichols and R. Jemison Jr., folder 6.1.1.9.22, RJ Papers.

12. "The Coming Sale: Twenty Choice Lots in Inman Park at Auction," *Atlanta Constitution*, 22 April 1890; Nichols, "Restrictions," 212. See also Fogelson, *Bourgeois Nightmares*, 46.

13. "Agreement Creating a Residential Retreat in River Oaks," p. 5, included with a letter from Hugh Potter to Robert Jemison, 12 July 1928, folder 6.1.32.31, RJ Papers.

14. Fogelson, *Bourgeois Nightmares*, 56; "Agreement Creating a Residential Retreat in River Oaks," p. 5, included with a letter from Hugh Potter to Robert Jemison, 12 July 1928, folder 6.1.32.31, RJ Papers.

15. Tocqueville, *Democracy in America*, 406; Nichols, "Financial Effect," 102; Hopkins, "Status, Mobility, and Dimensions," 226.

16. Joel Hurt to Olmsted Bros., 13 May 1905, Olmsted Associates Records, Series B—Job File #00071, Library of Congress Manuscript Division, transcribed in Druid Hills Olmsted Documentary Record, ed. Charles E. Beveridge, 135, accessed 26 June 2024, https://druidhills.org/resources/Documents/olmsted_firm_kirkwood_land_letters.pdf.

17. Cameron Park sales brochure (1914) reprinted in Charlotte V. Brown, "Three Raleigh Suburbs," 35; "I Simply Can't Afford It," Country Club District advertisement, *Kansas City Star*, 1 October 1922.

18. Nichols, "Restrictions," 212; Chester S. Chase, "A Well Planned and Well Planted Community," *House Beautiful*, September 1926, 264.

19. Hanchett, *Sorting Out*, 96–98. Ladd-Taylor, *Mother Work*, 49–50, 55–56, 62.

20. Richard H. Edmonds to Edward H. Bouton, letter, 27 July 1894, box 1, folder 13, RPC Records. See also Glotzer, *How the Suburbs*, 59.

21. "Home in Ansley Park," *Atlanta Journal*, 27 April 1909.

22. Advertisement for Peachtree Heights, *Atlanta Constitution*, 20 March 1914; advertisement for the Greater Wayne District, *Detroit Free Press*, 22 November 1925.

23. Advertisement for Cameron Park, *News and Observer*, 13 April 1913; R. Jemison Jr. to R. E. Calloway, 4 January 1924, RJ Papers; full-page advertisement from the *Birmingham News*, folder 6.1.13.19, RJ Papers; "Do It for the Kiddies," *Birmingham News*, 15 July 1923.

24. Advertisement for Palos Verdes, *Los Angeles Sunday Times*, 3 February 1924.

25. "A New Home * A New School * A New and Wholesome Environment for Your Children," advertisement; "Now—A Modern Public School in River Oaks," newspaper clipping, both in vol. 8, RO Scrapbook; Riddle, *River Oaks*.

26. Mintz, *Huck's Raft*, 215.

27. Advertisement for the Country Club District, *Kansas City Star*, 17 April 1910; advertisement for Cameron Park, *News and Observer*, 18 January 1913.

28. William P. Walthall, "East Lake Improvements Appeal to Suburb Dweller," *Atlanta Constitution*, 16 April 1916; Olmsted, "Planning Residential Subdivisions," 14–15.

29. "Stenographic Report of the Third Annual Conference of Developers of High-Class Residential Property" (1919), 238, Jemison Companies, Miscellany, #2838, Division of Rare and Manuscript Collections, Cornell University Library. See also "A Better School Environment an 'Added Value' That Materially Benefits Both You and Your Children," Palos Verdes Estates advertisement, *Los Angeles Times*, 26 April 1929; and "Every Shaker Village Home Is Near a Good School," Van Sweringen Company advertisement, undated, "Parent and Sex Instincts" Scrapbook, 1929–1934, box 279, vol. 4, RPC Records.

30. "A New School in Bloomfield Village," circa 1929, "Parent and Sex Instincts" Scrapbook, 1929–1934, box 279, vol. 4, RPC Records.

31. Advertisement for Buena Vista Annex, *Winston-Salem Journal*, 26 March 1922.

32. Gandolfo v. Hartman, 49 F. 181 (1892); George Whitelock to Edward H. Bouton, 5 October 1893, box 2, folder 8, RPC Records; Glotzer, *How the Suburbs*, 52–53, 95.

33. Advertisements for Boylan Heights, *Raleigh Times*, 7 May and 4 October 1909.

34. "Stenographic Report of the Third Annual Conference of Developers of High-Class Residential Property" (1919), 580, Jemison Companies, Miscellany, #2838, Division of Rare and Manuscript Collections, Cornell University Library. For two additional interpretations of this exchange, see Glotzer, *How the Suburbs*, 126–27; Fogelson, *Bourgeois Nightmares*, 96.

35. Pruitt, *Other Great Migration*; Hitt, "Peopling the City," 54–64; Steptoe, *Houston Bound*; Herbin-Triant, *Threatening Property*.

36. "Street Chat," *Raleigh Times*, 25 July 1900; "White Supremacy Clubs," *Morning Post*, 29 June 1900; "White Men Meet," *Morning Post*, 2 August 1900.

37. Forsyth County Property Deed Book #32, p. 345. This deed was dated 5 August 1889.

38. Forsyth County Property Deed Book #31, pp. 250 and 461; #32, p. 345. See also "H. E. Starbuck, grantor," "General Index to Real Estate Conveyances," Forsyth County,

North Carolina, 1849–1927, Forsyth County Register of Deeds Online Records Systems, accessed 20 May 2024, www.co.forsyth.nc.us/rod/online_lookup.aspx.

39. Gandolfo v. Hartman, 49 F. 181 (1892); Colin Gordon, "Dividing the City," 161; Wertheimer, *Law and Society*, 47.

40. Forsyth County Property Deed Book #25, pp. 281 and 395.

41. "Interesting to Everybody," *Twin-City Daily Sentinel*, 4 May 1893; "Wachovia Loan & Trust Company," advertisement, *Union Republican*, 28 November 1895; "Memoir to Late Hon. J. C. Buxton," *Twin-City Daily Sentinel*, 11 May 1917. See also the Winston-Salem city directories during this period, DigitalNC, www.digitalnc.org/collections/city-directories/.

42. "Notes from Blowing Rock," *Western Sentinel*, 22 August 1889.

43. "Local Notes," *People's Press*, 14 May 1891; promotional letter for West End, 15 September 1890, Historic West End, West End Neighborhood Association, http://historicwestend.org/wp-content/uploads/2014/09/WE-Hotel-and-Land-Co-1890.pdf; "State Legislature," *People's Press*, 5 February 1891; North Carolina Corporation Commission, *Third Annual Report*, 353; North Carolina Corporation Commission, *Fifth Annual Report*, 564; C. Sylvester Green, "John Cameron Buxton," NCpedia, accessed 15 June 2024, www.ncpedia.org/biography/buxton-john-cameron; Roger N. Kirkman, "Henry Elias Fries," NCpedia, accessed 15 June 2024, www.ncpedia.org/biography/fries-henry-elias; Tom E. Terrill, "Francis Henry Fries," NCpedia, accessed 15 June 2024, www.ncpedia.org/biography/fries-francis-henry. John C. Buxton's wife was the first cousin of the Fries brothers.

44. Forsyth County Deed Book #35, pp. 281 and 395; #38, pp. 46, 81, and 325; "Lots for Sale to Actual Settlers!," *Union Republican*, 5 November 1891; "Local Items," *People's Press*, 25 February 1892.

45. Advertisement for the Winston Development Company, *Union Republican*, 13 August 1891; Forsyth County Deed Book #46, p. 61.

46. "Assured Progress and Prosperity," *Western Sentinel*, 29 January 1891; "Local Items," *People's Press*, 23 April 1891; Forsyth County Deed Book #37, p. 529; #39, p. 162. The only racial covenants in this addition were for a group of six large lots sold together to a member of the interlocking directorate for a substantially greater sum than the surrounding property.

47. "Another Land Company Organized," *Western Sentinel*, 11 June 1891; Forsyth County Deed Book #39, p. 401; "Local News," *Union Republican*, 23 October 1890; Washington Park nomination form for the National Register of Historic Places, 4 December 1991, Winston-Salem/Forsyth County Planning and Development Services Department, "National Register of Historic Places," https://files.nc.gov/ncdcr/nr/FY2510.pdf.

48. See Forsyth County Deed Book #44, pp. 297 and 300; #47, p. 113; #57, p. 449; #119, p. 524; and #128, p. 98. Before Black families began moving onto East Fourth Street, property values in East Winston were stalled at about $400. See a sampling of real estate "deals" from that year in "Real Estate Deals," *Twin-City Daily Sentinel*, 6 December 1910, which contains recent sales for lots in East Winston and Columbia Heights.

49. "Raleigh Banks Show Progress," *Raleigh Times*, 8 January 1907; "For Greater Raleigh," *North Carolinian*, 13 June 1907; notice, Greater Raleigh Land Company, *North Carolinian*, 26 December 1907; Raleigh city directories between 1890 and 1910, DigitalNC,

www.digitalnc.org/collections/city-directories/. The three men involved in Cameron Park development were C. J. Hunter, B. S. Jerman, and H. E. Litchford.

50. Andrews was also vice president of the Citizens National Bank, which provided additional ties to H. E. Litchford, who was involved with both Boylan Heights and Cameron Park. Brown, "Three Raleigh Suburbs," 33; "Glenwood Lots," advertisement, *Raleigh Times*, 25 August 1906; "Now It Is Up to Raleigh's Aldermen," *Morning Post*, 30 May 1905; "Raleigh Banks Show Progress," *Raleigh Times*, 8 January 1907; "For Greater Raleigh," *North Carolinian*, 13 June 1907; notice, Greater Raleigh Land Company, *North Carolinian*, 26 December 1907; Raleigh city directories between 1890 and 1910, DigitalNC, www.digitalnc.org/collections/city-directories/.

51. Andrews-Duncan House nomination form for the National Register of Historic Places, "Andrews-Duncan House," Raleigh Historic Development Commission, accessed 5 August 2024, https://files.nc.gov/ncdcr/nr/WA0003.pdf; "The Big Land Sale," *Western Sentinel*, 9 October 1890. According to the *Western Sentinel* (Winston-Salem), A. B. Andrews and William Boylan, among others, participated in a lottery to distribute the first lots "sold" in West End. The deed record, however, suggests this "sale" was not a direct transfer of deeds for individual lots but a means to raise money to pay for the improvements. The investors then made a profit when the development company sold the improved lots. In 1896, William Boylan demanded a deed for his share of the property, but apparently, not every investor did. See Forsyth County Property Deed Book #51, p. 11. West End's investment "sale" was advertised in multiple Raleigh newspapers. "The Best Business Opportunity Yet Offered!," *Progressive Farmer* (Raleigh), 16 September 1890; West End Land Co. advertisement, *Raleigh News and Observer*, 13 September 1890. Raleigh's first racial covenant was recorded in Wake County Property Deed Book #212, p. 180, Wake County, NC, Register of Deeds Online Records Systems, Property Deed Books and Index, https://rodcrpi.wakegov.com/Booksweb/. See also Glenwood Land Co. incorporation papers, Wake County Property Deed Book 00000B, p. 212, Wake County, NC, Register of Deeds Online Records Systems, Property Deed Books and Index, https://rodcrpi.wakegov.com/Booksweb/. Additionally, A. B. Andrews was involved in other business ventures with West End's developers. For example, the Fries brothers and J. C. Buxton served as directors for Andrews's Northwestern North Carolina Railroad Company. "Annual Railroad Meeting," *Twin-City Daily Sentinel*, 2 September 1892.

52. Jones-Correa, "Origins and Diffusion," 545–47, 550; Gandolfo v. Hartman, 49 F. 181 (1892); Koehler v. Rowland, 205 S. W. 217 (1918). According to the Koehler decision, Wirtman Place used racial covenants in 1905. Kevin Fox Gotham suggests race restrictions in Kansas City date back as far as 1900. Gotham, "Urban Space, Restrictive Covenants," 623–24. According to Hanchett, the first race restriction used in Charlotte was in 1901. Hanchett, *Sorting Out*, 149–50.

53. "New Home Park for Gate City," *Atlanta Constitution*, 23 May 1909; "Post Yourself Thoroughly on Woodland Heights," *Houston Post*, 29 September 1907; William A. Wilson Realty Company, Woodland Heights promotional booklet, 1910, box 2, folder 10, HS Collection; advertisement for Eastwood, *Houston Post*, 29 September 1913; "Eastwood to Be Pretty Addition," *Houston Post*, 6 June 1912. See also Robert Fisher, "Protecting Community," 129–30.

54. Exclusion File of Frank Caozza, box 252, folder 12, RPC Records. See also Glotzer, *How the Suburbs*, 130–31.

55. Joel Hurt to Olmsted Associates, 4 April 1902, Olmsted Associates Records, Series B—Job File #00071, Library of Congress Manuscript Division, compiled in "Druid Hills Olmsted Documentary Record: Selected Texts," ed. Charles E. Beveridge, 130, https://druidhills.wordpress.com/wp-content/uploads/2011/07/letters-project-complete-text.pdf. See also Lands, *Culture of Property*, 55.

56. R. W. Marchant to Officer Jehu Rutledge, 18 April and 13 May 1908, box 32, folder 6, RPC Records. See also Fogelson, *Bourgeois Nightmares*, 196.

57. "On Our Fenceless State," *Atlantic Monthly*, August 1909, 283.

58. Wiese, *Places of Their Own*, 11–33; Glotzer, *How the Suburbs*, 60–69; Michney, *Surrogate Suburbs*; Rabinowitz, *Race Relations*, 97–124; Hanchett, *Sorting Out*, 134–35, 140–41; Henry Louis Taylor Jr., "Creating the Metropolis," 51–71.

59. "Seeing Raleigh in Automobile—Some Things Seen about City," *Raleigh Times*, 6 February 1909; Cauthen, *Historic Black Neighborhoods*, 93–98. See also Cauthen, *Raleigh's Black Community*.

60. Herbin-Triant, *Threatening Property*, 179–85; "Columbia Heights, Its Reception and Growth," anonymous letter to the editor, *Union Republican*, 26 March 1896; "Segregation by Common Consent," *Winston-Salem Journal*, 19 April 1914; "Salem Wants Improvements," *Winston-Salem Journal*, 3 June 1911; "How to Insure Segregation," *Winston-Salem Journal*, 22 April 1914; "Atkin's Outlines Negroes' Progress," *Winston-Salem Journal and Sentinel*, 10 February 1929.

61. I. McK. Pittenger, "A Much Needed Improvement," letter to the editor, *News and Observer*, 10 June 1920; "Wants Committee to Offer Extension Plans," *News and Observer*, 12 August 1920. See also Thomas Hanchett's discussion of Biddleville and Washington Heights, a Black residential park in Charlotte that was developed in 1912. Hanchett, *Sorting Out*, 134–35, 140–41.

62. "Independence Heights: Portrait of a Historic Neighborhood," Historic Independence Heights Neighborhood Council and Rice University, accessed 26 June 2024, http://indepheights.rice.edu/; Pruitt, *Other Great Migration*, 81; Steptoe, *Houston Bound*, 23, 30–31.

63. "House Divided against Itself," *Houston Informer*, 16 July 1927; "Thousands for Park Acreage, But—," *Houston Informer*, 29 December 1923; "North Carolina One Exception," *Houston Informer*, 26 January 1924; "High-Priced Colored Additions," *Houston Informer*, 10 November 1923.

64. Gwendolyn Wright, *Building the Dream*, 210; Lands, *Culture of Property*, 25.

65. Allen, *Mayor*, 30–31.

66. "Building Boom Starts in June," *News and Observer*, 11 July 1921.

67. Educators often refer to these networks as "social capital." Bourdieu, "Forms of Capital," 241–58. See also Rury, *Creating the Suburban*.

Chapter 3

1. E. S. Martin, "Children as an Incentive," *Harper's Weekly*, 10 December 1904, 29–31.

2. "Stenographic Report of the Third Annual Conference of Developers of High-Class Residential Property," 1919, 249, 344, Jemison Companies, Miscellany, #2838, Division

of Rare and Manuscript Collections, Cornell University Library; "Hi Cost Hits School Board," *Kansas City Times*, 7 May 1920; "School Site Deal Is Upheld," *Kansas City Star*, 14 March 1927.

3. William A. Wilson Realty Company, Woodland Heights brochure, 1910, HS Collection.

4. "Atlanta's Schools Menace to Health of Young Children," *Atlanta Constitution*, 8 October 1913.

5. Brian Wallstin, "Renovated Out of Existence," *Houston Press*, 6 July 2000. Booker T. Washington Elementary was renamed Brock Elementary in 1928 when "Colored High School" was renamed for Booker T. Washington. Houston city directories, 1912, 1923, and 1930, Houston City Directories collection, Houston History Research Center, Houston Public Library.

6. Eagles, *Jonathan Daniels*, 14–16; Charles W. Eagles, "Jonathan Worth Daniels," NCpedia, accessed 15 June 2024, www.ncpedia.org/biography/daniels-jonathan-worth.

7. See Rittenhouse, *Growing Up Jim Crow*.

8. Eagles, *Jonathan Daniels*, 14–16; Hirsch, "With or Without Jim Crow," 68–69.

9. Eagles, *Jonathan Daniels*, 15; Klarman, *From Jim Crow*, 212–17; Fogelson, *Bourgeois Nightmares*. See also Lassiter, *Silent Majority*, 1–19.

10. North Carolina Executive Mansion nomination form for the National Register of Historic Places, 22 April 1970, North Carolina Department of Natural and Cultural Resources, "National Register of Historic Places," https://files.nc.gov/ncdcr/nr/WA0015.pdf; "Another Graded School," *News and Observer*, 14 August 1886; Brown, "Three Raleigh Suburbs," 33; "Neighborhood History," Historic Oakwood, Society for the Preservation of Historic Oakwood, accessed 26 June 2024, www.historicoakwood.org/neighborhood-history.

11. "A Land Boom Right," *Raleigh News and Observer*, 27 July 1898; *Annual Report of the Mayor*, 141; "Two Thousand Dollars! Board of Alderman Appropriate to the Centennial," *State Chronicle*, 6 August 1892; "News of the City," *State Chronicle*, 13 July 1892; "The Raleigh Land Sale," advertisement, *Evening Visitor*, 3 July 1891; Raleigh city directories, 1885–1896, DigitalNC, www.digitalnc.org/collections/city-directories/; "College Park/Idlewild Neighborhood Plan" (public hearing draft), 22 April 1994, "Redevelopment Plans," City of Raleigh website, https://raleighnc.gov/planning/services/redevelopment-plans. The first residence was completed in 1892, surveying was completed in 1893, and the development was annexed to Raleigh in 1907.

12. Although the city's 1994 redevelopment plan (see note 11) claimed that Black property owners predominated after 1905, documents from the time describe a mixed-race housing area. "City in Brief," *Evening Visitor*, 9 May 1894; "City in Brief," *Press Visitor*, 7 October 1895; "Died," *Raleigh Times*, 4 November 1897; "A Land Boom Right," *News and Observer*, 27 July 1898; "Smallpox Breaks Out Again," *Farmer and Mechanic*, 27 June 1899; "A Destitute Family Pounded," *News and Observer*, 19 August 1899; "Sarah Irene Norman," *Raleigh Times*, 21 July 1900; "Death of Mrs. Martin," *Morning Post*, 14 August 1900; "Raleigh Visited by Severe Storms," *Morning Post*, 12 August 1902; "Capt L. W. Smith," *North Carolinian*, 28 January 1904; "Turned in False Alarm," *Morning Post*, 17 November 1904; "A Pathetic Death," *Raleigh News and Observer*, 9 May 1907; "Land Transfer," *Raleigh News and Observer*, 9 July 1907.

13. "Beautiful Building Lots for Sale," *State Chronicle*, 23 May 1891. The original streets

included Jones, Edenton, Lane, Swain, Seawell, and Idlewild. The blocks along New Bern Street remained all white from Swain Street, the eastern limit of Idlewild, to State Street, one block east of the addition's western border. The 1994 Idlewild Neighborhood Plan (see note 11) defined the borders of the community as Oakwood Ave to the north, New Bern to the south, Linden and Swain to the west, and Tarboro to the east, but the streets farther east were not fully developed in 1907. Raleigh city directories (street directories), 1908 and 1922, DigitalNC, www.digitalnc.org/collections/city-directories/.

14. This description was compiled from the Raleigh street directory for Hargett, Martin, and Davie Streets. Raleigh city directory, 1900, DigitalNC, https://lib.digitalnc.org/record/25786; Cauthen, *Historic Black Neighborhoods*, 112, 118–19, 148–52. See also Cauthen, *Raleigh's Black Community*.

15. Barbee, *Historical Sketches*, 39, 41; Fred Olds, "Educational," appendix in the Raleigh city directory, 1881, 195, DigitalNC, https://lib.digitalnc.org/record/25758. The Johnson High and Normal School was located three blocks west of the capitol and one block north of Hillsboro. For an analysis of Black parents' desire for an academic curriculum that would prepare their children for college, see Anderson, *Education of Blacks*.

16. Gibson and Jung, "Historical Census Statistics"; Raleigh city directory, 1900, DigitalNC, https://lib.digitalnc.org/record/25786. Garfield was located at the corner of Swain Street and E Davie Street (316 S Swain). The next block to the south on Swain Street, across from E Davie Street, was about 79 percent Black. According to Jennie Barbee, Garfield originally opened in 1878 in a church and then moved to the new location in 1880. Barbee, *Historical Sketches*, 51, 56; Olds, "Educational." Crosby School was located at 562 E Lenoir, and Chavis was located at 508 S West Street.

17. "The City Schools," *Raleigh News and Observer*, 9 September 1900; "The Wiley School," *Raleigh News and Observer*, 12 September 1900; Barbee, *Historical Sketches*, 46; advertisement for Cameron Park, *Raleigh Times*, 8 September 1910; advertisement for Cameron Park, *Raleigh News and Observer*, 18 January 1913.

18. "The Acreage Added over Doubles the Size," *Raleigh News and Observer*, 11 September 1907; "To the Voters of Raleigh," *Raleigh News and Observer*, 19 April 1908; Barbee, *Historical Sketches*, 52–53.

19. "Mayor Johnson's Annual Report," *Raleigh Times*, 13 October 1906; "Raleigh Township School Districts," *News and Observer*, 1 October 1907; Raleigh city directories, 1900, 1908, and 1922, DigitalNC, www.digitalnc.org/collections/city-directories/. Thompson School was located at the corner of Hargett and Swain Streets. Its address was on Hargett Street, which had a Black majority between Camden and State, two blocks south of Swain.

20. "To the Voters of Raleigh," *News and Observer*, 19 April 1908; "Chavis School to Close," *News and Observer*, 14 June 1908; "New Board Opens Up," *Raleigh Times*, 8 May 1909; "Auction Sale of City Property," *Raleigh Times*, 9 June 1909; "Raleigh Township Schools Report," *News and Observer*, 12 September 1909.

21. "The New Colored School," *Raleigh Times*, 30 July 1909; "Raleigh Township Schools Report," *News and Observer*, 12 September 1909. Haley, "Carolina Chameleon," 402; Simmons-Henry, *Culture Town*, 118–19. Although the Crosby and Garfield schools would not be officially combined until 1920, they already shared the same site and essentially the same children, with Crosby serving the primary grades and Garfield serving the older students.

22. "The Big Gin Mill Has Lost Its Fight: Raleigh Dispensary Overwhelmed at Polls,"

Raleigh Times, 26 December 1907; "Raleigh Public Schools," *Raleigh News and Observer*, 16 April 1908; "Schools Lose and Roads Also," *Raleigh News and Observer*, 22 April 1908.

23. "Association for Good Government," *Raleigh News and Observer*, 29 August 1908; "Good Government for Capitol City," *Raleigh News and Observer*, 12 November 1908; J. S. Wynne, "Mr. Wynne's View of the Tax Defeat," letter to the editor, *Raleigh Times*, 29 April 1908; "Reform Forces Take Charge of City Affairs," *Raleigh Times*, 5 May 1909. It is possible that the Panic of 1907 had a negative impact on the city, but the economic downturn was short-lived. Moreover, Raleigh's economy was rooted in the government sector, not in industry or finance, and none of the arguments made against the school tax mentioned concerns about the larger economy.

24. Advertisement for Boylan Heights, *Raleigh Times*, 7 May 1909.

25. "Wynne, Ellington, & Co.," *Morning Post*, 10 January 1901; want ads, *Morning Post*, 18 January 1901; "Annual Meeting Held," *Raleigh News and Observer*, 16 January 1909; "Raleigh Banking and Trust Company," advertisement, *Raleigh News and Observer*, 29 April 1906; "Parker-Hunter Realty Company," *Raleigh News and Observer*, 12 May 1910; "Street Chat," *Raleigh Times*, 25 July 1900; "White Supremacy Clubs," *Morning Post*, 29 June 1900; "White Men Meet," *Morning Post*, 2 August 1900; "New Insurance Company," *Raleigh Times*, 5 January 1905; "Chavis School to Close," *Raleigh News and Observer*, 14 June 1908; "Seeing Raleigh in Automobile—Some Things Seen About the City," *Raleigh Times*, 6 February 1909; advertisement for Boylan Heights, *Raleigh Times*, 21 May 1909; Raleigh city directories, 1908–1910, DigitalNC, www.digitalnc.org/collections/city-directories/. Initially, Ellington served as the vice president of Boylan Heights' development company. In 1908, the president of the company passed away, after which Ellington managed Boylan Heights through the real estate companies he shared with Wynne. The company's "Resolutions of Respect" for Fabius Busbee, the deceased, was signed by J. D. Turner, secretary of the company as well as secretary for Wynne and Ellington's Real Estate and Trust Company. "Resolutions of Respect," *Raleigh Times*, 9 September 1908.

26. "Observations," *Observer*, 17 February 1880; Raleigh city directories, 1881 and 1896, DigitalNC, www.digitalnc.org/collections/city-directories/. The St. Augustine's church school mentioned in the article is different from the private school run by St. Augustine's College. At that time, the school district still supported three public schools hosted by Black churches.

27. Raleigh Township Graded Schools, *Fortieth Annual Report*, 7–8, 15, 55. Unfortunately, when Wake County Public Schools moved from its location in downtown Raleigh to suburban Cary, it lost the microfilm containing the minutes for the Raleigh Township School Board. The only minutes that remain are the copies in my possession, but I did not make copies from 1916.

28. Blank, *Volume of Residential Construction*, 67. See also "More Home Building," *Atlanta Constitution*, 4 September 1921.

29. I. McK. Pittenger, "A Much Needed Improvement," letter to the editor, *Raleigh News and Observer*, 10 June 1920.

30. "Youths Arrested Under Suspicion," *Raleigh News and Observer*, 14 August 1914; "Will Erect New School Building," *Raleigh News and Observer*, 17 September 1915; "3550 Pupils Enrolled in Raleigh Schools," *Raleigh News and Observer*, 28 September 1915; "Glenwood Lots," *Raleigh Times*, 25 August 1906; "Murphey School Plans Accepted," *Raleigh News and Observer*, 29 October 1915; Brown, "Three Raleigh Suburbs," 33; Raleigh

Township Graded Schools, *Fortieth Annual Report*, 7–8, 16, 55. Lewis was completed in two stages: student enrollment rose by more than 250 percent between the fall of 1915, when the first five classrooms were built, and the spring of 1917, after the school was completed.

31. Wake County Property Deed Book #212, p. 180, Wake County, NC, Register of Deeds Online Records Systems, Property Deed Books and Index, https://rodcrpi.wakegov.com/Booksweb/. See also "Racially Restricted Covenants Project," Wake County Register of Deeds, accessed 11 August 2024, www.wake.gov/departments-government/register-deeds/racially-restrictive-covenants-project.

32. Legal scholar Sheryll Cashin examines a similar phenomenon in the more recent past. Scholars refer to this behavior as "opportunity hoarding." Cashin, *White Space, Black Hood*, 105–44; Tilly, *Durable Inequality*; Reeves, *Dream Hoarders*; Dougherty, "Shopping for Schools"; Rury and Rife, "Race, Schools and Opportunity Hoarding"; Rury, *Creating the Suburban*.

33. "Beautiful Modern Homes to Be Erected Where Dense Woods Stand on Peachtree," *Atlanta Constitution*, 27 April 1904; "Owners Give Stock to the Municipality," *Atlanta Constitution*, 1 May 1904; "Park Purchase to Be Discussed," *Atlanta Constitution*, 23 May 1904. According to historian Thomas Hanchett, "white-collar domination of urban politics" meant that the anti-annexation movement in the South was not as strong as it was elsewhere in the nation. Hanchett, *Sorting Out*, 213.

34. "Purchase of Piedmont Park by the City Will Result in Increased Interest in Park Situation, Benefiting All the Playgrounds," *Atlanta Constitution*, 25 May 1904; "Atlanta's Great Park System," *Atlanta Constitution*, 25 May 1904; "Mayor to Approve Extension of City and Park Purchase," *Atlanta Constitution*, 27 May 1904. Guano factories produced fertilizer from bird excrement, an industrial activity few would want adjacent to their neighborhoods.

35. "Mayor to Approve Extension of City and Park Purchase," *Atlanta Constitution*, 27 May 1904; "Will Make Terms for New District," *Atlanta Constitution*, 30 May 1904; "Limits of City Are Discussed," *Atlanta Constitution*, 31 May 1904; "Report Is Prepared on Park and Limits," *Atlanta Constitution*, 4 June 1904; "Hearing Given on City Bills," *Atlanta Constitution*, 21 July 1904; "City Charter Bills Again in Committee," *Atlanta Constitution*, 27 July 1904.

36. "Site Selection for New School," *Atlanta Constitution*, 29 November 1904; advertisement for Ansley Park, *Atlanta Constitution*, 12 March 1905; "For Extension Quick Action Will Be Taken," *Atlanta Constitution*, 17 June 1908; "Ansley Park: 14 Lots at Auction," *Atlanta Constitution*, 23 Sept 1908.

37. "Rainy Day Play Places, or Gymnasiums, Features of the Tenth Street School," *Atlanta Constitution*, 6 May 1906; "Attendance Increased," *Atlanta Constitution*, 8 September 1905; "Board of Education Reorganizes for Year," *Atlanta Constitution*, 4 January 1906; "Walker Street School—One of Atlanta's Oldest," *Atlanta Constitution*, 11 April 1909.

38. "Tenth Street School Patrons Ask City's Finance Committee for $15,000 for Improvements," *Atlanta Constitution*, 6 May 1915; "Ansley Park Lots Wanted," advertisement from E. Rivers Realty Co., *Atlanta Constitution*, 14 February 1909; Strayer and Engelhardt, *Survey*, 165.

39. "Needs of Schools Shown in Letter from Mr. Slaton," *Atlanta Constitution*, 14 October 1913; "School Campaign Gets Good Start at Mass Meeting," *Atlanta Constitution*,

7 February 1915; "Problems of Double Sessions in Schools Near Settlement by Equipping Rented House," *Atlanta Constitution*, 9 September 1917.

40. "School Board Will Ask Council for $1,500,000 to Erect More Schools," *Atlanta Constitution*, 25 November 1914; "School Situation Put Up to Council," *Atlanta Constitution*, 11 February 1915; "Ask Improvement of Many Schools," *Atlanta Constitution*, 13 May 1915. The councilman was Claude Ashley, who would introduce the city's first residential segregation ordinance, as discussed in chapter 5.

41. Minutes of the Atlanta Board of Education, 13 September 1911 and 23 May 1912; "Committee Is Named to Select School Site," *Atlanta Constitution*, 18 September 1910; "E. P. Ansley Offers Lot for School," *Atlanta Constitution*, 10 April 1910; "Ask City to Donate Lot for Ansley Park School," *Atlanta Constitution*, 24 May 1912; "Site for Eighth Ward School Is Becoming Imperative," *Atlanta Constitution*, 2 June 1912; "No School in Piedmont Park," *Atlanta Constitution*, 14 June 1912.

42. "Spring Street Work Will Be Hastened," *Atlanta Constitution*, 21 December 1913; "Ansley Park Residents Are Divided on Site of the Eighth Ward School," *Atlanta Constitution*, 27 March 1918. See also Pomerantz, *Where Peachtree Street*, 95–96.

43. "Spring Street School May Be Converted into Junior High," *Atlanta Constitution*, 8 March 1922; "Plans Are Made for Beautifying of Ansley Park," *Atlanta Constitution*, 10 March 1922; "Site for Eighth Ward School Is Becoming Imperative," *Atlanta Constitution*, 2 June 1912; "Tenth Street School Patrons Ask City's Finance Committee for $15,000 for Improvements," *Atlanta Constitution*, 6 May 1915.

44. "Bonds and Higher Tax Lose at Polls," *Atlanta Constitution*, 24 April 1919; "Atlanta Urged to Prepare for Population of 500,000 in Mayor Key's Message," *Atlanta Constitution*, 6 January 1920; "Mayor Key Re-Elected by 2742 Majority," *Atlanta Constitution*, 29 July 1920. Ansley Park residents were in Eighth Ward, Precinct A.

45. The three men were James Gray, Pleasant Hanes, and William Whitaker, who also served as president of the company. "Local Items," *People's Press*, 14 May 1891. The city directories also list the school board members and the occupations of residents. "School Notice," *Twin-City Daily Sentinel*, 22 October 1892; "Domestic Science Department Dinner," *Twin-City Daily Sentinel*, 27 February 1915; "Memoir to Late Hon. J. C. Buxton," *Twin-City Daily Sentinel*, 11 May 1917.

46. West End Land Co. advertisement, *Twin-City Sentinel*, 20 August 1892.

47. "Tenth Street School Patrons Ask City's Finance Committee for $15,000 for Improvements," *Atlanta Constitution*, 6 May 1915. Orme was one of the wealthy residents who lived on Peachtree Street. Advertisement for North Boulevard Park, *Atlanta Constitution*, 23 April 1916; "Orme Will Enter Race for Council from Eighth Ward," *Atlanta Constitution*, 20 May 1916; see also Garrett, *Atlanta and Environs*, 632.

48. "North Boulevard Park—Piedmont Park," advertisement, *Atlanta Constitution*, 19 May 1917.

49. "Able Leaders Named for Big Committees," *Atlanta Constitution*, 7 January 1919; "Board of Education Committees Named," *Atlanta Constitution*, 12 January 1919; "1918 City Council Committees," *Atlanta Constitution*, 8 January 1918; "Winburn Elected Head of Atlanta Education Board," *Atlanta Constitution*, 9 January 1920; Minutes of the Atlanta Board of Education, 23 August 1917, 17 January and 28 March 1918, and 31 December 1919. In January 1918, Virginia Avenue School was included in a list of fifteen Black schools. It had an enrollment of 184 for the 1917–18 academic year. According to the minutes for

December 1919, the district had fifteen Black schools, but that total included Ashby Street School, which had recently been converted to Black use. Nonetheless, Virginia Avenue School was still listed in the 1919 city directory, which means it remained open in late 1918, when the directory was printed.

50. "Mayor Key Announces 1921 School Program," *Atlanta Constitution*, 23 December 1920; "Lines Are Drawn for Fight on Tax," *Atlanta Constitution*, 2 January 1921.

51. "Trust Company Names Officers," *Atlanta Constitution*, 12 January 1922; "Atlanta Trust Company Adds Department," *Atlanta Constitution*, 22 January 1922; advertisement for Commercial National Bank, *News and Observer*, 5 November 1922; "Continuation of Boulevard Park Provides Attractive Home Sites," *Atlanta Constitution*, 18 January 1925.

52. W. C. Hogg to E. E. Oberholtzer, 15 December 1925; W. C. Hogg to H. L. Mills, 17 December 1925; H. L. Mills to W. C. Hogg, 19 December 1925; Hugh Potter to H. L. Mills, 27 April 1926; W. C. Hogg to Hugh Potter, "School Sites," 18 March 1926; W. C. Hogg, "Dickey School Site," memo, 11 January 1927. All in box 2J368, "Schools and School Sites, Houston, October 27, 1925—December 11, 1928," WH Papers.

53. Houston Independent School District, *Building Program*, 93; "River Oaks School Work Is Rushed," *Houston Chronicle*, 28 October 1928; Riddle, "'Homes to Last,'" 27; "Now—A Modern Public School in River Oaks," newspaper clipping, vol. 8, RO Scrapbook.

54. Invitation to a "public meeting" in the "interest of a Public School," 17 January 1901, "Bouton personal correspondence: S–Z, 1899–1901," box 205, folder 3, RPC Records; "Suburbs and County: Delegations Go to Towson to Ask for New Schools," *Baltimore Sun*, 31 January 1901; "Schoolhouse at Evergreen," *Baltimore Sun*, 26 January 1901. See also "Suburban Miscellany," *Baltimore Sun*, 4 March and 20 March 1901; and "Suburbs and County," *Baltimore Sun*, 18 April and 5 October 1901.

55. "Work on Peachtree Heights School Expected to Begin during January," *Atlanta Constitution*, 22 December 1916; "Peachtree School's Name Changed to Honor E. Rivers," *Atlanta Constitution*, 30 May 1926; "Move for High School in North Side Started," *Atlanta Constitution*, 14 November 1928.

56. For an analysis of increased per capita expenditures during the 1920s, see Amsterdam, *Roaring Metropolis*.

Chapter 4

1. Dashiell, *Dashiell Family Records*, 503, 540. For further information on Dashiell's daughters, see "Home Movies Enjoy After-Dinner Vogue," *Baltimore Sun*, 16 August 1931; and "Goes to Eastern Shore," *Baltimore Sun*, 28 August 1929. For the basic story behind Baltimore's segregation ordinance, see W. Ashbie Hawkins, "A Year of Segregation in Baltimore," *The Crisis*, November 1911, 28; and Power, "Apartheid Baltimore Style."

2. Other scholars have noted the connection between the rise of residential parks and the fall of property values in older, urban neighborhoods, but none have linked this phenomenon with child-rearing. LeeAnn Lands referred to the shift as a new "culture of property." Gretchen Boger and Kevin Fox Gotham analyzed the role that status played in the process, and Colin Gordon emphasized property values. But without including an analysis of child-rearing norms, neither the status argument nor the property value argument fully makes sense. Because families with small children were the largest market

for single-family homes, parenting decisions shaped the value of residential lots and imbued them with status. Clearly, some urban residential properties had high status and value before the existence of residential parks, and they maintained their status for homeowners without small children long after. Lands, *Culture of Property*; Boger, "Meaning of Neighborhood"; Gotham, "Urban Space, Restrictive Covenants," 618, 621, 629–30; Colin Gordon, "Dividing the City," 163, 165, 168, 172. See also Glotzer, *How the Suburbs*, 83–87.

3. "Cemetery Is Dead: Project Abandoned by the Promoters," *Atlanta Journal*, 10 March 1910.

4. Strayer and Engelhardt, *Survey*, 176.

5. Herbin-Triant, *Threatening Property*, 122. See also Hawkins, "Year of Segregation," 28; and Silver, "Racial Origins of Zoning," 192.

6. See William Henry Jones, *Housing of Negroes*, 72–80. This study examines the racial attitudes of white families who lived in mixed-race neighborhoods.

7. UK Board of Trade, *Cost of Living in American Towns*, 56.

8. Massey and Denton, *American Apartheid*, 17–26; Hanchett, *Sorting Out*, 3–8; Lands, *Culture of Property*, 29; Gotham, *Race, Real Estate*, 217.

9. UK Board of Trade, *Cost of Living in American Towns*, 250, 288, 388; Lands, *Culture of Property*, 33. See also William Henry Jones, *Housing of Negroes*, 80–81.

10. Beeth and Wintz, introduction to *Black Dixie*, 24; Gotham, *Race, Real Estate*, 27–30.

11. "New Water Mains Are Now Being Put Down," *Atlanta Journal*, 31 March 1910.

12. Shivery, "History," 47, 49, 70, 76, 79–81, 115; Shivery and Smythe, "Neighborhood Union," 151.

13. "An Open Letter to City Fathers," *Houston Informer*, 23 February 1924. See also "Some Startling Health Facts," *Houston Informer*, 28 May 1921; and "The Mirror: Do They Really Care?," *Houston Informer*, 15 March 1924.

14. Simmons, *Crescent City Girls*, 12–13; McMillen, *Dark Journey*; Rittenhouse, *Growing Up Jim Crow*.

15. Gordon-Reed, *Hemingses of Monticello*, 84–90; Cahn, *Sexual Reckonings*, 165. See also Robinson, *Dangerous Liaisons*; and Royster, *Southern Horrors*.

16. For a description of how southern white parents taught their children the etiquette of Jim Crow during the early twentieth century, see Smith, *Killers of the Dream*.

17. Wiese, *Places of Their Own*, 11–33; Glotzer, *How the Suburbs*, 60–69; Michney, *Surrogate Suburbs*; Rabinowitz, *Race Relations*, 97–124; Hanchett, *Sorting Out*, 134–35, 140–41.

18. Shivery, "History," 47, 49, 70, 79–81; Washington, "My View," 113–14. See also Garb, *City of American Dreams*, 181–82.

19. Boger, "Meaning of Neighborhood."

20. Hawkins, "Year of Segregation," 28; Silver, "Racial Origins of Zoning," 192.

21. Power, "Apartheid Baltimore Style," 29; "Baltimore Tries Drastic Plan of Race Segregation," *New York Times*, 25 December 1910; "Would Keep Out Negroes," *Baltimore Sun*, 13 July 1910; "Would Have a Black Belt: McCulloh Street Residents to Submit an Ordinance," *Baltimore Sun*, 14 September 1910.

22. "Would Have a Black Belt."

23. Dashiell, *Dashiell Family Records*, 503, 540.

24. "Baltimore Tries Drastic Plan"; Glotzer, *How the Suburbs*, 85; Hanchett, *Sorting Out*, 188.

25. Hawkins, "Year of Segregation," 27.

26. Advertisements for Roland Park, *Baltimore Sun*, 25 May, 30 May, and 25 July 1895; 18 June and 19 June 1896.

27. Glotzer, *How the Suburbs*, 49–54.

28. "Assured Progress and Prosperity," *Western Sentinel*, 29 January 1891; "Salem Wants Improvements," *Winston-Salem Journal*, 3 June 1911.

29. Forsyth County Property Deed Book #113, p. 51; "Bank Building Be Completed in Week [sic]," *Winston-Salem Journal*, 5 March 1913; "Forsyth Savings and Trust Company," *Winston-Salem Journal*, 22 June 1913; "Segregate Negroes in East Winston," *Winston-Salem Journal*, 14 June 1912; Winston-Salem city directory, 1912, DigitalNC, https://lib.digitalnc.org/record/25213.

30. Forsyth County Property Deed Book #96, p. 332; #98, p. 45.

31. "Segregate Negroes in East Winston," *Winston-Salem Journal*, 14 June 1912; "Segregation Ordinance," *Twin-City Daily Sentinel*, 6 July 1912; "Segregation in Whole City," *Winston-Salem Journal*, 6 July 1912.

32. "Oust Negroes from East 4th," *Winston-Salem Journal*, 29 December 1912.

33. Forsyth County Property Deed Book #32, p. 345; #73, p. 21.

34. Wertheimer, *Law and Society*, 47.

35. Forsyth County Property Deed Book #78, p. 219; #88, p. 141; #93, p. 10; #98, p. 20; #104, p. 278; #113, p. 51. Craver subdivided the property into three house lots, including one that faced Maple Street.

36. Forsyth County Property Deed Book #32, p. 290; #37, p. 454; #41, pp. 55, 87, and 334; #42, p. 413; #45, p. 47; #46, p. 517; #56, p. 540; #57, pp. 312 and 458; #60, p. 133; #78, p. 215; #82, p. 859; #96, p. 332; #98, p. 45; #113, p. 243. This property would also be divided into two additional lots on Linden Street. For the three race restrictions imposed by Starbuck in 1889, see Forsyth County Property Deed Book #31, pp. 250 and 461; and #32, p. 345. For a complete list of properties sold by Starbuck, see H. E. Starbuck, grantor, "General Index to Real Estate Conveyances," Forsyth County, 1849–1927, Forsyth County Register of Deeds Online Records Systems, accessed 20 May 2024, www.co.forsyth.nc.us/rod/online_lookup.aspx. Perhaps ironically, Starbuck sold Timlic his home lot on High Maple, where Timlic lived before moving to East Fourth Street.

37. Sanborn Fire Insurance Map from Winston-Salem, North Carolina, 1912, Library of Congress Digital Collections, accessed 15 June 2024, http://hdl.loc.gov/loc.gmd/g3904wm.g3904wm_g065221912; Winston-Salem city directory, 1912, DigitalNC, https://lib.digitalnc.org/record/25213; Forsyth County Property Deed Book #39, p. 401.

38. For falling property values, see Forsyth County Property Deed Book #56, pp. 82, 540, and 859. See also Winston-Salem city directories (street directories) between 1900 and 1910, DigitalNC, www.digitalnc.org/collections/city-directories/.

39. The conclusion that Watkins lost money on the sale of his property takes into consideration the fact that he built a house on the lot after he purchased it. Forsyth County Property Deed Book #98, p. 20; #96, p. 332; Winston-Salem city directories, 1908–1912, DigitalNC, www.digitalnc.org/collections/city-directories/. See also "Sudden Death of E. R. Watkins," *Union Republican*, 4 May 1911; and advertisement for Security Life and Annuity Company, *Western Sentinel*, 12 May 1911. Watkins also had an indirect tie to the Inside Land and Improvement Company since J. C. Bessent, the president of the Winston Development Company (1911), was a director for the Inside Land and Improvement Company when Columbia Heights was first developed.

40. Winston-Salem city directory, 1910, DigitalNC, https://lib.digitalnc.org/record/25201; Cox, Gwynn, and Lawrimore, *North Carolina Triad Beer*, 31; Forsyth County Property Deed Book #113, p. 51. The Renigars had been buying and selling property on the block since 1898. Forsyth County Property Deed Book #56, p. 540.

41. Winston-Salem city directories, 1906–1912, 1915, 1922, and 1924, DigitalNC, www.digitalnc.org/collections/city-directories/; Forsyth County Property Deed Book #113, p. 243; #82, p. 259; #152, p. 100; #56, p. 540; #82, pp. 259 and 292. It is possible the Renigars left Winston-Salem as early as 1911, since they no longer appear in the directories after that year. Moreover, I could not find an obituary for Theodore Renigar in the Winston-Salem press, even though he died in November 1927.

42. "Winston Segregation Ordinance Cannot Be Enforced, Says Court," *Twin-City Daily Sentinel*, 9 April 1914; "Colored Citizens Want Work Done on Two Streets," *Twin-City Daily Sentinel*, 18 March 1913; "Colored School Hearing Will Be Held on Tuesday," *Winston-Salem Journal*, 8 November 1913; "Oust Negroes from East Fourth," *Winston-Salem Journal*, 29 December 1912.

43. "Qualified Colored Voters Hold Meeting Here Tonight," *Winston-Salem Journal*, 1 November 1912; "Negroes Fight Mr. Bennett," *Winston-Salem Journal*, 5 November 1912; "All Democratic Candidates but One Victorious," *Twin-City Daily Sentinel*, 6 November 1912; Stephenson, "Segregation," 4.

44. Winston-Salem city directories, 1911–1922, DigitalNC, www.digitalnc.org/collections/city-directories/; Forsyth County Property Deed Book #160, p. 49; "Married in Charlotte," *Twin-City Daily Sentinel*, 6 September 1907.

45. "Segregation," *Atlanta Independent*, 14 June 1913; "Segregation Law Passes," *Atlanta Constitution*, 17 June 1913.

46. "Committee Favors Segregation Law," *Atlanta Constitution*, 13 June 1913; "Segregation," *Atlanta Independent*, 14 and 21 June 1913.

47. "Committee Favors Segregation Law," *Atlanta Constitution*, 13 June 1913; Atlanta city directories, 1908–1913, 1916, Atlanta City Directories collection, Kenan Research Center at the Atlanta History Center. The page with Eugene Mitchell's address is ripped out in the 1912 directory, but it is likely that this was the year Mitchell moved to Peachtree Street, since he still lived on Jackson in 1911, and his address was listed as Peachtree in 1913. For a description of Jackson Hill's former prestige, see Lands, *Culture of Property*, 76–77.

48. For example, see the real estate want ad in the *Atlanta Constitution* that sought to exchange a Jackson Street home for a lot near Tenth Street School, 30 December 1907; see also "Ansley Park Lots Wanted," advertisement from E. Rivers Realty Co., *Atlanta Constitution*, 14 February 1909.

49. For example, see Power, "Apartheid Baltimore Style"; Silver, "Racial Origins of Zoning"; Glotzer, *How the Suburbs*; Fennell, *Unbounded Home*; Brooks and Rose, *Saving the Neighborhood*; Lieb, "'Baltimore Idea'"; and Connerly, *Most Segregated City*.

50. "A Social Problem in Baltimore," *The Nation*, 24 December 1903, 497–98.

51. William Henry Jones, *Housing of Negroes*, 74–79.

52. "Would Have a Black Belt: McCulloh Street Residents to Submit an Ordinance," *Baltimore Sun*, 14 September 1910; "Baltimore Tries Drastic Plan of Race Segregation," *New York Times*, 25 December 1910.

53. "Baltimore Tries Drastic Plan."

54. "Residents Are Aroused," *Baltimore Sun*, 26 September 1910; "Section Is Up in Arms," *Baltimore Sun*, 16 July 1903.

55. "Baltimore Tries Drastic Plan"; "Segregation," *Atlanta Independent*, 21 June 1913; "Segregate Negroes in East Winston," *Winston-Salem Journal*, 14 June 1912.

56. For a discussion on the class standing of Baltimore's residents who sought the first segregation ordinance, see Boger, "Meaning of Neighborhood." Boger argues that the residents were prompted by a desire to protect the upward mobility they thought they had achieved when they first moved into the neighborhood.

57. "Segregate Negroes in East Winston," *Winston-Salem Journal*, 14 June 1912; "To Keep Out Negroes," *Baltimore Sun*, 8 November 1907. A possible ordinance was first discussed by a local improvement association in 1907, although action was not taken until 1910.

58. "Negro Invasion Grows," *Baltimore Sun*, 14 June 1913; "Thinks Mr. Dashiell Is Doing More Harm Than Good by Spreading Reports of the Negro Invasion of Prominent Streets," letter to the editor, *Baltimore Sun*, 17 June 1913. Dashiell's speech referenced in the letter to the editor was about the need to revise the segregation ordinance after earlier versions were declared unconstitutional.

59. Herbin-Triant, *Threatening Property*. Herbin-Triant argues that southern elites were much less supportive of the segregation ordinances than less affluent whites.

60. "Columbia Heights, Its Reception and Growth," anonymous letter to the editor, *Union Republican*, 26 March 1896; "Segregation by Common Consent," *Winston-Salem Journal*, 19 April 1914; "Statement of the Ownership, Management, Circulation, Etc.," *Winston-Salem Journal*, 13 October 1912. The year 1912 was the first year that a federal law required newspapers to reveal their ownership to the public. Historian Thomas Hanchett found the seeds of a similar idea in the creation of Washington Heights in Charlotte, North Carolina. Hanchett, *Sorting Out*, 143–44.

61. Forsyth County Deed Book #119, p. 524; #128, p. 98; "Salem Wants Improvements," *Winston-Salem Journal*, 3 June 1911; "Salem May Get Graded School," *Winston-Salem Journal*, 8 July 1911; "Some Improvement Work on East Fourth Street," *Western Sentinel*, 11 August 1911; "Teachers of City Schools," *Union Republican*, 11 July 1912.

62. "How to Insure Segregation," *Winston-Salem Journal*, 22 April 1914.

63. "How to Insure Segregation."

64. "Columbia Heights," *Winston-Salem Journal*, 24 April 1914. See also "Good Street Leading to Columbia Heights Needed," *Twin-City Daily Sentinel*, 24 April 1914; "Slater School May Get New Building Soon," *Winston-Salem Journal*, 29 April 1914; "Up to the Highway Commission," *Winston-Salem Journal*, 30 April 1914. In July, the improvements still had not taken place. See untitled note on the editorial page, *Winston-Salem Journal*, 21 July 1914; and "A Great Opportunity," *Winston-Salem Journal*, 22 July 1914. The citizens of the East Winston Improvement Association had a similar idea. They wanted to improve a single street in East Winston that would be set aside for affluent Black residents. "Citizens of East Winston Form Association," *Twin-City Daily Sentinel*, 20 June 1912; "Improvement Association," *Winston-Salem Journal*, 20 June 1912.

65. "Solid for West Law As It Is," *Baltimore Sun*, 21 January 1911.

66. Hawkins, "Year of Segregation," 30.

67. "Segregation," *Atlanta Independent*, 14 June 1913.

Chapter 5

1. A description of this controversy is included in Lieb, "'Shove Those Black Clouds.'"
2. "Against Negro School," *Baltimore Sun*, 13 October 1910.
3. Heather Andrea Williams, *Self-Taught*. See also Foner, *Short History*.
4. Consultant Service of the National Municipal League, *Governments of Atlanta and Fulton County*, 327, 350; Colin Gordon, "Dividing the City," 165.
5. For a local example, see "To Protest Once More," *Baltimore Sun*, 28 July 1903.
6. "Segregate Negroes in East Winston," *Winston-Salem Journal*, 14 June 1912.
7. "Against Negro School," *Baltimore Sun*, 13 October 1910; "To Combine Schools," *Baltimore Sun*, 9 May 1901; "Board Explains Why," *Baltimore Sun*, 29 June 1901.
8. "Protest to Board," *Baltimore Sun*, 20 June 1901; Power, "Apartheid Baltimore Style," 290–91.
9. Historian Gretchen Boger argues that the residents of northwest Baltimore were defending what the reputation of the street had been before affluent whites began leaving for the suburbs. Boger, "Meaning of Neighborhood."
10. "More Room for Pupils," *Baltimore Sun*, 29 July 1902; "Section Is Up in Arms," *Baltimore Sun*, 16 July 1903; "To Protest Once More," *Baltimore Sun*, 28 July 1903.
11. "To Protest Once More."
12. "Local Briefs," *Baltimore Sun*, 26 October 1877; "Buildings Improvements," *Baltimore Sun*, 1 September 1899; "The Schools Are Open," *Baltimore Sun*, 18 September 1900. The original Grammar School No. 6 / No. 46 received a new building in 1877 and then further "sanitary improvements" in 1899. The name Grammar School No. 6 was changed to No. 46 in 1901. The reasoning was explained in "Why Numbers Are Changed," *Baltimore Sun*, 21 February 1901.
13. "To Protest Once More"; "School 46 for Whites," *Baltimore Sun*, 30 July 1903.
14. "School 46 for Whites"; "Indignant at School Board," *Baltimore Sun*, 15 July 1903.
15. "Object to Colored School," *Baltimore Sun*, 10 September 1903.
16. "To Keep Out Negroes," *Baltimore Sun*, 8 November 1907.
17. Anderson, *Education of Blacks*, 238–78; W. G. Alexander, "Negro Colleges and Schools Are Best in the South," *Atlanta Constitution*, 23 October 1912; advertisement for Morris Brown College, *Atlanta Constitution*, 23 October 1912 and 12 May 1914.
18. "Morris Brown Torn into Two Factions As Result of Fire," *Atlanta Journal*, 28 January 1910; "Morris Brown May Purchase Site Near Spelman Seminary," *Atlanta Journal*, 1 March 1910; "Morris Brown College May Change Location," *Atlanta Journal*, 4 March 1910. See also Lands, *Culture of Property*, 81–92.
19. As quoted in Amsterdam, *Roaring Metropolis*, 44; "Resolutions Passed by Women Pledging Work for the Bonds," *Atlanta Constitution*, 29 January 1910.
20. Minutes of the Atlanta Board of Education, 12 March 1920. See also Benjamin Blackburn, "The Tax Rate and the Schools," letter to the editor, *Atlanta Journal*, 21 April 1919.
21. "Bond Election on December 15, for $3,465,800," *Atlanta Constitution*, 15 September 1909; "Negroes Pledge Aid to the Bonds," *Atlanta Constitution*, 27 January 1910; "Bond Campaign Gets Livelier," *Atlanta Constitution*, 27 January 1910; "Meetings Held for City Bonds," *Atlanta Constitution*, 1 February 1910; "How $3,000,000 of Bonds Will Be Used by City," *Atlanta Constitution*, 16 February 1910; "Mayor Maddox for a Second Term," *Atlanta Journal*, 16 February 1910.

22. "The Bond Issue," *Atlanta Independent*, 5 February 1910. Unfortunately, the issues between July 1910 and April 1913 are missing.

23. "West Side Citizens Make Plans to Beautify and Greatly Improve Their Section of the City," *Atlanta Journal*, 21 April 1909; "Make Those West Side Improvements!," *Atlanta Journal*, 21 April 1909; "Why the Bond Issue?," *Atlanta Journal*, 2 January 1910; "Will Hold Big Rally for West Side Viaduct," *Atlanta Journal*, 10 January 1910; "Build an Alabama Street Viaduct," *Atlanta Journal*, 18 January 1910; "Alabama Street Viaduct Can Be Built for $100,000," *Atlanta Constitution*, 23 January 1910; "Pushing the Viaduct Project," *Atlanta Journal*, 15 February 1910; "Keep Hammering for the Viaduct," *Atlanta Journal*, 23 February 1910.

24. "West Side Club Holds Meeting," *Atlanta Constitution*, 21 April 1909; "Bond Issue for Schools Is Scheduled," *Atlanta Constitution*, 1 October 1909; Strayer and Engelhardt, *Survey*, 165.

25. "Why Keep Them Apart?," political cartoon, *Atlanta Journal*, 20 January 1910. See also "A Protest!," political cartoon, *Atlanta Journal*, 2 February 1910.

26. "Why the Bond Issue?," *Atlanta Journal*, 2 January 1910.

27. "Build 2 Schools in Eighth Ward," *Atlanta Constitution*, 20 April 1910.

28. "Atlanta's Public Schools," *Atlanta Constitution*, 12 September 1900; "Board Elected City Teachers," *Atlanta Constitution*, 5 June 1904; "Site Is Selected for Negro School," *Atlanta Constitution*, 31 May 1910.

29. "Decatur Street," *Journal Magazine*, 18 May 1913, as reproduced in Garrett, *Atlanta and Environs*, 608–9. See also the debate in that book on pages 542–43.

30. Shivery, "History," 131.

31. Minutes of the Atlanta Board of Education, 22 September 1910 and 9 June 1911; "City of Atlanta Districted by Board of Education," *Atlanta Constitution*, 4 July 1912. Storrs School was even older than Houston Street School; it served as the overflow building for Houston's enormous attendance area.

32. Atlanta city directories, 1911–1913, Atlanta City Directories collection, Kenan Research Center at the Atlanta History Center; Minutes of the Atlanta Board of Education, 4 January 1912; "City of Atlanta Districted by Board of Education," *Atlanta Constitution*, 4 July 1912; "Twenty-Two New Teachers Fill Vacancies," *Atlanta Constitution*, 8 June 1913; US Census Bureau, *Abstract of the Thirteenth Census*. It is possible that Yonge Street School offered junior high–level classes that Houston did not, which explains why the Butlers' son attended Yonge. Even so, the Butlers were well known among government officials because of their social welfare work. In addition to his wife's activities as a prominent clubwoman, Dr. Butler served on the interracial committee following Atlanta's 1906 "riot" and was also involved in other charity work. "Negro Gives to Relief Fund," *Atlanta Constitution*, 1 October 1906; Shivery, "History," 104; Davis, *Lifting As They Climb*, 269–70; WHCCHP, Committee on the Infant and Preschool Child, *Young Child*, xi.

33. Atlanta city directories, 1908–1913, Atlanta City Directories collection, Kenan Research Center at the Atlanta History Center (Atlanta's directories were published in December. For example, the 1910 directory came out in December 1909); "Mayor Maddox Writes Hot Card," *Atlanta Constitution*, 13 October 1910. See also Lands, *Culture of Property*, 96–97.

34. Strayer and Engelhardt, *Survey*, 174, 177–78. The gain in Black residents in the

Walker Street School district is misleading because the survey did not adjust the data to reflect the fact that Ashby Street School had been converted to a Black school in 1919 (see chapter 7). Thus, the Black students attending Ashby were counted in the Walker Street district.

35. Atlanta city directories, 1913 and 1914, Atlanta City Directories collection, Kenan Research Center at the Atlanta History Center; "Negroes Planning to Build Hospital," *Atlanta Constitution*, 22 August 1915.

36. Minutes of the Atlanta Board of Education, 22 September 1910 and 9 June 1911; "Francis Will Build New 4th Ward School," *Atlanta Constitution*, 11 November 1910; "City of Atlanta Districted by Board of Education," *Atlanta Constitution*, 4 July 1912.

37. The official "elastic districting" policy, which was based on availability of seats, was implemented in 1914. Minutes of the Atlanta Board of Education, 22 April 1914 and 23 July 1914. See also the "Minority Report," dated 22 November 1913, in the minutes. The plan could not be enforced because of parent outrage at the board's hasty redistricting efforts.

38. "Atlanta's Schools Menace to Health of Young Children," *Atlanta Constitution*, 8 October 1913; "What Are the Facts?," *Atlanta Constitution*, 10 October 1913; "Woodward Will Probe Conditions in Six Schools," *Atlanta Constitution*, 10 October 1913.

39. "Woodward Will Probe Conditions in Six Schools," *Atlanta Constitution*, 10 October 1913; "Ashley Will Push Segregation Law: Sale of a Cottage on Houston Street to Negro Family Stirs People in Neighborhood," *Atlanta Constitution*, 11 June 1913; "Committee Favors Segregation Law," *Atlanta Constitution*, 13 June 1913; "Segregation," *Atlanta Independent*, 14 June 1913.

40. Holland D. McGahee, letter to the editor, *Atlanta Constitution*, 16 February 1913; Atlanta city directories, 1908, 1913, and 1914, Atlanta City Directories collection, Kenan Research Center at the Atlanta History Center. Claude Ashley first proposed the segregation ordinance in February 1913, but the corresponding directory was published in December 1912.

41. "Locals," *Winston Daily Pilot*, 13 September 1883. In 1882, there was evidently a case of smallpox in Bahnson Town. An article in the *People's Press* stated that the community could easily be quarantined because it had only sixty to seventy residents. "Local Items," *People's Press*, 5 January 1882. Moreover, the 1884 city directory lists about twenty households with an address in Bahnson Town while there were about 775 Black households listed in Winston and Salem at that time (mostly in Winston). According to my estimate, there were about 1,750 white households, so about one third of the residences were Black, while the census figure from 1890 identifies about 1,250 Black residents, meaning that fewer than 5 percent of the Black residents lived in Bahnson Town. Gibson and Jung, "Historical Census Statistics."

42. "Twin-City Topics," *Western Sentinel*, 5 June 1884.

43. Gibson and Jung, "Historical Census Statistics," table 34, "North Carolina—Race and Hispanic Origin for Selected Large Cities and Other Places: Earliest Census to 1990."

44. Sanborn Fire Insurance Map for Winston-Salem, North Carolina, 1885–1912, Library of Congress Digital Collections, www.loc.gov/item/sanborn06522_003/; Forsyth County Property Deed Book #113, p. 51; #58, p. 263.

45. "Teachers of City Schools," *Union Republican*, 11 July 1912; "Committee of Business Men to Select a Commissioner," *Twin-City Daily Sentinel*, 7 December 1912; "Oust

Negroes from East 4th," *Winston-Salem Journal*, 29 December 1912. Just one year earlier, J. W. Carter had hired "Ex-Judge Jones" to serve as his attorney in the racial covenant suit targeting James Timlic, as discussed in chapter 4.

46. "Appeal to Supreme Court in the Segregation Case," *Winston-Salem Journal*, 18 January 1914; "To Test Segregation Ordinance," *Union Republican*, 17 July 1913; "Favor Strict Enforcement of Segregation Law," *Winston-Salem Journal*, 17 May 1913. Buxton also represented William Darnell, whose case would ultimately lead to the demise of the ordinance. The appeals process for the Darnell case began in July 1913, although it is not clear that Buxton was representing him before January 1914.

47. "City Aldermen Elect the New City Officers," *Winston-Salem Journal*, 17 May 1913; "Atkin's Outlines Negroes' Progress," *Winston-Salem Journal and Sentinel*, 10 February 1929. In addition to serving as president of the Slater Industrial State and Normal School, Atkins was one of the incorporators of Forsyth Savings and Trust Company along with James Timlic and Charles Jones, who both owned homes on East Fourth Street. "Forsyth Savings and Trust Company," *Winston-Salem Journal*, 22 June 1913.

48. "Home, Sweet Home," advertisement, *Winston-Salem Journal*, 29 April 1917; "More Development on Southside," *Union Republican*, 11 July 1912; "To Establish a New Park," *Winston-Salem Journal*, 2 November 1912; "Interesting to Everybody," *Twin-City Daily Sentinel*, 4 May 1893; "Annual Report of Winston-Salem B & LA," *Twin-City Daily Sentinel*, 21 May 1913.

49. Tom E. Terrill, "Francis Henry Fries," NCpedia, accessed 15 June 2024, www.ncpedia.org/biography/fries-francis-henry; "1912 Was Good Year for Twin-City's Three Banks," *Twin-City Daily Sentinel*, 14 January 1913; advertisement for Wachovia Loan & Trust Company, *Union Republican*, 28 November 1895; "Our Banks and Bankers," *Western Sentinel*, 26 July 1900; "Memoir to Late Hon. J. C. Buxton," *Twin-City Daily Sentinel*, 11 May 1917; "Beautiful Dinner Party by Mr. and Mrs. Buxton," *Winston-Salem Journal*, 29 December 1910.

50. Winston-Salem city directories, 1911–1913, DigitalNC, www.digitalnc.org/collections/city-directories/.

51. "Statement of the Ownership, Management, Circulation, Etc.," *Winston-Salem Journal*, 11 October 1920; "Statement of the Ownership, Management, Circulation, Etc.," *Winston-Salem Journal*, 13 October 1912.

52. "Columbia Heights," *Winston-Salem Journal*, 24 April 1914. See also "Good Street Leading to Columbia Heights Needed," *Twin-City Daily Sentinel*, 24 April 1914; "Slater School May Get New Building Soon," *Winston-Salem Journal*, 29 April 1914; "Up to the Highway Commission," *Winston-Salem Journal*, 30 April 1914; untitled note on the editorial page, *Winston-Salem Journal*, 21 July 1914. In July 1914, no improvements had yet been made. See also "A Great Opportunity," *Winston-Salem Journal*, 22 July 1914.

53. "To Establish a New Park," *Winston-Salem Journal*, 2 November 1912; "City May Erect Modern Color'd School Building," *Winston-Salem Journal*, 28 October 1913; "Board to Discuss Sale of Property," *Winston-Salem Journal*, 7 November 1913; "Colored School Hearing Will Be Held on Tuesday," *Winston-Salem Journal*, 8 November 1913; "Removal Colored School Being Discussed," *Twin-City Daily Sentinel*, 28 October 1913.

54. "Mass-Meeting of Colored People Held Last Night," *Winston-Salem Journal*, 11 November 1913; "Board of Aldermen Defer Question," *Winston-Salem Journal*, 12 November

1913; "Colored Citizens Want Work Done on Two Streets," *Twin-City Daily Sentinel*, 18 March 1913.

55. "Colored Man Writes on Removal of School," letter to the editor, *Winston-Salem Journal*, 15 November 1913; "Qualified Colored Voters Hold Meeting Here Tonight," *Winston-Salem Journal*, 1 November 1912.

56. "To Establish a New Park," *Winston-Salem Journal*, 2 November 1912; "City Aldermen Elect the New City Officers," *Winston-Salem Journal*, 17 May 1913; "City May Erect Modern Color'd School Building," *Winston-Salem Journal*, 28 October 1913.

57. "Mass-Meeting of Colored People Held Last Night," *Winston-Salem Journal*, 11 November 1913; "Committee of Business Men to Select a Commissioner," *Twin-City Daily Sentinel*, 7 December 1912; "Colored School Hearing Will Be Held on Tuesday," *Winston-Salem Journal*, 8 November 1913; "Aldermen to Decide on School Matter Tonight," *Winston-Salem Journal*, 15 November 1913.

58. "Atlanta's Schools Menace to Health of Young Children," *Atlanta Constitution*, 8 October 1913.

59. Minutes of the Atlanta Board of Education, 12 January, 28 January, 9 March, 16 July, and 10 August 1926; "Education Board Approves Bonds," *Atlanta Constitution*, 10 March 1926; "Ira Street School Property for Sale," *Atlanta Constitution*, 1 August 1926; "Christian Council Urges Larger Portion of Bond Money for Negro Schools," *Atlanta Constitution*, 14 December 1927; Strayer and Engelhardt, *Survey*, 176; *Zone Map, Atlanta, Ga.*, 1922, file FF 339, folder 5, Atlanta City Maps, Kenan Research Center at the Atlanta History Center; ACC Minutes, 16 April 1923, vol. 28, "1923 January 2–1924 July," row 5, section B, shelf 1. Before the school was shuttered, the patrons successfully petitioned to change the area near the Ira Street School from a Black residential and industrial district to a white residential district. The original zoning ordinance designated much of the area a Black apartment district, even though the population that surrounded the school was more than 60 percent white in 1920. For a further discussion of racial zoning, see chapters 7 and 8.

60. Consultant Service of the National Municipal League, *Governments of Atlanta and Fulton County*, 91, 289, 339, 343; "The Parade of Youth," *Atlanta Constitution*, 17 March 1940; "Negroes Get Two Additional High Schools," *Atlanta Constitution*, 6 July 1947; "Improvements in Negro Education Here Outlined," *Atlanta Journal*, 6 July 1947; Atlanta Public Schools, Report of the Superintendent, 1947–1948, Historical Files, Hattie Mae White Educational Support Center, Houston Independent School District, Houston, Texas. For another example, see "Here's More about Schools: Race Problem," *Houston Press*, 30 December 1924.

61. "City May Vote $500,000 Bonds in Near Future," *Winston-Salem Journal*, 18 February 1914; "Committee Asks for Sum $150,000 for City Schools," *Winston-Salem Journal*, 7 March 1914; "Citizens to Vote on $175,000 Sewer Bonds; $125,000 Water; $50,000 School Bonds Mar. 27," *Winston-Salem Journal*, 27 January 1917; "Where Do We Stand Now?," *Twin-City Daily Sentinel*, 12 September 1921; R. O. Peacock, "The School Question," letter to the editor, *Twin-City Daily Sentinel*, 22 September 1921; "Plans Call for a Gradual Shifting School Centers [sic]," *Western Sentinel*, 14 February 1922.

62. See also Driskell, *Schooling Jim Crow*.

Chapter 6

1. Ryan, *Cradle*; Tyack, *One Best System*, 183; Mintz, *Huck's Raft*, 175. The number of high school students increased from 202,693 to 1,645,171.
2. Wright, *Old South, New South*, 14, 80.
3. "Ranking of the State Educational Systems," 167.
4. Plessy v. Ferguson, 163 U.S. 537 (1896); Cumming v. Richmond County Board of Education, 175 U.S. 528 (1899). See also Walsh, *Racial Taxation*, 36–39.
5. Shivery, "History," 230.
6. "Object to Colored School," *Baltimore Sun*, 10 September 1903; "Mount Street School," *Baltimore Afro-American*, 26 September 1903; "Too Old for School," *Baltimore Sun*, 15 October 1903; "City Hall Notes," *Baltimore Sun*, 18 December 1903.
7. Montague to Hunter, 9 September 1915, and Hunter to Underwood, 3 February 1923, CH Papers; "Public School Matters," *Evening Visitor*, 28 November 1890; Haley, *Charles N. Hunter*, 178–79; Barbee, *Historical Sketches*, 56. Before becoming principal of the school in Method, Hunter served as the principal for Raleigh's Garfield, Oberlin, and Chavis schools.
8. Simmons-Henry, *Culture Town*, 118–19.
9. "Raleigh's Population Will Be 50,000 in 10 Years," *Raleigh News and Observer*, 21 March 1923; "Notice of Sale," *State Journal*, 14 April 1916; "Parker-Hunter Realty Company," *News and Observer*, 12 May 1910; "Notice of Sale of Real Estate," *Union Herald*, 10 June 1920; "East College Park Redevelopment Plan," 21 October 1998, "Redevelopment Plans," City of Raleigh website, https://raleighnc.gov/planning/services/redevelopment-plans. James H. Pou and D. F. Fort, both developers of white residential parks, were also involved in the development of College Park. See "Sale of College Park Lots," *Union Herald*, 17 June 1920; "City Will Acquire New Water Main Extension," *News and Observer*, 2 July 1920; Minutes of the Raleigh Board of Commissioners, 1 July 1920, City of Raleigh, Minutes of the Governing Body, Book 1, M.509.10004, Municipal Records, State Archives of North Carolina.
10. Haley, "Carolina Chameleon," 402–3; B. F. Montague to C. N. Hunter, 9 September 1915, CH Papers; Raleigh Township Graded Schools, *Fortieth Annual Report*, 7–8, 15, 55. See also "Campaign Committee Shows Importance of All Voters Going to the Polls on Tuesday," *Atlanta Constitution*, 7 March 1921.
11. "Bond Election on December 15, for $3,465,800," *Atlanta Constitution*, 15 September 1909; "Negroes Pledge Aid to the Bonds," *Atlanta Constitution*, 27 January 1910; "Bond Campaign Gets Livelier," *Atlanta Constitution*, 27 January 1910; "Meetings Held for City Bonds," *Atlanta Constitution*, 1 February 1910. For a description of the Neighborhood Union's early work, see chapter 2.
12. Public School Campaign Monthly Time Book, 1913, box 4, folder 4, NU Collection; Petition to the Atlanta Board of Education, 19 August 1913, box 2, folder 20, NU Collection; Shivery, "History," 77; Shivery and Smythe, "Neighborhood Union," 152–53; Rouse, *Lugenia Burns Hope*, 65; "Ashley Will Push Segregation Law," *Atlanta Constitution*, 11 June 1913.
13. Shivery, "History," 93–100; Minutes of the Atlanta Board of Education, 23 January 1912 and 26 November 1913.
14. Shivery, "History," 96–97; Minutes of the Atlanta Board of Education, 26 November

1913; "$2,000,000 Bond Issue for Atlanta Schools Urged by Committee," *Atlanta Constitution*, 27 November 1913; "5,000,000 Bond Issue Proposed by Humphrey for City Improvements," *Atlanta Constitution*, 14 January 1914; "Fifth Ward Asks New Schoolhouse," *Atlanta Constitution*, 21 January 1914; "School Campaign Gets Good Start at Mass Meeting," *Atlanta Constitution*, 7 February 1915.

15. Strayer and Engelhardt, *Survey*, 176–77. During this time, more Black residents were moving into the neighborhood than white residents were moving out. The lack of housing meant that Black families were often forced to double up or to add additional dwellings to available lots.

16. "Atlanta's Worst Scandal!," *Atlanta Constitution*, 7 October 1913; "Even Basements Used to Afford Children Education," *Atlanta Constitution*, 9 October 1913; "What Are the Facts?," *Atlanta Constitution*, 10 October 1913; "Copenhill Park," *Atlanta Constitution*, 23 April 1890; "Why the Bond Issue?," *Atlanta Journal*, 2 January 1910.

17. "Atlanta's Schools Menace to Health of Young Children," *Atlanta Constitution*, 8 October 1913. See also Grable, "Other Side"; Consultant Service of the National Municipal League, *Governments of Atlanta and Fulton County*, 337.

18. Minutes of the Atlanta Board of Education, 26 November 1913; "Woodward Will Probe Conditions in Six Schools," *Atlanta Constitution*, 10 October 1913; "$2,000,000 Bond Issue for Atlanta Schools Urged by Committee," *Atlanta Constitution*, 27 November 1913; "Criticism Kills Bonds Says Cooper, Secretary Chamber of Commerce," letter to the editor, *Atlanta Constitution*, 8 September 1915; "Bonds and Criticism," *Atlanta Constitution*, 8 September 1915; "Postpone the Bond Election," *Atlanta Constitution*, 15 September 1915; "Shall We Fall Behind?," *Atlanta Constitution*, 7 June 1916; "Aroused by Exposures Education Board Names Investigation Committee," *Atlanta Constitution*, 24 October 1913.

19. Public School Campaign Monthly Time Book, 1913, box 4, folder 4, NU Collection; Shivery, "History," 96–97, 100–101.

20. Minutes of the Atlanta Board of Education, 26 November 1913; "$2,000,000 Bond Issue for Atlanta Schools Urged by Committee," *Atlanta Constitution*, 27 November 1913; "Needs of Schools Shown in Letter from Mr. Slaton," *Atlanta Constitution*, 14 October 1913; "Superintendent Slaton Submits Annual Report on City Schools," *Atlanta Constitution*, 30 December 1914; "What's to Be Done about It?," *Atlanta Constitution*, 8 October 1913.

21. Minutes of the Atlanta Board of Education, 22 November 1913, 10 January and 9 April 1918; "An Awakening Needed!," *Atlanta Constitution*, 3 September 1915; "Two Appeals to Atlanta," *Atlanta Constitution*, 6 August 1916; "If Not by Bonds—Then What?," *Atlanta Constitution*, 24 December 1916.

22. Shivery, "History," 102–5.

23. Shivery, "History," 98–99, 106; Minutes of the Atlanta Board of Education, 17 December 1914, 7 January, 25 March, and 7 August 1915; "Prospects Bright for City Schools," *Atlanta Constitution*, 28 May 1915; "Money Available, School Board Gets Busy on Buildings," *Atlanta Constitution*, 9 June 1915; Strayer and Engelhardt, *Survey*, 245–46.

24. "Ask Improvement of Many Schools," *Atlanta Constitution*, 13 May 1915; "Children to Get Spring Vacation," *Atlanta Constitution*, 27 August 1915; "List of Teachers for 1915 Revised," *Atlanta Constitution*, 5 September 1915; Strayer and Engelhardt, *Survey*, 244.

25. Pruitt, *Other Great Migration*; Hitt, "Peopling the City," 54–64. Cotton reached a high of 41.75 cents in April before skidding to 13.5 cents by the end of the year; tobacco

dropped from 44 cents to 21 cents. Cotton prices returned to half their inflated war values between 1922 and 1924—the best years during the decade—before falling once again. By 1929, tobacco, too, was again in crisis. Tindall, *Emergence*, 111–12, 355.

26. Superintendent's Annual Report, Minutes of the Atlanta Board of Education, 20 December 1916; Garrett, *Atlanta and Environs*, 673. Georgia's first compulsory attendance law went into effect on 1 January 1917. It required children between ages eight and fourteen to attend school for at least four months. Burgess, "Goddess," 201; Tyack, *One Best System*, 71. By 1885, sixteen of the thirty-eight states had passed compulsory attendance laws, and by 1900, thirty-one of forty-five.

27. Superintendent's Annual Report, Minutes of the Atlanta Board of Education, 24 January 1918 and 31 December 1920; "Housing Shortage Crippling Schools," *Atlanta Constitution*, 9 September 1921; "34,098 Students Seek Admission to Public Schools," *Atlanta Journal*, 13 September 1921; "Adopt Building Program for Raleigh Township's Schools," *Raleigh News and Observer*, 29 September 1921; Raleigh Minutes, 14 October 1920; Houston Independent School District, *Annual Report . . . 1919–20*, 9–23; "Houston's Efficient Teachers," *Houston Post*, 3 June 1924; "School Board Pleads for Bonds," *Houston Post*, 25 May 1924; "The Tax Rate Question Involves the Schools and Only the Schools," *Atlanta Journal*, 21 April 1919; "Public Schools Are Congested by Promotions," *Birmingham Age-Herald*, 29 January 1923; Birmingham Board of Education, *Birmingham School Survey, 1923*, 39; Wrenn, "Politics," 93.

28. "Adopt Building Program for Raleigh Township's Schools," *Raleigh News and Observer*, 29 September 1921; Birmingham Board of Education, *Birmingham School Survey, 1923*, 25–26, 39; Wrenn, "Politics of Memphis School Reform," 93.

29. "Everybody for Bonds," *Atlanta Constitution*, 23 February 1921; Strayer and Engelhardt, *Survey*, 8–10, 68–74; Minutes of the Atlanta Board of Education, 20 February 1918 and 3 May 1920.

30. "Our City," *Houston Chronicle*, 21 October 1924; "Name Broughton on School Board," *Raleigh News and Observer*, 12 February 1926. For a discussion of the "progressive" obsession with scientific expertise in government, see Leonard, *Illiberal Reformers*.

31. "Purpose of Bond Issue As Related to Schools Is Explained by Inman," *Atlanta Constitution*, 27 February 1921; "Leaders in Bond Movement Urging Big Vote Tuesday," *Atlanta Constitution*, 7 March 1921; "School Building Program Behind, Declares Sutton," *Atlanta Constitution*, 12 March 1922.

32. James R. Young, letter to the editor, *Raleigh Times*, 2 April 1922; "Our City," *Houston Chronicle*, 21 October 1924; "Greater Atlanta Drive Starts," *Atlanta Journal*, 17 January 1920.

33. Shivery, "History," 211; Driskell, *Schooling Jim Crow*; Meier and Rudwick, *From Plantation to Ghetto*, 232–36.

34. "Negroes Protest Jim Crow Laws," *Raleigh News and Observer*, 2 January 1919; "Don't Fail to Vote in City's Primary," *Raleigh News and Observer*, 21 April 1919; "Present Officials Lead in Municipal Primary," *Raleigh News and Observer*, 22 April 1919; "Col. Young Asks for an Apology," *Raleigh News and Observer*, 27 May 1919; Haley, *Charles N. Hunter*, 206–7. See also Zogry, "House That Dr. Pope Built." Dr. M. T. Pope ran for mayor, I. M. Cheek for commissioner of public safety, and C. E. Lightner for commissioner of public works.

35. "Big Welcome for Colored Soldiers," *Raleigh News and Observer*, 26 April 1919.

36. Minutes of the Atlanta Board of Education, 26 November 1913; "Prospects Bright for City Schools," *Atlanta Constitution*, 28 May 1915.

37. "Campaign Committee Shows Importance of All Voters Going to the Polls on Tuesday," *Atlanta Constitution*, 7 March 1921; "Success for Restoration of Old City Tax Rate and Bond Issue Is Prophesied," *Atlanta Journal*, 9 April 1919.

38. Petition of the Colored Teachers' Association, Minutes of the Atlanta Board of Education, 27 January 1919.

39. "Georgia's Chance," *Atlanta Constitution*, 6 June 1919; "Big Bond Rally Saturday Night," *Atlanta Constitution*, 11 February 1910. According to this article, there were 537 Black citizens registered to vote out of a total registration of 10,562. "Pay Taxes, Register—The Slogan," *Atlanta Independent*, 8 March 1919.

40. Undated letter to members, frame 0585, "1913–1917"; T. K. Gibson to James Weldon Johnson, 7 March 1919, frame 0734, "1919–1921," both in reel 9, group 1, box G-43, Atlanta, Georgia, Branch, *NAACP Branch Files*. See also Driskell, *Schooling Jim Crow*; and Bayor, *Race*, 17.

41. T. K. Gibson to James Weldon Johnson, 7 March 1919, frame 0734, "1919–1921," reel 9, group I, box G-43, Atlanta, Georgia, Branch, *NAACP Branch Files*; "Negroes Active for Bond Issue," *Atlanta Georgian*, 27 February 1919; "Bonds Declared in Danger—Don't Fail to Vote," *Atlanta Georgian*, 5 March 1919; "Big Negro Vote against Bonds Is Peril to Election," *Atlanta Georgian*, 5 March 1919; "McClelland Charges Plot to Defeat Bonds and Tax Raise," *Atlanta Journal*, 5 March 1919.

42. "Majority of White Voters Favor $1.50 Rate, Say Officials," *Atlanta Journal*, 6 March 1919.

43. "Our Neighbors Ought to Be Fair and Impartial," *Atlanta Independent*, 8 March 1919; "Negroes, Bonds, Taxation, and Mayor Pro Tem," *Atlanta Independent*, 8 March 1919.

44. Harry Pace to James Weldon Johnson, letter, 12 March 1919, frame 0734, "1919–1921," reel 9, group I, box G-43, Atlanta, Georgia, Branch, *NAACP Branch Files*.

45. "The Inconsistency of Our Morning Neighbor," *Atlanta Independent*, 29 March 1919.

46. "Negroes Are Told of Revenue Needs," *Atlanta Constitution*, 9 April 1919; "Success for Restoration of Old City Tax Rate and Bond Issue Is Prophesied," *Atlanta Journal*, 9 April 1919; Benjamin Blackburn, "The Tax Rate and the Schools," letter to the editor, *Atlanta Journal*, 21 April 1919; Minutes of the Atlanta Board of Education, 12 March 1920.

47. "The Negro Bonds and Increased Taxation," *Atlanta Independent*, 12 April 1919.

48. "Atlanta Schools Should Also Be Always Ahead," *Atlanta Journal*, 22 April 1919; "Urgent Necessity for Bonds and Tax Increase," *Atlanta Journal*, 22 April 1919; "Fine Schools City's Best Advertisements, Say Western Communities," letter to the editor, *Atlanta Constitution*, 10 April 1919. As the secretary of the West Side Improvement Club, W. H. Terrell had served on the "special committee on needed school improvements" that set the agenda for the 1910 bond issue, as discussed in chapter 5. His actions helped ensure that First Ward would receive no bond money for its aging Black schools but would acquire an additional white school it did not need.

49. "The Ballot Our Defense," *Atlanta Independent*, 19 April 1919. For a political analysis of these events, see Driskell, *Schooling Jim Crow*.

50. "Tax Increase and All Bond Issues Defeated: Big Vote in Few Wards against Raise," *Atlanta Georgian*, "Final Extra" edition, 23 April 1919.

51. "An Open Letter to the Editor of the *Atlanta Georgian*," *Atlanta Independent*, 3 May 1919.

52. "Disease, Death, Desolation, and Despair: Amidst Such Insanitary Conditions; Is Municipal Conscience Dormant?," *Houston Informer*, 7 February 1920; Cronin, "C. F. Richardson," 88.

53. "School Bond Issue for $3,000,000," *Houston Informer*, 21 April 1923.

54. "Forward or Backward?," *Houston Informer*, 5 May 1923; "Colored Citizen's Committee Favors $3,000,000 Bond Issue," *Houston Informer*, 5 May 1923; H. F. Edwards to Secretary of the NAACP, 28 June 1919, frame 0793, "1919–1923"; J. M. Adkins to Mr. Bagwell, 12 July 1923, frame 0877, "1923," both in reel 19, group I, box G-203, Houston, Texas, Branch, *NAACP Branch Files*.

55. "The Negro Vote Apparently 'Fixed,'" *Houston Post*, 5 May 1923; "A Great Step Forward for Houston Schools," *Houston Post*, 9 May 1923. The *Chronicle*, the *Press*, and the *Informer* all attempted to clear up the confusion about who could vote in bond elections (all who had paid their poll tax). Nevertheless, oral interviews have revealed that many African Americans remained convinced that they could not vote in any elections during the 1920s. Thelma Scott Bryant, interview by author, Houston, Texas, 25 July 2001; Hazel Hainsworth Young, interview by author, Houston, Texas, 28 July 2001. Both taught at Black high schools in Houston during the 1920s.

56. "Getting 'Em Told," *Houston Informer*, 12 May 1923; "Combating Negro Migration," *Houston Informer*, 12 May 1923; "Negro Exodus Stirs Dixie," *Houston Informer*, 19 May 1923; "North Carolina One Exception," *Houston Informer*, 26 January 1924.

57. "Southern City Erecting Many School Houses," *Houston Informer*, 19 May 1923. This last article was from the Associated Negro Press, demonstrating that the "labor shortage" argument extended beyond Houston and Atlanta. See also "Colored Americans Made Real History This Year," *Houston Informer*, 29 December 1923. According to the *Houston Press*, the migration had "struck Houston with full force" leading to an "acute shortage of laborers" in the city and surrounding area. "Labor Shortage Here," *Houston Press*, 16 May 1923.

58. "That Poll Tax Must Be Paid Right Now," *Houston Informer*, 26 January 1924; political advertisement, *Houston Informer*, 26 January 1924.

59. "That Bond Issue on April 26th, 1924," *Houston Informer*, 15 March 1924; "Another Big City Bond Issue," *Houston Informer*, 29 March 1924; "An Example of Minority Rule," *Houston Post*, 29 April 1924.

60. "School Board's Niggardly Policy," *Houston Informer*, 4 July 1925.

61. "Fate of Bond Issues Up to Voters Today," *Houston Post*, 10 June 1924; "Big Majority Approves All Bond Issues," *Houston Post*, 11 June 1924.

62. "Colored High School to House Only 300!!," *Houston Informer*, 18 July 1925; "'Houston Informer,' Negro Weekly, Hits City School Board," *Houston Post*, 13 September 1925.

63. "Getting Mathematics Somewhat Twisted Regarding Negro Junior High School," *Houston Informer*, 19 September 1925; "It Is Entirely Different in Houston!," *Houston Informer*, 3 October 1925; "Mammoth Crowd at Yates High School Left Disgusted," *Houston Informer*, 24 October 1925; "'Scat, Br'er Nat, We Won't Have That!," *Houston Informer*, 31 October 1925.

64. "New School Buildings for Colored Pupils," *Houston Informer*, 2 October 1926; "The Mirror: Public School Facilities," *Houston Informer*, 9 October 1926.

65. "School Bond Issue Gets Big Majority," *Houston Informer*, 7 November 1925; "New School Buildings for Colored Pupils," *Houston Informer*, 2 October 1926; "The Mirror: Public School Facilities," *Houston Informer*, 9 October 1926; "The Mirror: Another Milestone," *Houston Informer*, 19 May 1928. At the suggestion of the *Informer*, "Colored High School" was renamed Booker T. Washington High School.

66. Bryant, *Development*, 78; W. L. D. Johnson, "Organization," 62; Greene, "Sidelights on Houston Negroes," 149–50. Jesse O. Thomas, who established the Atlanta chapter of the National Urban League, also praised Houston's notable improvements in Black education. Thomas, "Negro Schools in Houston," 179.

67. "$8,850,000 Bonds Carry by Overwhelming Vote Assuring Urgently Needed Improvements," *Atlanta Constitution*, 9 March 1921; Shivery, "History," 211; Strayer and Engelhardt, *Survey*, 39.

68. Blank, *Volume of Residential Construction*, 67; "More Home Building," *Atlanta Constitution*, 4 September 1921.

69. "Segregation Law Killed by Decision of Supreme Court," *Atlanta Constitution*, 13 February 1915; "City Hall Gossip," *Atlanta Constitution*, 5 March 1916; "Segregation Law for City Planned," *Atlanta Constitution*, 2 April 1916; Buchanan v. Warley, 245 U.S. 60 (1917).

70. Minutes of the Atlanta Board of Education, 2 July, 9 July, and 5 August 1919; "To Make Ashby Street Negro School Beginning Next Year," *Atlanta Constitution*, 10 July 1919; "Negroes Will Get Ashby Street School," *Atlanta Constitution*, 6 August 1919; "Weekly Message from Churches of Atlanta to Appear on Constitution's Church Page," *Atlanta Constitution*, 13 December 1919; "Christian Council Urges Larger Portion of Bond Money for Negro Schools," *Atlanta Constitution*, 14 December 1927; "We Must Keep Faith," *Atlanta Constitution*, 14 December 1927. For other interracial efforts, see Ellis, "Crusade against 'Wretched Attitudes'"; Shivery, "History," 211, 412; Selig, *Americans All*.

71. "Fight in Council to End Committee Fails," *Atlanta Constitution*, 3 June 1919. The day after the board officially voted to convert Ashby, Edward G. Black and Clarence Constantine, the original developers of Sunset Park, donated a lot to the city for a Carnegie library for Black residents. "New Park for Colored to Allow No Tenants," *Atlanta Constitution*, 11 June 1919; "Life, Health, Happiness: Colored Now Know True Happiness in New Residential Section," *Atlanta Journal*, 11 August 1919; "Colored People Delighted over New Park," *Atlanta Journal*, 7 August 1919; "Colored Now Have Lovely Site for Homes," *Atlanta Constitution*, 4 August 1919; "Response of Colored to New Park Most Gratifying," *Atlanta Constitution*, 5 August 1919; "Colored People's Dream Come True," *Atlanta Constitution*, 6 August 1919; advertisement for West Hunter Park, *Atlanta Independent*, 26 July 1919. Edgar Craighead, the developer, worked for the L. W. Rogers Realty and Trust Co., which had developed Virginia-Highlands and Ponce de Leon Heights, both affluent, racially restricted developments in northeast Atlanta. "60 Lots for Sale in West Hunter Park," *Atlanta Independent*, 9 October 1920; "New Ashby Street Subdivision," *Atlanta Independent*, 26 June 1920; "Lots! Lots! Lots! Lots!," *Atlanta Independent*, 28 August 1920; Garrett, *Atlanta and Environs*, 797.

72. "Chief Bond Issue School for Negroes," *Atlanta Constitution*, 27 May 1923; "City Might Force Sale of Park Site for Girls' School," *Atlanta Constitution*, 14 June 1922; Floyd J. Calvin, "Heman Perry Started Atlanta on Its Home Building Program," *Pittsburgh Courier*, 1 October 1931. Calvin's article claimed that Heman Perry sold the school board the

site, but it also included other details that are incorrect. See Thompson, Lewis, and McEntire, "Atlanta and Birmingham," 18–19. This widely cited report used Calvin's article as the principal source for its otherwise unsupported conclusions about Heman Perry's role in the development of Atlanta's west side.

73. Kuhn, Joye, and West, *Living Atlanta*, 42–43; "Big Land Tract Tendered to City for Negro Parks," *Atlanta Constitution*, 21 October 1919; "Committee on Church Cooperation Plans" *Atlanta Constitution*, 2 April 1921. See also Speer, *John J. Eagan*, 75; "Edgar B. Craighead and John A. Manget Form Realty Firm," *Atlanta Constitution*, 17 February 1922; "'Moreland Heights,' New Residence Tract with 120 Lots for Moderate Priced Homes," *Atlanta Constitution*, 3 June 1923; "Georgia Committee on Interracial Cooperation White Section," membership list, box 12, folder 22, NU Collection.

74. Thomas Jesse Jones, *Negro Education*, 42; Caliver, *Secondary Education for Negroes*, 25–26. The figures for 1929–30 exclude South Carolina, although the state reported having 8,234 Black students enrolled in high school. Even though "urban" is defined as having more than 2,500 residents, cities were much more likely to provide accredited, four-year Black public high schools.

75. Benjamin, "Progressivism Meets Jim Crow," chapter 5.

76. Steptoe, *Houston Bound*, 38.

Chapter 7

1. Civic Development Department, Chamber of Commerce, "Supplement to City Planning and Zoning Accomplishments," 1929, box 11, DL22A2, RW Papers; Silver and Moeser, *Separate City*, 22.

2. For example, Silver, "Racial Origins of Zoning," 193; Fairbanks, *For the City*, 29.

3. Robert Whitten, "Atlanta Adopts Zoning," *American City*, 26 June 1922, 541; Committee on Best Methods of Land Subdivision, "Report of Conference Committee," 247; Whitten, "Zoning of Residence Sections," 34–39; Whitten, "Zoning and Living Conditions," 27–28; Ihlder, "Housing and the Regional Plan," 11. For a contemporary critique, see Bruno Lasker, "Unwalled Towns," *The Survey*, 6 March 1920, 675–80; and Bruno Lasker, response to Charles Cheney's "Removing Social Barriers by Zoning," *The Survey*, 22 May 1920, 279.

4. "Negro Construction Permits Are Issued: Plans for 100 Homes in Colored Subdivision Are Being Laid," *Atlanta Constitution*, 8 January 1922; "Zone Plan for Atlanta Ready for Meeting of Commissioners," *Atlanta Constitution*, 1 January 1922.

5. "Menaces to Our Community Life," *Houston Informer*, 8 December 1923.

6. "An Open Letter to City Fathers," *Houston Informer*, 23 February 1924.

7. Bowen v. City of Atlanta, 159 Ga. 145 (1924).

8. Law professor Philip Lee wrote, "Interest-convergence is not commonly applied to property law issues," although he acknowledged that *Buchanan v. Warley* (1917) and *Shelley v. Kraemer* (1948) can both be explained through Bell's theory. Lee, "Wall of Hate," 434–36. See also Godsil, "Race Nuisance," 544–45.

9. Bell, "Brown v. Board of Education," 523. For a class analysis of the segregation ordinances, see Herbin-Triant, *Threatening Property*, 161–74.

10. Hovenkamp, "Social Science," 661–62. For an influential example, see Napheys, *Physical Life of Woman*, 88–89.

11. Washington, "My View," 113–14; "Baltimore Tries Drastic Plan of Race Segregation," *New York Times*, 25 December 1910; McGuire, *At the Dark End*.

12. Roger L. Rice, "Residential Segregation by Law." See also evidence from Louisville, Kentucky: "Magistrates: Segregation Ordinance Again," *Kentucky Irish American*, 21 March 1914; and "Sides Heard," *Courier-Journal*, 19 March 1914. Additional evidence can be found in Fairbanks, *For the City*, 29.

13. As quoted in Herbin-Triant, *Threatening Property*, 158, 160.

14. Harris v. Louisville, 165 Ky. 559 (1915).

15. For Atlanta examples, see "Whites and Negroes May Be Segregated," *Atlanta Constitution*, 15 February 1913; "Segregation," *Atlanta Independent*, 14 and 21 June 1913. For Greensboro, North Carolina, see Herbin-Triant, *Threatening Property*, 160. For Louisville, Kentucky, see "Sides Heard," *Courier-Journal*, 19 March 1914. In this case, the president of the Real Estate Exchange claimed an ordinance was not needed to prevent violence because "there was no friction between the races at present."

16. "Segregation Law Passes Council," *Atlanta Constitution*, 17 June 1913; "Negro House Attacked," *Baltimore Sun*, 18 September 1913.

17. Harden v. City of Atlanta, 93 S. E. 338, 403 (Ga. 1917); "Residents Are Aroused," *Baltimore Sun*, 26 September 1910.

18. For a discussion of the six state cases, see Steil and Delgado, "Contested Values."

19. Power, "Apartheid Baltimore Style," 312–13; Rice, "Residential Segregation by Law," 185–86. See also Martin, "Segregation of Residences," 730.

20. Buchanan v. Warley, 245 U.S. 60 (1917). See also "Sides Heard," *Courier-Journal*, 19 March 1914.

21. Harris v. Louisville, 165 Ky. 559 (1915) and Lumpkin's concurring opinion in Carey v. City of Atlanta, 84 S. E. 338, 460 (Ga. 1915), which supported the constitutionality of property regulations limiting traditional property rights. See also Steil and Delgado, "Contested Values."

22. Hawkins, "Year of Segregation," 29. Hawkins was George McMechen's law partner who owned the house on McCulloh Street that triggered Baltimore's segregation ordinance.

23. Stephenson, "Segregation," 4. Segregation ordinances in Virginia came closest to actual racial zoning. Virginia was also the only state with an enabling law. See also Silver, "Racial Origins of Zoning," 28.

24. State v. Gurry, 121 Md. 534 (Md. 1913) 88 A 546.

25. For a local example, see "Race Segregation," *Union Republican*, 20 June 1912.

26. Carey v. City of Atlanta, 84 S. E. 338, 460 (Ga. 1915); "Segregation Law Killed by Decision of Supreme Court," *Atlanta Constitution*, 13 February 1915; "Segregation Law for City Planned," *Atlanta Constitution*, 2 April 1916.

27. "Court Issues Order Restraining Police in Segregation Suit," *Atlanta Constitution*, 12 August 1916; "Fined for Violations of Segregation Law," *Atlanta Constitution*, 3 September 1916; "Segregation Law Again under Fire," *Atlanta Constitution*, 26 July 1916; "Segregation Law to Be Given Test in Superior Court," *Atlanta Constitution*, 29 July 1916. See also William Henry Jones, *Housing of Negroes*, 80–81.

28. Harden v. City of Atlanta, 93 S. E. 338, 403 (Ga. 1917); "Race Segregation Ordinance Upheld by Supreme Court," *Atlanta Constitution*, 1 September 1917; "Segregation Law Declared Illegal," *Atlanta Constitution*, 6 November 1917.

29. Washington, "My View," 113–14.

30. "More Development on Southside," *Union Republican*, 11 July 1912; "To Establish a New Park," *Winston-Salem Journal*, 2 November 1912; "Annual Report of Winston-Salem B & LA," *Twin-City Daily Sentinel*, 21 May 1913; "Memoir to Late Hon. J. C. Buxton," *Twin-City Daily Sentinel*, 11 May 1917.

31. "Segregation Not Allowed by Law," *Farmer and Mechanic*, 14 April 1914. This article reprinted the decision in its entirety. See also Wertheimer, *Law and Society*, 52; Herbin-Triant, *Threatening Property*, 162.

32. "Winston Segregation Ordinance Cannot Be Enforced, Says Court," *Twin-City Daily Sentinel*, 9 April 1914. Louisville provides an additional example; see "Segregation of Races Urged," *Courier-Journal*, 15 November 1913; "Sides Heard," *Courier-Journal*, 19 March 1914; "Magistrates: Segregation Ordinance Again," *Kentucky Irish American*, 21 March 1914; and Rice, "Residential Segregation by Law," 184. The spokesman for those seeking an ordinance to protect their individual blocks was the superintendent of the mechanical department of the *Courier-Journal* and the *Louisville Times*. The leader of the white resistance against the ordinance was the president of the swanky Real Estate Exchange. According to the attorney representing those supporting the law, "It was not the intention of the ordinance to keep the negroes in the alleys and in the slums."

33. "Segregation," *Atlanta Independent*, 21 June 1913.

34. Garrett, *Atlanta and Environs*, 704; "A City Building Plan," *Atlanta Constitution*, 29 May 1917; "Rebuilding of Burned Area Planned," *Atlanta Constitution*, 23 May 1917; Burton Davis, "Cities of Texas Can Learn Lesson from Example of Atlanta," *Galveston Daily News*, 4 March 1923.

35. "A City Building Plan," *Atlanta Constitution*, 29 May 1917; "Fine Opportunity Offered Atlanta," *Atlanta Constitution*, 10 June 1917; "Atlanta's Big Fire Disaster May Be Turned into Benefit, Say City Planning Experts," *Atlanta Constitution*, 28 May 1917.

36. "Negro Section of Fire Zone to be Rebuilt on New and Broad Lines," *Atlanta Journal*, 22 June 1917; "Pledge Negroes Aid for Better Quarters; Plan Joint Meeting," *Atlanta Constitution*, 20 June 1917; "Don't Leave—Let's Stay Home," *Atlanta Independent*, 26 May 1917.

37. "Atlanta Leaders Placed on City Planning Board," *Atlanta Constitution*, 10 February 1920; "Indorsement Is Given Planning Campaign," *Atlanta Constitution*, 1 February 1920; "Plans to Beautify Fire-Swept Section Recited at Meeting," *Atlanta Constitution*, 17 June 1917; Lands, *Culture of Property*, 103.

38. "New Planning Board Announced by Mayor," *Atlanta Constitution*, 13 October 1920; Edge, *Joel Hurt and the Development of Atlanta*, 96–104; Tammy Galloway, "Joel Hurt," *New Georgia Encyclopedia*, last modified April 11, 2021, www.georgiaencyclopedia.org/articles/business-economy/joel-hurt-1850-1926/; "Charles A. Wickersham Dies; Southern Railroad Leader," *Atlanta Constitution*, 13 July 1949; "Headquarters for Homes," advertisement for Pittman Construction Company, *Atlanta Constitution*, 20 February 1910; "Homes for Sale," *Atlanta Constitution*, 22 January 1911; "F. J. Terry Dies after 17 Years with Newspaper," *Atlanta Constitution*, 7 March 1923; Brownell, "Commercial-Civic Elite," 170–71.

39. "Harry Goodhart Will Make Race for Mayor; Platform Is Outlined," *Atlanta Constitution*, 14 July 1920. Key rejected charter reform because it would weaken the powers of the mayor.

40. Grantham, *Hoke Smith*, 363.

41. Joel Hurt to F. L. Olmsted, 28 October 1920; Joel Hurt to F. L. Olmsted, 23 February 1921; F. L. Olmsted to Joel Hurt, 3 March 1921; F. L. Olmsted to Harold Buttenheim, 13 April 1921; Joel Hurt to F. L. Olmsted, 2 May 1921; "Report of the Special Committee to the City Planning Commission of Atlanta," 18 April 1921, all in Olmsted Associates Records, "Job Files, 1863–1971; Files; 2746; City plan; Atlanta, Ga., 1912–1921," Library of Congress Digital Collection, www.loc.gov/item/mss5257101672; Burton Davis, "Cities of Texas Can Learn Lesson from Example of Atlanta," *Galveston Daily News*, 4 March 1923; Lands, *Culture of Property*, 143. Otis was well known for developing the Peachtree Arcade, the nation's first fully indoor shopping center (1917).

42. Stephenson, "Segregation," 496–504; Atlanta's segregation ordinances, 1913 and 1916, box 12, DL22A3, "Race Segregation," RW Papers. Whitten kept these three documents in his files for Atlanta. Stephenson was the lawyer who had unsuccessfully defended Winston-Salem's segregation ordinance before the North Carolina Supreme Court.

43. Martin, "Segregation," 728–30.

44. "Need of Zoning System Shown," *Atlanta Constitution*, 16 February 1922.

45. "Plans Prepared for Organization of City Planners," *Atlanta Constitution*, 23 April 1921; "Zone Plan for Atlanta Ready for Meeting of Commissioners," *Atlanta Constitution*, 1 January 1922. Like the segregation ordinances, the law did not apply to live-in servants. "Zone Plan for Atlanta Ready for Meeting of Commissioners," *Atlanta Constitution*, 1 January 1922.

46. Minutes of the Atlanta Board of Education, 27 May 1927; *Tentative Zone Plan* map.

47. *Tentative Zone Plan* map. The westside colored district required only 2,500 square feet per family.

48. R. H. Whitten to Bruno Lasker, 28 April 1922, published in *The Survey*, 15 June 1922, box 12, DL22A3, "Race Segregation," RW Papers. See also Knight, *Negro Housing*, 137. Knight continued to make a similar argument even after Atlanta's racial zones were found unconstitutional.

49. Shivery, "History."

50. "The Colored Man Bottled In," *Atlanta Independent*, 30 August 1923; "Given Forty-Eight Hours to Move," *Atlanta Independent*, 19 October 1922.

51. "Given Forty-Eight Hours to Move"; "Colored Man Bottled In."

52. US Census Bureau, *Mortgages on Homes*, 69.

53. "Real Estate Men Denounce Zoning Plan for Atlanta," *Atlanta Constitution*, 10 March 1922; "Proposed Zoning Plan Denounced by Judge Kontz," *Atlanta Constitution*, 28 February 1922.

54. "City Zoning Plan Praised and Hit by Civic Leaders," *Atlanta Constitution*, 11 March 1922; Atlanta city directory, 1922, Atlanta City Directories collection, Kenan Research Center at the Atlanta History Center; ACC Minutes, 8 May 1924, vol. 28, "1923 January 2–1924 July," row 5, section B, shelf 1.

55. "Adair Declares Zone Plan Will Stabilize Values," *Atlanta Constitution*, 11 March 1922; "City Zoning Plan Praised and Hit by Civic Leaders" *Atlanta Constitution*, 11 March 1922.

56. "Committee Votes for Zoning Plan," *Atlanta Constitution*, 1 April 1922. Representative Watkins reflected the views of the chamber-of-commerce crowd while Representative Nutting reflected those who favored a ward-based system.

57. Strayer and Engelhardt, *Survey*, 176–77, 181–91. The school district's census divided the city into 350 house-count sections, with a population of about 550 people in each section. For population growth in Bellwood, see the statistics for the English Avenue School.

58. *Tentative Zone Plan* map; *Zone Map, Atlanta, Ga., 1922*, file FF 339, folder 5, Atlanta City Maps, Kenan Research Center at the Atlanta History Center. The revised draft was completed on 10 March, followed by two additional hearings. City council approved the final zone map by a vote of 24 to 3. ACC Minutes, 4 April 1922, vol. 26–27, "1917 July–1920 May; 1920 June 7–1923 January 1," row 5, section B, shelf 1. See also Lands, *Culture of Property*, 152–54.

59. For an examination of white residents' sense of loss during racial transition, see William Henry Jones, *Housing of Negroes*, 78–79.

60. Otis, *Atlanta's Plan*, 3; "Options Being Secured on New School Sites," *Atlanta Journal*, 17 March 1910; "Robert Whitten to Make Talks on Zoning Plan," *Atlanta Constitution*, 11 February 1922; "Robert Whitten Discusses Zoning Plan for Atlanta, *Atlanta Constitution*, 14 February 1922; "Civil Engineers and Realty Men Favor Zone Plan," *Atlanta Constitution*, 17 February 1922.

61. "Councilman Sims Urged for Mayor," *Atlanta Constitution*, 9 March 1922; "Simmons to Give Reception Today to Ku Klux Klan," *Atlanta Constitution*, 6 May 1922; "Labor Will Pass Today on Answer of School Board," *Atlanta Constitution*, 18 August 1921; Jackson, *Ku Klux Klan*, 37–38.

62. ACC Minutes, 20 August 1923, vol. 28, "1923 January 2–1924 July," row 5, section B, shelf 1; "Whitten Resigns; Mayor Accepts," *Atlanta Constitution*, 3 January 1923; "Planning Commission Members Deposed; Successors Are Named," *Atlanta Constitution*, 4 January 1923; "Mayor Walter Sims Names J. A. White for Planning Board," *Atlanta Constitution*, 7 January 1923; "White Honor-Guest at Real Estate Feed," *Atlanta Constitution*, 14 January 1923; "Sims Names Woman on Planning Board," *Atlanta Constitution*, 26 January 1923; "Expenses of City Must Be Lowered," *Atlanta Journal*, 8 May 1923; "Council to Get Plan for New Administration of City Zoning Law," *Atlanta Journal*, 10 June 1923; "Plan Board Workers Face Loss of Jobs," *Atlanta Journal*, 13 June 1923; "Planning Commission Engineer to Resign for Better Position," *Atlanta Journal*, 23 July 1923; "Torras Accepts Post as Engineer for City Planning Commission," *Atlanta Journal*, 24 June 1924; "Planner for Every Ward on City Board Is Couch Proposal," *Atlanta Journal*, 12 June 1923; "Proposed Increase of Planning Board Vetoed by Mayor," *Atlanta Journal*, 23 June 1923.

63. "City Planning Board Increase Vetoed by Sims," *Atlanta Constitution*, 24 June 1923; "Key Will Urge Paving Program," *Atlanta Constitution*, 27 December 1922; "Creation of Pay Ward at Grady Given Approval," *Atlanta Constitution*, 9 June 1923; "Majority Vote in Charter Election Demanded," *Atlanta Constitution*, 14 April 1922.

64. ACC Minutes, 19 June and 4 September 1922, vol. 26–27, "1917 July–1920 May; 1920 June 7–1923 January 1," and 2 April 1923, vol. 28, "1923 January 2–1924 July," both row 5, section B, shelf 1; advertisement for Sylvan Hills, *Atlanta Journal*, 4 June 1923; "Scenes in Morningside Park, Choice North Side Subdivision," *Atlanta Constitution*, 18 January 1925; "New Ashby Street Subdivision," advertisement, *Atlanta Independent*, 26 June 1920; "Lots! Lots! Lots! Lots!," *Atlanta Independent*, 28 August 1920.

65. ACC Minutes, 21 August, 2 October, 6 November, and 4 December 1922, vol. 26–27, "1917 July–1920 May; 1920 June 7–1923 January 1," row 5, section B, shelf 1; "Bachman Again Heads Atlanta Commercial Body," *Atlanta Constitution*, 18 January 1922; "Charter Election Runover Provided by Council," *Atlanta Constitution*, 18 April 1922; "Building

Permits," *Atlanta Journal*, 18 July 1922; "Negro Apartment Hearing Continues," *Atlanta Journal*, 23 August 1922; "Hearing on Negro Apartment House Fight Today," *Atlanta Constitution*, 23 August 1922.

66. ACC Minutes, 2 April, 16 April, 7 May, 3 September, 1 October, and 15 October 1923, 4 February, 8 May, 19 May, 5 June, 7 July, and 20 October 1924, vol. 28, "1923 January 2–1924 July," row 5, section B, shelf 1.

67. ACC Minutes, 27 November 1922, vol. 26–27, "1917 July–1920 May; 1920 June 7–1923 January 1," and 19 February, 16 April, and 21 May 1923, 19 May and 16 June 1924, vol. 28, "1923 January 2–1924 July," both row 5, section B, shelf 1; "Eleventh Ward Club Will Discuss Zoning Problem at Meeting," *Atlanta Constitution*, 2 May 1924.

68. ACC Minutes, 1 October 1923, vol. 28, "1923 January 2–1924 July," row 5, section B, shelf 1; *Tentative Zone Plan* map; *Zone Map, Atlanta, Ga., 1922*, file FF 339, folder 5, Atlanta City Maps, Kenan Research Center at the Atlanta History Center. See also "New Park for Colored to Allow No Tenants," *Atlanta Constitution*, 11 June 1919; Floyd J. Calvin, "Heman Perry Started Atlanta on Its Home Building Program," *Pittsburgh Courier*, 1 October 1931; Shivery, "History," 256, 270–74.

69. ACC Minutes, 21 May 1923, 16 August and 7 October 1924, vol. 28, "1923 January 2–1924 July," row 5, section B, shelf 1. The change made on 16 August was a single lot on a block that would be rezoned on 7 October. "Council Grants Zoning Changes of Minor Nature," *Atlanta Constitution*, 3 October 1924; "Council Committee Favors Zoning Change for Summit Avenue," *Atlanta Journal*, 3 October 1924.

70. ACC Minutes, 15 February and 8 May 1924, vol. 28, "1923 January 2–1924 July," row 5, section B, shelf 1; 7 October and 20 October 1924, vol. 29, row 5, section B, shelf 2. The change made on 15 February involved blocks that were originally included in an undetermined race district on the tentative zone map. See also Lands, *Culture of Property*, 153–54; Hanchett, *Sorting Out*.

71. "Key Will Urge Paving Program," *Atlanta Constitution*, 27 December 1922; "Complete Zone Plan, Recommended for City by Planning Commission, Adopted by Council," *Atlanta Constitution*, 11 April 1922; Whitten, "Zoning and Living Conditions," 25–26, 28. See also Kenneth Jackson, *Crabgrass Frontier*, 6–7.

72. "Great Enthusiasm Is Being Shown in the Banquet of Chamber Tonight," *Atlanta Constitution*, 16 January 1920; "Indorsement Is Given Planning Campaign," *Atlanta Constitution*, 1 Feb 1920; "Atlanta Leaders Placed on City Planning Board," *Atlanta Constitution*, 10 February 1920; "In the South," *Housing Betterment*.

73. For an analysis of housing and eugenics, see Lovett, "Eugenic Housing," 67–83. According to my research, the American Eugenics Society did not begin encouraging white Americans to raise larger families in federally subsidized suburban communities until the 1930s, but zoning policies of the 1920s did overlap with campaigns to promote "better babies" in residential parks. See chapter 10.

74. Toll, *Zoned American*, 157–59.

75. Bruno Lasker, "Unwalled Towns," *The Survey*, 6 March 1920, 675–80; Leonard, *Illiberal Reformers*, 158.

76. Bruno Lasker, response to Charles Cheney's "Removing Social Barriers by Zoning," *The Survey*, 22 May 1920, 279.

77. Lasker, "Unwalled Towns," 675–80.

78. "Plans Prepared for Organization of City Planners," *Atlanta Constitution*, 23 April 1921; Whitten, "Zoning and Living Conditions," 27–29. The conference began on 9 May 1921.

79. Whitten, "Zoning and Living Conditions," 29; Whitten, "Problems Involved in Zoning," 38.

80. Committee on Best Methods of Land Subdivision, "Report of Conference Committee," 247, 266.

81. Silver, "Racial Origins of Zoning," 192; Shah, *Contagious Divides*, 83, 87, 119.

82. "Stenographic Report of the Third Annual Conference of Developers of High-Class Residential Property" (1919), 568, 577, Jemison Companies, Miscellany, #2838, Division of Rare and Manuscript Collections, Cornell University Library. See also Fogelson, *Bourgeois Nightmares*, 129.

83. Anderson, "Zoning"; Woofter, *Negro Problems in Cities*; Silver, "Racial Origins of Zoning," 25.

84. Chicago Real Estate Board, *Chicago Real Estate Board Bulletin*, October 1917, 551. See also Philpott, *Slum and the Ghetto*, 164.

85. US Chamber of Commerce, "Supplement to City Planning and Zoning Accomplishments," November 1929, p. 7, box 11, DL22A2, RW Papers; Chicago Real Estate Board, *Chicago Real Estate Board Bulletin*, April 1917, 313, 315. See also Seligman, *Block by Block*.

86. Chicago Commission on Race Relations, *Negro in Chicago*, 123–24. "Plans Prepared for Organization of City Planners," *Atlanta Constitution*, 23 April 1921.

87. Hirsch, *Making the Second Ghetto*, 1; Grossman, *Land of Hope Chicago*, 179.

88. Chicago Commission on Race Relations, *Negro in Chicago*, 38; Bruno Lasker, "The Unmaking of a Myth," *The Survey*, October 1922, 46–49, box 12, DL22A3, "Race Segregation," RW Papers.

89. Garb, *City of American Dreams*, 179–95; Landry, *New Black Middle Class*, 21; Spear, *Black Chicago*, 14–15; Hirsch, *Making the Second Ghetto*, 4, 17. By 1940, three-quarters of Black residents lived in areas greater than 90 percent African American, and nearly half lived in exclusively Black census tracts.

90. Silver, "Racial Origins of Zoning," 25.

91. Kimball, "Brief Review of City Planning," 82; Kimball, "Survey of City and Regional Planning"; Hott, "Constitutionality of Municipal Zoning," 341–43; Bassett, *Zoning*.

92. Bruno Lasker, "The Atlanta Zoning Plan," *The Survey*, 22 April 1922, 114–15, box 12, DL22A3, "Race Segregation," RW Papers. Eight years earlier, the North Carolina Supreme Court had made a similar argument in the decision to overturn Winston-Salem's segregation ordinance. "Segregation Not Allowed by Law," *Farmer and Mechanic*, 14 April 1914.

93. R. H. Whitten to Bruno Lasker, 28 April 1922, box 12, DL22A3, "Race Segregation," RW Papers.

94. "Troops Fired on When New Fight Breaks Out After 85 Die in Tulsa," "Competition Gets Blame for Riots," and "Race Riots of Past Show Heavy Toll in Killed and Injured," newspaper clippings, box 12, DL22A3, "Race Segregation," RW Papers.

95. Crockett, *Black Towns*; "Competition Gets Blame for Riots," "Race Riots of Past Show Heavy Toll in Killed and Injured," box 12, DL22A3, "Race Segregation," RW Papers.

96. "Segregation Not Liked by Negroes," *Morning Tulsa Daily World*, 6 August 1916; "Negroes Protest Segregation Law," *Morning Tulsa Daily World*, 8 August 1916; "Administration Is Traitor to Negroes Who Elected Them," *Tulsa Democrat*, 5 August 1916; "Segregation Passes City Council," *Tulsa Star*, 5 August 1916; editorial page, *Tulsa Star*, 15 September 1916. As was true in most Jim Crow cities, Black Tulsans who worked for white

families often lived in alleys behind their employers' homes, which created an additional source of income for white property owners.

97. Oklahoma Commission to Study the Tulsa Race Riot of 1921, *Tulsa Race Riot*. See also Hannibal B. Johnson, *Black Wall Street*.

98. "Troops Fired on When New Fight Breaks Out After 85 Die in Tulsa," "Competition Gets Blame for Riots," box 12, DL22A3, "Race Segregation," RW Papers.

99. NAACP attorney Moorfield Storey argued in his brief for *Buchanan*, "No one outside a courtroom would imagine for an instant that the predominant purpose of this ordinance was not to prevent the negro citizens of Louisville, however industrious, thrifty and well-educated they might be, from approaching that condition vaguely described as 'social equality.'" Roger L. Rice, "Residential Segregation by Law," 190.

100. Godshalk, *Veiled Visions*; Gaines, *Uplifting the Race*, 49; White, *Man Called White*, 3–12; Driskell, *Schooling Jim Crow*, 78–79, 84–89, 94–96.

101. See Lassiter and Crespino, "De Jure/De Facto Segregation," 3–22.

102. Price-Spratlen and Guest, "Race and Population Change," 115; Whitten, "Zoning and Living Conditions," 22–24. See also Hirsch, "With or Without Jim Crow," 76.

103. Bowen v. City of Atlanta, 159 Ga. 145 (1924); ACC Minutes, 16 April 1923, vol. 28, "1923 January 2–1924 July," row 5, section B, shelf 1; "Ask Reargument in Zone Law Case," *Atlanta Constitution*, 21 October 1924.

104. "Segregation Section Is Unconstitutional," *Atlanta Constitution*, 18 October 1924; Bowen v. City of Atlanta, 159 Ga. 145 (1924); Lands, *Culture of Property*, 154.

Chapter 8

1. See also Flint, "Zoning and Residential Segregation," 207; West, "Black Atlanta."

2. Strayer and Engelhardt, *Survey*, 172–76.

3. Strayer, "School Building Program"; CBJ Snyder, discussion of Strayer's "School Building Program," 60; "Education Chiefs in Lively Session," *Atlanta Constitution*, 28 June 1922.

4. Olmsted, "Planning Residential Subdivisions," 14–15.

5. US Department of Labor Information and Education Service, *Suggestions for Own-Your-Own-Home Campaigns* (Washington, DC: Government Printing Office, 1919), box 6, folder 15, USHC Records; "'Educate Public to Build,' Says Secretary of Labor Wilson," *Build Now News*, April 1919, box 461, unprocessed, USHC Records.

6. Minutes of the Atlanta Board of Education, 3 May 1922; Ittner, "High Costs," 367; Holy, Arnold, and Anderson, "School Buildings." See also Tyack, *One Best System*.

7. Mintz, *Huck's Raft*, 175; "Text of Sutton's Address," *Atlanta Constitution*, 15 January 1927; Strayer, "School Building Program," 47. Atlanta's enrollment data is from 1915 and 1926.

8. Holy, Arnold, and Anderson, "School Buildings," 371–72; Caswell, *City School Surveys*, 86–87; Strayer, "School Building Program," 1.

9. Robert Whitten and Harold Weber, "Population, the City Plan, and the Schools," 6–7, unpublished manuscript, box 7, folder "Planning-Municipal-Schools," RW Papers; George B. Ford, "What Planning Has Done," 15–16; Bassett, *Zoning*, 70.

10. Strayer, "School Building Program," 52; Ford, "What Planning Has Done," 15–16; Moehlman, *Public School Plant Program*, 144, 180–82. Unfortunately, Moehlman did not identify which city he was referring to with a fifty-six-acre site.

11. Houston Independent School District, *Building Program*, 19, 29, 88, 108; Houston City Planning Commission, *Report*, 87.

12. Hanmer, discussion of Henry Hubbard's "Parks and Playgrounds," 35, 37. See also Hubbard, "Parks and Playgrounds,"17–18.

13. Whitten and Weber, "Population, the City Plan, and the Schools," 6–7, RW Papers.

14. George B. Ford, discussion of Strayer's "School Building Program," 63.

15. "School Building Program Behind, Declares Sutton," *Atlanta Constitution*, 12 March 1922; Hirsch, "With or Without Jim Crow"; Douglas, *Jim Crow Moves North*, 237–73. For a comparison of the educational expenditures in southern and northern cities, see Amsterdam, *Roaring Metropolis*.

16. Otis, *Atlanta's Plan*, 3; "Options Being Secured on New School Sites," *Atlanta Journal*, 17 March 1910; "Realtors and Bonds," *Atlanta Constitution*, 29 January 1921; "Education Board in Battle Royal over School Site," *Atlanta Constitution*, 9 November 1922; "Harry Goodhart Will Make Race for Mayor," *Atlanta Constitution*, 14 July 1920; "Present Charter Leads with Watkins' Second," *Atlanta Constitution*, 17 May 1922; Jackson, *Ku Klux Klan*, 262n19. Most of the support for the city manager plan came from Ansley Park and other Eighth Ward residential parks. For an analysis on commission-style governments in a southern context, see Hanchett, *Sorting Out*, 210; Brownell, "Urban South," 140–51.

17. Minutes of the Colored Women's Council, 19 February 1921, box 2, folder 12, Kate Richardson Lumpkin Papers, MSS 627, Kenan Research Center at the Atlanta History Center; "Give First Place to Urgent Needs," *Atlanta Constitution*, 11 March 1920; "Robert Whitten, Otis and Sutton Make Addresses," *Atlanta Constitution*, 19 November 1921; "Big Losses Laid to Lack of Zones," *Atlanta Constitution*, 15 February 1922; Shivery and Smythe, "Neighborhood Union," 158. See also E. Bernard West, "Black Atlanta." Engelhardt often appeared at meetings alongside Whitten.

18. "Negro Delegations of Atlanta Propose Three School Sites," *Atlanta Constitution*, 19 May 1922; Minutes of the Atlanta Board of Education, 3 May and 10 May 1922; Hickey, "From Auburn Avenue," 111.

19. Consultant Service of the National Municipal League, *Governments of Atlanta and Fulton County*, 349–50; "Negroes Get Two Additional High Schools," *Atlanta Constitution*, 6 July 1947; "Improvements in Negro Education Here Outlined," *Atlanta Journal*, 6 July 1947. That year, the board finally upgraded the Fourth Ward's equally overcrowded junior high to a Black high school, an action that represented a rare promotion—rather than the much more common *demotion*—of an existing school building. The other Black high school planned in 1947 was a vocational school operating out of the old Clark University campus on the southside.

20. "Council Approves Purchase of Site at Piedmont Park," *Atlanta Constitution*, 7 March 1922; "School Building Program Adopted by Board Friday," *Atlanta Constitution*, 25 March 1922; "Air View of New Boys' Senior School Site and Drawing of Plan," *Atlanta Constitution*, 12 March 1922. At the time of the building program, Atlanta still maintained separate high schools for white boys and girls. Grady was built to replace both the prestigious Boys High School and the popular Tech High School. The location for the new Girls High School was much more contentious. That battle is not analyzed here.

21. Strayer, "School Building Program," 51.

22. "Fifth Ward Gives Hearty Approval to Big Bond Issue," *Atlanta Constitution*, 10 February 1921.

23. Consultant Service of the National Municipal League, *Governments of Atlanta and Fulton County*, 91, 343; "Parent-Teachers Ask Junior High at Maddox Park," *Atlanta Constitution*, 14 March 1922; Minutes of the Atlanta Board of Education, 9 March and 19 October 1926, 14 February, 25 April, 12 June, and 10 July 1928; Strayer and Engelhardt, *Survey*, 221.

24. Minutes of the Atlanta Board of Education, 10 January 1921; "Winburn Elected Head of Atlanta Education Board," *Atlanta Constitution*, 9 January 1920. This article includes the first announcement of the board's plan to convert Davis Street School to Black use, even though Davis students had long been promised a new school. Although the Davis site was officially within the boundaries of First Ward, most of its students lived further north in Fifth Ward. Minutes of the Atlanta Board of Education, 22 May 1913, 16 December 1915, and 19 December 1917.

25. "Mayor Responsible for Her Discharge Miss Riordan Holds," *Atlanta Constitution*, 12 August 1921; "McCalley's Actions on Board Attacked," *Atlanta Constitution*, 30 August 1921; "Delegation from Davis School," *Atlanta Journal*, 13 January 1921; "Walter Sims Barely Misses Majority in Race for Mayor and Must Run Over with Woodward," *Atlanta Constitution*, 7 September 1922. Representative McCalley was from the Eighth Ward, where Ansley Park was located.

26. "Winburn Elected Head of Atlanta Education Board," *Atlanta Constitution*, 9 January 1920; "Hutcheson Explains Position on Negro," *Atlanta Constitution*, 29 May 1921; "McCalley Indorsed by Six Associations of Parent-Teachers," *Atlanta Constitution*, 27 August 1921; "New Key Cornerstone Laid with Ceremonies," *Atlanta Constitution*, 17 April 1923. The Summer Hill community had originally developed around the Summer Hill School, which opened at the end of the Civil War but had received little attention from the school board since then. Strayer and Engelhardt, *Survey*, 39, 133, 144, 149, 152.

27. "Men and Women Leaders of City to Handle Funds," *Atlanta Constitution*, 13 February 1921; "Leaders of Labor Speak for Bonds," *Atlanta Constitution*, 24 February 1921; "Presidents of Parent-Teacher Associations," *Atlanta Constitution*, 20 February 1921; Atlanta city directories, 1916–23, Atlanta City Directories collection, Kenan Research Center at the Atlanta History Center.

28. *Tentative Zone Plan* map; *Zone Map, Atlanta, Ga., 1922*, file FF 339, folder 5, Atlanta City Maps, Kenan Research Center at the Atlanta History Center; ACC Minutes, March and April 1922, vol. 26–27, "1917 July–1920 May; 1920 June 7–1923 January 1," row 5, section B, shelf 1.

29. Minutes of the Atlanta Board of Education, 6 January 1923; ACC Minutes, 18 December 1922, vol. 26–27, "1917 July–1920 May; 1920 June 7–1923 January 1," row 5, section B, shelf 1. Strayer and Engelhardt had recommended that a new Davis School be built and then eventually turned over to Black students, although a new school would have discouraged white residents from leaving the neighborhood. Strayer and Engelhardt, *Survey*, 226.

30. "$650,000 Building Permits Granted," *Atlanta Constitution*, 19 January 1928; Minutes of the Atlanta Board of Education, 29 June 1928.

31. ACC Minutes, 1 October 1923 and 8 May 1924, vol. 28, "1923 January 2–1924 July," row 5, section B, shelf 1; "Simpson Street Owners Seek Change in Zoning," *Atlanta Journal*, 2 March 1924. For later changes along Simpson Street, see ACC Minutes, 16 June 1924, vol. 28, "1923 January 2–1924 July," row 5, section B, shelf 1, and 7 October and 20 October 1924, vol. 29, row 5, section B, shelf 2. The quotes are from Flint, "Zoning and Residential Segregation," 331–32. Barbara Flint was able to access the more detailed records of the

planning commission, which were still being processed at the Kenan Research Center as I was finishing this manuscript.

32. Shivery and Smythe, "Neighborhood Union," 158; Shivery, "History," 222–31; "New Schools to Cost $4,964,679 Says Report," *Atlanta Independent*, 3 April 1924.

33. "Committee Reports on Public Schools for Negro Children," *Atlanta Independent*, 31 January 1924; Neighborhood Union school survey, 22 January 1924, box 7, folder 5, NU Collection; Shivery, "History," 229–30.

34. Advertisement for North Boulevard Park, *Atlanta Constitution*, 23 April 1916; "Orme Will Enter Race for Council from Eighth Ward," *Atlanta Constitution*, 20 May 1916; "School Building Program Adopted by Board Friday," *Atlanta Constitution*, 25 March 1922; "Continuation of Boulevard Park Provides Attractive Home Sites," *Atlanta Constitution*, 18 January 1925; "Inman and Gordon, Council Leaders, Resign Positions," *Atlanta Constitution*, 8 September 1925; "$8,000,000 Bond Issue Favored by Finance Body Schools to Get $3,000,000," *Atlanta Constitution*, 2 February 1926. See also Garrett, *Atlanta and Environs*, 632. The board purchased the site for North Boulevard Park's school only days after Strayer and Engelhardt's team had arrived in Atlanta to begin work on the survey. Minutes of the Atlanta Board of Education, 23 December 1921; "School Survey Headquarters Established," *Atlanta Constitution*, 21 December 1921.

35. "Realtors and Bonds," *Atlanta Constitution*, 29 January 1921; Minutes of the Atlanta Board of Education, 6 June 1913, 23 August 1917, 17 January and 28 March 1918, and 31 December 1919. In January 1918, Virginia Avenue School was included in a list of the district's fifteen Black schools. In December 1919, the minutes stated that the district had fifteen Black schools, but the total included Ashby Street School, which had recently been converted from white to Black use. Virginia Avenue School was still listed in the 1919 city directory, which means it still existed in late 1918 and then was closed the following year. "1918 City Council Committees," *Atlanta Constitution*, 8 January 1918; "Winburn Elected Head of Atlanta Education Board," *Atlanta Constitution*, 9 January 1920. The new Virginia Avenue School was named for developer Sam Inman, a fitting honor since the chair of the bond commission was Frank Inman, his son. Like almost all southern elites, the Inmans used their fortune to invest in residential park development.

36. "Inman and Gordon, Council Leaders, Resign Positions," *Atlanta Constitution*, 8 September 1925; "785,000 to Build Eight New Schools Asked of Council," *Atlanta Constitution*, 10 January 1926; "School Committee Warned of Crisis," *Atlanta Constitution*, 30 September 1926; "Issuance of Scrip to Avert Crisis in Schools Seen," *Atlanta Constitution*, 30 September 1926; "Fate of Atlanta's Schools Hinges on Mass Meeting of Citizens This Morning," *Atlanta Constitution*, 13 October 1926; "Text of Sutton's Address," *Atlanta Constitution*, 15 January 1927.

37. "$8,000,000 Bond Issue Favored by Finance Body Schools to Get $3,000,000," *Atlanta Constitution*, 2 February 1926; "Bonds and Higher Tax Lose at Polls," *Atlanta Constitution*, 24 April 1919; Jackson, *Ku Klux Klan*, 41–42; Preston, *Automobile Age Atlanta*, 79, 85. *Automobile Age Atlanta* contains maps from 1908 and 1920 that illustrate the movement of affluent families into Eighth Ward.

38. "Leaders of Labor Speak for Bonds," *Atlanta Constitution*, 24 February 1921; "Five Million Dollar Bond Issue? YES!: The Schools Require It; The Interests of Children Demand It," *Journal of Labor*, 5 February 1926; "$8,000,000 Bond Victory Foreseen in Voting Today," *Atlanta Constitution*, 24 March 1926.

39. "The School Muddle Grows More Complex," *Atlanta Independent*, 30 June 1927; "Christian Council Urges Larger Portion of Bond Money for Negro Schools," *Atlanta Constitution*, 14 December 1927; "We Must Keep Faith," *Atlanta Constitution*, 14 December 1927.

40. Minutes of the Atlanta Board of Education, 9 August, 30 August, 7 November, 22 November, and 28 November 1927, 10 April, 29 June, and 13 November 1928.

41. "Hartsfield Hits School Program," *Atlanta Constitution*, 2 March 1924; Dr. H. R. Butler, "Congratulates Negro for His Assistance in Educating the Whites," *Atlanta Independent*, March 6, 1924; "Mr. Hartsfield," *Atlanta Independent*, 6 March 1924. See also Louis Williams, "William Berry Hartsfield," 653.

42. After Boulevard School was sold to Morris Brown, Fourth Ward had only two remaining white schools. It is not clear whether the money to complete the small addition for the Forrest Avenue School was diverted from Howard Junior High, even though the board had agreed to do this. The construction company that completed Howard claimed that the total spent on the school was $350,000, including the $234,000 from the first bond issue, which would suggest that the amount from the second issue was reduced from $150,000 to $116,000. "Space Is Sought for Two Schools," *Atlanta Constitution*, 3 August 1928; "Fourth Warders Back 9-Hole Golf Course," *Atlanta Constitution*, 7 September 1928; "Plans for School Auditorium Opposed," *Atlanta Constitution*, 16 September 1928; "Fund Distribution Scored By White," *Atlanta Constitution*, 23 September 1928; "A Mighty Record of Construction," *Atlanta Constitution*, 3 November 1929. Earlier in 1926, the school board's Fifth Ward representative attempted to use $90,000 of the funds slated for Howard to build auditoriums for two white schools serving mostly working-class children. Minutes of the Atlanta Board of Education, 21 February 1922 and 26 October 1926.

43. "Fire Guts School on Ashby Street," *Atlanta Constitution*, 23 December 1926; "Atlanta Children Return to School Monday Morning," *Atlanta Constitution*, 3 January 1927; Minutes of the Atlanta Board of Education, 28 November 1927 and 29 June 1928; Shivery, "History," 224–25.

44. Minutes of the Atlanta Board of Education, 8 January 1920; "Reinstatement of W. F. Dykes Demanded," *Atlanta Journal*, 11 May 1921; "Sutton Optimistic on Taking Office," *Atlanta Journal*, 1 July 1921.

45. Lieb, "'Baltimore Idea,'" 114. Emily Lieb is currently working on a project to carefully lay out the connections between Baltimore schools and residential segregation.

46. Power, "Apartheid Baltimore Style," 316–17; Lieb, "'Baltimore Idea,'" 104–19; Lieb, "'Shove Those Black Clouds,'" 33.

47. Strayer, "School Building Program," 50; Grinnalds, discussion of Strayer's "School Building Program," 55–56; Strayer, *Abstract of a Survey*, 10.

48. "This City's Long Cherished Ambition for a City Plan Has at Last Been Realized," *Twin-City Daily Sentinel*, 8 January 1921; "Winston-Salem Will Have Good City Plan Made," *Winston-Salem Journal*, 9 January 1921; "Welcome Meeting for New City Officials," *Winston-Salem Journal*, 6 May 1921; James Howell Smith, "John Wesley Hanes," NCpedia, accessed 15 June 2024, www.ncpedia.org/biography/hanes-john-wesley.

49. "Well-Known City Plan Authority Talks of the Situation Here," *Twin-City Daily Sentinel*, 23 May 1921; "Town Topics," *Twin-City Daily Sentinel*, 30 December 1922.

50. "Solution Problem [sic] of Segregation Is Amicably Solved," *Western Sentinel*, 11 April 1922.

51. "Plans Call for a Gradual Shifting School Centers," *Western Sentinel*, 14 February 1922; "To Acquire Large Colored Park Area," *Twin-City Daily Sentinel*, 23 February 1922; "Plan for School and Park Reservations Shows Each Section to Be Supplied," *Twin-City Daily Sentinel*, 25 April 1922.

52. "Columbia Helps Twin City Plans," *Winston-Salem Journal*, 21 November 1919; "To Confer with School Board," *Winston-Salem Journal*, 4 February 1922; "Civitans Hold Weekly Meeting," *Winston-Salem Journal*, 2 September 1922; "Superintendent Latham Submits Annual Report," *Winston-Salem Journal*, 4 July 1922; "Plan for School and Park Reservations Shows Each Section to Be Supplied," *Twin-City Daily Sentinel*, 25 April 1922. The bond issue was for $1.8 million, but donations from local elites brought the total spent on the building program to well over $2 million.

53. "Half-Million Dollar Gift to City," *Winston-Salem Journal*, 4 July 1919; "Town Topics," *Twin-City Daily Sentinel*, 30 December 1922; "Notable Co-operative Spirit Was in Evidence at 'Forward' Meeting," *Twin-City Daily Sentinel*, 24 May 1921.

54. "Southside School Site Is under Fire," *Twin-City Daily Sentinel*, 8 December 1921; "Plan for School and Park Reservations Shows Each Section to Be Supplied," *Twin-City Daily Sentinel*, 25 April 1922; "Plans Call for a Gradual Shifting School Centers," *Western Sentinel*, 14 February 1922.

55. "How to Insure Segregation," *Winston-Salem Journal*, 22 April 1914; "Segregation by Common Consent," *Winston-Salem Journal*, 19 April 1914.

56. "Solution Problem [sic] of Segregation"; "Plan for School and Park Reservations"; "Superintendent Latham Submits"; "Three Million Dollar School Plant for City," *Western Sentinel*, 7 July 1922.

57. Minutes of the Raleigh Board of Commissioners, 7 March 1922, City of Raleigh, Minutes of the Governing Body, book 1, M.509.10004, Municipal Records, State Archives of North Carolina; "Raleigh Approves Million Dollars in School Bonds," *Raleigh News and Observer*, 5 April 1922; "Planning Board Named for City," *Raleigh News and Observer*, 8 March 1922; T. B. Eldridge, "What City Planning Means to Raleigh," *American City*, August 1922, 143–45; "Raleigh Is the Best Town and Dave Fort Proves It," *Raleigh News and Observer*, 30 July 1922; "Raleigh's Ideals and Real Estate," *Raleigh News and Observer*, 28 March 1923. See also Jack Alexander, "Raleigh," *Saturday Evening Post*, 12 April 1947, 20–21.

58. "Honor Memory of Dr. Withers," *Raleigh News and Observer*, 27 June 1924. For an analysis of commission-style governments within a southern context, see Hanchett, *Sorting Out*, 210; Brownell, "Urban South," 140–51.

59. "Zoning Ordinance of the City of Raleigh," 20 April 1923, Vertical File NAC 1620 Raleigh, Frances Loeb Library, Harvard Graduate School of Design, Cambridge, MA.

60. Minutes of the Raleigh Board of Commissioners, 2 March 1923, City of Raleigh, Minutes of the Governing Body, book 1, M.509.10004, Municipal Records, State Archives of North Carolina; "City Zoning Will Receive Wide Attention This Week," *Raleigh News and Observer*, 16 July 1922; "Planning Body to Determine Scope," *Raleigh News and Observer*, July 18, 1922; "Winston-Salem Purchases 25 Acres of Land for Negroes," *Raleigh News and Observer*, 11 April 1922; "New North School to Represent Outlay of Quarter Million," *Twin-City Daily Sentinel*, 27 October 1922; "C. V. York to Build New North School," *Twin-City Daily Sentinel*, 1 November 1922.

61. "City Plan Urged by Stephenson," *Raleigh News and Observer*, July 22, 1922; "James R. Weatherspoon Will Head Kiwanis Club," *Raleigh News and Observer*, 30 December 1922. Both C. V. York, a member of the Raleigh planning commission, and Gilbert Stephenson were members of the Kiwanis Club. Stephenson was appointed to the "committee to represent the club in conferences" with the planning commission.

62. C. N. Hunter to Superintendent Underwood, 3 February 1923, CH Papers.

63. Raleigh Minutes, 28 March and 22 June 1923; "Two New Schools Ready Opening on September 2," *Raleigh Times*, 20 August 1924; "High School Site Special Order Next Wednes.," *Raleigh Times*, 29 March 1923; "High School Site Question Now Up," *Raleigh News and Observer*, 29 March 1923; "Citizen's Group Report Points to School Need," *Carolinian*, 27 March 1948; Raleigh Minutes, 2 March 1948.

64. Clarence Poe to C. N. Hunter, 30 June 1923, CH Papers; Raleigh Minutes, 26 March 1924. Poe's popular magazine became better known as *Southern Living*.

65. "Decide to Submit Building Program in Full to Voters," *Raleigh News and Observer*, 25 February 1926. The total registration for the bond election was about 4,600. According to the numbers published in the *News and Observer*, the bonds carried by overwhelming majorities in both the fifteenth and sixteenth precincts (the two precincts with the largest share of Black voters). "Raleigh School Bond Issue Carries by Large Majority;" *Raleigh News and Observer*, 21 April 1926; "Heavy Morning Vote for School Bonds," *Raleigh Times*, 20 April 1926; Haley, "Carolina Chameleon," 581–82.

66. J. M. Broughton to C. N. Hunter, 20 February 1926, CH Papers; "Representative Negroes Ask Better School Site," letter to the editor, *Raleigh Times*, 24 July 1926; Haley, "Carolina Chameleon," 577; Raleigh Minutes, 13 May 1926; Barbee, *Historical Sketches*, 65.

67. S. J. Betts to C. N. Hunter, 26 July 1926, CH Papers; Charles Hunter, "Asks for Fair Dealing in Location of Negro School," letter to the editor, *Raleigh Times*, 16 July 1926.

68. "Representative Negroes Ask Better School Site," letter to the editor, *Raleigh Times*, 24 July 1926; "School Progress in Raleigh Now in Hands of 4631 Voters Registered for Election," *Raleigh News and Observer*, 18 April 1926; "Raleigh's Population Will Be 50,000 in Ten Years," *Raleigh News and Observer*, 21 March 1923; Amelia J. Hunter to C. N. Hunter, 16 August 1926, CH Papers.

69. Raleigh Minutes, 31 December 1930; "Raleigh School Bond Issue Carries by Large Majority," *Raleigh News and Observer*, 21 April 1926; "High School Site Special Order Next Wednes.," *Raleigh Times*, 29 March 1923. Although African Americans comprised about a third of the city's total population, Black students made up 40 percent of the district's elementary enrollment. Raleigh Minutes, 21 July 1931.

70. "Thompson School Wants to Know Who Gets Its Nickel," *Raleigh Times*, 17 March 1922; "Eight Schoolhouses Are Strongest Arguments for Million Dollar Bond Issue for Raleigh," *Raleigh News and Observer*, 19 March 1922; "School Bond Catechism Clears Local Situation," *Raleigh News and Observer*, 12 February 1922; "Thompson School to Cost $105,864," *Raleigh News and Observer*, 9 September 1922; "No Action Now on School Site," *Raleigh News and Observer*, 14 September 1922; Raleigh Minutes, 21 July and 9 September 1931.

71. "Committee Is Looking for New School Sites," *Raleigh Times*, 9 May 1922; "The Faces of Children," Cameron Park advertisement, *News and Observer*, 13 April 1913. Charles B. Park and John A. Park were the sons of Benjamin Park, a residential contractor in Raleigh.

Charles Park was also a professor of mechanical engineering at what would become North Carolina State. Amis, *Historical Raleigh*, 127–28; Raleigh city directory, 1921, DigitalNC, https://lib.digitalnc.org/record/25743.

72. "Proposed High School Site Draws Numerous Protests," *Raleigh News and Observer*, 23 July 1922; Fab Hunicutt, "Urges Central Location for High School," letter to the editor, *Raleigh News and Observer*, 24 July 1922; "New School Site Hearing Public," *Raleigh News and Observer*, 25 July 1922.

73. Raleigh Minutes, 15 August and 27 September 1922.

74. Longview Gardens promotional brochure, circa 1957, "History," Longview Gardens Neighborhood Association, www.longviewgardens.org/galleries/longviewad/index (site discontinued); "Longview Gardens Historic District," Raleigh Historic Development Commission, accessed 10 August 2022, https://rhdc.org/longview-gardens-historic-district; Raleigh city directory, 1924, DigitalNC, https://lib.digitalnc.org/record/25784.

75. Raleigh Minutes, 11 May 1923; "Print Zone Maps before Adoption City Ordinance," *Raleigh Times*, 17 March 1923.

76. "Way Made Clear for Two Schools," *Raleigh News and Observer*, 13 May 1923; "School Board Votes for Sites Two High Schools," *Raleigh Times*, 14 May 1923; Raleigh Minutes, 12 May 1923 and 18 March 1924. In 1924, John A. Park built his home at 1535 Carr Street in Hayes Barton. Raleigh city directories, 1921 and 1924, DigitalNC, www.digitalnc.org/collections/city-directories/.

77. "Smallwood Site for Senior High School Bought," *Raleigh Times*, 12 June 1924; "Morson High School," Vertical Files, Olivia Rainey Local History Library, Raleigh, North Carolina.

78. Raleigh Minutes, 24 February 1926 and 28 August 1929; "Mr. Betts Endorses C. N. Hunter's Views," letter to the editor, *Raleigh Times*, 19 July 1926; "Protest of Negro School Site Prima Facie Case," *Raleigh Times*, 24 July 1926.

79. See also Herbin-Triant, *Threatening Property*.

80. Atlanta Metropolitan Planning Commission, *Schools for Growing Atlanta: A Report to the Atlanta Board of Education on Estimating Classroom Needs in 1955–60*, unpublished report (Atlanta: 1952), pp. i, 69–70, Kenan Research Center at the Atlanta History Center, Atlanta, GA. The report was prominently stamped "confidential" in multiple places.

81. Strayer, "School Building Program," 54; "Raleigh School Bond Issue Carries by Large Majority," *Raleigh News and Observer*, 21 April 1926.

Chapter 9

1. Advertisement for the Country Club District, *Kansas City Star*, 17 March 1912.

2. WHCCHP, *Parent Education*, 5; WHCCHP, *Home and the Child*, 9–27.

3. WHCCHP, *Parent Education*, 13, 32–34; Leonard, *Illiberal Reformers*, 62–63; Herbert Hoover, "Statement Announcing the White House Conference on Home Building and Home Ownership," 15 September 1931, HH Collection.

4. E. S. Martin, "Children as an Incentive," *Harper's Weekly*, December 10, 1904, 29–31.

5. For example, the Neighborhood Union and Black PTAs were engaged in interracial work in the city, the state, and the region in hopes of improving Black housing, schools, and parks but also to promote parent education and interracial understanding. "Report of Sub-Committee Which Met Nov. 16, 1921 to Plan Inter-Racial Program," box 12, folder 3; minutes of the Atlanta Committee on Interracial Cooperation, 9 July 1925, box 11, folder

17; "Program for Annual Meeting, Georgia Committee on Interracial Cooperation, Central Y.M.C.A., Luckie Street, Atlanta, Georgia," 14 January 1931, box 10, folder 20; "Future Program," undated, box 12, folder 19; all in NU Collection.

6. Lynd and Lynd, *Middletown*, 146, 147, 151. For similar examples from mothers living in J. C. Nichols's Country Club District, see Worley, *J. C. Nichols*, 169–70, 238, 284–85.

7. Child Study Association of America, "The Purpose of the Federation for Child Study," 1913, Social Welfare History Project, Virginia Commonwealth University, https://socialwelfare.library.vcu.edu/programs/child-welfarechild-labor/child-study-association-of-america-statement-of-purpose-1913/; "The History of the Child Study Association of America: Its Growth and Activities, 1928," Social Welfare History Project, Virginia Commonwealth University, accessed 20 June 2024, https://socialwelfare.library.vcu.edu/programs/child-welfarechild-labor/child-study-association-history-1928/; Jack Hansan, "Child Study Association of America," Social Welfare History Project, Virginia Commonwealth University, 2013, accessed 20 June 2024, https://socialwelfare.library.vcu.edu/programs/child-welfarechild-labor/child-study-association-of-america-statement-of-purpose-1913/.

8. WHCCHP, *Parent Education*, 16, 32, 76–82; Sidonie Guerenberg, "Enlightened Parenthood," *Children: The Magazine for Parents*, November 1926, 3.

9. WHCCHP, *Parent Education*, 257–59. See also Mintz, *Huck's Raft*, 187.

10. Schoff, "National Congress," 140; Ladd-Taylor, *Mother-Work*, 4–5, 49; Leonard, *Illiberal Reformers*, xii, 4, 180; WHCCHP, *Parent Education*, 113, 116. The congress also successfully lobbied for a Home Education Division within the US Bureau of Education, and Schoff served as its director until 1919.

11. Schoff, "National Congress," 139–47. For a local example, see "Mrs. Spalding Reads Report at Atlanta Council Meeting," *Atlanta Constitution*, 29 May 1921; and "Historical Timelines," PTA.org, accessed 28 June 2024, www.pta.org/home/About-National-Parent-Teacher-Association/Mission-Values/National-PTA-History.

12. As quoted in "Do Parents Need Training?," *Raleigh Student*, 8 January 1926.

13. Davis, *Lifting As They Climb*, 129, 269–70; WHCCHP, *Young Child*, xi.

14. Minutes of the Neighborhood Union, 8 July, 23 July, 3 September, and 3 December 1908, 11 March, 9 September, 14 October, and 14 December 1909, 19 January and 25 February 1910, 10 August and 9 November 1911, box 4, folder 1; Charter of the Neighborhood Union, 1911, box 2, folder 3; Mrs. Edna E. Lamson to Mrs. Hope, box 2, folder 37, all in NU Collection; Shivery, "History," 58–59, 67, 71–72, 85, 120–21, 168, 175–76, 193, 207.

15. Austin, *Coming of Age*, 68–69.

16. Higginbotham, *Righteous Discontent*, 179–80.

17. Davis, *Lifting as They Climb*, 87–89, 98–99.

18. "The Gate City Free Kindergarten," circa 1917, box 12, folder 24, NU Collection. This undated fundraising speech explains the importance of the Gate City Free Kindergarten Association's work through a well-developed philosophy of parent education. The year 1917 is handwritten at the top. The document also mentions that, at the time, the association had been helping children and their mothers for twelve years (the association was established in 1905).

19. "Child Study Institute Closes," *Raleigh News and Observer*, 4 February 1921; "Child Study Club to Meet," *Raleigh News and Observer*, 9 November 1921; "Social Calendar," *Raleigh News and Observer*, 11 November 1923; "Parents Invited to Lectures in Durham," *Raleigh News and Observer*, 28 November 1925; "Pre-School Circle Program Announced,"

Atlanta Constitution, 8 June 1926; "Expert to Talk at Parent Meet," *Raleigh News and Observer*, 18 January 1928; "Children vs. Parent," *Raleigh News and Observer*, 14 February 1928; "School Status and Objective Outlined by Mrs. Clifford Walker," *Atlanta Constitution*, 14 October 1928; "Parents, Teachers to Hear Talk of Home Economics Worker," *Birmingham News*, 28 October 1928; "The Constitution's Parent-Teacher Page," *Atlanta Constitution*, 14 April 1929; "Parent Education Class Meets Friday," *Atlanta Constitution*, 7 January 1930.

20. "Plan Session on Parent Education," *Raleigh News and Observer*, 20 November 1927; "Looks to State Program for Parental Education," *Raleigh News and Observer*, 17 February 1928; "Makes Ready for New Institute Committee," *Raleigh News and Observer*, 24 February 1928; "State Association Sets Goal for Season's Work," *Raleigh News and Observer*, 19 October 1930.

21. "School Status and Objective Outlined by Mrs. Clifford Walker," *Atlanta Constitution*, 14 October 1928; Rury, *Creating the Suburban School Advantage*.

22. William A. Wilson Realty Company, Woodland Heights promotional booklet, 1910, box 2, folder 10, HS Collection.

23. "Home, Sweet Home," advertisement for Central Terrace, *Winston-Salem Journal*, 29 April 1917; "More Development on Southside," *Union Republican*, 11 July 1912; "To Establish a New Park," *Winston-Salem Journal*, 2 November 1912; advertisement for Ardmore, *Twin-City Daily Sentinel*, 29 March 1922.

24. Advertisement for "The Real Estate Columns" of the Sunpapers, *Baltimore Sun*, 3 November 1924.

25. Agran, *Herbert Hoover*, 146. According to Agran, Hoover's agenda reflected his two passions: "development of better homes" and "development of child welfare." For local examples, see "More Home Building," *Atlanta Constitution*, 4 September 1921; "Own-Your-Home Drive Is Showing Results," *Atlanta Constitution*, 19 March 1922; and "Raleigh's Great Expansion Began Less Than Ten Years Ago," *Raleigh News and Observer*, 26 October 1927.

26. Henry Holmes Company, OYOH advertisement, *National Real Estate Journal*, 27 February 1922; Henry Holmes Company, advertising materials, both in folder 6.1.4.2.1, RJ Papers.

27. During the red scare of 1919, it was less laughable to claim that homeownership would prevent the spread of communism, but the argument would not outlive the year; surely, it convinced few, if any, working people to buy a house. The following are all from the USHC Records: Bartholomew O'Toole to Woodrow Wilson, 12 December 1917, box 462, folder 4; Statement from Graham Taylor, "Noted Economist," on "Nation's Homes: Its Defense and Hope," circa 1917, box 462, folder 4; "The National 'Own Your Home' Movement: What It Is, Who Is Back of It, What It Means to You," no date, box 462, folder 5; Paul C. Murphy's office to Tom Ingersoll, 27 March 1919, box 462, folder 9; Tom Ingersoll to Paul C. Murphy's office, 1 April 1919, box 6, folder 11; US Department of Labor Information and Education Service, *Suggestions for Own-Your-Own-Home Campaigns* (Washington: Government Printing Office, 1919), box 6, folder 15; Southern Pine Service Association, "Build Your Home First," campaign pamphlet, 1919, box 6, folder 15; US Department of Labor Bureau of Industrial Housing and Transportation, memorandum, "What Inadequate Housing Means," no. 43, 10 June 1919, box 6, folder 11; OYOH advertisement, *Spokesman Review*,

16 March 1919, box 6, folder 5; "Own Your Home" Exposition advertisement, Philadelphia, no date, box 5, folder 7; Southern Pine Association, "Make Her Happier: Build a Home First," large advertising broadside, no date, box 464, folder 2; "Advertising Copy—Nos. 1–12," box 464, folder 3; *Build Now News*, April 1919, box 461, unprocessed.

28. Form letter from Paul Murphy's office to local women's clubs, 1919, box 464, folder 10; "Little Feet on the Stairway," Advertising Copy No. 6, circa 1919, box 464, folder 3; "A Letter to Little Boys and Girls—and Big Ones," Advertising Copy No. 3, circa 1919, box 464, folder 3; all in USHC Records. See also Luken and Vaughan, "Standardizing Child-Rearing," 271–76. Likewise, historian and policy analyst Eric Karolak argues that the USHC hoped to disseminate middle-class family values through the expansion of homeownership in suburban developments. Karolak, "'No Idea,'" 66–71.

29. "Value of Realty for Investment Shown by Adair," *Atlanta Constitution*, 13 January 1921; Blank, *Volume of Residential Construction*, 67; Gwendolyn Wright, *Building the Dream*, 150; Lands, *Culture of Property*, 113–14.

30. "Ask Reserve Bank to Aid Movement for Home-Owning," *Atlanta Constitution*, 15 January 1921; "Interest Grows in Home Show at Auditorium," *Atlanta Constitution*, 10 May 1922; Lands, *Culture of Property*, 125.

31. Birmingham's elaborate campaign was not surprising considering Hill Ferguson's leadership role in local residential park development and in the National Association of Real Estate Board's original "Own Your Home" campaign. See chapters 11 and 12 in this book. "The 'Own Your Home' Bulletin," no. 1, March 1918, box 295, folder 3; US Department of Labor Information and Education Service to H. K. Milner, 8 April 1919, box 463, folder 40; Department of Labor Information and Education Service to Hill Ferguson, 25 April 1919, box 463, folder 40; Hill Ferguson to John L. Weaver, 27 October 1917, box 462, folder 4, all in USHC Records.

32. "125,000 Expected to View Exhibit at Auditorium," *Birmingham Age-Herald*, 23 March 1925; "Home Exposition Opens in Gigantic Peach Bower," *Birmingham Age-Herald*, 24 March 1925; "Home Exposition Ends Sat: Special Plans Made for Children in Final Day," *Birmingham Age-Herald*, 28 March 1925.

33. Gries and Taylor, *How to Own*, v, 1, 9–11.

34. Agran, *Herbert Hoover*, 96.

35. Ford and Taylor, "Planning and Equipping," 194–98, 200; "George B. Ford Dies; Noted Architect," *New York Times*, 15 August 1930.

36. Hutchison, "Shaping Housing," 83–90; Hutchison, "Building for Babbitt," 184–87, 191; Agran, *Herbert Hoover*, 97; Calvin Coolidge to C. B. Crane, 5 July 1924, Caroline Bartlett Crane Collection, 1843–1935, A-92, Western Michigan Archives and Regional History Digital Collections, accessed 3 January 2024, https://cdm16259.contentdm.oclc.org/digital/collection/p4022coll10.

37. Crane, *Everyman's House*, 1, 44, 125, 129, 164–65; "Caroline Bartlett Crane Biography," Caroline Bartlett Crane Collection, 1843–1935, A-92, Western Michigan Archives and Regional History Digital Collections.

38. Hutchison, "Building for Babbitt," 194; Storrow, "Better Homes."

39. Shivery, "History," 256, 270–74.

40. Mrs. Lela. C. Lorenz to Mrs. John Hope, 27 May 1925, box 2, folder 45, NU Collection; "'Better Homes' Week Plans Taking on Definite Shape," *Atlanta Constitution*,

27 April 1924; "More Than 18,000 at 'Better Homes' Here Last Week," *Atlanta Constitution*, 20 May 1924; Shivery, "History," 256, 270–74; Minutes of the Atlanta Board of Education, 28 January 1926.

41. "'Better Homes' Week Plans Taking on Definite Shape," *Atlanta Constitution*, 27 April 1924. For another example of a southern demonstration house built in a racially restricted residential park, see "'Model Home' Is Opened with Tea," *Raleigh News and Observer*, 25 May 1926; Mrs. J. Henry Highsmith, "Women Attend Club Biennial," *Raleigh News and Observer*, 30 May 1926; advertisement for "Better Homes Week," *Raleigh News and Observer*, 23 November 1923. Although committees routinely claimed to be building affordable houses for families of modest means, the final cost almost always greatly exceeded the average home price at the time.

42. "Immense Throng Attends Cornerstone Ceremonies of First 'Better Home,'" *Atlanta Constitution*, 22 March 1926; "Samuel Inman PTA to Meet," *Atlanta Constitution*, 2 November 1924; "No. 1 Bungalow Located in Boulevard Park," *Atlanta Constitution*, 7 March 1926; "Local Civic Leaguers Sponsor Better Homes," *Atlanta Constitution*, 21 March 1926; Architects' Small House Service Bureau, *100 Bungalows*, 18.

43. Fass, *End of American Childhood*, 101, 111.

44. WHCCHP, *Parent Education*, 31–35, 303. For local examples, see Dr. Albert Loyal Crane, "Know Your Own Child," *Houston Post*, 25 November 1924; and "Radio Station to Have Full Week," *Raleigh News and Observer*, 12 February 1928.

45. WHCCHP, *Parent Education*, xi–xii, 302; table of contents, *Parents' Magazine*, October 1932, 4. *Parents' Magazine* first appeared in 1926 as *Children: The Magazine for Parents*. I refer to it by its more familiar name throughout the text.

46. Herbert Hoover, "America's Greatest Asset," *Children: The Magazine for Parents*, May 1927, 7; Jane Addams, "Your Child and Your Community," *Children: The Magazine for Parents*, March 1927, 7–8; George Hecht, "A Magazine for Parents," *Children: The Magazine for Parents*, October 1926, 4; WHCCHP, *Parent Education*, 3.

47. Ernest Groves, "Inside Tips for Fathers," *Children: The Magazine for Parents*, October 1926, 12–14; J. George Frederick, "Can a Tired Businessman Be a Good Father?," *Children: The Magazine for Parents*, April 1927, 15–16. For local examples see "Samuel Inman PTA to Meet," *Atlanta Constitution*, 2 November 1924; and "Institute Parental Education Will Meet in Raleigh Tuesday," *Raleigh News and Observer*, 12 February 1928.

48. Schlossman, "Perils of Popularization," 66.

49. Emma Kidd Hulburt, "Every Child Needs a Playroom," *Children: The Magazine for Parents*, November 1928, 24, 46; Helen Sprackling, "A Family Playroom," *Parents' Magazine*, October 1932, 22, 50–51.

50. WHCCHP, *Parent Education*, 302; Cross, *Kids' Stuff*, 54, 60–61, 71.

51. Charlotte Garrison, "What Toys for Your Children?," *Children: The Magazine for Parents*, November 1927, 21, 60–62; Minnetta Sammis Leonard, "Choose the Toy to Fit the Child," *Children: The Magazine for Parents*, November 1928, 18, 64–65.

52. Advertisement for StromBecKer Educational PlayThings, *Children: The Magazine for Parents*, January 1927, 61.

53. WHCCHP, *Parent Education*, 29, 239–40; Jacobson, *Raising Consumers*, 9–11. Examples include "Your Children Need Music," advertisement, *Winston-Salem Journal*, 12 November 1922; "A Mother's Duty," BH 1007, and "The Simple Charm of Childhood," BH 1006, Palmolive soap advertisements, Ad*Access Collection, Duke University Libraries Digital Repository, https://repository.duke.edu/dc/adaccess/BH1007 and https://

repository.duke.edu/dc/adaccess/BH1006; "The Food He Eats Is the Man He'll Be!," General Electric refrigerator advertisement, *Collier's Magazine*, 1929, accessed 29 June 2024, www.ebluejay.com/ads/item/6844402.

54. Selig, *Americans All*, 2–7, 44; Lasker, *Race Attitudes*, 10, 11, 108, 202, 286–87, 303, 308, 325, 331; "Seminar: Auspices Atlanta Committee of Women's Interracial Activities," circa 1931 (no date on original document), box 10, folder 20, NU Collection.

55. Lasker, *Race Attitudes in Children*, 122, 125.

56. Bruno Lasker, "How Children Acquire Race Prejudices," *Children: The Magazine for Parents*, March 1928, 23–24, 42; Helen L. Kaufman, "Should We Hand-Pick Our Children's Friends?," *Children: The Magazine for Parents*, August 1929, 17.

57. Selig, *Americans All*, 49, 51.

58. At that time, *Parents' Magazine* failed to capitalize the word "Negro" consistently, unlike all Black newspapers and the more liberal white ones.

59. Elizabeth McFadden, "Dey's All Got Debbils!," *Parents' Magazine*, October 1929, 22–23, 65–66.

60. McFadden, "Dey's All Got Debbils!" Emphasis in the original.

61. Ruth Sapin, "For Better or Worse—Servants Influence Children," *Children: The Magazine for Parents*, January 1929, 20–21, 42. According to Catharine Beecher, it was "to be regretted" when mothers relinquished influence "to domestics and playmates," who too frequently had a "pernicious" impact on children. Beecher, *Treatise on Domestic Economy*, 227–30.

62. Selig, *Americans All*, 44, 50; Lasker, *Race Attitudes in Children*. Lasker was especially cognizant of discrimination against Jewish immigrants because he was one; Gruenberg, too, was Jewish.

63. "Americans in the Making," *Children: The Magazine for Parents*, July 1927, 26–27.

64. Wilma King, *African American Childhoods*; Bernstein, *Racial Innocence*.

65. Wilma King, *African American Childhoods*, 123, 130.

66. Fleishman's Yeast trading card, 1 January 1899, Warshaw Collection of Business Americana, # 60, Yeast, box 1, folder 8, Archives Center, National Museum of American History, Smithsonian Institution, Washington, DC. See also Hale, *Making Whiteness*; and Scanlon, *Inarticulate Longings*.

67. "Little People of the Month," *Brownies' Book*, March 1920, 92; M. G. Allison, "Brownie Graduates," *Brownies' Book*, July 1920, 206–7. For an example of heroism within a mixed-race context, see "Little People of the Month," *Brownies' Book*, June 1920, 174. See also Brown, *New Brownies' Book*.

68. "Grown-Ups' Corner," *Brownies' Book*, January 1921, 25; Shivery, "History," 345; Wilkins, "Writing for Social Change," 26; Simmons, *Crescent City Girls*, 4–5, 9.

69. "Brownies' Book Special Offer," *Brownies' Book*, November 1921, 329.

70. "Grown-Ups' Corner," *Brownies' Book*, April 1921, 126.

71. Robert E. Simon, "Do You Know Your Child's Teacher?," *Children: The Magazine for Parents*, October 1926, 15–16.

72. Cahn, *Sexual Reckonings*, 76–78; Higginbotham, *Righteous Discontent*, 195–96; Selig, *Americans All*, 213–14.

73. Bruno Lasker, "Race Attitudes in Children: Every Day Older People Sow in Young Minds the Seeds for a Large Crop of Prejudices," *Woman's Press*, May 1926, 333.

74. Napheys, *Physical Life of Woman*, 88–89.

75. The South's interracial movement, which embraced the cultural gifts movement,

also failed to challenge segregation. For a critique, see "Future Program," undated, box 12, folder 19, NU Collection. For the impact of scientific racism on child study, see Bederman, *Manliness and Civilization*, 106; and Hilger, *Parent Trap*, 27. See also Selig, *Cultural Gifts*, 83, 212. The nation's first educational psychologist, G. Stanley Hall, had argued that *only* white adolescence should be lengthened since children of color would not be able to benefit from any additional advantages because of racial impediments. The child study movement had already rejected Hall's racist claims by the 1920s. Some evidence suggests that the parent education movement still influenced the eugenics movement, which located its efforts in suburban residential parks as the ideal place to raise a child. American Eugenics Society, *Report of the President of the American Eugenics Society*; Lovett, "Eugenic Housing."

76. Lasker, "Race Attitudes in Children," 332–33.

77. Gillis, "Islanding of Children," 321; Ladd-Taylor, *Mother-Work*, 54–55, 63–65; Coontz, *Social Origins*, 360. For a local example of this shift, see "Houston Heights Child Conservation League," *Houston Post*, 12 June 1921.

78. "Why Children Go Wrong," *Children: The Magazine for Parents*, June 1927, 19–20; "Back to the Home," *Raleigh News and Observer*, 27 November 1925; "Noted Speakers to Appear Here: Much Juvenile Crime Due to Parents," *Raleigh News and Observer*, 6 February 1928. For an earlier example, see Gotham, *Race, Real Estate*, 37.

79. WHCCHP, *Parent Education*, 29.

Chapter 10

1. Headley, "Citizen Rights and Community Rights," 12.

2. "Civitans Hear Zoning Expert," *Raleigh News and Observer*, 19 July 1922; "Need of Zoning System Shown," *Atlanta Constitution*, 16 February 1922; "Zone Scheme Faces Fight, Says Planners," *Houston Chronicle*, 13 December 1929.

3. Detroit Property Holders' Protective Association, anti-zoning pamphlet, undated, box 11, folder "Zoning—Opposition—Propaganda," RW Papers.

4. Brooks, "The Office File Box," 7; Metzenbaum, *Law of Zoning*, 125–26. See also Bassett, "Progressive South," 175–76.

5. Nichols, "Restrictions for the Small House Builder," 212–13; Elizabeth Cleveland, "'If Parents Only Knew___,'" *Children: The Parents' Magazine*, March 1928, 13; full-page advertisement for Palos Verdes Estates, *Los Angeles Sunday Times*, 3 February 1924.

6. J. C. Nichols, "Restrictions and Homes Associations," manuscript prepared for publication in the *National Real Estate Journal*, February 1939, p. 1, J.C. Nichols Company Records (K0106), Kansas City Manuscript Collections, State Historical Society of Missouri, accessed 15 May 2024, https://files.shsmo.org/manuscripts/kansas-city/nichols/JCN055.pdf.

7. Veiller, "Districting by Municipal Regulation," 151.

8. As quoted in Fogelson, *Bourgeois Nightmares*, 114–15; Riddle, "'Homes to Last,'" 21.

9. Riddle, "'Homes to Last,'" 25; Cook and Kaplan, "Civic Elites"; Riddle, *River Oaks*.

10. "A Real Homeplace for the Family of Modest Income," River Oaks advertisement, circa 1929, box 4, folder 19, HS Collection.

11. Olmsted Associates to Joel Hurt, 4 April 1902, Olmsted Associates Records, Series B—Job File #00071, Library of Congress Manuscript Division, compiled in "Druid Hills Olmsted

Documentary Record: Selected Texts," ed. Charles E. Beveridge, 135, https://druidhills.wordpress.com/wp-content/uploads/2011/07/letters-project-complete-text.pdf.

12. Shurtleff, "A.C.P.I. Notes," 133. For a local example, see "City Plan Board to Assert Power," *Atlanta Constitution*, 10 May 1922. See also, Freund, *Colored Property*, 65.

13. "Zoning Ordinance of the City of Raleigh," 20 April 1923, Vertical File NAC 1620 Raleigh, Frances Loeb Library, Harvard Graduate School of Design, Cambridge, MA. See also Steinberg, *Down to Earth*, 158–59.

14. Cheney, "Zoning in Practice," 171.

15. Hancock, "Planners," 297. According to Hancock, only 20 percent of the "thousand city planning, zoning, and housing reports" written during the 1920s "were actually followed through to any degree."

16. Detroit Property Holders' Protective Association, anti-zoning pamphlet, undated, box 11, folder "Zoning—Opposition—Propaganda," RW Papers; Headley, "Citizen Rights," 12; "Civitans Hear Zoning Expert," *Raleigh News and Observer*, 19 July 1922.

17. Metzenbaum, *Law of Zoning*, 114–15. See also Weiss, *Rise of the Community Builders*.

18. Whitten, "Five Illustrations," 3. For a description of the larger "intensive educational campaign" to "overcome" the "initial indifference or opposition," see "Atlanta Adopts Zoning," *Atlanta Constitution*, 23 June 1922.

19. Veiller, "Districting by Municipal Regulation," 151; Hooker, "Remarks at the Closing Dinner," 269; Eliot, "Letter," 33–34.

20. Kantor, "Benjamin C. Marsh," 50; Gwendolyn Wright, *Building the Dream*, 131.

21. George B. Ford, "Practical Planning," 79; "George B. Ford Dies; Noted Architect," *New York Times*, 15 August 1930.

22. American City Bureau, "City Planning Exhibition" booklet (1914), 12, 15, box 462, folder 21, USHC Records.

23. Freund, *Colored Property*, 52; Kantor, "Benjamin C. Marsh," 427; Weiss, *Rise of the Community Builders*, 186n41, 186n42.

24. Advisory Committee on Zoning, *Zoning Primer*; Advisory Committee on Zoning, *City Planning Primer*.

25. Advisory Committee on Zoning, *City Planning Primer*, 7–8.

26. Ihlder, "Housing and the Regional Plan," 11.

27. Charles H. Cheney, "Removing Social Barriers by Zoning," *The Survey*, 22 May 1920, 277–78. "Infestation" is Andrew Wright Crawford's word, but it was commonly used in the planning movement. Crawford, "What Zoning Is," 7; Crawford, discussion of H. M. Brinckerhoff's "Effect of Transportation," 67.

28. Advisory Committee on Zoning, *Zoning Primer*, 1.

29. "Second Ward League of Women Voters Hold Meeting," *Atlanta Journal*, 9 March 1923; "Mrs. M. C. Hardin Grateful for Planning Board Post," *Atlanta Journal*, 26 January 1923; "Mrs. M. C. Hardin, Prominent Atlanta Club Woman," *Atlanta Journal*, 28 January 1923; "Plan for Homes Week Celebration Here Are Pushed," *Atlanta Journal*, 27 May 1923; "Forestry Committee Chairman," *Atlanta Constitution*, 20 January 1924. The *Journal* claimed Hardin was the first woman to serve on a planning commission in the United States, although that assertion is difficult to substantiate.

30. Marsh and Ford, *Introduction to City Planning*, 1; Grinnalds, "Zoning Situation in Baltimore," 184–85. For another example, see Whitten, "Problems Involved," 39–40.

31. Smith v. City of Atlanta, 161 Ga. 769 (1926); "City Law against Building Stores in

Home Sections Invalid, High Court Rules," *Atlanta Journal*, 11 February 1926; "City Expected to Make Fight for Zone Law," *Atlanta Constitution*, 12 February 1926; "Atlanta Zoning Law Is Carried on Appeal to U.S. High Court," *Atlanta Journal*, 9 April 1926; "Atlanta Is Denied Zoning Act Review by Supreme Court," *Atlanta Journal*, 3 May 1926. During the appeals process, Corrine Smith was able to convince the planning commission to make the change, but council held steadfast in the face of strong opposition from Eighth Ward constituents. ACC Minutes, 20 August 1923 and 7 January 1924, vol. 28, "1923 January 2–1924 July," row 5, section B, shelf 1; "Committee Rejects Change in Zoning Law," *Atlanta Journal*, 22 December 1923; "Zoning Injunctions Asked," *Atlanta Journal*, 24 May 1924; "Injunction Hits Validity of Zone Ordinance," *Atlanta Constitution*, 28 January 1925; "City Zoning Law Upheld by Court," *Atlanta Constitution*, 12 March 1925. A similar case involving property on the opposite side of Piedmont Park ended differently because the owner was a powerful coal company rather than a female property owner. Plus, the original zone law had designated the property in question for industrial use. Thus, despite vociferous opposition, the residents of North Boulevard Park lost their appeal to prevent a coal yard—which was a far greater nuisance than a store—from being placed near the edge of their residential park. The lack of consistency in the petition process frustrated a growing number of residents, who increasingly moved to North Fulton County where a stricter zoning ordinance would better protect the area's many residential parks. ACC Minutes, 19 May 1924, vol. 28, "1923 January 2–1924 July," row 5, section B, shelf 1; "Board Refuses Piedmont Park Zoning Change," *Atlanta Constitution*, 22 April 1924; "Citizens Request Council to Halt Coal Yard Plans," *Atlanta Constitution*, 1 May 1924; "Women to Push Coal Yard Fight," *Atlanta Constitution*, 7 May 1924; "Clashes Looming on Zone Changes," *Atlanta Constitution*, 18 May 1924; "Fulton Zoning Act Passes Senate by Unanimous Vote," *Atlanta Journal*, 12 August 1925; Consultant Service of the National Municipal League, *Governments of Atlanta and Fulton County*, 347.

32. "Atlanta's Zoning Law, Its Great Worth to the People," *Atlanta Journal*, 18 April 1924; "The Worth of City Zoning," *Atlanta Journal*, 7 December 1925; "The Fame of City Zoning," *Atlanta Journal*, 30 April 1924.

33. "Engineer Urges Ratification of Zone Amendment," *Atlanta Journal*, 31 October 1928. Because the Georgia Supreme Court ruled that the Atlanta zoning ordinance violated the state constitution as well as the US Constitution, local officials still needed a state amendment even after the US Supreme Court declared residential zoning constitutional in *Euclid*.

34. Purdy, discussion of Whitten's "Zoning of Residence Sections," 41–42.

35. Kenneth Jackson, *Crabgrass Frontier*, 162–63; Fritz Blocki, "The Most Dangerous Job in the World," *Independent*, 30 May 1925, 605–6; Zelizer, *Pricing the Priceless Child*, 35.

36. Patri, "Death Toll," 31. See also Wallace, *Promise of Progressivism*.

37. Harmon, "Playgrounds in New Land Subdivisions," 85; Nichols, "Financial Effect," 95.

38. Illinois Chapter of the American Institute of Architects, "Need for Zoning," 21; Charles H. Cheney, "Removing Social Barriers by Zoning," *The Survey*, 22 May 1920, 278.

39. Stearns, *Anxious Parents*, 46; Swan, "Legality of Zoning," 29; Nichols, "Financial Effect," 102–3.

40. Brett v. Building Commission of Brookline, 250 Mass 73; 145 N.E. 269 (1924).

41. Miller v. Board of Public Works of Los Angeles, 195 Cal 477; 234 Pac. Rep 381 (1925).

42. Miller v. Board of Public Works of Los Angeles, 195 Cal 477; 234 Pac. Rep 381 (1925).
43. Pritz v. Messer, 112 Ohio St. 628; 148 N. E. 30 (1925).
44. Power, "Advocates at Cross Purposes," 82–83.
45. Euclid v. Ambler Co., 272 U.S. 365; 47 S. Ct. 114 (1926).
46. Metzenbaum, *Law of Zoning*, 125–26.
47. Marsh, *Introduction to City Planning*; Adams, "British Point of View," 29; Unwin, discussion of Veiller's "Buildings," 97–98; Unwin, "Remarks at the Dinner," 280; Hewitt, "Canada and the US," 181; Adams, "State, City, and Town Planning," 135; John Ihlder to Thomas Shallcross Jr., 3 March 1919, box 295, folder 5, USHC Records. See also Fairbanks, "From Better Dwellings," 34–39; Garner, "Garden City," 45, 48, 52; Radford, "Federal Government and Housing," 117.
48. "Stenographic Report of the Third Annual Conference of Developers of High-Class Residential Property," 1919, 233, Jemison Companies, Miscellany, #2838, Division of Rare and Manuscript Collections, Cornell University Library.
49. Marsh, *Introduction to City Planning*, 2; Kantor, "Benjamin C. Marsh," 424. See also American City Bureau, "City Planning Exhibition" booklet, 1914, 21–22, box 462, folder 21, USHC Records.
50. Veiller, "Buildings in Relation," 87–89.
51. Nichols, "Housing," 132–39.
52. Charles H. Cheney, "Removing Social Barriers by Zoning," *The Survey*, 22 May 1920, 275–78; Cheney, "Zoning in Practice," 32–33.
53. Hancock, "Planners," 298; Hurley, *Environmental Inequalities*.
54. Dougherty, "Shopping for Schools"; Rury and Rife, "Race, Schools and Opportunity Hoarding"; Rury, *Creating the Suburban*; Reeves, *Dream Hoarders*, 102–6.
55. Fogelson, *Bourgeois Nightmares*, 77.
56. Corrigan et al. v. Buckley, 271 U.S. 323 (1926); Bruce, "Racial Zoning," 709–10, 715; Monchow, *Use of Deed Restrictions*, 47–48; Kahen, "Validity of Anti-Negro Restrictive Covenants," 203–4; William Henry Jones, *Housing of Negroes*, 72, 78. See also Gonda, *Unjust Deeds*; and Brooks and Rose, *Saving the Neighborhood*, 3.

Chapter 11

1. Bowen v. City of Atlanta, 159 Ga. 145 (1924); Smith v. City of Atlanta, 161 Ga. 769 (1926). For a description of the Bowen case, see chapter 7. For a description of the Smith case, see chapter 10.
2. Because the Georgia Supreme Court had also declared Atlanta's zoning ordinance in violation of the state constitution, local officials needed an amendment expressly granting the power to zone cities with populations greater than 25,000. After the amendment was added in 1928, city council immediately passed a new zoning ordinance based on the original 1922 law but without race districts so as not to jeopardize the entire ordinance once again. Nevertheless, less than six months later, city council began passing old-school segregation laws, which were all declared unconstitutional. While the most enthusiastic supporters of the new zoning ordinance were affluent residents living in racially restricted neighborhoods, the advocates of the refurbished segregation ordinances lived in Fourth Ward, as had been true of the original 1913 segregation law. "City Law Against Building Stores in Home Sections Invalid, High Court Rules," *Atlanta Journal*, 11 February 1926;

"City Expected to Make Fight for Zone Law," *Atlanta Constitution*, 12 February 1926; "Atlanta Zoning Law Is Carried on Appeal to U.S. High Court," *Atlanta Journal*, 9 April 1926; "Atlanta Is Denied Zoning Act Review by Supreme Court," *Atlanta Journal*, 3 May 1926; "To Renew Effort to Enact Zoning Law for Atlanta," *Atlanta Constitution*, 23 November 1926; "Zone Act Clause Again Held Void by State Court," *Atlanta Journal*, 15 November 1927; "Ansley Parkers Go to Court to Protect Zoning," *Atlanta Journal*, 15 November 1928; "Zone Regulations Voted Tentative Council Approval," *Atlanta Journal*, 20 November 1928; "Zoning Ordinance Goes into Effect," *Atlanta Constitution*, 22 December 1928; "Segregation Law Passed in Council," *Atlanta Constitution*, 21 May 1929; Flint, "Zoning and Residential Segregation," 341.

3. Hott, "Constitutionality," 338, 347–48.

4. Ambler Realty Co. v. Village of Euclid, 297 F. 307 (1924).

5. Corrigan et al. v. Buckley, 271 U.S. 323 (1926); Bruce, "Racial Zoning," 709–10, 715; Monchow, *Use of Deed Restrictions*, 47–48; Kahen, "Validity of Anti-Negro Restrictive Covenants," 203, 204. See also William Henry Jones, *Housing of Negroes*, 72, 78; Brooks and Rose, *Saving the Neighborhood*, 3; Gonda, *Unjust Deeds*.

6. "Citizens Organize to Segregate Colored People in Baltimore," *Dallas Express*, 20 December 1919; Brooks and Rose, *Saving the Neighborhood*, 12; William Henry Jones, *Housing of Negroes*, 67; Monchow, *Use of Deed Restrictions*, 51; "Zone Ordinance to Boost Prices," *Birmingham News*, 1 August 1926.

7. Liberty Annex Corporation v. City of Dallas, et al., 289 S. W. (Tex. Civ. App. 1927).

8. For an examination of residential segregation and schooling in New Orleans, see Stern, *Race and Education*.

9. Omer S. Whiteman, letter to the editor, *Indianapolis News*, 27 November 1926; "Confirm Faith in Cause of Negro," *Indianapolis Star*, 23 June 1927; "Segregation Act Again Held Void," *Indianapolis Star*, 15 March 1927.

10. Harmon v. Tyler, 273 U.S. 668 (1927); Martin, "Segregation," 728–30.

11. Martin, "Segregation," 725–27. For a similar argument, see Knight, *Negro Housing*, 137.

12. Williams, "Legal Notes," 1927, 221; Bassett, "Zoning Roundtable," 1929, 194–95; Williams, "Legal Notes," 1930, 55–57.

13. Marcia Mead and George B. Ford, "As a Child Thinketh," *McCall's Magazine*, March 1927, Vertical file NAC 3570, France Loeb Library, Harvard Graduate School of Design, Cambridge, MA. For a local example, see "Realtors Issue 'Code of Ethics' on Construction," *Birmingham Age-Herald*, 15 March 1925; J. C. Hall, "Selecting the Site and Planning Your Home," in *Book of Homes* (*Birmingham News* Building and Home Service Department, 1928), folder 6.1.27.29; promotional brochure for Birmingham, Birmingham Chamber of Commerce, 1928, p. 5, folder 6.1.27.29, RJ Papers. Hall represented the subdivision department for Robert Jemison's real estate empire.

14. As quoted in Fogelson, *Bourgeois Nightmares*, 114–15; W. C. Hogg to J. C. Nichols, 5 February 1925, box 2J299, "City Planning #1, (1924–1926)," WH Papers; "Plan Estates Improvements," *Houston Post*, 10 August 1924; Society Page, *Houston Post*, 17 August 1924; "Country Club Estates Will Be Beautiful," *Houston Post*, 14 November 1924. The original name for the development was Country Club Estates. S. Herbert Hare had studied landscape architecture with Frederick Law Olmsted at Harvard University before joining his father's firm.

15. Spann v. City of Dallas, 111 Tex. 350, 212 S.W. 513 (Tex. 1921). See also Bassett, "Zoning Roundtable," 308; Kimball, "Brief Survey of City Planning Reports," 114; American Civic Association, "City Planning Progress in Dallas, Texas," *Civic Comment*, bulletin no. 5, 20 September 1920, 8, folder 6.1.11.20, RJ Papers. For an in-depth analysis of Dallas, see Fairbanks, *For the City*.

16. "City Planning Bills Get OK by Committee," *Houston Chronicle*, 2 February 1927; W. C. Hogg to Alex Weisberg of Dallas, 10 December 1926 and 16 January 1927; John Surratt of the Kessler Plan Association in Dallas to W. C. Hogg, 15 January and 25 February 1927; W. C. Hogg to John H. Kirby, member of Texas House of Representatives, 16 January 1927; John J. Simmons of the Dallas City Plan Commission, W. T Caswell of the Austin City Plan Commission, and John Surratt to W. C. Hogg, 3 February 1927; John Surratt, "Zoning Law Work Declared to Reside with City Plan Engineer and Commission," newspaper clipping, all in box 2J299, "City Planning #II (1927)," WH Papers. The Texas planners were clearly aware of events in Atlanta. "Texas, a State of 6,000,000 Souls: Enabling Acts Pending before Legislature Are Vital to the Growth of Beautiful Cities," *Austin American Statesman*, 20 February 1927; Burton Davis, "Cities of Texas Can Learn Lesson from Example of Atlanta," *Galveston Daily News*, 4 March 1923. Burton Davis was one of the correspondents assigned to Houston. In addition, members of the various Texas planning commissions attended the National Conference on City Planning each year.

17. Liberty Annex Corporation v. City of Dallas, et al., 289 S. W. (Tex. Civ. App. 1927); Kennedy England, field secretary of the Kessler Plan Association, to Miss Ethel Brosius, c/o Hogg Brothers; copy of the enabling legislation passed by the state on 16 April 1928, both in box 2J299, "City Planning #IV (1928-March thru June)," WH Papers.

18. "Zoning Ordinance Urged by Potter," *Houston Post-Dispatch*, 5 January 1927; "City Planner Group Will Be Reorganized," *Houston Chronicle*, 9 February 1927; "Memorial Park Is Abandoned as Site for City Airport," *Houston Chronicle*, 16 June 1927; W. C. Hogg to Mayor Oscar Holcombe, 22 June 1926; P. B. Timpson to W. C. Hogg, 2 November 1926; P. B. Timpson to W. C. Hogg, 21 October 1926, all in box 2J299, "City Planning #I (1924–1926)," WH Papers.

19. S. Herbert Hare to W. C. Hogg, 18 August 1927; W. C. Hogg to Mayor Oscar Holcombe, 16 April 1927; W. C. Hogg to John Staub, 8 July 1927; "City Planning Commission Is Created," *Houston Chronicle*, 29 June 1927, clipping with notes, all in box 2J299, "City Planning #II and #III (1927)," WH Papers.

20. "New City Plan Outline Given by Monteith," *Houston Chronicle*, 31 October 1929; "Country Club Estates," *Houston Post*, 7 December 1924; W. C. Hogg to Mayor Oscar Holcombe, 2 May, 25 July, and 17 November 1927; Mayor Oscar Holcombe to W. C. Hogg, 27 July and 16 November 1927, all in box 2J299, "City Planning #II (1927)," WH Papers. See also Monteith campaign flyer to "women voters," 10 January 1931; and campaign letter to Julia Ideson, 9 January 1931, both in box 1, folder 2, Political Campaigns Collection, MSS 115, Houston History Research Center, Houston Public Library. Monteith was one of the original directors of River Oaks as well as a director for the River Oaks Country Club.

21. "Potter Named on Commission," *Houston Press*, 21 May 1929; Cheryl Ferguson, *Highland Park*, 178–79, 201.

22. Wintz, "Emergence," 104–7; Malone, "Autonomy and Accommodation," 101; Passey, "Freedmantown"; "City Will Sue for Property," *Houston Press*, 22 May 1930, vol. 9, RO Scrapbook.

23. L. B. Ryon to W. C. Hogg, 30 June 1927, and L. B. Ryon to W. C. Hogg, 8 December 1927, both in box 2J299, "City Planning #II (1927)," WH Papers.

24. Kirkland, *Hogg Family and Houston*, 64–65; blank form, Survey of Negro Housing in Houston; Minutes of the Inter-Racial Committee, 10 November 1927; L. B. Ryon to W. C. Hogg, 26 April 1928; H. E. Brigham, secretary to W. C. Hogg, to S. W. Johnson, executive secretary of the Committee on Interracial Cooperation, 14 July 1927; handwritten note, H. E. Brigham to W. C. Hogg, 13 July 1927; blueprint of Race Distribution Map from 1924, all in box 2J339, "Inter-Racial Committee, April 4, 1927—November 10, 1927," WH Papers.

25. C. H. McGruder to W. C. Hogg, 6 January 1928; H. E. Brigham to C. H. McGruder, 3 February 1928; J. M. Burr to W. C. Hogg, 11 January 1928; H. E. Brigham to J. M. Burr, 3 February 1928, all in box 2J339, "Inter-Racial Committee, April 4, 1927–November 10, 1927," WH Papers. Hogg was unable to use eminent domain to fulfill his plans, and he ignored future requests to help fund Black residential park development, although he passed away in 1930. Minutes from the Committee on Interracial Cooperation, 5 July 1927; J. B. Grigsby to W. C. Hogg, 27 September 1929; handwritten note from H. E. Brigham, all in box 2J341, "Sundry, February 21, 1914–November 1, 1929," WH Papers. See also a similar letter from S. W. Johnson to W. C. Hogg, 26 September 1929, and handwritten notes exchanged between W. C. Hogg and H. E. Brigham, all in box 2J341, "Sundry, February 21, 1914–November 1, 1929," WH Papers.

26. "Cimbee's Ramblings," *Houston Informer*, 3 December 1927. See also Steptoe, *Houston Bound*, 46–47; Pruitt, *Other Great Migration*, 192–93.

27. Minutes from Committee on Interracial Cooperation, 10 November 1927; L. B. Ryon to W. C. Hogg, 26 April 1928, both in box 2J341, "Sundry, February 21, 1914–November 1, 1929," WH Papers. See also "The Survey Fund Is Complete," *Houston Informer*, 30 August 1930; and Henderson, "City Planning in Houston," 122–23.

28. Harmon v. Tyler, 273 U.S. 668 (1927). This court case was decided on 14 March 1927. D. M. Picton to W. C. Hogg, 2 July 1927, box 2J299, "City Planning #III (1927—July thru December)," WH Papers. This note was written in response to a letter Hogg sent to the mayor and copied to Picton: W. C. Hogg to Mayor Oscar Holcombe, 28 June 1927, box 2J299, "City Planning, 1924–1927," WH Papers.

29. O. H. Koch, *A City Plan for Austin, Texas* (Austin: City Plan Commission, 1928), 71–72, Austin History Center Archives, Austin Public Library. For an in-depth analysis of Austin, see Tretter, *Shadows*.

30. Hogg's letter was written only ten days after he learned of Austin's city plan. Walter Long to W. C. Hogg, 15 May 1929, box 2J341, "Sundry, February 21, 1914–November 1, 1929"; W. C. Hogg to Herbert Hare, 25 May 1929, box 2J299, "City Planning #V (1928–October thru March, 1930)," both in WH Papers. Planner John Nolen used similar language in his plans for Roanoke, Virginia, and Kingport, Tennessee, in 1928. Hanchett, *Sorting Out*, 169.

31. Herbert Hare to W. C. Hogg, 28 May 1929, box 2J299, "City Planning #V (1928-October thru March, 1930)," WH Papers.

32. "Houston to Fete Nation's Leading City Planners," *Houston Post*, 30 March 1924; "School Bonds up April 5: $3,000,000 Issue to Be Voted On," *Houston Press*, 3 March 1924; "Now up to the People of Houston," *Houston Post*, 26 March 1924; Minutes of the Houston

Independent School District Board of Education, 12 May 1924, Hattie Mae White Educational Support Center, Houston Independent School District, Houston, Texas.

33. Houston City Planning Commission, *Report*, 25–26, 87; "School Board Visits Sites Offered for Negro High School," *Houston Chronicle*, 28 May 1925.

34. "Forward or Backward?," *Houston Informer*, 5 May 1923; H. F. Edwards to Secretary of the NAACP, 28 June 1919, frame 0793, "1919–1923"; J. M. Adkins to Mr. Bagwell, frame 0877, "1923," both in reel 19, group I, box G-203, Houston, Texas, Branch, *NAACP Branch Files*; "North Carolina One Exception," *Houston Informer*, 26 January 1924. Houston's Colored High School originally opened in 1893.

35. "Colored Citizen's Committee Favors $3,000,000 Bond Issue," *Houston Informer*, 5 May 1923. For evidence that the school board originally agreed with the recommendations of the Colored Citizens Committee before the planning commission became involved, see Mrs. O. C. Castle, "Preliminary Survey and Recommendations for Building Program," filed along with the minutes of the Houston Independent School District Board of Education, 11 November 1924, Hattie Mae White Educational Support Center, Houston Independent School District, Houston, Texas. In 1915, Houston's city council had voted to eliminate the use of wards as political designations because they no longer made sense for the purpose of representation. The bayous hedged in the First, Second, and Sixth Wards while the other wards were free to grow exponentially. After 1928, wards were also no longer used to describe the various sectors of the city, although the Third, Fourth, and Fifth Wards continued to be used to designate the three key areas of Black concentration. The planning commission recommended shrinking the number of Black residents living in Fourth Ward while encouraging Black development in Third and Fifth Wards.

36. Houston City Planning Commission, *Reports*, 25; Houston Independent School District, *Building Program*, 71, 77, 120.

37. Scott, *American City Planning*, 11–12; "Thousands for Park Acreage, But—," *Houston Informer*, 29 December 1923.

38. "Local Blacks Need More Parks!," *Houston Informer*, 10 August 1929; "More Negro Park Acreage Asked," *Houston Informer*, 26 October 1929.

39. Houston Independent School District, *Building Program*, 71, 77; *Red Book of Houston*, 69; Steptoe, *Houston Bound*, 28; Thelma Scott Bryant, interview by author, Houston, Texas, 25 July 2001. St. Nicholas Catholic Church was originally founded in 1887 at the corner of Chenevert and Lamar Streets (the current location of the George R. Brown Convention Center). The church was moved further east in 1924.

40. Houston Independent School District, *Annual Reports . . . 1921–1922, 1922–1923*, 165, 167; Mrs. O. C. Castle, "Preliminary Survey and Recommendations for Building Program," filed along with the minutes of the Houston Independent School District's Board of Education, 11 November 1924, Hattie Mae White Educational Support Center, Houston Independent School District, Houston, Texas. Like that of most schools in sparsely populated areas, the total enrollment of Bowie was still below 200 in 1923.

41. Advertisement for Forest Home, *Houston Informer*, 21 April 1923 and 14 July 1923; "High-Priced Colored Additions," *Houston Informer*, 10 November 1923. For the names of the planning commission members, see Houston City Planning Commission, *Report*.

42. Houston Independent School District, *Building Program*, 63–75; "School Board's Niggardly Policy!," *Houston Informer*, 4 July 1925; "Houston's Cute Little High School

Building!," *Houston Informer*, 12 September 1925; "Another Big City Bond Issue," *Houston Informer*, 29 March 1924.

43. "Street Graveling Program and Sectionalism," *Houston Informer*, 28 August 1926.

44. Houston Independent School District, *Building Program*, 66, 76–77, 106; Houston Independent School District, *Annual Report . . . 1919–1920*, 102, 108–9.

45. A. Fletcher to J. S. Cullinan, 30 October 1923, and J. W. Slaughter to J. S. Cullinan, 24 January 1925, box 22, folder 1, Joseph Stephen Cullinan Family Papers, MSS 69, Houston History Research Center, Houston Public Library. In 1913, William Hogg became a director for Cullinan's Texas Oil Company (Texaco). He was also an investor in Cullinan's Farmers Petroleum Company. John O. King, *Joseph Stephen Cullinan*, 97, 119, 190n, 193, 197.

46. "1000 Acre Home Section Planned," *Houston Post*, 1 June 1924; W. C. Hogg to E. E. Oberholtzer, 15 December 1925; W. C. Hogg to H. L. Mills, 17 December 1925; H. L. Mills to W. C. Hogg, 19 December 1925; Hugh Potter to H. L. Mills, 27 April 1926; W. C. Hogg, "School Sites," memo, 18 March 1926; W. C. Hogg, "Dickey School Site," memo, 11 January 1927, all in box 2J368, "Schools and School Sites, Houston, October 27, 1925—December 11, 1928," WH Papers; Houston Independent School District, *Building Program*, 88.

47. "A New Home * A New School * A New and Wholesome Environment for Your Children," advertisement, vol. 8, RO Scrapbook; "Now—A Modern Public School in River Oaks," newspaper clipping, vol. 8, RO Scrapbook.

48. "Houston Parents Locate Near Public Schools Prior to Term Opening This Fall: Many Build," *Houston Post*, 28 July 1929.

49. Hubbard, "Brief Survey"; L. B. Ryon to W. C. Hogg, 22 October 1928, box 2J299, "City Planning #V (1928-October thru March, 1930)," WH Papers. Ryon's letter included a copy of the petition. "Zoning Action Delay Slated," *Houston Post*, 11 October 1928; "City Zoning," *Houston Press*, 30 January 1928.

50. Herbert Hare to W. C. Hogg, 29 October 1928, box 2J299, "City Planning #V (1928-October thru March, 1930)," WH Papers; "Draft of Zone Law Attacked," *Houston Post*, 10 October 1928.

51. "Zone Scheme Faces Fight, Says Planners," *Houston Chronicle*, 13 December 1929; "Zoning Law as Proposed by City Planning Commission Outlines Houston Districts," *Houston Press*, 13 December, 1929; "City Planning Chairman Gets Many Protests," *Houston Press*, 17 December 1929; "Realty Group Names Heads for New Year," *Houston Post*, 18 December 1929; "Realtors Hear City Planners," *Houston Post*, 18 December 1929; "Real Estate Board Holds Roundtable on City Zone Plan," *Houston Chronicle*, 22 December 1929; "Parley Set to Discuss Zoning Plan," *Houston Press*, 3 January 1930. These articles were also clipped for the RO Scrapbooks.

52. "Center Site Change Seen," *Houston Press*, 13 July 1926, clipping in Hogg's files, including threatening note about Ryon needing to keep his name out of the papers "if he expects to continue"; Henry W. Stude to W. C. Hogg (warning that Hogg lacked public support), 15 July 1927, all in box 2J299, "City Planning #I and #III," WH Papers; "Hogg Resigns Planning Post," *Houston Post*, 1 December 1929; "Our City," *Houston Chronicle*, 27 March 1928; "City Planning Body to Have Open Sessions," *Houston Chronicle*, 1 December 1929.

53. Mefo, "Why," *Houston Press*, 10 January 1930; Hugh Potter to W. C. Hogg, 13 January and 2 March 1929, and L. B. Ryon to W. C. Hogg, 18 February 1929, all in box 2J299, "City

Planning #V (1928–October thru March, 1930)," WH Papers. Ryon included the following clipping: "Real Estate Men Would Zone City Before Expansion," *Houston Chronicle*, 27 January 1929.

54. "200 Storm Council Session; Demand Zone Plan Be Killed," *Houston Post*, 19 May 1938.

55. Cheryl Ferguson, *Highland Park*, 23, 55, 169; "School Taxes Cut Two Cents," *Houston Press*, 29 May 1935; "School Site Is 'Regretted,'" *Houston Post*, 9 January 1936; "Parents to Protest Lack of Streets to New Lamar School," *Houston Chronicle*, 15 August 1937; "West University Club Will Seek Speedway Opening," *Houston Post*, 17 August 1937.

56. "Improve These Streets," *Houston Post*, 15 August 1937; "West Enders Ask Opening of Streets," *Houston Chronicle*, 17 August 1937; "West University Club Will Seek Speedway Opening," *Houston Post*, 17 August 1937; "Parents to Protest Lack of Streets to New Lamar School," *Houston Chronicle*, 15 August 1937.

57. W. C. Hogg to John Kirby, 1 May 1924; W. C. Hogg to Chester Bryan, 15 May 1925; W. C. Hogg to E. C. Barkley, 15 December 1927; W. C. Hogg to George Howard, 3 July 1927; W. C. Hogg to Mayor Oscar Holcombe, 27 October 1927; "Buffalo Drive Beautification Association" to L. B. Ryon, 9 December 1927; Herbert Hare to Jacob F. Wolters, chair of Buffalo Drive Association, 9 December 1927; E. C. Barkley to W. C. Hogg, 12 December 1927; W. C. Hogg to members of the planning commission, confidential memo, 18 March 1928, all in box 2J299, "City Planning #I and #III," WH Papers. Hogg wanted Kirby to serve as a "boulevard-around-the-town." In his letters to the mayor, he claimed he began advocating for Kirby Drive before he began developing River Oaks, and, therefore, improvements to the street did not advantage his development. See also "Planner Asks Widening of Kirby Drive," *Houston Press*, 4 July 1927; "Tubercular Hospital Will Stay on Drive," *Houston Chronicle*, 14 March 1928. River Oaks Shopping Center advertisement, *Gargoyle*, 15 December 1929; "Improve These Streets," *Houston Post*, 15 August 1937; "West Enders Ask Opening of Streets," *Houston Chronicle*, 17 August 1937; "Condemnation of Land for Street to School Asked," *Houston Chronicle*, 16 September 1937.

58. "Hugh Potter Hotly Denies He Dominates City Planning Groups," *Houston Chronicle*, 8 October 1937; Kaplan, "Race, Income, and Ethnicity." For further evidence that the critics of "River Oaks High School" were correct, see "City, School PWA Plans Submitted," *Houston Press*, 18 June 1935; and "Speakers for School Bond Issue Named," *Houston Chronicle*, 25 October 1935.

59. Houston Independent School District, *Building Program*, 32. For references to the petition for a high school in East End, see "School Tax Rate Is Cut Two Cents," *Houston Chronicle*, 29 May 1935; and "School Taxes Cut Two Cents," *Houston Press*, 29 May 1935.

60. Houston Independent School District, *Building Program*, 32; "Austin School Causes 'Kicks,'" *Houston Press*, 31 July 1937; "Is Lamar or Austin the Prettier School?," *Houston Post*, 3 August 1937; "Mills Denies East Enders' Accusations," *Houston Chronicle*, 2 August 1937; "Mills Says Jealousy Inspired East End and Lamar School Flareup," *Houston Post*, 3 August 1937; "East Ender Plan Rally over School," *Houston Press*, 3 August 1937; "East Enders to Continue School Probe," *Houston Chronicle*, 7 August 1937. The articles covering the controversy were clipped for the RO Scrapbooks. See also "School Board Protests Cut in U.S. Funds," *Houston Chronicle*, 19 November 1935; and "School Board Building Program Is Speeded Up," *Houston Press*, 13 December 1935.

61. Mary L. Johnson, "Jack Yates High School," box 3, folder 19, General and Mary

Johnson Papers, MSS 119, Houston History Research Center, Houston Public Library; US Census Bureau, *Fourteenth Census . . . State Compendium, Texas*, 80; Houston City Planning Commission, "Midtown-Fourth Ward," 1–15; Cary D. Wintz, "Fourth Ward, Houston," *Handbook of Texas*, Texas State Historical Society, updated 22 October 2020, www.tshaonline.org/handbook/entries/fourth-ward-houston; Cheryl Ferguson, *Highland Park*, 199–201. See also Bullard, "Housing Barriers."

62. Liberty Annex Corporation v. City of Dallas, et al., 289 S. W. (Tex. Civ. App. 1927); "Zone Ordinance to Boost Prices," *Birmingham News*, 1 August 1926; "Seeking Expert," *Birmingham News*, 14 March 1925; "Zoning Expert to Be Selected," *Birmingham Age-Herald*, 13 March 1925; "Pittsburg Man Named to Guide Plans," *Birmingham Age-Herald*, 28 March 1925. According to historian Charles Connerly, "In 1923, Whitten told the Birmingham city commissioners that Atlanta's racial zoning ordinance would probably not stand up in court." Connerly, *Most Segregated City*, 298n67. It is possible that, by this time, Whitten had soured on his experience with racial zoning in Atlanta and, therefore, advised Birmingham not to follow the same path, but I could find no evidence of this. Instead, it seems that the zoning commission had planned to hire Whitten until Robert Jemison intervened on Knowles's behalf.

63. M. Knowles to R. Jemison Jr., 5 November 1924; R. Jemison Jr. to M. Knowles, 19 December 1924; R. Jemison Jr. to J. H. Adams, chair of Zoning Commission, 19 December 1924; M. Knowles to R. Jemison Jr., 24 December 1924, all in folder 6.1.11.20, RJ Papers.

64. Flavel Shurtleff to R. Jemison Jr., 8 May 1925, folder 6.1.23.31, RJ Papers; C. M. Stanley, "Robt. Jemison Jr., Man of Many Achievements," *Advertiser*, 30 October 1960; Robert Jemison Jr., "Ensley Highlands" description, folder 17.2, HF Papers; Weiss, *Rise of the Community Builders*, 57.

65. Jerome Tucker to R. Jemison Jr., 7 July 1920, folder 6.1.11.20; George Yancey to R. Jemison Jr., 21 April 1923, folder 6.1.11.20; "A Bill to Be Entitled an Act," folder 6.1.11.20; Atlanta's Tentative Zoning Map among other planning materials, folder 6.1.11.21. All in RJ Papers.

66. "Negroes Object to Race Clause," *Birmingham News*, 18 January 1923; "Negroes Object to Race Clause," *Atlanta Independent*, 1 February 1923.

67. "Meetings Called on Zone Measure," *Birmingham News*, 13 May 1926; "Zoning Meetings Will End Friday," *Birmingham News*, 11 May 1926. Birmingham also had an Interracial Committee that advocated for better housing, better schools, and "better school house locations as to health and convenience" for Black residents. "State Leaders Hear Reports on Inter-racial Co-operation," *Birmingham Age-Herald*, 6 March 1925; "Dr. Dillard's Report Shows Inter-Racial Improvement," *Birmingham Age-Herald*, 8 March 1925.

68. *Zoning Ordinance of Birmingham, Alabama, Effective August 4, 1926*, Government Documents Department, Birmingham Public Library, Birmingham, Alabama; "Two Types Residences to Be Placed in Zones," *Birmingham News*, 24 March 1926.

69. "Zones Announced for Graymont by New Commission: First Regulations Made for Restricting Negro and White Residences," *Birmingham News*, 29 March 1925; "To Outline a Zoning Policy," *Birmingham Age-Herald*, 18 February 1925; "Pittsburg Man Named to Guide Plans," *Birmingham Age-Herald*, 28 March 1925. For a discussion of earlier demands for a segregation ordinance, see Connerly, *Most Segregated City*, 39, 42.

70. "Realtor Named to Zoning Board," *Birmingham Age-Herald*, 25 February 1925; "H. M. Henderson Is New President of the Realty Board," *Birmingham News*, 7 January

1926; "City Commission Places Approval on Zone Measure," *Birmingham News*, 13 July 1926; Sam Starke executive secretary of the Birmingham Real Estate Board, "New Zoning Law Goes into Effect," *Birmingham News*, 26 September 1926; Wallace Hopkins to Harold Henderson, 22 March 1927, folder 305.1.1.1.8, Harold Henderson Collection, MSS 1566, Department of Archives and Manuscripts, Birmingham Public Library. See also related documents in folder 7.3, HF Papers.

71. "Desert City Hall Plan for School Bonds," *Birmingham Age-Herald*, 22 January 1924; "Platoon System Works Wonders in City Schools," *Birmingham Age-Herald*, 24 February 1925; Glenn, *Report of Progress*, 130–31.

72. Glenn, *Report of Progress*, 171, 185, 194; "Zones Announced for Graymont by New Commission," *Birmingham News*, 29 March 1925; Birmingham Board of Education, *Birmingham School Survey, 1923*, 124; 1926 Zone Map, G3974.B5 1926 B68, Map Collection, Southern History Department, Birmingham Public Library, Birmingham, Alabama.

73. Birmingham Board of Education, *Birmingham School Survey, 1923*, 39, 126; Glenn, *Report of Progress*, 19–24, 171, 185, 194; 1926 Zone Map, G3974.B5 1926 B68, Map Collection, Southern History Department, Birmingham Public Library, Birmingham, Alabama.

74. "Redmont Property Makes New High Price Records," *Birmingham Age-Herald*, 1 March 1925; Redmont Park advertising brochure, circa 1925, folder 6.1.27.29, RJ Papers. Jemison was also a strong backer of the school bond issue. R. Jemison Jr. to W. D. Hoffman, 26 June 1922, folder 6.1.14.18, RJ Papers.

75. Brochure for Redmont Park, undated, HF Papers; Robert Jemison Jr., "Redmont Park" description, folder 17.2, HF Papers; advertisement for Redmont Park, *Birmingham Age-Herald*, 22 March 1925.

76. Hill Ferguson to Clyde Nelson, 8 September 1927, folder 10.39, HF Papers. Hill Ferguson was the vice president of Redmont's development company, and Clyde Nelson was the developer of Hollywood, a residential park that was Redmont Park's main competition during the 1920s, although Hollywood lots were more moderately priced. Robert Jemison Jr., "Mountain Brook Estates" description, folder 17.2, HF Papers. By 1927, 221 of Redmont's 275 lots had already been sold, and seventy-five homes had been constructed, although some homes occupied more than one lot.

77. "Where City Children Can Enjoy Real Country Life," Mountain Brook Estates advertisement, in "Parent and Sex Instincts" Scrapbook, 1929–1934, "Advertisements," box 279, vol. 4, RPC Records.

78. R. Jemison Jr. to Hill Ferguson, 13 July 1923, folder 6.1.14.19; Hill Ferguson to C. B. Glenn, school superintendent, 16 June 1923, folder 6.1.14.19; R. Jemison Jr. to R. G. Miles, 3 February 1927, folder 6.1.23.33, all in RJ Papers; "More Schools to Be Erected without Delay," *Birmingham Age-Herald*, 7 March 1925; Blackmon, *Slavery by Another Name*, 329–30.

79. Glenn, *Report of Progress*, 181–83; Birmingham Board of Education, *Birmingham School Survey, 1927*, 8.

80. "Real Estate Board Holds Installation," *Birmingham News*, 8 January 1926; Robert Jemison Jr., "Self-Government Must Be Deserved," *Nation's Business*, 5 June, 1926, 21–22; "An Address by Robert Jemison Jr. on Cleaner Business Ethics," *Birmingham News*, 22 August 1926.

81. For example, see J. C. Nichols to R. Jemison Jr., 29 December 1924, folder 6.1.13.9; personal correspondence, folder 6.1.1.9.22; Hugh Potter to R. Jemison Jr., 8 March 1928,

Hugh Potter to R. Jemison Jr., 30 October 1928, and R. Jemison Jr. to Hugh Potter, 21 November 1928, folder 6.1.32.31; River Oaks correspondence and miscellaneous correspondence with other developers, folder 6.1.41.17, all in RJ Papers. See also "Parent and Sex Instincts" Scrapbook, 1929–1934, "Advertisements," box 279, vol. 4, RPC Records. The scrapbook was a collection of child-centered advertisements from other residential parks.

82. R. Jemison Jr. to Morris Knowles, 21 July 1926; J. H. Adams, chair of the Zoning Commission, to R. Jemison Jr., 2 August 1926; R. Jemison Jr. to Hill Ferguson, et al., 5 August 1926, all in folder 6.1.34.35, RJ Papers.

83. "Atkin's Outlines Negroes' Progress," *Winston-Salem Journal and Sentinel*, 10 February 1929; Herbin-Triant, *Threatening Property*, 182–83.

84. T. J. Woofter Jr., "Negro Housing in Winston-Salem, North Carolina," circa 1925, p. 4, Union Station History Collection, Digital Collections, Winston-Salem State University Archives, https://wssu.contentdm.oclc.org/digital/collection/p17140coll12/id/30/rec/1; "Superintendent Latham Submits Annual Report," *Winston-Salem Journal*, 4 July 1922.

85. Woofter, "Negro Housing," 4–5, 7–9.

86. Woofter, "Negro Housing," 1–2, 7.

87. "City of Winston-Salem Government Meeting Notes, 1920–1929," City of Winston-Salem website, accessed 15 May 2024, www.cityofws.org/DocumentCenter/View/2713/Winston-Salem-1920-to-1929-PDF; Morris Knowles, *City of Winston-Salem, North Carolina, Zoning Ordinance*, adopted 12 December 1930, North Carolina Collection, Forsyth County Public Library, Winston-Salem, North Carolina. The Winston-Salem zoning ordinance included a "two-family" district between the single-family district and apartment district.

88. "City of Winston-Salem Government Meeting Notes, 1920–1929"; Atkins High School registration form for the National Register of Historic Places, pp. 1, 12–13, Winston-Salem/Forsyth County Planning and Development Services Department, "National Register of Historic Places," accessed 30 June 2024, https://files.nc.gov/ncdcr/nr/FY1295.pdf; Winston-Salem city directories, 1931 and 1932, DigitalNC, www.digitalnc.org/collections/city-directories/; City of Winston-Salem Zone Map, 1930, North Carolina Maps project, University of North Carolina, accessed 15 June 2024, https://web.lib.unc.edu/nc-maps/.

89. City of Winston-Salem Zone Map, 1930; Clinard v. Winston-Salem, 6 S. E. 2d 867 (N.C. 1940).

90. Winston-Salem city directories, 1930–1940, DigitalNC, www.digitalnc.org/collections/city-directories/; Clinard v. Winston-Salem, 6 S. E. 2d 867 (N.C. 1940). Birmingham's racial zoning map would not be overturned until 1951. See Connerly, *Most Segregated City*, 3.

91. Clinard v. Winston-Salem, 6 S. E. 2d 867 (N.C. 1940).

92. "City of Winston-Salem Government Meeting Notes, 1930–1939," City of Winston-Salem website, accessed 15 May 2024, www.cityofws.org/DocumentCenter/View/2717/Winston-Salem-1930-to-1939-PDF; Freund, "Some Inadequately Discussed Problems," 136–37, 146–47.

93. Freund, "Some Inadequately Discussed Problems," 137; Monchow, *Use of Deed Restrictions*, preface; Weiss, *Rise of Community Builders*, 50.

94. Knowles, *Report*, 14, 17–18, 20, 29, 34. For a more in-depth analysis of Charleston, see Weyeneth, *Historic Preservation*, 13–14.
95. Knowles, "Trends in Present-Day City Planning," 102.

Chapter 12

1. William Henry Jones, *Housing of Negroes*, 74–79.
2. Boger, "Meaning of Neighborhood," 236–58.
3. Gwendolyn Wright, *Building the Dream*, 150.
4. Riddle, "'Homes to Last,'" 21.
5. Robert Whitten, "Probable Future Population and School Requirements of the Dobbs Ferry School District," report to the Board of Education of School District Number Three, Town of Greenburgh, New York, 1932, box 13, DL 22A4, RW Papers.
6. James, *Land Planning*, 204–6; Flavel Shurtleff to "Members of the Institute" / directors of the National Conference on City Planning, 7 February 1927, folder 6.1.23.33, RJ Papers; Alice Barrows, "School Building Survey and Program for Warwick, Rhode Island: A Study of a Town in the Path of an Expanding Metropolitan Area," United States Office of Education, Bulletin No. 33, 1930 (Washington, DC: Government Printing Office, 1931), box 7, DL229W, RW Papers.
7. Monchow, *Use of Deed Restrictions*, 13; Robert Whitten, "How a Self-Contained Neighborhood Unit Might Be Planned," *American City*, March 1927, 287–93; Shelby Harrison, introduction, 24.
8. Brody, "Constructing Professional Knowledge," 38, 39, 42, 48, 53, 70.
9. Perry moved to Forest Hills Gardens in 1912. At the time, it was a suburban community of single-family homes, although apartments would be added later. It was designed by Frederick Law Olmsted Jr. and was at least partially funded by the Russell Sage Foundation. Brody, "Constructing Professional Knowledge," 38; Gillette, "Evolution of Neighborhood Planning," 422. See also Garner, "Garden City," 47–48.
10. Perry, "Neighborhood Unit," 45, 126, 128. In 1924, Perry presented similar ideas at the National Conference of Social Work. See also Gillette, "Evolution of Neighborhood Planning," 425–27.
11. Robert Whitten, "Family Types and Community Relations in Determining Housing Needs," undated report, circa 1932, p. 36, box 4, DL229T, RW Papers. Perry's "Neighborhood Unit" had a far larger impact on the superblock development of public housing, with terrible results. His work was reborn in 1948 when it was rediscovered and then adopted by the Committee on the Hygiene of Housing of the American Public Health Association. Gillette, "Evolution of Neighborhood Planning," 427. See also Silver, "Neighborhood Planning," 161–74; Robert Whitten, "How a Self-Contained Neighborhood Unit Might Be Planned," *American City*, March 1927, 287–93; Perry, "Neighborhood Unit," 123; and Brody, "Constructing Professional Knowledge," 77–78.
12. Whitten and Andrews, *Neighborhoods of Small Homes*, 75–83. For a local example that attempts to discount both class and race, see D. A. Crane, "The Black Heart of Atlanta," *Georgia Tech Engineer* 10, no. 4, May 1949, reprinted by the Atlanta Urban League, box 73, folder 12, Atlanta Urban League Papers, MSS 0025, Archives Research Center, Robert W. Woodruff Library of the Atlanta University Center.

13. It appears that the influence of Perry's "Neighborhood Unit" became somewhat inflated in the secondary literature, with scholars, advocates, and critics sometimes ascribing any general description of the attributes of a residential park to Perry, even when the original documents did not reference Perry or even use the term "neighborhood unit." His most innovative ideas regarding urban redevelopment, community building, and the scale of individual communities had far less impact. Brody, "Constructing Professional Knowledge," 1, 14, 51, 85, 87; Gillette, "Evolution of Neighborhood Planning," 421–44; Silver, "Neighborhood Planning," 161–74; Erickson and Highsmith, "Neighborhood Unit."

14. Purdy, discussion of Whitten's "Zoning of Residence Sections," 41–42; Dan Wheeler, *General Index*; Gries and Ford, *Planning for Residential Districts*, vii–viii, 6; Gries and Ford, *Housing and the Community*, v. Hoover's WHCCHP also published reports that discussed the type of neighborhoods best suited to child-rearing. Their analysis promoted residential parks with no mention of Perry's neighborhood unit. WHCCHP, *Home and the Child*, 9–27.

15. Weiss, *Rise of the Community Builders*, 57; Hornstein, *Nation of Realtors*, 148–49; Gwendolyn Wright, *Building the Dream*, 205.

16. Glotzer, *How the Suburbs*, 157; Weiss, *Rise of the Community Builders*, 29, 47–48; Tauber and Tauber, *Negroes in Cities*.

17. Hill Ferguson's biography was taken from *Library of Alabama Lives* (1961), folder 17.2, HF Papers. In 1933, the newly established Home Owners Loan Corporation (HOLC) tasked local appraisers with making maps to guide its mortgage program, which was designed to help family's keep their homes despite the avalanche of defaults during the Depression. The FHA's land planning division "worked closely with leading subdividers," and its field office was in Jemison's building. Brody, "Constructing Professional Knowledge," 78–79. For an examination of the infamous HOLC security maps, see Michney, "How the City Survey's"; and Winling and Michney, "Roots of Redlining." See also Lands, *Culture of Property*, 157–58.

18. "Realtors Fete Zoning Board," *Birmingham News*, 26 March 1926; Flavel Shurtleff to R. Jemison Jr., 8 May 1925, folder 6.1.23.31, RJ Papers; C. M. Stanley, "Robt. Jemison Jr., Man of Many Achievements," *Advertiser*, 30 October 1960, folder 17.2, HF Papers; "The 'Own Your Home' Bulletin," no. 1, March 1918, box 295, folder 3; US Department of Labor Information and Education Service, "Financing the Prospective Home Owner," 25 April 1919, Press Release no. 4–23A, "Own-Your-Own Home," box 295, folder 3; US Department of Labor Information and Education Service, *Suggestions for Own-Your-Own-Home Campaigns* (Washington: Government Printing Office, 1919), box 6, folder 15; US Department of Labor Information and Education Service to H. K. Milner, 8 April 1919; Department of Labor Information and Education Service to Hill Ferguson, 25 April 1919, box 463, folder 40, "Alabama"; Hill Ferguson to John L. Weaver, 27 October 1917, box 462, folder 4, all in USHC Records; "Value of Realty for Investment Shown by Adair," *Atlanta Constitution*, 13 January 1921.

19. Hornstein, *Nation of Realtors*, 150–51; Weiss, *Rise of the Community Builders*, 8.

20. River Oaks advertisement, "More School Children Means We Need More Homes," *Houston Post*, 5 July 1935.

21. "Segregation Law Passed in Council," *Atlanta Constitution*, 21 May 1929; "Segregation Law Veto Under Fire," *Atlanta Constitution*, 23 May 1929; "Segregation Act Passed over Veto," *Atlanta Constitution*, 4 June 1929; "Council Passes Segregation Law," *Atlanta*

Constitution, 17 March 1931; "Key to Talk with Beavers on Police Demotion Cases before He Approves Paper," *Atlanta Journal*, 17 March 1931; "Atlanta Segregation Ordinance Attacked," *Atlanta Constitution*, 14 April 1931. For reports on the bombings of Black residences, see "Cross Sections of Life in Gate City of South," *Atlanta Constitution*, 26 February 1932; "Bomb Found on Porch of Negro's Residence," *Atlanta Constitution*, 16 July 1932; "Cross Sections of Life in Gate City of South," *Atlanta Constitution*, 26 August 1932; "Blast Damages Home," *Atlanta Constitution*, 8 November 1932; "House Is Dynamited on Manigault Street," *Atlanta Constitution*, 2 February 1933. In 1930, city council passed a third law that was intended to act as an indirect segregation ordinance. It required moving companies to obtain a permit before moving residents from one house to another. Black residents were denied permits if they planned to move into racially contested areas. This law, too, was declared unconstitutional. "Atlanta Council Reorganized for Year's Work," *Atlanta Constitution*, 7 January 1930; "Moving Law Attacked in Mandamus Action," *Atlanta Constitution*, 7 February 1933; Lands, *Culture of Property*, 155.

22. Federal Housing Administration, Better Housing News Flashes No. 9, 1936, Motion Picture Films, Records of the Federal Housing Administration, Records Group 31, National Archives and Records Administration, College Park, Maryland.

23. Ewen, *Immigrant Women*, 98; Hubbard, "Annual Survey," 116–18; Cheryl Ferguson, *Highland Park*, 4–5; "Home Show Sets Children's Day," *Birmingham Age-Herald*, 27 March 1925; Moody, *Wacker's Manual*; Kimball, *Our City—Dallas*. See also "Money Being Pledged for Plan Session," *Dallas Morning News*, 27 April 1928; Nolen, "Getting Action in City Planning," 165–71; US Department of Labor Information and Education Service, *Suggestions for Own-Your-Own-Home Campaigns*, box 6, folder 15; Southern Pine Service Association, "Build Your Home First" Campaign pamphlet, 1919, box 6, folder 15; Southern Pine Association, "Make Her Happier: Build a Home First," large advertising broadside, no date, box 464, folder 2, all in USHC Records. See also Luken and Vaughan, "Standardizing Child-Rearing," 125.

24. Mintz, *Huck's Raft*, 277. The literature on child-centered postwar suburbs includes Fass, *End of American Childhood*; Coontz, *Way We Never Were*; Cohen, *Consumer's Republic*; Clark, *American Family Home*; May, *Homeward Bound*; Ehrenreich, *Fear of Falling*; and Stearns, *Anxious Parents*.

25. Piketty, Saez, and Zucman, "Distributional National Accounts," 577. See also Piketty, Saez, and Zucman, "Economic Growth in the US."

26. Stearns, *Anxious Parents*, 2, 72; Cross, *Kids' Stuff*; Jacobson, *Raising Consumers*; Engelhardt, *End of Victory Culture*.

27. Nolen, "Importance of Citizens' Committees," 34–35; Federal Housing Administration, *Underwriting Manual*, section 284 and 285; Chetty, Hendren, Kline, and Saez, "Where Is the Land"; Justin Wolfers, "Why the New Research on Mobility Matters: An Economist's View," *New York Times*, 4 May 2015; Gregor Aisch, Eric Buth, Matthew Bloch, Amanda Cox, and Kevin Quealy, "The Best and Worst Places to Grow Up: How Your Area Compares," *New York Times*, 4 May 2015; Paul Krugman, "Stranded by Sprawl," *New York Times*, 28 July 2013.

28. Edward Franklin Frazier, "Neighborhood Union in Atlanta," *Southern Workman*, September 1923, 442.

29. Dollard, *Caste and Class*, 359. See also McGuire, *At the Dark End*; Cahn, *Sexual Reckonings*; Chatelain, *South Side Girls*; Hine, "Rape and the Inner Lives."

30. "Negro Additions in Houston," *Houston Informer*, 20 September 1930. See also Power, "Apartheid Baltimore Style," 317; "The Ghetto," *Crisis*, March 1915, 220; Herbin-Triant, *Threatening Property*; Hillier, "Who Received Loans?"

31. "Given Forty-Eight Hours to Move," *Atlanta Independent*, 19 October 1922. See also Power, "Apartheid Baltimore Style," 290–91; Boger, "Meaning of Neighborhood," 236–58; and Glotzer, *How the Suburbs*, 85.

32. "A Survey of the Opinions of a Hundred Heads of Families Respecting Washington Park Made Jointly by Neighborhood Union and Atlanta School of Social Work," December 1924, box 7, folder 5; Petition to Mayor Key and the Park Commission, 1922, box 2, folder 41; Minutes of the Neighborhood Union, 7 October 1922, box 4, folder 14, all in NU Collection; Shivery, "History," 254–56, 381.

33. Rabin, "Expulsive Zoning," 102, 118–19. Rabin largely assumed that local planning commissions intentionally designated Black districts as industrial areas, but in many cases, white property owners demanded the changes be made, much to the chagrin of planners. Either way, Black residents did not have the political power to stop it. See also Shertzer, Twinam, and Walsh, "Race, Ethnicity," 244–45.

34. Minutes of the Neighborhood Union, 7 October 1922, box 4, folder 14, NU Collection; Flint, "Zoning and Residential Segregation," 331–32, 337.

35. ACC Minutes, 4 September 1922, vol. 26–27, "1917 July–1920 May; 1920 June 7–1923 January 1," row 5, section B, shelf 1; 2 July, 15 October, and 19 November 1923, 17 March, 19 May, and 7 July, vol. 28, "1923 January 2–1924 July," row 5, section B, shelf 1; and 16 August 1924, vol. 29, row 5, section B, shelf 2. For the lone exception, see ACC Minutes, 16 June 1924, vol. 28, "1923 January 2–1924 July," row 5, section B, shelf 1. The pharmacist was Dr. O. E. Collum. See also ACC Minutes, 5 May 1924, vol. 28, "1923 January 2–1924 July," row 5, section B, shelf 1; Atlanta city directory, 1923, Atlanta City Directories collection, Kenan Research Center at the Atlanta History Center; "West End People Victors in Zoning Change Contest," *Atlanta Constitution*, 8 July 1924. For descriptions of the new Black residential parks west of Ashby, see "New Park for Colored to Allow No Tenants," *Atlanta Constitution*, 11 June 1919; "Life, Health, Happiness: Colored Now Know True Happiness in New Residential Section," *Atlanta Journal*, 11 August 1919; "Colored People's Dream Come True," *Atlanta Constitution*, 6 August 1919; advertisement for West Hunter Park, *Atlanta Independent*, 26 July 1919; "60 Lots for Sale in West Hunter Park," *Atlanta Independent*, 9 October 1920; and "New Ashby Street Subdivision," *Atlanta Independent*, 26 June 1920.

36. "Land of Economic Opportunity and Inadequate Housing Facilities," *Atlanta Independent*, 20 September 1923.

37. "Negro Sections Neglect," *Houston Post*, 4 January 1939.

38. Sarah Ginnsberg and the Students of the Atlanta School of Social Work, "Negro Families in Need," a report prepared for the Neighborhood Union, 1933, box 13, folder 35, NU Collection; Shivery, "History," 372; Michney, *Surrogate Suburbs*, 53; Wye, "New Deal," 634–36; Hirsch, "Choosing Segregation," 209–14.

39. For me, Arnold Hirsch's classic *Making the Second Ghetto* remains the single most useful volume for explaining how public housing policy produced residential segregation. For a more recent analysis of Hirsch's impact, see Keeanga-Yamahtta Taylor, "Banality of Segregation," 490–93; and Balto, "White Rage, White Liberals," 511–15. See also Hirsch,

"Choosing Segregation," 214–18; Radford, "Federal Government," 102–18; Biles, "Public Housing," 147–52; Reed, *Not Alms but Opportunity*, 186–87. For an examination of public housing from the perspective of those who lived there, see Rhonda Williams, *Politics of Public Housing*.

40. Robert Murray Haig, Clarence Arthur Perry, and Robert Whitten, "Report of Sub-Committee on Housing Projects in Relation to City Plan," 1934, box 4, DL229T, RW Papers. Whitten served as chair of the committee. See also Perry, *Rebuilding of Blighted Areas*; Von Hoffman, "Why They Built Pruitt-Igoe," 186–87; Stern, *Race and Education*, 195–229.

41. Hunt, *Blueprint for Disaster*, 147–51. See also Vale, *Purging the Poorest*; Von Hoffman, "Why They Built Pruitt-Igoe," 193–97, 199; Radford, "Federal Government," 102–18; Biles, "Public Housing," 147–49.

42. Sampson, *Great American City*, 149–79.

43. Cashin, *White Space, Black Hood*; Dorceta Taylor, *Toxic Communities*; Sampson, *Great American City*; Sharkey, *Stuck in Place*; Sharkey, *Neighborhoods*; Jenkins, *Bonds of Inequality*; Seligman, *Block by Block*; Cutler, Glaeser, and Vigdor, "Rise and Decline," 456, 470, 487; Markley et al., "Limits of Homeownership"; Massey, "Still the Linchpin."

44. Benjamin, "Suburbanizing Jim Crow"; Houston Model City Department, *In-Depth View of Third Ward*; Bullard, "Housing Barriers," 6–7, 10; Chetty, Hendren, Kline, and Saez, "Where Is the Land"; Justin Wolfers, "Why the New Research on Mobility Matters: An Economist's View," *New York Times*, 4 May 2015; Gregor Aisch, Eric Buth, Matthew Bloch, Amanda Cox, and Kevin Quealy, "The Best and Worst Places to Grow Up: How Your Area Compares," *New York Times*, 4 May 2015; Paul Krugman, "Stranded by Sprawl," *New York Times*, 28 July 2013; Hobson, *Legend of the Black Mecca*.

45. Radford, "Federal Government," 116; Gillette, "Evolution of Neighborhood Planning," 38; Brody, "Constructing Professional Knowledge," 86, 94, 99.

46. Urban Land Institute, *Community Builders Handbook*, 92.

47. Rome, *Bulldozer in the Countryside*, 119–52; Duany, Plater-Zyberk, and Speck, *Suburban Nation*; Hurley, *Environmental Inequalities*.

48. Wood, *Housing*.

49. Ladd-Taylor, *Mother-Work*, 54–55, 63–65; Gillis, "Islanding of Children," 321; Coontz, *Social Origins*, 360; WHCCHP, *Parent Education*, 29; Lasker, *Race Attitudes in Children*.

50. Donald Trump, "Remarks by President Trump in Press Conference," 14 July 2020, Trump White House Archives, https://trumpwhitehouse.archives.gov/briefings-statements/remarks-president-trump-press-conference-071420.

51. For an overview of the role of government in residential segregation, see Rothstein, *Color of Law*.

Afterword

1. Florida, *New Urban Crisis*; Duany, Plater-Zyberk, and Speck, *Suburban Nation*; Chaskin and Joseph, *Integrating the City*; Goetz, *New Deal Ruins*; Rothstein and Rothstein, *Just Action*.

2. Stephen Menedian, Samir Gambhir, and Arthur Gailes, "Twenty-First Century Racial

Residential Segregation in the U.S.," 30 June 2021, Roots of Structural Racism Project, University of California, Berkeley, accessed 16 May 2024, https://belonging.berkeley.edu/roots-structural-racism; Yung Chun, Tyler Haupert, Stephen Roll, Sophia R. Fox-Dichter, and Michal Grinstein-Weiss, "Did the Pandemic Advance New Suburbanization?," Brookings Institution, 23 May 2022, www.brookings.edu/articles/did-the-pandemic-advance-new-suburbanization/.

3. Bell, "Brown v. Board of Education," 523; Ifill, "Focus on the Costs," 32–35; Desmond King, "Keeping the American," 259–61; Havekes, Bader, and Krysan, "Realizing Racial and Ethnic"; Lands, *Culture of Property*, 215–16; Steffes, *Structuring Inequality*, 18, 119; Reeves, *Dream Hoarders*, 1–15.

4. Ramey and Ramey, "Rug Rat Race"; Philip N. Cohen, "Fertility Trends Explained," 2017 edition, *Family Inequality Blog*, 22 May 2018, https://familyinequality.wordpress.com/2018/05/22/fertility-trends-explained/; Doepke and Zilibotti, *Love, Money and Parenting*, 54–57. See also Florida, *New Urban Crisis*.

5. Kornrich and Furstenberg, "Investing in Children"; Reeves, *Dream Hoarders*, 50–56; Selingo, *Who Gets In*, 72–73. See also "How Diverse Are Student Populations on College Campuses in the U.S.?," *Chronicle of Higher Education*, 17 May 2024, www.chronicle.com/article/student-diversity/. The Chronicle of Higher Education and *Inside Higher Ed* routinely publish articles about program elimination and campus closures. For example, see Scott Carlson, "The Endangered Small College: Many Are on the Brink, but They've Never Been More Vital," *Chronicle of Higher Education*, 26 June 2024, www.chronicle.com/article/the-endangered-small-college; Josh Moody, "More Campus Cuts in March," *Inside Higher Ed*, 29 March 2024, www.insidehighered.com/news/business/cost-cutting/2024/03/29/more-campus-cuts-march; Lee Garder, "Flagships Prosper, While Regionals Suffer," *Chronicle of Higher Education*, 13 February 2023, www.chronicle.com/article/flagships-prosper-while-regionals-suffer; and Robert Kelchen, "Are Colleges Really on the Brink? A Recent Book Says More Institutions Should Declare Financial Exigency," *Chronicle of Higher Education*, 13 March 2024, www.chronicle.com/article/are-colleges-really-on-the-brink. Many of the humanities programs that are being targeted for elimination immerse students in critical reading, writing, research, ethics, and logical thinking. Although critics of higher education frequently quote students who complain that their courses have little to do with their professional or daily life, that critique often refers to professional coursework rather than courses in the liberal arts. Moreover, many colleges that are experiencing economic strain have served as crucial engines of upward mobility because lower income students must often attend school closer to home. They cannot afford to travel far away to college, and they have more responsibilities outside of school than affluent students. Lower costs, a tighter-knit campus, and closer relationships with faculty along with fewer graduate students and smaller class sizes create a more welcoming environment, which is why lower income students frequently choose small, regional schools. This has been true even as tuition-driven institutions struggle to provide a strong academic foundation for their students, due to a greater vulnerability to minor changes in the economy or to student demand.

6. Madeleine Levine, *Teach Your Children Well*; Doepke and Zilibotti, *Love, Money, and Parenting*; Claire Cain Miller, "The Relentlessness of Modern Parenting," *New York Times*, 25 December 2018, www.nytimes.com/2018/12/25/upshot/the-relentlessness-of-modern-parenting.html; David Brooks, "The Age of Coddling Is Over," *New York Times*,

16 April 2020, www.nytimes.com/2020/04/16/opinion/coronavirus-medical-training.html; Kate Julian, "The Anxious Child and the Crisis of Modern Parenting," *The Atlantic*, 14 April 2020, www.theatlantic.com/press-releases/archive/2020/04/the-anxious-child-and-the-crisis-of-modern-parenting/609901/.

7. Piketty, Saez, and Zucman, "Economic Growth"; Piketty, Saez, and Zucman, "Distributional National Accounts."

8. Chetty et al., "Fading American Dream."

9. Bound, Hershbein, and Long, "Playing the Admissions Game."

10. Reeves, *Dream Hoarders*, 72.

11. Julian, "Anxious Child." More psychologists are blaming smartphones for increased anxiety and depression among the young. The competition they engender along with the outright bullying are certainly important factors, but the push for more childhood accomplishments started before social media rose to the fore. Moreover, kids who rarely use social media have experienced increased anxiety while those who are addicted to their phones don't always experience negative outcomes. Thus, increased expectations for genuine accomplishments at younger ages along with our tendency to ignore obvious problems that the next generation will need to address should not be overlooked as factors that are stressing even affluent, highly privileged children.

12. For examples of concern over "helicopter parenting," see Claire Cain Miller and Jonah Engel Bromwich, "How Parents Are Robbing Their Children of Adulthood," *New York Times*, 16 March 2019, www.nytimes.com/2019/03/16/style/snowplow-parenting-scandal.html; Madeleine Levine, *Teach Your Children Well*.

13. Doepke and Zilibotti, *Love, Money, and Parenting*, 40–41, 73–75. Their data is from 2012. For more on exhausted parents, see Westervelt, *Forget "Having It All."*

14. Pamela Druckerman, "The Bad News about Helicopter Parenting: It Works," *New York Times*, 7 February 2019, www.nytimes.com/2019/02/07/opinion/helicopter-parents-economy.html. See also Nate G. Hilger, "Stop Pretending That Intensive Parenting Doesn't Work," *The Atlantic*, 10 October 2022, www.theatlantic.com/ideas/archive/2022/10/intensive-parenting-kids-happiness-health/671782/.

15. "Relax, Your Kids Will Be Fine," *The Economist*, 26 July 2014, www.economist.com/leaders/2014/07/26/relax-your-kids-will-be-fine. See also Reeves, *Dream Hoarders*, 41–46, 123–52.

16. Hilger, *Parent Trap*, 195–97.

17. Doepke and Zilibotti, *Love, Money and Parenting*, 153–56.

18. Sard and Tegeler, "Children and Housing Vouchers," 299; Hendren, "Effects of Moving," 280; Hilger, *Parent Trap*, 131, 195–97; Carter and Welner, *Closing the Opportunity Gap*.

19. Kimberly Jones, *How We Can Win*.

BIBLIOGRAPHY

Primary Sources

Archives

ALABAMA

Birmingham Public Library
    Department of Archives and Manuscripts
        Hill Ferguson Papers
        Harold Henderson Collection
        Robert Jemison Jr. Papers
    Government Documents Department
    Southern History Department
        Map Collection

CALIFORNIA

The American Presidency Project, University of California, Santa Barbara
    Herbert Hoover Collection, www.presidency.ucsb.edu/people/president/herbert-hoover

GEORGIA

Archives Research Center, Robert W. Woodruff Library, Atlanta University Center
    Atlanta University Printed and Published Materials
    Atlanta Urban League Papers
    Neighborhood Union Collection
Atlanta Board of Education Archives and Museum, Atlanta Public Schools' Center for Leadership and Learning
    Minutes of the Atlanta Board of Education
Kenan Research Center at the Atlanta History Center
    Atlanta City Directories
    Atlanta City Maps
    City of Atlanta Records
    Kate Richardson Lumpkin Papers

MARYLAND

Johns Hopkins University Sheridan Libraries, Baltimore
    Special Collections
        Roland Park Company Records
National Archives and Records Administration, College Park
    Records of the Federal Home Loan Bank Board
    Records of the Federal Housing Administration

380 | Bibliography

MASSACHUSETTS
Frances Loeb Library, Harvard University Graduate School of Design, Cambridge
    Special Collections
        Papers of Robert Harvey Whitten, 1920–1935

MICHIGAN
Western Michigan Archives and Regional History Digital Collections
    Caroline Bartlett Crane Collection, https://cdm16259.contentdm.oclc.org/digital/collection/p4022coll10

MISSOURI
State Historical Society of Missouri
    Kansas City Manuscript Collections
        J. C. Nichols Company Records, https://collections.shsmo.org/manuscripts/kansas-city

NEW YORK
Cornell University Library, Ithaca
    Division of Rare and Manuscript Collections
        Jemison Companies, Miscellany

NORTH CAROLINA
DigitalNC
    Raleigh city directories, www.digitalnc.org/collections/city-directories/
    Winston-Salem city directories, www.digitalnc.org/collections/city-directories/
Duke University, Durham
    David M. Rubenstein Rare Book and Manuscript Library
        Charles N. Hunter Papers
    Duke University Libraries Digital Repository
        Ad*Access Collection, https://repository.duke.edu/dc/adaccess
Forsyth County, NC, Register of Deeds Online Records Systems
    Property Deed Books and Index, www.co.forsyth.nc.us/rod/online_lookup.aspx
Forsyth County Public Library, Winston-Salem
    North Carolina Collection
Louis Round Wilson Special Collections Library, University of North Carolina at Chapel Hill
    North Carolina Map Collection
Olivia Rainey Local History Library, Raleigh
    Vertical Files
State Archives of North Carolina, Raleigh
    City of Raleigh: Municipal Records
    Department of Public Instruction: Division of Negro Education (Interracial Commission)
Wake County, NC, Register of Deeds Online Records Systems
    Property Deed Books and Index, https://rodcrpi.wakegov.com/Booksweb/
Winston-Salem State University Archives
    Digital Collections
        Union Station History Collection, https://cdm17140.contentdm.oclc.org/digital/collection/p17140coll12/search

TEXAS
Austin History Center Archives, Austin Public Library
Dolph Briscoe Center for American History, University of Texas at Austin
    William Clifford Hogg Papers
Hattie Mae White Educational Support Center, Houston Independent School District
    Historical Files
    Minutes of the Houston Independent School District Board of Education
Houston History Research Center, Houston Public Library
    General and Mary Johnson Papers
    Hare and Hare Collection
    Houston City Directories
    Houston Map Collection
    Houston Parks Collection
    Houston Subdivision Collection
    Joseph Stephen Cullinan Family Papers
    Local History Collection
    Political Campaigns Collection
    River Oaks Collection

WASHINGTON, DC
Library of Congress Digital Collections
    Olmsted Associates Records, www.loc.gov/collections/olmsted-associates-records/about-this-collection/
    Sanborn Fire Insurance Maps, Winston-Salem, www.loc.gov/item/sanborn06522_003/
National Museum of American History, Smithsonian Institution
    Archives Center
        Warshaw Collection of Business Americana—Yeast

Periodicals

American City
Atlanta Constitution
Atlanta Georgian
Atlanta Independent
Atlanta Journal
Atlanta Constitution
Atlantic Monthly
Austin (TX) American Statesman
Baltimore Afro-American
Baltimore Sun
Birmingham (AL) Age-Herald
Birmingham (AL) News
Brownies' Book
Carolinian (Raleigh, NC)
Chatham (NJ) Press
Chicago Real Estate Board Bulletin
Children: The Magazine for Parents / Parents' Magazine
Collier's Magazine
Courier-Journal (Louisville, KY)
The Crisis
Dallas Express
Dallas Morning News
Detroit Free Press
Evening Visitor (Raleigh, NC)
Farmer and Mechanic (Raleigh, NC)
Fitchburg (MA) Sentinel
Galveston (TX) Daily News
Gargoyle (Houston, TX)
Harper's Weekly
House Beautiful
Houston Informer

Houston Chronicle
Houston Post and *Houston Post-Dispatch*
Houston Press
The Independent
Indianapolis News
Indianapolis Star
Ithaca (NY) Journal
Journal Magazine
Journal of Labor (Atlanta, GA)
Kansas City (MO) Star
Kansas City (MO) Times
Kentucky Irish American (Louisville, KY)
Liberator
Lincoln (NE) Star
Literary Digest
Los Angeles Times
Los Angeles Sunday Times
McCall's Magazine
Monroe (LA) News-Star
Morning Post (Raleigh, NC)
Morning Tulsa (OK) Daily World
The Nation
Nation's Business
New York Times
News and Observer (Raleigh, NC)
North Carolinian (Raleigh, NC)
Observer (Raleigh, NC)
The Outlook
People's Press (Winston-Salem, NC)
Pittsburgh (PA) Courier
Post-Star (Glen Falls, NY)
Press Visitor (Raleigh, NC)
Progressive Farmer (Raleigh, NC)
Raleigh Student
Raleigh Times
Salem (OH) News
Saturday Evening Post
Southern Workman
State Chronicle (Raleigh, NC)
State Journal (Raleigh, NC)
The Survey
Times (Munster, IN)
Times (Shreveport, LA)
Tulsa (OK) Democrat
Tulsa (OK) Star
Twin City Sentinel (Winston-Salem, NC)
Union Herald (Raleigh, NC)
Union Republican (Winston-Salem, NC)
Waco (TX) News-Tribune
Western Sentinel (Winston-Salem, NC)
Winston (NC) Daily Pilot
Winston-Salem (NC) Journal
Winston-Salem (NC) Journal and Sentinel
Woman's Press

Texts in Conference Proceedings

Adams, Thomas. "The British Point of View." In *Proceedings of the Third National Conference on City Planning*, 27–37. Boston: National Conference on City Planning, 1911.

———. "State, City, and Town Planning." In *Proceedings of the Eighth National Conference on City Planning*, 119–39. Boston: National Conference on City Planning, 1916.

Cheney, Charles. "Zoning in Practice." In *Proceedings of the Eleventh National Conference on City Planning*, 162–85. Boston: National Conference on City Planning, 1919.

Committee on Best Methods of Land Subdivision. "Report of Conference Committee on 'Best Methods of Land Subdivision.'" In *Proceedings of the Seventh National Conference on City Planning*, Appendix A, 247–73. Boston: National Conference on City Planning, 1915.

Crawford, Andrew. Discussion of H. M. Brinckerhoff's "The Effect of Transportation upon the Distribution of the Population in Large Cities." In *Proceedings of the Thirteenth National Conference on City Planning*, 67–69. Boston: National Conference on City Planning, 1921.

Davis, Otto. "Shall We Encourage or Discourage the Apartment House?" In *Housing Problems in America: Proceedings of the Fifth National Conference on Housing*, 328–39. New York: American Housing Association, 1916.

Ford, George B. Discussion of George Strayer's "The School Building Program an Important Part of the City Plan." In *Proceedings of the Fourteenth National Conference on City Planning*, 62–64. Boston: National Conference on City Planning, 1922.

———. "Practical Planning of Residential Streets." In *Proceedings of the First National Conference on City Planning*, 79–81. Boston: National Conference on City Planning, 1909.

———. "What Planning Has Done for Cities," In *Proceedings of the Sixteenth National Conference on City Planning*, 1–23. Boston: National Conference on City Planning, 1924.

Grinnalds, Jefferson. Discussion of George Strayer's "The School Building Program an Important Part of the City Plan." In *Proceedings of the Fourteenth National Conference on City Planning*, 55–56. Boston: National Conference on City Planning, 1922.

Hanmer, Lee. Discussion of Henry Hubbard's "Parks and Playgrounds: Their Requirements for Distribution as Elements in the City Play." In *Proceedings of the Fourteenth National Conference on City Planning*, 33–38. Boston: National Conference on City Planning, 1922.

Harper, Frances Ellen Watkins. "The Afro-American Mother." In *The Work and Words of the National Congress of Mothers First Annual Session*, 67–71. New York: D. Appleton, 1897.

Hewitt, C. Trafford. "Canada and the US as a Field for the Garden City Movement." In *Proceedings of the Sixth National Conference on City Planning*, 180–89. Boston: National Conference on City Planning, 1914.

Hooker, George. "Remarks at the Closing Dinner." In *Proceedings of the Eighth National Conference on City Planning*, 265–72. Boston: National Conference on City Planning, 1916.

Hubbard, Henry V. "Parks and Playgrounds: Their Requirements and Distribution as Elements in the City Plan." In *Proceedings of the Fourteenth National Conference on City Planning*, 1–33. Boston: National Conference on City Planning, 1922.

Hurty, J. N. "The State and Housing." In *Housing Problems in America: Proceedings of the Fifth National Conference on Housing*, 167–89. New York: American Housing Association, 1916.

Ihlder, John. Discussion of Henry Hubbard's "The Size and Distribution of Playgrounds and Similar Recreation Facilities in American Cities." In *Proceedings of the Sixth National Conference on City Planning*, 296–300. Boston: National Conference on City Planning, 1914.

Nichols, J. C. "Financial Effect of Good Planning in Land Subdivision." In *Proceedings of the Eighth National Conference on City Planning*, 91–106. Boston: National Conference on City Planning, 1916.

———. "Restrictions for the Small House Builder." In *Home Building and Subdividing: Proceedings and Reports of the Home Builders and Subdividers Division*, 212–13. Chicago: National Association of Real Estate Boards, 1925.

Nolen, John. "Getting Action in City Planning." In *Proceedings of the Thirteenth National Conference on City Planning*, 162–75. Boston: National Conference on City Planning, 1921.

———. "The Importance of Citizens' Committees in Securing Public Support for a City Planning Program." In *Proceedings of the Sixteenth National Conference on City Planning*, 28–52. Boston: National Conference on City Planning, 1924.

Olmsted, Frederick Law, Jr. "Planning Residential Subdivisions: President's Address." In *Proceedings of the Eleventh National Conference on City Planning*, 1–21. Boston: National Conference on City Planning, 1919.

Purdy, Lawson. Discussion of Robert Whitten's "The Zoning of Residence Sections." In *Proceedings of the Tenth National Conference on City Planning*, 41–42. Boston: National Conference on City Planning, 1918.

Snyder, C. B. J. Discussion of George Strayer's "The School Building Program an Important Part of the City Plan." In *Proceedings of the Fourteenth National Conference on City Planning*, 53–54, 60. Boston: National Conference on City Planning, 1922.

Strayer, George. "The School Building Program an Important Part of the City Plan." In *Proceedings of the Fourteenth National Conference on City Planning*, 46–53. Boston: National Conference on City Planning, 1922.

Unwin, Raymond. Discussion of Lawrence Veiller's "Buildings in Relation to Street and Site." In *Proceedings of the Third National Conference on City Planning*, 97–107. Boston: NCCP, 1911.

———. "Remarks at the Dinner Given by the City Club of Philadelphia." In *Proceedings of the Third National Conference on City Planning*, 280–84. Boston: National Conference on City Planning, 1911.

Veiller, Lawrence. "Buildings in Relation to Street and Site." In *Proceedings of the Third National Conference on City Planning*, 80–96. Boston: National Conference on City Planning, 1911.

———. "Districting by Municipal Regulation." In *Proceedings of the Eighth National Conference on City Planning*, 147–58. Boston: National Conference on City Planning, 1916.

Whitten, Robert H. "Zoning and Living Conditions." In *Proceedings of the Thirteenth Annual National Conference on City Planning*, 22–30. Boston: National Conference on City Planning, 1921.

———. "The Zoning of Residence Sections." In *Proceedings of the Tenth National Conference on City Planning*, 34–39. Boston: National Conference on City Planning, 1918.

Government Documents

Adams, Thomas, ed. *Neighborhood and Community Planning*. New York: Regional Plan of New York and Its Environs, 1929.

Advisory Committee on Zoning. *A City Planning Primer*. Washington, DC: US Government Printing Office, 1928.

———. *A Zoning Primer*. Washington, DC: US Government Printing Office, 1922.

Annual Report of the Mayor and Officers of the City of Raleigh, N.C., for the Fiscal Year Ending February 28, 1890. Raleigh, NC: E. M. Uzzel, 1890.

Birmingham Board of Education. *The Birmingham School Survey, 1923*. Birmingham, AL: Birmingham Print, 1923.

———. *The Birmingham School Survey, 1927*. Birmingham, AL: Roberts & Son, 1927.

Chicago Commission on Race Relations. *The Negro in Chicago: A Study of Race Relations and a Race Riot*. Chicago: University of Chicago Press, 1922.

Federal Housing Administration. *Underwriting Manual: Underwriting Analysis under Title II, Section 203 of the National Housing Act*. Washington, DC: Government Printing Office, 1936.

Gibson, Campbell, and Kay Jung. "Historical Census Statistics on Population Totals by Race, 1790–1990, and by Hispanic Origin, 1970 to 1990, for Large Cities and Other Urban Places in the United States." Working Paper No. 76. US Census Bureau, February 2005. www.census.gov/content/dam/Census/library/working-papers/2005/demo/POP-twps0076.pdf.

Glenn, C. B. *Report of Progress: Birmingham Public Schools, September 1, 1921 to August 31, 1931.* Birmingham, AL: Birmingham Board of Education, 1931.

Gries, John, and James Ford, eds. *Homemaking, Home Furnishing, and Information Services.* Washington, DC: White House Conference on Home Building and Home Ownership, 1932.

———. *Housing and the Community—Home Repair and Remodeling.* Washington, DC: White House Conference on Home Building and Home Ownership, 1932.

———. *Negro Housing.* Washington, DC: White House Conference on Home Building and Home Ownership, 1932.

———. *Planning for Residential Districts.* Washington, DC: White House Conference on Home Building and Home Ownership, 1932.

Gries, John M., and James S. Taylor. *How to Own Your Own Home: A Handbook for Prospective Home Owners.* Washington, DC: Government Printing Office, 1923.

Harrison, Shelby. Introduction to Perry, "Neighborhood Unit."

Houston City Planning Commission. "Midtown-Fourth Ward Neighborhood Improvement Plan." Houston, TX: Houston City Planning Department, 1975.

———. *Report of the City Planning Commission, Houston, Texas.* Houston: The Forum of Civics, 1929.

Houston Independent School District. *Annual Report of the Public Schools of the Independent School District of the City of Houston, Texas, 1919–1920.* Houston: Houston Board of Education, 1920.

———. *Annual Report of the Public Schools of the Independent School District, Houston, Texas, 1921–1922, 1922–1923.* Houston: Houston Board of Education, 1923.

———. *The Building Program of the Houston Independent School District, 1924–1930.* Houston: Press of Morin and Maes, 1931.

Houston Model City Department. *An In-Depth View of Third Ward.* Houston: Progressive Environmental Planners, 1973.

Indiana Constitutional Convention. *Report of the Debates and Proceedings of the Convention for the Revision of the Constitution of the State of Indiana, 1850.* Vol. 1. Indianapolis: A. H. Brown, 1850.

Knowles, Morris. *Report of the City Planning and Zoning Commission upon a Program for the Development of a City Plan with Specific Studies of Certain Features Thereof.* Charleston, 1931.

North Carolina Corporation Commission. *Fifth Annual Report of the North Carolina Corporation Commission for the Year Ending December 31, 1903.* Raleigh, NC: E. M. Uzzell, 1904. North Carolina Digital State Publications Collection, North Carolina Digital Collections. https://digital.ncdcr.gov/Documents/Detail/annual-report-of-the-north-carolina-corporation-commission-for-the-year-ending-...-1903/2807925.

———. *Fourth Annual Report of the North Carolina Corporation Commission for the Year Ending December 31, 1902.* Raleigh, NC: Edwards & Broughton, 1903. North Carolina Digital State Publications Collection, North Carolina Digital Collections.

https://digital.ncdcr.gov/Documents/Detail/annual-report-of-the-north-carolina-corporation-commission-for-the-year-ending-...-1902/2807926.

———. *Sixth Annual Report of the North Carolina Corporation Commission for the Year Ending December 31, 1904*. Raleigh, NC: E. M. Uzzell, 1904. North Carolina Digital State Publications Collection, North Carolina Digital Collections. https://digital.ncdcr.gov/Documents/Detail/annual-report-of-the-north-carolina-corporation-commission-for-the-year-ending-...-1904/2807929.

———. *Third Annual Report of the North Carolina Corporation Commission for the Year Ending December 31, 1901*. Raleigh, NC: Edwards & Broughton, and E. M. Uzell, 1902. North Carolina Digital State Publications Collection, North Carolina Digital Collections. https://digital.ncdcr.gov/Documents/Detail/annual-report-of-the-north-carolina-corporation-commission-for-the-year-ending-...-1901/2807924.

Perry, Clarence. "The Neighborhood Unit: A Scheme of Arrangement for the Family-Life Community." In *Neighborhood and Community Planning*, edited by Thomas Adams, 22–140. New York: Regional Plan of New York and Its Environs, 1929.

———. *The Rebuilding of Blighted Areas: A Study of the Neighborhood Unit in Replanning and Plot Assemblage*. New York: Regional Plan Association, 1933.

Raleigh Township Graded Schools. *Fortieth Annual Report of the Raleigh Township Graded Schools: Session 1916–1917*. Raleigh, NC: Edwards & Broughton, 1917. https://digital.ncdcr.gov/Documents/Detail/annual-report-of-the-raleigh-township-graded-schools-raleigh-north-carolina-1917/408436.

Strayer, George. *Abstract of a Survey of the Baltimore Public Schools, 1920–1921*. Baltimore: Board of School Commissioners, 1921.

Strayer, George, and N. L. Engelhardt. *Survey of the Public School Buildings and the School Building Program for Atlanta, Georgia*. New York: Teachers College, 1922.

Tocqueville, Alexis de. *Democracy in America*. Abridged. Translated by Henry Reeve. Edited by Henry Steele Commager. London: Oxford University Press, 1952.

UK Board of Trade. *Cost of Living in American Towns: Report of an Enquiry by the Board of Trade into Working Class Rents, Housing and Retail Prices, Together with the Rates of Wages in Certain Occupations in the Principal Industrial Towns of the United States of America*. London: His Majesty's Stationery Office, 1911.

US Census Bureau. *Abstract of the Thirteenth Census, 1910*. Washington, DC: Government Printing Office, 1913. https://www2.census.gov/library/publications/decennial/1910/abstract/abstract-1910-p3.pdf.

———. *Fourteenth Census of the United States: State Compendium, Texas*. Washington, DC: Government Printing Office, 1925. https://www2.census.gov/library/publications/decennial/1920/state-compendium/06229686v38-43ch5.pdf.

———. *Mortgages on Homes: A Report on the Results of the Inquiry as to the Mortgage Debt on Homes Other Than Farm Homes at the Fourteenth Census, 1920*. Census Monographs 11. Washington, DC: Government Printing Office, 1923. https://www2.census.gov/library/publications/decennial/1920/monograph-2/00551139n02.pdf.

West, Mary Mills. *Child Care: Part 1; The Preschool Age*. Care of Children Series 3. Children's Bureau, Department of Labor. Washington, DC: Government Printing Office, 1918.

Wheeler, Dan. *General Index to the Final Reports of the President's Conference on Home*

Building and Home Ownership. Washington, DC: President's Conference on Home Building and Home Ownership, 1933.

White House Conference of Child Health and Protection, Committee on the Family and Parent Education. *The Home and the Child: Housing, Furnishing, Management, Income, Clothing*. New York: Century, 1931.

———. *Parent Education: Types, Content, and Method*. New York: Century, 1932.

White House Conference on Child Health and Protection, Committee on the Infant and Preschool Child. *The Young Child in the Home: A Survey of Three Thousand American Families*. New York: D. Appleton-Century, 1936.

Whitten, Robert. "Five Illustrations of the Need for Zoning." *Atlanta Zone Plan: Report Outlining a Tentative Zone Plan for Atlanta*. Atlanta City Planning Commission, 1922.

Wood, Edith Elmer. *The Housing of the Unskilled Wage Earner: America's Next Problem*. New York: Macmillan, 1919.

Books, Articles, and Master's Theses

Abdy, Edward Strutt. *Journal of a Residence and Tour in the United States of North America: From April 1833 to October 1834*. Vol. 1. London: John Murray, 1835.

Allen, Ivan. *Mayor: Notes on the Sixties*. New York: Simon and Schuster, 1971.

Amis, Moses. *Historical Raleigh with Sketches of Wake County and Its Important Towns*. Raleigh, NC: Commercial Printing Company, 1913.

Anderson, Nels. "Zoning and the Mobility of Urban Population." *City Planning* 1, no. 3 (October 1925): 155–59.

Architects' Small House Service Bureau of the United States. *100 Bungalows of Frame and Masonry Construction*. Minneapolis, MN: Architects' Small House Service Bureau, 1927.

Arthur, Timothy Shay. *The Mother's Rule; or, The Right Way and the Wrong Way*. Philadelphia: Smith and Peters, 1856.

Atwell, Ernest T. "Playgrounds for Colored America." *The Playground* 15, no. 1 (April 1921): 84–89.

Bannerman, Helen. *The Story of Little Black Sambo*. Chicago: Reilly and Britton, 1908.

Bassett, Edward. "The Progressive South." *City Planning* 8, no. 3 (July 1932): 175–77.

———. *Zoning: The Laws, Administration, and Court Decisions during the First Twenty Years*. New York: Russell Sage Foundation, 1936.

———. "Zoning Roundtable." *City Planning* 3, no. 4 (October 1927): 307–11.

———. "Zoning Roundtable: Race Zoning." *City Planning* 5, no. 3 (July 1929): 194–97.

Beecher, Catharine. *A Treatise on Domestic Economy, for the Use of Young Ladies at Home, and at School*. New York: Harper, 1848. https://archive.org/details/treatiseondomestoobeec/page/n225.

Beecher, Catharine, and Harriet Beecher Stowe. *The American Woman's Home; or, Principles of Domestic Science: Being a Guide to the Formation and Maintenance of Economical, Healthful, Beautiful, and Christian Homes*. New York: J. B. Ford, 1869.

Blake, William. *Songs of Innocence*. London: William Blake, 1789. Lessing J. Rosenwald Collection, Library of Congress. www.loc.gov/item/48031328/.

Bracey, John H., Jr., and August Meier, eds. *Papers of the NAACP: Part 12. Selected*

Branch Files, 1913–1939. Series A, *The South.* Black Studies Research Sources: Microfilms from Major Archival and Manuscript Collections. Bethesda, MD: University Publications of America, 1991. Microfilm.

Brissot de Warville, Jacques Pierre. *New Travels in the United States of America.* Boston: J. Bumstead, 1788.

Bruce, Andrew A. "Racial Zoning by Private Contract in the Light of the Constitutions and the Rule Against Restraints on Alienation." *Illinois Law Review* 21, no. 7 (1926–27): 704–17.

Bryant, Ira B. *The Development of Houston Negro Schools.* Houston: Informer, 1935.

Caliver, Ambrose. *Secondary Education for Negroes.* 1932. Reprint, New York: Negro Universities Press, 1969.

Campbell, Helen. *Household Economics: A Course of Lectures in the School of Economics of the University of Wisconsin.* New York: G. P. Putnam's Sons, 1896.

———. "Is American Domesticity Decreasing, and If So, Why?" *Arena* 19 (January 1898): 96.

Caswell, Hollis. *City School Surveys: An Interpretation and Appraisal.* New York: Teachers College, Bureau of Publications, 1929.

Cheney, Charles H. "Zoning in Practice." *National Municipal Review* 9, no. 1 (January 1920): 31–43.

Consultant Service of the National Municipal League. *The Governments of Atlanta and Fulton County Georgia: A Report of a Complete Administrative and Financial Survey of the Several Departments and Activities of the City of Atlanta and Fulton County.* Atlanta: Atlanta Chamber of Commerce, 1938.

Cope, Henry F. "The Conservation of the Modern Home." In *The Child Welfare Manual: A Handbook of Child Nature and Nurture for Parents and Teachers,* edited by The Editorial Board of the University Society, 20–22. New York: University Society, 1915.

Crane, Caroline Bartlett. *Everyman's House.* Garden City, NY: Doubleday, 1925.

Crawford, Andrew Wright. "What Zoning Is." In *Zoning: As an Element in City Planning, and for Protection of Property Values, Public Safety, and Public Health,* edited by Lawson Purdy, Harland Bartholomew, Edward Bassett, Andrew Wright Crawford, and Herbert Swan, 1–8. Washington, DC: American Civic Association, 1920.

Dashiell, Benjamin. *Dashiell Family Records.* Vol. 2. Baltimore: Sun Printing Office, 1929. https://archive.org/details/dashiellfamilyreoodash_0.

Davis, Elizabeth Lindsey. *Lifting as They Climb.* 1933. Reprint, New York: G. K. Hall, 1996.

Davis, Michael. *The Exploitation of Pleasure: A Study of Commercial Recreation in New York City.* New York City: Department of Child Hygiene of the Russell Sage Foundation, 1911.

Eliot, Charles. "A Letter from President Emeritus Eliot." *City Planning* 1, no. 1 (April 1925): 33–34.

Fisher, Ernest McKinley. *Principles of Real Estate Practice.* New York: MacMillan, 1923.

Ford, James. "Planning and Equipping the Home for Children." In *The Better Homes Manual,* edited by Blanche Halbert, 194–203. Chicago: University of Chicago Press, 1931.

Frazier, Edward Franklin. "The American Negro's New Leaders." *Current History* 29 (April 1928): 56–59. www.jstor.org/stable/45332830.

Freund, Ernst. "Some Inadequately Discussed Problems of the Law of City Planning and Zoning." *Illinois Law Review* 24, no. 2 (June 1929): 136–47.

Gifford, Ward C. *Real Estate Advertising.* New York: MacMillan, 1925.

Greene, Lorenzo D. "Sidelights on Houston Negroes as Seen by an Associate of Dr. Carter G. Woodson in 1930." In *Black Dixie: Afro-Texan History and Culture in Houston,* edited by Howard Beeth and Cary D. Wintz, 134–54. College Station: Texas A&M University Press, 1992.

Grinnalds, Jefferson. "The Zoning Situation in Baltimore." *City Planning* 1, no. 3 (October 1925): 184–85.

Grund, Francis J. *The Americans in Their Moral, Social and Political Relations.* London: Longman, Rees, Orme, Brown, Green, & Longman, 1837.

Harmon, William. "Playgrounds in New Land Subdivisions." *City Planning* 2, no. 2 (April 1926): 85–86.

Headley, Madge. "Citizen Rights and Community Rights: What a Zoning Plan Is and Its Relation to Negro Housing." *Opportunity* 1, no. 1 (January 1923): 12–14.

Holland, Endesha Ida Mae. *From the Mississippi Delta: A Memoir.* Chicago: Lawrence Hill Books, 1997.

Holy, T. C., William E. Arnold, and H. W. Anderson. "School Buildings." *Review of Educational Research* 2, no. 5 (December 1932): 370–86. https://doi.org/10.2307/1167705.

Hott, George D. "Constitutionality of Municipal Zoning and Segregation Ordinances." *West Virginia Law Review* 33, no. 4 (June 1927): 333–49. https://researchrepository.wvu.edu/wvlr/vol33/iss4/3.

Hubbard, Theodora Kimball. "Annual Survey of City and Regional Planning in the United States, 1926." *City Planning* 3, no. 2 (April 1927): 111–54.

———. "A Brief Survey of City and Regional Planning in the United States, 1929." *City Planning* 6, no. 3 (July 1930): 199–224.

Ihlder, John. "Housing and the Regional Plan." *City Planning* 3, no. 1 (January 1927): 1–16.

Illinois Chapter of the American Institute of Architects. "The Illinois Chapter of the American Institute of Architects on the Need for Zoning." In *Zoning: As an Element in City Planning, and for Protection of Property Values, Public Safety, and Public Health,* edited by Lawson Purdy, Harland Bartholomew, Edward Bassett, Andrew Wright Crawford, and Herbert Swan, 21–24. Washington, DC: American Civic Association, 1920.

"In the South." *Housing Betterment* 11, no. 2 (April 1922): 189.

Ittner, W. B. "High Costs and Sane Economies in the Building of Schools." *Elementary School Journal* 24, no. 5 (January 1924): 365–67. www.jstor.org/stable/994533.

James, Harlean. *Land Planning in the United States for City, State, and Nation.* New York: MacMillan, 1926.

Jones, Thomas Jesse. *Negro Education: A Study of the Private and Higher Schools for Colored People in the United States.* Washington, DC: Government Printing Office, 1917.

———. *A Study of the Social Welfare Status of the Negroes in Houston, Texas.* Houston: Webster-Richardson, 1929.

Jones, William Henry. *The Housing of Negroes in Washington, DC: A Study in Human Ecology.* Washington, DC: Howard University Press, 1929.

Kahen, Harold. "Validity of Anti-Negro Restrictive Covenants: A Reconsideration of the Problem." *University of Chicago Law Review* 12, no. 2 (February 1945): 198–213. https://doi.org/10.2307/1597187.

Kimball, Justin F. *Our City—Dallas*. Dallas: Kessler Plan Association of Dallas, 1927.

Kimball, Theodora. "A Brief Review of City Planning in the United States, 1921–1922." *National Municipal Review* 12, no. 2 (February 1923): 77–82.

———. "A Brief Survey of City Planning Reports in the United States, 1921." *Landscape Architecture* 12 (1922): 112–16.

———. "Survey of City and Regional Planning in the United States, 1922 with a List of Plan Reports 1921–1922." *Landscape Architecture* 13, no. 2 (January 1923): 122–39.

Knight, Charles. *Negro Housing in Certain Virginia Cities*. Richmond, VA: William Byrd, 1927.

Knowles, Morris. "Trends in Present-Day City Planning in the United States, 1931." *City Planning* 8, no. 2 (April 1932): 102.

Lasker, Bruno. *Race Attitudes in Children*. 1929. Reprint, New York: Greenwood, 1968.

Lee, Yan Phou. "Why I Am Not a Heathen: A Rejoinder to Wong Chin Foo." *North American Review* 145, no. 370 (September 1887): 306–12.

Locke, John. *Some Thoughts Concerning Education*. 1693. Reprint, London: Cambridge University Press, 1934.

Lynd, Robert S., and Helen Merrell Lynd. *Middletown: A Study in Modern American Culture*. New York: Harcourt, Brace, 1929.

MacChesney, Nathan William. *The Principles of Real Estate Law: Real Property, Real Estate Documents and Transactions*. New York: Macmillan, 1927.

Marsh, Benjamin, and George B. Ford. *An Introduction to City Planning: Democracy's Challenge and the American City*. New York: Self-published, 1909.

Martin, Arthur T. "Segregation of Residences of Negroes." *Michigan Law Review* 32, no. 6 (April 1934): 721–42. https://doi.org/10.2307/1281531.

Metzenbaum, James. *The Law of Zoning*. New York: Baker, Voorhis, 1930.

Moehlman, Arthur B. *Public School Plant Program*. New York: Rand McNally, 1929.

Monchow, Helen. *The Use of Deed Restrictions in Subdivision Development*. Chicago: The Institute for Research in Land Economics and Public Utilities, 1928.

Moody, Walter D. *Wacker's Manual of the Plan of Chicago*. Chicago: Henneberry, 1911.

Napheys, George. *The Physical Life of Woman: Advice to the Maiden, Wife, and Mother*. Philadelphia: David McKay, 1890.

National Association of Real Estate Boards. *Session by Session Outline of a Course in Real Estate Fundamentals*. Chicago: National Association of Real Estate Boards, 1926.

Nichols, J. C. "Housing and the Real Estate Problem." *Annals of the American Academy of Political and Social Science* 51 (January 1914): 132–39.

Olmsted, Frederick Law. *A Journey in the Back Country: Our Slave States*. New York: Mason, 1860.

Olmsted, Vaux & Co. *Preliminary Report upon the Proposed Suburban Village at Riverside, near Chicago*. New York: Sutton, Brown, 1868.

Otis, Robert R. *Atlanta's Plan, 1909–1932*. Atlanta, 1932.

Patri, Angelo. "The Death Toll." *The Playground* 17, no. 1 (April 1923): 31.

Purdy, Lawson. "Land Values and Social Values." *City Planning* 3, no. 4 (October 1927): 253–62.

Purdy, Lawson, Harland Bartholomew, Edward Bassett, Andrew Wright Crawford, and Herbert Swan, eds. *Zoning: As an Element in City Planning, and for Protection of Property Values, Public Safety, and Public Health*. Washington, DC: American Civic Association, 1920.

"A Ranking of the State Educational Systems." *School and Society* 24 (August 1926): 167.

The Red Book of Houston: A Compendium of Social, Professional, Religious, Educational, and Industrial Interests of Houston's Colored Population. Houston: Sotex, 1915.

Riddle, Don. "'Homes to Last for All Time': The Story of Houston's River Oaks." *National Real Estate Journal* (4 March 1929): 21–28.

———. *River Oaks: A Pictorial Presentation of Houston's Residential Park*. Houston: River Oaks Corporation, 1929.

Rousseau, Jean Jacques. *Emile, or On Education*. 1763. Reprint, New York: Basic Books, 1979.

Schoff, Hannah Kent. "The National Congress of Mothers and Parent-Teacher Associations." *The Annals of the American Academy of Political and Social Science* 67 (September 1916): 139–47.

Sedgwick, Elizabeth Dwight. "The Game at Jackstraws and the Christmas Box." In *The Pearl or Affection's Gift*, edited by Thomas T. Ash, 17–52. Philadelphia: Thomas T. Ash, 1834.

Shivery, Louie Delphia Davis. "The History of Organized Social Work among Atlanta Negroes, 1890–1935." Master's thesis, Atlanta University, 1936.

Shurtleff, Flavel. "A.C.P.I. Notes." *Landscape Architecture* 15, no. 2 (January 1925): 133–34.

Smith, Lillian. *Killers of the Dream*. New York: W. W. Norton, 1949.

Stephenson, Gilbert T. "The Segregation of the White and Negro Races in Cities." *South Atlantic Quarterly* 13, no. 1 (January 1914): 1–18.

Storrow, Helen. "Better Homes for Negroes in America." *Opportunity* 9, no. 6 (June 1931): 174–77.

Stowe, Harriet Beecher. *Uncle Tom's Cabin*. 1852. Reprint, New York: Signet, 1981.

Swan, Herbert. "The Legality of Zoning." In *Zoning: As an Element in City Planning, and for Protection of Property Values, Public Safety, and Public Health*, edited by Lawson Purdy, Harland Bartholomew, Edward Bassett, Andrew Wright Crawford, and Herbert Swan, 26–33. Washington, DC: American Civic Association, 1920.

Thomas, Jesse O. "Negro Schools in Houston." *Opportunity* 8 (June 1930): 179.

Urban Land Institute. *The Community Builders Handbook*. Washington, DC: Urban Land Institute, 1947.

Wallick, Ekin. *The Small House for a Moderate Income*. New York: Hearst's International Library, 1915.

Ware, John F. W. *Home Life: What It Is, and What It Needs*. Boston: Wm. V. Spencer, 1864.

Washington, Booker T. "My View of Segregation Laws." *New Republic* 5 (4 December 1915): 113–14.

Weber, A. F. "Suburban Annexations." *North American Review* 166, no. 498 (May 1898): 612–17.

Wheeler, Gervase. *Rural Homes: Or, Sketches or Houses Suited to American Country Life, with Original Plans, Designs, &c.* New York: C. Scribner, 1851.
White, Walter. *A Man Called White: The Autobiography of Walter White.* New York: Viking, 1948.
Whitten, Robert. "Problems Involved in Zoning a Large City Like Chicago." In *Zoning in Chicago*, edited by Charles Nichols, 37–48. Chicago: Cook County Real Estate Board, 1919.
Whitten, Robert, and Thomas Andrews. *Neighborhoods of Small Homes: Economic Density of Low-Cost Housing in America and England.* Cambridge, MA: Harvard University Press, 1931.
Williams, Frank Backus. "Legal Notes." *City Planning* 3, no. 3 (July 1927): 216–23.
———. "Legal Notes." *City Planning* 6, no. 1 (January 1930): 55–58.
Wilson, Henry. *The Bungalow Book.* Chicago: Henry Wilson, 1910.
Woofter, Thomas J., Jr., ed. *Negro Problems in Cities.* New York: Doubleday, Doran, 1928.
Wordsworth, William. "Ode: Intimations of Immortality from Recollections of Early Childhood." In *William Wordsworth: The Poems*, vol. 1, edited by John O. Hayden, 523–29. New Haven, CT: Yale University Press, 1981.

Secondary Sources

Books

Agran, Edward Gale. *Herbert Hoover and the Commodification of Middle-Class America.* Lanham, MD: Lexington Books, 2016.
Amsterdam, Daniel. *Roaring Metropolis: Businessmen's Campaign for a Civic Welfare State.* Philadelphia: University of Pennsylvania Press, 2016.
Anderson, James. *The Education of Blacks in the South, 1860–1935.* Chapel Hill: University of North Carolina Press, 1988.
Austin, Paula. *Coming of Age in Jim Crow DC: Navigating the Politics of Everyday Life.* New York: New York University Press, 2019.
Barbee, Jennie M. *Historical Sketches of the Raleigh Public Schools, 1876–1942.* Raleigh, NC: Barbee Pupils' Association, 1943.
Bayor, Ronald. *Race and the Shaping of Twentieth-Century Atlanta.* Chapel Hill: University of North Carolina Press, 1996.
Bederman, Gail. *Manliness and Civilization: A Cultural History of Gender and Race in the United States, 1880–1917.* Chicago: University of Chicago Press, 1995.
Bernstein, Robin. *Racial Innocence: Performing American Childhood from Slavery to Civil Rights.* New York: New York University Press, 2011.
Blackmon, Douglas A. *Slavery by Another Name: The Re-enslavement of Black Americans from the Civil War to World War II.* New York: Anchor Books, 2008.
Blank, David M. *The Volume of Residential Construction, 1889–1950.* New York: National Bureau of Economic Research, 1954.
Boydston, Jeanne. *Home and Work: Housework, Wages, and the Ideology of Labor in the Early Republic.* New York: Oxford University Press, 1990.
Brooks, Richard R. W., and Carol M. Rose, *Saving the Neighborhood: Racially Restrictive Covenants, Law, and Social Norms.* Cambridge, MA: Harvard University Press, 2013.

Brown, Karida L. *The New Brownies' Book: A Love Letter to Black Families.* San Francisco: Chronicle Books, 2023.
Brown, Lawrence T. *The Black Butterfly: The Harmful Politics of Race and Space in America.* Baltimore: Johns Hopkins University Press, 2021.
Bryant, Ira B. *Texas Southern University: Its Antecedents, Political Origin, and Future.* Houston: Bryant, 1975.
Butler, George D. *Pioneers in Public Recreation.* Minneapolis, MN: Burgess, 1965.
Cahn, Susan K. *Sexual Reckonings: Southern Girls in a Troubling Age.* Cambridge, MA: Harvard University Press, 2007.
Carter, Prudence L., and Kevin G. Welner. *Closing the Opportunity Gap: What America Must Do to Give Every Child an Even Chance.* New York: Oxford University Press, 2013.
Carter, Wilmoth A. *Shaw's Universe: A Monument to Educational Innovation.* Raleigh: Shaw University, 1973.
Cashin, Sheryll. *White Space, Black Hood: Opportunity Hoarding and Segregation in the Age of Inequality.* Boston: Beacon Press, 2021.
Cauthen, Carmen Wimberley. *Historic Black Neighborhoods of Raleigh.* Charleston, SC: The History Press, 2023.
———. *Raleigh's Black Community in the Reconstruction Era.* Charleston, SC: The History Press, forthcoming.
Cell, John Whitson. *The Highest Stage of White Supremacy: The Origins of Segregation in South Africa and the American South.* Cambridge, UK: Cambridge University Press, 1982.
Chaskin, Robert J., and Mark L. Joseph. *Integrating the Inner City: The Promise and Perils of Mixed-Income Public Housing Transformation.* Chicago: University of Chicago Press, 2015.
Chatelain, Marcia. *South Side Girls: Growing Up in the Great Migration.* Durham, NC: Duke University Press, 2015.
Chudacoff, Howard. *Children at Play: An American History.* New York: New York University Press, 2007.
Clark, Clifford Edward, Jr. *The American Family Home, 1800–1960.* Chapel Hill: University of North Carolina Press, 1986.
Cohen, Lizabeth. *A Consumer's Republic: The Politics of Mass Consumption in Postwar America.* New York: Knopf, 2003.
Connerly, Charles. *The Most Segregated City in America: City Planning and Civil Rights in Birmingham, 1920–1980.* Charlottesville: University of Virginia Press, 2005.
Connolly, N. D. B. *A World More Concrete: Real-Estate and the Remaking of Jim Crow South Florida.* Chicago: University of Chicago Press, 2014.
Coontz, Stephanie. *The Social Origins of Private Life: A History of American Families, 1600–1900.* London: Verso, 1988.
———. *The Way We Never Were: American Families and the Nostalgia Trap.* New York: Basic Books, 1992.
Cox, Richard, David Gwynn, and Erin Lawrimore. *North Carolina Triad Beer: A History.* Charleston, SC: The History Press, 2021.
Crockett, Norman. *The Black Towns.* Lawrence: University Press of Kansas, 1979.
Cronon, William. *Changes in the Land: Indians, Colonists, and the Ecology of New England.* Rev. ed. New York: Hill and Wang, 2003.

Cross, Gary. *Kids' Stuff: Toys and the Changing World of American Childhood.* Cambridge, MA: Harvard University Press, 1997.
Dahir, James. *The Neighborhood Unit Plan: Its Spread and Acceptance.* New York: Russell Sage Foundation, 1947.
Danielson, Michael N. *The Politics of Exclusion.* New York: Columbia University Press, 1976.
Degler, Carl. *At Odds: Women and the Family in America from the Revolution to the Present.* New York: Oxford University Press, 1980.
Demos, John. *Past, Present, and Personal: The Family and the Life Course in American History.* New York: Oxford University Press, 1986.
Doepke, Matthias, and Fabrizio Zilibotti. *Love, Money and Parenting: How Economics Explains the Way We Raise Our Kids.* Princeton, NJ: Princeton University Press, 2019.
Dollard, John. *Caste and Class in a Southern Town.* New Haven, CT: Pub. for the Institute of Human Relations by Yale University Press, 1937.
Dorsey, Allison. *To Build Our Lives Together: Community Formation in Black Atlanta, 1875–1906.* Athens: University of Georgia Press, 2004.
Douglas, Davison M. *Jim Crow Moves North: The Battle over Northern School Segregation, 1865–1954.* New York: Cambridge University Press, 2005.
Doyle, Don. *New Men, New Cities, New South: Atlanta, Nashville, Charleston, Mobile, 1860–1910.* Chapel Hill: University of North Carolina Press, 1985.
Driskell, Jay Winston, Jr. *Schooling Jim Crow: The Fight for Atlanta's Booker T. Washington High School and the Roots of Black Protest Politics.* Charlottesville: University of Virginia Press, 2014.
Duany, Andres, Elizabeth Plater-Zyberk, and Jeff Speck. *Suburban Nation: The Rise of Sprawl and the Decline of the American Dream.* New York: North Point, 2010.
Du Bois, W. E. B. *Black Reconstruction in America.* 1935. Reprint, New York: Atheneum, 1992.
Duneier, Mitchell. *Ghetto: The Invention of a Place, the History of an Idea.* New York: Farrar, Straus and Giroux, 2016.
Eagles, Charles. *Jonathan Daniels and Race Relations: The Evolution of a Southern Liberal.* Knoxville: University of Tennessee Press, 1982.
Edge, Sarah Simms. *Joel Hurt and the Development of Atlanta.* Atlanta: Atlanta Historical Society, 1955.
Ehrenreich, Barbara. *Fear of Falling: The Inner Life of the Middle Class.* New York: Pantheon, 1989.
Ellen, Ingrid Gould, and Justin Peter Steil, eds. *The Dream Revisited: Contemporary Debates about Housing, Segregation, and Opportunity.* New York: Columbia University Press, 2019.
Engelhardt, Tom. *The End of Victory Culture: Cold War America and the Disillusioning of a Generation.* Rev. ed. Amherst: University of Massachusetts Press, 2007.
Erickson, Ansley. *Making the Unequal Metropolis: School Desegregation and Its Limits.* Chicago: University of Chicago Press, 2016.
Ewen, Elizabeth. *Immigrant Women in the Land of Dollars: Life and Culture on the Lower East Side, 1890–1925.* New York: Monthly Review Press, 1985.
Fairbanks, Robert. *For the City as a Whole: Planning, Politics, and the Public Interest in Dallas, Texas, 1900–1965.* Columbus: Ohio State University Press, 1998.

Fass, Paula. *The End of American Childhood: A History of Parenting from Life on the Frontier to the Managed Child*. Princeton, NJ: Princeton University Press, 2016.
Fennell, Lee Anne. *The Unbounded Home: Property Values beyond Property Lines*. New Haven, CT: Yale University Press, 2009.
Ferguson, Cheryl. *Highland Park and River Oaks: The Origins of Garden Suburban Community Planning in Texas*. Austin: University of Texas Press, 2014.
Ferguson, Karen. *Black Politics in New Deal Atlanta*. Chapel Hill: University of North Carolina Press, 2002.
Fishman, Robert. *Bourgeois Utopias: The Rise and Fall of Suburbia*. New York: Basic Books, 1987.
Fitzpatrick, Ellen. *Endless Crusade: Women Social Scientists and Progressive Reform*. New York: Oxford University Press, 1990.
Florida, Richard. *The New Urban Crisis: How Our Cities Are Increasing Inequality, Deepening Segregation, and Failing the Middle Class—And What We Can Do about It*. New York: Basic Books, 2017.
Fogelson, Robert. *Bourgeois Nightmares: Suburbia, 1870–1930*. New Haven, CT: Yale University Press, 2005.
Foner, Eric. *A Short History of Reconstruction, 1863–1877*. New York: Harper and Row, 1990.
Freund, David. *Colored Property: State Policy and White Racial Politics in Suburban America*. Chicago: University of Chicago Press, 2007.
Gaines, Kevin. *Uplifting the Race: Black Leadership, Politics, and Culture in the Twentieth Century*. Chapel Hill: University of North Carolina Press, 1996.
Garb, Margaret. *City of American Dreams: A History of Home Ownership*. Chicago: University of Chicago Press, 2005.
García, David G. *Strategies of Segregation: Race, Residence, and the Struggle for Educational Equality*. Oakland: University of California Press, 2018.
Garrett, Franklin M. *Atlanta and Environs: A Chronicle of Its People and Events*. Vol. 2. Athens: University of Georgia Press, 1969.
Gilmore, Glenda Elizabeth. *Gender and Jim Crow: Women and the Politics of White Supremacy in North Carolina, 1896–1920*. Chapel Hill: University of North Carolina Press, 1996.
Glazer, Nathan, and Davis McEntire, eds. *Studies in Housing and Minority Groups*. Berkeley: University of California Press, 1960.
Glotzer, Paige. *How the Suburbs Were Segregated: Developers and the Business of Exclusionary Housing, 1890–1960*. New York: Columbia University Press, 2020.
Godshalk, David Fort. *Veiled Visions: The 1906 Atlanta Race Riot and the Reshaping of American Race Relations*. Chapel Hill: University of North Carolina Press, 2005.
Goetz, Edward. *New Deal Ruins: Race, Economic Justice, and Public Housing Policy*. Ithaca, NY: Cornell University Press, 2013.
Gonda, Jeffrey. *Unjust Deeds: The Restrictive Covenant Cases and the Making of the Civil Rights Movement*. Chapel Hill: University of North Carolina Press, 2015.
Gordon, Colin. *Mapping Decline: St. Louis and the Fate of the American City*. Philadelphia: University of Pennsylvania Press, 2008.
Gordon, Linda. *The Second Coming of the KKK: The Ku Klux Klan of the 1920s and the American Political Tradition*. New York: Liveright Publishing Corporation, 2017.

Gordon-Reed, Annette. *The Hemingses of Monticello: An American Family.* New York: W. W. Norton, 2008.
Gotham, Kevin Fox. *Race, Real Estate, and Uneven Development: The Kansas City Experience, 1900–2010.* 2nd ed. Albany: State University of New York Press, 2014.
Graff, Harvey J. *The Dallas Myth: The Making and Unmaking or an American City.* Minneapolis: University of Minnesota Press, 2008.
Grantham, Dewey. *Hoke Smith and the Politics of the New South.* Baton Rouge: Louisiana State University Press, 1958.
Grossman, James. *Land of Hope: Chicago, Black Southerners, and the Great Migration.* Chicago: University of Chicago Press, 1989.
Gutman, Marta. *A City for Children: Women, Architecture, and the Charitable Landscapes of Oakland, 1850–1950.* Chicago: University of Chicago Press, 2014.
Hale, Grace Elizabeth. *Making Whiteness: The Culture of Segregation in the South, 1890–1940.* New York: Vintage Books, 1999.
Haley, John. *Charles N. Hunter and Race Relations in North Carolina.* Chapel Hill: University of North Carolina Press, 1987.
Hanchett, Thomas. *Sorting Out the New South City: Race, Class, and Urban Development in Charlotte, 1875–1975.* Chapel Hill: University of North Carolina Press, 1998.
Harris, Linda, ed. *Early Raleigh Neighborhoods and Buildings.* Raleigh: Raleigh City Council, 1983.
Hayden, Dolores. *Building Suburbia: Green Fields and Urban Growth, 1820—2000.* New York: Pantheon Books, 2003.
Haynes, Robert V. *A Night of Violence: The Houston Riot of 1917.* Baton Rouge: Louisiana State University Press, 1976.
Hendricks, Wanda A. *Fannie Barrier Williams: Crossing the Borders of Region and Race.* Urbana: University of Illinois Press, 2014.
———. *Gender, Race, and Politics in the Midwest: Black Club Women in Illinois.* Bloomington: Indiana University Press, 1998.
Herbin-Triant, Elizabeth A. *Threatening Property: Race, Class, and Campaigns to Legislate Jim Crow Neighborhoods.* New York: Columbia University Press, 2019.
Higginbotham, Evelyn Brooks. *Righteous Discontent: The Women's Movement in the Black Baptist Church, 1880–1920.* Cambridge, MA: Harvard University Press, 1994.
Highsmith, Andrew. *Demolition Means Progress: Flint, Michigan, and the Fate of the American Metropolis.* Chicago: University of Chicago Press, 2016.
Hilger, Nate G. *The Parent Trap: How to Stop Overloading Parents and Fix Our Inequality Crisis.* Cambridge, MA: MIT Press, 2022.
Hobson, Maurice J. *The Legend of the Black Mecca: Politics and Class in the Making of Modern Atlanta.* Chapel Hill: University of North Carolina Press, 2017.
Hornstein, Jeffrey M. *A Nation of Realtors: A Cultural History of the Twentieth-Century American Middle Class.* Durham, NC: Duke University Press, 2005.
Howell, Ocean. *Making the Mission: Planning and Ethnicity in San Francisco.* Chicago: University of Chicago Press, 2015.
Hunt, D. Bradford. *Blueprint for Disaster: The Unraveling of Chicago Public Housing.* Chicago: University of Chicago Press, 2009.
Hurley, Andrew. *Environmental Inequalities: Class, Race, and Industrial Pollution in Gary, Indiana, 1945–1980.* Chapel Hill: University of North Carolina Press, 1995.

Jackson, Kenneth T. *Crabgrass Frontier: The Suburbanization of the United States.* New York: Oxford University Press, 1985.
———. *The Ku Klux Klan in the City, 1915–1930.* New York: Oxford University Press, 1967.
Jacobson, Lisa. *Raising Consumers: Children in the American Mass Market in the Early Twentieth Century.* New York: Columbia University Press, 2004.
Jenkins, Destin. *The Bonds of Inequality: Debt and the Making of the American City.* Chicago: University of Chicago Press, 2021.
Johnson, Charles Spurgeon. *Into the Main Stream: A Survey of Best Practices in Race Relations in the South.* Chapel Hill: University of North Carolina Press, 1947.
———. *Patterns of Negro Segregation.* 4th ed. New York: Harper, 1943.
Johnson, Hannibal B. *Black Wall Street: From Riot to Renaissance in Tulsa's Historic Greenwood District.* Austin: Eakin Press, 1998.
Jones, Kimberly. *How We Can Win: Race, History, and Changing the Money Game That's Rigged.* New York: Henry Holt, 2022.
Kett, Joseph F. *Rites of Passage: Adolescence in America, 1790 to the Present.* New York: Basic Books, 1977.
Kevles, Daniel. *In the Name of Eugenics: Genetics and the Uses of Human Heredity.* Cambridge, MA: Harvard University Press, 1998.
King, John O. *Joseph Stephen Cullinan: A Study of Leadership in the Texas Petroleum Industry, 1897–1923.* Nashville: Vanderbilt University Press, 1970.
King, Shannon. *Whose Harlem Is This, Anyway? Community Politics and Grassroots Activism During the New Negro Era.* New York: New York University Press, 2015.
King, Wilma. *African American Childhoods: Historical Perspectives from Slavery to Civil Rights.* New York: Palgrave MacMillan, 2005.
Kirby, Jack Temple. *Darkness at the Dawning: Race and Reform in the Progressive South.* Philadelphia: J. B. Lippincott, 1972.
Kirkland, Kate Sayen. *The Hogg Family and Houston: Philanthropy and the Civic Ideal.* Austin: University of Texas Press, 2009.
Klarman, Michael J. *From Jim Crow to Civil Rights: The Supreme Court and the Struggle for Racial Equality.* New York: Oxford University Press, 2004.
Klepp, Susan. *Revolutionary Conceptions: Women, Fertility, and Family Limitation in America, 1760–1820.* Chapel Hill: University of North Carolina Press, 2009.
Knupfer, Anne Meis. *Toward a Tenderer Humanity and a Nobler Womanhood: African American Women's Clubs in Turn-of-the-Century Chicago.* New York: New York University Press, 1996.
Kousser, J. Morgan. *The Shaping of Southern Politics: Suffrage Restriction and the Establishment of the One-Party South, 1880–1910.* New Haven, CT: Yale University Press, 1974.
Kruse, Kevin. *White Flight: Atlanta and the Making of Modern Conservatism.* Princeton, NJ: Princeton University Press, 2005.
Krysan, Maria, and Kyle Crowder. *Cycle of Segregation: Social Processes and Residential Stratification.* New York: Russell Sage Foundation, 2017.
Kuhn, Clifford M., Harlon E. Joye, and E. Bernard West. *Living Atlanta: An Oral History of the City, 1914–1948.* Athens: University of Georgia Press, 1990.
Kusmer, Kenneth L. *A Ghetto Takes Shape: Black Cleveland, 1870–1930.* Urbana: University of Illinois Press, 1976.

Ladd-Taylor, Molly. *Mother Work: Women, Child Welfare, and the State, 1890–1930*. Urbana: University of Illinois Press, 1995.

Landry, Bart. *The New Black Middle Class*. Berkeley: University of California Press, 1987.

Lands, LeeAnn. *Culture of Property: Race, Class, and Housing Landscapes in Atlanta, 1880–1950*. Athens: University of Georgia Press, 2009.

Larson, John Lauritz. *The Market Revolution in America: Liberty, Ambition, and the Eclipse of the Common Good*. New York: Cambridge University Press, 2010.

Lasch, Christopher. *Haven in a Heartless World: The Family Besieged*. New York: Basic Books, 1977.

Lassiter, Matthew D. *The Silent Majority: Suburban Politics in the Sunbelt South*. Princeton, NJ: Princeton University Press, 2006.

Leavitt, Judith Walzer. *The Healthiest City: Milwaukee and the Politics of Health Reform*. Princeton, NJ: Princeton University Press, 1982.

Leonard, Thomas C. *Illiberal Reformers: Race, Eugenics, and American Economics in the Progressive Era*. Princeton, NJ: Princeton University Press, 2017.

Levine, David Allan. *Internal Combustion: The Races in Detroit, 1915–1926*. Westport, CT: Greenwood, 1976.

Levine, Madeleine. *Teach Your Children Well: Parenting for Authentic Success*. New York: Harper, 2012.

Lewis, Earl. *In Their Own Interests: Race, Class, and Power in Twentieth-Century Norfolk, Virginia*. Berkeley: University of California Press, 1991.

Litwack, Leon F. *North of Slavery: The Negro in the Free States, 1790–1860*. Chicago: University of Chicago Press, 1961.

Marable, Manning. *How Capitalism Underdeveloped Black America: Problems in Race, Political Economy, and Society*. Boston: South End Press, 1983.

Massey, Douglas S., and Nancy Denton. *American Apartheid: Segregation and the Making of the Underclass*. Cambridge, MA: Harvard University Press, 1998.

May, Elaine Tyler. *Homeward Bound: American Families in the Cold War Era*. New York: Basic Books, 1988.

McCabe, Brian J. *No Place Like Home: Wealth, Community, and the Politics of Homeownership*. New York: Oxford University Press, 2016.

McGuire, Danielle. *At the Dark End of the Street: Black Women, Rape, and Resistance—a New History of the Civil Rights Movement from Rosa Parks to the Rise of Black Power*. New York: Alfred A. Knopf, 2010.

McMillen, Neil. *Dark Journey: Black Mississippians in the Age of Jim Crow*. Urbana: University of Illinois, 1990.

McRae, Elizabeth Gillespie. *Mothers of Massive Resistance: White Women and the Politics of White Supremacy*. New York: Oxford University Press, 2018.

Meier, August, and Elliott Rudwick. *From Plantation to Ghetto*. 3rd ed. New York: Hill and Wang, 1976.

Meyer, Stephen. *As Long As They Don't Move Next Door: Segregation and Racial Conflict in American Neighborhoods*. Lanham, MD: Rowman & Littlefield, 1999.

Michney, Todd. *Surrogate Suburbs: Black Upward Mobility and Neighborhood Change in Cleveland, 1900–1980*. Chapel Hill: University of North Carolina Press, 2017.

Mintz, Steven. *Huck's Raft: A History of American Childhood*. Cambridge, MA: Belknap Press of Harvard University Press, 2004.
Mixon, Gregory. *The Atlanta Riot: Race, Class, and Violence in a New South City*. Gainesville: University Press of Florida, 2005.
Mohl, James. *Abortion in America: The Origins and Evolution of National Policy, 1800–1900*. New York: Oxford University Press, 1978.
Morgan, Jennifer. *Laboring Women: Reproduction and Gender in New World Slavery*. Philadelphia: University of Pennsylvania Press, 2004.
Myrdal, Gunnar. *An American Dilemma: The Negro Problem and Modern Democracy*. New York: Harper, 1944.
Nissenbaum, Stephen. *The Battle for Christmas: A Social and Cultural History of Our Most Cherished Holiday*. New York: Vintage, 1997.
Norton, Mary Beth. *Liberty's Daughters: The Revolutionary Experience of American Women, 1750–1800*. Boston: Scott, Foresman, 1980.
Odem, Mary E. *Delinquent Daughters: Protesting and Policing Adolescent Female Sexuality in the US, 1885–1920*. Chapel Hill: University of North Carolina Press, 1995.
Orfield, Gary. *Must We Bus? Segregated Schools and National Policy*. Washington, DC: Brookings Institution Press, 1978.
———. *The Walls Around Opportunity: The Failure of Colorblind Policy for Higher Education*. Princeton, NJ: Princeton University Press, 2022.
Peterson, Jon A. *The Birth of City Planning in the United States, 1840–1917*. Baltimore: Johns Hopkins University Press, 2003.
Philpott, Thomas. *The Slum and the Ghetto: Neighborhood Deterioration and Middle-Class Reform, Chicago, 1880–1930*. New York: Oxford University Press, 1978.
Pietila, Antero. *Not in My Neighborhood: How Bigotry Shaped a Great American City*. Chicago: Ivan R. Dee, 2010.
Platt, Harold L. *City Building in the New South: The Growth of Public Services in Houston, Texas, 1830–1915*. Philadelphia: Temple University Press, 1983.
Pomerantz, Gary. *Where Peachtree Street Meets Sweet Auburn: The Saga of Two Families and the Making of Atlanta*. New York: Scribner, 1996.
Preston, Howard. *Automobile Age Atlanta: The Making of a Southern Metropolis, 1900–1935*. Athens: University of Georgia Press, 1979.
Pruitt, Bernadette. *The Other Great Migration: The Movement of Rural African Americans to Houston, 1900–1941*. College Station: Texas A&M University Press, 2013.
Putnam, Robert. *Our Kids: The American Dream in Crisis*. New York: Simon & Schuster, 2015.
Rabinowitz, Howard. *Race Relations in the Urban South, 1865–1890*. Athens: University of Georgia Press, 1996.
Radford, Gail. *Modern Housing for America: Policy Struggles in the New Deal Era*. Chicago: University of Chicago Press, 1996.
Reed, Touré F. *Not Alms but Opportunity: The Urban League and the Politics of Racial Uplift, 1910–1950*. Chapel Hill: University of North Carolina Press, 2008.
Reese, William. *The Origins of the American High School*. New Haven, CT: Yale University Press, 1995.
Reeves, Richard V. *Dream Hoarders: How the Upper Middle Class Is Leaving Everyone*

Else in the Dust, Why That Is a Problem, and What to Do about It. Brookings Institution Press: Washington, DC, 2018.

Rittenhouse, Jennifer. *Growing Up Jim Crow: How Black and White Southern Children Learned Race.* Chapel Hill: University of North Carolina Press, 2006.

Robinson, Charles F., II. *Dangerous Liaisons: Sex and Love in the Segregated South.* Fayetteville: University of Arkansas Press, 2003.

Rome, Adam. *The Bulldozer in the Countryside: Suburban Sprawl and the Rise of American Environmentalism.* New York: Cambridge University Press, 2001.

Rothstein, Leah, and Richard Rothstein. *Just Action: How to Challenge Segregation Enacted under the Color of Law.* New York: Liverlight, 2023.

Rothstein, Richard. *The Color of Law: A Forgotten History of How Our Government Segregated America.* New York: Liveright Publishing, 2017.

Rouse, Jacqueline Anne. *Lugenia Burns Hope: Black Southern Reformer.* Athens: University of Georgia Press, 1998.

Royster, Jacqueline Jones, ed. *Southern Horrors and Other Writings: The Anti-Lynching Campaign of Ida B. Wells, 1892–1900.* Boston: Bedford Books, 1997.

Rury, John L. *Creating the Suburban School Advantage: Race, Localism, and Inequality in an American Metropolis.* Ithaca, NY: Cornell University Press, 2020.

Ryan, Mary P. *Cradle of the Middle Class: The Family in Oneida County, New York, 1790–1865.* Cambridge: Cambridge University Press, 1981.

Sampson, Robert. *Great American City: Chicago and the Enduring Neighborhood Effect.* Chicago: University of Chicago Press, 2012.

San Miguel, Guadalupe, Jr. *Brown Not White: School Integration and the Chicano Movement in Houston.* College Station: Texas A&M University Press, 2001.

Scanlon, Jennifer. *Inarticulate Longings: The Ladies' Home Journal, Gender, and the Promises of Consumer Culture.* New York: Routledge, 1995.

Scott, Mel. *American City Planning Since 1890.* Berkeley: University of California Press, 1969.

Selig, Diana. *Americans All: The Cultural Gifts Movement.* Cambridge, MA: Harvard University Press, 2008.

Seligman, Amanda. *Block by Block: Neighborhoods and Public Policy on Chicago's West Side.* Chicago: University of Chicago Press, 2005.

Selingo, Jeffrey. *Who Gets In and Why: A Year Inside College Admission.* New York: Scribner, 2020.

Shah, Nayan. *Contagious Divides: Epidemics and Race in San Francisco's Chinatown.* Berkeley: University of California Press, 2002.

Sharkey, Patrick. *Neighborhoods and the Black-White Mobility Gap.* Washington, DC: Economic Mobility Project, 2009.

———. *Stuck in Place: Urban Neighborhoods and the End of Progress Toward Racial Equality.* Chicago: University of Chicago Press, 2013.

Silver, Christopher, and John V. Moeser. *The Separate City: Black Communities in the Urban South, 1940–1980.* Lexington: University Press of Kentucky, 1995.

Simmons, LaKisha Michelle. *Crescent City Girls: The Lives of Young Black Women in Segregated New Orleans.* Chapel Hill: University of North Carolina Press, 2015. https://doi.org/10.5149/northcarolina/9781469622804.001.0001.

Simmons-Henry, Linda. *Culture Town: Life in Raleigh's African American Communities.* Raleigh, NC: Raleigh Historic Districts, 1993.
Sklar, Kathryn Kish. *Catharine Beecher: A Study in American Domesticity.* New York: W. W. Norton, 1976.
Smith, Preston H., II. *Racial Democracy and the Black Metropolis: Housing Policy in Postwar Chicago.* Minneapolis: University of Minnesota Press, 2012.
Spear, Allan. *Black Chicago: The Making of a Negro Ghetto.* Chicago: University of Chicago Press, 1967.
Speer, Robert E. *John J. Eagan: A Memoir of an Adventurer for the Kingdom of God on Earth.* Birmingham, AL: American Cost Iron Pipe Company, 1939.
Stearns, Peter N. *Anxious Parents: A History of Modern Childrearing in America.* New York: New York University Press, 2003.
Steffes, Tracy L. *Structuring Inequality: How Schooling, Housing, and Tax Policies Shaped Metropolitan Development and Education.* Chicago: University of Chicago Press, 2024.
Steinberg, Ted. *Down to Earth: Nature's Role in American History.* 4th ed. New York: Oxford University Press, 2019.
Steptoe, Tyina. *Houston Bound: Culture and Color in a Jim Crow City.* Oakland: University of California Press, 2016.
Stern, Walter. *Race and Education in New Orleans: Creating the Segregated City, 1764–1960.* Baton Rouge: Louisiana State University Press, 2018.
Straus, Emily E. *Death of a Suburban Dream: Race and Schools in Compton, California.* Philadelphia: University of Pennsylvania Press, 2014.
Suggs, Henry Lewis, eds. *The Black Press in the South, 1865–1979.* Westport, CT: Greenwood, 1983.
Sugrue, Thomas. *The Origins of the Urban Crisis: Race and Inequality in Postwar Detroit.* Princeton, NJ: Princeton University Press, 1996.
Tauber, Karl E., and Alma F. Tauber. *Negroes in Cities: Residential Segregation and Neighborhood Change.* New York: Atheneum, 1969.
Taylor, Dorceta E. *Toxic Communities: Environmental Racism, Industrial Pollution, and Residential Mobility.* New York: New York University Press, 2014.
Taylor, Keeanga-Yamahtta. *Race for Profit: How Banks and the Real Estate Industry Undermined Black Homeownership.* Chapel Hill: University of North Carolina Press, 2019.
Taylor, Quintard. *In Search of the Racial Frontier: African Americans in the American West, 1528–1990.* New York: W. W. Norton, 1998.
Thomas, June Manning, and Marsha Ritzdorf, eds. *Urban Planning and the African American Community: In the Shadows.* Thousand Oaks, CA: Sage, 1997.
Thuesen, Sarah Caroline. *Greater than Equal: African American Struggles for Schools and Citizenship in North Carolina, 1919–1965.* Chapel Hill: University of North Carolina Press, 2013.
Tilly, Charles. *Durable Inequality.* Berkeley: University of California Press, 1998.
Tindall, George Brown. *The Emergence of the New South, 1913–1945.* Baton Rouge: Louisiana State University Press, 1967.
Todd-Breland, Elizabeth. *A Political Education: Black Politics and Education Reform in Chicago since the 1960s.* Chapel Hill: University of North Carolina Press, 2018.

Toll, Seymour I. *Zoned American*. New York: Grossman, 1969.
Tretter, Eliot M. *Shadows of a Sunbelt City: The Environment, Racism, and the Knowledge Economy in Austin*. Athens: University of Georgia Press, 2016.
Trounstine, Jessica. *Segregation by Design: Local Politics and Inequality in American Cities*. New York: Cambridge University Press, 2018.
Tyack, David. *The One Best System: A History of American Urban Education*. Cambridge, MA: Harvard University Press, 1974.
Vale, Lawrence J. *Purging the Poorest: Public Housing and the Design Politics of Twice-Cleared Communities*. Chicago: University of Chicago Press, 2013.
Wallace, James. *The Promise of Progressivism: Angelo Patri and Urban Education*. New York: Peter Lang, 2006.
Walsh, Camille. *Racial Taxation: Schools, Segregation, and Taxpayer Citizenship, 1869–1973*. Chapel Hill: University of North Carolina Press, 2018.
Webster, Crystal Lynn. *Beyond the Boundaries of Childhood: African American Children in the Antebellum North*. Chapel Hill: University of North Carolina Press, 2021.
Weiss, Marc. *The Rise of the Community Builders: The American Real Estate Industry and Urban Land Planning*. New York: Columbia University Press, 1987.
Wellman, Judith. *The Road to Seneca Falls: Elizabeth Cady Stanton and the First Women's Rights Convention*. Urbana: University of Illinois Press, 2004.
Wertheimer, John. *Law and Society in the South: A History of North Carolina Court Cases*. Lexington: University Press of Kentucky, 2009.
Westervelt, Amy. *Forget "Having It All": How America Messed Up Motherhood—and How to Fix It*. New York: Seal Press, 2018.
Weyeneth, Robert R. *Historic Preservation for a Living City: Historic Charleston Foundation, 1947–1997*. Columbia: University of South Carolina Press, 2000.
White, Dana F., and Victor A. Kramer, eds. *Olmsted South: Old South Critic / New South Planner*. Westport, CT: Greenwood, 1979.
Wiese, Andrew. *Places of Their Own: African American Suburbanization in the Twentieth Century*. Chicago: University of Chicago Press, 2004.
Williams, Heather Andrea. *Self-Taught: African American Education in Slavery and Freedom*. Chapel Hill: University of North Carolina Press, 2005.
Williams, Rhonda Y. *The Politics of Public Housing: Black Women's Struggles against Urban Inequality*. New York: Oxford University Press, 2005.
Wolcott, Victoria. *Remaking Respectability: African American Women in Interwar Detroit*. Chapel Hill: University of North Carolina Press, 2001.
Woodward, C. Vann. *Origins of the New South, 1877–1913*. Baton Rouge: Louisiana State University Press, 1971.
———. *The Strange Career of Jim Crow*. New York: Oxford University Press, 1957.
Worley, William S. *J. C. Nichols and the Shaping of Kansas City: Innovation in Planned Residential Communities*. Columbia: University of Missouri Press, 1993.
Wright, Gavin. *Old South, New South: Revolutions in the Southern Economy since the Civil War*. Baton Rouge: Louisiana State University Press, 1996.
Wright, Gwendolyn. *Building the Dream: A Social History of Housing in America*. Cambridge, MA: MIT Press, 1983.
Zelizer, Viviana A. *Pricing the Priceless Child: The Changing Social Value of Children*. Princeton, NJ: Princeton University Press, 1985.

Articles, Chapters, Reports, and Working Papers

American Eugenics Society. *Report of the President of the American Eugenics Society, Inc.* New Haven, CT: American Eugenics Society, June 26, 1926. www.eugenicsarchive.org/html/eugenics/static/images/635.html.

Balto, Simon. "White Rage, White Liberals, and the Making of the Second Ghetto." *Journal of Urban History* 46, no. 3 (January 2020): 511–15. https://doi.org/10.1177/0096144219891151.

Bauman, Mark K. "Centripetal and Centrifugal Forces Facing the People of Many Communities: Atlanta Jewry from the Frank Case to the Great Depression." *Atlanta Historical Journal* 23, no. 3 (Fall 1979): 25–54.

Beard, Rick. "From Suburb to Defended Neighborhood: The Evolution of Inman Park and Ansley Park, 1890–1980." *Atlanta Historical Journal* 26, no. 2 (Summer 1982): 113–40.

Beeth, Howard, and Cary D. Wintz. Introduction to *Black Dixie: Afro-Texan History and Culture in Houston*, edited by Howard Beeth and Cary D. Wintz, 13–31. College Station: Texas A&M University Press, 1992.

Bell, Derrick A., Jr. "Brown v. Board of Education and the Interest-Convergence Dilemma." *Harvard Law Review* 93, no. 3 (January 1980): 518–33. https://doi.org/10.2307/1340546.

Benjamin, Karen. "Suburbanizing Jim Crow: The Impact of School Policy on Residential Segregation in Raleigh." *Journal of Urban History* 30, no. 2 (March 2012): 225–46. https://doi.org/10.1177/0096144211427114.

Biles, Roger. "Public Housing and the Postwar Urban Renaissance, 1949–1973." In *From Tenements to the Taylor Homes: In Search of an Urban Housing Policy in Twentieth-Century America*, edited by John F. Bauman, Roger Biles, and Kristin M. Szylvian, 143–162. University Park: Pennsylvania State University Press, 2000.

Boger, Gretchen. "The Meaning of Neighborhood in the Modern City." *Journal of Urban History* 35, no. 2 (January 2009): 236–58. https://doi.org/10.1177/0096144208327915.

Boris, Eileen. "The Power of Motherhood: Black and White Activist Women Redefine the 'Political.'" *Yale Journal of Law and Feminism* 2 (1989): 25–49.

Bound, John, Brad Hershbein, and Bridget Terry Long. "Playing the Admissions Game: Student Reactions to Increasing College Competition." National Bureau of Economic Research, Working Paper 15272. www.nber.org/papers/w15272.pdf.

Bourdieu, Pierre. "The Forms of Capital." In *Handbook of Theory and Research for the Sociology of Education*, edited by John Richardson, 241–58. New York: Greenwood, 1986.

Brooks, Arthur V. N. "The Office File Box—Emanations from the Battlefield." In *Zoning and the American Dream: Promises Still to Keep*, edited by Charles M. Haar and Jerold S. Kayden, 3–30. Chicago: American Planning Association, 1989.

Brown, Charlotte V. "Three Raleigh Suburbs: Glenwood, Boylan Heights, Cameron Park." In *Early Twentieth-Century Suburbs in North Carolina*, edited by Catherine W. Bishir and Lawrence S. Earley, 31–38. Raleigh: Division of Archives and History, North Carolina Department of Cultural Resources, 1985.

Brownell, Blaine A. "The Commercial-Civic Elite and City Planning in Atlanta, Memphis, and New Orleans in the 1920s." In *The Physical City: Public Space and Infrastructure*, edited by Neil Shumsky, 165–94. New York: Routledge, 1996.

———. "The Urban South Comes of Age, 1900–1940." In *The City in Southern History: The Growth of Urban Civilization in the South*, edited by Blaine A. Brownell and David R. Goldfield, 123–58. Port Washington, NY: Kennikat Press, 1977.

Bullard, Robert D. "Housing Barriers: Trends in the Nation's Fourth Largest City." *Journal of Black Studies* 21, no. 1 (September 1990): 4–14. www.jstor.org/stable/2784350.

Burgess, Charles. "The Goddess, the School Book, and Compulsion." *Harvard Educational Review* 46, no. 2 (1976): 199–216. https://doi.org/10.17763/haer.46.2.ml3122571205596t.

Chetty, Raj, David Grusky, Maximilian Hell, Nathaniel Hendren, Robert Manduca, and Jimmy Narang. "The Fading American Dream: Trends in Absolute Income Mobility since 1940." *Science* 356, no. 6336 (April 2017): 398–406. https://doi.org/10.1126/science.aal4617.

Chetty, Raj, Nathaniel Hendren, Patrick Kline, and Emmanuel Saez. "Where Is the Land of Opportunity? The Geography of Intergenerational Mobility in the United States." *Quarterly Journal of Economics* 129, no. 4 (2014): 1553–623. www.jstor.org/stable/26372582.

Chused, Richard H. "Euclid's Historical Imagery Symposium on the Seventy-Fifth Anniversary of Village of Euclid v. Ambler Realty Co." *Case Western Reserve Law Review* 51 (2000): 597–616. https://digitalcommons.nyls.edu/fac_articles_chapters/270/.

Clapper, Michael. "School Design, Site Selection, and the Political Geography of Race in Postwar Philadelphia." *Journal of Planning History* 5, no. 3 (2006): 241–63. https://doi.org/10.1177/1538513206289235.

Cook, Charles, and Barry Kaplan. "Civic Elites and Urban Planning: Houston's River Oaks." *East Texas Historical Journal* 15, no. 2 (1977): 29–37.

Crimmins, Timothy J. "West End: Metamorphosis from Suburban Town to Intown Neighborhood." *Atlanta Historical Journal* 26, no. 2 (Summer 1982): 33–45.

Cronin, Mary M. "C. F. Richardson and the Houston Informer's Fight for Racial Equality in the 1920s." *American Journalism* 23, no. 3 (2006): 79–103. https://doi.org/10.1080/08821127.2006.10678026.

Cutler, David M., Edward L. Glaeser, and Jacob L. Vigdor. "The Rise and Decline of the American Ghetto." *Journal of Political Economy* 107, no. 3 (June 1999): 455–506. https://doi.org/10.1086/250069.

Dougherty, Jack. "Shopping for Schools: How Public Education and Private Housing Shaped Suburban Connecticut." *Journal of Urban History* 38, no. 2 (March 2012): 205–24.

Ellis, Ann Wells. "A Crusade Against 'Wretched Attitudes': The Commission on Interracial Cooperation's Activities in Atlanta." *Atlanta Historical Journal* 23, no. 1 (Spring 1979): 21–44.

Erickson, Ansley. "Building Inequality: The Spatial Organization of Schooling in Nashville, Tennessee, after Brown." *Journal of Urban History* 38, no. 2 (March 2012): 247–70. https://doi.org/10.1177/0096144211427115.

Erickson, Ansley, and Andrew H. Highsmith. "The Neighborhood Unit: Schools, Segregation, and the Shaping of the Modern Metropolitan Landscape." *Teachers College Record* 120, no. 3 (March 2018): 1–36. https://doi.org/10.1177/016146811812000308.

Fairbanks, Robert. "From Better Dwellings to Better Neighborhoods: The Rise and Fall of the First National Housing Movement." In *From Tenements to the Taylor Homes: In Search of an Urban Housing Policy in Twentieth-Century America*, edited by John F. Bauman, Roger Biles, and Kristin M. Szylvian, 21–42. University Park: Pennsylvania State University Press, 2000.

Field, Corinne T., and LaKisha Michelle Simmons. "Introduction to Special Issue: Black Girlhood and Kinship." *Women, Gender, and Families of Color* 7, no. 1 (Spring 2019): 1–11. www.muse.jhu.edu/article/733520.

Fisher, Robert. "Protecting Community and Property Values: Civic Clubs in Houston, 1909–1970." In *Urban Texas: Politics and Development*, edited by Char Miller and Heywood T. Sanders, 128–37. College Station: Texas A&M University Press, 1990.

Garlitz, Barbara. "The Immortality Ode: Its Cultural Progeny." *Studies in English Literature, 1500–1900* 6, no. 4 (Autumn 1966): 639–49. https://doi.org/10.2307/449359.

Garner, John S. "The Garden City and Planned Industrial Suburbs: Housing and Planning on the Eve of World War I." In *From Tenements to the Taylor Homes: In Search of an Urban Housing Policy in Twentieth-Century America*, edited by John F. Bauman, Roger Biles, and Kristin M. Szylvian, 43–59. University Park: Pennsylvania State University Press, 2000.

Gillette, Howard, Jr. "The Evolution of Neighborhood Planning: From the Progressive Era to the 1949 Housing Act." *Journal of Urban History* 9, no. 4 (August 1983): 421–44. https://doi.org/10.1177/009614428300900402.

Gillis, John R. "The Islanding of Children—Reshaping the Mythical Landscapes of Childhood." In *Designing Modern Childhoods: History, Space, and the Material Culture of Children*, edited by Marta Gutman and Ning De Coninck-Smith, 316–30. New Brunswick, NJ: Rutgers University Press, 2008.

Godsil, Rachel D. "Race Nuisance: The Politics of Law in the Jim Crow Era." *Michigan Law Review* 105, no. 3 (December 2006): 505–57. www.jstor.org/stable/40041527.

Gordon, Colin. "Dividing the City: Race-Restrictive Covenants and the Architecture of Segregation in St. Louis." *Journal of Urban History* 49, no. 1 (2023): 160–82. https://doi.org/10.1177/0096144221999641.

Gotham, Kevin Fox. "Urban Space, Restrictive Covenants and the Origins of Racial Residential Segregation in a US City, 1900–50." *International Journal of Urban and Regional Research* 24, no. 3 (September 2000): 616–33. https://doi.org/10.1111/1468-2427.00268.

Grable, Stephen. "The Other Side of the Tracks: Cabbagetown—A Working-Class Neighborhood in Transition during the Early Twentieth Century." *Atlanta Historical Journal* 26, no. 2 (Summer 1982): 51–66.

Greene, Casey. "Guardians against Change: The Ku Klux Klan in Houston and Harris County, 1920–1925." *Houston Review* 10, no. 1 (1988): 3–20.

Gutman, Marta, and Ning De Coninck-Smith. "Good to Think With: History, Space, and Modern Childhood." In *Designing Modern Childhoods: History, Space, and the Material Culture of Children*, edited by Marta Gutman and Ning De Coninck-Smith, 1–19. New Brunswick, NJ: Rutgers University Press, 2008.

Hancock, John L. "Planners in the Changing American City, 1900–1940." *Journal of the American Institute of Planners* 33, no. 5 (November 2007): 290–304.

Havekes, Esther, Michael Bader, and Maria Krysan. "Realizing Racial and Ethnic

Neighborhood Preferences? Exploring the Mismatches between What People Want, Where They Search, and Where They Live." *Population Research and Policy Review* 35 (2016): 101–26. https://doi.org/10.1007/s11113-015-9369-6.

Henderson, Archie. "City Planning in Houston, 1920–1930." *Houston Review* 9, no. 3 (Fall 1987): 107–36.

Hendren, Nathaniel. "Effects of Moving to Opportunity: Both Statistically and Socially Significant." In *The Dream Revisited: Contemporary Debates about Housing, Segregation, and Opportunity*, edited by Ingrid Gould Ellen and Justin Peter Steil, 280–82. New York: Columbia University Press, 2019.

Hickey, Georgina. "From Auburn Avenue to Buttermilk Bottom: Class and Community Dynamics among Atlanta's Blacks." In *Historical Roots of the Urban Crisis: African Americans in the Industrial City, 1900–1950*, edited by Henry Louis Taylor Jr. and Walter Hill, 109–43. New York: Garland, 2000.

Highsmith, Andrew, and Ansley Erickson. "Segregation as Splitting, Segregation as Joining: Schools, Housing, and the Many Modes of Jim Crow." *American Journal of Education* 21, no. 4 (August 2015): 563–95. https://doi.org/10.1086/681942.

Hillier, Amy E. "Redlining and the Home Owners' Loan Corporation." *Journal of Urban History* 29, no. 4 (May 2003): 394–420. https://doi.org/10.1177/0096144203029004002.

———. "Spatial Analysis of Historical Redlining: A Methodological Exploration." *Journal of Housing Research* 14, no. 1 (2003): 137–67. www.jstor.org/stable/44944777.

———. "Who Received Loans? Home Owners' Loan Corporation Lending and Discrimination in Philadelphia in the 1930s." *Journal of Planning History* 2, no. 1 (February 2003): 3–24. https://doi.org/10.1177/1538513202239694.

Hine, Darlene Clark. "Rape and the Inner Lives of Black Women in the Middle West." *Signs* 14, no. 4 (Summer 1989): 912–20. www.jstor.org/stable/3174692.

Hirsch, Arnold R. "Choosing Segregation: Federal Housing Policy Between Shelley and Brown." In *From Tenements to the Taylor Homes: In Search of an Urban Housing Policy in Twentieth-Century America*, edited by John F. Bauman, Roger Biles, and Kristin M. Szylvian, 206–25. University Park: Pennsylvania State University Press, 2000.

———. "With or Without Jim Crow: Black Residential Segregation in the United States." In *Urban Policy in Twentieth-Century America*, edited by Arnold R. Hirsch and Raymond A. Mohl, 65–99. New Brunswick, NJ: Rutgers University Press, 1993.

Hitt, Homer L. "Peopling the City: Migration." In *The Urban South*, edited by Rupert B. Vance and Nicholas J. Demerath, 54–77. Chapel Hill: University of North Carolina Press, 1954.

Hopkins, Richard. "Status, Mobility, and Dimensions of Change in a Southern City: Atlanta, 1870–1910." In *Cities in American History*, edited by Kenneth T. Jackson and Stanley K. Schultz, 216–31. New York: Alfred A. Knopf, 1972.

Hovenkamp, Herbert. "Social Science and Segregation Before *Brown*." *Duke Law Journal* 1985, no. 3/4 (1985): 624–72. https://doi.org/10.2307/1372373.

Huggins, Kay Haire. "City Planning in North Carolina, 1900–1929." *North Carolina Historical Review* 46, no. 4 (October 1969): 377–97. www.jstor.org/stable/23518279.

Hurley, Andrew. "Shaping Housing and Enhancing Consumption: Hoover's Interwar Housing Policy." In *From Tenements to the Taylor Homes: In Search of an Urban Housing Policy in Twentieth-Century America*, edited by John F. Bauman, Roger Biles, and

Kristin M. Szylvian, 81–101. University Park: Pennsylvania State University Press, 2000.
Hutchison, Janet. "Building for Babbitt: The State and the Suburban Ideal." *Journal of Policy History* 9, no. 2 (1997): 184–210.
Ifill, Sherrilyn. "Focus on the Costs of Segregation for All." In *The Dream Revisited: Contemporary Debates about Housing, Segregation, and Opportunity*, edited by Ingrid Gould Ellen and Justin Peter Steil, 32–35. New York: Columbia University Press, 2019.
Jenkins, Destin. "Ghosts of the Past: Debt, the New South, and the Propaganda of History." In *Histories of Racial Capitalism*, edited by Destin Jenkins and Justin Leroy, 185–213. New York: Columbia University Press, 2021.
Jones-Correa, Michael. "The Origins and Diffusion of Racial Restrictive Covenants." *Political Science Quarterly* 115, no. 4 (Winter 2000): 541–68. https://doi.org/10.2307/2657609.
Kantor, Harvey. "Benjamin C. Marsh and the Fight over Population Congestion." *Journal of the American Institute of Planners* 40, no. 6 (1974): 422–29.
Kaplan, Barry J. "Race, Income, and Ethnicity: Residential Change in a Houston Community, 1920–1970." *Houston Review* 3, no. 1 (Winter 1981): 178–202.
Karolak, Eric J. "'No Idea of Doing Anything Wonderful': The Labor-Crisis Origins of National Housing Policy and the Reconstruction of the Working-Class Community, 1917–1919." In *From Tenements to the Taylor Homes: In Search of an Urban Housing Policy in Twentieth-Century America*, edited by John F. Bauman, Roger Biles, and Kristin M. Szylvian, 60–80. University Park: Pennsylvania State University Press, 2000.
Kelly, Michael T. "Land Speculation and Suburban Covenants: Racial Capitalism and the Pre-Redlining Roots of Housing Segregation in Syracuse, New York." *Antipode* 54, no. 5 (May 2022): 1629–49. https://doi.org/10.1111/anti.12845.
Kerber, Linda K. "Separate Spheres, Female Worlds, Woman's Place: The Rhetoric of Women's History." *Journal of American History* 75, no. 1 (June 1988): 9–39. https://doi.org/10.2307/1889653.
King, Desmond. "Keeping the American Federal State Active: The Imperative of 'Race-Sensitive' Policy." In *The Dream Revisited: Contemporary Debates about Housing, Segregation, and Opportunity*, edited by Ingrid Gould Ellen and Justin Peter Steil, 259–61. New York: Columbia University Press, 2019.
Klima, Don. L. "Breaking Out: Streetcars and Suburban Development, 1872–1900." *Atlanta Historical Journal* 26, no. 2 (Summer 1982): 67–82.
Kornrich, Sabino, and Frank Furstenberg. "Investing in Children: Changes in Parental Spending on Children, 1972–2007." *Demography* 50, no. 1 (2013): 1–23. www.jstor.org/stable/23358830.
Kunkle, Camille. "Piedmont Park: Atlanta's Urban Backyard." *Atlanta History* 34, no. 2 (Summer 1990): 28–42.
Lassiter, Matthew D., and Joseph Crespino. "De Jure/De Facto Segregation: The Long Shadow of a National Myth." In *The Myth of Southern Exceptionalism*, eds. Matthew Lassiter and Joseph Crespino, 3–22. New York: Oxford, 2009.
Lee, Philip. "A Wall of Hate: Eminent Domain and Interest Convergence." *Brooklyn Law Review* 84, no. 2 (May 2019): 421–74. https://brooklynworks.brooklaw.edu/blr/vol84/iss2/3.

Lieb, Emily. "The 'Baltimore Idea' and the Cities It Built." *Southern Cultures* 25, no. 2 (July 2019): 104–19. www.jstor.org/stable/26696401.

———. "'Shove Those Black Clouds Away!': Jim Crow Schools and Jim Crow Neighborhoods in Baltimore before Brown." In *Baltimore Revisited: Stories of Inequality and Resistance in a U.S. City*, edited by P. Nicole King, Kate Drabinski, and Joshua Clark Davis, 24–36. New Brunswick, NJ: Rutgers University Press, 2019.

Light, Jennifer S. "Nationality and Neighborhood Risk at the Origins of FHA Underwriting." *Journal of Urban History* 36, no. 5 (September 2010): 634–71. https://doi.org/10.1177/0096144210365677.

Lovett, Laura L. "Eugenic Housing: Redlining, Reproductive Regulation, and Suburban Development in the United States." *Women's Studies Quarterly* 48, no. 1/2 (Spring/Summer 2020): 67–83. www.jstor.org/stable/26979202.

Luken, Paul C., and Suzanne Vaughan. "'Be a Genuine Homemaker in Your Own Home': Gender and Familial Relations in State Housing Practices, 1917–1922." *Social Forces* 83, no. 4 (June 2005): 1603–25. www.jstor.org/stable/3598405.

———. "Standardizing Child-Rearing Through Housing." In *Incorporating Texts into Institutional Ethnographies*, edited by Dorothy E. Smith and Susan Marie Turner, 255–304. Toronto: University of Toronto Press, 2014.

Malone, Cheryl Knott. "Autonomy and Accommodation: Houston's Colored Carnegie Library, 1907–1922." *Libraries and Culture* 34, no 2 (Spring 1999): 95–112. www.jstor.org/stable/25548712.

Markley, Scott N., Taylor J. Hafley, Coleman A. Allums, Steven R. Holloway, and Hee Cheol Chung. "The Limits of Homeownership: Racial Capitalism, Black Wealth, and the Appreciation Gap in Atlanta." *International Journal of Urban and Regional Research* 44, no. 2 (2020): 310–28. https://doi.org/10.1111/1468-2427.12873.

Massey, Douglas S. "Still the Linchpin: Segregation and Stratification in the USA." *Race and Social Problems* 12 (January 2020): 1–12. https://doi.org/10.1007/s12552-019-09280-1.

Maxwell, Louise Passey. "Freedmantown: The Origins of a Black Neighborhood in Houston, 1865–1880." In *Bricks without Straw: A Comprehensive History of African Americans in Texas*, edited by David A Williams, 125–52. Austin, TX: Eakin Press, 1997.

Michney, Todd. "How the City Survey's Redlining Maps Were Made: A Closer Look at HOLC's Mortgage Rehabilitation Division." *Journal of Planning History* 21, no. 4 (November 2022): 316–44. https://doi.org/10.1177/15385132211013361.

Oklahoma Commission to Study the Tulsa Race Riot of 1921. *Tulsa Race Riot: A Report by the Oklahoma Committee to Study the Tulsa Race Riot of 1921.* February 28, 2001. Oklahoma Historical Society. www.okhistory.org/research/forms/freport.pdf.

Papademetriou, Peter C. "Urban Development and Public Policy in the Progressive Era, 1890–1940." *Houston Review* 5, no. 3 (Fall 1983): 117–26.

Piketty, Thomas, Emmanuel Saez, and Gabriel Zucman. "Distributional National Accounts: Methods and Estimates for the United States." *Quarterly Journal of Economics* 133, no. 2 (May 2018): 553–609. https://doi.org/10.1093/qje/qjx043.

———. "Economic Growth in the US: A Tale of Two Countries." *VOX*, CEPR Policy Portal, 29 March 2017. https://voxeu.org/article/economic-growth-us-tale-two-countries.

Power, Garrett. "Advocates at Cross Purposes: The Briefs on Behalf of Zoning in the Supreme Court." *Journal of Supreme Court History* 22, no. 2 (1997): 79–87.

———. "Apartheid Baltimore Style: The Residential Segregation Ordinance of 1910–1913." *Maryland Law Review* 42, no. 2 (1983): 289–323. https://digitalcommons.law.umaryland.edu/mlr/vol42/iss2/4.

Price-Spratlen, Townsand, and Avery M. Guest. "Race and Population Change: A Longitudinal Look at Cleveland Neighborhoods." *Sociological Forum* 17, no. 1 (March 2002): 105–36. www.jstor.org/stable/685089.

Pruitt, Bernadette. "'For the Advancement of the Race:' The Great Migrations to Houston, Texas, 1914–1941." *Journal of Urban History* 31, no. 4 (May 2005): 435–78.

Rabin, Yale. "Expulsive Zoning: The Inequitable Legacy of Euclid." In *Zoning and the American Dream: Promises Still to Keep*, edited by Charles Haar and Jerold Kayden, 101–21. Chicago: American Planning Association, 1989.

Radford, Gail. "The Federal Government and Housing during the Depression." In *From Tenements to the Taylor Homes: In Search of an Urban Housing Policy in Twentieth-Century America*, edited by John F. Bauman, Roger Biles, and Kristin M. Szylvian, 102–20. University Park: Pennsylvania State University Press, 2000.

Ramey, Garey, and Valerie A. Ramey. "The Rug Rat Race." *Brookings Papers on Economic Activity* 41, no. 1 (Spring 2010): 129–99. www.brookings.edu/articles/the-rug-rat-race/.

Rice, Bradley R. "The Battle of Buckhead: The Plan of Improvement and Atlanta's Last Big Annexation." *Atlanta Historical Journal* 25, no. 4 (Winter 1981): 5–22.

Rice, Roger L. "Residential Segregation by Law, 1910–1917." *Journal of Southern History* 34, no. 2 (May 1968): 179–99. https://doi.org/10.2307/2204656.

Rosales, F. Arturo. "Mexicans in Houston: The Struggle to Survive, 1908–1975." *Houston Review* 3, no. 2 (Summer 1981): 224–48.

Rury, John L., and Aaron Tyler Rife. "Race, Schools and Opportunity Hoarding: Evidence from a Post-War American Metropolis." *History of Education Quarterly* 47, no. 1 (2018): 87–107. https://doi.org/10.1080/0046760X.2017.1353142.

Sard, Barbara, and Phillip Tegeler. "Children and Housing Vouchers." In *The Dream Revisited: Contemporary Debates about Housing, Segregation, and Opportunity*, edited by Ingrid Gould Ellen and Justin Peter Steil, 297–303. New York: Columbia University Press, 2019.

Schlossman, Steven. "Perils of Popularization: The Founding of Parents' Magazine." *Monographs of the Society for Research in Child Development* 50, no. 4/5 (1985): 65–77. https://doi.org/10.2307/3333864.

Schuler, Edgar A. "The Houston Race Riot, 1917." *Journal of Negro History* 29, no. 3 (July 1944): 300–38. https://doi.org/10.2307/2714820.

Shertzer, Allison, Tate Twinam, and Randall P. Walsh. "Race, Ethnicity, and Discriminatory Zoning." *American Economic Journal: Applied Economics* 8, no. 3 (2016): 217–46. www.jstor.org/stable/24739134.

Shivery, Louie Davis, and Hugh H. Smythe. "The Neighborhood Union: A Survey of the Beginnings of Social Welfare Movements among Negroes in Atlanta." *Phylon* 3, no. 2 (1942): 149–62. https://doi.org/10.2307/271522.

Silver, Christopher. "Neighborhood Planning in Historical Perspective." *Journal of the*

American Planning Association 51, no. 2 (1985): 161–74. https://doi.org/10.1080/01944368508976207.

———. "The Racial Origins of Zoning: Southern Cities from 1910–40." *Planning Perspective* 6, no. 2 (1991): 189–205. https://doi.org/10.1080/02665439108725726.

Smith, T. Lynn. "The Emergence of Cities." In *The Urban South*, edited by Rupert B. Vance and Nicholas J. Demerath, 24–37. Chapel Hill: University of North Carolina Press, 1954.

Steil, Justin, and Laura Delgado. "Contested Values: How Jim Crow Segregation Ordinances Redefined Property Rights." In *Global Perspectives on Urban Law*, edited by N. Davidson and G. Tewari, 7–26. London: Routledge, 2018.

Sundue, Sharon Braslaw. "Beyond the Time of White Children: African American Emancipation, Age, and Ascribed Neoteny in Early National Pennsylvania." In *Age in America: The Colonial Era to the Present*, edited by Corinne T. Field and Nicholas L. Syrett, 47–66. New York: NYU Press, 2015. DOI:10.18574/nyu/9781479870011.001.0001.

Taylor, Henry Louis, Jr. "Creating the Metropolis in Black and White: Black Suburbanization and the Planning Movement in Cincinnati, 1900–1950. In *Historical Roots of the Urban Crisis: African Americans in the Industrial City, 1900–1950*, edited by Henry Louis Taylor Jr. and Walter Hill, 51–71. New York: Garland, 2000.

Taylor, Keeanga-Yamahtta. "The Banality of Segregation: Why Hirsch Still Helps Us Understand Our Racial Geography." *Journal of Urban History* 46, no. 3 (January 2020): 490–93. https://doi.org/10.1177/0096144219896575.

Thompson, Robert A., Hylan Lewis, and Davis McEntire. "Atlanta and Birmingham: A Comparative Study in Negro Housing." In *Studies in Housing and Minority Groups*, edited by Nathan Glazer and Davis McEntire, 13–83. Berkeley: University of California Press, 1960.

Trachtenberg, Alan. Review of *Building the Dream: A Social History of Housing in America*, by Gwendolyn Wright. *Journal of American History* 69, no. 3 (December 1982): 670.

Ulrich, Laurel Thatcher. "The Ways of Her Household." In *Women's America: Refocusing the Past*, edited by Linda K. Kerber and Jane Sherron De Hart, 39–48. New York: Oxford University Press, 2000.

Von Hoffman, Alexander. "Why They Built Pruitt-Igoe." In *From Tenements to the Taylor Homes: In Search of an Urban Housing Policy in Twentieth-Century America*, edited by John F. Bauman, Roger Biles, and Kristin M. Szylvian, 180–205. University Park: Pennsylvania State University Press, 2000.

Wilkins, Ebony Joy. "Writing for Social Change: Using the Brownies' Book as a Model Platform to Nurture a New Generation." *Black History Bulletin* 75, no. 1 (Winter/Spring 2012): 26–30. www.jstor.org/stable/24759717.

Williams, Louis. "William Berry Hartsfield and Atlanta Politics: The Formative Years of an Urban Reformer, 1920–1936." *Georgia Historical Quarterly* 84, no. 4 (Winter 2000): 651–76.

Wilson, Bobby M. "Black Housing Opportunities in Birmingham, Alabama." *Southeastern Geographer* 17, No. 1 (May 1977): 49–57. www.jstor.org/stable/44370653.

Winling, LaDale C., and Todd M. Michney. "The Roots of Redlining: Academic, Governmental and Professional Networks in the Making of the New Deal Lending

Regime." *Journal of American History* 108, no. 1 (June 2021): 42–69. https://doi.org/10.1093/jahist/jaab066.

Wintz, Cary D. "The Emergence of a Black Neighborhood: Houston's Fourth Ward, 1865–1915." In *Urban Texas: Politics and Development*, edited by Char Miller and Heywood T. Sanders, 96–109. College Station: Texas A&M University Press, 1990.

Wrenn, Lynette Boney. "The Politics of Memphis School Reform, 1883–1927." In *Southern Cities, Southern Schools: Public Education in the Urban South*, edited by David N. Plank and Rick Ginsberg, 81–108. New York: Greenwood, 1990.

Wye, Christopher G. "The New Deal and the Negro Community: Toward a Broader Conceptualization." *Journal of American History* 59, no. 3 (December 1972): 621–38. https://doi.org/10.2307/1900661.

Dissertations and Master's Theses

Benjamin, Karen. "Progressivism Meets Jim Crow: Segregation, School Reform, and Urbanization in the Interwar South." Ph.D. diss., University of Wisconsin, 2007.

Brody, Jason S. "Constructing Professional Knowledge: The Neighborhood Unit Concept in the Community Builder's Handbook." Ph.D. diss., University of Illinois, 2009.

Flint, Barbara. "Zoning and Residential Segregation: A Social and Physical History, 1910–1940." Ph.D. diss., University of Chicago, 1977.

Haley, John. "The Carolina Chameleon: Charles N. Hunter and Race Relations in North Carolina, 1865–1931." Ph.D. diss., University of North Carolina at Chapel Hill, 1981.

Jackson, Robena Estelle. "A Socio-Historical View of a Segregated Community." Master's thesis, University of Texas at Austin, 1979.

Johnson, W. L. D. "Organization of the Public Schools in Houston, Texas, 1905–1940." Master's thesis, Prairie View State Normal and Industrial College, 1943.

Mikkelsen, Vincent. "Coming from Battle to Face a War: The Lynching of Black Soldiers in the World War I Era." Ph.D. diss., Florida State University, 2007.

Slaten, Ellen Leah. "Development without Constraint: The Prolonged Battle over Zoning in Houston, 1927–1990." Master's thesis, University of Texas at Austin, 1990.

SoRelle, James M. "The Darker Side of 'Heaven': The Black Community in Houston, Texas, 1917–1945." Ph.D. diss., Kent State University, 1980.

Sudheendran, Kesavan. "Community Power Structure in Atlanta: A Study in Decision Making, 1920–1939." Ph.D. diss., Georgia State University, 1982.

West, E. Bernard. "Black Atlanta: Struggle for Development, 1915–1925." Master's thesis, Atlanta University, 1976.

Zogry, Kenneth. "The House That Dr. Pope Built: Race, Politics, Memory, and the Early Struggle for Civil Rights in North Carolina." Ph.D. diss., University of North Carolina, 2008.

INDEX

Abbott, Grace, 218, 220
affluent Black families: and Black schools, 12, 25–26, 104, 112, 114, 119, 124, 147, 149, 163, 187, 198, 200–201, 204, 259, 261, 286; child-rearing style of, 10, 15, 25; and children's education on segregation, 85; discrimination faced by, 173; and housing selection, 9, 25, 59, 79, 82, 82, 86, 87–96, 99–100, 104, 108, 114, 120, 146, 149, 152, 153, 163, 169, 187, 260–61, 267; intensive child-rearing strategies of, 18, 25, 29, 39, 120, 163, 208, 229, 280, 296, 297; lack of political power, 13, 39, 94; and parent education, 211, 227, 229; and property values, 13, 290; and racial uplift, 208, 231; and residential parks, 57, 58, 90, 150, 163, 187, 256, 261, 274, 279–80, 287, 314n48, 364n25; and segregation ordinances, 173; and single-family homes, 261, 286; and upward mobility, 26–27, 86, 157affluent white families: and automobile risks, 35; and child study movement, 209; child-rearing standards of, 9, 17, 31, 81, 98, 100, 105, 157, 160, 179, 189, 190, 236, 240, 249, 277, 278, 279, 281; city services for, 99; and dominance of middle-class norms, 2; intensive child-rearing strategies of, 17–18, 19, 22–24, 291, 294–95, 296; older neighborhoods, views on, 79, 87; and parent education, 4–5, 210, 231, 233; and property rights, 233; and property values, 11, 96; and residential parks, 1–2, 7–9, 12, 41–42, 49, 61, 62, 76, 81, 82, 101, 105, 230, 262, 265, 281, 290; and school building programs, 187; and school quality, 11, 12, 63–64, 72, 76, 78, 105, 120, 129, 133, 181, 197, 250; and segregation ordinances, 9, 87–89, 61, 62, 154, 269, 306n27; and suburban developments, 38–39, 41, 79, 240; and upward mobility, 12, 13–14, 17–18, 25, 39, 41, 250; urban apartments of, 37, 89; and zoning ordinances, 5, 249, 278; and upward mobility, 63, 295

Allen, Ivan, Jr., 61–62, 75
amalgamation, 2, 25, 85–86, 151, 152–56, 174, 230
Ambler Realty Co. v. Village of Euclid (1924), 251
American City Planning Institute, 175, 239, 268, 284
American dream, 3, 13–14, 173, 295
Ansley, Edwin, 45, 72–73, 75–76
antimiscegenation laws, 2, 85–86, 151, 153, 160, 174, 284
apartments, 37–38, 89, 169, 216, 240–41, 246, 248, 273, 370n87
Ashley, Claude, 113, 153, 168–69, 193, 321n40, 329n40
Atkins, Simon, 60, 117, 274, 277, 330n47
Atlanta, Georgia: Ansley Park, 45, 47, 58, 72–76, 82, 95, 159, 168, 188, 192, 243, 346n16; Ashby Heights, 146; Bellwood, 165, 168, 169, 188, 190; Berkeley Park, 164; Black housing options in, 82, 112–13, 328n34; and Black out-migration, 141, 336n57; Black schools of, 103, 108, 110, 111–12, 120–22, 127–31, 132, 134, 135, 137, 141, 143, 145, 147, 192–94, 205, 321n49, 328n31, 329n34, 331n59; Boulevard Park, 136; business class of, 61–62, 95, 268; and charter reform, 159, 187, 192, 340n39, 346n16; city services in, 84, 137, 158; Copenhill Park, 129; Druid Hills, 46, 58–59, 95, 96, 159, 164, 168, 236–37, 252; Fourth Ward, 74, 95–96, 108, 110–14, 131, 138–39, 145, 153, 157–58, 162–63, 165, 168–69, 187, 191, 193–94, 284–85, 346n19, 349n42, 361n2; Garden Hills, 45; homeownership rates in, 5; Inman Park, 45, 95, 111, 129, 159, 161; intergenerational inequality in, 290; Jackson Hill, 95–96; and mixed-race neighborhoods, 121–22, 155–56; Morningside Park, 146, 168; NAACP of, 135–38, 139, 141, 191; National Urban League of, 337n66; Neighborhood Union of, 29–30, 33, 84, 124, 127–30, 131, 187, 191, 210–11, 219, 222, 286–88, 298, 309–n47, 352n5;

414 | Index

Atlanta, Georgia (*continued*)
North Atlanta, 72–74; North Boulevard Park, 76–77, 164, 168, 188, 191–92, 219–20, 348n34, 360n31; Peachtree Heights, 47, 58, 78, 95; Piedmont Park, 72, 73, 75, 77, 159, 188, 194, 360n31; playgrounds of, 33–34, 158, 310n65; Ponce de Leon Heights, 337n71; population characteristics of, 165, 342n57; and racial zoning, 10, 149, 150, 158–65, 168, 174, 176, 178–79, 181, 182, 188, 193, 194, 196, 216, 222, 242, 251, 253, 254, 268, 269, 270, 282, 288, 331n59, 341n47, 342n58, 368n62; residential patterns in, 83; school bond elections of, 117, 126–27, 135–38, 139, 140, 143, 164, 186, 335n48; school building program of, 179, 181–82, 186–94, 204–5, 216, 282, 346n20, 348n34; segregated schools in, 64, 72–78, 103–4, 108, 110–13, 120–22, 127–31, 132–34, 135, 137, 141, 143, 145, 147, 192–94, 205, 321n49, 328n31, 329n34, 331n59; segregation ordinances of, 15, 95–96, 103, 104, 108, 113–14, 120, 127, 139, 145, 152, 153, 155–56, 157, 160, 161, 168, 169, 173, 190, 193, 199, 284–85, 329n40, 361n2, 373n21; Summer Hill, 189–90, 347n26; Sunset Park, 145, 146, 337n71; Sylvan Hills, 168–69; Virginia-Highlands, 337n71; ward-based political system of, 73, 165, 168, 284; Washington Park, 146, 162, 163, 287; West Hunter Park, 146; zoning ordinances of, 242–43, 360n33, 361n2
Atlanta Metropolitan Planning Commission, 204, 352n80
Atlanta Real Estate Board, 149–50, 157, 159, 164, 186
Atlanta University, 29, 145, 162, 165, 187
Austin, Texas, 5, 257–58, 267, 364n30
automobiles, 32, 34–35, 47, 244–45

Baltimore, Maryland: Guilford, 58; and property values, 96; racial transition in, 9, 98, 195, 327n9; and residential segregation, 199, 349n45; Roland Park, 47, 54, 59–60, 77–78, 89, 252, 274, 282; school building program of, 182, 194–95; segregated schools in, 103–8, 125, 194; segregation ordinances of, 9, 81, 88–90, 95, 98, 100, 103–5, 107, 120, 152, 153, 155, 194, 199, 326n57, 339n22
Bassett, Edward, 184, 258, 283

Beecher, Catharine, 21, 23–24, 225, 357n61
Bell, Derrick, 151, 293, 338n8
Bennett, Silas, 94, 119
Better Homes in America movement (BHA), 5, 207, 217–21, 234, 240–42, 356n41
Bickett, Thomas, 134–35
biracial children, 85, 151, 230
Birmingham, Alabama: Black migration from, 269; business class of, 269, 275; Hollywood, 369n76; homeownership rates in, 5; Interracial Committee of, 368n67; lopsided growth in, 290; Mountain Brook Estates, 273; "Own-Your-Own-Home" (OYOH) campaign in, 216, 285, 355n31; and racial zoning, 267–70, 271, 274, 275; Redmont Park, 49, 273, 369n76; and residential parks, 268, 271, 273; school bond elections of, 273, 369n74; school building program of, 133, 270–73; segregated schools in, 132–33, 269–73, 368n67
Black activists: and Black homeownership survey, 256–57; and Black schools, 118–19, 122, 124, 125–30, 135–38, 139, 140–42, 146, 149, 192–93, 201, 259; "child-saving" campaigns of, 18; death threats against, 147; on equal investment, 13, 84, 85; and Great Migration, 134, 141; and interracial networks, 124, 127, 129, 134, 145, 146, 199, 219; on racial zoning, 150, 268; on segregation ordinances, 85, 87, 95, 99; and voting blocs, 124, 126, 135–38, 141; and white conflict, 114–15, 117–20; on white supremacy, 151–52
Black Americans: and coalitions across color line, 30–31; educational access of, 134; equal citizenship for, 2, 25, 124; and medical care, 66; passing for white, 152; political actions of, 94, 104, 110; racial covenants restricting, 42; racial stereotypes of, 223, 225; threat of violence controlling movement of, 54, 134–35, 174–75; and tobacco industry employment, 115; voting rights of, 55, 136, 335n39; and white supremacy campaigns, 55
Black churches, 67, 69, 71, 318n16, 319n26
Black clubwomen, 30, 211, 223, 291; and racial uplift, 231
Black colleges, 29, 33, 64–66, 68, 70, 108, 112–14, 125–27, 131, 157, 161–62, 187, 145, 162, 165, 187, 274, 286, 319n26, 330n47, 346n19,

349n42. *See also* Atlanta University; Clark University; Morehouse College; Morris Brown College; St. Augustine's College; Shaw University; Slater Industrial State and Normal School; Spelman College

Black communities: apartments for, 169; and Black businesses, 87, 91, 94–95, 112, 117, 118, 177, 202–3, 259, 275, 287, 288; city services for, 60–61, 82, 84–85, 90, 94, 99–100, 115, 118, 125, 137, 139–41, 150, 158, 196, 258, 261–62, 288, 326n64; and environmental hazards, 280, 288, 289–91; location of Black homes, 83–87, 95, 153, 262, 340n32, 344–45n96; location of Black schools, 59–60, 67, 112, 189, 262, 347n26; and public housing, 289, 374n39; and racial zoning, 161–62, 163, 168, 169, 287, 288, 341n47; single-family homes in, 59, 261; white encroachment in, 59–60, 189–90. *See also* Black schools

Black development: areas set aside for, 13, 186, 365n35; Black schools located in, 11, 12, 259–60; and economic growth, 290; local officials' control of, 149; and racial zoning, 163, 165, 253; and unenforced zoning protections, 13, 288; and voluntary segregation, 275

Black elites: and Black schools, 15, 112, 117–19, 147, 259–61; as homebuyers, 87, 91; residential developments of, 146, 261, 274; and segregation ordinances, 94, 95, 119

Black families: and Black school locations, 65; and deed restrictions, 39; effect of racial subjugation of, 225; housing needs of, 4, 39, 149, 150, 164, 288; housing opportunities of, 10, 86–87, 98, 112, 120, 149, 154, 164, 169, 170, 179, 204, 333n15; living conditions of, 84; and parent education movement, 15, 225; and racial covenants, 8; racial zoning facilitating needs of, 149–50; and residential parks, 89, 90, 312n2; and segregation ordinances, 88, 149–50; and single-family homes, 13, 150, 211; white property owners selling to, 98–99, 114, 326n56; white residents' violence against, 9–10, 26. *See also* affluent Black families; Black middle-class families; Black working-class families

Black homebuyers, 94, 95, 98, 114, 287, 307n46

Black libraries, 137, 139, 141, 143, 256, 337n71

Black schools: access to high schools, 104–6, 108, 114, 118–19, 124, 131, 135, 136, 137, 139–42, 143, 145, 146, 187, 190, 193, 200–202, 204, 256, 259, 261, 262, 271, 277, 286, 338n74, 365n34; and Black activists, 118–19, 122, 124, 125–30, 135–38, 139, 140–42, 146, 192–93, 201, 259; Black elites' negotiation for, 15, 112, 117–19, 147, 259–61; condition of, 67, 69, 71, 122, 124, 127–30, 131, 132, 134, 135, 138–41, 149, 190–91, 204, 259, 271, 272, 273; consolidation of, 69–70, 71, 125; location of, 11, 12, 59–60, 64–67, 69, 71, 76, 89, 99, 103–4, 107, 108, 110–12, 114–15, 117–19, 120, 124, 181, 189, 203–4, 258, 262, 318n16, 318n21, 347n26, 348n35; overcrowding of, 11, 75, 111–12, 122, 124, 127, 131, 132, 137, 145, 187, 193, 346n19; playgrounds of, 137, 139, 258, 310n65; school boards' closing of, 65, 66, 76–77, 124, 190–91, 321–22n49; and school quality, 79, 86, 103, 104, 125, 135, 137, 139–41, 147, 149, 179, 187, 194, 259; and segregation ordinances, 103, 104–5, 120, 150; white schools converted to, 103–8, 120–22, 125, 131, 138, 145–46, 158, 189, 194, 259, 285, 327n12, 329n34, 337n71, 347n24

Black veterans, 10, 134–35, 136

Black working class, 82, 83, 124, 131, 134

Black working-class families, 11, 18, 39, 124, 198, 259, 272–73

Bouton, Edward, 77, 274, 282

Bowen, Annie, 178–79

Bowen v. Atlanta (1924), 178–79, 181, 251

Brett v. Building Commission of Brookline (1924), 245–46

Brookline, Massachusetts, 42, 245

Buchanan v. Warley (1917): and alienation, 250; and property rights, 153–54, 252; and property values, 160; and racial zoning, 10, 151, 175, 178, 179, 252, 269; and residential segregation, 9; and restrictive covenants, 307n43; and segregation ordinances, 103, 145, 147, 151, 156, 157, 160, 173, 194, 199, 252, 269, 284; Moorfield Storey on, 345n99; and theory of interest convergence, 151, 338n8

business class, 1, 61–62, 70, 78, 134, 164–65, 269

Butler, Henry Rutherford, 112–13, 193, 328n32

Butler, Selena Sloan, 112–13, 193, 210, 211, 328n32
Buxton, John C., 56, 76, 117, 156–57, 197, 315n51, 330n46

Carey v. City of Atlanta (1915), 155–56
Caswell, Hollis, 183–84
Charleston, South Carolina, 267, 279
Charlotte, North Carolina, 315n52, 326n60
charter reform, 159, 187, 192, 340n39, 346n16
Chase, Arthur Minturn, 32, 35
Cheney, Charles, 238, 241, 245, 248–49
Chetty, Raj, 290, 295
Chicago, Illinois, 5, 44, 45, 172–75, 289, 344n89
child labor, 18, 19, 31–32
child-rearing: and Black middle class, 10, 15, 25; citizenship tied to, 1, 17, 18, 25, 30–31, 39, 207–8; and collective efficacy, 289, 298; and deed restrictions, 7, 46–47, 234; and housing market, 2, 3–4, 5, 14; intensive strategies of, 13, 17–18, 19, 20–23, 24, 25–32, 34–35, 38–39, 61, 207, 208–9, 291, 294–96, 308n3; and property values, 3–4, 11, 81, 239, 323n2; in residential developers' advertising, 6–7, 41–42, 49, 52–53, 61, 76–77, 87, 89, 101, 207, 211–12, 234, 235, 273, 312n2, 370n81; and single-family homes, 4–5, 19, 24, 25, 35–38, 39, 41, 207, 216, 218, 221, 239–40, 245, 247, 264, 281, 285, 322–23n2; and suburban development, 41, 235, 285, 286, 290–91, 312n2; undesirable areas for, 9, 12, 14, 96. *See also* parenting
children: anxiety of, 296, 377n11; childish antics of, 59; child-rearing standards for, 81; and consumerism, 208, 221–22, 225–27; environment for, 4, 62, 88; extension of childhood through adolescence, 21, 358n75; free-range children, 32, 221; health of, 47, 49; and innocence, 19, 20; as national resource, 2; as nucleus of middle-class domesticity, 23, 24, 172–73; playmates of, 7–9, 34–36, 42, 49, 52–53, 58–59, 65, 81, 216, 229–30, 357n61; public investments in, 297; racial and ethnic stereotypes of, 26–27, 29, 58–59, 85, 107–8, 124, 223, 225; and racial violence, 26, 27, 29, 287; residential parks centered on, 3–13, 49, 52, 61, 307n45; of servants, 58–59; and upward mobility, 1, 5, 7, 10, 15, 17–18, 21–22, 49, 63, 88, 105, 230, 293; and white supremacy, 29, 85, 225. *See also* playgrounds
Child Study Association (CSA), 209–10, 220, 221–23
child study movement, 207–10, 358n75
Chinese Americans, 8, 54, 55, 172–73
cities, 5, 8, 25, 35, 170, 174–75, 252. *See also* Jim Crow cities
citizenship: and affluent white families, 25; child-rearing tied to, 1, 17, 18, 25, 30–31, 39, 207–8; equal citizenship for Black Americans, 2, 25, 124; and Fourteenth Amendment, 124; and racial zoning, 163, 341n48; and single-family homes, 5, 39; and social class, 172; virtuous citizenship rhetoric, 20, 21
City Federation of Women's Clubs, 108, 110
City of Birmingham v. Monk (1951), 270–71
city planning, 183–86, 205. *See also* National Conference on City Planning (NCCP); planning commissions; planning movement
Clark University, 127, 131, 346n19
Cleveland, Ohio, 133, 159, 176, 178, 184, 247
Clinard v. Winston-Salem (1940), 277–78
colonial period, 19, 20, 22
Columbus, Ohio, Upper Arlington, 52
Committee on Church Cooperation (CCC), 145, 146
consumerism, 21, 23, 208, 210, 221–22, 225–27, 235, 286
Corrigan v. Buckley (1926), 12, 13, 44, 250, 251–52, 279
cotton, collapse of, 131, 333n25
Crane, Caroline Bartlett, 218, 221
Crawford, Andrew Wright, 241, 359n27
Cullinan, Joseph, 262, 366n45
cultural gifts movement, 222–23, 229, 230, 357n75
Cumming v. Richmond County Board of Education (1899), 124

Dallas, Texas, 54, 142, 173, 252, 254, 274, 363n16
Daniels, Jonathan, 64–66
Daniels, Josephus, 64, 65, 66–67
Darnell, William, 157, 330n46
Dashiell, Milton, 81, 88–89, 97–100, 104–5, 326n58
Davis, Benjamin: on Black schools, 110, 192,

193; on mixed-use neighborhoods, 288; on poll taxes, 136; on property values, 98; on racial zoning, 150, 163, 170, 269, 287; on school bond election, 137, 138, 139; on segregation ordinances, 95, 100, 114, 150, 158; on upwardly mobile Black families, 157; on white hatred of Black Americans, 10
deed restrictions: acceptance of, 1, 2, 7, 47, 231, 233; and child-rearing, 7, 46–47, 234; and race restriction, 55; and racial transition, 90; of residential parks, 7, 8–9, 41, 42, 54, 58–59, 65, 66, 71, 83, 91, 101, 178, 186, 230, 235, 237; and suburban development, 39, 45, 236; and zoning ordinances, 234–38
de jure segregation: and Black children, 2; and Chinese immigrants, 172; experimentation with, 250; failure of judicial test of, 10, 11; forms of, 279; and Great Migration, 9; and improvement associations, 88, 89, 326n57; and limits on modern schools, 78; in North, 25, 170; and property rights, 160; and racial transition, 14; racial zoning as, 150, 175, 269; and school building programs, 253; US Supreme Court on, 252
Detroit, Michigan, 47, 52–53, 184, 290
Doepke, Matthias, 294, 296
domestic help, 21, 29, 83, 152, 225, 357n61
domesticity, 13–14, 21, 23–24, 34–36, 44, 172–73
Du Bois, W. E. B., 177, 227, 229
duplexes, 5, 245, 246, 247, 269, 305n14

economic panics, 22, 45
Engelhardt, N. L., 181, 183, 194–95, 197, 346n17, 347n29, 348n34
Enlightenment, 17, 20, 22
Euclid v. Ambler (1926), 5, 233–35, 238, 246–47, 249–52, 254, 274, 278–79, 360n33
eugenics, 170, 343n73, 358n75

Federal Housing Administration (FHA), 3–4, 13, 122, 283–86, 288, 291, 307n46, 372n17
federal housing policy, 3, 6, 12–13, 284, 286, 307n48
Ferguson, Hill, 283, 355n31, 369n76
fertility rate, 20, 22, 24, 27, 31
Ford, George B., 184, 185–86, 217, 240, 253, 258
Ford, James, 217, 240, 242, 372n14

Forsyth Savings and Trust Company, 90, 330n47
Fourteenth Amendment, 8, 9, 42, 54, 55, 124, 151, 153–54, 172
Fries, Henry, 117–19, 275
Fries brothers, 56, 315n51

Gandolfo v. Hartman (1892), 8, 54–55, 58, 305n22, 313n32, 314n39, 315n52
gender roles, 14, 20, 21–24, 36, 138, 221, 242
General Federation of Women's Clubs, 215, 217, 218
Georgia Supreme Court, 10, 145, 150–51, 153, 155–56, 178, 242–43, 251, 360n33, 361n2
ghetto formation, 12, 15
Gordon, Colin, 55, 322n2
Great Depression, 6, 45, 220–21, 263, 280, 287, 288, 372n17
Great Migration, 9, 11–12, 54, 58, 134, 141, 158, 173–75, 186, 269
Gries, John, 216–18, 372n14
Grinnalds, Jefferson, 182, 195, 199, 203, 238, 242
Gruenberg, Sidonie, 209, 220, 222, 231, 291

Hall, G. Stanley, 209, 358n75
Hanes, James G., 196, 199, 274–75
Hanes family, 56, 196–97, 321n45
Hanmer, Lee, 34, 185–86
Harden v. City of Atlanta (1917), 153, 156
Hare, S. Herbert, 254, 258, 262, 264
Harmon v. Tyler (1927), 252, 254, 364n28
Harris v. City of Louisville (1915), 152–53, 339n21
Hawkins, W. Ashbie, 88–89, 97, 100, 154–55, 339n22
Headley, Madge, 233, 238
Herbin-Triant, Elizabeth, 82, 152, 306n27, 326n59
higher education, 295–96, 376n5
Hogg, William, 77, 253–62, 264, 266–67, 364n25, 364n28, 364n30, 366n45, 366n52, 367n57
Holcombe, Oscar, 254, 288, 364n28
home economics, 36, 218, 220
homeownership, 4–5, 212, 215–20, 242, 256–57, 283, 285–86, 355n28, 372n14. *See also* single-family homes
Home Owners Loan Corporation (HOLC), 283, 307n46, 372n17

Hoover, Herbert: on child-rearing and single-family homes, 4–5, 6, 207, 212, 216–18, 220, 246, 283, 292; and public-private partnerships, 274; and zoning advisory committee, 235, 240–42, 246, 268, 283
housing market, 2–6, 14, 78, 81–82, 96, 284
Houston, Texas: airport site for, 254; and Black homeownership survey, 256–57; and Black out-migration, 141–42, 336n57; Braeswood, 266; Cinco Ranch, 290; Colored Citizens Committee of, 259; conversion of white schools to Black schools in, 121; and de jure segregation, 267; Eastwood, 58; Emancipation Park, 259, 260, 261, 262; and eminent domain, 256, 264n25; Forest Home, 261, 262; Fourth Ward, 256–57, 259–62, 284–85, 365n35; Hermann Park, 265; Independence Heights, 60–61; Memorial Park, 253–54; NAACP of, 140, 259; and park facilities for Black residents, 260; planning commission of, 234, 253, 254–59, 261, 262, 263–67, 365n35; race distribution map of, 256; and racial zoning, 253, 254, 256, 257–58, 259; residential patterns of, 84–85, 260–61, 268; and residential segregation, 256; Rice Institute, 265; River Oaks, 44, 45, 49, 60, 77, 236, 253–67, 274, 283, 284, 290, 363n20, 367n57; Riverside Terrace, 266; San Felipe District, 60, 253, 255–56, 259, 261, 262, 267; school board of, 258–59, 262; school bond elections of, 140, 141–42, 143, 258–59, 261, 265, 336n55; school building program of, 185, 253, 259, 262–67; School Property Committee, 259; and school sites, 259–61; segregated schools in, 132, 133–34, 139–42, 143, 256, 259, 262–67, 337n65, 337n66, 365n34; St. Nicholas Catholic Church, 261, 365n39; ward system of, 365n35; Woodland Heights, 41, 58, 63, 212; zoning ordinance of, 254–55, 267
Hunter, Charles, 125–27, 147, 199–202, 204, 332n7
Hurt, Joel, 46, 58–59, 111, 129, 159, 168, 236–37

Ihlder, John, 35, 218, 241
immigration laws, 173
improvement associations, 88, 89, 104, 107, 326n57
income inequality, 17, 183, 294, 295–96, 297

Indiana, 26, 252
Indigenous people, 135, 225
industrialization, 17, 31, 123, 133
interest convergence theory, 151, 154, 293, 338n8
interracial cooperation, 124, 127, 129, 134, 145, 146, 199, 208, 219
interracial relationships: and mixed-race neighborhoods, 103–4, 105, 107–8, 115, 281; and playmates, 35, 58–59, 65–66, 81, 229–30; and residential segregation, 86, 230; and segregation ordinances, 88, 152–53, 154; and social equality, 58–59, 61, 85, 104, 178, 345n99; taboos against, 9, 85, 230; and views on race relations, 65–66, 108, 222–23, 229–30; white supremacy on, 85, 86, 145, 151–52, 230

Jemison, Robert, Jr.: and Birmingham, 270, 271, 273, 283; and FHA land planning division, 372n17; and Morris Knowles, 268, 274, 368n62; and planning movement, 240, 268, 284; on property valuation, 4, 6; real estate interests of, 273–74, 362n13, 370n81; and Redmont Park, 49, 273; and Urban Land Institute, 290
Jewish Americans, 173, 223
Jim Crow cities: and Black development, 149; Black schools in, 103; block-level segregation patterns of, 8–9, 10, 62, 64, 66, 78, 79, 81, 82; cash-strapped school districts of, 11–12, 65, 123; and child-rearing standards for white children, 81; de jure segregation in, 78, 252; and industrial economy, 133; lack of city services for Black communities, 60–61; and racial covenants, 8, 11, 42, 44, 54–55, 57, 58, 63; residential patterns in, 83–87, 91; and residential segregation, 15, 186, 204; school districts of, 65–72, 123
Jim Crow laws. See white supremacy
Jones, Charles, 90–91, 93, 94, 330n47
Julius Rosenwald Fund, 277
juvenile delinquency, 34, 192, 211, 282

Kansas City, Missouri: Country Club District of, 7, 44, 46–47, 52, 207, 235–36, 254, 274, 282, 362n14; racial covenants of, 58, 315n52
Kelly, William A., Jr., 277–78

Kessler, George, 157–58
Key, James, 129, 158–59, 164, 187, 188, 189, 194, 340n39
Kimball, Theodora, 175–76
Klepp, Susan, 20, 22
Knowles, Morris, 196–97, 267–69, 274–75, 279, 368n62
Koehler v. Rowland (1918), 315n52
Kornrich, Sabino, 294–95
Ku Klux Klan, 168, 179, 187, 190, 192

Lasker, Bruno, 171–72, 176, 222, 229–30, 248, 249–50, 291
Laura Spelman Rockefeller Memorial, 209, 217, 220
Liberty Annex Corp. v. Dallas (1927), 252
Locke, John, 19, 20, 209
Los Angeles, California, 44, 49, 58, 235, 238
lynchings, 27, 85, 86, 134, 177, 287

market revolution, 17–18, 21–22, 31, 123, 208
Marsh, Benjamin, 240, 242, 248
Martin, E. S., 63, 208
McMechen, George, 81, 88–89, 97–98, 103–4, 152, 339n22
Memphis, Tennessee, 83, 132
Metzenbaum, James, 234, 238, 247
Miller v. Board of Public Works of Los Angeles (1925), 246
Mitchell, Eugene, 95–96, 325n47
mixed-race neighborhoods: and Black homes, 83, 84, 86; Black schools in, 64, 103, 105, 112–13, 115, 117, 120, 197–98, 261; and city services, 84, 99, 120, 158; decline in desirability of, 8; housing patterns of, 15, 83, 156, 190, 271; and interracial relationships, 103–4, 105, 107–8, 115, 281; and racial zoning, 160, 269, 277; in Raleigh, 67, 69, 71, 317n12; and school locations, 65, 188, 202–3, 204; and segregation ordinances, 88, 100, 114, 154, 155–56; shifting white residents from, 11, 88–89, 154; and social equality, 61, 104; and traditional urban development, 67, 86, 145, 155, 188, 233; white families remaining in, 82–83, 84, 104, 120, 253, 269, 281, 323n6; white schools in, 64, 104, 112–13, 120, 261, 365n40
mixed-use neighborhoods: decline in desirability of, 8, 89, 96, 107; and segregation ordinances, 154; shifting white residents from, 11, 86, 154, 285; and traditional urban development, 83, 89, 111, 145, 233, 288, 293; and white absentee landlords, 253, 277, 287
Moehlman, Arthur, 184–85, 345n10
Monteith, Walter, 254, 258, 263, 363n20
Morehouse College, 187, 286
Morris Brown College, 108, 112, 113, 114, 157, 161–62, 187, 349n42
mortgage market, 5
multifamily housing, 38, 234, 238, 240–41, 244–47, 251, 264, 269

NAACP, 15, 134–39, 154, 158, 187, 250, 259
National Association of Colored Women (NACW), 30–31, 211
National Association of Real Estate Boards (NAREB): and Robert Jemison Jr., 273–74, 284; and mandatory real estate courses, 6, 238; "Own-Your-Own-Home" (OYOH) campaign of, 212, 216, 355n31; and planning movement, 240; and Hugh Potter, 283; and residential park developers, 5, 12
National Conference on City Planning (NCCP): and Robert Jemison Jr., 268, 274, 284; and playgrounds, 34; and school building programs, 182; and school sites, 52, 184, 186, 195; and single-family zoning, 44, 171–72, 178, 238, 239–40, 243, 248, 278, 283; and Texas planning commissions, 258, 363n16
National Congress of Mothers, 30–31, 210, 310n50
National Housing Act, 283, 285
National Parent Teacher Association, 30, 210, 220, 222, 310n50
Neighborhood Union, 29–30, 33, 84, 124, 127–30, 131, 187, 191, 210–11, 219, 222, 286–88, 298, 309n47, 352n5
neighborhoods: Black public investment in, 150; high-poverty neighborhoods, 297; neighborhood unit concept, 282–83, 371n11, 372n13, 372n14; older neighborhoods, 12, 63, 70, 72, 79, 81, 82, 86, 87, 89, 100, 108, 149, 154, 194, 202, 204, 249, 252, 267, 282–84, 322n2; realtors' selling of, 61; transitional neighborhoods, 82, 91, 100, 101, 145, 275; turnover in, 46. *See also* mixed-race neighborhoods; mixed-use neighborhoods

neighbors: and mixed-race blocks, 155, 156, 160; and property values, 25, 96, 97, 98, 154; and residential parks, 49, 58, 59, 81, 229; social equality suggested by proximity, 61, 104; white opposition to Black next-door neighbors, 281
New Deal, 3, 12, 13, 284, 307n48
New Orleans, Louisiana, 83, 252, 254, 285
New York City, 10, 149, 170, 182, 233, 243
Nichols, J. C.: on children's needs, 245; Country Club District of, 7, 207, 235, 236, 254, 274, 282; on deed restrictions, 45, 46–47, 235–36; and planning movement, 240; on property valuation, 4, 6, 44, 236; and racial covenants, 57–58; on school quality, 63; single-family zoning, 248; and Urban Land Institute, 290
Nolen, John, 258, 286, 364n30
North Carolina Supreme Court, 117, 153, 156–57, 196, 199, 277–78, 341n42, 344n92
northern cities, 8, 25, 170, 174–75, 252
North Harlem, New York, 33

Oberlin, North Carolina, 59–60
Olmsted, Frederick Law, 44, 46
Olmsted, Frederick Law, Jr., 46, 52, 58–59, 159, 182, 236–37, 254, 371n9
Olmsted, John Charles, 46, 58–59, 159, 236–37
Oregon, 248–49
Orme, Aquilla, 76–77, 136, 191–92, 194, 219, 321n47
Otis, Robert, 159–60, 165, 168, 170, 341n41
"Own-Your-Own-Home" (OYOH) campaigns, 5, 207, 212, 215–20, 275, 283, 285–86, 355n31

Palos Verdes, California, 185
panic of 1873, 45
panic of 1893, 45
panic of 1907, 45, 70, 319n23
parent education movement: and Black domestic help, 225, 357n61; and Black families, 15, 225; and child-rearing experts, 245, 249; and child study movement, 207–10, 220, 358n75; and eugenics movement, 358n75; and Gate City Free Kindergarten Association, 353n18; impact of, 208–12; and Neighborhood Union, 210, 211; and *Parents' Magazine*, 220–30; and Parent-Teacher Associations, 210, 211, 222, 229; and public housing, 289; and racial attitudes, 222–23; and residential parks, 207, 208, 211–12, 216, 230, 233, 253; rhetoric of, 7, 205, 207, 208, 217, 230; and single-family homes, 207, 212, 217, 221, 230, 234, 281–82; standards of, 14; and white middle class, 4–5, 210, 231, 233

parenting: American style of, 17; cultural ideas about, 1–3, 7, 13–14, 207, 281–82, 292; goals of, 19–25; and informal mothers' groups, 220; intelligent parenting, 38, 207, 233; racialized limits of intensive parenting, 25–31; and upward mobility, 208; and urban development, 14, 231, 233. *See also* child-rearing
Parents' Magazine, 220–30, 235, 356n45, 357n58
Parent-Teacher Associations (PTAs), 34, 35, 74, 210–11, 229, 242, 352n5
Park, Charles, 202–4, 351n71
Park, John A., 203–4, 351n71, 352n76
Perry, Clarence, 282–83, 289, 371n9, 371n10, 372n13, 372n14
Perry, Heman, 146, 150, 187, 219, 337n72
Philadelphia, Pennsylvania, 172, 173
planning commissions: and city planning, 183–86; and local clubwomen, 242, 359n29; and racial zoning, 158–61, 164–65, 168–69, 175–76, 179, 188, 234, 374n33; residential park developers serving on, 63, 77; and school boards, 11, 181, 186, 204; and schools, 6, 11, 12, 77, 184
planning movement: and housing reform, 218; and Robert Jemison Jr., 240, 268, 284; and property rights, 160; rhetoric of, 149, 240, 241, 249, 286, 359n27; and school sites, 181, 184; and single-family zoning, 5, 172, 233, 234, 239–41, 243–45, 247–48
playgrounds: backyard playgrounds, 35; Black children's access to, 32–33, 34, 85, 134, 140, 310n65; lack of, 211; location of, 182; and Neighborhood Union, 127; planning commissions on, 3; and racial zoning, 10, 11, 181; and residential developers, 6, 7; and residential parks, 8, 52, 63, 244, 307n45; and school sites, 185–86, 197, 282; supervision of, 18, 32–35, 310n67
Plessy v. Ferguson (1896), 9, 123–24, 151, 154, 160
Poe, Clarence, 201, 203–4, 351n64

police power: and multifamily housing, 246–47; and property rights, 238, 243; and property values, 234, 242; and racial covenants, 10, 149, 254; and segregation laws, 8, 10, 91, 149, 152, 251; and single-family zoning, 278
poll taxes, 126, 135–36, 141, 336n55
Portland, Oregon, 171, 285–86
Potter, Hugh, 4, 6, 254, 264, 266, 274, 283–84, 290
Prather, Hugh, 54, 173, 274, 290
Pritz v. Messer (1925), 246
Progressive Era, 19, 36–38, 133, 170–72, 210, 230, 239–40
property rights, 45–46, 153–55, 160, 233–35, 238, 243, 252, 259n15, 339n21
property values: and adjacent properties, 236–37, 243, 253–54, 258, 278, 284, 360n31; and affluent Black families, 13, 290; and affluent white families, 11, 96; in Black neighborhoods, 25; and Black schools, 104–8; and child-rearing, 3–4, 11, 81, 239, 323n2; and commercial and industrial usage, 233; exclusion associated with, 7, 11; in older neighborhoods, 81, 89, 322n2; and property evolution, 82–83; and racial covenants, 279; and racial segregation, 2, 62, 290, 306n24; and racial transition, 91, 96–99, 327n9; and racial zoning, 160, 164, 176, 179; and residential park developers, 4, 6; and school sites, 182, 186, 203; and segregation ordinances, 96–100, 153, 154, 326n58; and single-family zoning, 234, 236, 239, 243–44, 247, 249; and traditional urban development, 82, 96; in transitional neighborhoods, 91; and white middle-class child-rearing, 14, 81, 179
Pruitt, Bernadette, 54–55
public housing, 289, 371n11, 374n39
public-private partnerships, 3, 274, 307–8n49
public schools, 18, 22, 52–54, 123, 124, 131–34
Purdy, Lawson, 10–11, 243–44, 283

race relations, 65–66, 108, 134, 222–23, 229, 229–30. *See also* interracial cooperation; interracial relationships
race suicide, 36, 210, 234
racial covenants: and Black children, 2, 250; Black people targeted by, 8–9, 306n27; Chinese immigrants targeted by, 8; *Corrigan v. Buckley* on, 12, 13, 44, 250, 251–52; and Jim Crow cities, 8, 11, 42, 44, 54–55, 57, 58, 63; legality of, 97; and police power, 10, 149, 254; and racial transition, 14, 307n43; and residential park developers, 55–56, 58, 60, 89, 101, 156; and residential parks, 54–62, 66, 70, 71, 83, 86, 89, 93, 252; and segregation ordinances, 101, 251–52; and unsalable properties, 12, 252; in urban environment, 42; white ethnic immigrants targeted by, 8
racial districting maps, 10, 11
racial hierarchy, 2, 4, 9–10, 18, 25–31, 78, 85–87, 222
racial stereotypes, 26, 27, 29, 223, 225
racial tolerance, 229–30, 291
racial transition: and Black schools, 103, 104, 112; and property values, 91, 96–99, 281, 327n9; racial covenants failing to prevent, 14, 307n43; and racial zoning, 160, 169, 267, 269, 275, 277; and schools, 108, 110–14, 120; and segregation ordinances, 88, 89–90, 94, 95, 100, 104, 113–14, 139, 145, 155, 160, 253, 269; and white middle-class child-rearing standards, 9, 105
racial violence, 25; Atlanta 1906 riot, 178; Rosewood, Florida, massacre, 135; threats of, 134–35, 174–75, 176; Tulsa massacre, 135, 176–78
racial zoning: and Atlanta's school building program, 186–94; and Black communities, 161–62, 163, 168, 169, 287, 288, 341n47; as de jure segregation, 150, 175, 269; and equal treatment under the law, 150, 163; and housing conditions for Black people, 150, 169, 170, 343n70; judicial tests of, 10, 11, 145, 150–51, 176, 250, 251, 252, 254, 282; national debate over, 170–78; and planning commissions, 158–61, 164–65, 168–69, 175–76, 179, 374n33; and playgrounds, 10, 11, 181; and racial covenants, 252; and racial transition, 160, 169, 267, 269, 275; real estate industry on, 149–50; and schools, 10, 11, 181, 182, 187, 193, 234, 279, 331n59; segregation ordinances compared to, 150–51, 163; segregation ordinances distinguished from, 149, 160, 161, 163, 252–53; as unconstitutional, 163, 164, 186, 188, 341n48; and unsalable property, 160, 170, 179, 190, 269, 278; and white absentee landlords, 253, 277, 287

Raleigh, North Carolina: and Black veterans, 134–35; Boylan Heights, 54, 57, 70–71, 202, 203, 315n50, 319n25; business class of, 70, 268; Cameron Park, 46, 47, 49, 52, 57, 60, 67, 69, 127, 202, 203, 315n50; College Park, 125–27, 199, 201, 332n9; Glenwood-Brooklyn, 71, 72; Hayes Barton, 66, 67, 203; Idlewild, 67, 69, 199, 202, 317n11, 317–18n13; interlocking directorate of, 57, 315n50, 315n51; Longview Gardens, 203–4; lopsided growth in, 290; NAACP Emancipation Day celebration, 134; Oakwood, 66; Oberlin Village, 67; planning commission of, 182; and racial concentration, 119; racial covenants in, 57, 72; racial segregation in, 62, 66; redevelopment plan of, 317n12; residential segregation in, 198–99, 203–4; school bond elections of, 201, 202, 351n65; school building program of, 182, 198–203, 205; segregated schools in, 64, 65–72, 77, 125–27, 132, 133, 147, 182, 199–203, 318nn15–16, 318n19, 320n30; South Park, 71; "White Supremacy Clubs" of, 55; Wilmont, 202

Real Estate Exchange, 339n15, 340n32

real estate industry, 6, 71–72, 145, 149–50, 154–55, 306n24, 307n46

Reconstruction period, 26–27, 60, 103, 110, 115, 122, 123, 189

redlining, 13, 307n46, 307n48, 307–8n49

red scare of 1919, 354n27

"Red Summer" of 1919, 135, 174

reformers, 18–19, 30–32, 34–37, 46, 311n86

religion, 19, 22, 67, 69, 71, 145–46, 318n16, 319n26

residential park developers: amenities of, 82; annexation of, 73–74; capital outlay of, 44–45; child-rearing references in advertising of, 6–7, 41–42, 49, 52–53, 61, 76–77, 87, 89, 101, 207, 211–12, 234, 235, 273, 312n2, 370n81; and deed restrictions, 45, 46–47, 72, 83, 186, 233, 274; and exclusivity, 54; and FHA's mortgage insurance program, 283; impact on older neighborhoods, 249; miscegenation prevented by, 86; and National Association of Real Estate Boards, 5, 12; profits of, 14, 61; and property valuation, 4, 6, 45; and racial covenants, 55–56, 58, 60, 89, 101, 156; and racial demographics of surrounding property, 65, 66; role in segregation process, 13; and school boards, 63, 65, 67, 77–78, 117; and school quality, 2, 63, 67, 72, 73–74, 75, 76–77, 182; and school sites, 270–71; and single-family zoning, 278; and speculators, 42, 44–46, 52, 61, 74, 233, 238; and streetcar companies, 159; and white schools, 11

residential parks: aesthetics regulated in, 235; and affluent Black families, 57, 58, 90, 150, 163, 187, 256, 261, 274, 279–80, 287, 314n48, 364n25; and affluent white families, 1–2, 7, 12, 41–42, 49, 61, 62, 76, 81, 101, 105, 230, 262, 265, 281, 290; and charter reform, 187, 346n16; child-centered amenities of, 3–13, 49, 52, 61, 69, 81, 91, 100, 101, 150, 164, 202, 207, 234, 235, 244–45, 252, 267, 273, 278, 279, 281–82, 284, 290, 307n45, 343n73, 358n75; deed restrictions of, 7, 8–9, 41, 42, 54, 58–59, 65, 66, 71, 83, 91, 101, 178, 186, 230, 235, 237; demand for, 12, 96; expansion of, 5–6; financial resources needed for, 14, 54; and housing market, 284; improvements invested in, 6, 7, 42, 44, 45, 74, 315n51; and lack of interracial relationships, 7, 42, 52–54, 65; and minimum house values, 42, 45, 56, 57; modern housing in, 183; and older neighborhoods, 282–83; and parent education, 207, 208, 211–12, 216, 230, 233, 253; and park-neighborhood ideology, 305n24; and playgrounds, 8, 52, 63, 244, 307n45; and property values, 236, 237; and racial covenants, 54–62, 66, 70, 71, 83, 86, 89, 93, 252; racial restrictions of, 4, 13, 42, 64, 72, 78, 81, 103, 114, 125, 146, 168–69, 175, 195, 204, 208, 253, 287; and residential segregation, 3–13, 62, 100, 188, 285; and schools, 8, 11–14, 52–54, 62, 65, 70, 71, 72–78, 120, 131, 136, 182, 184, 187–88, 194, 197, 199, 202, 207, 267, 270–71; and segregation ordinances, 97, 101, 154; and single-family zoning, 5, 41, 195, 234, 278, 279; and social class, 81; and suburban development, 8, 41, 311n74; success of, 98; traditional urban development altered by, 61, 81, 82, 91, 101, 103, 108; as voluntary segregation, 99

residential property, 3–4, 12, 14, 323n2

residential segregation: and Black schools, 147, 186; and child-centered residential parks, 3–13, 62, 100, 188, 285; expansion of, 19, 87–96, 286–87; government's role in, 292; and Houston, 256; and interracial relationships, 86, 230; and Morris Knowles, 279; Bruno Lasker on, 222; motivation behind, 2, 3; ordinances of, 9, 10, 306n27; and public housing, 374n39; and redlining, 307n46; and school building programs, 182, 183, 204, 253; and school sites, 181, 184, 186, 201–2, 270–71, 282; single-family homes tied to, 81; and social class, 13–15, 41, 54, 63, 66, 171, 172, 176, 183, 188, 197, 306n27. *See also* segregation ordinances

respectability, 25, 36, 173, 229

Revolutionary period, 13, 17, 19, 20, 295

Reynolds, R. J., 56, 197

Richardson, Clifton, 60–61, 84–85, 139–42, 143, 147, 150–51, 259–62, 287

River Oaks Corporation, 77, 254, 266, 281

Roanoke, Virginia, 155, 339n23, 364n30

Roberts v. Boston (1849), 26

Rosewood, Florida, massacre of 1923, 135

Rousseau, Jean Jacques, 19, 209

Russell Sage Foundation, 34, 371n9

Ryon, Lewis, 234, 256, 366n52

St. Augustine's College, 66, 68, 125–26, 201, 204, 319n26

St. Louis, Missouri, 55, 103

Schoff, Hannah, 210, 353n10

school boards: Black schools closed by, 65, 66, 76–77, 124, 190–91, 321–22n49; Black schools opened by, 104–5; conversion of white schools to Black schools, 103–7, 120–21, 189, 194, 327n12, 347n24; and planning commissions, 11, 181, 186, 204; and residential park developers, 63, 65, 67, 77–78, 117; and school quality, 74–75, 76, 77, 78, 142; and school sites, 181, 185, 186

schools: access to high schools, 22, 122, 123, 183; compulsory school attendance, 18, 32, 131–32, 334n26; double and triple sessions of, 33; "elastic districting" policy of, 329n37; fireproof construction of, 64, 71, 72, 131, 141, 192, 204; funding of, 11, 33, 123; ideal schools, 24–25, 52; inequality of, 70, 72–78, 123–24, 131; modern school buildings, 11, 12, 63, 64, 73, 74, 78, 79, 120, 122, 131–34, 135, 137, 179, 181, 282; and opportunity hoarding, 320n32; and planning commissions, 6, 11, 12, 77, 184; playgrounds supplied by, 34; racial segregation of, 9, 25–26, 63, 64, 65–72, 86, 88, 156, 222; and racial transition, 108, 110–14, 120; and racial zoning, 10, 11, 181, 182, 187, 193, 234, 279, 331n59; and residential parks, 8, 11–14, 52–54, 62, 65, 70, 71, 72–78, 120, 131, 136, 182, 184, 187–88, 194, 197, 199, 202, 207, 267, 270–71; and site selection, 11–12, 64–66, 181, 183–86, 201–2, 270–71, 279; and socioeconomic status, 4, 12, 14, 41, 63–64, 72–76, 78, 105, 113, 120, 129, 133, 181, 197, 250; and suburban development, 39, 41, 253; tax-supported expenditures on, 123; travel distance to, 11–12, 63, 65, 69, 70, 74, 103, 105, 118, 119, 125, 128, 181, 187, 188, 197, 200–201, 266; and voluntary segregation, 114. *See also* Black schools; public schools; white schools

school survey movement, 183–88, 194, 197, 282, 348n34

scientific racism, 18, 151–52, 230, 358n75

segregation: Black activists on, 85, 87, 95, 99; block-level segregation patterns, 8–9, 10, 62, 64, 66, 78, 79, 81, 82, 83–87, 88, 100, 103, 104, 107, 108, 110, 114, 115, 119, 120, 125, 145, 147, 149–50, 154–55, 156, 165, 176, 189, 194, 269, 275, 277; and child-rearing standards, 279; costs of maintaining of, 297; entrenchment of, 2, 293–94; long-term effects of, 61–62; and public housing, 289; in public spaces, 55; by race and class, 3, 39; rationale for, 2, 251, 293; and real estate ideology, 311n86; and school location, 65, 182; "self-help" within context of, 4; state-required segregation, 11; voluntary segregation, 99, 114, 118, 120, 177, 196, 198, 199, 258, 267, 274, 275, 277, 286; white children's unearned advantages from, 230; white northerners' support for, 25; widespread nature of, 39, 293; zoning connected to, 171. *See also* de jure segregation; residential segregation

segregation laws, 8, 10, 91, 149, 151, 152, 251

segregation ordinances: and affluent white families, 61, 62, 269, 306n27; and amalgamation, 152–53, 154, 155, 156; and Black schools, 103, 104–5, 120, 150; and interracial relationships, 88, 152–53, 154; judicial review of, 99, 252; and police power, 8, 10, 91, 149, 152, 251; and property rights, 153–54, 155, 160, 252, 339n21; and property values, 96–100, 153, 154, 326n58; and public health and safety assertions, 153, 339n15; and racial covenants, 101, 251–52;

424 | Index

segregation ordinances (*continued*)
  and racial transition, 88, 89–90, 94, 95, 100, 104, 113–14, 139, 145, 155, 160, 253, 269; racial zoning compared to, 150–51, 163; racial zoning distinguished from, 149, 160, 161, 163, 252–53; and traditional urban development, 82, 145; and unsalable property, 149, 160; US Supreme Court on, 9, 100, 103, 145, 151, 153, 156, 157, 164, 268; and white middle class, 9, 87–88, 89, 154, 306n27
servants, 56, 58–59, 152, 269, 341n45. *See also* domestic help
Service Realty Company, 169, 219
sexual assault: and the sexualization of Black girls, 27, 29; targeting Black women and girls, 85, 86, 152, 287
Shaw University, 64–65, 68
Shelley v. Kraemer (1948), 338n8
Shivery, Louie, 29, 33, 39, 111, 127, 131, 210–11, 309n47
Sims, Walter, 168–69, 179, 190–93
single-family homes: affordability of, 5, 245–46; backyard play structures and, 35, 42; in Black communities, 59, 261; and Black families, 13, 15, 25, 87–96, 150, 163, 211; as ideal for child-rearing, 4–5, 19, 24, 25, 35–38, 39, 41, 207, 216, 218, 221, 239–40, 245, 247, 264, 281, 322–23n2; and parent education, 207, 212, 217, 221, 230, 234, 281–82; and play space, 36, 38, 218, 221, 245; racial segregation tied to, 81; and racial zoning, 160, 162, 165, 171–72, 176; realtors on, 6; and school sites, 186; servants' housing and, 59; superiority of, 2–3; and zoning ordinances, 237–38
single-family zoning: acceptance of, 1, 2; and child-centered planning, 5, 239–42, 243, 244–49, 291; and deed restrictions, 230, 237; discriminatory nature of, 176; and planning movement, 5, 172, 233, 234, 239–41, 243–45, 247–48; and property values, 234, 236, 239, 243–44, 247, 249; and public amenities, 237–38, 247; racial zoning compared to, 251; and residential parks, 5, 41, 195, 234, 278, 279; and school building programs, 253; US Supreme Court on, 5, 233, 246–47, 251, 254, 360n33; Robert Whitten on, 171–72, 178
Slater Industrial State and Normal School, 274, 330n47
slavery, 18, 25, 27, 312n7

smartphones, 377n11
Smith, Corrine, 243, 360n31
Smith, Hoke, 158–59, 168, 178
Smith v. Atlanta (1926), 242–43, 251, 360n31
social capital, 316n67
social class, 12–14, 41, 73–74, 113, 323n2; business class, 1, 61–62, 70, 78, 134, 164–65, 269; and children's playmates, 35, 36, 42, 49, 52–53, 216; and deed restrictions, 7, 45, 58, 59; integration of, 292; and parenting styles, 297; and racial hierarchy, 78, 222; and residential parks, 81; and residential segregation, 13–15, 41, 54, 63, 66, 171, 172, 176, 183, 186, 197, 306n27; and school quality, 4, 41, 63–64, 72, 74–76, 78, 105, 113, 120, 129, 133, 181, 197, 250; and school sites, 188; and single-family zoning, 278; and white schools converted to Black schools, 105–6
South: anti-annexation movement in, 320n33; Black residents living outside of, 10, 269; and cultural gifts movement, 357n75; fertility during antebellum period, 22; low-wage economy of, 123, 136; New South, 132; per capita spending on education in, 78; public school system of, 27, 103, 123, 131, 132; racial covenants of, 8, 10, 42, 44, 54–55, 58, 63, 306n27; urbanization of, 11, 131
South Carolina, 338n74
Spann v. City of Dallas (1921), 254
Spelman College, 33, 108, 187
Starbuck, Henry, 55–56, 90–91, 324n36
State v. Gurry (1913), 155
Staub, John, 254, 267
Stephenson, Gilbert, 160, 199, 341n42, 351n61
Stowe, Harriet Beecher, 23, 26
Strayer, George, 181–83, 185, 187–88, 191, 194–95, 197, 205, 347n29, 348n34
suburban development: and affluent parents, 38–39, 41; and child-rearing, 41, 235, 285, 286, 290–91, 312n2; and children's health, 47, 49; and deed restrictions, 39, 45, 236; and domesticity, 36, 44; expansion of, 1, 5–6; and federal housing policies, 12; and middle-class families, 37; and moderately priced subdivisions, 12–13, 307n45; and national progress, 36, 38; and Progressive Era, 37–38; and racial exclusion, 13, 281; and schools, 39, 41, 253; socioeconomic

status framing disputes over, 13–14. *See also* residential parks
suburban environmentalists, 291

Terrell, Mary Church, 31
Timlic, James, 90–91, 94, 99, 115, 118, 324n36, 330n45, 330n47
tobacco, collapse of, 333–34n25
Tocqueville, Alexis de, 46
Toledo, Ohio, Ottawa Hills, 248
toy industry, 36, 221–22, 225
traditional urban development: block-by-block nature of, 61, 103; European feudalism compared to, 172; and mixed-income neighborhoods, 293; and mixed-race neighborhoods, 67, 86, 145, 155, 188, 233; and mixed-use neighborhoods, 83, 89, 111, 145, 233, 288, 293; and property values, 82, 96; and racial covenants, 12, 252; residential parks altering, 61, 81, 82, 91, 101, 103, 108; and segregation ordinances, 82, 145; and Tulsa massacre, 177
Tulsa, Oklahoma, 135, 176–78, 344n96
Twentieth Century Voter's Club, 134, 334n34
Twenty-Fourth Amendment, 135

upward mobility: and Black families, 26–27, 86, 157; and children, 1, 5, 7, 10, 17–18, 21–22, 49, 63, 88, 105, 230, 293; education as means to, 22, 24; and parenting, 208; and white families, 3, 12, 13–14, 17–18, 25, 39, 41, 81, 87, 88–89, 105, 108, 250
urban development: and deed restrictions, 45; hodgepodge growth patterns of, 41, 236; and parenting, 14, 231, 233; urban redevelopment, 283; white elites' control of, 14, 158–59, 236, 249; and white supremacy campaigns, 55. *See also* traditional urban development
urban environment, 8, 11, 21–22, 31–35, 39, 41–42, 47, 49, 61
Urban Land Institute (ULI), 290
US Chamber of Commerce, 218, 274
US Children's Bureau, 38, 220
US Commerce Department, 216, 274
US Housing Corporation (USHC), 212, 215, 217, 240, 355n28
US Supreme Court: on antimiscegenation laws, 284; on de jure segregation, 252; on property rights, 153–54; on racial covenants, 12, 44, 250, 251–52; on school inequality, 124; on segregation ordinances, 9, 100, 103, 145, 151, 153, 156, 157, 164, 268; on single-family zoning regulations, 5, 233, 246–47, 251, 254, 360n33

Veiller, Lawrence, 218, 235, 239, 248
Ventura, California, 54, 55, 58
voting rights, of Black people, 55, 136, 335n39

Washington, Booker T., 87, 156
Washington, DC, Willow Tree Playground, 33
Wheeler, Gervase, 24–25
white elites: and Great Migration, 134; leadership positions of, 15; and racial zoning, 170; and segregation ordinances, 98, 99, 100, 117, 156–57, 326n59, 340n32; urban development controlled by, 14, 158–59, 236, 249
white ethnic immigrants, 8, 18, 20, 170–71, 173, 225
white families: and acquisition of public resources, 15; ambitions of, 1, 3; and block-level segregation patterns, 79, 81, 87; and competitive parenting, 208; exclusion of Black children's access to housing and schools, 29, 124; and interracial relationships, 103–4; liberal attitudes of, 229; in mixed-race neighborhoods, 82–83, 84, 104, 120, 253, 269, 281, 323n6; upward mobility of, 3, 81, 87, 88–89, 105, 108. *See also* affluent white families; white working-class families
White House Conference on Child Health and Protection, 4–5
White House Conference on Home Building and Home Ownership, 4–5, 217, 242, 283, 372n14
white liberalism, 220–30
white people: and preservation of racial hierarchy, 2, 9–10, 85–87; as property owners, 98–99, 100, 114, 326n56; and race suicide fears, 210
white schools: access to high schools, 69, 131, 138, 139, 142; conversion to Black schools, 103–8, 120–22, 125, 131, 138, 145–46, 158, 189, 194, 259, 285, 327n12, 329n34, 337n71, 347n24; fireproof construction of, 71;

426 | Index

white schools (*continued*)
inferior white schools, 12, 120, 123, 128–29, 131, 146–47; location of, 181; in mixed-race neighborhoods, 104, 112–13, 120, 261, 365n40; overcrowding of, 11, 64, 69, 72, 113, 129, 193

white supremacy: on biracial children, 85, 151; and Black children, 29, 85, 225; and Black middle class, 15; and Black social equality, 178, 345n99; boundaries of, 86, 97; campaigns on, 55, 65; dictates of, 9; and inferior Black homes of mixed-race housing, 83, 84, 86; on interracial relationships, 85, 86, 145, 151–52, 230; and lynchings, 27, 85, 86; Frederick Law Olmsted on, 312n7; on racial separation, 151–52; and segregation ordinances, 94; and threats of violence, 134–35, 174–75; and Tulsa massacre, 135, 176–78

white working-class families: and child labor, 18–19, 31–32; child-rearing strategies of, 14, 18, 32, 295; domesticity of, 34, 35; homes of, 32, 179; and modern school buildings, 11, 39, 124, 128–29, 192, 202, 349n42; and racial zoning, 165, 168, 170, 189, 275

Whitten, Robert: and Atlanta, 10, 149, 159–61, 163, 165, 168, 169–70, 174, 176, 178, 179, 239, 253, 268, 282, 341n42, 368n62; and Birmingham, 267–68, 368n62; and Cleveland, 178; and Dallas, 254; and New York City, 10, 149, 170; and New York regional plan, 282–83; and planning commissions, 258; on playgrounds, 186; and public housing, 289, 375n40; and school sites, 187, 346n17; on school survey movement, 184, 282; on single-family zoning, 171–72, 178; and Tulsa massacre, 177

Wilson, Woodrow, 64, 217

Winston, North Carolina, 55–56, 114–15, 156–57, 329n41. *See also* Winston-Salem, North Carolina

Winston Development Company, 93, 324n39

Winston-Salem, North Carolina: Ardmore, 212; Buena Vista, 42, 53–54; Central Terrace, 117, 157, 197, 212, 275; Columbia Heights, 57, 60, 90, 99, 100, 117, 118, 119, 198, 274–75, 324n39, 326n64, 330n52; coordinated residential development in, 56–57, 268; East Winston, 56–57, 90, 93, 275, 277, 278, 314n48, 326n64; Inside Land and Improvement Company, 57; interlocking directorate of, 56, 57, 196, 314n46; Kimberly Park, 275; and racial covenants, 55–57, 89–91, 93, 94, 314n46; and racial zoning, 196, 199, 267, 268, 274, 275, 277–78, 370n87; school bond elections of, 277, 350n52; school building program of, 182, 195–98, 199, 202, 268, 274, 275, 277; segregated schools in, 103–4, 114–15, 120, 122, 196, 277; segregation ordinance of, 90, 94, 98–99, 100, 103, 104, 114, 115, 117, 119, 120, 152, 196, 199, 258, 277, 278, 330n46, 341n42, 344n92; Slater Normal School, 274; and voluntary segregation, 274, 275, 277; Washington Park, 56, 57; West End, 55–56, 57, 76, 197, 315n51

Wordsworth, William, 22–23
World War I, 45, 54, 64, 131–34, 174, 268
World War II, 12, 286

Zilibotti, Fabrizio, 294, 296, 308n3
zoning ordinances: and Advisory Committee on Zoning, 5; and affluent white families, 249; and assumptions of parent education, 231; and child-centered appeals, 234–35, 243; and deed restrictions, 234–38; judicial review of, 149–50, 240, 253; and property rights, 233, 234, 238, 259n15; and separation of industrial, commercial, and residential areas, 149, 238, 360n31; single-family zoning, 1, 2, 5, 171–72, 176, 178, 230, 233, 234, 237–38, 239, 240–42, 245, 247–48, 251, 253–54, 278–79, 291; in southern cities, 11; and speculators, 238; and state enabling laws, 94, 179, 240, 248, 254, 268–69, 339n23; unenforced zoning protections for Black development, 13, 288. *See also* racial zoning

www.ingramcontent.com/pod-product-compliance
Lightning Source LLC
Chambersburg PA
CBHW020217240426
43672CB00006B/335